Discretion and the Quest for Controlled Freedom

"Discretion is an inevitable yet controversial feature in public policy and law, but it is several years since a comprehensive and coherent analysis appeared in the literature. This collection of original essays, written from different disciplinary perspectives, explores this protean and elusive phenomenon in a variety of ways. The papers have been well organised and closely edited and raise our understanding of the meaning and place of discretion to a new level."

—Keith Hawkins,
Professor Emeritus of Law and Society, Oxford University, UK

"This volume addresses some of the very important practice dilemmas for professionals in our time. It provides a road map for navigating the contours of working the spaces between the restrictions of rules and the responsiveness to people in shifting contexts. It gives us hope and ways to move forward. A must-read for every professional."

—Jan Fook,
Professor and Chair, Department of Social Work, University of Vermont, USA

Tony Evans • Peter Hupe
Editors

Discretion and the Quest for Controlled Freedom

palgrave
macmillan

Editors
Tony Evans
Department of Social Work
Royal Holloway, University of London
Egham, UK

Peter Hupe
Public Governance Institute
Catholic University of Leuven
Leuven, Belgium

ISBN 978-3-030-19565-6 ISBN 978-3-030-19566-3 (eBook)
https://doi.org/10.1007/978-3-030-19566-3

Cover credit: ilbusca / Getty Images

This Palgrave Macmillan imprint is published by the registered company Springer Nature Switzerland AG
The registered company address is: Gewerbestrasse 11, 6330 Cham, Switzerland

Preface

Discretion embodies a dynamic balance in the tension between freedom and control. Even if the relationship is a hierarchical one, some degree of 'letting go' is always involved. The carpenter may hang the painting on the wall, but perhaps at a lower height than the owner of the painting might prefer. Unlike the painting's owner, the carpenter is aware of electricity cables hidden under the plaster and the importance of avoiding them.

The process of the making of this interdisciplinary edited collection could be characterized in similar terms. While no hierarchy was involved, the dynamics in the relationship between the publisher and the editors, between the editors and the contributors and also between the editors themselves showed elements of an ongoing search for an appropriate balance between freedom and control. In the end, we feel that this creative tension has produced a valuable collective contribution to the study of discretion.

The origins of this monograph go back to a conversation over a cup of coffee in Grenoble in 2013. Having participated in a conference panel, we exchanged ideas about our respective research agendas and agreed that we would be interested in jointly editing a volume of essays on discretion. Eventually, the 'implementation' of this agreement following up on the publisher's invitation but particularly all contributors' work, has led to the present collection.

Many chapters in this volume were first presented at an authors' meeting held on September 7–8, 2017, at All Souls College, Oxford. We would like to thank Christopher Hood for hosting this meeting and the participants for making it an inspiring and fruitful event. The Warden, fellows and staff of All Souls College are acknowledged for the hospitality offered. Particular thanks are due to Kate Hitchman and Irini Hatzimichali, the successive events managers. For Peter, who was a visiting fellow at the College in 2012–2013, it was a special pleasure to return to All Souls.

From the beginning on, the publisher gave us continuous support. Over the years we were in touch with several persons. By mentioning—in alphabetical order—Anne-Kathrin Birchley-Brun, Ambra Finotello, Imogen Gordon Clark and Katelyn Zingg, we would like to thank Palgrave Macmillan for their support in the process of bringing this interdisciplinary edited collection about.

Egham, UK	Tony Evans
Leuven, Belgium	Peter Hupe

Contents

Notes on Contributors

Victor Bekkers is Professor of Public Administration and Public Policy at Erasmus University Rotterdam, the Netherlands. His research interest primarily focuses on how the introduction of information and communication technology and media as well as (co-creative) innovation processes influence the shaping of different public policy processes and public services. He is also the dean of the Erasmus School of Social and Behavioural Sciences.

Antoinette de Bont is an endowed professor at the Erasmus School of Health Policy & Management, Erasmus University Rotterdam, the Netherlands. Her research focuses on new roles for citizens, professionals and policymakers in digital health. She is currently studying the governance of big data technologies in European health care.

Mark Bovens is Professor of Public Administration at the Utrecht University School of Governance in the Netherlands. One of his main research topics is public accountability. On this topic he has published several books, such as *The Quest for Responsibility* (1998), *The Real World of EU Accountability* (with Deirdre Curtin and Paul 't Hart, 2010) and *The Oxford Handbook of Public Accountability* (with Robert Goodin and Thomas Schillemans, 2014).

Evelyn Z. Brodkin has published widely on street-level organizations, welfare state politics, public policy and management, with a particular interest in issues of poverty, inequality and marginalization. Recent work includes her co-edited book, *Work and the Welfare State: Street-Level Organizations and Workfare Politics*, tracing the advance of workfare-style policies in six countries. She leads an international collaboration, *The State at the Street*, investigating Nordic welfare state responses to the European refugee crisis from state level to street level. Brodkin is an associate professor at the University of Chicago, USA, and a visiting professor at Aalborg University and the University of Gothenburg.

Gideon Calder is Senior Lecturer in Social Sciences and Social Policy at Swansea University, UK. He is author or editor of ten books, most recently *The Routledge Handbook of the Philosophy of Childhood and Children* (2018) and has a particular interest in the application of philosophy to matters of policy and practice—social justice for children; and co-production. He co-edits the journal *Ethics and Social Welfare*.

Danielle Davidson is Lecturer in Social Work and Human Services at the School of Public Health and Social Work, Queensland University of Technology, Australia. She has a multi-disciplinary background, with degrees in the areas of criminology, psychology; and social work and human services. She has extensive social research experience across these three disciplines and non-face-to-face practice experience with young people. In addition to a continued interest in distance practice modalities, her research focuses on the experiences and well-being of human services practitioners, through the lenses of street-level bureaucracy, as well as complexity and organizational theories.

Marlies van Eck is an assistant professor and researcher at eLaw—Center for Law and Digital Technologies, Leiden University. She is specialized in information and communication technology and administrative law and interested in the impact of new technology and its use by the government on citizens and legal protection. In her thesis 'Automated Administrative Chain Decisions and Legal Protection' (2018) she has performed legal and empirical research to observe and assess the execution of tasks by public administration: https://pure.uvt.nl/ws/portalfiles/portal/20399771/Van_Eck_Geautomatiseerde_ketenbesluiten.pdf. She is also interested in enabling constructive and informed discussions on the use of artificial intelligence.

Tony Evans is Professor of Social Work at the Department of Social Work at Royal Holloway, University of London, UK. His research focuses on exploring ideas of expertise and ethics at the interface of policy and professional practice.

Paul du Gay is a professor in the Department of Organization (IOA) at Copenhagen Business School (CBS) and professor and director of research at the School of Management, Royal Holloway, University of London. His books include *In Praise of Bureaucracy* (2000), *The Values of Bureaucracy* (ed.) (2005), *Organizing Identity* (2008) and *For Formal Organization: The Past in the Present and Future of Organization Theory* (with Signe Vikkelsø, 2017). At CBS, he directs the Velux Foundation project 'Office as a Vocation: Re-instating an Ethics of Office in Public Service'.

Mark Hardy is a senior lecturer in the Department of Social Policy and Social Work at the University of York, UK. There he teaches a mixture of social work theory, research methods and philosophy; and criminology. He is the author of *Evidence and Knowledge for Practice* (with Tony Evans, 2010) and *Governing Risk* (Palgrave Macmillan, 2015); and is co-editing *Mental Health Social Work: The Art and Science of Practice* (with Martin Webber, forthcoming, Routledge).

Michael Hill is Emeritus Professor of Social Policy at the University of Newcastle, UK. Before entering academic life he was a street-level bureaucrat in a local social assistance office. He wrote an article based on that experience and moved on to research at the Universities of Oxford and Bristol on the implementation of social policy. He has worked closely with Peter Hupe on various articles and a book, *Implementing Public Policy* (third edition, 2014). His long-standing text *The Public Policy Process* reached its seventh edition in 2017 in a joint version with Frédéric Varone of the University of Geneva.

Christopher Hood has been a fellow at All Souls College, Oxford, since 2001 and has been a visiting professor at the Blavatnik School of Government in Oxford since 2015. He specializes in the study of executive government, regulation and public-sector reform; has taught public administration and government on three continents over more than four decades; has published some 28 books and is working on a study of the planning and control of public spending.

Peter Hupe is Visiting Professor at the Public Governance Institute, Catholic University of Leuven, Belgium, and Honorary Senior Research Fellow at the School of Social Policy, University of Birmingham, UK. While teaching public administration at Erasmus University Rotterdam, he had academic affiliations in Leiden, Leuven, London, Oxford and Potsdam. His research focuses on the theoretical-empirical study of policy processes, particularly policy implementation and street-level bureaucracy. He discovered the relevance of the latter during an earlier career as a policymaker in the Dutch national civil service.

Hannah Jobling is Lecturer in Social Work at the University of York, UK. She is interested in the varying ways social work is conceptualized in different times and places; and how knowledge transmission shapes contextualized practices. She researches and writes on the history of social work, the policy/practice relationship, critical realism and theories of power.

Michael Luntley is Emeritus Professor of Philosophy at the University of Warwick and has written extensively on Wittgenstein and on issues in the philosophy of education, including expertise. Recent publications include *Opening Investigations* (2015); 'What's the problem with Dewey?', *European Journal of Pragmatism and American Philosophy*, Special number on centenary of Dewey's *Education and Democracy*, 2016, Vol. VIII, No. 1, 77–99; 'Forgetski Vygotsky', *Educational Philosophy and Theory,* 2017, Vol. 49, No. 10, 957–970; and 'Wittgenstein and the path of learning', for J. Stickney & M. Peters (eds.) *A Companion to Wittgenstein on Education: Pedagogical Investigations* (2016).

Greg Marston is Professor of Social Policy and Head of Department, School of Social Science at the University of Queensland, Australia. His research interests include poverty and inequality, the politics of policymaking and social service delivery models. He is undertaking the Australian Research Council-funded research into conditional welfare, climate change, automation and work futures.

Peter Mascini holds a chair in Empirical Legal Studies at the Erasmus School of Law and is an associate professor at the Erasmus School of Social and Behavioural Sciences, Erasmus University Rotterdam, the Netherlands. He manages the research programme 'Behavioural Approaches to Contract and Tort'. He studies the legitimization, implementation and enforcement of legal and policy instruments on a range of domains such as health and safety, crime-fighting, torts, education and the labour market. He is particularly interested in studying the tenability of behavioural assumptions underlying policies and policy theories. In his research, he uses both quantitative and qualitative methods.

Catherine Needham is Professor of Public Policy and Public Management at the Health Services Management Centre, University of Birmingham, UK. She has published a wide range of articles, chapters and books for academic and practitioner audiences. Her most recent book entitled *Reimaging the Public Service Workforce* was published in 2018. She tweets as @DrCNeedham.

Zachary W. Oberfield is Associate Professor of Political Science at Haverford College. His research interests include schools, leadership and street-level bureaucracy. He is the author of two books—*Are Charters Different? Public Education, Teachers, and the Charter School Debate* (2017) and *Becoming Bureaucrats: Socialization at the Front Lines of Government Service* (2014)—and a winner of the 2015 Best Book Award from the Public and Nonprofit Division of the Academy of Management. He holds a PhD in Political Science from the University of Wisconsin-Madison.

Kirstine Zinck Pedersen is an associate professor in the Department of Organization, Copenhagen Business School, Denmark. Her research attends to the organizational, practical and ethical implications of transformations of the public sector. In her recent book *Organizing Patient Safety: Failsafe Fantasies and Pragmatic Practices* (Palgrave Macmillan, 2018) she enquires into the international preoccupation with patient safety and its consequences for organizational routines, medical professionalism and discretionary practices in hospital settings.

Suzanne Rutz is an assistant professor at the Erasmus School of Health Policy & Management, Erasmus University Rotterdam, the Netherlands. She also works as an inspector at the Netherlands Health and Youth Care Inspectorate. Her research focuses on reflexivity in regulatory practice, participation of citizens and providers in inspections; and quality improvement of regulated services from the inspectors' perspective.

Lars Tummers is Professor of Public Management and Behaviour at Utrecht University, the Netherlands. His research interests are public management, leadership and citizen/state interactions. Related to this, he has developed an interdisciplinary field combining psychology and Public Administration called 'Behavioural Public Administration'.

Hendrik Wagenaar is a senior academic advisor to the International School for Government at King's College, London and an adjunct professor at the University of Canberra, Australia. He publishes in the areas of participatory democracy, interpretive policy analysis, deliberative policy analysis, prostitution policy and practice theory. He is the author of *Meaning in Action: Interpretation and Dialogue in Policy Analysis* (2011) and editor of *Deliberative Policy Analysis* (with M. Hajer, 2003). In the area of prostitution research he has published *Designing Prostitution Policy: Intention and Reality in Regulating the Sex Trade* (with Helga Amesberger and Sietske Altink, 2017).

Dirk J. Wolfson has served with the International Monetary Fund and as the director of economic policy in the Dutch Treasury, before joining Erasmus University Rotterdam, the Netherlands, as Professor of Public Finance and member of the Scientific Council for Government Policy. Upon retirement, he served a term in the Senate (Labour Party) and joined Erasmus University again as a visiting scholar in the Department of Public Administration. He is a member of the Dutch Royal Academy of Sciences.

Stavros Zouridis is Professor of Public Administration and Law at Tilburg University, the Netherlands. His research focuses on the rule of law as a mode of government, risk regulation and law enforcement. He has developed a multidisciplinary framework for the analysis of the constitutional state and the rule of law. In a recent book he used this framework to analyse the institutional crisis of the rule of law in Europe. In September 2018 the Dutch government appointed him as a member of the Dutch Safety Board.

List of Figures

List of Tables

CHAPTER 1

Conceptualizing Discretion

Tony Evans and Peter Hupe

1.1 The Illusion of Total Control

Discretion presumes some form of hierarchical relationship. A body or person grants a degree of circumscribed freedom to another body or person, to be exercised in a particular setting according to particular standards. As such, the phenomenon of discretion is generic and ubiquitous—although its occurrence is pluriform and dynamic.

Once there was a time in which life had a quiet pace. When men came home after a hard day's work, their wives offered them a drink. The children were doing their homework, enabling the maid to prepare the evening meal. All were looking forward to the family outing on Sunday afternoon, with a car ride after church attendance.

This could be a scene from an early episode of *Mad Men*. It seems an idyllic picture—but only if seen from a very particular perspective of white heterosexual male privilege. The scene is a complete caricature which cannot be read without irony or, for that matter, retrospective indignation. At most we may watch re-runs of *Happy Days* or similar television series cherishing the 1950s, as a form of nostalgia (Halberstam 1993). The picture above suggests a stable order, in which everyone knows his and her place. What seems at stake here is an illusion of total control, as well as the current demise of that illusion.

As with any illusion, the picture is one-sided. The image of the happy family ignores the shadow-sides: harsh class relationships, segregation and discrimination, violence and abuse, oppression of counter-voices. The hierarchical

T. Evans (✉)
Department of Social Work, Royal Holloway, University of London, Egham, UK
e-mail: Tony.Evans@rhul.ac.uk

P. Hupe
Public Governance Institute, Catholic University of Leuven, Leuven, Belgium
e-mail: pieter.hupe@kuleuven.be

T. Evans, P. Hupe (eds.), *Discretion and the Quest for Controlled Freedom*, https://doi.org/10.1007/978-3-030-19566-3_1

relationships pictured above, the hegemonic status of a particular cultural orientation and submissiveness as a standard mode of conduct, no longer prevail. Of course, these features, to a smaller or larger extent, in various contexts do remain reality. In contrasting then and now, here and there, while we have to recognize the differences, we also need to acknowledge continuities. At least, however, the mentioned features have lost their self-evident character.

Giving an assessment of 'modern times', Hupe and Edwards (2012) speak of de-centring, multi-sourced sense-making and autonomization as characteristics of the current era. *De-centring* means that a variety of action locations set the stage for all kinds of 'political' activities outside the formal locus of politics in its narrow sense. *Multi-sourced sense-making* implies that giving meaning to one's life in terms of common interests, concerns and identities may be based on the intersection of different aspects of social characteristics, such as class position, ethnicity and gender. As Hupe and Edwards (2012: 181) point out, people 'draw eclectically from a variety of sources' to give meaning to their lives. *Autonomization* refers to an extended number and range of autonomous or quasi-autonomous actors, constituting a plurality of publics. Contemporary individuals believe that they are in charge of their own lives; they define their identity and mutual relationships in their own terms.

It is against this background that discretion is a topic more than ever worthwhile studying. The occurrence of a multi-dimensional diversity and the recognition of a range of perspectives—and potential insights from these different perspectives—invite thorough reflection on the subject of discretion. If power relationships cannot be taken for granted as hierarchies, if orientations cannot be assumed as monochrome and hegemonic, while actors serve in all kinds of representational roles, then the ideas of control and freedom suggested by the very term 'discretion' need to be reflected upon. Furthermore, the macro setting in which discretion in the public sphere is being formulated and practised shows dualistic developments, tending towards both enhanced discretion and more freedom and diminished discretion and greater control.

Information and communication technologies can enlarge the freedom of action. The internet, for instance, has turned the world into a global village, allowing individual actors to directly interact with each other and access and exchange information at speed. At the same time, search engines monitor and direct behaviour, while algorithms channel processes such as trading across a range of commodities and currencies, amplifying problems (and occasionally creating 'flash crashes'). The result is diminished freedom and increased surveillance. Where freedom does exist it can be abused in destructive ways—as hate speech, abusive images, 'fake news'. These in turn lead to calls for more human supervision, judgement and discretion to bring a sense of perspective and control to unbounded systems.

This interdisciplinary edited collection provides a state-of-the-art account of scholarly analysis of discretion—we have asked authors to bring their insights on this topic of shared concern from a range of disciplinary perspectives. Discretion tends to be a central topic in disciplines such as law and sub-disciplines such as the sociology of professionals and policy implementation. Amongst these disciplines and sub-disciplines, to a greater or smaller extent, there has been a history of exchange of ideas and debates about discretion. Currently, discretion is re-emerging as an area of study. As it shows, there are also novel insights into discretion as a concept and as an empirical phenomenon.

1.2 Disciplines on Discretion

The Renaissance essayist Montaigne, in the essay 'A trait of certain ambassadors', reflects on the idea that it is better that servants obey the instructions of their masters, rather than challenge them. Looking back to classical antiquity, he describes the case of the Roman general Crassus, who, having seen a ship's mast in the harbour, instructed an engineer to get it for him to use as a battering ram. The engineer saw a better mast, more suited to the task and brought that instead. Crassus had the engineer whipped for disobeying orders.

Montaigne reflects on this event, pointing out that commanders often have to ignore the letter of the instruction in order to better achieve the aim in ever-changing circumstances. The risk of waiting for new instructions is that nothing will be done. In a rhetorical question Montaigne observes: '[D]id not Crassus, when he wrote to an expert and advised him of the use for which that mast was destined, seem to consult his judgement and invite him to interpose his opinion?' (Montaigne trans Frame 1958: 51).

Montaigne, writing in the late sixteenth century, draws on the classical idea of discretion as judgement and anticipates the predominant modern idea of discretion as the freedom to act on judgement. Two centuries later, the German philosopher Hegel (1977) explored the relationship between knowledge and power in his seminal exposition of the master/servant relationship. Hegel helps us to understand the dynamic and unstable relationship of knowledge, freedom and power in the operation of control and delegation. The imposition of control and a particular world view by a master on a servant paradoxically creates power and freedom for the servant. The master imposes and continues to occupy this world view uncritically. For the servant, his/her view of the world is confronted with another perspective which he/she has to incorporate and in this process, moves to create a new, richer and more productive understanding of the world that supersedes that of his/her master.

More recently, the philosopher Baier (1986) has directed our attention to the social ecology of formal relationships that entail discretion such as delegation, principal/agent agreements and contractual powers and obligations. Discretion does not merely exist in the contract that established a principal/agent relationship; for instance, it assumes broader social conventions and norms that ground the trust that makes sense of these relationships—the broader network of social expectations, assumptions and conventions that support the conditions of trust that allow contracts and formal agreements to operate. For Baier, these background conditions reflect ideas of justice and fairness that facilitate the trust that underpins discretion, allow it to operate and also provide criteria against which to evaluate and challenge its abuse.

Contemporary ideas of discretion elide the ideas of judgement, trust and freedom to act. The nature of the judgement that is to be exercised and the extent of the freedom within which it can operate are open questions. They regard issues about power as a constraint on and potential within discretionary roles. Different academic disciplines have approached these questions and the term 'discretion' itself in varying ways.

In a review of disciplinary approaches to discretion, one of the present authors made a comparison of theoretical lenses through which discretion is examined (Hupe 2013). In law, for example, discretion refers to the appropriate exercise of legitimate authority within limits specified by legislators. In studies of public administration, public management and public policy, 'discretion' tends to be used to describe and evaluate the freedom of public officials—particularly of those working at the street level of government. In this context, the term indicates the legitimate space for the officials to make their own decisions and exercise their own judgement about how public services are delivered and the degree of freedom from external control they have in doing this. In economics, sociology and other social sciences, the idea of discretion is more widely deployed, but often to refer to a particular locus of research. In economics, discretion is often viewed through the lens of a principal/agent relationship focusing on questions of costs and hazards of delegation, conflicting interests and trust. In sociology discretion is associated with the study of occupations, particularly professionals and public officials, and the interpretations and enforcement of rules and conventions in everyday interactions.

While there are particular disciplinary 'takes' on discretion, there are also often debates within disciplines about the ideas and phenomena to which 'discretion' refers. Within the study of law, for instance, a number of influential but very different approaches to discretion were developed in American jurisprudence in the late sixties/early seventies. Davis (1969) presented a formulation of discretion as a deficit—and a fundamental problem: in the absence of control and the specification of work, discretion is the freedom left to public officials to make their own decisions beyond effective control. Underpinning this view is the idea that discretion is fundamentally illegitimate and, ideally, laws and procedures should be formulated as tightly as possible to constrain the freedom of public officials to as great a degree as possible. In a sense, Baier's call to understand discretion not merely as a formal, legalistic relationship but as a role interacting with broader but often implicit social conventions and assumptions can be seen in two alternative legal characterizations of discretion. Dworkin (1977), for instance, offers a view of discretion as nested in sets of rules. It is about freedom, but within more or less formal systems of rules and expectations. Dworkin was concerned to argue that discretion is never absolute—it is never unbounded autonomy—even in situations where the law seems to be silent, the discretion (to be valid) has to be based on basic background rules of rational judgement. Kadish and Kadish (1973) provide another picture of discretion: as a corrective to overly literal approaches to rules. For them, discretion permeates public bodies; it is about understanding the point behind a rule and having the freedom to ignore the letter of the law to better achieve its purpose. Discretion, they argue, requires actors to think about what they have been told to do to make sense of it and be thoughtful rather than just obedient in handling obligations.

Similarly, within economics, the characterization of actors and their approach to discretion has changed. The classical idea of the *homo economicus* has been re-evaluated by behavioural economists. The classic economist models operate on an assumption of human agency as individual, rational, geared to adapt behaviour in response to incentives to maximize their material interests. The economic agent is best placed to make judgements about the most effective choices, but when he or she is acting on behalf of an another—as in a principal and agent relationship—they cannot be trusted to make the best judgement for their principal. Instead, the assumption is that they will use the freedom they have been afforded to advance their own rational self- interests. However, over the past decades behavioural economists have challenged this assumption, arguing that most people, most of the time, act habitually and make decisions on the basis of assumptions and guesswork. They have to be 'nudged' to make more economically rational choices (Thaler and Sunstein 2008). From this point of view, the problem of agents is primarily their ignorance and laziness, while they can be encouraged to conform to their principal's goals by creating an architecture of choices—such as user-friendly forms and processes—that nudge them to make the right decisions (Cabinet Office/Institute for Government 2010). However, thinking back to Hegel's observation of the master/servant dialectic we should not jump to the conclusion that the principal always knows best—the agent's experience of working on the ground can provide greater insights into what is possible and what can actually be done.

Furthermore, disciplinary approaches to discretion—ideas from disciplines—are not hermetically sealed. Ideas move across disciplines and can develop and change in the process. Legal ideas of discretion, for instance, permeate the literature, often providing key definitions and jumping-off points for further analysis: Davis (1969) is often cited in public administration and political analysis of discretion. Economic ideas of discretion have become highly influential across many disciplines. Public choice theory, for instance, has brought a hard-edged idea of motivation and behaviour—basically the classic economic model of human actors as self-interested, rational calculators—to the study of policy implementation and the examination of the behaviour of discretionary actors (e.g. Niskanen 1971). In the sociology of professions, Johnson (1972) analyses the achievement of professional power in terms of a market model of seller and buyer relations to understand the extent of freedom and control of professional practice in any particular situation.

Certain disciplinary approaches can be seen to set and shift the agenda of interest in discretion, often in a way that has extended and developed the debate, not least by stimulating critical perspectives. Historically, legal ideas of discretion have tended to be influential and used widely to conceptualize and pin down the phenomenon of discretion. More recently, economic perspectives, particularly ideas from economics of firms and management, have come to dominate debates about discretion in terms of seeing it in a range of fields through the lens of agency theory, economic motivation and the problems of control, self-interest and entrepreneurialism (Ulohi 2007). A particularly influential approach in health policy that draws on this framework is Bossert's idea of 'decision-spaces'—an idea that also draws on public administration ideas of discretion (1998: 1518 fn). The decision space approach is very much concerned with de-centralization and approaches the issue from within a principal/agent perspective (Roman, Cleary and McIntyre 2017), focusing on the delegation of decision-making authority down from the centre to the periphery. Bossert wants to develop an approach that specifies both the nature and extent of formal authority and an actor's ability to exercise that authority—an approach that echoes the well-established distinction between *de jure* discretion and *de facto* discretion. Decision space describes not only the delegation of formal authority but also the capacities of actors to make decisions such as the control of appropriate resources. In identifying these two aspects of discretion, the idea provides tools to explore the mismatch that can occur between the formal accounts of discretion and what discretion looks like on the ground. However, the dominance of certain paradigms of discretion risks crowding out other perspectives and imposing a 'normal science' (Kuhn 1970) of discretion research, assuming certain problems to be the right ones to be solved and requiring a specific approach to understanding these questions. We should keep in mind that any 'normal science' is a construct that eventually breaks down; the imposition of a way of seeing and researching a phenomenon is doomed to unravel, as its limitations become increasingly apparent and the effort of shoring up the paradigm becomes increasingly costly. In fact, it is often at the margins beyond 'normal science' that limitations are most clearly articulated and challenged and new insights and alternatives to the conventional wisdom developed.

For instance, the influence of agency theory and its assumptions in framing approaches to discretion is challenged from a range of perspectives that point to the value and potential for multi-disciplinary approaches and debates. Street-level bureaucracy theory, for instance, questions the assumption that discretion is simply devolved from the centre (Lipsky 1980/2010). It points out that, even if it were, discretion cannot be managed and directed straightforwardly in line with the principal's priorities. The nature of street-level work is that front-line workers know more about their work and the people they work with than their managers. This fact enables them to control the upward flow of information to influence how situations are seen and decisions are made to manage their managers. Furthermore, systems of top-down control are necessarily rickety, with imprecise and sometimes contradictory procedures open to interpretation and flexible application.

The different but connected ways in which discretion is conceived are intriguing. In this interdisciplinary edited collection, we want to explore these differences, similarities and connections in the tension between freedom and control across social and political practices, as well as their implications in different disciplines and contexts. In short, this collection provides a contemporary review of the state of knowledge about the phenomenon of 'discretion'. The academically dispersed treatment of discretion and contemporary developments in the real world underline the need to address the topic of discretion by bringing together different insights and views in a collection aimed to address interest in this subject matter.

In the next section of this chapter, the meaning of the central concept is explored. What kind of empirical phenomena are referred to when the term 'discretion' is used? Discretion has to do with both the usage of freedom and the exercise of control. In the third section, the various scholarly views on discretion are highlighted. If discretion is broadly conceived as the exercise of judgement and freedom to act within externally controlled limits, from which angles has it been studied so far? The chapter ends with an outline of the structure of the edited collection.

1.3 Localizing Discretion

As noted above, there are several widely used definitions of discretion that scholars tend to deploy, often drawn from the realm of law and justice. Perhaps the most widely quoted definition, particularly in the public administration literature, is Davis' (1969: 4), for whom

> [a] public officer has discretion wherever the effective limits on his power leave him free to make a choice among possible courses of action and inaction.

Davis' definition describes the extent of discretion and is formulated within a perspective from which discretion is viewed as a problem, particularly in terms of a democratic deficit of lack of (public) control. In order to characterize discretion Dworkin (1977: 31) introduced the metaphor of the 'hole in the donut'. It links to a concern to understand the ways legal actors operate and the law works in the real world (Hawkins Ed. 1992). Basically, the metaphor points to the question whether discretion begins (the 'hole') where rule application ends (the 'dough'). Discretion, in this view, is exercised in a hierarchical relationship of control between a (single) rule maker 'M' and a (single) rule applier 'A'. Within a set of rules, M specifies when and to what extent A can use his or her own judgement when making decisions in line with the rules formulated in the set.

An alternative view sees 'discretion' as synonymous with the actions of actor A as such. In that alternative view, exercising discretion stands for balancing action prescriptions stemming from *various* sources. 'Action prescriptions' include not only formal rules, but also professional norms and societal expectations; sometimes even market requisites are involved (Hupe and Hill 2007; Thomann, Hupe and Sager 2018). And these prescriptions arise from multiple sources. While M may assume that only his or her rules are to be applied by A, in fact, A has to juggle a plurality of action demands. Using the freedom at hand then not only is inevitable, it is necessary. And the freedom available to actors is in part constituted by the multiple requirements and the elaboration of requirements (Evans and Harris 2004).

Discretion exists within a network of actors—in direct relationships between people and roles, while often mediated by documents, resources and the like. To understand discretion in any situation one has to understand how it operates within its context—the cross-cutting and asymmetrical network of relationships that reflect different dimensions of power. While one actor is afforded freedom, this is a freedom that is subject to control by another actor. At the same time, such control is limited by the very delegation of freedom. The need to allow someone else to act enables the other actor to extend and alter the extent and nature of that freedom. This relationship involves tensions, constraints and elasticities in which the scope to act may be prescribed but cannot be predetermined. The nature of the relationship is much less one between a puppeteer and a puppet than one between a director and actors in a theatre play or film. The director, or *regisseur*, can instruct and advise and can impose sanctions off-stage. *On* stage, however, it is the actors who act and decide. While being on their own, at that moment they cannot be controlled remotely.

Montaigne's story of the Roman General Crassus and the engineer illustrates the essentially relational nature of discretion and its cross-cutting asymmetries of power. It alerts us to the ways in which power can constrain or enable the exercise of discretion as judgement, as well as to the idea of judgement itself as a notion that can reflect power.

The discretionary relationship is often expressed in terms of a principal who instructs and an agent who is instructed. However, the nature of the relationship of control and freedom can be animated by different concerns (e.g. Duska 1992). The idea of principal and agent has a long history in law, where it was characterized as a trusting engagement of an agent by a principal to carry out instructions or act in their best interest. Within the constraints set by the principal, the agent was free to act and it was assumed that the agent would be motivated by loyalty. If the principal had concerns, redress was available through the courts. An alternative characterization of the agent/principal relationship developed in economics and management. Here, the relationship was characterized by distrust. It emphasized the need to control and monitor agents. Principals may have to delegate a task, but they should do this in the expectation that the agent is likely to stint in responsibility; to avoid this, they would need to monitor what the agent does and use control to limit action.

As we explore the characterization of discretion as a relationship of freedom and control between two parties we increasingly recognize the complexity that is likely to arise in organizational situations. In most organizations, there is a significant distance between the first principal—the senior policy-maker, for instance, who delegates the original task—and the final agent—the public worker at the street level, who carries it out. The space is filled with layers of managers and officials, whose decisions and actions are likely to have an effect on the nature and character of discretion as it passes down the line (Evans 2016). They will also be acting alongside systems of remote control, such as procedures and policies, interpreting and prioritizing these. Increasingly, such systems of control take more immediate forms, like in the case of information and communication technologies. The ultimate consequence may be the replacement of these intermediaries.

However, the relationship between principal and agent is not just one way. The knowledge and judgement of agents is an important counterweight to the power of principals. At its most basic, the agents know more about what is going on at that moment in that place than the principals. They have a more immediate understanding of the situation at hand, because of their location in that situation. They understand what will work within it and are aware of what the challenges are of putting it into effect. Another source of knowledge that agents might have is the experience they have built up from being in situations. Their power is not just the access to information they have from being in the place, but also how they have come to understand the nature of the job, how their work relates to broader background circumstances that enables them to exercise judgement about what is needed and, practically, how to achieve a goal or task. As situational knowledge blurs into expertise, expertise blurs into a more formal body of occupational knowledge and expertise that some workers have acquired through training and qualification; a characteristic that we most often associate with the idea of professionals—occupations with formal training and qualifications. From each of these positions—and agents may occupy more than one at any one time—agents have information, skills and judgement that enable them to understand and act in the situation in a way which their principal cannot second-guess.

Even from this very short outline of the uses of discretion as a concept and area of study, it is evident that it is an idea and concern that runs across a range of disciplines within the social sciences and beyond. This, we would argue, is the case because it is an idea that is activated by fundamental concerns about actors' freedom and capacity to act (agency) and an awareness, simultaneously, that this freedom also entails constraint and regulation (control). Freedom and control mutually restrain each other. There may be an urge for freedom, but there is also a 'quest for control' (van Gunsteren 1976). At the same time, total control is an illusion. The tension between these two fundamental concerns engages ideas about the basis upon which freedom and control are necessary and possible (e.g. permission, accountability and trust). It is between the extremes of these two, complete freedom and total control, that discretion can be localized.

Different disciplines bring different concerns to the study of the subject matter central in this edited collection. Discussions of discretion can entail ideas of authority and rules (law) and normative concerns about justice, virtue and rights (ethics); the pursuit of material interests (economics); judgement and its limitations (psychology); the role of social structures and dynamics (sociology) and power (politics). While each discipline foregrounds certain concerns, each one also draws on—sometimes disguised or assumed—ideas about the context of discretion and the nature and motivation of actors. One of the fundamental aims of this book is to explore these underlying ideas and examine how they make sense of disciplinary approaches, while connecting and linking apparently different ideas of discretion in various disciplines.

1.4 The Structure of the Edited Collection

This monograph consists of four parts. After the present introductory chapter, institutional settings get attention in the first part of the volume, titled 'Discretion in Context'. Next, an exploration of the variety of (disciplinary) views is central: 'Perspectives on Discretion'. In the third part, 'Discretion in Governance', the focus is on aspects of the ways in which discretion is investigated in the study of public policy, public administration and public management. In the final part, 'Practising Freedom and Control', the floor is given to reflections on particular subjects in their relationships to discretion.

Part I ('Discretion in Context') provides an empirical frame establishing the profile of discretion as a contemporary object of scholarly enquiry across disciplines. After an introduction, the first five chapters set the scene by exploring key aspects of the state as the context of discretion in social welfare. Chapter 3 considers discretion as a strategy of blame avoidance. We often think of discretion as a prized attribute of public bodies, but, as Hood points out, with power comes responsibility. In looking at how discretion is distributed across public services we need to consider how shifting discretion can be used to manage exposure to criticism and potentially blame. Another influential view of the state is a system of surveillance and control. From this perspective, as Hardy outlines in Chap. 4, discretion deploys underlying logics—often contained in bodies of expertise—that serve to organize and control members of society. Brodkin, in Chap. 5, considers discretion as politics by other means. Looking at the sclerotic state of federal politics in the United States, she argues that political decision-making about priorities and rationing has been shifted to organizational actors in the administration of services. In Chap. 6 Hill considers historical debates in the UK about the use of discretion as a means of providing welfare benefits to citizens and the complex relationship of administrative discretion and welfare rights. In Chap. 7, the final chapter in this first part of the edited collection, Marston and Davidson critically explore the uses of discretion from the point of view of citizen empowerment.

The scholarly treatment of discretion has tended to be concentrated in a narrow range of disciplines, particularly law and economics. Policy studies and political science have also been concerned with discretion, especially in research on street-level bureaucracy, as has the sociology of professions. However, this interest has not been an exclusive concern of these (sub-)disciplines and we need to look across the range to get a sense of perspectives—as suggested above (Hupe 2013). Part II ('Perspectives on Discretion') provides an overview of (disciplinary) perspectives on discretion.

In the law, discretion is treated as the translation of rules into action. Rules are seen as circumscribing the limits within which judgement is legitimated. As far as rule application implies behaviour, the latter is considered to be predominantly rule-guided. After an introductory chapter, Mascini, in Chap. 9, looks beyond 'the hole in the donut' (Dworkin 1977) and considers the broader social networks within which legal decision-making is located. In Chap. 10 the economic perspective on discretion is examined by Wolfson. While the relationship between a 'principal' and an 'agent' is focused on concerns about compliance, he argues that discretion has the potential to offer creativity and responsiveness in service provision.

Chapter 11 provides an overview of insights from the psychological perspective on discretion. Tummers and Bekkers focus on the role of alienation and associated psychological pressures as important insights into understanding how actors approach organizational rules and deploy discretion. Being trained and socialized into a specific occupation may be an ongoing process but is this also a matter of learning how to use discretion? What does discretion mean in developing occupational craftsmanship? How does discretion in the workplace work, given the nature of socialization processes? Oberfield addresses these questions from a sociological perspective in Chap. 12. Finally, Jobling, in Chap. 13, considers discretion from a critical perspective that questions how power within the state is used and asks in whose interests it is deployed. She does this through an examination of discretion in mental health practice. The idea of discretion is often discussed in terms of judgement on choices to be made. However, she points out, forms of knowledge can structure and, in a way, 'control' judgement. Particular authority hence can be used to control and curtail discretionary behaviour.

Part III ('Discretion in Governance') considers a range of perspectives on the role of discretion in governance. In public policy, public administration and public management, discretion has been—and will remain—a contentious issue. Here discretion tends to be seen as a problem—for instance, the ***implementation gap***—and as a phenomenon to be restricted or at least to be specified, within boundaries of legitimate authority. However, when we look more closely at the discussion of discretion, there is a growing range of perspectives identifying discretion as a potentially positive and dynamic force, often linked to a variety of discretionary actors. After an introductory chapter, the first chapter in this part of the edited collection deals with discretion and the requisites of bureaucracy (Chap. 15). In contrast to the caricature of bureaucracies as organizations devoid of discretion, du Gay and Pedersen argue that discretion is an inherent and dynamic characteristic of bureaucracies. In Chap. 16, Hupe and Hill look at discretion in the policy process and explore its role horizontally and vertically across the range of organizations and actors involved in developing and implementing public policy. Wagenaar, in Chap. 17, looks at discretion as the practice of government at the street level. Local practices flesh out the bare bones of policy and reflect local experience and the accumulated expertise of service delivery. Rutz and de Bont (Chap. 18) focus on discretion as an organized and officially sanctioned space in which the rules that usually structure discretion are open to question, challenge and review. Managers have significant discretion in their work, but Needham argues this discretion needs to be understood as situated within a network of formal and informal accountabilities, in which cross-cutting responsibilities challenge the idea of managers as simply organizational actors (Chap. 19). In the final chapter (Chap. 20) of this part of the edited collection, Zouridis, van Eck and Bovens look at digitalization and discretion. They argue that increasingly discretion has to be understood as a function of information technology systems and procedures and the central role of algorithms in systems of decision-making. System designers now have become critical discretionary actors in organizations.

Finally, Part IV ('Practising Freedom and Control') focuses on the dilemmas, challenges and opportunities of freedom and control in practices of discretion. Chapter 22 is a philosophical exploration of discretion as an aesthetic accomplishment. In this chapter Luntley considers discretion at the margins—where the rules give out—focusing on the role discretion plays in imagining and crafting new thinking and innovative response to situations. Rather than being a specialist trained attribute, discretion in this sense reflects curiosity, creativity and imagination. Professional work is almost synonymous with discretion. In Chap. 23 Evans argues that professional expertise and freedom are closely related; discretion is not a fixed attribute of professions. Professional discretion can vary in its extent and nature. It is located in a dynamic matrix of forms of expertise, relationships of control and power, in which the broader needs, interests and concerns of organizations, as well as wider political and social interests, play a role. In Chap. 24 Evans approaches discretion as a site of creativity. In the same way that theatre actors and musicians perform a text or score, front-line actors, he argues, have to interpret and extemporize policy. Practitioners have to bring policy to life, recognizing policy as both a limitation on what they can do and, at the same time, a resource that can be used to open up different avenues in providing responsive services. Ethical decision-making is also central to the idea of discretion. Calder, in Chap. 25, explores the relationship between standards and professional freedom as a productive tension resolved by practical reason in practice settings. He argues that discretion is a locus for ethical judgement and considers an approach to ethical analysis that focuses on human flourishing as the basis for negotiating the ethical opportunities, tensions and dilemmas of discretion. In the concluding chapter (Chap. 26) the editors identify key themes and use these to draw conclusions about developing debates and interdisciplinary approaches to discretion.

References

Baier, A. (1986). Trust and anti trust. *Ethics*, 96(2), 231–260.

Bossert, T. (1998). Analysing the decentralisation of health systems in developing countries: Decision space, innovation and performance. *Social Science and Medicine*, 47(10), 1513–1527.

Cabinet Office/Institute for Government. (2010). *MINDSPACE—Influencing behaviour through public policy*. London: Institute for Government.
Davis, K.C. (1969). *Discretionary justice: A preliminary inquiry*. Baton Rouge, LA: Louisiana State University Press.
Duska, R. (1992). Why be a loyal agent? A systematic ethical analysis. In N. Bowie & E. Freeman (Eds), *Ethics and agency* (pp. 143–168). New York: Oxford University Press.
Dworkin, R.M. (1977). *Taking rights seriously*. Cambridge, MA: Harvard University Press.
Evans, T. (2016). Street-level bureaucracy, management and the corrupted world of service. *European Journal of Social Work*, 19, 602–615.
Evans, T. & Harris, J. (2004). Street-level bureaucracy, social work and the (exaggerated) death of discretion. *British Journal of Social Work*, 34, 871–889.
Halberstam, D. (1993). *The fifties*. New York: Villard Books.
Hawkins, K.O. (Ed.) (1992). *The uses of discretion*. Oxford: Clarendon Press.
Hegel, G. (1977). *Phenomenology of spirit* (A. Miller, Trans.). Oxford: Oxford University Press.
Hupe, P.L. (2013). Dimensions of discretion: Specifying the object of street-level bureaucracy research. *Der Moderne Staat. Zeitschrift für Public Policy, Recht und Management*, 6(2), 425–440.
Hupe, P.L. & Edwards, A.R. (2012). The accountability of power: Democracy and governance in modern times. *European Political Science Review*, 4(2), 177–194.
Hupe, P.L. & Hill, M.J. (2007). Street-level bureaucracy and public accountability. *Public Administration*, 82(2), 279–299.
Johnson, T. (1972). *Professions and power*. London: Macmillan.
Kadish, M. & Kadish, S. (1973). *Discretion to disobey*. Stanford, CA: Stanford University Press.
Kuhn, T. (1970). *The structure of scientific revolutions*. Chicago: University of Chicago Press.
Lipsky, M. (1980/2010). *Street-level bureaucracy. Dilemmas of the individual in public service*. New York: Russell Sage Foundation.
Montaigne, M. (1958). *The complete essays of Montaigne* (Frame, Trans.). Stanford, CA: Stanford University Press.
Niskanen, W.A. Jr. (1971). *Bureaucracy and representative government*. Chicago and New York: Aldine-Atherton.
Roman, T.E., Cleary, S. & McIntyre, D. (2017). Exploring the functioning of decision space: A review of the available health systems literature. *International Journal of Health Policy and Management*, 6(7), 365–376
Thaler, R. & Sunstein, C. (2008). *Nudge*. Newhaven: Yale UP.
Thomann, E., Hupe, P.L. & Sager, F. (2018). Serving many masters: Public accountability in private policy implementation. *Governance*, 31, 299–319.
Ulohi (2007). Revisiting the principal-agent theory of agency: Comments on the firm-level and cross-national embeddedness theses. *Journal of Organizational Behaviour*, 28, 75–80.
van Gunsteren, H.R. (1976). *The quest for control: A critique of the rational-central-rule approach in central affairs*. London: John Wiley & Sons.

PART I

Discretion in Context

CHAPTER 2

Discretion in Context: An Introduction

Peter Hupe and Tony Evans

2.1 Introduction

In the first part of this edited collection discretion is placed in context. The latter word may suggest some form of geographical positioning in terms of the physical background of the five chapters presented. Then indeed a topographical bias may be observed: all authors come from and write, to a greater or smaller extent, about phenomena observed in the Commonwealth—or at least Anglo-Saxon—countries they are residents of.

However, the arguments developed in the five chapters have a broader reach. Each addresses a particular kind of 'context' of discretion as generic phenomenon. Christopher Hood focuses on the relationship between discretion and blame avoidance in government (Chap. 3). Mark Hardy problematizes the ways modern government tries to monitor the behaviour of its functionaries as well as of its citizens, while trying to control the freedom of both (Chap. 4). Evelyn Brodkin explores the ways in which street-level organizations *de facto*, rather than intendedly, function as political actors (Chap. 5). Michael Hill overviews the evolutionary dynamics of the debate about granting or withholding discretion in British social assistance (Chap. 6). And Greg Marston and Danielle Davidson critically examine empowerment in theory and practice (Chap. 7).

This selection of chapters shows that 'context' entails a variety of dimensions. This variety comprises, among others, levels of analysis (macro/meso/micro), layers of public administration (supra-national/national/local and all

P. Hupe (✉)
Public Governance Institute, Catholic University of Leuven, Leuven, Belgium
e-mail: pieter.hupe@kuleuven.be

T. Evans
Department of Social Work, Royal Holloway, University of London, Egham, UK
e-mail: Tony.Evans@rhul.ac.uk

T. Evans, P. Hupe (eds.), *Discretion and the Quest for Controlled Freedom*, https://doi.org/10.1007/978-3-030-19566-3_2

in between) and *structure* versus *agency* (institutions/individuals). Apart from anything else, the five chapters share a substantially empirical focus, in the sense that the authors in their descriptive analysis stress what actually happens, to a certain extent beyond good intentions laid down in some formal policy document. Rather than at what normatively may be expected, the authors hence look at what they observe in empirical reality. At the same time it is clear that they do so from a greater or smaller dispositional distance towards government and with a more or less critical view on the ways discretion is practised.

2.2 Discretion and Blame Avoidance

Christopher Hood observes discretion as an element of power struggles within governments, bureaucracies and organizations. There, groups or individuals are trying to reduce or restrict the discretion of others, while increasing or maintaining their own discretionary space. On the other hand, actors in public administration also frequently accept and even initiate arrangements that seem to limit their *own* discretion. Hood mentions the introduction of expert advisory committees as example at the higher policy level, as well as the usage of formalized decision algorithms, at the field or operational level. Where do such limitations on discretion come from?

A first possibility may be to see such developments as part of some long-term Weberian-style process of rational-legal modernization producing ever more rule-bound bureaucracy. A second possible factor is technological development enabling remote monitoring and surveillance of individuals in ways and at a scale thus far unforeseen. Mentioning a third possibility, Hood sees as key that the pursuit or maintenance of discretion may court excessive risk of blame when the wrong choices or actions are chosen. At that point a contradictory logic of blame avoidance by shunning or limiting discretion can be expected to operate. That clash or trade-off between the contradictory desiderata of blame avoidance and the pursuit of discretion is central in Hood's chapter.

Less because of some compelling overall logic of rational-legal modernization or because of technological change, it seems because of the associated blame risk that discretion may be voluntarily restricted. This being so, Hood sees at least two complications in the idea of an ineluctable trade-off between the risk of incurring blame and the ability to exercise discretion in politics and bureaucracy. One is that such a trade-off seems to apply only in specific contexts or conditions. The other complication is that in at least some times and places it may be possible to 'have it all'. A combination of blame risk and the exercise of discretion occurs when forms of organization or behaviour are adopted that can *both* deliver some measure of discretion and, at the same time, serve as a bureaucratic or political blame shield.

With the first complication, failure to exercise discretion itself is seen as a culpable act of discretion. Hood gives several examples of conditions in which the idea of a blame/discretion trade-off can break down. Those conditions imply that blame can come to attach to officeholders or organizations that fail to act with discretion, while equally credit can go to those who seize or apply discretion even for apparently high-blame actions. A pertinent example of the former is Adolf Eichmann's role in the Holocaust.

In some situations however, combining blame avoidance and discretion seems possible. Hood sketches three variants of this second complication: pooling discretion, semi-delegated discretion and validated discretion. One possible way to retain discretion in the sense of latitude for decision and action but at the same time to manage the associated blame, is to pool the exercise of discretionary powers across multiple actors or organizations—a device that means spreading or sharing rather than completely avoiding blame.

While pooled decision-making arrangements serve to share but not completely avoid blame, a related approach is one of fudged or plastic delegation of the exercise of discretion to disavowable agents. The latter term refers to the various advisory, adversary and policy delivery organizations that officially operate at some distance from ministers or the core of executive government and for which the latter can therefore try to disclaim at least some degree of responsibility.

A third possible variant of combining discretion with blame avoidance implies the use of external (or semi-external) validation in the form of endorsement or approval of the way discretion is used by outside authority of one kind or another. Securing approval then can be used as a partial blame shield. Hood observes that in some conditions, then, blame avoidance can go along with the exercise of discretion, at the least when independent or semi-independent enquiries are delayed, inconclusive or diverted away from key issues.

2.3 Discretion in the Surveillance State

Mark Hardy reflects on the effectiveness of state intervention against the background of a growing awareness of the inherent epistemological limitations of the modernist project. In his chapter he reviews debates regarding the role of practitioner discretion across the contested arena of the social state. He does so by examining the ways in which technological change has enabled the development and deployment of surveillance as a strategy of government. The term 'social state' refers to the rationalities, activities and practices of workers employed to contribute to the achievement of the social goals of the state in areas such as health care, social work, criminal justice and welfare.

Practitioners are required to make judgements and to differentiate between citizens. Knowledge generated via surveillance is an important source here. It is in making these distinctions and judgements that practitioners exercise discretion. Discretion has traditionally been recognized as a defining feature of professionalism. However, within the social state, practitioner discretion has come to be problematized, increasingly designated as the weak link in professional practice. As such, its exercise is subject to various strategies of oversight, constraint and regulation. The ideal which motivates these constraints is an approach to decision-making in which knowledge diminishes uncertainty by replacing the vagaries of individual subjectivity with the presumed certainties of generalized objectivity. Surveillance as a technique of government is utilized across a variety of domains of state activity, including national security, espionage and policing; and also health, welfare and criminal justice. Surveillance activities across the social state arguably represent a means of remedying the limits of knowledge. Via the elimination of uncertainty, risk can be effectively managed and thus security achieved.

The ability of managers to check the activities of staff accentuates anxieties regarding decision-making, as scrutiny of processes and choices often does. Enhanced technological capabilities may also affect the culture of practice within the agencies of the social state. Foucault's concept of biopower offers a way of thinking about the development and use of surveillance through the prism of power. The concept entails a way of theorizing the use of power towards securing the health and well-being of both individuals and the population as a whole. Central are the more diffuse modes of governing directed at human biological capacities. Foucault's approach is critical of modernity and thus of the ways of knowing aimed at with biopower. While it is not obvious how biopower might enable either more effective or more ethical practice, exploring discretion through such a lens seems worthwhile.

2.4 Discretion in the Welfare State

Evelyn Brodkin focuses on the politics of discretion in the context of the welfare state. It is in the discretionary micro-practices in street-level organizations that the meta-politics of the welfare state indirectly is being shaped. Those practices affect the boundaries of the possible for advancing contested policy projects, for claiming rights and for negotiating socio-political status. Within those boundaries, street-level organizations function as political institutions when they shape social provision, specifically access to and distribution of benefits and services. Those organizations also structure opportunities for voice, claiming and assertion of rights. And they manage the consequences of their practices, using strategies of legitimation, symbolism and blame-shifting.

Building on two theoretical perspectives, political institutionalism and street-level bureaucracy, Brodkin stresses that her theoretical approach conceptualizes the organizational *practices* as political. Street-level organizations may be institutionally positioned to be mediators of welfare state politics, but they are not seen as purposeful political actors as such. The politics of discretion is not necessarily negative or harmful; discretion can be used in ways that advance normative goals of social justice, equality or democracy. In a similar vein, discretion is not treated as an individual-level phenomenon.

Rather, Brodkin's approach identifies the elements of discretionary practices through which organizations perform latent political functions that are largely indirect. It directs attention to the ways in which discretion is structured in specific organizational and political contexts. The political significance of discretionary behaviours derives from their effects, regardless of ascribed or imputed purposes or individual motivation. The politics of discretion, conceptualized in this way, should be understood as operating systematically, but indirectly, making it a type of politics that is not obvious. The analytical challenge is to reveal the conditions under which discretion is patterned and to assess its consequences for 'who gets what, when and how'.

2.5 Discretion and Welfare Rights in a British Context

Michael Hill addresses discretion in the context of the provision of cash benefits in the UK. The wider debate is between the arguments for selectivity and those for universalism in social policy. With universalism, the norm of equal treatment of equal cases is stressed, while selectivity enables treatment 'made to measure' in the circumstances at hand. In the political reality of the welfare state, considerations like cutting public expenditures versus meeting the needs of the poor may be important drivers of what remains an ongoing debate.

Looking at the evolution of discretion in UK social assistance, Hill identifies two issues as particularly salient. One concerns the feasibility of eliminating discretion in this activity, the other the desirability of doing so. Hill's historical account makes clear that eliminating discretion *is* difficult. He gives an overview of the search in post-war British social security policy for ways to eliminate means testing by crafting selectivity in ways involving 'criteria' which minimize discretion. Hill highlights that replacing discretion by much more specific rules about entitlement had to mean what was then called 'rough justice'.

This dynamic evolution so far has resulted in a situation in which substantial areas show a high level of regulatory activity, often elaborately codified. Inasmuch as officials are engaged in making judgements about efforts to obtain work or training and may apply sanctions if dissatisfied with these efforts, this situation clearly involves forms of discretion.

Apart from this development, technological change fuels a tendency towards the routinization of decision-making accompanied by the elimination of face-to-face contacts. Important for the analysis of the implications of discretion are the possible negative consequences of such forms of automatization. While routinization may contribute to the reduction of biased behaviour by public officials, citizen-clients have to cope with complicated forms and hard-to-understand outcomes. These issues are particularly salient where claimants have low levels of literacy or English as not their first language. Thus Hill suggests that it is important not to lose sight of the way in which the application of rules may imply a less visible exercise of discretion, particularly where they are applied to complex situations.

2.6 Discretion and Empowerment

Greg Marston and Danielle Davidson aim to critically examine the discourses of empowerment and the institutional contexts in which they are deployed, contested and reframed. Their argument is that empowerment, depending on its discursive usage, can work out in two contrasting ways. On one hand, it may provide an important justification for professional discretion on the front line of social services to act in the interests of individual or collective freedom. Conversely, when defined and deployed in terms of marketized choice and personal responsibility, empowerment can be a hollow term, functioning as a de-politicizing force.

Based on a discussion of academic debates and professional discourses, Marston and Davidson distinguish three different meanings of empowerment: a form of community development, a means of coproducing needs and marketized choice. They illustrate their argument with a case study of empowerment constructed in the context of workfare, particularly the case management within a non-profit social service organization in Australia aimed at the 'activation' of welfare recipients.

Given their findings, the authors are critical about empowerment. The case study demonstrates that empowerment is applicable to both workers and clients of services. Workers need to be trusted that they can meet client needs without too tightly prescribed pathways and outcomes. However, addressing patterns of disadvantage in the local communities concerned through community development initiatives was not a prominent part of the empowerment imagination for the social service agency managers or the case managers. Despite the espoused aim of the studied workfare project to address the causes of poverty, this goal was never elevated to a more macro political strategy of lobbying political-administrative authorities for more public housing, public transport, income security or job creation.

Marston and Davidson conclude that working towards self-improvement obviously is not the same as working towards social and economic justice. Addressing matters of justice and equity at a collective level through a more inclusive polity might mean that less is demanded from the individuals working 'at the front line', but more attention is given to the organizational and socio-political environment they are working in.

CHAPTER 3

Discretion and Blame Avoidance

Christopher Hood

3.1 Introduction: The Discretion/Blame Risk Trade-Off

In Chap. 1, the editors describe discretion, 're-emerging as an area of study', as 'the exercise of judgement and freedom to act within externally controlled limits'. Indeed, in an organizational or bureaucratic context, discretion has often been equated with a form of power. That is because in normal speech the word connotes the ability—sometimes the duty—of an individual or group to exercise judgement in choosing one course of action rather than another (e.g. over what to pay attention to, how to use time, which of a set of multiple rules or guidelines to apply, who to appoint or elect to a given office or position, even when to use a weapon and against whom). That ability or duty can be restricted or constrained in various ways, for example, in the form of formal decision prompts, vetoes, post hoc reviews, even physical constraints.

Discretion in that sense can also come in formal or informal variants, according to whether the ability or duty to exercise judgement is enshrined (or forbidden) in law or enacted rules. Michel Crozier (1964), in his classic account of power in organizations, saw such power as residing in whatever groups have effective discretion over the supply of critical resources or processes and in Crozier's analysis those in that position are not necessarily those at the upper hierarchical levels. Indeed the *de facto* discretion available to street-level bureaucrats or field staff has long been acknowledged in the literature on bureaucracy (Lipsky 1980). Crozier, however, also identified other groups, such as key support functionaries, who could also possess de facto discretionary power over significant resources. In their recent study of the politics of representation in

C. Hood (✉)
All Souls College, Oxford, UK
e-mail: christopher.hood@all-souls.ox.ac.uk

T. Evans, P. Hupe (eds.), *Discretion and the Quest for Controlled Freedom*, https://doi.org/10.1007/978-3-030-19566-3_3

African-American education in the United States, Kenneth Meier and Amanda Rutherford (2017: 187) noted some of the different zones of discretion possessed by the different players in the US education system:

> School board members [...] have discretion over funding issues [...] but far less, if any influence over assignments [...]. School administrators have extensive influence over teacher hiring and the application of discipline but less discretion in the day-to-day interaction of teachers with students. Teachers exercise vast discretion over student referrals for discipline or for grouping assignments [...] but any influence they have over school funding policy will be indirect.

That link between discretion and power means that discretion is one of the elements (along with items such as reputation and core budgets) that can be taken as a bureaucratic maximand in rational-choice-style reasoning about what drives bureaucratic behaviour, on the assumption that individuals normally want more rather than less power. For example, Patrick Dunleavy's (1991: 202) classic account of 'bureau-shaping' conceives high levels of discretion as a key goal for higher-level bureaucrats. Indeed, in the passage quoted in the previous paragraph, Meier and Rutherford (2017) use the words 'discretion' and 'influence' as if they were interchangeable. And following that sort of logic, power struggles within governments, bureaucracies and organizations might normally be expected to consist of groups or individuals trying to reduce or restrict the discretion of others, while increasing or maintaining their own discretionary space.

And yet it is a matter of common observation that governments, ministers, bureaucracies, other organizations—even parliaments or legislatures—frequently accept and even initiate arrangements that at least appear to have the effect of limiting their discretion. At the higher or policy levels, common examples include the introduction of expert advisory committees that must be consulted over matters of policy or regulation, the adoption of more or less prescriptive codes of conduct or legal requirements to replace more fluid custom-and-practice arrangements; or the application of automatic funding formulae in place of case-by-case bargaining over resource allocation. At the field or operational levels of bureaucracy and public services, common examples include formalized decision algorithms replacing more open-ended exercises of judgement, physical systems that preclude (or all but preclude) certain courses of action that would otherwise be possible, as in the classical story of Ulysses tied to the mast of his ship to prevent him from changing course in succumbing to the lure of the Sirens. The modern equivalent is found in a host of failsafe devices, single-use medical instruments or 'zero tolerance' obligations that preclude choices not to take action on certain types of cases for *de minimis* or similar reasons.

There is more than one way of accounting for the development of such limitations on discretion and probably several factors are at work. One possible line of explanation would be to see such developments as part of some long-term

Weberian-style process of rational-legal modernization producing ever more rule-bound bureaucracy—with the rules increasingly embedded into the software through which modern bureaucracy works—that has the effect of increasingly constraining free choice by officeholders at all levels. That is a familiar dynamic in studies of bureaucratization, although the micro-foundations of such dynamics are not always easy to identify and, as Bernard Silberman (1993: ix) and others have pointed out, 'Weber's expectations with regard to the convergence of bureaucratic structure throughout modern industrial societies [...] have been disappointed'.

Another possible explanatory factor, which can be closely related to that Weberian theme of ever-increasing quantification and legal rationalism, is the striking development of technological systems that can enable remote monitoring and surveillance of individuals who in earlier eras were beyond the effective day-to-day reach of superordinates or reviewers. Almost six decades ago, Herbert Kaufman (1960) published a classic account of forest rangers in the United States, as far-flung field agents of the federal government who had to operate for much of the time beyond the reach of observation by, or ready communication with, their hierarchical supervisors. His careful research brought out all the mechanisms, including socialization and the keeping of journals, that helped to enable the Forest Service to achieve a remarkable degree of uniformity in its policies and procedures despite the centrifugal effects that might be expected to result from that organization's vast terrain. Almost 60 years later, however, in an age when security forces (or other organizations) can track and indeed assassinate individuals in remote places with often unnerving accuracy by drones controlled from computers on the other side of the planet (Gusterson 2016), many field workers can now be continually followed and communicated with in ways that could scarcely have been dreamt of in 1960. And beyond that classic 'field agent' relationship within bureaucracies, caseworkers of many kinds across public services (from those who grade the quality of student examination papers to social workers risk-assessing vulnerable people) now do much of their work on-screen through online IT systems whose architecture both restricts their choices and monitors their performance. Such technological limitations on discretion are rather more redolent of the work of Michel Foucault and his forerunner Jeremy Bentham, with their emphasis on the efficacy of systems of disciplinary order that do not rely on 'ostentatious signs of sovereignty' (Ferguson 1984: 32).

This being so, there is at least one other factor that can account for limits on discretion in political and bureaucratic life, despite the apparent desirability of such discretion for many individuals as a means to power, freedom and self-actualization. That is because the pursuit or maintenance of discretion can in some times and places be seen as courting excessive risk of blame when the wrong choices or actions are chosen and, at that point, a contradictory logic of blame avoidance by shunning or limiting discretion can be expected to operate. It is that clash or trade-off between the contradictory desiderata of blame avoidance and the pursuit of discretion that this chapter aims to explore.

The idea of such a trade-off can be traced back a long way in that strain of writing about bureaucracy that stresses tendencies to defensiveness, detachment and risk aversion. For example, Sir Edwin Chadwick (1854: 190), an energetic advocate of reform in the mid-nineteenth-century British civil service, strongly condemned what he saw as the deleterious effects of the pursuit of safety in public office by individuals seeking to avoid individual responsibility and without any strong sense of mission.[1] In modern Western political science, the idea of such a trade-off has been notably expounded by Kent Weaver (1986, 1988) in his classic work on blame avoidance in the design of public policy. Weaver's theme has been echoed in the work of others using a similar perspective, such as Paul Pierson (1994) in his account of what constrained welfare state retrenchment in the United States and the UK in the 1980s, Richard Rose with various collaborators in stressing the politically defensive role played by inertia in tax policy and public policy more generally (Rose 1990; Rose and Karran 1987; Rose and Davies 1994) and the present author (Hood 2011) extending the argument to bureaucratic behaviour and structure as well as to policy (re)design.

The underlying idea in Weaver's (and Rose's) analysis is that legislators will tend to choose to forego discretion in circumstances where the expected blame risk from retaining or applying discretion outweighs what would otherwise be the attractions of exercising the power of autonomous choice. And Weaver argued that such circumstances increasingly applied to the United States in the 1980s (and he thought to some other Western countries too), with a strong negativity bias in electoral politics meaning that electoral credit-claiming possibilities from positive exercise of discretion were outweighed by the corresponding blame risks on the downside and that public policy in many domains consequently tended to be so tilted to blame avoidance that opportunities for political credit-claiming were often not taken up.

Perhaps the most familiar example of discretion being voluntarily restricted less because of technological change or some compelling overall logic of rational-legal modernization than because of the associated blame risk is the frequent phenomenon of elected politicians choosing a range of institutional devices to restrict or abandon discretion over the determination of their own salaries (a common 'blame magnet' for disgruntled voters). Frequently observed variants include efforts to link elected politicians' salaries to those of specified grades in the public service, the outsourcing of decisions over increases in politicians' pay or other benefits to independent pay commissions and ingenious decision rules such as the one adopted by Representative Vic Fazio in the US Congress in the 1980s, which incorporated a procedure by which increases in Congressional salaries were adopted automatically unless voted down by the House, giving members of Congress the opportunity to signal virtue and mollify their indignant constituents by voting against pay increases only after the formal deadline for opposition had passed (King and Peters 1994: 149–50).

A second well-known instance of 'discretion avoidance' by legislators is the much-discussed long-term decline in the proportion of so-called discretionary spending in the US federal budget (i.e. that part of federal spending that requires an annual appropriation bill to go through the Congress), as against mandatory spending (see Posner 2016: 6). The latter category of spending does not require annual appropriation bills and mostly consists of entitlement programmes such as social security and health benefits that are 'automatically' funded outside the annual budgeting process and the discrete log-rolling deals that were so much emphasized by the 'serial disjointed incrementalism' analysts of American budgetary and legislative behaviour in the 1960s (such as Wildavsky 1964; Lindblom 1965).

A third example is the much-discussed and widespread tendency in the 1980s and 1990s towards interest rate-setting by independent central banks (themselves often acting on the votes of 'independent' experts on rate-setting committees) rather than directly by governments or finance ministries (Blancheton 2016). For example, the first major act of nationalization by the UK's post-World War II Labour government in early 1946 was that of the Bank of England, on the grounds that effective economic management and avoidance of what were seen as the economic policy errors of the 1930s required the exercise of monetary policy by central banks to be under close day-to-day government control (Williamson 1984).[2] Half a century later, one of the first acts of Tony Blair's 'New Labour' government (elected in 1997 by a landslide of similar proportions to that of its 1945 predecessor) was to announce 'independence' for the Bank of England on precisely opposite grounds, namely that putting a measure of formal distance between the central bank and political leaders would be more likely to deliver better economic performance by insulating interest-rate-setting decisions from the cycle of electoral politics. The technical arguments for central bank independence have been much debated by scholars; the political pay-offs of (at least apparently) outsourcing discretion and consequent blame from elected officeholders over monetary policy decisions[3] less so.

However, there are at least two complications in the idea of an ineluctable trade-off between the risk of incurring blame and the ability to exercise discretion in politics and bureaucracy. One is that such a trade-off only seems to apply in some contexts or conditions and can break down at the point where officeholders come to face blame from voters or citizens if they fail to exercise discretion in conditions that seem to call for positive and direct choice rather than following automatic rules or outsourcing decisions to others. At this point, the decision to follow rules or obey orders may itself be seen as a potentially culpable act of discretion, on the 'not to act is to act' principle.

The other complication about the idea of a basic trade-off between blame risk and the exercise of discretion is that in at least some times and places it may be possible to 'have it all' by adopting forms of organization or behaviour that can *both* deliver a measure of discretion (of a kind, anyway) and, at the same time, serve as a bureaucratic or political blame shield. After all, one of the standard criticisms of central bank 'independence' in practice (just as applied to public corporations in the heyday of nationalized industries) is that it enables substantial behind-the-scenes political interference by governments to influence central bank decisions (e.g. through powers of appointment or reappointment of central bank governors or members of monetary policy committees), but enables those governments to avoid formal political accountability for such decisions. This chapter will discuss each of these complications in the following sections.

3.2 *Damned If You Do and Damned If You Don't*: When Failure to Exercise Discretion Is Itself Seen as a Culpable Act of Discretion

The idea of a blame/discretion trade-off can break down in those conditions where blame can come to attach to officeholders or organizations that fail to act with discretion and equally credit can go to those who seize or apply discretion even for apparently high-blame actions.

Examples at the high policy level are not hard to find. The biggest-ever electoral landslide in twentieth-century British history, in October 1931, was secured by an emergency coalition government, the three-party National Government headed by former Labour Prime Minister Ramsay MacDonald. That government was formed in August 1931 without an election, worked through a ten-member cabinet modelled on the War Cabinet of World War I, gave itself special powers to change primary legislation by Orders in Council (secondary legislation), while in the month before the election began to enact a major fiscal squeeze that would impact on a wide swathe of voters, including a sharp increase in the then social security tax coupled with emergency spending cuts. Those spending cuts included a ten-per cent cut in unemployment benefits in the middle of the deepest recession in the twentieth century and immediate pay cuts for all public sector workers, including the armed forces and police (see Hood and Himaz 2017: 61 and 66–7). A serious naval mutiny against those pay cuts in Scotland the month before the election spooked the financial markets to the extent that the defence of the currency exchange rate (the main justification given by the emergency government for applying the fiscal squeeze) became impossible and the pound had to be taken off the Gold Standard anyway. Contrary to the standard suite of modern political-science assumptions about voter behaviour (i.e. a tendency to retrospective voting focused on past track record rather than future promises, linked with a bias towards negativity and high salience of 'pocket book' preoccupations in shaping voters' choices), the incumbents who had chosen to impose such significant losses on the electorate were overwhelmingly rewarded rather than punished by the voters (though admittedly the fortunes of the different parties within the coalition were not the same).

Again, 70 years later, in 2001, during the worst episode in the twentieth century of foot-and-mouth cattle disease, a social and financial catastrophe that led to the compulsory slaughter by the armed forces of over ten million sheep and cows in the UK by measures whose legality was disputed, the incumbent

Prime Minister Tony Blair was re-elected by a landslide (in an election that had to be delayed for a month because of the disease). Blair's approach to handling the blame over the epidemic before the election at first involved handing over control of the epidemic to 'experts', including the government's Chief Scientist and a team of academic epidemiologists from Imperial College, but he then chose to go onto the opposite tack in blame management during the month before the election by assuming 'personal responsibility' for the measures to eradicate the disease.

Such cases show that in some (perhaps extraordinary) circumstances, major loss imposition through the exercise of discretion can attract credit as much as blame, if enough voters or citizens can be persuaded—as many seem to have been in the two cases mentioned above—that the alternatives to the painful actions the incumbents had enacted were worse. Indeed, a study of all the fiscal squeezes in the UK over a century showed that such squeezes were by no means always followed by electoral loss for incumbents (Hood and Himaz 2017), contrary to what retrospective voting theory might suggest. A similar conclusion was drawn from a cross-national comparative study of nine fiscal squeezes in different times and places (Hood, Heald and Himaz 2014).

Something similar can apply at lower levels of bureaucracy or public services as well. In extreme circumstances it can be failure to exercise discretion by abandoning standard operating rules or official styles, which itself comes to be seen as a culpable act of discretion and attracts blame. Probably the most famous—in a dark way, 'exemplary'—case is the 'only following orders' defence offered by Adolf Eichmann (SS-*Obersturmbahnführer* who was one of the chief organizers of the Holocaust under the Nazi regime in Germany during World War II) in his trial for war crimes in Jerusalem in 1961–1962. Such a defence can break down, as it did in that case, when simply following orders or guidelines rather than rejecting them as unconscionable is what comes to be seen as blameworthy (for the best-known but controversial interpretation of the Eichmann trial see Arendt 1963).

The same can happen when officeholders choose to act in a narrow official style rather than applying discretion to go beyond a 'see no evil' approach. That happened to the shortest-serving Director-General of the BBC, George Entwistle, whose resignation after only 54 days in his job in 2012 was triggered by a BBC documentary programme incorrectly implicating a senior Conservative politician in a major child sex abuse scandal (Entwistle claimed to have been unaware of the programme in question until after it had been broadcast). His resignation was also prompted by criticisms of his choice not to read emails from colleagues and to disregard unofficial hints and gossip about sexual abuse of children by one of the BBC's major stars, Sir Jimmy Savile, well before Entwistle took the allegations against Savile to the police in October 2012, subsequent to Savile's death in 2011 (Halliday 2012). Even, perhaps especially, at 'street bureaucrat' level, the same potential exists for blame to arise from failure to exercise discretion, as happens, for instance, when standard procedures for imposing parking penalty charges are (legally but insensitively) applied by parking police to emergency service vehicles or vehicles left stranded after a terror attack, as was reported to have happened in London after such an attack on London Bridge in June 2017 (Wiseman 2017). Robotic behaviour that aims to avoid conscious exercise of discretion is not always a successful way of avoiding blame and that raises a central question for the analysis in this edited collection as to whether 'discretion' is to be conceived as starting where 'rule application' ends or applies to human behaviour in the round, meaning that almost all behaviour involves 'discretion'.

3.3 *Having It All?* Combining Blame Avoidance and Discretion

The idea of a blame/discretion trade-off may also be problematic to the extent that officeholders can and often do adopt arrangements intended to deflect or at least diffuse blame without (completely) surrendering discretionary power. Indeed, decades of literature in public administration (e.g. on quangos, public corporations, statutory boards, regulators and similar 'arms-length' bodies) have much to say about institutional arrangements that at least on the surface seem to have the properties of 'having it all' and thus avoiding the discretion/blame trade-off, in that the political centre somehow contrives to surrender formal responsibility while continuing to exercise discretion by pulling the strings in the background. Here we will discuss three selected arrangements that all operate on the 'responsibility' aspect of blame, namely the pooling of discretion to share blame, the partial or apparent delegation of discretion in order to transfer or diffuse blame and the validation of discretion as another means of spreading or sharing blame.

Hanging Together: *Pooled Discretion*

One possible way to retain discretion in the sense of latitude for decision and action but at the same time to manage the associated blame is to pool the exercise of discretionary powers across multiple actors or organizations—a device that means spreading or sharing rather than completely avoiding blame. In this way a group of actors opt to 'hang together to avoid being hanged separately', in the well-known saying often said to have been uttered by Benjamin Franklin before signing the American Declaration of Independence.[4] At the higher political level, such pooling arrangements are institutionalized in the familiar arrangements for Cabinet decision-making in those parliamentary systems where individual ministers' votes in Cabinet (to the extent that formal votes are taken) are not officially disclosed. And perhaps the ultimate form of pooling at the higher political level is the phenomenon of all-party 'grand coalition' national governments in especially challenging political circumstances.

Analogous arrangements for spreading the blame by attempting to collectivize decision-making or responsibility can be found all down the institutional food chain. The utilitarian philosopher Jeremy Bentham famously made 'single-seatedness' as a route to individual accountability a central theme in all his various sets of 'principles' for maximizing efficacy and minimizing expense in public management (see, e.g., Hume 1981: 4, 46). He dismissed all collegial arrangements in public administration as 'screens' allowing individuals to dodge blame and shirk responsibility ('It is the nature of a board to serve as a screen from responsibility [...] a screen from [...] punishment or disrepute' (Bentham 1843, vol. 6: 558)). Even Bentham, however, had to make some exceptions to his single-seatedness principle (Hume 1981: 158), and although Germany and some other European countries replaced board-type arrangements with individual responsibility in a bureaucratic line of command of the kind favoured by Bentham in their nineteenth-century public administration reforms, board-type or other collective arrangements are still commonly found in public administration at all levels. One of the consequences of such arrangements is to collectivize responsibility and share blame for the exercise of discretion. Familiar everyday examples include letters and emails sent from 'teams' rather than named individuals and awarding or disciplinary bodies that normally only act collectively, such as boards of examiners and bodies like case committees in social work when they work in a similar way.

A notable case in point that shows bureaucratic collectivization in response to blame risk is the arrangement adopted by police in England to legislation in 1997 which required the police to keep a register of the names and addresses of convicted sex offenders released from custody who were living in each police district—and by that simple, apparently innocuous, requirement exposed police to significant risk of blame if such individuals reoffended without defensible arrangements for risk assessment and monitoring. The blame risk led police into joining forces with probation officers and municipal social housing bureaucrats in elaborate joint-decision arrangements to agree and record quantified risk classifications (relating to the estimated likelihood of reoffending) of sex offenders released from custody in their areas. The effect of these arrangements was to 'share blame and minimize the ability of organizations to blame one another after a tragedy for not passing on crucial information' (Hood, Rothstein and Baldwin 2001: 158). Indeed, this 'hang together' approach to managing blame extended to other organizations in the field, such as 'third sector' voluntary organizations. The collectivization process was linked to the development and adoption of formal checklists for risk assessment and management of ex-offenders, to act as a further blame shield.

However, the Benthamite view that collective arrangements can function as a 'blame shield' for their individual or organizational members assumes some degree of confidentiality that prevents the views or votes of individual members of such a collectivity from being publicly recorded, such that such people or entities can disown individual responsibility for any decisions that attract blame. Once such individualized records are kept and made public, the 'shield' of collectivity largely disappears and blame hangs on which group members spoke or voted in what way. We noted earlier the contrast between two UK Labour governments 50 years apart, one of which nationalized the Bank of England in

1946 and the other of which gave 'independence' to the Bank over the setting of interest rates in 1997, but there was at least one important intermediate step between those two events. Kenneth Clarke, Conservative Chancellor of the Exchequer (Finance Minister) from 1993 to 1997, recounted in his memoirs that

> [r]esponsibility for the sensitive subject of interest rates left me dangerously politically exposed and I rapidly made some changes. Norman Lamont [*Clarke's predecessor as Chancellor of the Exchequer*] had introduced monthly meetings for Treasury ministers and senior officials to discuss monetary policy with the governor and chief economist of the Bank. Without consulting anyone, I announced that the minutes of these meetings would henceforth be published (Clarke 2016: 323–4).

Clarke's move meant that the recorded advice of civil servants and the Governor of the Bank of England was publicly available for the first time, making it harder for those players to avoid sharing the blame over interest rate policy with the Chancellor. That collectivization arrangement was a half-way house on the way towards the complete outsourcing and individualization of blame for interest rate-setting by Clarke's Labour successor, Gordon Brown, in 1997, which finally resulted in an independent monetary policy committee to decide on interest rates through a procedure in which each individual member's vote was registered and published. So transparency—another of Jeremy Bentham's recurrent preoccupations and one of his key principles for good government—is crucial in determining the extent to which the group exercise of discretion will collectivize or individualize blame. In the case of the potentially blame-magnetic power to decide central bank interest rates, there is an important distinction between those interest-rate-setting central bank monetary committees where the votes of each member are separately published (which inevitably individualizes blame) and those where only the collective decision is made public.

Passing the Buck: *Semi-Delegated Discretion*

While pooled decision-making arrangements serve to share but not completely avoid blame, a related approach is one of fudged or plastic delegation of the exercise of discretion to disavowable agents. Such agents comprise the extensive and messy world of quagos, quangos, para-government bodies and all the other terms used in the public administration literature to denote the various advisory, adversary and policy delivery organizations that officially operate at some distance from ministers or the core of executive government and for which the latter can therefore try to disclaim at least some degree of responsibility. Well-known examples include the independent public corporation much favoured in the Progressive era and the early twentieth century, independent regulators of business of the type created in the United States in the late nineteenth century and (mostly in some watered-down form) by other countries in the later twentieth century, the marketing boards for food and agricultural produce that were so widely adopted in the middle years of the twentieth century in developed and developing countries, adversary bodies such as public auditors and ombudsmen, agencies with delegated functions operating at arms' length from government and all the many advisory and standard-setting bodies in different policy domains.

Each of these semi-state bodies tends to incorporate its own delicate form of blame-avoidance architecture and each of them commonly involves 'no man's land' areas where responsibility is unavoidably vague, disputed or shared as between the 'independent' and 'core' parts of public administration. This phenomenon of semi-delegated responsibility (and consequent blurring of boundaries for blame) is familiar in the business sector, for example, in the case of those airlines that formally contract out their baggage-handling operations to separate companies, meaning that disgruntled passengers with lost baggage find they are directed to vent their spleen elsewhere, whereas the airlines' advertisements often imply that they look after the whole 'travel experience'.

The same phenomenon is observable in public administration as well. For example, after the privatization of the former telecommunication monopoly in the UK in the mid-1980s, the 'independent' regulator of telecommunications (then called Oftel or the Office of Telecommunications) was dependent on a government department, the then Department of Trade and Industry, for many of its staff (and at first for the exercise of all its personnel functions). Some of the key regulatory powers in telecommunications at that time, such as the issuance of licences and official representation of the UK in international telecommunications bodies, rested with the department rather than Oftel. Only those steeped both in the small print of the 1984 Telecommunications Act and in the details of bureaucratic practice could possibly know who exactly was responsible for exercising what kind of discretion (Hall, Scott and Hood 2000).

In addition to that familiar and extensive institutional terrain are 'quangos' in the original sense of the word, as coined by Alan Pifer (1967), President of the Carnegie Corporation of New York, over 50 years ago to denote quasi-*non*-governmental organizations, meaning organizations that seem to be private firms, non-profit organizations or voluntary bodies but are in fact funded and/or created by government. (In common parlance, however, the term 'quango' soon came to be used as a synonym for arms-length public bodies in general, completely obscuring the distinction Pifer originally intended to draw by coining the term.)

In military operations, espionage and international relations more generally, 'unacknowledgeable means' have a long history because of their convenient deniability when it comes to actions that may prove to be violations of international law or to be potential sources of diplomatic incidents. A case in point is the apparently private aircraft, said to be registered to dummy American corporations, used for 'extraordinary rendition' flights in the extra-judicial movement of prisoners to other countries for 'interrogation', as applied by the US government to suspected Al-Qaeda militants after the 9/11 attacks on the United States in 2001 (Mayer 2005). The point Pifer was making in the 1960s, however, was that somewhat similar institutional arrangements were to be found in the sphere of domestic politics and government in the United States at that time. This was the case, for example, in the form of the ostensibly voluntary community bodies brought into existence by the federal Office of Economic Opportunity in the 'War against Poverty' programme under the presidency of Lyndon Johnson in the 1960s (Moynihan 1969).

Bodies that had the same characteristics of being apparently private or independent but in practice acting as an instrument of government were not far to seek in other countries too, as in the classic case of the Irish Hospitals Sweepstake, a body created in the 1920s to help fund the nascent healthcare system of the newly independent Irish Free State. It was constituted as an ostensibly private company separate from the government to avoid diplomatic incidents because much of its ticket revenue came from sales in other countries where lotteries were illegal at that time (Hood and Mackenzie 1975: 417). And since Pifer made his observations half a century ago, the privatization of utilities in the UK and some other countries has made more common that kind of quasi-non-government organization that takes the form of national state owned enterprises (SOEs) operating in other countries in the guise of 'private' operators or contractors (e.g. running rail services or building and operating nuclear power plants).

Securing Approval: *Validated Discretion*

A third possible variant of 'having it all' in combining discretion with blame avoidance is by the use of external (or semi-external) validation in the form of endorsement or approval of the way discretion is used by outside authority of one kind or another, which can then be used as a partial blame shield.

Over two decades ago, Michael Power (1994; see also Power 1997) pointed to the development of what he termed an 'audit explosion' in the UK, a country that he saw as developing into an 'audit society'. The audit explosion Power claimed to be developing was manifested in the spread of arrangements for external or semi-external validation of a range of systems and policies operated by public and private organizations and loosely modelled on financial audit (for a study that aimed to chart the growth of arms-length regulation of public sector bodies in the UK at that time, see Hood, Scott, James, Jones, and Travers (1999)). Power saw this development of 'rituals of verification' as part of an ultimately fruitless search for what he termed 'assurance' of soundness and good conduct. The 'audit society' phenomenon Power pointed to can also be interpreted from a blame-management perspective as a set of devices to avoid or limit blame by scrutiny and reports from external assessors that validate the conduct of organizations as meeting 'best practice' standards not only in their financial affairs but also in other policies and practices. How far Power's vision of the audit society represented excessive 'conceptual stretching' of the concept of audit and how far the developments he pointed to at that time were specific to the UK or more widespread are matters of scholarly debate. However, the point here is simply that such arrangements offer a way of validating discretion and thus some protection from blame.

External validation as a blame shield for the exercise of discretion can come in forms that are not closely based on the 'audit' model. A case in point relates to the validation of official economic forecasting, an activity that unavoidably involves the exercise of judgement and is notoriously error-prone and therefore blame-attracting. In the early 1990s the then UK Conservative government was under heavy political fire over its conduct of economic policy, including the production of official forecasts of recovery from recession that proved to be embarrassingly optimistic or premature. In an effort to spread or limit the blame, the then Chancellor of the Exchequer (Norman Lamont) created a panel of independent economic forecasters, announced with a flourish in 1992 and operating from 1993 to 1997 (Budd 1999). This panel comprised experts (originally seven) chosen from across the whole wide spectrum of opinion in economics, ranging from ultra-Keynesians to those espousing the strictest variant of monetarism and from those associated with the political left to those firmly on the right. The seven experts were tasked with providing and publishing individual economic forecasts three times (later twice) a year. Given their composition it was inevitable that their forecasts and views would be so divergent that any forecast from the official Treasury could be shown to be well within the range of what those independent experts foresaw.

After 1997 (with the election of Tony Blair's New Labour government and the granting of 'independence' to the Bank of England, as noted earlier) the Panel of Independent Forecasters was abandoned and replaced by a different approach to validation more in line with Power's 'audit society' model. The main public audit body, the National Audit Office (NAO), was tasked with 'auditing' the UK Treasury's official economic forecasts (which were crucial to the Labour government's claim to economic competence) and thus provided the government with the political defence that its economic and financial forecasts had been independently audited. When it came down to the small print of the arrangements (always crucial for the analysis of blame avoidance), what the public audit body was being asked to do was to validate the 'reasonableness' of the assumptions underlying the official forecasts. Many of those in the National Audit Office had no enthusiasm for picking up this political hot potato, not least because the institution had no real expertise in economic forecasting.[5] Moreover, as with the Panel of Independent Forecasters that preceded the 'audit validation', the very wide range of views within the economics profession about how the economy works and what might be plausible future scenarios for economic performance, it was all but impossible for the public auditor to brand any official assumption as patently 'unreasonable'.

After a decade of operation, this validation system lost much of its political 'blame shield' utility in the (largely un-forecasted) international financial crash of 2008 and subsequent deep recession, but in that case it was not just economic forecasting within government that was discredited, but the economic forecasting community more broadly. The NAO validation system continued to exist in some sort of limbo for two more years, until 2010, when after another change of government, the next move within the UK was to follow a tendency adopted by some other OECD (Organisation for Economic Co-operation and Development) countries to offload the task (and associated blame risks) of economic forecasting and assessment of the state of the public finances to separate non-partisan 'Fiscal Councils' (OECD 2010). In the UK case that involved creating the reassuringly titled Office of Budget Responsibility, an organization that described itself as a 'watchdog' but was constituted as an executive non-departmental public body sponsored by the Treasury. Therefore its remit and staffing was under the control of the executive rather than the legislature (Kaffash 2010).

A further form of validation of the exercise of discretion comes in the form of independent or semi-independent enquiries or reviews, another set of institutional devices on which there is a substantial public administration literature and which are often said in political folklore to be devices for at least postponing blame because of their potential to move the issues they are dealing with 'into the long grass' (but see Sulitzeanu-Kenan 2007 for a more sceptical view of the 'long grass' effect of enquiries). Such enquiries or reviews can in some cases also serve to dissipate blame for the way discretion is exercised as a result of the remit they are given and the way they are structured. There is a rich literature on the way such issues can shape blame (for instance, Rhodes 1975; Prasser 1985; Resodihardjo 2009). For example, in the case of the UK government's contentious handling of the serious 2001 foot-and-mouth epidemic, as mentioned earlier, the post hoc review took the form of no less than three separate underlapping enquiries, one into the future of British farming, one into the government's management of the crisis and one into the future handling of animal diseases in general (the latter led by the Royal Society, the UK's premier science academy, several of whose members had been leading players in the handling of the crisis, for example, in the adoption of a much-criticized 'contiguous cull' policy to kill millions of uninfected animals). Many of the politically awkward questions about the handling of the crisis were liable to fall into the cracks between this apparent plethora of enquiries. In some conditions, then, blame avoidance can go along with the exercise of discretion, at the least when independent or semi-independent enquiries are delayed, inconclusive or diverted away from key issues.

3.4 Some Concluding Comments

The three types of 'half-way house' between discretion and blame avoidance that have been discussed here are certainly not intended as a complete inventory of types of blame avoidance. They broadly constitute what in earlier work I have termed 'agency' and 'policy' approaches to blame avoidance (Hood 2011). They all operate on the responsibility part of the 'blame equation' (who knew or did what when)—leaving aside all the artistry of political or corporate spin and presentational approaches that operate on the 'perceived loss or harm' part of that equation (how much suffering or damage was incurred). Even then, the trio of types discussed here excludes some important forms of response affecting the use of discretion, such as complete withdrawal from provision of some kinds of blame-magnetic services (such as the provision of advice) or major switches of policy instruments (as with the United States' move from its post-9/11 policy of capturing suspected Al-Qaeda insurgents and moving them to other countries for interrogation, as mentioned earlier, to greater emphasis on targeted killings of such individuals by drone strikes (Gusterson 2016: 159)). The aim of these examples is simply to demonstrate that the exercise of discretion can be combined with significant blame-avoidance activity at least in some circumstances. Three points can therefore tentatively be made in conclusion.

First, the discussion above indicates that the idea that there is an ineluctable trade-off between the avoidance of blame and the exercise of discretion, while undoubtedly powerful as an analytical starting point, seems to have at least two kinds of limits. One is that the political (or micro-political) process may produce circumstances in which officeholders, governments or other organizations face blame risk for *not* exercising discretion (in the ordinary sense) in some way, by inaction such as following rules that can be seen as inappropriate for the situation in hand or by relying on others (experts or other delegates) for the exercise of discretion. The other limit to the trade-off idea is that the exercise of discretion can in some circumstances be combined with institutional arrangements calculated to share or shift the associated blame, for example, by collective decision-making. While this chapter has not directly looked at blame-avoidance *outcomes*, the examples given earlier suggest that there is at least some circumstantial evidence for the proposition that blame-avoidance outcomes as well as activity can sometimes be combined with exercise of discretion. However, systematic empirical validation or qualification of these propositions is certainly needed.

Second, however, each of the potentially 'have it all' approaches to mixing discretion and blame avoidance that have been discussed here seems likely to be unstable, as many of the examples given earlier show. Indeed, the likely instability of 'quangos' in the original sense was stressed by Alan Pifer (1967) in his original discussion of that phenomenon, as discussed earlier. Again, this proposition needs systematic empirical enquiry, but there are several likely sources of instability. One is the imperative to keep bureaucratic plates spinning so that critics can always be rebuffed with the standard claim that any culpable failings have been overcome by later restructuring or reorganization. A related source is the tendency for such arrangements to wear out with use and familiarity. Yet another is the vulnerability of any hybrid to collapse under contradictory pressures and the fact—noted in some of the 1980s literature on delegation as a route to blame avoidance (e.g. Fiorina 1982, 1986)—that the blame-deflecting effects of delegation arrangements are often only sufficient to muddy the waters during relatively short 'blame firestorms' (before the issue-attention cycle in public opinion moves on to some other issue) rather than to withstand continuous pounding over a long period.

Third and relatedly, it seems possible that periods of severe or sustained crisis are likely to be points at which the trade-off between blame avoidance and the exercise of discretion that was posited at the outset of this chapter are particularly likely to break down. The apparently 'anomalous' examples given earlier all came from situations in which one issue had become all-dominant (coping with a terror attack, a major epidemic or a natural disaster, dealing with dire economic or fiscal crisis, as in the example of the UK 1931 general election). And those seem to be cases in which the various approaches that may keep blame at bay for long enough in circumstances where public and political attention is more labile (shifting from one issue to another) will fail to produce the desired blame-avoidance outcome.

Notes

1. Chadwick (1854: 190) saw too many public officeholders as following the fatalistic maxim: '*Fungi officio taliter qualiter; numquam male loqui de superioribus; sinere insanum mundum vadere quo vult* [...]' ('Perform your duties tolerably, or so-so; never speak ill of superiors; allow the mad world to go where it wants [...]').
2. However, the organization continued to be funded up to the early 1980s by interest on deposits placed with it by private banks and is said to have continued to enjoy a degree of independence from the government in its regulatory capacity (Reid 1988: 205–6).
3. And those monetary decisions may themselves be framed or indeed pre-empted by the fiscal decisions or non-decisions made by elected politicians.
4. Franklin's utterance of this famous dictum is disputed by historians and the saying is anyway traceable to much earlier sources.
5. Nevertheless the NAO chose to accept this role, and indeed in 2006 also accepted another role that might be interpreted as having 'blame shield' characteristics, namely that of 'sleaze czar' (as the role was dubbed) or, more precisely, independent adviser on ministerial conflicts of interest (Hencke 2006).

References

Arendt, H. (1963). *Eichmann in Jerusalem: A report on the banality of evil*. New York: Penguin.

Bentham, J. (1843). *The works of Jeremy Bentham* (published under the superintendence of his executor, John Bowring, Vol. 6). Edinburgh: William Tait.

Blancheton, B. (2016). Central Bank independence in a historical perspective: Myth, lessons and a new model. *Economic Modelling*, 52(Part A), 101–107.

Budd, A. (1999). Learning from the wise people. *The Manchester School*, supplement 1999 1463–6786, 36–48.

Chadwick, E. (1854). *Papers relating to the reorganization of the civil service*. London: HMSO.

Clarke, K. (2016). *Kind of blue: A political memoir*. London: Pan Macmillan.
Crozier, M. (1964). *The bureaucratic phenomenon*. Chicago: Chicago University Press.
Dunleavy, P.J. (1991). *Democracy, bureaucracy and public choice: Economic explanations in Political Science*. New York: Harvester-Wheatsheaf.
Ferguson, K.E. (1984). *The feminist case against bureaucracy*. Philadelphia: Temple University Press.
Fiorina, M. (1982). Legislative choice of regulatory reform: Legal process or administrative process? *Public Choice*, 39(1), 33–66.
Fiorina, M. (1986). Legislator uncertainty, legislator control and the delegation of legislative power. *Journal of Law, Economics and Organization*, 2(1), 133–151.
Gusterson, H. (2016). *Drone: Remote control warfare*. Cambridge, MA: MIT Press.
Hall, C., Scott, C. & Hood, C. (2000). *Telecommunications regulation: Culture, chaos and interdependence inside the regulatory process*. London: Routledge.
Halliday, J. (2012, 19 December). Pollard Report: George Entwistle 'did not read emails' about Jimmy Savile. *The Guardian*. Retrieved July, 2017, from https://www.theguardian.com/media/2012/dec/19/pollard-report-george-entwistle-jimmy-savile.
Hencke, D. (2006, 24 March). Blair names audit chief as anti-sleaze adviser. *The Guardian*. Retrieved August, 2017, from https://www.theguardian.com/politics/2006/mar/24/uk.labour.
Hood, C. (2011). *The blame game: Spin, bureaucracy and self-preservation in government*. Princeton, NJ: Princeton University Press.
Hood, C. & Himaz, R. (2017). *A century of fiscal squeeze politics: A hundred years of austerity, politics and bureaucracy in Britain*. Oxford: Oxford University Press.
Hood, C. & Mackenzie, W. (1975). Appendix III: The problem of classifying institutions. In D. Hague, W. Mackenzie & A. Barker (Eds), *Public policy and private interests: The institutions of compromise* (pp. 409–423). London: Macmillan.
Hood, C., Scott, C., James, O., Jones, G.W. & Travers, T. (1999). *Regulation inside government: Waste-watchers, quality police and sleaze-busters*. Oxford: Oxford University Press.
Hood, C., Rothstein, H. & Baldwin, R. (2001). *The government of risk: Understanding risk regulation regimes*. Oxford: Oxford University Press.
Hood, C., Heald, D. & Himaz, R. (Eds) (2014). *When the party's over: The politics of fiscal squeeze in perspective*. Oxford: Oxford University Press for the British Academy.
Hume, L.J. (1981). *Bentham and bureaucracy*. Cambridge: Cambridge University Press.
Kaffash, J. (2010, 17 May). Mixed reaction to Office of Budget responsibility. *Public Finance*. Retrieved August, 2017, from http://www.publicfinance.co.uk/news/2010/05/mixed-reaction-office-budget-responsibility.
Kaufman, H. (1960). *The forest ranger: A study of administrative behaviour*. Baltimore, MD: Johns Hopkins University Press.
King, D. & Peters, B.G. (1994). The United States. Ch 9 in C. Hood, C. & B.G. Peters (Eds), *Rewards at the top: A comparative study of high public office* (pp. 146–165). London: Sage.
Lindblom, C. (1965). *The intelligence of democracy: Decision-making through mutual adjustment*. New York: Free Press.
Lipsky, M. (1980). *Street-level bureaucracy. Dilemmas of the individual in public service*. New York: Russell Sage Foundation.
Mayer, J. (2005). Outsourcing torture. *New Yorker*. Magazine, February 2005.

Meier, K.J. & Rutherford, A. (2017). *The politics of African-American education: Representation, partisanship and educational equity.* Cambridge: Cambridge University Press.
Moynihan, D.P. (1969). *Maximum feasible misunderstanding: Community action in the war on poverty.* New York: Collier Macmillan.
OECD (2010). *Making reform happen: Lessons from OECD countries.* Paris: OECD.
Pierson, P. (1994). *Dismantling the welfare state: Reagan, Thatcher and the politics of retrenchment.* Cambridge: Cambridge University Press.
Pifer, A. (1967). *The quasi nongovernmental organization* (Reprinted from the 1967 Annual report of the Carnegie Corporation). New York: Carnegie Corporation of New York.
Posner, P. (2016). *Portfolio budgeting: A new strategy for budgeting.* Statement for hearing before the Committee on the Budget, US Senate. Retrieved August, 2017, from https://www.budget.senate.gov/imo/media/doc/senate-budget-test-april%2D%2D%2D%2Dfinal-Posner.pdf.
Power, M. (1994). *The audit explosion.* London: Demos.
Power, M. (1997). *The audit society: Rituals of verification.* Oxford: Oxford University Press.
Prasser, S. (1985). Public inquiries in Australia: An overview. *Australian Journal of Public Administration*, XL(1), 1–15.
Reid, M. (1988). *All-change at the City.* London: Macmillan.
Resodihardjo, S. (2009). *Crisis and change in British and Dutch prison services: Understanding crisis-Reform processes.* Burlington, VT: Ashgate.
Rhodes, G. (1975). *Committees of inquiry.* London: George Allen and Unwin.
Rose, R. (1990). Inheritance before choice in public policy. *Journal of Theoretical Politics*, 2(3), 263–291.
Rose, R. & Davies, P. (1994). *Inheritance in public policy: Change without choice in Britain.* New Haven: Yale University Press.
Rose, R. & Karran, T. (1987). *Taxation by political inertia.* London: Allen and Unwin.
Silberman, B.S. (1993). *Cages of reason: The rise of the rational state in France, Japan, the United States and Great Britain.* Chicago: Chicago University Press.
Sulitzeanu-Kenan, R. (2007). Scything the grass: Agenda setting consequences of appointing public inquiries in the UK. A longitudinal analysis. *Policy and Politics*, 35(4), 629–650.
Weaver, K. (1986). The politics of blame avoidance. *Journal of Public Policy*, 6(4), 371–398.
Weaver, R.K. (1988). *Automatic government: The politics of indexation.* Washington, DC: Brookings.
Wildavsky, A. (1964). *The politics of the budgetary process.* Boston: Little, Brown.
Williamson, P. (1984). 'A Bankers' Ramp'? Financiers and the British political crisis of August 1931. *English Historical Review*, 99(393), 770–806.
Wiseman, E. (2017, 8 June). 'Disgusting': Outrage as parking wardens issue £130 fines to cars caught up in London Bridge attack. *The Telegraph.* Retrieved July, 2017, from http://www.telegraph.co.uk/cars/news/traffic-wardens-issue-terror-tickets-motorists-whose-cars-stranded/.

CHAPTER 4

Discretion in the Surveillance State

Mark Hardy

4.1 Introduction

Practitioner discretion is a corollary of uncertainty across 'the social state' and the means via which professionals exercise both function and authority. But what happens to this discretion as knowledge and understanding increase and uncertainty declines? Changes in the extent and capabilities of surveillance technologies hold significant potential (as well as possible pitfalls) to enhance the accuracy and effectiveness of professional practitioner judgements and decision making. In this chapter I will review debates regarding the role of practitioner discretion across the contested arena of the social state by examining the ways in which technological change has enabled the development and deployment of surveillance as a strategy of government.

My central argument is that the use of surveillance by broadly defined state actors to generate data, information, evidence or knowledge pertaining to 'social' questions and problems is hampered by inherent epistemological issues when applied to the judgements and decisions of practitioners. In theory, at least, knowledge generated via surveillance enhances the ability of state actors, including professional practitioners, to make the 'right' decision, by strengthening the robustness of the knowledge on which such judgements are made, thus promoting security in its broadest sense. Technological changes, however, are occurring in a context in which the decisions we all make are subject to intense scrutiny and critique, while concerns regarding harm, risk and security have become conflated; so their character reflects these concerns. I draw on the notion of biopolitics to help make sense of how shifts in the means and extent

M. Hardy (✉)
Department of Social Policy and Social Work, University of York, York, UK
e-mail: mark.hardy@york.ac.uk

T. Evans, P. Hupe (eds.), *Discretion and the Quest for Controlled Freedom*, https://doi.org/10.1007/978-3-030-19566-3_4

of surveillance are impacting on practitioner discretion, situating current concerns within enduring debates regarding the proper role and limits of the state. As an analytical frame, this enables us to trace shifts in state practices and the knowledge which underpins them, as well as the practical and political value attached to professional expertise. The fulcrum for such discussions is the notion of risk, a concept in danger of overuse but nevertheless helpful in thinking through the ways in which knowledge and power intersect in the discretionary spaces where health, justice and welfare professionals navigate the intersections between certainty and uncertainty as they endeavour to make the 'right' decision.

In this chapter I use the catch-all term 'the social state' to refer to the related rationalities, activities and practices of workers employed to contribute to the achievement of the social goals of the state. I include in this classification diverse activities such as health care, social work, criminal justice and welfare, which collectively comprise 'a *particular sector* in which very diverse problems are categorized as needed, special cases, specific institutions, a category of qualified personnel' (Deleuze 2007: 113). Like all such configurations, this is an imprecise term which does not do justice to the complexity of each different specialism, nor to the effects of changing contexts on the contours of practice within this 'hybrid domain' (Deleuze 2007: 114). The arguments in this chapter therefore have three caveats.

Firstly, I do not dwell on recent and ongoing transformations in the organization and funding of the domains which comprise the social state—marketization, contracting-out, public-private partnerships, privatization—each of which problematizes both 'the state' and 'the social' (Donzelot 1979) as coherent entities. Indeed, the impact of these changes has been addressed at length elsewhere (e.g. Clarke 2004; Dardot and Laval 2013) with inconclusive results. Here, my position is that although significantly reconfigured, the notion of the social state still retains enough traction for us to engage in meaningful discussion of its activities.

Secondly and relatedly, the sheer diversity of professional roles, tasks, groupings and grades means that, of necessity, my focus is general rather than context specific. Clearly, it would not be possible to discuss the variable effects of shifts in mentalities, practices and techniques of government across such a wide plethora of roles and activities in one chapter. Thus I make no claims to comprehensiveness here and, in any case, the nature of the arguments I will be making lend themselves to a more general approach, despite the limitations which therefore accrue.

Finally, although occasionally I refer to occurrences from further afield, in the main my focus is restricted to UK developments; so readers are advised to think critically in assessing relevance to other contexts and jurisdictions.

4.2 Discretion

The cases for and against practitioner discretion as a defining trait of professionalism in all its variants have been well rehearsed (e.g. Abbott 1988; Evans 2010; Cribb and Gewirtz 2015; Hupe, Hill and Buffat Eds 2015). On one hand, the status and legitimacy of professionalism derive from knowledge and expertise gained through education, experience and authority. On the other, problems stem from the lack of accountability that accrues by virtue of the power and status of expertise, which protect professionalism from challenge and leave its subjects open to inaccurate decision making or ineffective intervention. Traditionally, such discussions have been conducted in terms of the respective merits of clinical and administrative models of practice. The former attaches significance to lived experience, subjectivity and creative relational meaning making. The latter, by contrast, privileges objective processes, consistency and the use of formalized knowledge according to established protocols, often developed and implemented in a top-down fashion (Fook and Gardner 2007; see also Schön 1983). More recently, growing public and political awareness of the limitations inherent within the knowledge bases underpinning practice has undermined faith in professionalism, with a knock-on effect on the legitimacy of state actors more generally, especially given the positioning of many professionals within the state apparatus post 1945 and scepticism regarding the motives and competence of politics more generally. This is particularly the case with regard to those state activities which concern the welfare and security of the citizenry and the presumed role of the state to preserve and enhance these under the terms of the social contract (Beetham 1991). Thus, in the broad areas of welfare, health care, criminal justice and social care, for example, a notable lack of confidence in the ability of the state to achieve these aims has developed over the last few decades, in stark contrast to the confidence that previously underpinned commitment to the social state.

It seems to me that, at heart, concerns regarding the effectiveness of state intervention reflect growing awareness of the inherent epistemological limitations of the modernist project (O'Brien and Penna 1998). The decline in faith in the capacity of the state and its agents to ensure the security of the citizenry in its broadest sense has nevertheless provoked a response from both state and professions. In many ways developments in policy and practice across this arena over the last quarter-century represent efforts to restate the capacity of the state to fulfil modernist ambitions. Changing models of management, accountability and governance (Power 1997; Newman 2001); knowledge-based initiatives and concerted attempts to enhance the quality of both decisions and outcomes (Sackett, Rosenberg, Gray, Haynes and Richardson 1996; Munro 2011) are all part of an effort to reinvigorate state legitimacy (Garland 1996). The centrality of epistemological concerns is clear in the strategic emphasis placed on knowledge-based practices—including in understanding and addressing risk—within contemporary legitimation strategies.

Surveillance, Knowledge and Risk

Surveillance—watching, for the purposes of government, so as to further the aims of those in power—is a long-standing activity with origins that reflect deep-seated human needs for reassurance, stability and peace. MacNish (2018) suggests that although its origins preceded the emergence of formalized nation-states, surveillance has come to represent a fairly standard technique of government, utilized across a variety of domains of state activity. He references historical exemplars and techniques from the Old Testament, ancient Greece, imperial Rome and medieval Europe, including confession, the Inquisition and the panopticon, all of which contribute to 'the sustained monitoring of a person or people' (2018: 10), for 'the purposes of influencing or managing those whose data have been garnered' (Lyon 2001). In liberal democracies, however, the use of surveillance by state actors has gradually come to be associated by many with the pursuit of social order by government or control, whereby the state engages in 'managing, shaping, even creating its constituent population' (Pierson 2004: 44). Key here is the role of knowledge in Enlightenment thought and the entire modernist project it underpins.

Garland (2001) argues that the apparent decline in faith in the modernist ideal can be traced to a number of related developments. These include: research findings pointing to the ineffectiveness of intervention by state professionals to address either general social problems or the individual cases they are comprised of; developments in mass media, which ensure wider awareness of local failings, thus impacting on public (particularly middle class) confidence; and the impact of the sociological critique of coercive state power—'under the cover of kindness' (Margolis 1997: 3)—on the welfare ideal and the rise to prominence of neoliberal thinking, with its emphasis on individualism, autonomy and efficiency in the structures and institutions of the state from the mid-1970s onwards. These factors coalesced to impact politically and practically in what Rose (1996) influentially but controversially described as 'the death of the social'.

It is clear from this reading that the decline of the social has an epistemological root (Hardy 2016). High-profile service failures generally involve judgements and decisions by practitioners which, with the benefit of hindsight, are perceived to have been wrong—inaccurate, unjust, disempowering, ineffective—and contributed to someone suffering harm or the diminishment of well-being. Such failings are sometimes deemed indicative of individual practitioner incompetence, while on other occasions regarded as reflecting the inadequacy of the knowledge base underpinning practice, undermining faith in the generalized ability of professionals to practise effectively and thus fulfil the state's responsibility to protect its citizens (Butler and Drakeford 2003; Heyman, Shaw, Alaszewski and Titterton 2010; Dingwall and Hillier 2016).

Consequently, initiatives to counter this trend and strengthen the robustness of this knowledge base are twofold, sometimes focused on individualized practice, sometimes much wider. For example, the emphasis on evidence- or knowledge-based policy and practice across the social state, whatever its limitations (Evans and Hardy 2010), represents an attempt to ensure that practitioner decision making is based on 'objective evidence' rather than 'subjective opinion'.

Similarly, the rise to prominence of both risk thinking and associated risk assessment policies, protocols and practices seeks to enhance the scientific reliability of judgements pertaining to the harm that particular individuals may suffer or cause via the privileging and incorporation of actuarially generated data. Traditional skills and knowledge are downplayed here by a shift 'from the gaze to the objective accumulation of facts' (Castel 1991: 282), as practice is reconstituted as 'a *new mode of surveillance*: that of systematic predetection' (1991: 288). The relationship between practitioner and subject is less important because the subject has been supplanted and reconstructed from risk factors. Risks can be imputed from statistical correlations. Initiatives such as these have generated controversy, as a focus on risk is generally seen as undermining concerns regarding individual need and welfare; and an emphasis on robust scientific knowledge as countering holistic, intuitive professional expertise. At the same time, managerial initiatives have utilized the rubric of efficiency, effectiveness and accountability to tighten constraints on the ability of practitioners to exercise untrammelled professional discretion. These strategies have attracted sustained scrutiny and critique (see Hardy 2015 for an overview), as they entail the taking of 'strong positions' within the long-standing debate in the philosophy of knowledge regarding the respective merits of nomothetic versus idiographic knowledge and—in political philosophy—the ethics of state intervention, particularly the level of confidence we ought to have in professional judgement as a form of delegated authority.

Surveillance, Security and the State

Surveillance as a technique of government is utilized across a variety of domains of state activity, including national security, espionage and policing, as well as health, welfare and criminal justice. There are various ways in which surveillance might contribute to security. Surveillance is often thought of as conducted directly via the observation of actions and behaviours of individuals and/or groups which undermine security. This enables the use of power to inhibit these individuals and/or groups via preventative, inhibitory mechanisms, up to and including incapacitation. Additionally, the prospect of these measures—punishment, in effect—has a deterrent effect. However, surveillance also operates in a broader way by extending the idea of security to what Schuilenburg (2015) refers to as 'safe existence', whereby everyday low-level concerns with health and well-being are often accommodated and so a variety of practitioners and professions have historically been involved in the achievement of security, broadly defined.

More recently, technological developments over the last century, particularly radio, telecommunications and then the development of the internet, have altered the foci and methods of surveillance activities. In 2013, concerns regarding the extent of state monitoring of email and web traffic, reflecting ongoing changes in our standard means of communication, were highlighted by the US government employee Edward Snowden, whose disclosures confirmed that government authorities worldwide secretly harvest, store and mine communications data. To a significant extent, contemporary 'surveillance state' activities involve the monitoring of computers by computers and the stockpiling of information for possible further, deeper interrogation. For some, this revelation confirmed and heightened fears associated with the idea of an all-seeing, all-powerful state, a long-standing issue in political thought (Neocleous 2000). Significantly, however, for a large proportion of the populace it provoked little response, leading to concerns that as a collective, we are sleepwalking into a surveillance society, entailing the ubiquitous use of state surveillance capacities to further what Deleuze (1992) characterized as the 'control society'.

Against this background, surveillance-related activities and responsibilities fall upon contemporary practitioners, including the numerous and diverse sectors which characterize the outsourced, partially privatized social state. In health, welfare and criminal justice and related areas such as welfare benefits, pensions and housing, practitioners make decisions about their fellow citizens which are intended to achieve diverse objectives. At heart, however, health, welfare and justice are concerned with human security and, to this end, practitioners have established traditions of involvement in surveillance activities. Examples are numerous—trailing and observation of possible benefit fraud suspects, home visits in social work, the collation of patient records by General Practitioners, electronic monitoring of ex-offenders subject to supervision in the community, the use of CCTV evidence in criminal cases—such that surveillance represents a standard strategy in case work across the social state.

In pursuit of this end, in all of these settings, practitioners are required to make judgements which differentiate those who do from those who don't, those who can from those who can't, those who will from those who won't, with knowledge generated via surveillance as a potentially key source. It is in making these distinctions and judgements that practitioners exercise discretion (Evans and Harris 2004). Discretion takes various forms and has traditionally been recognized as an inherent and defining feature of professionalism, the mechanism via which autonomous decision making has effect. But practitioner discretion within the social state has come to be problematized, increasingly designated as the weak link in professional practice. As such, its exercise is subject to various strategies of oversight, constraint and regulation. The ideal which motivates these constraints is an approach to decision making in which knowledge undermines uncertainty by replacing the vagaries of individual subjectivity with the presumed certainties of generalized objectivity. Surveillance activities across the social state arguably represent a means of remedying the (partial, variable, imprecise) limits of knowledge (Lyon 2001). It is only via the elimination of uncertainty that risk can be effectively managed and thus security achieved—a logic which legitimates a plethora of state activities, including arguably illegal surveillance.

Like any strategy of government, surveillance has both strengths and limitations. At a general level, advocates of surveillance emphasize the need sometimes to access information that is otherwise unavailable to achieve protective or investigative ends. Traditionally, this has mainly been where rules, norms or laws are at stake and harm a potential outcome. More generally the inclusion of information generated via surveillance ensures that relevant details are taken into account in arriving at a judgement. It is important to stress that practitioner decisions often have an enabling or empowering potential and so data garnered via surveillance may contribute to actions which enhance well-being or diminish harm. Stoddart highlights 'surveillance as potentially an act of care' (2018: 57–8) and undoubtedly the quality of care within the social state is dependent on the extent, nature and quality of the knowledge base which underpins it (Glasby 2011; see also Holmboe, Lipner and Greiner 2008).

On the other hand, surveillance can be used as a means of enabling the state to better control the citizenry via disproportionate intervention, which undermines individual rights in the name of the greater good, the utilitarian ethos writ large and applied widely. It is this oppressive potential which critics tend to emphasize when they stress the potential for surveillance to violate codes of privacy and confidentiality, undermine consent and trust; and promote disproportionate or precipitative intervention. Although it varies by role and context, each of these possibilities is important in the social state, where practitioner education, training and experience tend to emphasize that efficacy is connected and in some cases dependent on positive, enduring relationships with service users. Additionally, despite claims of objectivity and accuracy, there is concern that surveillance activities contribute to social sorting (Lyon 2002) based on profiling techniques which highlight the experience of disadvantage and disempowerment as indicators of risk (Henman and Marston 2008). Categorization and classification—processes underpinning the exercise of discretion—are therefore necessary and have a constitutive effect. Knowledge, then, although often flagged as the remedy for ignorance, is nothing of the sort where surveillance activities are directed at 'the usual suspects'. The balance between privacy and security is evident here, easily articulated but difficult to achieve in practice.

Surveillance and Technology

Developments in surveillance clearly reflect technological change. Heidegger (1977) suggested that our inability to fully comprehend the implications of technological agency mean that we rarely foresee the extent to which, by our actions, we prohibit our own freedom until it is too late. Contemporary surveillance activities are dependent upon constantly expanding computing processing power to store and access information, investigate and identify patterns, divine correlations and undertake calculations according to mathematical formula embedded within the algorithms which characterize the tools used to analyse contemporary surveillance data (see also Chap. 20 of this handbook). The ability of computers to collect and collate data for the purpose of calculations (their *raison d'être*) has the spin-off effect of enabling mass surveillance of online activities, thus arguably rendering confession redundant, as our 'true selves' are revealed.

In the realm of the social state, the role of technology in accelerating changes in how knowledge informs professional practice is an important area of theoretical debate. For some, technological developments are the driver of social progress. For others, ostensibly progressive technological processes and calculations have sometimes detrimental social effects (Beer 2017). Thus surveillance has shifted from a human activity to one which is mediated via particular technology but has potent unforeseen consequences. Franko Aas (2005a) analysed the ways in which developments in information technology initially impacted on sentencing practice in criminal courts. Subsequently, this focus expanded to incorporate the role, content and function of changing forms of knowledge within decision making across domains and jurisdictions (Amoore 2013; see also Henman 2010; Hornqvist 2010). Parton (2008) suggests that these developments have impacted significantly on the nature and form of knowledge drawn upon, how this is represented and thus the perception of the nature and effects of practice. Practitioner decision making is positioned as an objective process based upon factual knowledge. Case formulations and risk assessments become 'artefact' phenomena which 'exist [s] in the formulae, theorems or assessments which construct them' (Parton 1996: 111). Certain presumptions underpin faith in the basis for and accuracy of calculation: firstly, that it is possible to predict *future* behaviour of individuals on the basis of *past* behaviour of populations, using statistical aggregates of 'risk factors'. Next, these judgements, regarding what is going on, what will happen and if and how best to intervene, are more likely to be accurate when based on *objective* rather than *subjective* knowledge—numbers 'act as technical mechanisms for making judgments' (Rose 1999: 198). Finally, outcomes will be improved if decision making draws on actuarial rather than clinical sources, based on formal rather than informal knowledge. Data and information are privileged ahead of relational understanding such that 'complex explanatory narratives tend to be compressed into shorter, instantly understandable messages' (Franko Aas 2005b: 152). Holism becomes redundant, as 'master categories [...] obscure any ambiguities' (Parton and Kirk 2010: 33). Individuals are 'reduced to end oriented practices that are configured by a form of political arithmetic' (Webb 2009: 223). Thus 'routine procedures of classification and categorization are readily translated into [...] proactive practices of security [...] to prevent the occurrence of dangers in the future' (Aradau, Lobo-Guerrero and van Munster 2008: 149).

Surveillance, then, accentuates the strategies associated with risk and security in the social state. Changing capabilities—innovations, if you like—enable new possibilities. Developments in technology emphasize both the potential and pitfalls of risk thinking more generally—the diminishment of traditional concerns with justice, proportionality, confidentiality and privacy, for example. With computing capabilities increasing exponentially, we have seen the ability of the state to harvest, store and analyse data expand massively. Where effective, the positive potential of surveillance will be maximized, as more accurate decision making and precise allocation enables health, well-being and security. In other cases, the concerns expressed regarding 'the rise of risk' (Garland 2003; Webb 2006) will be magnified. For example, information generated via surveillance is used to pre-emptively and sometimes inappropriately target preventative interventions against marginal populations (Garrett 2009; Schinkel 2011; Harcourt 2015).

Clearly, practical and ethical concerns flow from such developments. Simplistic dichotomies—clinical or actuarial, subjective or objective—arguably represent an unrealistic portrayal of the complex and ambiguous situations which practitioners in the social state are required to address. Despite claims to robustness and accuracy, are these formulations—artefacts of reality and predictions regarding the future—actually 'factual'? To what extent is it appropriate—fair, just—to characterize and make judgements about other people in the here and now using what they have done in the past as a guide to what they will do in the future? Amoore (2013) questions the basis for what she terms 'ontological associations' derived from patterns in data which bear little resemblance to 'breathing, sweating anxious and creative human beings struggling to find their way out of the darkness' (Bernstein 1998: 230). To what extent ought the exercise of power be connected to the quality and accuracy of the knowledge which underpins it or the expertise of those in positions to judge? Such questions are hardly novel. Rather, they reflect enduring issues in political philosophy regarding the basis on which authoritative figures exercise power.

4.3 Theorizing Surveillance

Surveillance, then, is best regarded as one strand within the wider epistemological strategy which underpins the operation of the social state. To fully understand the implications of its development, it is necessary to locate its use within a wider understanding of the relationship between forms of power and strategies of government, not least as these apply to the goal of achieving security. Here, the work of the philosopher Michel Foucault comes to the fore.

Biopower

Foucault's main analytical concern was the operation of power within society, a concern which manifested across various substantive objects of enquiry—medicine, madness, criminality, sexuality—each of which to a greater or lesser extent remains part of the evolving state's retinue of responsibilities. A principal concern in his work was how the subject is impacted and so constituted via both power and knowledge. Foucault's neat elision 'power/knowledge' emphasizes the intersection between practice and rationality and was central to his analysis of the establishment of the human sciences. Here, contingency enables the establishment of sites for the development of disciplinary knowledge and techniques (the clinic, asylum or prison), a more nuanced and reflexive account than those which privilege the progressive accumulation of objectively derived scientific facts (Dean 1994). Foucault tracked the evolution and operation of power within society over time—from a sovereign approach, then a more dispersed disciplinary model (to which surveillance was a key strategy) and to a biopolitical orientation.[1]

Although biopower remains conceptually fuzzy, nevertheless it represents a helpful way of thinking about the development and use of surveillance through the prism of power. It is best understood as a way of theorizing the use of power towards securing the health and well-being of both individuals and—significantly—the population as a whole via approaches which relied not on the direct application of power but, instead, more diffuse approaches to governing directed at human biological capacities. The traditional tendency for sovereign power to be used coercively and oppressively in a top-down fashion was supplemented (and to some extent replaced) by an approach which privileged the role of authority in fostering and promoting life (the 'bio' of biopolitics) through population-level initiatives, such as public hygiene and large-scale public health, as well as through attempts at moral training—'managing, controlling and optimising' (Villasden and Wahlberg 2015). Key here was surveillance as a technique for gathering knowledge which would enable the classification of groups within the social body on the basis of some clear population-level trait and thus as governable bodies within a territorial context (Elden 2007). Through ongoing collation of information, the 'nature' of the group could be better defined, understood and governed. Eventually, this understanding of group traits would enable security to be worked towards based upon forecasts and probabilities of risks, thus insuring against danger via insurance (O'Malley 2004). Strategies of government based on knowledge derived from demographic, medical and biological sources thus took on an explicitly social function. In an increasingly complex society, the sovereign operation of power, top-down and authority based, was recognized as ineffective in terms of accuracy and implementation, and so amended to incorporate alternative forms of knowledge and dispersed networks of power.

Foucault's work on biopolitics was subsumed within his later iteration of the functioning of power, governmentality (Dean 1999), but the concept has retained theoretical and analytical purchase amongst other theorists. It has attracted a lot of attention lately, partly due to posthumous publications (Foucault 2004, 2008) and is now regarded as an important element in a fully constituted appraisal of how power functions in society (Lemke 2011; Mills 2018). However, the Italian philosopher Agamben (1998) has been critical of Foucault's relegation of the sovereign model to the history books. He argues that biopolitics should not be conflated with modernity either as an historical epoch or as characteristically liberal approaches to government, as its concerns were evident prior to the latter's emergence and because core sovereign functions remain evident today. Here, Agamben highlights the significance of sovereign power in drawing the lines which authoritatively distinguish full, involved politically engaged living, from its marginal opposite, which he terms 'bare life': the life lived and experienced by those rejected and excluded from the wider community. In this analysis, the progressive, rights-based initiatives which characterize contemporary liberal Western democracy disguise the power of sovereign figures, most notably their inherent capacity to constitute and declare the parameters of an emergency and so initiate what he designates as a 'state of exception' (Agamben 2005), in which presumed distinctions regarding who and what are acceptable manifest via sovereign providence.

These core concepts—'bare life' and 'the state of exception'—have been explored and critiqued at length in social and political philosophy, as they clearly resonate and demonstrate theoretical utility in attempts to make sense of both historical and contemporary manifestations of the operation of power within society (Campbell and Sitze 2013; Cisney and Morar 2016). Indeed, it is evident that our understanding of recent shifts in the operation of state power, including the intersection of risk and security, might be enhanced via the application of these core concepts. We can see how contemporary attributions of high-risk status, for example, are dependent on the use of power by a figure with authority, through the exercise of judgement, to designate an individual as different from the norm. Such judgements have consequences, in terms of formal and informal restrictions on the ability to fully participate in social life. Although such designation may be legitimate, in the sense that it is applied by a practitioner with the necessary delegated authority, we can also see that the direction of travel with regard to state security activities increasingly slackens restrictions on the application of such designations, widens the domains within which their application has utility and uses claims to objectivity to disguise inherent subjectivity in decisions regarding risk status. The acceptance of the threat to individual rights that these changes signify is dependent on both overt and covert changes in what is deemed acceptable, legally and culturally, which in a meaningful sense draw upon and contribute to a risk-driven consensus that when it comes to security, the rules of the game have changed. Very easily, *a* 'state of exception' becomes *the* 'new normal'. With regard to surveillance practices in particular, we can see how taken-for-granted norms about privacy, trust and confidentiality are abandoned in the name of security: 'what counts now is no longer evidence [...] because "we know their true nature"' (Aradau *et al.* 2008: 152).

This theme has been expanded on by Esposito (2008), who developed the notion of the immunitary paradigm, whereby contemporary politics'—indeed, modernity more generally—emphasis on security is analogous to the biological model of disease in that the desire for secure community living is dependent on the exclusion of contaminatory elements. And for Aradau *et al.*: 'The specification of an enemy is the very condition of possibility for the deployment of security' (2008: 151). Surveillance, separation and segregation are thus significant strategies in the pursuit of the security on which community depends. Similarly, Jean-Luc Nancy emphasizes the extent to which biopolitics 'designates the order of a politics devoted to the managing and control of life' (2007: 15), a form of management dependent on technology. It seems that in seeking to secure life, biopolitics has a tendency to sacrifice the individual for the greater good, a decidedly utilitarian rationality seemingly at odds with the conventions associated with Western liberal society. Here there are parallels with the defence of sovereignty mounted by the political philosopher Carl Schmitt, who's illiberal 'political theology' (1934/2010) originated the notion of the sovereign exception and utilizes the distinction between 'friend' and 'enemy' as a criterion for decision making in the public realm (Lilla 2016). The right of the sovereign to make this distinction is the essence of politics, while all life is political. There is no place here for the codification of norms via the rational processes associated with liberal legal reasoning as protection against the inadequacies or abuses of state power (Bernstein 2013).

4.4 Contemporary Surveillance

As should be clear by now, surveillance has an established heritage as a strategy of government. There is clearly, then, no direct relationship between expressed anxieties regarding surveillance and the novelty of technology used. Additionally, historical analysis highlights that fears regarding surveillance have a track record of not coming to pass, at least in extreme, dystopian versions. Although long-established practices, surveillance implementation has been variable and partial, whether by accident or design. Notwithstanding revelations regarding the illegal monitoring of communications there is also a healthy and vigorous debate regarding the legal framework within which state surveillance is undertaken (Travis 2018). That said, however, very recent developments may well render this sanguine view redundant. Here, I am referring to the impact of 'big data'. There has been a growing awareness of late of the potential ways in which the large-scale collection, storage and analysis of data (data gathered in the main via electronic surveillance techniques) concerning individual behaviour, actions and views might lead to new and significant insights at both the general and specific levels. The hope is that big data predictive analytics—the use of constantly evolving algorithms to analyse correlations within and between very large, often disparate sets of data—will '"unlock" the blockages and limitations of disciplinary and biopolitical techniques of government' via 'the detection of previously unknown patterns and the discovery of surprising hidden knowledge' (Aradau and Blanke 2017: 374–5). 'Big data' represents the key that will unlock the potential of predictive analytics in improving the accuracy of judgements regarding the future which are made in the here and now—'near-time'—(McCue 2015) on the basis of what Amoore (2013) refers to as 'ontological associations'. Here, patterns revealed within data via algorithms are presumed 'real' and so the associations derived and the conclusions drawn from them are substantively accurate as a representation of reality. In the social state, such potentialities are only just beginning to manifest and be explored, but there is considerable optimism that by analysing the links between large, diverse data sets, various 'wicked' issues may prove resolvable (Cook 2014; Grimer 2015). The assumption is that the sheer quantity and diversity of available information, combined with ever-advancing processing power will enable insights previously hidden within the intersections between knowledge derived from multiple sources to be brought to the fore and integrated. These sources include both publicly available data but also that which is routinely gathered via surveillance techniques used in both the overt and covert monitoring of computers, digital devices, internet records, social media posts and commercially held data. Predictive data analytics promise that the future will be knowable, as the logic of risk is scaled up significantly. Optimistically, not only might such analysis enable more accurate judgements in both policy and practice, it could also subvert hierarchal relations of domination because it makes the basis of decision making more transparent, thus enabling ground-level challenges to the authority of unsubstantiated or oppressive decision making (Hannah-Moffat 2018).

Difficulties are also anticipated, however. The notion that we all have a 'data double' or 'digital doppelgänger' (Haggerty and Ericson 2000; Stephens-Davidowitz 2017) has provoked significant disquiet within which we can discern the inherent ambivalence which characterizes attitudes to surveillance in contemporary society. On one hand, enhanced technological developments—progress—potentially enable the 'better' achievement of collective goals: safety and security. On the other, the capability to 'know' more accurately and precisely provokes concerns about 'being' known. There is clearly a tension here, 'between knowing too much and not knowing enough' (MacNish 2018: 14), which at heart concerns issues of identity and freedom.

There are also less prosaic concerns. Whereas knowledge is traditionally the province of the research community, the collection of data by commercial operators raises issues regarding the ethical and methodological robustness of the knowledge claims made by actors with a financial stake in the circulation of the knowledge they generate. Additionally, there is little expectation that big data will transcend value-based bias. In fact, the non-academic basis of much predictive analysis makes both ethical and reflexive considerations less likely. As Hannah-Moffat (2018) points out, analysts are used to dealing with data, not people. Beer (2016, 2018), however, reminds us that such analysis has social impact. Thus predictive analysis has the less optimistic potential to replicate the inadequacies of risk-based decision making on a larger scale, with all that this entails in terms of solidifying deviant identities and accentuating risk aversion as a blame avoidance strategy (Hardy 2016; see also Hood 2011 and Chap. 3 of this handbook).

Discretion in the Contemporary Social State

As always, time will tell whether or not these dystopian scenarios come to pass. At the moment, the use of these technologies by practitioners of the social state remains limited. Social work organizations, for example, are still grappling with the issue of whether or not publicly available social media ought to be accessed by staff undertaking assessments of particular individuals or families, including children, with contradictory policy guidance within localities. The internet records of perpetrators of child sexual abuse—an important source of knowledge, one would presume, for practitioners undertaking risk assessments—are not accessible to staff. The capacity of records of GPS-enabled phones to be used to track individuals subject to restrictions on movement, perhaps due to domestic violence, has not been utilized other than in a reactive fashion. Computer systems to enable the accessibility and transferability of medical records routinely demonstrate via their failings the complexity of seemingly straightforward knowledge integration tasks. Elsewhere, technology has had a more sustained impact—the use of biometric technology by immigration officers monitoring asylum seekers is a helpful example, although not necessarily a helpful practice (Ajana 2013, 2015). Additionally, the 'Prevent' initiative asks that practitioners across the social state (including higher education) be proactively alert to signs of radicalization amongst young people, particularly Muslims (Thomas 2016; Stanley, Guru and Gupta 2018) via monitoring, surveillance and engagement. But (for whatever reason) wider roll-out remains relatively limited and much of the potential—whether good or ill—of such developments, although clearly technically realizable, remains hypothetical.

Even so, there are ways in which recent developments in surveillance technology have affected professional discretion in the social state. This is because the self-same technical capacities that enable the monitoring of the population *by* state actors can also be applied *to monitor* practitioners. The noted shift to 'knowledge work' (Ericson and Haggerty 1997) and the use of computer-aided assessment and decision support tools (Berg 1997), combined with a clear emphasis in managerial discourse on transparency and accountability, mean that it is possible to scrutinize the activities of practitioners in much more detail and depth than previously (see Chap. 20). Whereas Pithouse (1987) described social work as an 'invisible trade', the rapid and wide roll-out of information technology across the intervening decades for recording, assessment and communication activities means that social work—or large swathes of it, at least—has become highly visible. Indeed, there is significant evidence to suggest that apparent tendencies towards risk-averse decision making amongst social professionals owe something to the ways in which shifts to electronic information systems render practitioners potentially liable for 'mistakes' and blame in ways that their previous low visibility protected against. The ability of managers to check the activities of staff arguably accentuates anxieties regarding decision making, as scrutiny of processes and choices often does (Gillingham 2011, 2015). This is by no means clear-cut, as Evans (2010, 2011) reminds us, and there are—as always—notable exceptions. But it is a clear trend, with real effects (Webb 2006; Deering 2011; Hood 2011).

It is also the case that enhanced technological capabilities may affect the culture of practice within the agencies of the social state. Many of these agencies retain, for want of a better way of expressing it, a public sector ethos, which manifests in the sort of principled resilience identified and theorized by Lipsky (1980/2010) and Foucault (1982), respectively (see also Mawby and Worrall 2013). Zedner (2011) highlights the sometimes paradoxical effect that an emphasis on the goal of security can have upon institutional ethos. As security becomes explicitly ingrained as an organizational objective and one which it appears successful in achieving, culture shifts to accommodate this success.[2] Gros (2012) similarly argues that this tendency is accentuated where security is tainted by overtly political or financial considerations, which subvert its role in maintaining equilibrium and so foster 'catastrophe'. The logic of security merges with the logic of risk in ways that hinder the supposed goals of safety.[3]

Clearly, there is a risk here of replicating the pessimism that characterizes more critical, dystopian analysis. In reality, 'it is likely that big data technologies will function similar to other forms of risk prediction [...] in that they will be used for diverse and sometimes contradictory ends—with both meaningful and problematic outcomes' (Hannah-Moffat 2018: 14). Following O'Malley (2004), empirical reality challenges rhetorical discourse regarding the practical effects of risk thinking, which generally take the form of hybrid assemblages rather than catastrophic transformations. There is sometimes a tendency to reify untrammelled professional discretion unduly—whereby the 'dark side' to discretion—its role in facilitating injustice, unfairness or oppression—is side-stepped (Hardy 2016). Significantly, however, in the playing out of possibilities associated with the advance of the surveillant assemblage (Haggerty and Ericson 2000), certainty remains a distant goal. Various necessary steps—from data to information, from information to knowledge, from knowledge to meaning, from meaning to prediction, from prediction to action and from action to outcomes (adapted from Lorenz 2017)—require the subjective negotiation of complex and ambiguous terrain. As long as such epistemological uncertainty remains, discretion will prevail and practitioners of the social state will retain a significant 'frontline' role in determining how practice develops and is implemented—for better or worse.

4.5 Conclusion

Arguably, surveillance has always been an element of professional activity. As Foucault has demonstrated, the biopolitical impulse of government requires categorization via dividing practices, while both overt and covert means of gathering information and generating knowledge have played a critical role in these. Under the (unwritten) terms of the social contract, citizens sacrifice freedom in return for security. In order to provide that security, the state makes judgements regarding the threat levels that particular individuals and groups pose to others, themselves or collective well-being, as a basis for both proactive and reactive measures. The work of the social state has always entailed distinguishing between the deserving and the undeserving in one form or another, and in order to make this distinction, organizations and practitioners have engaged in the identification and accumulation of information, data and knowledge. Ongoing technological developments may change the means via which this occurs, but do little to alter the fundamental character or principles of surveillance. Practice does not occur in a vacuum, with changes in technology and society impacting on standard working routines. As things stand, we are only at the very early stages of exploring the impact of big data upon practitioner decision making and discretion. But although the social effects of technology are meaningful, practice appears resilient. That said, anxieties regarding contemporary technologies of surveillance do appear to be of a different nature and magnitude to those that surveillance has previously provoked, reflecting changes in *volume*, *velocity* and *variety* (Hannah-Moffat 2018). These technological innovations arguably enable effectiveness but in the process raise significant questions regarding the settlement which characterizes the relationship between citizen and state in liberal democracies. Enduring debates regarding liberty and security and freedom and justice take on a different character, given awareness of what the state is willing to do and may well—soon—have the capacity to achieve. Key technological developments—particularly the capacity to collate, mine and integrate information from email and internet—have the potential to accentuate and accelerate more general issues regarding the ways in which concerns regarding risk and security are impacting on the nature, form and function of practitioner discretion.

The epistemology of biopower is the predominant epistemology of modernity, and so although exploring discretion through such a lens is revealing, it is not obvious how it might enable either more effective or more ethical practice in the social state. But Foucault's own epistemology—that which is embedded within his parallel methodological strategies of archaeology and genealogy—is critical of modernity and thus of the ways of knowing associated with biopower. His work highlights the point that it is via claims to knowledge that power is secured and via access to power that claims to knowledge are validated and thus 'truth' constructed. His interrogation of biopower reminds us of the necessity for a critical sensibility regarding the contested authority of knowledge claims and of discretion. By emphasizing the contingency of power/knowledge we are reminded that claims-makers—including practitioners of the social state—utilize the technological character of assessment practice to disguise the contested nature of the substance of their judgements and decisions. Their true character—'best guesses' (Hardy 2016)—is rarely acknowledged, perhaps because their actual accuracy is so difficult to capture. 'Big data', which promises to utilize 'collective intelligence' to enhance the state's 'superior capacity to make judgments' (Mulgan 2018: 156), exemplifies and magnifies the thinking and methods associated with modernity, with little recognition of potential pitfalls. For example, its utilization might well undermine the ability of practitioners to develop and apply knowledge in practice and thus limit the cultivation and exercise of practical wisdom, the professional's traditional remedy for uncertainty.[4] For now, however, there remains considerable ambivalence regarding the potential 'price to be paid' in achieving security. How real such concerns are and how they might affect the nature and extent of discretion amongst decision makers within the continually and rapidly evolving roles and responsibilities of the social state remain—for now—unknowns.

Notes

1. It is important to appreciate that this was a descriptive rather than a normative undertaking and so Foucault is not expressing a preference here for a particular model of political organization.

2. Following this logic, sometimes it is failure that promotes institutional resilience.
3. There are echoes here of Beck's (1992) acknowledgement of the paradoxical roots of risk, namely that the safer we are, the more concerned we are that we might become unsafe. Evans explains, 'Danger is the hidden potential or the unknowable in that which is knowable. It cannot be known, otherwise it would be a calculable problem that could be overcome—hence no danger' (2013: 28). Here, we can see the links between biopolitics and thanatopolitics, a scaling-up of the death impulse that so fascinated Foucault (Eribon 1991) and via which death—killing at the behest of sovereign power—becomes the ultimate guarantor of life. The power over life which characterizes Agamben's state of exception is also the power of death (Murray 2006; Vatter 2011). In this way, the modernist dream becomes a potential nightmare.
4. The same logic underpins concerns that the advent of self-driving cars may mean that passengers will not develop the necessary evasive driving skills to navigate potentially dangerous situations. The assumption is that there will be far fewer accidents, but inevitably, dangerous situations will nevertheless arise. Where accidents are imminent is seems unlikely that a passenger who has never driven before will be able to avoid these.

References

Abbott, A. (1988). *The system of professions: An essay on the division of expert labor*. Chicago: University of Chicago Press.

Agamben, G. (1998). *Homo sacer: Sovereign power and bare life*. Stanford, CA: Stanford University Press.

Agamben, G. (2005). *State of exception*. Chicago: University of Chicago Press.

Ajana, B. (2013). *Governing through biometrics: The biopolitics of identity*. Basingstoke: Palgrave Macmillan.

Ajana, B. (2015). Augmented borders: Big data and the ethics of immigration control. *Journal of Information, Communication and Ethics in Society*, 13(1), 58–78.

Amoore, L. (2013). *The politics of possibility: Risk and security beyond probability*. Durham: Duke University Press.

Aradau, C. & Blanke, T. (2017). Politics of prediction: Security and the time/space of governmentality in the age of big data. *European Journal of Social Theory*, 20(3), 373–391.

Aradau, C., Lobo-Guerrero, L. & van Munster, R. (2008). Security, technologies of risk and the political: Guest editors' introduction. *Security Dialogue*, 39(2–3), 147–154.

Beck, U. (1992). *Risk society: Towards a new modernity*. London: Sage.

Beer, D. (2016). *Metric power*. Basingstoke: Palgrave Macmillan.

Beer, D. (2017). The social power of algorithms. *Information, Communication and Society*, 20(1), 1–13.

Beer, D. (2018). Envisioning the power of data analytics. *Information, Communication and Society*, 21(3), 465–479.

Beetham, D. (1991). *The legitimation of power*. Basingstoke: Macmillan.

Berg, M. (1997). *Rationalising medical work: Decision support techniques and medical practices*. Cambridge: MIT Press.

Bernstein, P. (1998). *Against the gods: The remarkable story of risk*. London: John Wiley.
Bernstein, R. (2013. *Violence: Thinking without bannisters*. Cambridge: Polity Press.
Butler, I. & Drakeford, M. (2003). *Scandal, social policy and social welfare*. Bristol: Policy Press/BASW.
Campbell, T. & Sitze, A. (Eds) (2013). *Biopolitics: A reader*. Westchester: Duke University Press.
Castel, R. (1991). From dangerousness to risk. In G. Burchell, C. Gordon & P. Miller (Eds), *The Foucault effect: Studies in governmentality* (pp. 281–298). Hemel Hempstead: Harvester Wheatsheaf.
Cisney, V.W. & Morar, N. (Eds) (2016). *Biopower: Foucault and beyond*. Chicago: Chicago University Press.
Clarke, J. (2004). *Changing welfare, changing states: New directions in social policy*. London: Sage.
Cook, T.D. (2014). 'Big data' in research on social policy. *Journal of Policy Analysis and Management*, Spring 2014, 544–547.
Cribb, A. & Gewirtz, S. (2015). *Professionalism*. Cambridge: Polity.
Dardot, P. & Laval, C. (2013). *The new way of the world: On neo-liberal society*. London: Verso.
Dean, M. (1994). *Critical and effective histories: Foucault's methods and historical sociology*. London: Routledge.
Dean, M. (1999). *Governmentality: Power and rule in modern society*. London: Sage.
Deering, J. (2011). *Probation practice and the new penology*. Farnham: Ashgate.
Deleuze, G. (1992). Postscript on societies of control. *October*, 59(Winter), 3–7.
Deleuze, G. (2007). *Negotiations*. New York: Columbia University Press.
Dingwall, G. & Hillier, T. (2016). *Blamestorming, blamemongers and scapegoats: Allocating blame in the criminal justice process*. Bristol: Policy Press.
Donzelot, J. (1979). *The policing of families*. New York: Pantheon.
Elden, S. (2007). Governmentality, calculation, territory. *Environment and Planning D: Society and Space*, 25(3), 562–580.
Eribon, D. (1991). *Michel Foucault*. Cambridge: Harvard University Press.
Ericson, R. & Haggerty, K.D. (1997). *Policing the risk society*. Oxford: Oxford University Press.
Esposito, R. (2008). *Bios: Biopolitics and philosophy*. Minneapolis, MN: University of Minnesota Press.
Evans, T. (2010). *Professional discretion in welfare services: Beyond street-level bureaucracy*. Farnham: Ashgate.
Evans, T. (2011). Professionals, managers and discretion: Critiquing street-level bureaucracy. *British Journal of Social Work*, 41(2), 368–386.
Evans, B. (2013). *Liberal terror*. Cambridge: Polity Press.
Evans, T. & Hardy, M. (2010). *Evidence and knowledge for practice*. Cambridge: Polity Press.
Evans, T. & Harris, J. (2004). Street level bureaucracy, social work and the (exaggerated) death of discretion. *British Journal of Social Work*, 34, 871–895.
Fook, J. & Gardner, F. (2007). *Practising critical reflection: A resource handbook*. Maidenhead: Open University Press.
Foucault, M. (1982). The subject and power. In L. Dreyfus & P. Rabinow, *Michel Foucault: Beyond structuralism and hermeneutics* (pp. 208–226). Chicago: Chicago University Press.
Foucault, M. (2004). *Society must be defended*. London: Penguin Books.

Foucault, M. (2008). *The birth of biopolitics: Lectures at the College de France 1978–1979.* Basingstoke: Palgrave Macmillan.

Franko Aas, K. (2005a). *Sentencing in the age of information: From Faust to Macintosh.* London: Glass House Press.

Franko Aas, K. (2005b). The ad and the form: Punitiveness and technological culture. In J. Pratt, D. Brown, M. Brown, S. Hallsworth & W. Morrison (Eds), *The new punitiveness: Trends, theories, perspectives* (pp. 150–166). Cullompton: Willan.

Garland, D. (1996). The limits of the sovereign state: Strategies of control in contemporary society. *British Journal of Criminology*, 36(4), 445–471.

Garland, D. (2001). *The culture of control.* Oxford: Oxford University Press.

Garland, D. (2003). The rise of risk. In R.V. Erikson & A Doyle (Eds), *Risk and morality* (pp. 48–86). London: University of Toronto.

Garrett, P.M. (2009). *Transforming' children's services: Social work, neoliberalism and the 'modern' world.* Maidenhead: Open University Press.

Gillingham, P. (2011) Computer based information systems and human service organizations: Emerging problems and future possibilities. *Australian Social Work*, 64 (3), 299–312.

Gillingham, P. (2015) Electronic information systems in human service organisations: the what, who, why and how of information. *The British Journal of Social Work*, 45(5), 1598–1613.

Glasby, J. (2011). From evidence based to knowledge based policy and practice. In J. Glasby (Ed.) *Evidence, policy and practice: Critical perspectives in health and social care* (pp. 85–98). Bristol: Policy Press.

Grimer, J. (2015). 'We are all social scientists now': How big data, machine learning and causal influence work together. *PS: Political Science and Politics*, 48(1), 80–83.

Gros, F. (2012). *Le principe securité.* Paris: Gallimard.

Haggerty, K. & Ericson, R. (2000). The surveillant assemblage. *British Journal of Sociology*, 51(4), 605–622.

Hannah-Moffat, K (2018). Algorithmic risk governance: Big data analytics, race and information activism in criminal justice debates. *Theoretical Criminology*, advance access 1–18.

Harcourt, B. (2015). *Exposed: Desire and disobedience in the digital age.* Cambridge: Harvard University Press.

Hardy, M. (2015). *Governing risk: Care and control in contemporary social work.* Basingstoke: Palgrave Macmillan.

Hardy, M. (2016). 'I know what I like and I like what I know': Epistemology in practice and theory and practice again *Qualitative Social Work*, 15(5–6), 762–778.

Heidegger, M. (1977). *The question concerning technology and other essays.* New York: Harper Row.

Henman, P. (2010). *Governing electronically: E-government and the reconfiguration of public administration, policy and power.* Basingstoke: Palgrave Macmillan.

Henman, P. & Marston, G. (2008). The social division of welfare surveillance. *Journal of social policy*, 37(2), 187–205.

Heyman, B., Shaw, M., Alaszewski, A. & Titterton, M. (2010). *Risk, safety and clinical practice: Health care through the lens of risk.* Oxford: Oxford University Press.

Holmboe, E.S., Lipner, R. & Greiner, A. (2008) Assessing quality of care: Knowledge matters. *JAMA*, 299(3), 338–340.

Hood, C. (2011). *The blame game: Spin bureaucracy and self-preservation in government.* New Jersey: Princeton University Press.

Hornqvist, M. (2010). *Risk, power and the state: After Foucault.* Abingdon: Glasshouse.

Hupe, P., Hill, M. & Buffat, A. (Eds) (2015). *Understanding street-level bureaucracy.* Bristol: Policy Press.

Lemke, T. (2011). *Biopolitics: An advanced introduction.* London: New York University Press.

Lilla, M. (2016). *The reckless mind: Intellectuals in politics.* New York: New York Review of Books.

Lipsky, M. (1980/2010). *Street-level bureaucracy: Dilemmas of the individual in public services.* New York: Russell Sage Foundation.

Lorenz, W. (2017, 19–21 April). Social work research and accountable practice. Challenging dogma in uncertain times. Keynote address. In *7th European Conference for Social Work Research*, Aalborg, Denmark.

Lyon, D. (2001). *Surveillance society: Monitoring everyday life.* Maidenhead: Open University Press.

Lyon, D. (2002). Everyday surveillance: Personal data and social classifications. *Information, Communication and Society*, 5(2), 242–257.

MacNish, K. (2018). *The ethics of surveillance: An introduction.* Abingdon: Routledge.

Margolis, L. (1997). *Under the cover of kindness: The invention of social work.* Charlottesville: University of Virginia Press.

Mawby, R. & Worrall, A. (2013). *Doing probation work: Identity in a criminal justice occupation.* Abingdon: Routledge.

McCue, C. (2015). *Data mining and predictive analysis.* Oxford: Butterworth-Heinemann

Mills, C. (2018). *Biopolitics.* Abingdon: Routledge.

Mulgan, G. (2018). *Big mind: How collective intelligence can change our world.* New Jersey: Princeton University Press.

Munro, E. (2011). *The Munro report of child protection: Final report: A child centred system.* London: Department of Education.

Murray, S.J. (2006). Thanatopolitics: On the use of death for mobilizing political life. *Polygraph*, 18, 192–215.

Nancy, J.L. (2007). *The creation of the world: Or globalization.* New York: SUNY Press.

Neocleous, M. (2000). *The fabrication of social order: A critical theory of police power.* London: Pluto Press.

Newman, J. (2001). *Modernising governance: New labour, policy and society.* London: Sage.

O'Brien, M. & Penna, S. (1998). *Theorising welfare: Enlightenment and modern society.* London: Sage.

O'Malley, P. (2004). *Risk, uncertainty and government.* London: Glasshouse.

Parton, N. (1996). Social work, risk and the 'blaming system'. In N. Parton (Ed.) *Social theory, social change and social work* (pp. 98–114). London: Routledge.

Parton, N. (2008). Changes in the form of knowledge in social work: From the social to the 'informational'? *British Journal of Social Work*, 38, 253–269.

Parton, N. & Kirk, S. (2010). The nature and purposes of social work. In I. Shaw, K. Briar-Lawson, J. Orme & R. Ruckdeschel (Eds), *The SAGE handbook of social work research* (pp. 23–36). London: Sage.

Pierson, C. (2004). *The modern state* (2nd ed.). London: Routledge.

Pithouse, A. (1987). *Social work: The social organisation of an invisible trade.* Aldershot: Avebury.

Power, M. (1997). *The audit society: Rituals of verification.* Oxford: Oxford University Press.

Rose, N. (1996). The death of the social? Reconfiguring the territory of government. *Economy and Society*, 25, 327–356.

Rose, N. (1999). *Powers of freedom: Reframing political thought*. Cambridge: Cambridge University Press.

Sackett, D.L., Rosenberg, W.M., Gray, J.A., Haynes, R.B. & Richardson, W.S. (1996). Evidence based medicine: What it is and what it isn't. *British Medical Journal*, 312, 71–72.

Schinkel, W. (2011). Prepression: The actuarial archive and new technologies of security. *Theoretical Criminology*, 15(4), 365–380.

Schmitt, C. (1934/2010). *Political theology: Four chapters on the concept of the sovereignty*. Chicago: Chicago University Press.

Schön, D. (1983). *The reflective practitioner: How professionals think in action*. Farnham: Ashgate.

Schuilenburg, M. (2015). *The securitization of society: Crime, risk and social order*. New York: New York University Press.

Stanley, T., Guru, S. & Gupta, A. (2018). Working with PREVENT: Social work options for cases of 'radicalisation risk'. *Practice*, 30(2), 131–146.

Stephens-Davidowitz, S. (2017). *Everybody lies: Big data, new data and what the internet can tell us about who we really are*. London: Harper Collins.

Stoddart, E. (2018). Wolves in the airport: Jesus critique of purity as a challenge to 21st century surveillance. *Practical Theology*, 11(1), 54–66.

Thomas, P. (2016). Youth, terrorism and education: British Prevent programme. *International Journal of Lifelong Education*, 16(2), 171–187.

Travis, A. (2018). UK mass digital surveillance regime ruled unlawful. *The Guardian*, January 30th.

Vatter, M. (2011). Eternal life and biopower. *CR: The New Centennial Review*, 10(3), 217–250.

Villasden, K. & Wahlberg, A. (2015). The government of life: Managing populations, health and scarcity. *Economy and Society*, 44(1), 1–15.

Webb, S. (2006). *Social work in a risk society: Social and political perspectives*. Basingstoke: Palgrave Macmillan.

Webb, S. (2009). Risk, governmentality and insurance: The actuarial recasting of social work. In H.W. Otto, A. Polutto & H. Ziegler (Eds), *Evidence based practice: Modernising the knowledge base of social work* (pp. 211–226), Opanden and Farmington Hills, MI: Barbara Budrick Publishers.

Zedner, L. (2011). Epilogue: The inescapable insecurity of security technologies? In K.F. Aas, H.E. Oppen Gundhus & H.M. Lovell (Eds), *Technologies of insecurity: The surveillance of everyday life* (pp. 257–270), Abingdon: Glasshouse.

CHAPTER 5

Discrection in the Welfare State

Evelyn Z. Brodkin

5.1 Introduction

Street-level organizations are critical sites for welfare state politics. They occupy a structural position in the welfare state, where they effectively mediate between individuals and the state and, in more practical terms, between formal policy and informal provision (Lipsky 1980; Brodkin 2013). Positioned between policy rhetoric and reality, street-level organizations function as locations for a distinctive form of welfare state politics, one that is constituted through the exercise of discretion in everyday practice. In a broad sense, it is the discretionary micro-practices within these organizations that indirectly shape the meta-politics of the welfare state by affecting the boundaries of the possible for advancing contested policy projects, claiming rights and negotiating sociopolitical status.

As contributors to this edited collection attest and as Evans and Hupe (in their introduction) and Hupe (2013) have laid out in some detail, discretion as a concept may be considered in a wide variety of ways. In this chapter, I specifically tackle the politics of discretion as a matter of relevance to political-institutional theories of the welfare state, advancing a street-level perspective that highlights the critical role of discretion in welfare state politics and locates analysis of discretion *in place*. From this perspective, the political significance of discretion derives largely from its indirect effects; that is, from how the discretionary practices of street-level organizations, effectively, mediate policy and politics.

E. Z. Brodkin (✉)
University of Chicago, Chicago, IL, USA

Aalborg University, Aalborg, Denmark

University of Gothenburg, Gothenburg, Sweden
e-mail: e-brodkin@uchicago.edu

T. Evans, P. Hupe (eds.), *Discretion and the Quest for Controlled Freedom*, https://doi.org/10.1007/978-3-030-19566-3_5

In contrast to other approaches, this perspective does not require ascribing purposeful political intent to street-level practitioners nor does it rule out purposeful behaviour. In addition, rather than treating discretion as an individual-level phenomenon, it directs attention to the ways in which discretion is structured in specific organizational and political contexts. The politics of discretion, conceptualized in this way, should be understood as operating systematically, but indirectly, making it a type of politics that is difficult to discern and assess.

In fact, this lack of transparency, at times, can be exploited to political advantage; for example, when governance reforms are promoted to improve efficiency or accountability but invisibly create conditions that shift patterns of discretion, resulting in limiting access to social benefits or skewing responsiveness to marginalized populations (Brodkin and Marston 2013; see also Van Slyke 2003; Soss, Fording and Schram 2011; van Berkel, Caswell, Larsen and Kupka 2017). From this perspective, managerial reforms may be understood as a form of politics by indirection. They change where discretion in policy delivery is exercised (e.g., whether implementing organizations are public, nonprofit or for-profit and whether they are federal, state or municipal) and under what organizational conditions it is exercised (e.g., through various contract incentives, fiscal arrangements, performance monitoring and so forth). To rephrase Harold Lasswell's (1936) classic formulation: Managerial reform is political because it changes who does what and how.

This is not to say that all forms of discretion are political. Rather, discretion can be understood to be political when its exercise becomes systematized and produces patterns of practice that have consequences for 'who gets what, when [and] how' and also for who gets *heard*, when and how. It is important to note that the politics of discretion is not necessarily negative or harmful, at least, in terms of normative judgements about its effects. It is possible that discretion can be used in ways that advance normative goals of social justice, equality or democracy. The analytical challenge is to reveal the conditions under which discretion is systematized and to assess its effects.

This chapter considers discretion in the context of welfare state politics. It argues that, as a conceptual matter, the discretionary practices of street-level organizations can be understood as political to the extent that they shape social provision, structure opportunities for claiming and voice and manage the consequences of conflicts inherent in their practices. The discussion places discretion within a theoretical framework that recognizes that institutions matter to welfare state politics (Pierson 1994; see also Evans, Rueschemeyer and Skocpol 1985) and then extends institutional theory to move beyond disembodied accounts of 'the state' to take account of the street-level organizations that form its operational core. It is here where the practical work of the state takes place and welfare state politics effectively continues—albeit outside of recognized channels for making politics.[1]

5.2 Why Organizations Matter to Welfare State Politics

This discussion builds on two well-known theoretical perspectives, political institutionalism and street-level bureaucracy. Although a full review of these perspectives is beyond the scope of this chapter, a brief discussion highlights some relevant theoretical insights. Generally, analysis grounded in political institutionalism places structural arrangements at the centre of explanations for welfare state politics and the development of the welfare state; see, for example, March and Olsen (1983), Evans *et al.* (1985), Skocpol (1992), Robertson (1993) and Pierson (1994). Much of this research is historical and it has generated insights into both the historical and contemporary effects of particular types of political institutions.

For example, in her foundational work in this area, Skocpol (1992) directed attention to ways in which institutional arrangements affected 'policy possibilities' and, subsequently, how 'policies shape politics'. A key analytical concern involved the structuring effects of higher-order institutions, among them electoral arrangements, party systems and broadly defined policy regimes. At times, this perspective also has led to consideration of the implications of broad institutional arrangements for smaller-order institutions, specifically advocacy organizations. For example, Skocpol (1992) has argued that the exclusion of women from US electoral institutions in the early twentieth century (before suffrage) gave special importance to women's organizations as locations for the pursuit of 'women's issues' and women's political voice.

Building on the institutionalist perspective, Pierson (1994, 2005) has emphasized the importance of 'policy feedback', arguing that differences in welfare state policy regimes affect both the political stability and the vulnerability of specific policies. He has identified ways in which policy arrangements effectively obscure welfare state cutbacks, for example, when public benefit programmes shrink invisibly simply because they are not automatically indexed to keep up with inflation. Pierson suggests that these types of 'untraceable' cuts can reduce the potential for political backlash to retrenchment strategies that might generate more opposition if more readily visible. This is similar to a line of argument in the organizational literature suggesting that organizational mechanisms may play an important but indirect role in expanding and restricting social welfare provision. However, analyses adopting the perspective of political institutionalism, generally, have not drilled down to the organizational level, leaving the specific role of street-level organizations in welfare state politics inadequately explored.

In contrast, the organizations that deliver social policy are central to street-level bureaucracy theory (Lipsky 1980). This theory places public agencies in a central position of indirectly mediating between citizens and the state as they engage directly in the business of providing public benefits and services. Lipsky hypothesized that conditions of work that tend to prevail in public bureaucracies—multiple and conflicting objectives, limited resources, unlimited demand and problematic accountability—effectively privilege front-line staff to use their discretion in policy delivery. However, these conditions also lead them to create informal patterns of behaviour or coping mechanisms, through which they manage the contradictions of their work and, ultimately, skew access to benefits and services, shape policy content and control client populations.

This chapter focuses on discretion within *street-level organizations*, of which large, public bureaucracies are a subset. Building on Lipsky's seminal work, the study of street-level organizations recognizes that the policy world has changed dramatically since the 1980s. Large public bureaucracies are no longer the only, nor even necessarily the dominant, locations for the work of the welfare state. Policy may be delivered through a variety of other forms, including non-governmental organizations, for-profit firms and mixed public-private arrangements. In addition, the conditions under which policy delivery occurs in these diverse settings have been transformed by governance and managerial reforms, among them devolution, contracting and performance management. The study of street-level organizations recognizes these important shifts.

The study of street-level organizations also broadens the scope of analysis to consider how discretionary practices do more than simply implement policy. They also, effectively, make welfare state politics (Brodkin 2015). This approach brings the organizational insights of street-level theory to the welfarist understandings of political institutionalism. This chapter lays the foundation for a conceptual map of the linkages between street-level discretion and welfare state politics.

5.3 The State, the Street and Welfare Politics

If, as argued here, street-level organizations play an important role in welfare state politics, what positions them to do this? In part, the structural position of human service organizations derives from the limitations of the formal policymaking process, particularly the difficulties of crafting legislation that can surmount obstacles to enactment and produce authoritative action. These limitations are arguably, particularly acute in the US case, but by no means limited to it. It is a well-remarked feature of US policymaking that it is constituted by bargaining, a process necessary to create a winning coalition. The idealized notion of authoritative policymaking is vitiated by the conditions under which it occurs, conditions in which compromise and logrolling are a price of passage. As Kingdon points out: 'We [...] do not usually clarify our goals; indeed this is often counterproductive because constructing a political coalition involves persuading people to agree on a specific proposal when they might not agree on a set of goals to be achieved' (Kingdon 1984: 82).

It follows that one might expect legislative indeterminacy, rather than authoritativeness, when issues are essentially contested. As a strategic matter, legislation that presents broad and ambiguous goals or contains multiple and conflicting objectives may diffuse or deflect conflict, albeit at the cost of coherence or definitiveness (Lowi 1979). Others take a more sanguine view, allowing that law may at times express more of a hope than a pragmatic solution

(Lindblom 1959; Price 1981; Arnold 1990). It is not necessarily the case that legislators do not wish for clearer and better-conceived legislation, but that it is difficult to accomplish. As Kingdon explains: 'Action is often facilitated by fuzzing over what one is trying to accomplish. When participants do define their preferences with a modicum of precision, they conflict' (Kingdon 1984: 84). This 'logic of congressional action' is captured by the oft-repeated maxim: 'Don't let the best drive out the good' (Arnold 1990).

The difficulties of legislative coalition-building multiply when policymaking involves highly contested areas of state activity. Social welfare policymaking is particularly contentious when it raises difficult questions about the scope of the state, as well as social, racial, gender and class relations. Under these circumstances, it becomes strategic to legislate broad goals and evade the devilish details that ultimately determine how policies will be operationalized in practice. These practices are consistent with rational choice models of legislative behaviour that demonstrate the importance of credit-claiming, blame-avoiding and evading traceable choices that might later be used by electoral opponents (Arnold 1990; see also Price 1981). These limitations may take a different form in other western democracies, producing, for example, framework laws that leave the pesky implementation details to be sorted following the legislative process, as if implementation and policymaking were truly distinctive enterprises.

Despite these and other national differences, as a general matter, the institutional limitations of lawmaking have critical implications for street-level organizations. One consequence of legislative indeterminacy is that it tacitly delegates down the political task of operationalizing conflicting goals and balancing policy's grand rhetorical ambitions against the practicalities of the possible. Charged with the task of translating indeterminate policy into determinate action, street-level organizations become a location for the continuation of welfare state politics by administrative means.

If policy conflicts were as overt in street-level organizations as they are in the legislative arena, one would expect replication of the battles, stalemates and, perhaps, evasions common to formal lawmaking. However, street-level organizations have certain institutional advantages as mediators of political conflict. A key advantage can be found in the discretionary nature of human services provision. Discretion is commonly regarded as a highly problematic feature of human services work, at least from a managerial perspective. Paradoxically, what is managerially problematic may be politically functional under some circumstances. This dual view of discretion requires some explanation.

First, discretion is inherent in many aspects of policy provision, especially in areas of social welfare. This occurs, in part, because individual judgement and flexibility is necessary to determine individual or community needs and fashion appropriate responses to them. To a degree, this aspect of discretion is recognized and authorized. However, there is also an element of irreducible discretion in human services work, because much of it occurs outside of direct observation and managerial control (Lipsky 1980).

In practice, lower-level discretion may be only loosely related to formal policy provisions or may even be contrary to them. Despite the persistent efforts of managers to control them, street-level practices remain problematic. In contrast to hierarchical notions of practice, Lipsky's model suggests that discretion introduces considerable uncertainty into policy delivery, as front-line practitioners use their discretion to respond not to formal directives, but to the conditions of work. Their adaptive behaviours, when systematic, effectively produce what people come to experience as 'policy'.

From this vantage point, it follows that the structural position of street-level organizations as mediators of welfare state politics derives jointly from the indeterminacy of formal policy and law *and* the discretionary nature of much policy work. Together they place street-level organizations in a position that effectively requires and enables them to be part of welfare state politics. In this sense, the discretionary activities of these organizations may be understood as political when they operationalize social policy in specific ways that have bearing on who gets what and how.

It is important to note that discretion is regarded here as an analytical construct of interest because it introduces uncertainty and flexibility into the production of policy. Analysis should not presume how discretion will be exercised and, thus, whether its effects are positive or negative, which are normative judgements. Rather, investigation into the uses of discretion is treated as an empirical matter. Patterns of informal practice, the conditions that produce them and their effects are the subject of enquiry.

As I have argued elsewhere (Brodkin 2013, 2015), when social policy is unclear, open to interpretation or requires judgement in the course of its implementation, it creates the space for welfare state politics to continue in the discretionary work of street-level organizations. It is here that policy meaning is effectively constructed in everyday practice. Discretion gives fluidity to this work and provides the space for welfare state politics to continue, albeit through manifestly nonpolitical means.

5.4 On the Politics of Discretion

If street-level organizations are institutionally positioned to be mediators of welfare state politics, how do they function in this role? What gives them their *political* significance? First, it is important to stress that the theoretical framework outlined here conceptualizes the organizational *practices* as political. In contrast to other analyses discussed earlier, the approach described here does not treat these organizations as purposeful political actors, although at times they certainly may be. Rather, it identifies the elements of discretionary practices through which organizations perform latent political functions that are largely indirect and only loosely related to their manifest functions. Specifically, street-level organizations function as political institutions when they

- shape social provision, specifically access to and distribution of, as well as the content of, benefits and services;
- structure opportunities for voice, claiming and assertion of rights; and
- manage the consequences of their practices, using strategies of legitimation, symbolism and blame-shifting.

The following subsections briefly discuss each of these dimensions.

Shaping Provision

Formal social policy establishes the explicit terms of provision, among them eligibility standards, catchment areas and specific criteria for the distribution of benefits and services. When street-level organizations operate according to law and formal rules, they effectively are operating as 'authorized' gatekeepers to benefits and services. However, formal rules and standards do not in themselves fully determine who gets what, when and how. Organizational arrangements and informal practices independently affect access and distribution. This makes street-level organizations gatekeepers in a different sense in that their gatekeeping practices extend beyond formal rules. As informal gatekeepers, they may skew access and distribution in systematic ways that are inconsistent with formal law.

Often, these kinds of 'skewing effects' are not readily observable in practice nor are they made visible through administrative data and many types of routine programme evaluation. The political significance of street-level organizations derives not only from their role in informally determining who gets what, but also from their role in obscuring extra-legal or nonlegal patterns of distribution. When distributive effects are obscure and hard to trace, political accountability is highly problematic. In a sense, street-level organizations may be said to engage in a form of 'stealth' political activity when they influence social provision through informal, even invisible, organizational practices.

One classic example can be found in Stone's (1984) insightful study of disability policy. She showed that informal gatekeeping practices effectively expanded or narrowed access to disability benefits in periods in which formal requirements were unchanged. At times, these practices responded to tinkering with administrative criteria for defining disability, but at other times they were apparently independent of explicit alterations in policy. For example, Stone describes how a relatively technical requirement for consultative disability examinations became an indirect mechanism for restricting the provision of disability benefits. Disability status became harder to get when discretion for assessments moved from individual medical doctors (who took a relatively expansive view) to 'volume contract providers' who virtually mass-produced assessments that were less attentive to individual circumstances and, as an indirect consequence, more restrictive in their disability determinations (Stone 1984: 121–4).

Street-level practices were politically significant because they provided an indirect means of adjusting policies regulating work to changing economic conditions, but without generating political conflict associated with explicit policy shifts. Stone argues that informal gatekeeping practices effectively reduced 'the pressures of unemployed workers on the work-based distributive system at the same time preserve[ing] the legitimacy of the work ideology' (Stone 1984: 168).

However, discretion alone does not determine whether informal practices will change systematically nor can it predict the direction of change—whether restrictive or expansive. As Evans and Hupe point out in their introduction, efforts to 'control' discretion or at least shape its exercise, have been an important underlying element in so-called new public management reforms with sometimes unpredicted (although perhaps predictable) consequences. Without going into detail, there is now a sizeable literature illuminating how performance management has been used to shape discretion and, indirectly, restrict access to social benefit programmes and how procedural demands on street-level practitioners can reshape the contours of access and responsiveness, too often leaving marginalized groups out in the cold (Adler 2006; Brodkin and Majmundar 2010; Soss *et al.* 2011; Brodkin and Marston 2013; Lens 2013; van Berkel *et al.* 2017).

This literature, more generally, points to the structuring effects of organizational conditions on discretion and their systemic consequences. For example, research on child welfare practices has shown that, despite policy edicts and professional training ostensibly intended to assure that social workers assist parents in reuniting with their children, organizational conditions may discourage caseworkers from making an effort to work closely with parents. Smith and Donovan (2003) found that social workers developed informal patterns of practice that favoured investing in meaningless exercises of documentation, paper-pushing and standardized (rather than individualized) assignment to services. Moreover, in typical street-level fashion, social workers coped with the disjuncture between what they ***should*** have done and what they ***actually*** did by defining their clients as undeserving of their help. As Smith and Donovan (2003: 549) describe:

> A […] common view is that parents warrant a low priority among the factors competing for a caseworkers' time […]. [O]ne caseworker described how, given her low expectations for parental involvement, she invests little time or effort in engaging parents, saying: 'I'd have to say that biological parents, in most cases, take a very low priority. Because, like I said, for the most part, they don't do much, so I don't have to spend a lot of time'.

The larger political significance of these systematized, discretionary practices is underscored by studies that both show their effects and that place them in larger, macro-political context. These studies are part of a broader line of enquiry linking the micro-practices of street-level organizations with the macro-politics of the welfare state. From this perspective, organizations are understood to operate 'as if' they were intended to perform functions quite different from those explicitly articulated, but relevant to larger conflicts over the scope and content of the welfare state (Brodkin 2013, 2015; see also Stone 1984; Herd and Lightman 2005; Soss, Schram and Fording 2011).

Although street-level organizations do the work of the welfare state, research on their informal practices shows that they are neither controlled by the administrative hierarchy of the state nor fully autonomous. Yet their discretionary practices should be understood analytically as constitutive of the state and as deeply embedded in the larger political economy. From a political perspective, discretion can be understood to be politically significant to the extent that its exercise both reflects and refracts the broader political environment, sometimes in unanticipated ways.

The challenge for enquiry is to examine the relationship between welfare state politics and street-level organizations. Although much recent literature documents ways in which street-level organizations have been instrumental in welfare state cutbacks and the advance of neo-liberal restrictions on social protections, this does not mean that street-level organizations cannot shape provision in more expansive ways or in ways that advance social and economic equality (see, for example, Andersen, Caswell and Larsen 2017; see also Spitzmueller 2014). As a political matter, one would hypothesize that variation in the practices of street-level organizations, in part, would be contingent on the dynamics of social conflict in the broader political economy. If these organizations function as political mediators and provide a location for conflict over welfare state politics, one would expect to find variation over time and in different national settings. Precisely how organizational practices vary and the factors that produce variation are the key subjects for investigation.

Structuring Voice

A second political dimension of organizational practice involves structuring opportunities for voice, claiming and assertion of rights. Street-level organizations function politically when they shape the prospects for articulating and pursuing interests, that is, for 'naming, blaming, and claiming' (Felstiner, Abel and Sarat 1980: 81). Studies have shown various ways that these organizations informally set the conditions for making claims and asserting rights, thus facilitating or restricting possibilities for voice and resistance. Studies have shown that control may be exercised by structuring interactions, signalling the secondary status of service claimants, arranging office encounters to be more or less hospitable and penalizing claimants for overstepping informal bureaucratic boundaries (Miller 1983; Bennett 1995; Soss 1999; Morgen 2001; Brodkin 2011; Watkins-Hayes 2013; Zacka 2017).

These structuring practices may occur, for example, when caseworkers simplify their jobs by sticking to a script and deflecting or ignoring efforts of claimants to assert needs or explain complex situations that might be difficult to resolve (Brodkin 2011; Zacka 2017). Within the domain of street-level organizations, individuals who assert demands may be regarded as 'frustrating, demanding, and uncooperative—"a pain in the ass"' (Maynard-Moody and Musheno 2003: 132). Human services workers may informally subject individuals to 'little tests' of moral worth through which they determine for whom they will stretch the rules and who they will punish by strict enforcement of them (2003: 133).

These practices may be understood generally as varieties of the coping mechanisms street-level practitioners develop to manage the unwieldy demands of their jobs (Lipsky 1980). Although individuals arguably gravitate to these jobs because of an interest in the helping professions, the conditions under which they operate may undermine good intentions. In certain contexts, those who exercise voice, assert claims and resist efforts to control them may be labelled 'trouble', subject to threats and bureaucratic forms of punishment (Brodkin 2013; see also McCleary 1978; Miller 1983; Watkins-Hayes 2013).

Alternatively, in a different organizational context, discretion might be used in ways that enlarge possibilities for voice. For example, Small (2006) discovered that some private, nonprofit organizations became a place for brokering resources through informal interactions among clients and staff and with other organizations. He found that this is more likely to occur in those organizations distinguished by their stability, capacity and resilience. Similarly, Spitzmueller (2014) illuminated how staff at a small community mental health centre struggled to maintain the space for forms of discretion that they saw as responsive and inclusive, while coming under intense pressure to operate differently by an increasingly efficiency-promoting health insurance system.

Analytically, what is important is that this work goes on in organizations structurally positioned between overt welfare state politics and an invisible politics of discretion. Regardless of intent, organizational practices are functionally political when they affect possibilities for voice, claiming and assertion of rights. This is the case whether the organizations are public bureaucracies, nonprofits or private for-profit agencies. However, it is also the case that it is important, analytically, to consider whether discretion functions differently in different organizational contexts. To the extent that differences are systematic, institutional arrangements for policy delivery—that is, choices about which organizations will function as mediators and under what conditions—have profound implications for the politics of discretion and the welfare state, more broadly.

Are there types of organizations, perhaps those that are community-based or formed from the grassroots, that operate differently, essentially, that mediate welfare state politics differently and may even expand opportunities for voice? Or are there differences in the ways organizations shape voice that are affected by either the capacity of the organizations or the relative status of their client/members? These questions, nominally about organizational form, are fundamentally about the political functions of their practices.

Managing the Consequences of Organizational Practice

The practices of street-level organizations, to the extent that they are visibly at odds with the interests of their clients-constituents, could create problems for the legitimacy of these organizations. In the more egregious cases, it could even make them battlegrounds for resistance to practice and policy. At times, street-level organizations do indeed suffer crises of legitimacy and precipitate urgent demands for administrative reform (Hasenfeld 1992: 10–1; Brodkin 2013).

In order to function effectively as political institutions, they must have the capacity to manage the consequences of their practices, such that crises are the exception, not the rule. Are there ways in which these organizations are able to manage the contradictions between their manifest functions as 'helpers' and 'providers' and their latent political functions in shaping provision and structuring voice?

First, as discussed, systemic effects of the organizational practices highlighted here are indirect and difficult to discern. Even when individuals experience interactions negatively, they do so in the singular. In the absence of highly organized social service claimant groups (akin to the welfare rights organizations of the 1960s), individual encounters with street-level organizations tend to remain exactly that, individualized. They may object to their own treatment, but have little opportunity to link their own experience to those of others or the organization as a whole. In addition, individuals dissatisfied with what they receive from these organizations may absolve their caseworkers and (reasonably enough) blame circumstances beyond their control (Soss 1999).

Second, organizations may have formal processes for complaint and redress, such as fair hearings or administrative appeals that provide an outlet for individual objections and buffer the potential for broader mobilization against organizational practices. Research on formal complaint processes suggests that, in some circumstances, appeal arrangements may operate partly as a safety valve that allows problems to be individualized while leaving organizational routines largely untouched (Adler 2013; Lens 2013). Even when individual problems are acknowledged, they may be regarded as 'mistakes' or 'errors' in discretion, giving redress to individuals and legitimating grievance processes, while at the same time leaving patterns of discretion largely undisturbed.

Third, the consequences of problematic organizational practices may be managed, in part, by administrative strategies that purport to advance accountability, transparency and responsiveness. Research on aspects of the so-new managerialism is suggestive on this point. For example, performance measurement is a widely used new managerial strategy of particular relevance to street-level organizations. In effect, performance measures selectively identify dimensions of organizational practice and attach them to financial incentives and disincentives as a way of advancing accountability for attending to manifest policy objectives. Of course, this does not mean that all manifest goals receive attention, particularly given the breadth and ambiguity of goals as formally articulated in law or mission statements. In practice, performance measures give primacy to some goals and aspects of performance over others. As a technical matter, it is very difficult to construct performance measures for human services that depend on individualized judgement, discretion and other aspects. Quantity is easier to measure than quality, particularly when there are no agreed-upon criteria for quality. However, this is more than a technical concern. It is also a political concern.

Absent measures for responsiveness to individual needs, for service quality or for broader outcomes relevant to improved well-being, performance measurement can create a type of rudimentary accountability that may have perverse effects with respect to service quality and responsiveness (Hasenfeld 2000; Cutler and Waine 2000; Morgen 2001; Hasenfeld and Powell 2004; Considine 2005; Dias and Maynard-Moody 2006). For example, a study of welfare-to-work contracts in Chicago showed that pay-for-performance measures rewarded agencies for placing clients in jobs but largely indifferent to how that was done. Although ostensibly intended to promote better-'quality' placements, performance measures were designed in ways that, in practice, created organizational incentives to push clients into the most readily available jobs, namely, lower-wage, unstable, short-term jobs (Brodkin 2007). In effect, performance measures created incentives for street-level staff to develop informal practices favouring a quick-in, quick-out job strategy, effectively undermining the prospects for sustained improvements in family economic or social well-being.

Analytically, one must be cautious about reifying either vision of managerialism; that is, as a strategy for accountability or as a device to legitimate human services practices that are oriented more towards efficiency and social regulation than towards quality or responsiveness. To the extent that new managerial strategies manifestly suggest transparency and political accountability while, in practice, operating in contradiction to both, they may serve a latent function in managing the contradictions of informal organizational practices.

Fourth, the capacity of street-level organizations to manage the consequences of their practices may derive, in part, from the 'myth and ceremony' of human services work. Hasenfeld contends that human services organizations, in their discretionary practices, may reflect and enforce moral categories that place the poor and disadvantaged outside of prevailing social norms (Hasenfeld 1992, 2000; Hasenfeld and Powell 2004). However, the potentially contentious nature of this so-called moral work (essentially, *political* work) is obscured when it occurs under the rubric of administration and with the imprimatur of professional human services provision.

In order for street-level organizations to function effectively as political institutions, they must have the capacity to manage the conflicts that are inherent in this role. Viewed from this perspective, formal accountability measures, such as complaint processes, performance measurement and so forth, may be understood, in part, as symbolic devices. They confer legitimacy on organizations by suggesting a modicum of democratic transparency and managerial responsiveness, while in practice delivering less than they appear to offer (Edelman 1964, 1977). This is not to say that managerial efforts to improve practices and accountability are necessarily inauthentic or cynical. Rather, it is to suggest that managerial strategies may perform other functions that are inconsistent with or indifferent to the good intentions of practitioners. As Edelman advises, administration, like law, should be understood as a 'symbol and ritual which, among other functions, serves as a legitimizer of elite objectives' (Edelman 1964: 68). To the extent that these types of mechanisms enable street-level organizations to manage conflict over social provision, they should be understood as part of the politics of discretion.

Fifth, to some extent, the costs of managing the contradictions of street-level work may devolve to the practitioners themselves. Zacka offers a probing examination of the moral dilemmas that occur at the interface of organizational conditions and moral disposition. He advises, 'For most people, inhabiting a role is not something one can keep at arm's length [...]. When "impossible situations" force agents to take actions that are irreconcilable with their role conception, they [...] put workers in conflict with their own selves. An impossible situation threatens one's sense of moral integrity' (Zacka 2017: 228). His analysis suggests that the potential political implications of these internalized harms merit serious consideration.

5.5 Conclusion: Street-Level Organizations, Discretion and Welfare State Politics

Street-level organizations occupy an important and problematic structural position within welfare state politics, where they, effectively, mediate between citizens and state and between policy and practice. Within their boundaries, a politics of discretion takes shape as everyday discretionary practices influence social provision, structure opportunities for claiming and voice; and manage the consequences of conflicts inherent in organizational practices.

The everyday practices that indirectly produce these effects tend to be opaque, their patterns difficult to discern, and their effects even more difficult to ascertain. Thus, the politics of discretion largely occurs at a remove both from managerial instruments of accountability and oversight and also from democratic mechanisms of accountability and responsiveness. Certainly, it is difficult to contest what one cannot readily see.

The discretionary practices of street-level organizations merit attention as an object of study that can illuminate otherwise hidden domains of welfare state politics where struggles for rights, recognition and relief take place in everyday organizational life.

Note

1. The arguments outlined here are adapted from and draw on Brodkin (2009) and (2013).

References

Adler, M. (2013). Sanctions and the absence of redress in British New Deal programs. In E.Z. Brodkin & G. Marston (Eds), *Work and the welfare state* (pp. 229–248). Washington, DC: Georgetown University Press.

Adler, M.E. (2006, December). Fairness in context. *Journal of Law and Society*, 33(4), 615–638.

Andersen, N., Caswell, D. & Larsen, F. (2017). A new approach to helping the hard to place unemployed: The promise of developing new knowledge in an interactive and collaborative process. *European Journal of Social Security*, 19(4), 335–352.

Arnold, R.D. (1990). *The logic of congressional action*. New Haven, CT: Yale University Press.

Bennett, S.D. (1995). No relief but upon the terms of coming into the house: Controlled Spaces, Invisible Disentitlements, and Homelessness in an Urban Shelter System. *Yale LJ*, 104, 2157.

Brodkin, E.Z. (2007). Bureaucracy redux: Management reformism and the welfare state. *Journal of Public Administration Research and Theory*, 17(1), 1–17.

———. (2009). The politics and governance of workfare in the US. In F. Larsen & R. van Berkel (Eds), *The new governance and implementation of labour market policies* (pp. 139–165). Copenhagen: DJOF Publishing.

———. (2011). Policy work: Street-level organizations under New Managerialism. *Journal of Public Administration Research and Theory*, 21(suppl 2), i253–i277.

———. (2013). Street-level organizations and the welfare state. In E. Brodkin & G. Marston (Eds), *Work and the welfare state* (pp. 143–166). Washington, DC: Georgetown University Press.

———. (2015). The inside story: Street-level research in the US and beyond. In P. Hupe, M. Hill & A. Buffat (Eds), *Understanding street-level bureaucracy* (pp. 25–42). Bristol: Policy Press.

Brodkin, E.Z. & Majmundar, M. (2010). Administrative exclusion: Organizations and the hidden costs of welfare claiming. *Journal of Public Administration Research and Theory*, 20(4), 827–848.

Brodkin, E.Z. & Marston, G. (Eds). (2013). *Work and the welfare state*. Washington, DC: Georgetown University Press.

Considine, M. (2005). The reform that never ends: Quasi-markets and employment services in Australia. In E. Sol & M. Westerveld (Eds), *Contractualism in employment service: A new form of welfare state governance* (pp. 41–71). The Hague, The Netherlands: Kluwer Law International.

Cutler, T. & Waine, B. (2000). Managerialism reformed? New Labour and public sector management. *Social Policy and Administration*, 34(3), 318–332.

Dias, J.J. & Maynard-Moody, S. (2006). For-profit welfare: Contracts, conflicts, and the performance paradox. *Journal of Public Admin. Research and Theory*, 17(2), 189–211.

Edelman, M. (1964). *The symbolic uses of politics*. Urbana, IL: University of Illinois Press.

———. (1977). *Political language: Words that succeed and policies that fail*. New York: Academic Press.

Evans, P.B., Rueschemeyer, D. & Skocpol, T. (1985). *Bringing the state back in*. Cambridge: Cambridge University Press.

Felstiner, W., Abel, R. & Sarat, A. (1980–1981). The emergence and transformation of disputes: Naming, blaming, claiming … *Law & Society R*, 15, (3/4), 631–654.

Hasenfeld, Y. (1992). The nature of human service organizations. In Y. Hasenfeld (Ed.), *Human services as complex organizations* (pp. 24–44). Newbury Park, CA: Sage Publications.

———. (2000). Organizational forms and moral practices: The case of welfare departments. *Social Service R*, 74(3), 329–351.

Hasenfeld, Y. & Powell, L.E. (2004). The role of non-profit agencies in the provision of welfare-to-work services. *Administration in Social Work*, 28(3/4), 91–110.

Herd, D. & Lightman, E. (2005). Rituals of degradation: Administration as policy in the Ontario Works programme. *Social Policy and Administration*, 39(1), 65–79.

Hupe, P.L. (2013) Dimensions of discretion: Specifying the object of street-level bureaucracy research. *Der Moderne Staat. Zeitschrift für Public Policy, Recht und Management*, 6(2), 425–440.

Kingdon, J.W. (1984). *Agendas, alternatives, and public policies.* Glenview, IL: Scotts, Foresman & Company.

Lasswell, H.D. (1936). *Politics: Who gets what, when, how.* New York: McGraw Hill.

Lens, V. (2013). Redress and Accountability in Work Activation Policies in the US. In E.Z. Brodkin & G. Marston (Eds), *Work and the welfare state* (pp. 249–267). Washington, DC: Georgetown University Press.

Lindblom, C.E. (1959). The science of muddling through. *Public Administration Review*, 19, 79–88.

Lipsky, M. (1980). *Street-level bureaucracy: Dilemmas of the individual in public services.* New York: Russell Sage Foundation.

Lowi, T.J. (1979). *The end of liberalism: The second republic of the United States* (2nd ed.). New York: W.W. Norton.

March, J.G. & Olsen, J.P. (1983). The New Institutionalism: Organizational factors in political life. *American Political Science* Review, 78(3), 734–749.

Maynard-Moody, S. & Musheno, M. (2003). *Cops, teachers, counselors: Stories from the front lines of public service.* Ann Arbor: University of Michigan Press.

McCleary, R. (1978). On becoming a client. *Journal of Social Issues*, 34, 57–75.

Miller, G. (1983). Holding clients accountable: The micro-politics of trouble in a work incentive program. *Social Problems*, 31(2), 139–151.

Morgen, S. (2001). The agency of welfare workers: Negotiating devolution, privatization, and the meaning of self-sufficiency. *American Anthropologist*, 103 (3), 747–761.

Pierson, P. (1994). *Dismantling the welfare state? Reagan, Thatcher, and the politics of retrenchment.* Cambridge: Cambridge University Press.

———. (2005). The study of policy development. *Journal of Policy History*, 17(1), 34–51.

Price, D.E. (1981). Policy making in congressional committees. *American Political Science Review*, 72(2), 548–574.

Robertson, D.B. (1993). The return to history and the new institutionalism in American political science. *Social Science History*, 17(1), 1–36.

Skocpol, T. (1992). *Protecting soldiers and mothers.* Cambridge, MA: Harvard University Press.

Small, M.L. (2006). Neighborhood institutions as resource brokers: Childcare centers, inter-organizational ties, and resource access among the poor. *Social Problems*, 53(2), 274–292.

Smith, B.D. & Donovan, S. (2003). Child welfare practice in organizational and institutional context. *Social Service Review*, 77(4), 541–563.

Soss, J. (1999). Welfare application encounters: Subordination, satisfaction, and the puzzle of client evaluations. *Administration and Society*, 31(1), 50–94.

Soss, J., Fording, R. & Schram, S. (2011). *Disciplining the poor: Neoliberal paternalism and the persistent power of race.* Chicago: University of Chicago Press.

Spitzmueller, M. (2014). *The making of community mental health policy in everyday street-level practice: An organizational ethnography.* Ph.D. dissertation, University of Chicago.

Stone, D. (1984). *The disabled state.* Philadelphia, PA: Temple University Press.

van Berkel, R., Caswell, D., Larsen, F. & Kupka, P. (Eds). (2017). *The front-line delivery of welfare-to-work in the EU.* London: Routledge.

Van Slyke, D.M. (2003). The mythology of privatization in contracting for social services. *Public Administration Review*, 63(5), 296–315.

Watkins-Hayes, C. (2013). Race, respect, and red tape: Inside the black box of racially representative bureaucracies. In E.Z. Brodkin & G. Marston (Eds), *Work and the welfare state* (pp. 167–184). Washington, DC: Georgetown University Press.

Zacka, B. (2017). *When the state meets the street: Public service and moral agency.* Cambridge: Harvard University Press.

CHAPTER 6

Discretion and Welfare Rights in a British Context

Michael Hill

6.1 Introduction

When discretion is seen as policy problem, context will be important. Particularly salient here is the substantive policy area involved. One particular area where debates about discretion have occurred is in the provision of cash benefits. In this context concerns about how discretion is exercised are embedded in a wider debate between the arguments for selectivity and those for universalism in social policy, driven forward by activists and scholars who emphasize the importance of welfare rights.

Rothstein (1998: 160–1) argues:

> [S]elective programs present serious problems of implementation, for they allow administrators a wide field for discretionary action. There is often no solution to this problem (within the limits of such programs). The difficulty of finding useable criteria for selecting recipients can often become unmanageable. This creates a 'black hole of democracy' in which citizens find themselves faced with an administration or system of rules which no one really understands and in which no one can be held responsible.

Rothstein goes on to echo an argument found in the conclusion of Titmuss' (1958) treatment of this subject: a need to minimize discretion through the elimination of means testing in favour of more universalist social security programmes. There is a long-standing theme here about how to replace the Poor Law. Winston Churchill, in his days as a social reformer, argued in 1909 for the introduction of unemployment insurance in terms of its simple qualifying rules: 'I do not like mixing up moralities and mathematics' (quoted in Fulbrook 1978: 137–8).

M. Hill (✉)
University of Newcastle, Newcastle upon Tyne, UK

T. Evans, P. Hupe (eds.), *Discretion and the Quest for Controlled Freedom*, https://doi.org/10.1007/978-3-030-19566-3_6

However, if discretionary action is *the problem*, it may be argued that it is one that needs not be solved by the elimination of means testing but rather that selectivity may be designed in ways involving 'criteria' which minimize it. In this chapter using illustrations from the debate about discretion in social assistance in the UK, it will be argued that this is something very hard to achieve.

The case for centring this argument around a particular debate in a specific country is that it has occupied a salient role in the development of both welfare rights action and the study of social policy in the UK. This goes aside from the fact that a short chapter cannot range too widely and the fact that the present author, having been heavily involved in it during his early career, is better qualified to explore the UK debate than to attempt a more wide-ranging analysis. This being so, it may be noted that aspects of this debate have been explored in a comparative study of social assistance (Eardley, Bradshaw, Ditch, Gough and Whiteford 1996) and that Jewell (2007) has brilliantly highlighted some of the problems about achieving a balance between rules and discretion in social administration in a comparative study of Germany, Sweden and the United States.

This chapter will start with a brief account of the way in which the UK system was shaped after the Beveridge Report by the 1948 National Assistance Act. It will proceed from that to the discussion of the debate about the discretionary powers under the Act developed in the 1960s and 1970. Then attention will be given to the 1980 and 1986 Acts, which eliminated the powers to give discretionary additions and restricted the availability of single payments. But these changes left behind difficult issues about the interpretation of rules restricting the availability of benefits ('discretion' in the terms used in this edited collection). Aspects of these—the restriction of rent payments, the treatment of single parents and the administration of benefits to people out of work—are explored. This leads to discussions of the difficulties inherent in the framing of rules for complex situations and of the implications of decision-making without face-to-face contact and then a final summing-up section.

6.2 Discretion in the National Assistance Board

The National Assistance Act of 1948 was the last step in the demolition of the British Poor Law. It gave responsibility for residential care for the aged or disabled poor to the local authorities, but set up a national body to administer cash payments to meet need, the National Assistance Board (NAB). That organization, staffed by civil servants and ultimately responsible to the government through the Ministry of Pensions and National Insurance, was given a measure of autonomy with a government-appointed Board. It inherited duties given to the Unemployment Assistance Board in 1934, whose role was further extended in 1940. When the Beveridge Report (1942) recommended the establishment of a comprehensive system of social insurance, it recognized the need for a residual body to meet needs not covered by insurance (para. 369) and that there would be a transitional period before contributory benefits (particularly pensions) reached subsistence level.

While the National Assistance Act was claimed to represent the abolition of the Poor Law, the absence here of a clean break from the stigma of means testing meant that suspicion particularly attached to the discretionary provisions in the legislation. However, in the House of Commons debate on the 1948 National Assistance Act, the Minister of National Insurance, James Griffiths, offered an argument for discretion that would be unlikely to hear from a politician today:

> In the field in which the Assistance Board will make cash payments after July, there will be an infinite variety of human needs to meet—such an infinite variety that I am certain it cannot be met by any general scale or special standard scales, however generous. It is, therefore, essential that from the beginning the Board should realise that they will not be able to fulfil their tasks adequately unless they exercise a wide measure of discretion in their payments over and above the standard scales (Hansard 1947: 1172).

That statement highlights powers to provide extra; these took two forms: regular weekly additions to benefits, mostly provided to older people for exceptional extra costs arising from heating, laundry and special dietary needs and one-off payments for exceptional needs for clothing replacements, removal costs, house maintenance and so forth These both steadily grew in importance across the life of the NAB, and it was certainly the case that their arbitrary nature was an important facet of the critique of discretion. The NAB was replaced by the Supplementary Benefits Commission in 1969 and there were some efforts to strengthen the rule structure. Legislation in 1980 took this process further (see Walker 1983, 2015) and will be discussed below. Since then there have been various name changes to the extent that, to avoid confusion, the generic expression 'social assistance' is used in much of the rest of this discussion.

There were also powers to reduce benefits below what might, from a superficial look at the rules, be considered standard entitlements. They included powers to restrict the following:

- Rent payments where rent were considered excessive, a rule that included considerations about whether it was reasonable for the claimant to live in such accommodation (note that later legislation shifted the onus for assistance with housing costs to the local authorities).
- Payments to unemployed people if the entitlement determined by the standard rules was deemed to be above the wage level the claimant was likely to be able to achieve. This provision was described as a 'wage stop'.
- Payments restricted to below the standard allowance where individuals were deemed to have left jobs voluntarily or been sacked for forms of misconduct (these provisions followed from more explicit rules contained in the National Insurance Act and therefore involved a complex and sometimes fraught interaction with the local Department of Employment office).

There was also a particularly difficult issue about what was then called 'cohabitation', about claims from single or deserted women in situations in which they were living with men (see Marsden 1973). The salience of this issue particularly derived from the fact that the means test was a 'family' one with provisions (as in fact was the case with national insurance) assuming that two can live more cheaply than one.

6.3 The Debate About Discretion in Social Assistance

The present author wrote an article based upon his own experience of working in the NAB in which he sought to analyse the factors that influenced the way discretion was used (Hill 1969). The article attracted attention, since it came out at a time when a lively debate was emerging about the need for more effective government action to alleviate poverty. A pressure group that remains the most effective lobby group on poverty, the Child Poverty Action Group, was founded in 1965 (see McCarthy 1986). Alongside arguments about the need for substantive policy change an emergent 'welfare rights' movement began to raise issues about the role of discretion.

The author found his article used by both sides of the argument about this. One particular contribution came from an academic who was also the Vice-chairman of the new Supplementary Benefits Commission, Richard Titmuss. He used the evidence on the minutiae of decision as material for a controversial essay attacking the emergent welfare rights movement that seemed to be arguing that all social assistance entitlements could be codified as 'rights'. Titmuss (1971: 124–5), after reviewing the American literature on the subject (including notably Davis' [1969] arguments against discretion), argued against

> the 'pathology of legalism' rules based on precedent and responsive only very slowly to rapidly changing human needs and circumstances. The increasing application of 'legalism' to the public assistance system combined with rising demands for 'welfare rights' has led, all over the United States, to a massive fragmentation of entitlement. Itemised legal entitlements, in the assessment of needs and resources, now embrace hundreds of visible articles and objects—practically everything that bedrooms, living-rooms, kitchens and lavatories may contain.

Titmuss' view was contested by those who, whilst sharing his view on the need to maximize right to 'universalist' benefits, considered he took too complacent a view of residual discretion (see Townsend 1975).

In the mid-1970s the debate about discretion in social assistance led to a substantial internal review of the system initiated in 1976, conducted with comparatively open participation (for the history of this initiative see Walker 1983). A key actor here was the Chairman of the Supplementary Benefits Commission appointed in 1975: David Donnison. In exploring the case for reform he made a distinction between 'judgement' and 'discretion' (Donnison 1977). Judging by his later discussion of this (Donnison 1982) he seems to recognize that this is a difficult distinction to make—discretionary decisions depend upon judgement. However, what he seemed to be aiming at was a narrowing of the area of discretionary decision-making to highlight the exceptional. This was done in the 1980 Act by embodying in the basic legal framework a provision making a distinction between rates payable to long-term and short-term claimants so that the discretionary additions were, roughly speaking, integrated into the long-term rate payable to elderly people and the long-term sick. The issue of discretionary single payments was tackled by provisions making them, other than in certain special situations, only available as loans. These were provided from a cash-limited Social Fund. That is of course a simplified account of two Acts of Parliament enacted in 1980 and 1986.

The important point for this chapter is to highlight that replacing discretion by much more specific rules about entitlement had to mean what was, in the debate at the time about gainers and losers, called 'rough justice'. The new rules guaranteed additional benefits to some who had previously depended upon discretionary decisions in their favour but also excluded some from consideration. Drawing a firm line between categories of claims instead of discretion imposed a much more explicit politically driven approach to a state-protected minimum than that implied in the quotation from James Griffiths set out above. However, the 1980 and 1986 Acts left broadly untouched the issues about discretion that could involve the refusal or cutting of benefits. The next section explores these.

6.4 Discretion and the Restriction of Benefits

Rent Additions

It is pertinent to note that the Beveridge Report considered how to include an element to cover housing costs in the payment scales it recommended for National Insurance. Because it found this too difficult, a rent addition provision was included in National Assistance, generating as, noted above, the possibility of discretionary adjustment if the rent was deemed to be too high. In the early days variations between rent levels were not substantial, with subsidies to local authority housing providers contributing to minimizing the need for specific benefit restrictions. Various government housing policies undermined that situation, notably the weakening of controls on private rents and encouragement to local authorities to consider schemes that means-tested rent.

The most significant developments on this issue however occurred under the Conservative government led by Margaret Thatcher in the 1980s. The support of rental costs was shifted from the social assistance scheme to a national Housing Benefit scheme, run by local authorities. At the same time subsidies to local authority housing schemes were shifted in ways which increased rent differentials. The central government's aim was to subsidize renters rather than houses, shifting housing costs onto high-income tenants and supporting low-income ones by way of benefits. Furthermore, a sequence of measures encouraged the sale of local authority houses to their tenants and the transfer of the remaining housing stock to housing associations. In effect, the changes summarized here amounted to what was in fact a revolution in the public support for the housing of the poor, generating a range of new issues about the benefit subsidy of housing. These included ones about the treatment of people in high-value houses or seen as under-occupying larger and more expensive houses (when the children had left home) or in situations in which their landlords could increase rent assured that the benefit scheme would take on the additional cost.

These developments brought to a head, in respect of the housing costs, the *discretion* versus *rough justice* issue discussed above. Should extensive local discretion, perhaps at local cost, be relied upon to deal with these issues or should rules be developed that placed ceilings on the levels of cost to be met. It has, across a series of recent measures, been the latter approach that has been adopted. The hardship consequent upon this forced those affected tenants to try to solve the problem by moving or otherwise experience inroads into their disposable income. Here again then is a situation in which the imposition of rules has had negative consequences.

The Treatment of Single Parents and Other Issues About Household Composition

The National Assistance scheme had to deal with two related policy problems in respect of the treatment of single parents: the expectation that absent parents (almost always of course fathers) should contribute to the costs of their children (including perhaps the living costs of the parent carer) and the fact that there might be grounds for disputing the 'single' status of the claimant. The salience of these issues has been affected, over time, by changes in social behaviour.

In the 1960s most single parents were divorced or separated; there were very few claims from unmarried mothers. The NAB employed 'liable relative officers' with a role to try either to see that there were court settlements in place with payments being made or to encourage voluntary settlements (under the threat that the NAB had powers to secure court orders) (see Marsden 1973 for an account of this activity from the recipients' point of view). In the 1980s the government became dissatisfied with this situation, hence tried to replace a quasi-discretionary approach with a more formal one. This was a formula-driven scheme to replace both the assessments made as part of the administration of the existing means-tested benefits and the assessments made by the courts in determining maintenance on the breakdown of a relationship. The Child Support Act was enacted in 1991, but ran into severe implementation problems from its ambition not merely to strengthen the search for support of benefit claimants, but also to take over the role of the courts. But perhaps the point most relevant to this chapter is that a rather loose system, depending on a combination of the capacity of the relief agency to take action and the (discretionary?) decisions taken by the courts, was replaced by an elaborate formula which looked at the resources available on both sides (parent carer and absent parent) and therefore had to adjust as these varied. The workload of the new Child Support Agency was heavy and the disputes many (particularly in the light of the significance of post-split family arrangements aiming to ensure contact on both sides). Eventually there was a return to a system not widely dissimilar to that which prevailed before it. The discussion returns to this below.

The other issue arises particularly from interaction between the assumptions mentioned above about support from absent parents and the operation in the benefits system (also in UK insurance benefits) of the assumption that two can live more cheaply than one. A couple (living together as man and wife) secure less in benefits than two separate single people. While the UK system can be accused of having a particular obsession with sexual relationships, there is an issue here about any rules in which benefit entitlements are dependent upon household arrangements. Not only do sharing arrangements in respect of daily living, heating and lighting make a difference, so do those in respect of payment of rent. As an issue about discretion this comes down principally to an issue about the interpretation of specific situations (and perhaps the detection of fraud through non-disclosure). However, there are issues about how readily rules can be devised to deal with marginal cases, intermittent residency in particular. In the contemporary situation with respect to alleged under-occupation affecting Housing Benefit entitlement, hard cases about the availability of spare rooms for returning adult children have secured media attention.

The Treatment of Unemployed Claimants

The provisions in the National Assistance scheme to enforce labour market attachment have a history going back to the introduction of measures to supply benefits to unemployed people in the UK at the beginning of the twentieth century, and have equivalents in many countries. In the UK Unemployment Insurance scheme operating in the early 1960s there were safeguards, inserted to reassure the trades unions, designed to protect workers from arbitrary action by employers (see Fulbrook 1978), specifying the rules relating to denial of benefits and linking these to an appeal system. The NAB broadly followed these, except inasmuch as its powers included the 'wage stop' provision described above. Like its successor body, it was not confined to these options and one innovation it tried was a procedure in which time limits were imposed on the continued receipt of support. That measure did not survive into the period of much higher unemployment which started in the late 1970s. However, what also came with higher unemployment was the development of a continuing succession of schemes to train and support unemployed people. The word 'coerce' might also have been used in that last sentence; benefit penalties might be applied to failure to participate in these developments (space limitations prevent an extension of this discussion into this area of public policy where discretionary elements are widespread); see, for example, May and Winter (2009) on Denmark and Osiander and Steinke (2016) on Germany.

Again, as in the earlier discussion of changing housing policy, it is difficult to fully explain the evolution of discretionary powers without a long digression into the wider context of policy change. From the 1970s onwards the system of both financial support and help with job-seeking or training to unemployed people in the UK changed dramatically in a context of higher unemployment and government policies which increasing stigmatized the workless (see, for example, Green Ed. 1990). The fact that the insurance benefit for unemployed people depended on a sustained period of contributions before losing a job and was exhausted after a period, meant that a high proportion of workless people were supported by mean-tested benefits. Another change has been the increased incidence of female labour market participation. Social assistance rules that specifically excluded women with school-age children from any requirement to seek work have been successively altered to force all but the mothers of children under 1 to be subject to the regulation of behaviour linked to receipt of the benefit now called 'job seekers allowance'.

The intention here is not to suggest that unemployed people in the UK are now subject to a control regime characterized as uncontrolled discretion, but rather that a substantial area of regulatory activity—much of it quite elaborately codified—involves forms of discretion inasmuch as officials are engaged in making judgements about efforts to obtain work or training and may apply sanctions if dissatisfied with these efforts. There are close parallels here with the US welfare administration practices described by Brodkin (2011; see also Chap. 5 of this edited collection).

Alongside the development of ways of receipt of social assistance for people below retirement age to labour market participation has come increasing attention to the validity of claims to be unfit for work. The UK, in common with other European countries, encountered increased levels of claims for benefits available to long-term sick and disabled people. It is not the concern of this chapter to explain this development, except to say that one governmental response to it was to look increasingly critically at people's claims to be unfit for work. The consequence was the increase in the testing of these claims, a form of discretion not absent in the NAB but unmentioned in the 1969 article. The arbitrary nature of this activity has attracted attention in the press, particularly inasmuch as it has been contracted out to private agencies, who are alleged to work with specific performance targets, setting goals for numbers of claims disallowed. The implications of having a claim to be unfit to work disallowed are both a reduction to a low level of benefit entitlement and exposure to the sanctioning regime described in the last sub-section.

6.5 When Making Rules Is Difficult

The attack on discretion in social assistance in the UK came in the first place as an argument about a lack of enforceable rights, involving therefore unfairness. Its intellectual roots were in Davis' (1969: 215) attack on the 'unpleasant areas of discretionary determinations'. This was taken up by people concerned about poverty in the form of a two-pronged attack: one against the discretionary power of the system, the other against individual decisions by that system. The second wing of that attack therefore involved 'welfare rights' work supporting claimants' efforts to secure more through advocacy at the 'street level' but also at the appeal tribunals. This second wing produced the paradoxical effect that it became seen as problematical to the funder of the system, the government. During the 1960s the numbers of discretionary additions to benefits, both weekly supplements and single payments, increased rapidly (see Walker 1983, Chap. 3). There was also a steady increase in the number of claims taken to appeal tribunals. Moreover this discretion was costly, not just in terms of amounts added to benefits but also in terms of staff costs. Hence where the welfare rights movement criticized the discretionary provisions for doing too little to relieve poverty, the government attacked them for doing too much.

The attack on discretionary additions was naturally then at the centre of the 'reform' debate in the 1970s. Hence the distinction made above between this aspect of social assistance policy where discretion has been curbed effectively and the other aspects which have continued unresolved and on and off the policy change agenda ever since. What this seems to do is to highlight issues about complexity at the heart of the need for discretion. An important point about the discretionary additions was that they are explicitly quantifiable; the decisions involved are about amounts of money. This is particularly clear as far as the weekly additions were concerned. Reform meant building them into the basic weekly allowance for some and conversely denying this to others. The advocates for the poor, like the Child Poverty Action Group (McCarthy 1986), had to accept that there were winners and losers in the 'victory' against discretionary additions.

The other element in the debate about additions to benefit, single payments for exceptional needs, has been the subject of suggestions that perhaps they can be handled better if the decision-makers are in some sense trained 'specialists'. A brief digression on this issue is justified by the role of that argument in respect to the exercise of discretionary powers.

In the debate about social assistance reform in the 1970s one option to deal with this issue was seen as involving local-authority-employed social workers in benefit administration. As social work increasingly focused, in the 1950s and 1960s, on preventative work designed to support children in their own homes, social workers became increasingly dissatisfied that they could not make cash payments themselves. Legislation in the 1960s permitted such payments (Packman 1975). Research on how this power was used indicated that its use varied erratically between different local authorities (Lister and Emmett 1976; Hill and Laing 1979; Valencia, Jackson and Bland 1979). This actually had the effect of taking some of the pressure off the central social assistance budget.

This issue was given a new twist by the limitation imposed on the use of social assistance by the 1986 Social Security Act. The local authorities did not want to find that these budgets had to grow rapidly to meet needs the Department of Social Security was unprepared to meet (Jones 1989). But the position of local authority social workers was further complicated by assumptions made by the Department of Social Security (and embodied in the Social Fund guidelines for their staff) that social workers would co-operate in the assessment of need for Social Fund help and in particular in sorting out cases where Community Care Grants might help people to leave or remain out of institutional care. The local authority associations, the main social worker organization (British Association of Social Workers) and the main local government trade union (NALGO) all refused to accept the role the Department of Social Security had identified for social workers. The preference was for what was called 'determined advocacy', in essence involving agreeing to help clients fight the Social Fund for the best possible deal and not cooperating with the Social Fund to vet claims, to sort out budgeting problems or to cool out 'undeserving' claimants. This added a dimension to the already heavy demands on social workers (Wilson and Hill 1988) and one response at that time was the appointment of 'welfare rights' officers in local authority departments to undertake this task. In practice, in the face of cuts to local government finance, this work has withered away.

The point of this digression therefore is to note that two idea currents in the period 1960–1980—either that social work and social assistance might become integrated or that the exercise of discretionary powers might come under adversarial scrutiny by the local authority departments that employ social workers—were de facto rejected. This left both exceptional material provision (by way, for example, of food banks) and welfare rights advocacy to voluntary organizations.

Modern controversy about social assistance discretion has thus particularly centred upon issues other than the exceptional enhancement of benefits, that is, rules that have particularly defeated efforts to routinize because of their complexity. This is particularly evident in the case of the Child Support Act. King and Crewe (2013) call their chapter on this, in their book *Blunders of our governments*, 'Support for children—or taxpayers?' Here, of course, quantification was possible; there was scope for developing a formula to determine amounts of money paid. However:

> The new child-maintenance formula was laid out across four pages of closely typed algebra and could require up to 144 separate computations. If either parent requested a review, the initial maintenance assessment could be recalculated as often as four times a year (King and Crewe 2013: Kindle loc. 1646).

An important point about this attempt to limit discretion (as noted above, not just the discretion of social assistance officials but also that exercised by the courts) is that it occurred at a time when dramatic changes were occurring in family life in the UK. Relatively stable marriage (exceptionally punctuated by separation or divorce) as the norm for the procreation of children was being replaced by a diversity of arrangements between couples. Concerns for the welfare of children meant that the formal (in the case of marriage breakdown) and informal (in other cases) arrangements made between parents needed to be flexible and ideally consensual. The heavy hand of a government agency working with an elaborate formula could easily be a counterproductive force in these circumstances. But even when the new child support system was looked at from a conventional, money-oriented, public management point of view:

> The National Audit Office (NAO) [...] revealed that CSA officials spent 90 per cent of their time in calculating maintenance assessments and only 10 per cent on collecting actual money [...]. The CSA [...] was still taking more than six months to process close to half of all its cases. Two in five of its assessments were wrong. A backlog of 570,000 cases were still outstanding, and more than half of them had been for more than a year (King and Crewe 2013: Kindle loc. 1655).

The issues about the treatment of single parents differ from the other areas in which continuing issues about the exercise of discretion have been identified—housing support, benefits for unemployed people, disability—in that an effort to reduce discretion could be based upon a formula. In all the other cases the money issues come down to ones about the refusal or limitation of benefit.

It is also pertinent that all the issues—including the treatment of single parents—are ones where there were strong political pressures for policy development and considerable controversy related to those pressures. Policy initiatives were driven by arguments that the so-called welfare state had created opportunities for the exploitation of the system. Payments to single mothers, public support for rents and tolerance of scroungers unwilling to work or feigning disability featured in this discourse (Boyson 1971). Whilst many accounts of the impact of this process then feature explicit cuts to benefits and it is not the purpose of this discussion to deny the significance of these, it may be argued that the continuation of a variety of forms of discretion was a product of compromises in which there was a wish to be able to show that punitive measures might be mitigated in specific circumstances.

6.6 Dispensing with Face-to-Face Contact

An important theme in the attack upon discretion is that it personalizes decision-making in ways which mean that the race, class or gender biases of the decision-makers influence who gets what. Once again then, as noted in the last section, a concern that face-to-face decision-making is costly finds an ally amongst those whose concerns are not about that but about social justice. It may also be noted that the UK developments discussed here have occurred against the background of computing techniques that make the mass handling of complex decisions easier. The questions that follow, important for the analysis of the implications of discretion, are therefore about the negative consequences of the elimination of face-to-face contacts consequent upon the routinization of decision-making.

At the same time, too much should not be made of the issue about face-to-face encounters. Obviously there are activities where discretion and face-to-face engagement go hand in hand. If, for example, issues about teaching are discussed then there will be strong linked arguments against an impersonal distance learning system with mechanical marking procedures. In the case of social assistance the exercise of discretion without face-to-face contact may be feasible and desirable. A discussion of student grants in the Netherlands by Bovens and Zouridis (2002) provides a cognate example where a very personalized system, with very apparent arbitrary features, has been replaced by a system in which the discretionary elements are embedded in a questionnaire and its interpretation (see also Chap. 20 of this edited collection). On the other hand it may be argued that some of the problems about the child support scheme discussed above might have been avoided with provisions to enable an element of face-to-face negotiation about how to resolve conflicting approaches. Part of the case against the scheme is that it was introduced just at the time when efforts were being made to increase the use of mediation in divorce settlements. It may similarly be suggested that the benefit issues about the so-called under-occupation of houses could be tackled by discretionary powers linked with face-to-face examination of the hard cases. Indeed one can perhaps go further and suggest that the under-occupation of social housing is an issue best tackled by means other than arbitrary benefit cuts.

The policies to encourage labour market participation amongst unemployed and disabled people do still involve both discretionary powers and face-to-face contacts. A question that certainly troubles researchers here is whether the kinds of routinization developed in these fields reduce or enhance biases (Wright 2016).

Relevant to the whole issue of the use of face-to-face contact in the exercise of discretion in social assistance is the fact that many of the people likely to be affected by adverse decisions may face difficulties in understanding and completing forms. Amongst claimants there may be low levels of literacy, while many may not have English as their first language.

6.7 Conclusion

There are two issues that are particularly salient in this account of the evolution of discretion in UK social assistance. One concerns the feasibility of eliminating discretion in this activity, the other the desirability of doing so. In practice these two questions are linked because issues about whether it is desirable to eliminate comes to a head when that elimination is particularly difficult.

On the first question Carol Walker's (2016: 60) summing-up of her account of the history of discretionary payments in social assistance is pertinent:

> As the primary concern of British social security policy has shifted from meeting the needs of the poor and vulnerable to cutting total spending, regardless of the consequences for claimants, so the role of the street-level bureaucrat has been transformed. Their scope for discretion has been virtually eliminated as computerized assessments have replaced the exercising of individual skill and judgement. The scope for officials on the ground to exercise 'inherent discretion, […] func-

tion as policy co-makers, and [...] show a certain craftsmanship in fulfilling their tasks' no longer exists.[1]

This chapter takes a broader view of discretion in this field of activity inasmuch as it explores its role in relation to a wider range of issues than discretionary *payments*. It therefore suggests that it is important not to lose sight of the way in which the application of rules may imply a less visible exercise of discretion, particularly where the rules are applied to complex situations. In a sense, in a context in which there is an under-resourced administration and low levels of direct communication with benefit applicants, inaccurate rule application becomes the functional alternative to thoughtless or prejudiced discretion. This is particularly evident in the story of the Child Support Act.

On the other hand, the discussion, in the early part of the chapter, about discretionary additions and single payments focussed on what may be regarded as a dated debate. Titmuss' (1971) defence of discretion was expressed in the context in the belief that social assistance formed a 'withering safety net' to fade in importance as the social insurance system grew. Now it is the case that social insurance is of minimal significance in the UK for income support for anyone except those over pension age. The alternative of broadly framed rule systems for the main means-tested benefits may be defended as the 'least worst' option in the absence of social insurance. But as a consequence the welfare rights issues for modern advocates of the poor are harsh and arbitrary rules administered in pressurized benefit offices, where contact with the public is minimal and quantitative performance norms are salient. A latter-day Titmuss might not argue for discretion as an everyday feature of social assistance (as it was when the present author worked in the system), but surely might still have argued that discretionary interventions would be appropriate to handle complex issues. Among them are those associated with contemporary family changes, the search for accommodation in an under-supplied housing market for the poor or the difficulties facing disabled people when they seek work.

Note

1. In this quote Walker refers to the three elements of the working definition of street-level bureaucrats formulated by Hupe, Hill and Buffat in the introductory chapter of their edited volume (Hupe *et al.* 2015: 16).

References

Beveridge, W. (1942). *Social insurance and allied services*. Cmd.6404, London: HMSO.

Bovens, M. & Zouridis, S. (2002). From street-level to system-level bureaucracies: How information and communication technology is transforming administrative discretion and constitutional control. *Public Administration Review*, 62(2), 174–184.

Boyson, R. (1971). *Down with the poor*. London: Churchill.

Brodkin, E.Z. (2011). Policy work: Street-level organizations under new managerialism. *Journal of Public Administration and Research*, 21(2), 253–277.

Davis, K.C. (1969). *Discretionary justice*. Baton Rouge: Louisiana State University Press.
Donnison, D.V. (1977, September 15). Against Discretion. *New Society*, pp. 534–536.
Donnison, D. (1982). *The politics of poverty*. Oxford: Martin Robertson.
Eardley, T., Bradshaw, J., Ditch, J., Gough, I. & Whiteford, P. (1996). *Social assistance in OECD countries: Synthesis report*. London: HMSO.
Fulbrook, J. (1978). *Administrative justice and the unemployed*. London: Mansell.
Green, D. (Ed.) (1990). *The emerging British underclass*. London: IEA.
Hansard (1947). *Second reading of the National Assistance Bill*. Hansard 24 November 1947, vol. 444, cc 1603–716.
Hill, M.J. (1969). The exercise of discretion in the National Assistance Board. *Public Administration*, 47, 75–90.
Hill, M. & Laing, P. (1979). *Social work and money*. London: Allen and Unwin.
Hupe, P., Hill, M. & Buffat, A. (2015) Introduction: Defining and understanding street-level bureaucracy. In P. Hupe, M. Hill & A. Buffat (Eds), *Understanding street-level bureaucracy* (pp. 3–24). Bristol: Policy Press.
Jewell, C.J. (2007). *Agents of the welfare state. How caseworkers respond to need in the United States, Germany and Sweden*. New York: Palgrave Macmillan.
Jones, B. (1989). Section one: At the crossroads. *Benefits Research*, 3, 22–25.
King, A. & Crewe, I. (2013). *The blunders of our governments*. London: One World
Lister, R. & Emmett, T. (1976). *Under the safety net*. London: Child Poverty Action Group.
Marsden, D. (1973). *Mothers alone*. Harmondsworth: Penguin Books.
May, P.J. & Winter, S.C. (2009): Politicians, managers, and street-level bureaucrats: Influences on policy implementation. *Journal of Public Administration Research and Theory*, 19(3), 453–476.
McCarthy, M. (1986). *Campaigning for the poor*. Beckenham: Croom Helm.
Osiander, C. & Steinke, J. (2016) The moment of street-level bureaucrats in a public employment service. In P. Hupe, M. Hill & A. Buffat (Eds), *Understanding street-level bureaucracy* (pp. 295–312). Bristol: Policy Press.
Packman, J. (1975). *The child's generation*. Oxford: Blackwell.
Rothstein, B. (1998). *Just institutions matter*. Cambridge: Cambridge University Press.
Titmuss, R.M. (1958). *Essays on the welfare state*. London: Allen and Unwin.
Titmuss, R.M. (1971). Welfare rights, law and discretion. *Political Quarterly*, 42(2), 113–132.
Townsend, P. (1975). *Sociology and social policy*. London: Allen Lane.
Valencia, M., Jackson, M. & Bland, R. (1979). Variations in provision of financial aid through social work. *Policy and Politics*, 7(1), 69–81.
Walker, C. (1983). *Changing social policy*. London: Bedford Square Press.
Walker, C. (2016). Discretionary payments in social assistance. In P. Hupe, M. Hill & A. Buffat (Eds), *Understanding street-level bureaucracy* (pp. 45–60). Bristol: Policy Press.
Wilson, A. & Hill, M. (1988). Social workers and welfare rights. *Social Services Research*, 5.
Wright, S. (2016). Conceptualising the active welfare subject: Welfare reform in discourse, policy and lived experience. *Policy and Politics*, 44(2), 235–252.

CHAPTER 7

Discretion and Empowerment

Greg Marston and Danielle Davidson

7.1 Introduction

Empowerment is a polyvocal term with a range of normative meanings. Individuals may be empowered when they have a sufficient level of autonomy to be self-determining in regard to basic liberties enshrined in law. Individuals may also be empowered when they have knowledge and material resources to make an informed choice about where to live, when and what to study, where to work and what to do with their discretionary time. In political terms, geographical- or identity-based communities are empowered when they successfully make claims on the state in regard to securing human rights. The meaning of empowerment can as well be defined by its opposite. Coercion is considered antithetical to a liberal interpretation of empowerment. When the state or another external authority exercises unreasonable control, then the possibility of the self-determining subject is substantially weakened. In the middle of this continuum is a 'grey area' where various state and non-state actors, including the helping professions, are situated in a mix of care and control discourses and practices. The profession of social work, for example, explicitly draws on empowerment as a principle that defines and informs their ethical practice. In this context, the idea of empowerment implies that something or someone needs to change for individual well-being to be improved, often through the redistribution of material resources, knowledge or some other valued resource. These descriptions illustrate the difficulty of pinning down the meaning of empowerment, particularly when it comes to professional practice and policy

G. Marston (✉)
School of Social Science, The University of Queensland, Brisbane, QLD, Australia
e-mail: g.marston@uq.edu.au

D. Davidson
School of Public Health and Social Work, Queensland University of Technology, Brisbane, QLD, Australia

T. Evans, P. Hupe (eds.), *Discretion and the Quest for Controlled Freedom*, https://doi.org/10.1007/978-3-030-19566-3_7

implementation, where empowerment is frequently espoused but rarely questioned.

In her seminal work on the concept of empowerment, *The will to empower*, the political scientist Barbara Cruikshank (1999) makes the argument that empowerment can be both liberating and coercive at the same time. Cruikshank's (1999: 68) thesis poses a challenge to a normative discourse where 'empowerment is unquestionably viewed to be a "noble or radical political strategy"'. Cruikshank (1999: 67) argues that 'the political logic and techniques of empowerment developed in social programmes and reform movements produce a technology of citizenship—a method of constituting citizens out of subjects and maximising their political participation'. Cruikshank's framework is closely aligned with Foucault's analysis of government as the 'conduct of conduct', where programmes designed to empower clients are a form of politics, a strategy to act upon others by getting them to act in their own self-interest. The art of liberal government depends on technologies of citizenship developed in social movements, public policy, the professions and social science research to produce active and empowered citizens. These technologies rarely emerge from parliamentary democracy; they tend to be cultivated in social work discourses and therapeutic social service programmes, and their common goal is to get the citizen to act as his or her own master (Cruikshank 1999: 102). The goals of the programme or policy become the goals of the subject. The empowerment strategy relies on a complex interplay of personal autonomy, organizational interests and identities that promote an improved state of individual and collective well-being (Hand 2017: 20).

The chapter asks three questions about the politics and practice of the empowerment project. First, at the local level of social service organizations what does empowerment mean in an age of welfare retrenchment and conditional citizenship where citizens have less choice about determining the means and ends of welfare and well-being? Second, has our understanding of empowerment changed much since Cruikshank published her seminal work in 1999? And third, how does empowerment and discretion play out in service user-worker interactions? The first part of the chapter maps some of the context for understanding the ideal subject of 'welfare reform' and outlines the competing definitions of empowerment. The second part of the chapter looks at a case study of empowerment in a social service organization that has been seeking to redefine its goals and move away from a charitable and paternalistic approach to 'lifting people out of poverty', to a model where the means and ends of empowerment are coproduced through the practice of what the agency refers to as 'relational case management'. The case study illustrates the more nuanced way in which empowerment can be understood in contemporary human services practice, at the level of policy implementation.

The overall aim of the chapter is to critically examine the discourses of empowerment and the institutional contexts in which they are deployed, contested and reframed. As will be shown, depending on how it is defined, empowerment can provide an important justification for professional discretion on the front line of social services to act in the interests of individual or collective freedom. Conversely, empowerment can be a hollow term or a de-politicizing force when defined and deployed in terms of marketized choice and personal responsibility.

7.2 'Activating' Citizens: Empowerment Through Welfare Reform

Welfare states, as they have developed in English-speaking countries like Australia, the US, the UK and Canada during the twentieth and twenty-first centuries, pursued multiple objectives, some of which are highly contradictory. A country like Australia has weak forms of welfare universalism in the form of healthcare and primary and secondary education, while simultaneously pursuing market-orientated housing policies and income support systems in the form of 'workfare'. The latter is about making welfare subjects responsible for their own welfare through a combination of state discipline and human capital investment in preparation for maximizing participation in markets. Social services traditionally provided by the state are also outsourced through government contracts in quasi-market employment services. In Australia, this trend accelerated in the late 1990s when the Commonwealth (the national) Employment Service, which used to directly provide employment assistance to the unemployed, was put out to tender to for-profit and non-profit agencies that now provide these services on behalf of government (initially under the name of Job Network, now JobActive). Sanctions for individuals on income support payments for failure to comply with these new participation measures were also introduced. Under this model 'welfare reform' became a policy narrative that defines empowerment in terms of reducing caseloads for front-line workers, providing 'choice' for service users through market models of social service delivery and reducing the government's 'welfare bill' (Morgen and Maskovsky 2003).

Conditional welfare associated with the withdrawal of benefits for not undertaking compulsory training or attending job interviews for any work of any duration has been in place for more than two decades. It is these policy settings that give rise to the mantra that 'work is the best form of welfare', a political message that seeks to construct market dependency as the 'natural order', while demonizing state dependency in the form of welfare receipt. Thus, it is 'passive' welfare recipients that must be 'activated', rather than the state or employers in this representation of human agency and action. Consequently, the problem of unemployment becomes the problem of the unemployed. Lack of empowerment in this version is equated with lack of market engagement (Shaver 2002). Responsibility for addressing unemployment is devolved from the realm of the political to the realm of the technical, as something to be 'fixed' in either the individual or in the funding contract between the government and the third-party provider.

The scale of the problem moves from a national discussion about the mismatch between demand and supply in the labour market (put simply as there are not enough paid jobs for those who want them) to the local level of assessment and diagnosis, training and job coaching. Front-line professionals are the key agents of change at the local level of activation. As Considine (2001) argues, in advanced liberal welfare states, case management has become the principal mode of engaging with and empowering unemployed citizens. Case management in this context has a conditional and paternalistic rationality. Pre-defined engagement activities and employment opportunities are offered, but at the same time failure to undertake prescribed activities can result in a financial penalty being applied in the form of withdrawal of some or all of the unemployment benefit (McDonald and Marston 2005). This version of 'pre-packaged empowerment' becomes possible by accepting the authority of the state, assuming the local actors located in street-level organizations are willing to play along with the 'activation' script.

Within this contracted social services model it seems there is little room for either front-line workers or clients to shape the means and ends of welfare. However, opportunities for coproduction, adaptation and resistance are still possible, residing in the spaces of local welfare offices where these policies are implemented. As numerous studies have shown there are varying responses on the part of workers as to how they appropriate or resist dominant discourse about devalued welfare subjectivities and the need for 'strong paternalism' in order to prepare unemployed citizens for paid work (Thomas and Buckmaster 2010). What is common to these contexts are a range of constraints, such as contracted performance targets, computerized assessments, high caseloads that in and of themselves reduce the capacity for worker discretion, client autonomy and self-determination. In these environments, the pathway to empowerment is tightly prescribed and regulated for both front-line workers and the clients they work with.

What we know from classic studies of street-level bureaucracy (Lipsky 1980/2010) and more fine-grained ethnographic analysis is that there are multiple rationalities at play at the local level of policy practice that are mediated by organizational culture, professional discretion and available resources. Although hegemonic discourses about welfare and the 'empowered' welfare subject shape the perspectives of policy makers and managers, front-line workers can construct different meanings and express different perspectives about what it means to be an empowered subject (Morgen and Maskovsky 2003).

In the context of the introduction of Personal Responsibility and Work Opportunity Reconciliation Act (PRWORA) in the US in the mid-1990s, Riccucci (2005: 115) found that an eligibility-compliance culture pervaded the front line of welfare bureaucracies, despite efforts by management to redirect some of the behaviours and actions of managers. Analytical perspectives that treat welfare bureaucracy and third-party organizations contracted by the state to deliver welfare services as a site of institutional struggle have shown how worker/client relations are shaped in these local settings by dominant norms about the causes and consequences of poverty:

> Neoliberal ideologies about poverty promoted by welfare agencies foster hierarchical, often adversarial relationships between workers and recipients, undermining potential alliances, even though both groups contend with unrealistic agency expectations (Morgen and Maskovsky 2003: 5).

However, it is also important not to take an over-unified or determinist view. Treating welfare reform as a set of unstable, hybrid forms of governmental practices opens up new areas of ethnographic enquiry (Morgen and Maskovsky 2003). In these local relations, subjectivity can be conceptualized as the socially reinforced conceptualization of self that informs action, while subjectivity is also an object of others' actions (e.g. case managers, department officials) (Korteweg 2003). For example, in the context of welfare reform in the US during the mid- to late 1990s, the achievement of self-sufficiency, defined as financial independence from the welfare state, became the expressed goal of the Personal Responsibility and Work Opportunity Reconciliation Act (PRWORA). Two main avenues were promoted to women to realize this goal: marriage and paid employment (Korteweg 2003: 450). These subjectivities were promoted through various participation requirements and sanctions for non-compliance. For those subject to the reforms learning how to 'do interviews' was a central means by which the image of the idealized paid worker was fleshed out. In her analysis of these policy changes Korteweg (2003) argues that policy makers failed to support women's caring labour at home, as there was an absence of provision for adequate child care. Motherhood was given some recognition, but only in terms of a 'good mother' being a 'working mother'. This and other studies have demonstrated how women and other categories of welfare recipients resist these strategic and selective interpretations of their subjectivity and relations of dependence (Fraser and Gordon 1994).

What is also striking is the absence of a strong counter-discourse to coercive state power as operationalized in workfare programmes. In effect, this may mean that the concerns raised by Barbara Cruikshank in her book on empowerment have intensified since her work was published in 1999. Cruikshank was concerned that 'self-help' empowerment techniques, coupled with coaching in practices such as Job Clubs, would de-politicize class and gender relations over time. Although well intentioned, Cruikshank argues empowerment 'is a strategy for constituting and regulating the political subjectivities of the "empowered"' (Cruikshank 1999: 69). As such, programmes that are activated by social policy makers to empower service users' work as technologies of citizenship, in that they are aim to develop and promote 'good citizenship' (McDonald and Marston 2005: 6), which is constructed in a one-dimensional mode around the centrality of the paid work ethic. The key mode of being included in the social citizenry is through participation in the labour market.

In the context of welfare reform, the pathway to this idea of 'good citizenship' focuses on people developing high levels of 'human capital' to become independent economic actors. Hence, empowerment acts as the conduit towards enhanced market participation (production, work, consumption) and lower costs to the state in terms of welfare provision. This is achieved through 'technologies of agency' that are ever present in programmes designed to assist the 'disadvantaged' (Dean 1999). According to Morgen and Maskovsky (2003), neoliberal welfare policies have had a particularly insidious impact on collective action, placing expectations on human services organizations to demonstrate individualized and autonomous client outcomes. In a neoliberal political vision the empowered subject is one whose autonomy is measured by market independence, rather than dependency on the state for material well-being. This model assumes that adults are failed subjects who no longer have a moral compass to determine right from wrong or good from bad actions. As such, these failed subjects must be morally retrained to become 'self-regulating' subjects through what Lawrence Mead (1997) refers to as 'help and hassle' in his defence of paternalism in the everyday delivery of income support and welfare services. The tension between care and control that is at the core of paternalism is pushed down to the local level of social service delivery.

This discussion has highlighted how the empowered subject is a subject who participates in their own moral and material remaking, but their empowerment is never entirely of their own making. Governing through freedom means that citizens are not simply free to choose, but obliged to be free (Pawson 2011: 120). The empowered subject is therefore always about more than individual freedom, it is about shaping human conduct towards forms of emancipation that can only be realized through participation in certain practices and rituals, such as counselling, consumption or participation in labour and housing markets. In a marketized version of the ideal self the individual is required to invest in themselves to improve their chances of becoming 'self-reliant'. Conversely, if individuals are unable or unwilling to adopt a marketized subjectivity they find themselves on the wrong side of a moral binary, which legitimizes the state taking corrective action through increasingly punitive conditions and penalties. Workfare programmes in countries such as the US, Australia, the UK and New Zealand work in precisely this way in terms of their 'activation' and empowerment logic in that the means and ends of welfare are pre-determined. There is little room in this version of empowerment for coproducing ends and means.

Empowerment and Governing Together

There are other variants of the empowered subject that have a stronger foundation in liberation and communitarian philosophy, particularly those developed in community development and more radical traditions of social work teaching and practice. It is important to briefly outline some of these differences, as they highlight the variety of empowerment logics that inform decision-making and discretion in social services. Strengths-based social work practice, for example, emphasizes developing people's capacities and challenging the social and structural origins of 'client problems' (Maidment and Egan 2009). From this perspective, empowerment aims to achieve the social justice objectives of radical social work (Payne 2014: 294). Here, empowerment is concerned with improving the control individuals have over their lives, and implementing practice approaches that directly benefit service users (Payne 2014: 296), while not overlooking the importance of structural social change for the long-term empowerment of disadvantaged peoples. From a community development perspective, the approach to empowerment is aimed at the broader structural level, that is, '*empowerment aims to increase the power of the disadvantaged*' (Ife 2013: 63, italics in original). Ife (2013: 63) espouses that empowerment is inevitably about power as something that can be quantified, 'giving power to individuals or groups, taking power into their own hands, redistributing power from the "haves" to the "have nots", and so on', all of which accords with a theory of power as something that can be possessed and redistributed.

Within this paradigm the empowerment of disadvantaged groups at the meta-level is approached through strategies such as policy and planning (development or change of structures and institutions that generate more equitable services and opportunities for participation in community life), social and political action (importance of political struggle and change to increase effective power); and education and consciousness-raising (improving power through improving access to and quality of education). At the meso-level the concept of coproduction from the public administration and community development literature is relevant to thinking about this more democratic version of empowerment as a form of social and political action (Hupe 1993). Coproduction can take several forms. Collective coproduction refers to citizen involvement in design and delivery of social services whose benefits may be enjoyed by the entire community (Nabatchi, Sancino and Sicilia, cited by Hand 2017). Individual coproduction can be defined as a case where citizens contribute to service delivery through mutual agreement with front-line workers about the nature of their problems and how to address them. This model stands in contrast to the 'strong paternalism' of state workfare policies described earlier where the means and ends are pre-determined and where the choices frequently boil down to acquiescence or rejection of the programme or policy goals. Community development and coproduction frameworks represent an approach to empowerment that seeks to reframe policy problems, to educate the public in order to depose the myth of the 'welfare queen' or the 'scrounger' or to highlight disparities in wealth and income as the mark of an unhealthy or immoral society (see Wilkinson and Pickett 2009). The insights from Cruikshank (1999: 107) on the empowerment project suggest that as a political strategy this approach does not necessarily point the right course towards transformative and long-lasting emancipation:

> To start from the fact of political exclusion and then argue for the inclusion of poor women's voices in debates over welfare reform, to argue for their self-representation, is already to take the welfare queen for granted, to take her for real.

Cruikshank is concerned with how an economic calculus is used to estimate need or standardized assessments are applied to determine categorical eligibility for welfare benefit. Once classified, these citizens are constructed as categories demanding one form of intervention or another by the state or a third party contracted on behalf of the state to provide a range of services. The capacity for agency in this form of citizenship is minimal, reduced to a notion of choice in a mixed economy of welfare where the citizen is theoretically able to take their custom elsewhere if they are unhappy with the service provided. Public services are not immune from conflating consumer sovereignty with choice. Empowerment through choice became central to modernizing the public service in countries such as the UK, the US and Australia during much of the 1990s (Clarke 2005). Public services were reformed to empower citizens through expanding 'choice and voice'. Contestability and competition principles were applied to dismantle and unsettle the idea that government should be both the funder and the provider of social services. Competition and a 'consumer culture' were used to generate citizen 'experiences and expectations of individualized choice' (Clarke 2005: 449). Public services were positioned as inflexible, 'backward, inadequate and paternalistic' (Clarke 2005: 449). There have been numerous studies of the managerial push into the public realm and its intended and unintended consequences. Critics suggested consumer choice in the context of public social services de-collectivizes the very notion of the public, as citizens are constructed as individual agents pursuing self-interest (Needham 2011).

This discussion has sketched the construction of empowerment in the context of workfare and welfare retrenchment and some of the variants of empowerment in academic debates and professional discourses where empowerment can be defined as a form of community development, as a means of coproducing needs or as marketized choice. The next section will explore an empirical case study of empowerment that represents a version of empowerment aimed at addressing poverty, which is an attempt to steer a course between individual responsibility, therapeutic discourses of empowerment; and community-based solutions and social action. The case study highlights how discretion, defined here as a form of knowledge judgement and constrained action, opens up a degree of indeterminacy when it comes to setting goals about what ought to be done in the name of empowerment at the local level of service delivery.

7.3 A Case Study of Empowerment in Action

The case study analysed in the second section of this chapter is drawn from a case management service within a large multi-site non-profit Australia social service organization. This agency has traditionally provided material assistance in the form of 'emergency relief' to individuals (cash assistance and food parcels to people in poverty), but it has over the past five years adopted a complementary case management model where professionally qualified staff work with voluntary clients (self-referral from emergency relief programme) to identify personal goals and the means of achieving them. The programme known as 'Doorways' uses terms like 'positive action planning', a 'positive lifestyle program' and a 'strengths-based approach' where the case manager seeks to 'build relationships with clients that have a focus on the underlying issues contributing to their need to access Emergency Relief' (The Salvation Army 2017). The Doorways model is quite different to the mode of case management found in the JobActive (formerly the Job Network) programme, as the former has small caseloads and minimal pre-determined means and ends, whereas the latter is characterized by high caseloads, contractual targets relating to job placement, narrowly defined key performance indicators and low levels of trust between the stakeholders (Considine *et al.* 2015).

The authors were involved in a process evaluation of the Doorways Service model in 2014, which included identifying the impact of a case management model in relation to meeting client needs and improving the lives of people experiencing poverty and social disadvantage. Qualitative research was selected as the primary data collection method involving face-to-face and phone interviews and observation. Participant voices included in this chapter include clients and case management staff. Seven service sites were involved in this study spanning New South Wales (five sites), Queensland (two sites) and the Australian Capital Territory (ACT) (one site). Data collection occurred over a three-month duration in 2015. Collecting data at each site involved conducting semi-structured interviews, observation, immersion in the setting and writing field notes. Across all seven sites, a total of 45 client interviews and 9 Doorways case managers' interviews were conducted. Observations of case management meetings and interviews also took place. In the research Doorway's clients were asked to reflect on their experiences of the case management process, such as the types of assistance and support received and initial outcomes in relation to their finances, support networks and level of well-being. The research team carried out thematic analysis of the interview and observation data to identify the most common and divergent points about the case management experience.

7.4 The Role of Empowerment in Case Management Service Provision

The case management service of Doorways is explicitly defined as 'client centred' and it emphasizes ongoing and intensive support in order to address long-term, complex and multi-faceted client needs. The empowerment approach adopted by the service is similar to the therapeutic approach to empowerment outlined by Cruikshank (1999): that is, one where services are focused on promoting client self-sufficiency through self-reflection towards an end that is broadly defined as self-improvement and independence. The impetus for introducing the Doorways model was the organization identifying a need to reduce the long-term reliance on Emergency Relief in the form of material and financial assistance. The service wanted to stop the 'revolving door', by providing 'no wrong door' in the form of material assistance, counselling, interviewing skills and, if necessary, referral for people living in poverty.

One of the first tasks of the early face-to-face case management sessions was to produce a list of 'life goals' and the steps to achieving them.

'Self-reliance', particularly in terms of financial independence, from both Emergency Relief and state welfare was one of the overriding aims, as described by one of the case managers during the research interview:

> We're not giving that handout, we're giving a hand up. Because somebody needs help, we're not going to hand it out and here you go, see you later, good luck with that. We're going here you go, let us try and help you, if we can't we will find somebody who can. So that's the hand up.... (Case manager_Urban, 1).

Emphasis is placed on promoting client 'self-sufficiency' through providing budgeting counselling and enhancing job readiness. Case management here is aimed at developing and promoting 'self-reliant' citizens (McDonald and Marston 2005). Clients were also sometimes constructed as 'highly vulnerable' by case managers; a group that needed to be taken care of, unable to take care of themselves without intensive support. Some case managers engaged in what they described as 'gentle coercion' of long-term Emergency Relief recipients by making future financial and material support contingent upon participation in Doorways case management. However, most case managers were reluctant to go down this path, insisting that trust and the voluntary nature of the case management were critical to a successful engagement with clients. For these agencies and their workers 'relational case management', with a high degree of discretion over client goals and how to achieve them, was perceived as the conduit through which client empowerment could be achieved. In these interactions the principle of voice and coproduction were seen to be fundamental values and principles:

> Doorways is a measured and responsible approach to helping people get out of a state of welfare or a state of poverty. Rather than say, this is how it is, you've got to feel the pinch. We're saying, what approaches can we work with you? What issues are occurring? What underlying purposes are there to the reasons behind what's happening? (Case manager_Urban, 2).

In this excerpt there is a sense in which client understandings of the causes of poverty can be linked to insights from the workers to identifying 'underlying purposes'. In this sense there is a democratization of knowledge about the problems and how to address them. There is also an acknowledgement that different ways of working are necessary and beneficial. A high level of positive discretion occurs in all the interactions observed, as the programme architecture is less constrained by strict targets and limited resources. These interactions can be contrasted with transactional case management relationships in contracted Job Active sites where the client is provided with little or no autonomy to determine the ends or means of empowerment (McDonald and Marston 2005: 381). The Doorways case managers emphasized empathy engagement and relationship-building techniques or respect to enhance self-confidence. As one case manager commented:

> The capacity building is huge. I think that's just—that's a lovely moment when you can see people realising—especially when—from the very beginning when we're doing intake and we're looking at where they're at and then where they want to be in three months. Actually, what are you good at? What can you actually do? For some of them it's the first time they've ever realised that they are actually capable of doing this stuff (Case manager_Regional, 1).

The case manager's belief in the potential and ability of clients to set goals and make the time to work towards them helped in developing a relationship of trust and respect based on a 'strengths-based' perspective. In this sense, discretion combined with small caseloads provided the 'room to move', which has been regularly identified as a key marker of successful professional practice at the street level (Brodkin and Marston 2015). The clients of the services that were interviewed felt respected by their workers:

> [I]t's just been really, really difficult navigating our way through all the different sort of social systems, like the education system or even a workplace. It's very, very difficult. My son has a learning disability, so accessing that support there, it's been really hard when you—I don't have that social capital. I'm not married to anyone important, I have coloured skin and I've got no money. So I think people—I'm easily ignored and pushed aside, or swept through the cracks.

Flexibility in service provision was a key characteristic of the service approach that provided high levels of job satisfaction among the case managers. As one case manager commented:

> This is at the coalface [...] at the frontline. It's generalist. It's so flexible in a way that it doesn't matter whether you're here for one visit or 20 visits. It doesn't matter whether you're here for mental health or just because you need someone who could provide you with support on a hobby [...]. This is what's so fantastic about it. It's so broad and flexible that it gives every client some way of achieving at least some goal. Now it's just about getting more powerful (Case manager_Urban, 2).

This quote illustrates how the case managers had discretion to tailor service delivery to the individual needs of clients at a pace that is set by the client. This ability to tailor service provision to client needs was perceived by the majority of case managers to be essential for improving client empowerment, in terms of enhancing self-confidence to work towards goals. Addressing these issues takes time, as such the model resists short-term measures of success that are associated with more marketized models of case management where empowerment is superficially tied to short-term job placements and a range of other 'tick and flick' measures of success:

> [T]his program may take a little while to see its full benefits. A lot of the work that I do here and plus the referrals and information that I give I think that it's not something that will necessarily have an outcome overnight. With some things it may but long-term work is what will be able to be fully assessed (Case manager_Urban, 5).

The ultimate goal for many of the case managers was for the client to be empowered through knowledge and skills to the point of being self-governing:

> So we put it in the context of men have got a toolbox in their shed, they've got a tool for fixing everything, a hammer to fix this or a screwdriver to fix that. We have to do a toolbox of life, and for everything that we put in it, is going to help with some situation in our lives. So if it's mental health, it's a GP or a service that they're aware of or they choose. If it's child counselling, families counselling as such, we have Salvation Army counselling. So all the things that we put in, or services, budgets, life skills, health skills [...] when we're coming to the end of the casework journey, we can actually get a box with these cards in it. Or we can do an emergency box, so when we're coming to the end of it, something happens down the track, they don't panic. I can't pay the rent, what do I do? I look in the box and these are the services that are available to help me (Case manager_Urban, 4).

This aim for autonomy is balanced with an emphasis on building client capacity and self-belief:

> It's pretty special that you get—when you do this kind of work, that you get to see that so often in people that just someone to get the spark of belief back, like believing in themselves and believing in their capability, that they can actually do something. Because by the time we get them they're—by the time people are engaging in Emergency Services and then Doorways, a lot of them are so far down and just have lost all self-confidence, self-esteem or belief. They're just really eking out a living, just trying to survive week to week (Case manager_Urban, 4).

The definition of success here is personal transformation from a state of 'bare life', with the idea that that personal transformation will result in material improvement in one's circumstances. Promoting self-efficacy through respectful, friendly, encouraging professional relations is ultimately focused on aligning individual behaviour with dominant social norms, in relation to work, family and education. The difference is that the goals of the society in a socio-cultural sense become the goals of the individual (Hand 2017). To refuse the broader project of what constitutes a meaningful life in a hegemonic sense is a more radical proposition that is seemingly beyond the scope of what is possible in the local Doorways office.

The limits of discretionary freedom within the Doorways project are more or less constrained to a refusal to be the sort of 'welfare recipient' that dominant welfare discourses construct; that is, as a passive subject of professional help. It is this model of empowerment that comes closer to political action in terms of the framework put forward by Cruikshank (1999: 121): 'Resistance must take the form of a refusal to act as a *recipient*, a refusal to be what our relations to the state have made us'. This refusal can apply as much to workers as it can to clients. Case managers commented that they occasionally needed to go outside their mandated role in order to adequately support clients with complex needs. For instance, at times they needed to support clients outside of work hours and to bend some of the 'rules' (in terms of seeing clients outside of the workplace) in order for clients to fit the requirements for aid:

> We're here to help you out in this time of need, if that time of need is an hour today, or an hour once, twice, three times a week, until you're able to walk on your own again, then that's what we'll do. I am happy to see people on weekends, down the street to make change happen (Case manager_Urban, 3).

This level of discretion as a form of autonomy is distinct from the amount of discretion possible in government-contracted case management provided by mainstream services like the Job Network, where workers must meet pre-defined targets and client outcomes. Considine *et al.* (2015: 55–6) illustrate that the discretionary power of Job Network case managers in Australia has become more constrained over time in response to proceduralization and tight regulation of service implementation, accompanied by high caseloads and less time to respond to expressed needs. The extent to which workers are encouraged to use their own professional judgement and experience to advise clients or refer complex problems up the line impacts the flexibility of service delivery. This reduction in discretionary practice contrasts markedly from the original intention of these Job Networks when they were originally set up in the late 1990s in Australia, to provide service users with 'flexible service delivery', where there was some ability to tailor responses to individual needs. This capacity to be responsive has diminished in direct proportion to how much the dominant welfare discourse has come to define citizens for what they lack, rather than for what strengths and capabilities they have.

In contrast, the construction of citizens in Doorways case management model is at least a partial attempt to not accept the deficiency model of the 'passive subject' of welfare reform. And for Cruikshank (1999) this refusal allows us to see the political in the 'strategic field of small things' as she refers to it, to acknowledge the potential of new interventions that can disrupt taken-for-granted assumptions about what those subject to 'welfarist' discourses are capable of. Clearly, the Doorways case management model does not manage to entirely escape the individualized construction of empowerment that atomizes subjects and their actions; however, there are moments where both workers and clients are able to keep both structure and agency in the frame of understanding poverty as they negotiate goals and the means to achieve them. There is also a more generous allocation of time built into the Doorways model, which goes against the grain of instrumental welfare service delivery where milestones and unrealistic key performance targets shape what should be achieved and by when. These models, which have almost become an accounting exercise, leave little room for serendipity, or what the anthropologist Gillian Tett (2015) refers to as 'slackness', which she argues has largely been lost in human services systems defined by a quest for hyper-efficiency and financial accountability.

In contrast, what the Doorways case management model seeks to rework in its implicit rejection of 'one size fits all' service delivery is a version of empowerment where the pace of personal and political change is determined by the client and the front-line worker through a mix of mutual negotiation and 'soft paternalism'. The slowing down of case management practice allows the relational dimension to come to fore in a way that is more authentic and genuine for both sides of the human services encounter. A capacity to have the time to coproduce problems and solutions is central to versions of discretion where power-knowledge relations not only promote social norms as being synonymous with ideal constructions of self-identity, but open up new ways of thinking about and acting on issues such as poverty that defy simplistic binaries between structure and agency.

At the same time there are obvious limits in these street-level encounters to realizing what Weeks (2011) calls collective freedom, where the meaning of what constitutes a 'good life' is radically rethought in terms of how people construct their identities and spend their time. Street-level policy actors are members of organizations that for the most part remain committed to a normative project around an ethic of paid work and family. Opening more possibilities for 'post-work' politics and moving beyond a disciplinary mode of poverty governance would require reimagining the role of non-profits and their relationship with governments. One way forward suggested by Soss, Fording and Schram (2011: 306) is for a form of public accountability where non-profit organizations are freed from the commodity relations of neoliberal poverty governance:

> Strong civil society organisations can be vital collaborators in poverty governance, supporting a deeper and more inclusive form of democracy for the disadvantaged in a variety of ways [...]. Reformers should strive not to tie the hands of frontline workers, but to restructure decision making around mutual engagement and interdependence, ensuring that power is shared on terms that are subject to renegotiation.

Another institutional step to realize a more ambitious empowerment agenda, which, as frequently noted by feminists in their analysis of care work, is to focus on the industrial conditions of front-line workers. De-skilled case managers at the front line who are not appropriately remunerated for their complex work or provided with appropriate training and skills are simply unable to work effectively in a transformative mode of poverty governance and engagement. Over-worked and underpaid front-line workers have little time to think about emancipatory processes as they pursue narrowly defined outcomes. It is difficult to imagine how disenfranchised front-line staff will ever deliver a model of empowerment that is genuinely transformative. It is for all these reasons that discretion remains the 'wild card' (Brodkin 2003) of public and social services. Individual abuses of street-level authority are in many cases the predictable consequences of the structures, routines and incentives that shape and discipline the use of discretion (Soss, Fording and Schram 2011: 205). Clearly institutional settings matter, but at the same time we should be careful about inferring that what happens upstream over-determines what happens downstream in policy development.

Unlike a statutory setting where rules and regulations are more tightly prescribed, the Doorways model of decision-making authority was highly devolved. Apart from a general philosophy about 'developing strategies and skills to achieve more sustainable outcomes' there were no prescribed pathways for client empowerment. Nonetheless, being more in control and having greater autonomy were frequently interpreted in case plans in terms of economic security, typically as either getting a job, getting a house, reducing debt, 'getting off welfare' or going back to school. The model of empowerment is largely associated with self-improvement and meeting presenting needs, such as material well-being. Arguably, these are the very conditions that are required before being able to consider more ambitious interpretations of empowerment as a form of collective action to address structural inequalities and systemic forms of exclusion. Added to this are the specific concerns that non-profits and civil society groups in Australia have had their advocacy role muted in their preparedness to accept government contracts to deliver services and policies in ways that leave little room to autonomously define the means and ends of welfare. In this prescriptive contractual environment the positive effects of professional discretion tend to be limited to making workfare policies less punitive than they might otherwise be, rather than challenging the way in which poverty and unemployment are understood and acted upon at a socio-cultural level.

7.5 Conclusion

The discussion covered in this chapter has sought to critically examine empowerment in theory and practice. As demonstrated in the Doorways case study, empowerment is applicable to both workers and clients of services; that is, workers need to be trusted that they can meet client needs without tightly prescribed pathways and outcomes. However, addressing patterns of disadvantage in these local communities through community development initiatives or other group-based interventions was not a prominent part of the empowerment imagination for the social service agency managers or the case managers. This is likely to reflect the material nature of the case management encounter where workers are meeting one on one with multiple clients to address a range of individualized goals over the course of any given day. Despite the espoused aim of Doorways to address the causes of poverty, this goal was never elevated to a more macro political strategy of lobbying local authorities and politicians for more public housing, public transport, income security or job creation. All of the workers who participated in the study were able to list these structural causes of poverty when interviewed, but they did not consider it part of their formal role and professional identity to work at this level of collective agency. Consequently, the concern that political theorists like Cruikshank (1999) have is that as long as empowerment projects remain within the confines of individual case management encounters, then its political framing as a form of community activism will be diminished.

Like Cruikshank (1999), our intention in this chapter has not been to destroy or discount the concept of empowerment, but to bring out both its dangers and its promises to light. The fate of empowerment as a more ambitious political project is closely linked to how social problems are interpreted and how individual professionals and citizens think and act upon themselves and others. Working towards self-improvement is not the same as working towards social and economic justice. As Iris Marion Young (2011: 132) explains:

> The forces of capital and commodification have colonized what used to be off limits to the social and political [...] subjecting all of life to scheduling, producing, connecting, messaging, immersing oneself in the quotidian and therefore losing sight of the bigger picture.

Under these circumstances, the self-sufficiency and self-reliance discourse that infuses income support and employment policies in countries like Australia becomes a kind of comfort zone when it comes to contemplating political action against social injustice. Nancy Rosenblaum (cited by Young 2011: 40) argues that part of the reason a self-sufficiency discourse thrives in present conditions is because we have a declining faith in our own political agency and 'the less confidence we have in our own democratic political agency the more we demand of others'. Consequently, citizens come to passively regard the complex workings of society whose effects are fortunate for some individuals and unfortunate for others as solely the result of individual effort and not a matter of justice for which all citizens should take collective responsibility (Young 2011).

Addressing these matters of justice and equity at a collective level through a more inclusive polity might mean we demand less from those at the front line who are attempting to use professional discretion and coproduction of needs as tools to humanize an indifferent or hostile bureaucracy, or to reconcile contradictory and contested policy principles and ethics. This task becomes even more challenging in the marketized context of contractual service delivery where high caseloads are frequently the norm and key performance indicators are promoted that reward short-term job placement outcomes. This organizational environment certainly limits the capacity for the development of an empowerment model that promotes job satisfaction for front-line workers and which is genuinely transformative in the lives of ordinary people who use these services. An important resource for the realization of a more authentic form of empowerment is discretionary time for individual workers. A higher degree of temporal autonomy, which is consistent with the foundations of professionalism, can help to facilitate individual reflection, collaboration with other agencies and free-flowing dialogue with colleagues, all of which can get lost in the quest for hyper-efficiency in modern organizations, where an ethos of managerialism is dominant (Tett 2015). Other authors in this edited collection note that a degree of indeterminacy at the street level is also a requirement for good practice, as it allows for creative solutions that can, over time, reshape policies and laws in ways that promote justice and self-determination. But at the same time if the pendulum between control and freedom over knowledge, material resources, rules and regulations is not carefully calibrated, the result can be unaccountable decision-making, prejudice and discrimination. It would seem the nature of the socio-political ecosystem (including power dynamics and professional and disciplinary knowledge) ultimately determines whether discretion is an empowering or disempowering force in the lives of ordinary citizens.

References

Brodkin, E. (2003). Street level research: Policy at the frontlines. In M. Lennon & T. Corbett (Eds), *Policy in action: Implementation research and welfare reform* (pp. 145–164). Washington, DC: Urban Institute Press.

Clarke, J. (2005). New Labour's citizens: Activated, empowered, responsibilised, abandoned? *Critical Social Policy*, 25 (4), 447–463.

Considine, M. (2001). *Enterprising state: The public management of welfare to work.* Cambridge: Cambridge University Press.

Considine, M. Lewis, J.M. O'Sullivan, S. & Sol, E. (2015). *Getting welfare to work: Street-level governance in Australia, the UK, and the Netherlands.* Oxford: Oxford University Press.

Cruikshank, B. (1999). *The will to empower: Democratic citizens and other subjects.* Ithaca, NY: Cornell University Press.

Dean, M. (1999). *Governmentality: Power and rule in modern society.* London: Sage.

Fraser, N. & Gordon, L. (1994). A genealogy of dependency: Tracing a keyword of the U.S. welfare state. *Journal of Women and Culture in Society*, 19(2), 309–336.

Hand, L. (2017). Producing a vision of the self-governing mother: A study of street-level bureaucrat behavior in coproductive interactions. *Administration and Society*, 50(8), 1–27.

Hupe, P.L. (1993). The politics of implementation: Individual, organizational and political co-production in social services delivery. In: Hill, M. (Ed.), *New agendas in the study of the policy process* (pp. 130–151). Hemel Hempstead: Harvester Wheatsheaf.

Ife, J. (2013). *Community development in an uncertain world: Vision, analysis and practice.* Port Melbourne: Cambridge University Press.

Korteweg, A.C. (2003). Welfare reform and the subject of the working mother: 'Get a job, then a career'. *Theory and Society*, 32, 445–480.

Lipsky, M. (1980/2010). *Street-level bureaucracy: Dilemmas of the individual in public services.* New York: Russell Sage Foundation.

Maidment, J. & Egan, R. (Ed.) (2009). *Practice skills in social work and welfare: More than just common sense* (2nd ed.). Crows Nest: Allen & Unwin.

McDonald, C. & Marston, G. (2005). Workfare as welfare: Governing unemployment in the advanced liberal state. *Critical Social Policy*, 84(3), 374–401.

Mead, L. (1997). *The New Paternalism: Supervisory approaches to poverty.* Washington, DC: Brookings Institution Press.

Morgen, S. & Maskovsky, J. (2003). The anthropology of welfare 'reform': New perspectives on U.S. urban poverty in the Post-Welfare Era. *Annual Review of Anthropology*, 32, 315–338.

Needham, C. (2011) Personalization: From story-line to practice. *Social Policy and Administration*, 45(1), 54–68.

Pawson, H. (2011). Governing independence and expertise: The business of housing associations. *Housing Studies*, 26, 301–303.

Payne, M. (2014). *Modern social work theory* (4th ed.). Basingstoke, Hampshire: Palgrave Macmillan.

Riccucci, N. (2005). *How management matters: Street-level bureaucrats and welfare reform.* Washington, DC: Georgetown University Press.

Shaver S. (2002). Australian welfare reform: From citizenship to supervision. *Social Policy and Administration*, 36, 331–345.

Soss, J. Fording, R. & Schram, S. (2011). *Disciplining the poor: Neoliberal paternalism and the persistent power of race.* Chicago: The University of Chicago Press.

Tett, G. (2015). *The silo effect.* New York: Simon and Schuster.

The Salvation Army (2017). *Doorways: Emergency relief handbook.* http://www.sarmy.org.au/en/Social/Doorways-Handbook/Introduction/ [accessed 30/03/17].

Thomas, M. & Buckmaster, L. (2010). *Paternalism in social policy: When is it justifiable.* Research Paper No 8, Canberra, Commonwealth Parliament.

Weeks, K. (2011). *The problem with work: Feminism, Marxism, Antiwork Politics, and Postwork imaginaries.* Durham: Duke University Press.

Wilkinson, R. & Pickett, K. (2009). *Why more equal societies almost always do better.* London: Penguin Books.

Young, I. (2011). *Responsibility for justice.* Oxford: Oxford University Press.

PART II

Perspectives on Discretion

CHAPTER 8

Perspectives on Discretion: An Introduction

Tony Evans and Peter Hupe

8.1 Introduction

The second part of this edited collection explores discretion from a range of different disciplinary perspectives. The first two chapters consider perspectives—law and economics—that traditionally have been highly influential. The authors of these two chapters identify and challenge the assumptions of what they see as the traditional disciplinary approach of these perspectives and propose more research-informed conceptions of discretion in their place. The other three chapters bring newer perspectives to bear on the analysis of discretion—from the fields of sociology, psychology and critical studies.

One of the advantages of presenting insights from different disciplines on discretion is that we come to see that often people, while working within a particular discipline, draw on insights from other disciplines in their work. Dirk Wolfson's analysis, for instance, draws on insights from the psychology of judgement and decision-making to extend the economic perspective, while Zachary Oberfield uses the ideas of logics of appropriateness, as well as approaches associated with political science, to explore socialization and discretion. Furthermore, these chapters also show how authors recognize the need to extend their work into other areas to enrich their discipline. Lars Tummers and Victor Bekkers, for instance, identify the need for further research to explore processes of socialization and cultural practices in how people use discretion, while Peter Mascini argues that the value of insights from sociology is to extend the analysis of legal decision-making and understanding of key legal

T. Evans (✉)
Department of Social Work, Royal Holloway, University of London, Egham, UK
e-mail: Tony.Evans@rhul.ac.uk

P. Hupe
Public Governance Institute, Catholic University of Leuven, Leuven, Belgium
e-mail: pieter.hupe@kuleuven.be

T. Evans, P. Hupe (eds.), *Discretion and the Quest for Controlled Freedom*, https://doi.org/10.1007/978-3-030-19566-3_8

actors such as judges. These chapters underline the point that, while we may talk about disciplinary perspectives, we need to recognize that the boundaries of disciplines are often porous. However, as Hannah Jobling argues in her chapter, flexibility and creativity on the ground can often be masked by our assumptions of the approaches that disciplines should take.

8.2 Discretion from a Legal Perspective

In the first chapter in Part II of this edited collection, Peter Mascini argues for a more inclusive socio-legal perspective to discretion to replace a narrow legal approach. The legal approach, he explains, regards discretion as operating outside the system of rules and authority constituted by the formal legal system. That approach contrasts discretionary decision-making with legal decision-making, which is characterized as interpreting and applying rules. As such, discretion is seen as uncontrolled, arbitrary and capricious. It is a problem for the law, because it is considered as a threat to the legal order, which should be constrained by the development of increasingly coherent and extensive rules.

In contrast, Mascini argues that a broader socio-legal approach provides a more realistic understanding of discretion. This approach is less concerned with the legal rules and formally specified roles in understanding discretion. It is more interested in understanding discretion through the way it is used in practice. This shift from the traditional perspective, he argues, involves recognizing the role of informal systems and broader social factors and recognizing the way they influence the shape and deployment of discretion in action.

At the core of this approach is a challenge to the exceptionalism of the legal method. Judges, for instance, are one amongst many other groups of actors involved in discretionary decision-making. Legal actors are not hermetically sealed in a legal universe, but are social actors whose assumptions, commitments and biases are deeply implicated in their decision-making and their approaches to discretion. Furthermore, discretion is not an aberration but a fundamental aspect of legal practice that reflects the imprecision and incoherence of the legal system. The legal approach, in drawing a line between law and society, denies the fact that law is part of a broader political-administrative system. Judges, for instance, do not operate in *splendid isolation*; they act and make decisions within a network of other actors.

Mascini argues that shifting from a legal perspective to a socio-legal perspective gives rise to a more fruitful approach to analysing discretion that directs our attention to the influence of actors' attitudes, interpretations and practices. Cases, for instance, are not natural entities. A case is an assemblage of facts, which can be assembled in a way that makes the matter a legal concern or ordered in another, that makes it a social issue. Facts do not speak for themselves; they are ordered and arranged by actors for a purpose. Social and ethical commitments, as well as legal principles, also affect 'legal' decision-making. Furthermore, judges do not make decisions in isolation. Other actors—who may or may not be recognized by legal scholars—are also influential and important. Judges make decisions at the end of a process in which other actors—by the exercise of their discretion—have structured, constrained or extended subsequent judicial choices.

For Mascini, the value of a socio-legal perspective is that it recognizes the breadth of factors that influence and structure legal decisions beyond the narrow focus on formal rules and the boundaries of specific legal roles. Discretion is not an aberration or the closed preserve of judges. Instead, it is a widespread phenomenon, a set of organized and organizing socio-legal practices.

8.3 Discretion from an Economic Perspective

In the next chapter, Dirk Wolfson considers discretion from an economic perspective. Economics is often caricatured as the dismal science, concerned only with the allocation of scarce resources, the costs and benefits of choices and efficient outcomes. But for Wolfson, its remit is wider. It is also concerned with ethical issues such as fairness and equality, recognizing diverse needs and interests and striking balances between their competing claims. For Wolfson, discretion is a way in which economics can navigate this terrain of competing demands and claims, sensitizing itself to the tension in public services between the demands of obedience and accountability to policymakers on one hand and calls for responsiveness and flexibility in providing services to citizens, on the other.

Discretion has always had a role to play in the economics of organizations. Traditionally this has meant a focus on the tension between the value of delegation by managers and the costs of control of employees. This concern is formulated in the idea of the principal/agent relationship, which draws on a broad-brush set of assumptions that actors are simply instrumental, rational and self-interested, pursuing their material interests in a marketplace made up of similar self-interested actors. However, Wolfson points out, the characterization of actors as homogenous, simply driven by means/ends thinking and a conception of narrow self-interested motives, has increasingly come to look problematic, particularly in the light of research in the behavioural sciences. The latter suggests that decision-making is more nuanced than simple means/end calculation and that human motives and concerns are more diverse and complex than traditional economics allow.

Diversity is not only a social but also now a political reality, recognized by policymakers in the rhetoric of personalized and customized public services. However, within this rhetoric, Wolfson identifies a tension between accountability to policy and flexibility in delivering services. He sees professionals as having a central role to play in holding this tension. They work with citizens to tailor services to particular needs and, to do this, need freedom within policy. Principals should stand back and allow their local agents freedom to make appropriate local decisions. But for Wolfson, discretion is not being given free rein. Rather, it is freedom within a reconfiguration of the principal/agent model. Drawing on insights from behavioural economics, principals, he argues, steer and guide agents rather than expect them to follow detailed instructions. Using nudges, rewards and sanctions, principals can encourage agents to be accountable vertically within the policy hierarchy and horizontally across service networks.

Against this background, Wolfson puts forward the idea of 'situational contracting'—which allows for the local co-production of services within networks of accountability—to describe the operation and management of discretion in professional/citizen encounters. Characterizing discretion in this way, allows public servants to be creative and to develop interactive relationships with citizens, while also enabling executive oversight and monitoring. This also entails a shift, Wolfson argues, from seeing discretion exclusively as a problem of compliance to recognizing it as a process of creativity and responsiveness allowing the customization of services.

8.4 Discretion from a Psychological Perspective

In the next chapter, Lars Tummers and Victor Bekkers look too at actors' approaches to discretion in the context of bureaucracy. The frame they use to examine this is psychological. They consider the operation of discretion at the level of individual practitioners, particularly addressing the attitude of workers to policy and the behaviours these workers adopt. In looking at this, they draw on two key ideas: 'policy alienation' and 'coping'.

Policy alienation is an attitudinal concept that conveys a sense of disconnection between the practitioners' aspirations and policy. The disconnect may be because practitioners feel that what they are being asked to do is impossible, perhaps because of insufficient resources, or it may be because they see the policy as unhelpful, meaningless or detrimental to the people with whom they work; or because they disagree. Coping refers to how people behave, what they do, in the process of public service delivery. For Tummers and Bekkers this is a behavioural idea focusing on what actors do rather than what they feel.

They deploy these ideas to consider how street-level bureaucrats who experience policy alienation respond and the behaviours those actors tend to adopt to cope. They seek to build on Lipsky's deployment of the idea of coping (as a response to stress) and seek to explain the link between feelings of alienation and patterns of behaviour. They identify three broad families of coping amongst practitioners. Examining frontline responses to organizational rules, they recognize different attitudes to rules which, in turn, expand or contract discretion, reflecting different strategies and commitments. One strategy is bending the rules. Practitioners who bend the rules strive for flexibility and responsiveness to the interests of the people they work with. Those street-level bureaucrats then seek to move towards the interests of their clients. Another pro-client strategy is breaking the rules. This approach is illustrated with the example of a teacher who, disagreeing with a new testing regime, simply passes students even when they do not meet the new requirements. A third strategy concerns rigid rule enforcement. The authors see this as an anti-client strategy and associate it with a punitive attitude to clients, making work more manageable by controlling pressures experienced by workers.

The identification of this range of strategies, Tummers and Bekkers suggest, illustrates the value of a psychologically informed research agenda for the study of discretion and street-level bureaucratic practices. One area they identify for further consideration is the role of socialization in developing (or reducing) the range of coping behaviours that street-level bureaucrats may use. They also point to the need to consider policy alienation and coping as a more widespread phenomenon through organizations. Senior managers and frontline practitioners, they point out, are subject to similar stresses, and managers' coping strategies need to be examined as well. The idea of coping, they suggest, would also be valuable in studying the interaction of practitioners and users: how characteristics of clients may interact with, and possibly change, the coping strategies of staff. They argue that further work is needed to consider the possible influence of different cultural characteristics on strategies of coping. Additional research, the authors conclude, may not only spread new light on the micro aspects of policy work but can also inform its design and implementation.

8.5 Discretion from a Sociological Perspective

In his chapter, Zachary Oberfield uses a sociological lens to consider the discretion of the organizational actor. His particular focus is the relative influence of the adoption of an organizational role and actors' biography in constructing approaches to discretion. In contrast to the individualistic focus of the economic view of actors driven by means/ends and costs/benefits calculations, Oberfield adopts a different perspective, which locates actors' decision-making within socially located ideas of identity, perception and judgement. Specifically, he draws on the idea of the logic of appropriateness to explore the discretion of organizational actors. From this point of view, identity is fuzzy rather than clearly fixed and single; it is a repertoire of roles and ideas of who they are. This repertoire allows them to recognize and respond to the range of different situations they may encounter. Situations can be understood in different ways, depending on what particular aspect of one's identity one draws on as appropriate in that setting. This, in turn, brings to bear the set of whichever motives and concerns are felt to be salient to acting appropriately in that situation. We often do this automatically, but there are also times when these habitual scripts of role, situation and action spark off against each other and when whatever used to fit now grates. When this happens, we become aware of the way we tend to understand what we do, how we focus on certain things and act. It is then that we have to re-examine what we have tended to see as appropriate in the situation.

Oberfield is interested in how discretion, as an aspect of a bureaucratic role, is formed and sustained. He identifies two classic sociological approaches to this. One focuses on individual dispositions, how actors impose their biography on the role they occupy; the other on organizations' ability to make people fit into the position they occupy. The first idea draws on the observation that individual dispositions tend to be relatively stable. From this point of view, people with a propensity to be bureaucrats are selected by organizations and slot into the role. They are round pegs in round holes. The second perspective is that identities are more malleable. It is possible to round off square pegs to fit in round holes; through training and induction, they ingest organization culture and bend to peer pressure. Hence, they become actors who fit the roles to which they have been recruited.

In the main body of the chapter, Oberfield outlines findings from his research which explored the influence of disposition and socialization in early career police officers and welfare workers' attitudes to discretion. Unlike office-holders who come to their bureaucratic role thoroughly trained and with an existing professional identity, police cadets and welfare workers come to their role without prior training. They are bureaucrats whose idea of what their work involves comes both from who they are and from the training they have received. In this research, Oberfield found that both groups of workers came to their new positions with an idea of public servants as actors who follow rules (although they also recognized that things may differ on a case-to-case basis). He followed the training received by both groups of workers in their new roles. Police cadets were told in their training that discretion is part of the job, but at the same time, there was a definite undertone in this message that common-sense judgement should be employed in the use of discretion on the ground. Welfare officers' training played down the role of discretion. However, alongside the emphasis in training on rules and policy prescription, there was a strong message that rules and policies are open to interpretation. Oberfield observed the effect of induction on these workers. He found that the police cadets, for instance, were increasingly receptive to the idea that not everything can be done by the book; and that the welfare workers increasingly recognized their role in interpreting rules and embraced this discretion. Institutional factors were significant, but they modified existing dispositions rather than fundamentally transforming them.

The author returned to some of his original interviewees—the police cadets—ten years after the original study. Reviewing his findings, he found that the police officers had sustained but not significantly changed their approach. For Oberfield, a sociological perspective points to the value of considering both agent biography and organizational influences in understanding bureaucrats' approaches to discretion. Furthermore, he points out, it is unlikely that one of these factors alone explains what is going on; rather, research needs to explore the interplay of the two.

8.6 Discretion from a Critical Perspective

In the final chapter of this part of the edited collection, Hannah Jobling looks at discretion from a critical perspective. This is a perspective that stands outside specific disciplines to consider how particular forms of knowledge are interwoven with power. Using mental health as a case study, she focuses on discretion as judgement and how forms of knowledge animate decision-making; how particular approaches to knowing are taken for granted and in turn influence the latitude of freedom available to different actors.

The nature of expertise in mental health is contested. There is no consensus regarding the nature of mental ill health or how best to help. However, despite this, the biomedical approach—one approach to understanding mental ill health, which is closely associated with psychiatry—has become dominant. Alternative perspectives, often associated with other professional groups (and service users) may be acknowledged, but they are often marginalized.

Jobling considers how the biomedical approach became so influential and particularly how it has insinuated itself into policy and service delivery. In policy, the diagnostic categories and abstract systems of disease and strategies of disease management characteristic of the biomedical approach, are fundamental to the way in which mental health services are planned and delivered. Ideas about mental health, to be seen as legitimate, have to be translated and transformed through the biomedical lens to count. For instance, the notion of recovery which was developed by service users (as a challenge to the idea of psychiatric pathology) has now been transformed within mental health services into an idea about patients' acceptance of their responsibility to self-manage their condition within a biomedical frame. Jobling also points to the way in which biomedical knowledge—despite the talk of multidisciplinary working—sets the terms of trade of inter-professional interaction and tends to push other perspectives on mental health to the margins.

Jobling draws on an empirical study, to explore the scope and operation of discretion in the context of the dominance of the biomedical perspective in policy and practice. Her research involved both practitioners and service users and examined discretionary decision-making on the frontline. She found that, while biomedical language was pervasive—both in the way people talk about mental health and in the policies they have to operate—it is not a perspective that is simply accepted and left unquestioned. In fact, for many of the people she interviewed, there was a dissonance between the concerns of this perspective and a quieter but compelling ethical discourse focusing on a commitment to fuller cooperation with service users rather than compulsion, while also a sense of partnership and human obligations to the citizens with whom practitioners work could be observed. Practitioners, she found, were concerned about the corrosive impact on relationships and the punitive nature of risk management strategies that emphasize compliance with medication. Jobling also found that practitioners sought to use their discretion to craft a space in which they could work with service users to develop a shared understanding of mental health and cooperative working, to identify more creative interventions than merely relying on medication. Here practitioners, she noted, sought to take advantage of the liminal space between professionally prescribed roles and the organizationally prescribed role of care coordinator to shift the boundaries of their position and recalibrate the register of their judgement. This enabled practitioners to create the spaces within which they could work cooperatively with service users, sharing the freedom to make decisions and enriching the idea of judgement by combining perspectives to challenge the policy and epistemic constraints of the biomedical perspective.

CHAPTER 9

Discretion from a Legal Perspective

Peter Mascini

9.1 Introduction

Is there such a thing as a legal approach to discretion? I will argue that, yes, a specific legal approach to discretion can be distinguished. This particular legal approach is even occasionally referred to as 'the legal paradigm', assuming the existence of a specific framework of concepts, results and procedures within which subsequent research is structured (Kuhn 1970). In this paradigm, discretion is viewed as behaviour that is not prescribed by rules and that therefore is believed to be unpredictable and posing a potential threat to the consistency and legitimacy of rulings. This conception implies that discretion can and ought to be constrained by filling gaps in statutory standards and by using legal control instruments.

While the work of several legal scholars and legal practitioners clearly does not fit neatly in the legal paradigm, the latter is often attributed to them. The idea of the legal paradigm is used by socio-legal scholars to contrast it to their own approach to the study of discretion. In their view, discretion is not to be defined as decision-making that is not guided by rules, but by the manner in which general rules are applied to concrete cases in practice (Hawkins 2001). In a socio-legal approach, discretion is viewed as unavoidable rather than controllable by legal instruments, variable rather than fixed by the reach of legal rules and patterned by other factors than the law rather than unpredictable. A socio-legal approach also broadly studies the use of discretion by all professionals and officials that have the authority to apply general rules to concrete cases rather than focusing on judges only. Moreover, attempts to curtail discretion are not necessarily viewed as more preferable than

P. Mascini (✉)
Erasmus School of Law, Erasmus University Rotterdam, Rotterdam, The Netherlands

Erasmus School of Social and Behavioural Sciences, Erasmus University Rotterdam, Rotterdam, The Netherlands

T. Evans, P. Hupe (eds.), *Discretion and the Quest for Controlled Freedom*, https://doi.org/10.1007/978-3-030-19566-3_9

allowing discretion. Using the alleged legal paradigm as a strawman may be useful for socio-legal scholars in flashing out the distinctive characteristics of their own approach and carving out a niche for themselves (see, more generally, Goldfinch and Wallis 2010), it may also come at a cost. It involves the risk of overlooking potential heterogeneity amongst legal scholars and legal practitioners in their approach of discretion by suggesting more unity in it than might be justified. After all, as I will argue, there are many legal scholars and legal practitioners who acknowledge the limitations of approaching discretion in a purely formal and legal matter and whose views fall outside the scope of the legal paradigm.

I will indeed argue that although the work on discretion of some legal scholars and legal practitioners may be appropriately characterized as paradigmatic, I even do not exclude the possibility that the so-called legal paradigm represents the majority of the legal scholarship and legal practice; this characterization also ignores major differences of opinion between legal scholars and legal practitioners in their approach to discretion and their consciousness of the constraints that adhere to the legal paradigm. Consequently, differences may be overstated between the manner in which discretion is studied by legal scholars and legal practitioners, on one hand, and socio-legal scholars who contrast their own work to the legal paradigm, on the other hand. As a result, potential for dialogue, mutual recognition and collaboration may be missed. Providing this specific line of argumentation implies that I am approaching the legal perspective from a particular angle rather than providing a comprehensive discipline overview.

In this chapter, I will first set out the four main characteristics of the so-called legal paradigm. Subsequently, I will discuss some important dissenting views of legal scholars and legal practitioners on all of these characteristics of the legal paradigm. I will then discuss how certain socio-legal scholars who study discretion contrast their own work to the main characteristics that they attribute to the legal paradigm. In addition, I will use the way in which judges in lower courts use discretion as a case study to illustrate that such a socio-legal approach can indeed yield insights that could not be obtained from an ideal typical legal paradigmatic approach. In doing so, I will argue that the socio-legal approach proves invaluable for the study of discretion but also shares a lot with legal scholars and legal practitioners whose work falls outside the scope of the legal paradigm.

9.2 A Legal Paradigm?

Four interrelated features are attributed to a legal approach to rules and discretion or the so-called legal paradigm. Firstly, that it is possible to make a clear distinction between rule-directed behaviour and discretion. Discretion then refers to the decision space that exceeds the limits of the formal authority of public officers: 'a public officer has discretion whenever the effective limits on his power leave him free to make a choice among possible courses of action or inaction' (Davis 1969). This starting point also underlies the well-known metaphor of the donut which Dworkin (1977) uses for discretion: 'An area left over by a surrounding belt of restriction'. The dough stands for decisions prescribed by the rules; the hole in the donut stands for the decisions that relate to situations to which the rules do not apply. Both definitions are based on the assumption that, based on statutory rules, it can be clearly identified where the authority of a public officer begins and where it ends. The scope of discretion is thereby primarily motivated by formal rules 'This terminology seems to clearly communicate that discretion should be understood as a constant, rather than a variable, feature of the study. It is neither being explained, nor being used to explain anything else. It simply is, and therefore stands outside of inquiry' (Nickels 2007: 571).

The second feature attributed to the legal paradigm more or less automatically follows from the starting point that discretion is not an independent study object. It means that behaviour that is not steered by rules is presented as unstructured: 'according to the division between discretionary *or* ordered by rules, decision-making is *either* informal and thus essentially lacking in structure, arbitrary and capricious, *or* it is governed by legal rules, principles and policies' (Tata 2007: 428, italics in original). In legal practice, not only social behaviour but also legally non-binding rules, or 'soft law', fall outside the focus of the legal paradigm: 'Judicial review of discretionary decision-making continues to focus myopically on whether decisions comport with statutes and regulations. Administrative culture, administrative practices, and the administrative structures in which and through which discretion is exercised are even more remote from the judicial perspective than guidelines' (Pottie and Sossin 2005). In the legal paradigm the emphasis is thus on behaviour that is governed by legal rules and on the control of discretion by means of legal instruments. 'The legal paradigm is exemplified by a belief in the importance of the law and of courts and court-like procedures in dealing with the existence of discretion. This is evidenced by a tendency to regulate discretion by means of general rules and standards and by subjecting its exercise to legal scrutiny, for example by way of allowing challenge by way of appeal to tribunals or judicial review. Moreover, the importance of fair procedures is emphasized' (Lacey 2001: 372).

The third feature that is ascribed to the legal paradigm is that discretion is considered 'technically unnecessary'. In this respect, reference is usually made again to Dworkin (1977), who makes a distinction between weak and strong discretion. Weak discretion is attributed to the imprecision or ambiguity of the law, the scope of freedom judges have to determine the material facts of a case (with references) or the nature of decisions that are not subject to further review (i.e. the higher courts). Strong discretion refers to not being bound by standards set by any authority. Dworkin claims that disagreement about the meaning of words does not imply an absence of right answer. Neither does disagreement on the sources of law imply such an absence (Vila 2001). Instead, Dworkin argued that ultimately there is always only one right decision, if only approximately, which is the decision that fits best with the legal system as a whole—with its rules ('all or nothing standards'), precedents and legal principles (inconclusive standards, which nonetheless lend justificatory support to courses of action) that make the legal order coherent. This implies that in his approach, discretion is viewed as technically unnecessary, since discretion involves the possibility of choosing between alternative courses of action or inaction when deciding.

Fourthly, discretion is presented as a threat to the rule of law in the sense that it enables judges to take decisions that are not democratically legitimized (see also in this volume, Chap. 16 of Hupe & Hill, particularly subsection 'Discretion and Delegation'). The connection between discretion and the rule of law further gives rise to making a fundamental distinction between discretion allotted to judges and other officers. According to the ideal of the separation of powers, judges occupy an independent position, while other officers are subject to hierarchical control: 'the judiciary is usually granted a high degree of autonomy: due to the principle of judicial independence, horizontal self-regulation takes precedence over external and vertical authority' (Biland and Steinmetz 2017: 3). Because of the independent position judges occupy in systems of separated powers, it is believed to be dangerous for judges to exercise discretion and attempt to repair the law (Shapiro 2007: 33); judges are expected to enforce legislation, not to make it (see also, de Jong, Faure, Giesen and Mascini 2018).

Incidentally, it is not just influential legal scholars like Davis (1969) who plead for limiting democratic deficits that originate from judicial discretion by filling gaps in statutory standards and by using legal control instruments. Sometimes legal practitioners recommend this themselves. In the Netherlands, for example, lawyers have been dissatisfied for years about the lack of clarity provided by the Supreme Court's guidelines (*gezichtspuntencatalogus*) when assessing the principles of reasonableness and fairness (Article 6 paragraph 2 of the Dutch Civil Code) concerning the decision to waive the time limit for mesothelioma asbestos claims that relate to damage that has only become apparent after the time limit. This dissatisfaction has led to numerous recommendations by legal scholars and legal practitioners to further limit the discretion of judges when reviewing this rule of exception (Hebly 2017). To give another example from the Netherlands, when judging the open norm 'conflicting with societal decency' (Article 6: 162 paragraph 2 of the Civil Code), judges deliberately try to make decisions look objective by seeking guidance in external sources such as the Supreme Court's jurisprudence, legislation, professional standards, disciplinary law and expert judgments (Smeehuijzen 2017).

In summary, supposedly in the legal paradigm, discretion is considered as behaviour that is unpredictable because it is not directed by rules and that therefore poses a threat to the consistency and legitimacy of judgments so that discretion can and should be avoided as much as possible by filling gaps in statutory standards and by using legal control instruments. Moreover, it focuses primarily on judges, courts and legal procedures. Although this characterization covers part of the legal scholarship and legal practice, it also ignores significant differences of opinion within the legal study of discretion.

9.3 Dissenting Views

To begin with, legal scholars have frequently criticized Dworkin's approach to discretion. For instance, for excluding semantic problems from his characterization of strong discretion as if such problems can be solved unambiguously (Vila 2001). In addition, in relation to strong discretion, Dworkin would not only wrongly assume that the law consists of a coherent and consistent system of rules and principles, but also that there is consensus on how decisions can be derived from this. Instead, in practice, legal systems appear to be a patchwork rather than a coherent system of rules. In addition, often there are several competing doctrines from which different decisions can be derived (Galligan 1990: 12–3). This means that in practice, even in situations where legal standards *are* available, multiple decisions are often possible. This implies that it is not possible to make a clear distinction between rule steered behaviour and discretion: 'in the clearest and strongest cases of discretion that division may be clear, but more typically the two are interwoven, with discretion occurring where there are gaps in the standards, or where the standards are vague, abstract, or in conflict' (Galligan 1990: 22).

Apart from the contention of Dworkin's analytical legal approach to discretion, legal scholars have offered alternative views on discretion. In Hart's positivist approach, for example, discretion is viewed not only as inevitable, but also as necessary for the proper functioning of the rule of law (Shaw 2013). Hart considers discretion as inevitable because the language on which law is based is sometimes indeterminate (linguistic indeterminacy), because rules can impossibly predict everything (relative ignorance of fact) and because it is not possible to objectively weigh goals (relative indeterminacy of aim): 'We are men not gods' (Shaw 2013: 703). However, this does not mean that discretion by definition is arbitrary. On the contrary, Hart distinguishes discretion explicitly from arbitrary decisions (and from determined decisions). 'A choice, he argued, counts as an exercise of discretion only if it invites a reasoned defense grounded in principles "deserving of rational approval"' (Shaw 2013: 699). According to Hart, discretion applies when a decision meets the following six characteristics: (1) There is no clear 'correct' decision, (2) No goal is formulated at a concrete level, (3) The consequences of all possible decisions are unclear, (4) Different values are at stake without their mutual priority being clear, (5) 'Wise' or 'sensible' are more meaningful distinctions than 'good' or 'wrong', (6) Decisions can be legitimized in two ways—(a) by justifying the arguments which are the basis of the decision and (b) by referring to the outcome of the decision. Making careful rationally determined decisions provides, according to Hart, for the indeterminacy of law and is in accordance with the rule of law: 'it is the job to be done when indeterminacy inevitably arises'. Kadish and Kadish (1973) go even further by arguing that even if clear rules exist, officials may hold the power and the right to deviate from law in certain contexts and yet not act illegally in a sense—because law itself contains standards of adaptations to its own departures—if this enables them to attain the general objectives and values that are central to the roles these officials fulfil within the community.

A second alternative to Dworkin's analytical approach to discretion is provided by Posner (2008; see also Smith 2010). Like Galligan, he argues that legal methods, such as the use of precedents, can lead to very different outcomes. This is due to the fact that precedents can be interpreted in many different ways, for example, because different aspects are highlighted as decisive for the precedent, while the degree of comparability between the precedent and the present case may also be controversial. All explanations, according to Posner, depend on circumstances, including institutional factors such as the motives and methods of judges. Yet judicial decisions show a remarkably high degree of predictability and consistency, despite the unavailability of an unequivocal methodology that leads to unanimous results. The reason for this is that judges' decisions are determined not only by their personal background and preferences but also by factors concerning the profession of the judge. Institutional factors such as the appointment for life, the statutory salary and the premise that judges are not accountable to politics undoubtedly contribute to the ideal of impartial decision-making. Also, the behaviour of judges is determined by the appreciation that they reap for their functioning from the legal community. According to Posner, this means that the absence of unambiguously interpretable rules does not in any way prevent judges from using their discretion predictably and legitimately.

Finally, some representatives of the ideal-typical legal paradigm show consciousness of the need to transcend its limitations. This applies, for example, to Davis who advocated the restriction of discretion by legal control instruments. He stated, 'Jurisprudence misses many realities about justice because it is much too concerned with judges and legislators and not enough with administrators, executives, police and prosecutors. Furthermore, jurisprudence acknowledges the law-discretion dichotomy and then spends itself almost entirely on the law half… We need a new jurisprudence that will encompass all of justice, not just the easy half of it' (cited by Lacey 2001: 361).

Thus, there are also legal scholars who problematize the clear distinction between rules and discretion that is made in the legal paradigm, who consider discretion as an inevitable and useful part of the rule of law rather than a 'technical unnecessity' that poses a threat to consistent and legitimate rulings; and who advocate to pay more attention to the contingencies in the use of discretion rather than concentrating on the limitations of existing legislation and case law as inputs to judicial decision-making. Most views on legal scholarship and legal practice generally recognize that there are differences of opinion within this field of research, but without questioning the existence of a dominant legal paradigm. Views that differ from this ideal type are presented as marginal or deviant. The result is that legal scholars and legal practitioners who advocate doing more empirical research on the use of discretion and affording more attention to the other side of the rule/discretion divide are ignored and that no connection is sought with them.

9.4 A Socio-legal Approach to Discretion

Emphasizing the dominance of a homogenous paradigm also helps to contrast it with a socio-legal approach to discretion. The latter approach indeed offers in all respects an alternative to the features attributed to the legal paradigm.

Firstly, in a socio-legal approach, the question of how discretion is formally defined is substituted with the question of how officials use discretion in practice. 'Identifying the formal locus of discretion is best seen as a preliminary, if the task is to understand actual decision practices, and what shapes them' (Hawkins 2011: 188–9). Also, allegedly, the normative reflection about what the role of discretionary power should be cannot be answered satisfactorily without establishing first how officials use their discretion in practice (Lacey 2001: 386). A logical consequence of studying discretion empirically is that it is considered a variable rather than a constant. After all, in practice, the scope of discretion is not given, but context dependent. For example, the extent to which a judge has discretion in the deliberations of the council chamber will depend on the space she appropriates and the authority that her colleagues allow her. An experienced judge with much authority will have more discretion in an identical situation than an inexperienced temporary judge who still has to establish her reputation (Nickels 2007).

Secondly, a socio-legal approach does not assume that behaviour that is not regulated is unpredictable and arbitrary. '[T]he key critical point is that the [legal] perspective is founded on the assumption that to exercise discretion is to exercise free choice, constrained only by legal limits (Davis 1969: 4). From a jurist's vantage point, without legal limits, this "freedom" remains unconstrained and unstructured, and choices will be made on the basis of individual, arbitrary and intuitive standards. [...] There is no room within this paradigm to consider how far individual "free choice" may be already, collective, ordered, routinized and structured by phenomena other than the law itself. From a social scientific standpoint, human agency is rarely, if ever, voluntary' (Campbell 1999: 80).

Baumgartner (2001: 130) even goes so far as to argue that sociological laws steer behaviour more than the law: 'Legal codes vary across jurisdictions, changing with the passage of time and geographical distance. The sociological laws that determine the use of discretion, however, are general and unchanging'. Baumgartner refers to the dependence of the outcomes of legal disputes on the relational distance between the actors who are involved in these disputes. Feldman (2001: 183) likens the difference between formal and social constraints to the difference between a wall and a rushing stream of water. The wall is firm, clearly delineated and hurts when you run into it, but it can also be assaulted and broken down. The rushing stream, however, moves, its speed varies and it may at times even be pleasurable, but it also rushes on creating a path for itself against the mightiest resistance. 'The stream and the social context have influence not because of their absolute strength but because of their insidious natures and their sheer persistence'.

Thirdly, the socio-legal approach challenges the assumption that the use of legal control instruments automatically helps to protect the legal order from the alleged threat posed to it by discretion. The use of legal control instruments may raise thresholds that reduce access to justice, substitute formalistic styles of reasoning for purposive reasoning and they may be accompanied with over-indulgent rulemaking and disproportional and unreasonable sanctions, which may undermine the legitimacy of the law. Judicial review strengthens the hand of lawyers as opposed to experts in deciding specialist issues which are translated into legal terms and it may lead to defensive behaviour and inefficiency of administrative agencies (Baldwin and Hawkins 1984). Also, non-legal control mechanisms such as the intensification of accountability measures, hierarchical and parliamentary control and the introduction of knowledge expert systems can induce resistance, evasive behaviour, retention and manipulation of data, shifting responsibilities and reducing sight of the way in which officials use their discretion in practice (Ringeling 1986; Jorna and Wagenaar 2007).

Fourthly, a socio-legal approach relinquishes the automatic link between discretion and rule of law. Thus, it is not assumed in advance that there is a fundamental difference between the way in which judges and other officers use discretion. In fact, Biland and Steinmetz (2017: 321) conclude that the differences in the way in which family judges use their discretion in two jurisdictions—France and Quebec—are more pertinent than those between judges and street-level bureaucrats. 'As a result, regarding decision making, the boundary is more between judiciaries than between judicial and administrative actors'. Moreover, they refer to Mileski's study of a state criminal court in the United States which 'led her to show similarities between judicial and bureaucratic work and to conclude that "the patterns of judicial demeanor may be very close to those for bureaucratic workers in other legal or even non-legal settings"' (Biland and Steinmetz 2017: 300).

Relaxing the link between discretion and the rule of law can also lead to a problematization of the distinction between the status that is attributed to legislation and policy. After all, in their study of social welfare administration in Canada, Pottie and Sossin (2005) show that while in practice both implementing agencies and beneficiaries do not distinguish between legislation and policy—in fact, executives are only inclined to consult statutes if policy instruments do not provide a solution—administrative judges remain far more comfortable reviewing policies expressed in statutes than those expressed in guidelines, directives or other informal instruments of soft law and administrative communication. One reason for this hesitancy is the separation of powers, by which the business of governing, policymaking and policy implementation is reserved to the executive branch of government. However, in settings such as social welfare, public law cannot fulfil the purpose of governing the interaction between government decision-makers and affected parties in order to ensure fair and reasonable outcomes that are consistent with the legitimate interests of government and the rights of those affected until and unless the decision-making process is first seen as an integrated whole and not as the sum of artificially discrete realms of law, policy and administration (Pottie and Sossin 2005).

Even more fundamental is that a socio-legal approach problematizes the ideal type of the independent judge who takes decisions on individual cases. 'What may on the surface appear to be one simple discretionary decision quite often involves a rather more complex series of decisions' (Hawkins 2001: 27). A holistic or systemic approach towards discretion not only implies that decision-making in law to a large extent is a collective enterprise. It also draws attention to the fact that effective powers to decide are frequently assumed by actors other than the person allocated formal authority to exercise discretion and are diffused among a variety of actors who all play a part in the handling of an individual case. Moreover, the one-sided focus on case discretion—the exercise of discretion in the handling or disposal of cases—in the legal paradigm ignores the fact that 'a good deal of decision-making in legal bureaucracies is concerned with matters of policy—deciding in general how to decide in specific cases' (Hawkins 2001: 28). Policy discretion—the ability to create rules and policies—can be used to limit and shape case discretion, and there is often a tension between the rules set by actors and the discretion available to lower-level actors within those rules (Bushway and Forst 2013).

This can be illustrated by a study on the implementation of border controls in countries affiliated to the Schengen Convention (van der Woude and van der Leun 2017). The EU left it to the discretion of individual countries to determine how to guarantee that border controls comply with the Schengen Convention. This allowed the Dutch government to expand the monitor that was originally intended to check for illegal residence in such a way that the monitor could now also be used to detect crime. This goal expansion was also expressed in the change of name from the Mobile *Alien* Monitor to the Mobile *Security* Monitor. This institutional development has enabled military police officers to define their task more widely. Consequently, the military police no longer controlled only illegal immigration but also human trafficking, identity fraud and drug trafficking. A socio-legal approach thus understands the manner in which individual officials use their discretion in terms of the broader social context in which they operate.

In summary, it can be said that a socio-legal approach to discretion drops a number of fundamental principles that are attributed to the dominant legal paradigm. Discretion is conceived as a variable rather than a constant. Behaviour that is not steered by legal rules is not ignored. Rather, the patterns and regularities in the way social factors influence the use of discretion are precisely the central subject of research. In addition, the socio-legal approach pays attention to the intended and unintended consequences of legal and non-legal control instruments. Furthermore, it eliminates the automatic link between judicial discretion and the rule of law, so that similarities in the way judges and other officials use their discretion become a potential study topic, just as the similarities of how legislation and policy; or 'hard' and 'soft' law, affect decision-making processes.

9.5 A Socio-legal Analytical Framework

Abandoning these principles gives rise to a more open, practice-oriented approach to discretion than is attributed to the ideal-typical legal paradigm. A successful socio-legal analytical framework is developed by Hawkins (2011: 189–91). It focuses on criminal law but can be applied more broadly to the uses of discretion. The starting point of his analytical framework is that decisions can only be understood by reference to their embeddedness in interpretative practices, frames, fields and surrounds. *Interpretative practices* concern the gradual process of linking the construction of a case by selecting, eliciting, valuing and weighing bits and pieces of information to the selection of the rules that are deemed relevant to apply to the emergent case. '*The frame* is the means by which the everyday world is linked with the legal world. It describes how features in a particular problem or case are understood, placed and accorded relevance'. '*A decision field* describes the legally and organizationally defined setting in which decision-makers work'. While the field is something defined by and acted on by the organization, in contrast, events in the surround are not open to control. '*The surround* is the broad setting in which decision-making activity takes place, serving as an environment both for individual decision-making, and for the activities of the criminal justice bureaucracies in which such decision-making occurs'. The different elements of the practices of decision-making and their contexts are inextricably linked. Therefore, in order to be able to understand the nature of judicial decision-making, 'a connection needs to be forged between the interpretive processes that individuals engage in when deciding a particular case, and forces in the decision-making environment'.[1]

The remainder of this chapter consists of an illustration of the application of the socio-legal approach based on insights from studies of judges' use or non-use of discretion in sentencing in lower courts. These studies have been chosen with the intention of showing that a socio-legal approach to discretion can also provide valuable insights regarding the main subject of the legal paradigm—determining the scope of legally acceptable outcomes—that could not have been achieved had it only been studied from within the legal paradigm. In the legal paradigm the focus is on law rather than on the judge as a distinct actor; the judge is the means through which any rules or principles would be given effect (Anleu, Brewer and Mack 2016: 49). Discretion is supposed to be identical for all judges because the same legal sources apply to them. The analysis of discretion ends by describing the scope for legally correct—or at least legally acceptable—outputs. However, from a socio-legal approach the analysis of discretion begins where the legal paradigm ends. The focus is on the application of legislation and legal principles in practice rather than on the theoretical and jurisprudential discussion of the legal sources. As we will see, this offers a more social, relational and interactive understanding of the judge in sentencing, extending and complementing, the valuable, but necessarily limited, insights of the legal paradigm (Anleu *et al.* 2016: 46). If the socio-legal approach can demonstrate its value when it comes to the heart of the study topic of the legal paradigm, it is even more likely to be of added value when it comes to topics that usually lie outside the scope of attention of the legal paradigm.

9.6 Judges' Use of Discretion

Interpretative Work on 'Facts' and 'Cases'

The point of departure of a socio-legal approach to the way in which judges use discretion is that it involves interpretative work. This interpretative work relates to three questions: what is the case the judge has to decide on, what rules are applicable to this case and how should the relevant rules be applied? Each of these three decision steps involves substantial discretion (Galligan 1990).

> 'First, a judge must find facts, and fact-finding is inevitably a partly discretionary process, since it requires making complicated judgments whose components cannot be foretold and resolved in advance. Deciding what actually happened always involves some discretionary judgments about what evidence to hear, what evidence to regard as relevant, and what evidence to regard as reliable, to say nothing about drawing final conclusions about what actually happened'. […] 'A second reason [a judge] often has great discretion is that someone must decide what the relevant rules are, and in the first instance this must effectively be the fact-finder, since it is impossible to know what facts are relevant until the rules to which the facts are relevant have been identified'. […] 'A third source of the initial decision-makers' discretionary authority arises from his power to decide how to apply the rule to the facts. […] These decisions require the decision-maker to exercise the discretion of both an interpreter of law and a finder of facts'. '[S]ince, as regularly happens in litigation of any real complexity, multiplicitous and uncertain facts must be applied to broadly written rules, the scope for discretion is obviously substantial' (Schneider 2001: 66–7).

What is more: fact-finding and rule-finding discretion cannot be separated: Before the law can be applied the facts must be categorized, but before the facts can be categorized the law must be applied. Facts are selected and marshalled to fit perceived rules of law, but the rules themselves change in response to facts, often by deploying concepts and categories that had not formerly been supposed to be applicable (Samuel 2017). One particular discretion judges have in relation to rule application is that they 'may define their scope for discretion permissively and expansively *or* restrictively, even to the point of denying any discretion at all' (Tata 2007: 430). Tata proceeds by giving a poignant example of self-denial of discretion, which he derived from Cover's (1975) historical study of the Fugitive Slave Act: 'Time and again the judiciary paraded its helplessness before the law; lamented its harsh results yet nonetheless declined to use their legal discretion to make "ameliorist" solutions possible (5–6). Thus, in selectively denying or expanding the scope of "rules" and "discretion", judges *are* exercising discretion' (Tata 2007: 430).

Several empirical studies have given more concrete attention to the interpretative constitution of the facts of the case and the person of the defendant. Some of these studies suggest that judges rely on their interpretation of signs of hope and remorse to arrive at a sentence type. Defendants who neither display signs of remorse nor signs of hope are generally thought of as irredeemable. In such cases, judges tend to opt for detention, while they tend to choose for an alternative sentence—for example, fine or community service—in case judges believe defendants do display at least some signs of hope and remorse (e.g. Tombs and Jagger 2006; Beyens and Scheirs 2010). Judges' interpretive work in relation to creating an image about the redeemability or irredeemability of the defendant can manifest itself in at least three ways (Mascini, van Oorschot, Weenink and Schippers 2016). First, judges assemble different cues from what they see as the facts of the case to create an image of the defendant. In their interpretative practices, judges may encounter various cues that they may interpret as signs of hope or remorse and others that point to the contrary. In weighing these signs, and against the background of the available sentence types, judges try to arrive at an image of the redeemability of the defendant. When they do not find the available clues conclusive, they may actively elicit various clues as signs of hope or remorse. The selecting, weighing and eliciting of signs of hope and remorse show the complexity of judges' interpretative practices.

What contributes to this complexity is the fact that the meanings that judges give to defendants' personal, social and even legal characteristics are not fixed (see also, Tata 1997: 406). Being employed, having a partner and permanent residency are not always interpreted as positive signs, even though judges usually indicate that they perceive the three W's of *Wonen, werken, en wijf* (a house, a job and a wife) to be stabilizing factors. For instance, in one case, a judge did not consider the defendant's married status, his pregnant wife and his full-time employment as positive signs since these factors had also been present at the time of the offence. Consequently, the judge doubted whether the defendant would refrain from breaking the law in the future since his wife with a child on the way and his job had not prevented him from doing so in the past. This example shows that judges do not consider these cues in isolation but try to relate them to one another in the context of the case.

Yet another contribution to the complexity of judges' interpretative work when it comes to 'facts' and 'cases' can be derived from a study about the manner in which family judges deal with accusations of sexual child abuse in divorce cases (Smit, Bijleveld and Antokolskaia 2017). Family judges take the view that they generally cannot (and should not) determine the legitimacy or merit of allegations of sexual child abuse in divorce cases, yet they almost always try to estimate them, and these estimates nevertheless steer them in their consideration of certain decisions. If the mother has not declared the accusation to the police, the allegation is often not taken seriously. Besides, the timing of the accusation is an indicator of perceived validity. Very old accusations that are being retrieved, or accusations invoked in the heat of a custodial battle, are circumstances that may negatively affect credibility. Conversely, mothers who maintain an accusation, or mothers who were not reluctant to allow contact between the child and the father prior to the accusation, are interpreted as cues that could confirm the validity of the accusation. Although judges cannot refer to these cues in their judgments because they prove nothing, in the background, they do make a difference in their decisions. This shows that the interpretative work of judges can also impact their sentencing implicitly.

What these socio-legal studies show is that legal rules cannot be applied mechanically. Without active interpretative work, judges cannot determine what is the case about which to decide, what rules apply to the case and how to apply the rules. This interpretative work also shows that 'the scope of what is called "discretion" and "rules" is inescapably indeterminate in daily practice (even if an abstract analysis might suggest greater precision). Rather "rules" are inherently malleable, indeterminate and discretionary while "discretion" is inherently patterned, ordered, and rule-governed [...]. To put it in Dworkinian terms: the dough is always full of discretion and the holes are replete with codes, expectations and cultural-cum-organizational rules' (Tata 2007: 429–30).

Frames (and Surround)

In the preceding section, we have seen that determining what the 'facts' and the 'cases' are about, which judges must decide upon, cannot be understood in isolation from the interpretative work that it involves. Subsequently, how judges select, weigh and elicit data cannot be understood properly without knowing how judges frame data. 'Facts and frames are reflexive: facts narrow the potential frame while the frame provisionally applied may cause some facts to be discarded or disabled, others to be introduced and yet others reinterpreted. Put another way, frames are reflexive in the sense that they both constitute reality and they selectively identify the facts that sustain a social reality' (Hawkins 2011).

The role that frames play in the way in which judges use their discretion can be illustrated by research that builds on the previously mentioned research on signs of remorse (van Oorschot, Mascini and Weenink 2017). The presence or absence of signs of remorse is often understood to have consequences for judges' sentencing decisions. However, remorse does not play a uniform role across offender types. In an ethnographic study in a Dutch criminal court, three different frames were identified, within which defendants' performances of remorse assume differential levels of importance. Defendants' performances of remorse tend to be doomed to fail altogether in the frame of the drugs addict. Drug-addicted defendants are often denied the very status of a moral subject as their performances of remorse are judged as empty promises or inauthentic, strategically apologizing. In the angry young man frame, performances of remorse require the denial of distributed responsibility. While judges know very well that responsibility is distributed over participants in situations of violence in public places, defendant's factual accounts should downplay or neglect this. Defendants who note the distributed nature of responsibility in their efforts to provide a temporal and causal coherent story of what happened, run the risk of damaging their remorseful impression, as it suggests that they are not taking responsibility for their actions. In the explosive couple frame, performances of distributing responsibility and suspending remorse may still result in mitigated sentences. In domestic abuse cases, the perceived messiness of human relationships in which violence takes place does not always translate into the demand that defendants display remorse, that is, take full responsibility and seek help. What prevails is the idea that these relationships are characterized by a dynamic between two explosive partners. Situating performances of remorse within these three frames shows that performances of remorse that 'check the boxes' may nevertheless fail to mitigate a sentence—in the case of 'typical' drug addicts—and that sentences may be mitigated in the very absence of performances of remorse—in the case of 'explosive couples'.

Furthermore, and importantly, this study also shows that frames interact with their surround. The notion that addiction discards moral responsibility is part of a wider societal discourse. In this discourse, addiction, particularly concerning the most criminalized substances, is seen as dangerous mainly because it means a loss of independence, which in turn threatens prevailing ideas about persons as autonomous individuals responsible for their own life trajectories. The narrative of the angry young man is again not uniquely tied to sentencing practices but is part of a wider discourse that links violence and aggression to masculinity. Central is the idea that young males, notably from working-class origins, cannot remain passive when they are provoked and challenged by other males. Finally, the explosive couple narrative is also related to a discourse about the role of the state as guardian of *public* safety, as it is in public space that citizens might unwillingly encounter other citizens that may harm them, whereas encounters between citizens in the domestic sphere is seen as a matter of individual choices. This shows that the three frames are not uniquely tied to the sentencing practices of judges, but interact with social attitudes, which are widely diffused in society. In other words, these frames can interact with classifications of deservingness, worthiness and responsibility prevailing in broader sections of the population (Lipsky 1980: 155).

What we have seen is that frames play a crucial role in how judges use their discretion. The present case as a whole, rather than the constructed facts or the legal rules, is the starting point of the judges' decision-making process (Hartendorp and Wagenaar 2004). A judge first looks for the most appropriate outcome in each particular case, a decision that best fits the case and only then checks whether a logical justification for the judgment can be derived from a rule that satisfies him for the time being because it fits the case. 'Routine decision-making can therefore be best understood as a process of gradual affirmation or denial of a provisional solution to a problem by informally employing typical or typical whole case stories built up through comparative experience' (Tata 1997: 407).

Fields

A decision field describes the legally and organizationally defined setting in which decision-makers work. It is 'anchored by the fixed occupational roles and tasks sanctioned by the legal bureaucracy, and the routine ways in which people make sense of what they encounter [...]' (Hawkins 2011: 190). The positioning of judges within the field in which they are active, shows that the ideal of the independent judge is remote from the practice of decision-making. This can be illustrated by the example of the sentencing process in criminal cases. 'The account of unique and complex behaviour which may have led to an arrest is necessarily normalized, standardized and simplified by the criminal process. Information about criminal behaviour before the judge is represented as one of a selection of typical stories which judges are able to recognize quickly by scanning the file and listening to "the evidence". [...] Judges may recognize and respond to the cues and expectations provided by decisions made earlier in the criminal process and predict decisions downstream' (Tata and Hutton 1998: 353). '[Thus,] the effective disposal of "streams of cases" depends on the ability of the criminal process to communicate expectations and cues which guide judges in answering the question "what type of case is this?" [...] [I]f it is true that whole case stories are largely constructed and typified by the criminal process before they even reach the judge, then it is also true that the agenda for judicial sentencing is in practice largely circumscribed by the construction, cues, and expectations of earlier and later points in the criminal process' (Tata 1997: 403, 413).

Positioning judges' decisions in the field can render visible the effective power of other actors than the official allocated formal legal authority to exercise discretion. This is also demonstrated, for instance, by the role judicial clerks fulfil in the decision-making by judges in the Netherlands (Holvast 2017). A discrepancy is observed between the formal position of judicial assistants and the wide variation in their actual involvement. In regulations and policy documents the administrative and secretarial role is emphasized, while little is regulated regarding the potential advisory and discussion-related duties of assistants. This presents the image of the judicial assistant as a mainly administrative figure who has only limited involvement in the judicial decision-making. In fact, judicial assistants' involvement affects the judicial decision-making practice in three ways. First, judicial assistants control the progression of a case within the court, for instance, by determining whether or not an administrative case should be heard. Thus, judicial assistants play a key role in assuring that the judicial procedure runs smoothly and by performing their administrative duties they can indirectly affect the working methods of judges.

Second, judicial assistants steer the judges in a certain direction. This is particularly done through memos in which judicial assistants might emphasize certain information which concurrently can affect the judges' decision-making. The drafting of judgments can additionally also steer judges' decision-making especially when few instructions are given for writing a judgment. Third, judicial assistants provide judges with additional views to consider. This last practice particularly occurs when judicial assistants provide judges with advice, or when they function as discussion partners. This means that, potentially, the influence that judicial clerks have on the decisions taken by judges goes beyond their formal job description. Taking into account the fact that judicial clerks are only one of the many actors that engage in the collective decision-making process, this suggests that the discretion of the judge is influenced by all other actors involved in the decision-making process.

Holvast (2017) also shows that the relationship between clerks and judges differs between jurisdictions. She has compared the position of clerks in Dutch district courts with the law clerk model in the US, the magistrates' clerks in the system of lay adjudication in England and Wales and the judicial assistants who are currently employed at the English and Welsh Court of Appeal and the UK Supreme Court. The exploration of the different assistance models shows that all judiciaries struggle with the issue of how to make the best use of judicial assistants, while concomitantly attempting to diminish the risk of assistants being too influential. Yet each model includes its own individual mix of features to deal with this dilemma. For instance, in the US, clerks are allowed to actively participate in the preparation and negotiations of briefs while their participation in deliberation sessions is particularly inconceivable. And whereas magistrates' clerks play an important role in informing lay judges, English and Welsh judges consider judicial assistants' participation in judgement drafting in the higher courts as inappropriate. It can be assumed that these differences in the relationship between judicial clerks and judges influence the manner in which the latter use their discretion.

The hypothesis that national differences indeed impact how judges use their discretion, has been convincingly demonstrated by Biland and Steinmetz (2017: 312) in their above mentioned comparative research on family judges. Whereas 'French judges have discretion to "mold" the encounters with clients, and especially to speak up to them, Canadian judges use their granted discretion to decide in a case-by-case treatment of family affairs'. These differences in judges' attitudes and uses of discretion depend on group status, practical concerns and legal culture. French judges hear all cases filed in family courts. The intense work pressure that this entails causes judges to handle individual cases routinely. Legal culture increases the tendency of French judges to exert little discretion when it comes to decision-making. The civil law tradition to which they belong denies the judiciary any form of rulemaking by case law and officially restricts its jurisdiction to law enforcement. Besides, the codification process, which is key in this legal culture, has been justified by the will to create 'rules for all possible cases', thereby limiting judges' room for discretion. This legal culture was reflected in judges' own view of their prerogatives. However, the inquisitorial system that prevailed in the French family court, empowered French judges to use their discretion by leading the hearings and expressing their point of view during judicial encounters. In Quebec, family judges are under less time pressure because they only deal with the most complex and contentious cases. As part of the common law culture, case law sets some standards but legitimizes judges' ability to apply them in a particular case. Therefore, these judges feel confident and legitimized to use their discretion in complex custodial cases. However, they also preserve a more neutral and impartial façade than the French judges during the hearings, which is in line with the common law legal culture that values judges' formally passive role. The judges' awareness of the trial as an adversarial process induces self-restraint.

This means that the way in which judges use their discretion is constrained by the interpretative work and decisions of other actors in the decision-making process as well as by the specificities of the organization and the division of responsibilities in national settings. This shows the importance of 'an understanding of the sentencing process which is not overwhelmingly focused on the judge as the decision maker, but rather as part of a sequence in a decision process, where the judge is a member (albeit the most central) of a collaborative sentencing world. Consequently, [such an approach] focuses our attention on sentencing as a social process, rather than simply as an individual judicial exercise chiefly based on the application of principles to case facts' (Tata 2007: 442).

9.7 Conclusion

In this chapter I have problematized the concept of the legal paradigm. While some legal scholars and legal practitioners view judicial discretion as unpredictable behaviour that is not prescribed by rules and that can and should be avoided as much as possible with statutory rules and legal control instruments, other legal scholars and legal practitioners consider judicial discretion an inevitable and useful part of the rule of law and argue that more attention should be paid to the way in which judges use their discretion in practice. In addition, I have argued that the application of a socio-legal approach to what is preeminently a study object of the alleged legal paradigm—legal outcomes of individual court cases—can provide insights that remain invisible when discretion is conceived as a formal and strictly legal matter. Rather than determining the scope of judicial choices that is or ought to be allowed by the existing legal sources, a socio-legal approach offers an understanding of how professionals and officials who have the authority to apply general rules to specific cases—which encompasses many other professions than judges alone—actually use their discretion in specific contexts. When focusing on judicial sentencing in lower courts, the socio-legal approach shows that the way in which judges use their discretion involves interpretative work and framing; and is interconnected with organizational fields and social surroundings.

This conclusion is certainly not new. Not only has the socio-legal approach proven its value for a long time already, it is also likely to be of lasting value because the context in which judges operate is constantly undergoing change. Changes in, for example, types of offences, workload, decision-making powers, legislation and punitive climate can affect judges' use of discretion, while, conversely, changing patterns in the way in which judges use their discretion can affect the frames, fields and surrounds in which judges are embedded. These cross-level interactions are an inexhaustible source of research. Characteristic of the current context in which judges in most developed countries operate is, for example, that media, politicians and administrative departments closely monitor, and sometimes challenge, the neutrality, substance and productivity of their decisions. Whether and how the scrutiny by different audiences affects the way in which judges use their discretion is a research question that is in line with the current context in which judges operate. Another example of how a changing context may affect the use of discretion pertains to the evolving expectations and role definitions of judges. Like in other countries, in the Netherlands stakeholders and judges alike increasingly expect the judiciary to put more effort into addressing the conflicts that underlie legal disputes (Grootelaar, Mascini and van Rossum 2017). The initiatives that have resulted from this, such as a new procedure in administrative law (*de nieuwe zaaksbehandeling*), codes of conduct for personal injury lawyers and insurers, and subsidies for alternative dispute resolution, may impact the manner in which judges use their discretion.

As a socio-legal approach has acquired a full and hopefully lasting position when it comes to the study of discretion, it may no longer be necessary to contrast this approach to an assumed dominant legal paradigm. Rather more work can be made of forging bridges with legal scholars and legal practitioners who acknowledge the limitations of studying discretion in a purely formal and legal matter.

Note

1. A possibly less known but equally useful theoretical framework is advanced by Wagenaar (2004; see also Chap. 17 of this volume). His focus is on the social micromechanics of work to explain how administrative workers negotiate practical problems in the context of a large, complex bureaucracy. Specifically, he discusses four issues that, taken together, outline a useful theory of administrative practice: *situatedness* (work always takes place in a context that influences how it is understood and carried out), *knowing* (the application of knowledge in the carrying out of work tasks), *action* (the prime vehicle for negotiating the world) and *interaction* (the centrality of interaction for work). He attributes a central role to practical judgement as the sense-making activity that binds the other elements of a theory of practice into a meaningful whole.

References

Anleu, S.R., Brewer, R. & Mack, K. (2016). Locating the judge within sentencing research. *International Journal for Crime, Justice and Social Democracy*, 6(2), 46–63.

Baldwin, R. & Hawkins, K. (1984). Discretionary justice: Davis reconsidered. *Public Law*, 580, 570–599.

Baumgartner, M. P. (2001). The myth of discretion. *The uses of discretion* (2nd edition, pp. 129–162). Oxford: Clarendon Press.

Beyens, K. & Scheirs, V. (2010). Encounters of a different kind: Social enquiry and sentencing in Belgium. *Punishment & Society*, 12(3), 309–328.

Biland, É. & Steinmetz, H. (2017). Are judges street-level bureaucrats? Evidence from French and Canadian family courts. *Law & Social Inquiry*, 42(2), 298–324.

Bushway, S. D. & Forst, B. (2013). Studying discretion in the processes that generate criminal sanctions. *Justice Quarterly*, 30(2), 199–222.

Campbell, E. (1999). Towards a sociological theory of discretion. *International Journal of the Sociology of Law*, 22, 79–101.

Cover, R. (1975). *Justice accused: Antislavery and the judicial process.* New Haven, CT: Yale University Press.

Davis, K. (1969). *Discretionary justice: A preliminary inquiry.* Baton Rouge, Louisiana: Louisiana State University.

de Jong, E.R., Faure, M.G., Giesen, I. & Mascini, P. (2018). Judge-made risk regulation and tort law: An introduction. *European Journal of Risk and Regulation*, 9, 6–13.

Dworkin, R. (1977). *Taking rights seriously.* London: Duckworth.

Feldman, M. (2001). Social limits to discretion: An organizational perspective. In K. Hawkins (Ed.), *The uses of discretion* (2nd ed., pp. 163–183). Oxford: Clarendon Press.

Galligan, D.J. (1990). Senses of discretion. In *Discretionary powers: A legal study of official discretion* (pp. 2–55) Oxford Scholarship Online.

Goldfinch, S. & Wallis, J. (2010). Two myths of convergence in public management reform. *Public Administration*, 88(4), 1099–1116.

Grootelaar, H., Mascini, P. & Van Rossum, W. (2017). Recht als probleemoplossing? [The law as solution to problems?] *Recht der Werkelijkheid*, 38(2), 3–8.

Hartendorp, R.C. & Wagenaar, H. (2004). De praktische rechter: De opmerkelijke relevantie van Paul Scholten voor een eigentijdse rechtsvindingstheorie [The practical judge: The remarkable relevance of Paul Scholten for a contemporary legal decision-making theory]. *Netherlands Journal of Legal Philosophy*, (1): 60–89.

Hawkins, K. (2001). The use of legal discretion: Perspectives from law and social science. In K. Hawkins (Ed.), *The uses of discretion* (2nd ed., pp. 11–46). Oxford: Clarendon Press.

Hawkins, K. (2011). Order, rationality and silence: Some reflections on criminal justice decision-making. In L. Gelsthorpe & N. Padfield (Eds), *Exercising discretion: Decision-making in the criminal justice system and beyond* (pp. 186–219). London and New York: Routledge.

Hebly, M.R. (2017). Geen beweging in het verjaringsregime voor mesothelioomclaims [No movement in the limitation regime for mesothelioma claims]. *Nederlands Tijdschrift voor Burgerlijk recht*, 32(7), 220–230.

Holvast, N.L. (2017). *In the shadow of the judge: The involvement of judicial assistants in Dutch district courts.* Amsterdam: University of Amsterdam.

Jorna, F. & Wagenaar, P. (2007). The 'iron cage' strengthened? Discretion and digital discipline. *Public Administration*, 85(1), 189–214.

Kadish, M.R. & Kadish, S.H. (1973). *Discretion to disobey: A study of lawful departures front legal rules*. Stanford, CA: Stanford University Press.

Kuhn, T. (1970). *The structure of scientific revolutions* (2nd ed.). Chicago, IL and London: Chicago University Press.

Lacey, N. (2001). The jurisprudence of discretion: Escaping the legal paradigm. In K. Hawkins (Ed.), *The uses of discretion* (2nd ed., pp. 361–388). Oxford: Clarendon Press.

Lipsky, M. (1980). *Street-level bureaucracy: Dilemmas of the individual in public services*. New York: Russell Sage Foundation.

Mascini, P., van Oorschot, I., Weenink, D. & Schippers, G. (2016). Understanding judges' choices of sentence types as interpretative work: An explorative study in a Dutch police court. *Recht Der Werkelijkheid*, 37(1), 32–49.

Nickels, E.L. (2007). A note on the status of discretion in police research. *Journal of Criminal Justice*, 35, 570–578.

Posner, R.A. (2008). *How judges think*. Cambridge, MA: Harvard University Press.

Pottie, L. & Sossin, L. (2005). Demystifying the boundaries of public law: Policy, discretion, and social welfare. *University of British Columbia Law Review*, 38(1), 147–188.

Ringeling, A.B. (1986). Beleidsvrijheid opnieuw bezien [Discretion reconsidered]. In A.F.A. Korsten & W. Derksen (Eds), *Uitvoering van overheidsbeleid. Gemeenten en ambtelijk gedrag belicht* (pp. 213–224). Leiden, etc.: Stenfert Kroese.

Samuel, G. (2017). *A short introduction to judging and to legal reasoning*. Cheltenham and Northampton, MA: Edward Elgar.

Schneider, C.E. (2001). Discretion and rules: A lawyer's view. In K. Hawkins (Ed.), *The uses of discretion* (2nd ed., pp. 47–88). Oxford: Clarendon Press.

Shapiro, S.J. (2007). The "Hart-Dworkin" debate: A short guide for the perplexed. *SSRN*, 1–54.

Shaw, G. C. (2013). H. L. A. Hart's lost essay: Discretion and the legal process school. *Harvard Law Review*, 127, 666–727.

Smeehuijzen, J.L. (2017). Hoe oordeelt de feitenrechter over strijd met de maatschappelijke betamelijkheid in de zin van art. 6:162 lid 2 BW? Een jurisprudentieonderzoek [How does the judge assess the conflict with societal decency in the sense of art. 6: 162 paragraph 2 of the Dutch Civil Code? A jurisprudence investigation]. *Vermogensrecht*, 125.

Smit, A.E., Bijleveld, C.C.J.H. & Antokolskaia, M.V. (2017). Het besluitvormingsproces van civiele rechters in procedures over de gevolgen van een (echt)scheiding met een beschuldiging van seksueel kindermisbruik [The decision process of civil judges in procedures about the effects of divorce cases with an accusation of sexual abuse]. *Recht Der Werkelijkheid*.

Smith, C. (2010). Rechters maken eigen regels: En toch is de rechtspraak onpartijdig [Judges make their own rules, and yet judicial decision-making is impartial]. *Academische Boekengids*, (March), 13–15.

Tata, C. (1997). Conceptions and representations of the sentencing decision process. *Journal of Law and Society*, 24(3), 395–420.

Tata, C. (2007). Sentencing as craftwork and the binary epistemologies of the discretionary decision process. *Social & Legal Studies*, 16(3), 425–447.

Tata, C. & Hutton, N. (1998). What 'rules' in sentencing? Consistency and disparity in the absence of 'rules'. *International Journal of the Sociology of Law*, 26(3), 339–364.

Tombs, J. & Jagger, E. (2006). Denying responsibility. Sentencers' accounts of their decisions to imprison. *British Journal of Criminology*, 46(5), 803–821.

van Oorschot, I., Mascini, P. & Weenink, D. (2017). Remorse in context(s): A qualitative exploration of the negotiation of remorse and its consequences. *Social & Legal Studies*. https://doi.org/10.1177/0964663

van der Woude, M. & van der Leun, J. (2017). Crimmigration checks in the internal border areas of the EU: Finding the discretion that matters. *European Journal of Criminology*, 14(1), 27–45.

Vila, M.I. (2001). The concept of judicial discretion. In *Facing judicial discretion: Legal knowledge and right answers revisited* (pp. 1–36) Kluwer.

Wagenaar, H. (2004). 'Knowing' the rules: Administrative work as practice. *Public Administration Review*, 64(6), 643–655.

CHAPTER 10

Discretion from an Economic Perspective

Dirk J. Wolfson

10.1 Introduction

People are not alike: not in their *preferences* and *capabilities* when dealing with adversities and opportunities, not in their *needs* and not in *understanding* of what is hitting them in terms of globalization, technological development, job security, income distribution and environmental threats. Many are insecure and trust in governance appears to be on the wane, making way for a 'national populism' in the US and large parts of Europe. All this calls for a new deal in which diversity is addressed with discretion and a strengthening of the human service element.

Section 10.2 introduces an economic perspective on discretion by offering a brief survey of the state of the art in the methodology of economics, the theory of economic policy and its underlying behavioural assumptions (Sent 2004). Section 10.3 shows how a growing professionalism of the civil service and of street-level case workers in particular, creates scope for discretion in dealing with diversity and to close the gap between top-down and bottom-up approaches in policymaking and implementation.

Section 10.4 pleads the case for a mode of contextual or situational contracting that draws on recent insights from an emerging field of behavioural economics into the potential of principal/agent relationships in public governance. It will be shown how the situational mode accommodates diversity, matches demand and supply of public services, deals with information asymmetries, reveals the potential and preferences of the contracting parties and fosters trust in the political process by integrating bottom-up and top-down approaches. Within a legal framework that sets the stage, throughout the entire chain of policymaking and delivery and in network management as well,

D. J. Wolfson (✉)
Erasmus University Rotterdam, Rotterdam, The Netherlands

T. Evans, P. Hupe (eds.), *Discretion and the Quest for Controlled Freedom*, https://doi.org/10.1007/978-3-030-19566-3_10

professional agents submit mandates to their principals for further detailed implementation. Approval grants them legitimate space on the basis of comply-or-explain to deal with diversity and to use discretion in customizing benefits and matching efforts required from their counterparts.

Note that transactions concluded *reveal* the trade-offs between criteria of good governance and suggest their *acceptability*. The process of situational contracting clarifies *who* pays for, gets or does *what, when, where, how* and *why*, as the normative issues in political intervention. Outcomes are monitored and feed-back is provided for responsive policymaking, implementation and control.

Section 10.5 shows how the situational mode reveals prevailing ideologies and preferences. Section 10.6 introduces evidence from early applications and suggestions for rolling out this new mechanism design. Section 10.7 offers a summary and discussion and Sect. 10.8 rounds up with a conclusion.

10.2 An Economic Perspective on Diversity and Discretion

Economists analyse how people manage their welfare in a world where time, individual energy, money and natural resources are scarce. *Scarcity* implies the need to make choices; it is the key-concept of economics, which offers insights about the way individual or collective choices in dealing with scarcity work out. In short, economics tries to answer the question: *what happens*, if we do something with scarce resources. That helps to find least-cost (efficient) solutions for the aims that people pursue, on their own, through their political system or by way of their voluntary organizations. In this process, costs are defined as 'the benefits forgone by not using resources in their most valued alternative use' (Culyer 1985: 147).

Efficiency is measured with the *'Pareto criterion'*, which holds that the optimal or 'best achievable' use of scarce resources is reached if there is no alternative which will leave some people better off without worsening the position of others (Just, Hueth and Schmitz 2004: 6). Concentrating on efficiency provides a *benchmark* that allows us to trade this criterion with possibly rival concerns that are dimensions of our welfare as well, such as (1) upholding the *rule of law*, (2) *fairness* in the prevailing distribution of income and opportunity and (3) environmental *sustainability* over time. These additional concerns are largely dealt with by bargaining in the political and administrative process and may be supplemented by non-governmental organizations (NGOs) or private philanthropy.

Economic theory, political theory and political practice meet in the design of economic *policy*; that reverses the analytical line of thought of economic theory in order to find out what we ourselves, our voluntary organizations or our political agents *should* do, if we *want* a particular social result (Hennipman 1995: 5–58). In the context of policy, the question is now no longer just *what happens?* but *what can we do about it?* How do we strike a balance between efficiency and concerns such as fairness and sustainability, once we have identified the scarcities and costs at stake?

In short, economic *policy* tries to balance the 'least-cost' perspectives of economic *analysis* with our more comprehensive normative preferences regarding rights, fairness and sustainability, as aspects of our welfare that are inspired by political theory and by what Adam Smith (1759) already called our 'moral sentiments'.

In a democracy, politicians are supposed to base policies on individual preference and consumer's and citizen's *sovereignty* as the drivers or independent variables in dealing with scarcity: '*Wir sind das Volk*' ('We are the people') chanted the Berliners at the fall of the Wall. But how does the policy process align the 'technical', *descriptive* and evidence-based least-cost analysis of economic theory with the leading normative or *prescriptive* preferences of the people? It does this by using an *if… then* methodology: '*if* so and so are your convictions and preferences, *then* this and that are your options, costs and possible results' (Yew-Kwang Ng 1979). In actual practice, however, the individual convictions, preferences and capabilities of people *differ* and this diversity makes the case for *discretion*, in an appeal for *leeway* as the basis of freedom for actors to act within legitimized limits in the delivery of public goods and services.

Figure 10.1 shows how the choice between markets, public provision and regulation in managing our welfare is conditioned by degrees—from 0 to 100 per cent—of *indivisibility of scale, excludability* and *rivalry in demand* and by normative considerations about human rights, fairness in the distribution of opportunity and income. *Indivisibility* implies that the scale of what we want is given and cannot be broken down in bits and pieces; *excludability* that acquisition requires consideration in return; and *rivalry* that what *you* have *I* can't have at the same time.

Cell 1 of the matrix denotes, for example, the case of protection against a rising sea-level. The Netherlands is a low-lying country that is protected from the incursion of the sea by dikes. Dikes come in one *indivisible* piece and once a large-scale coastal defence is built, everyone behind it is protected, without *rivalry* and with no possibility of individual *exclusion*, meaning, also, that commercial exploitation would not be able to recoup costs. Hence, social efficiency requires public funding of what is called a (pure) public good.

Cell 2 covers situations of rival demand, as in the case of overgrazing and a risk of desertification, when open access may lead to what environmentalists call a 'tragedy of the commons', a public *bad* that may require—where possible—the introduction of individual property rights or public regulation.

Cell 3 shows a mixed bag of indirect market goods (commercial radio, paid for by advertisers and with free access for listeners); quasi-public goods (non-rival weather forecasts, excludable and payable by copy right, but often provided as a public service and paid for by taxation); and private philanthropy, such as NGOs which may cover both non-rival and rival demand.

Indivisibility of scale / *Excludability*		Non-rival demand 0 %	Rival demand .... 100 %
Individual exclusion or rejection costly or even impossible	0 %	**Open access** 1. ***(pure) public good*** (protection against rising sea-level)	2. ***(pure) public bad*** (tragedy of the commons)
Individual exclusion or rejection possible	100 %	**Controllable access** 3a ***indirect market good*** (commercial radio) 3b ***quasi-public good*** (weather forecast?) 3c ***private philanthropy and NGO's***	4a ***typical market good*** (shelter and food) 4b ***quasi-public good*** (education, public health) 4c ***private philanthropy and NGO's***

Fig. 10.1 The case for public intervention

When demand is ***rival***, user rights or ownership need to be exclusive, if possible, as in the case of typical market goods (Cell 4a in the scheme). Yet, excludable access in areas such as education and health care may be provided in *Open Access* when either governments or private philanthropy are prepared to foot the bill for an adequate supply, creating quasi-public goods, for instance to redistribute opportunities or income (Cells 4b and 4c).

In terms of behavioural and technical assumptions, the economic perspective was traditionally based on deductions from rather crude assumptions; the first four below, for example, do not really hold up well under closer scrutiny:

1. 'Economic Man' (*homo economicus*) is well-informed, rational and self-interested; yet, he is an ***artificial construct*** and does not exist in real life. Modern behavioural economics recognizes that information may be unreliable and that people have social and altruistic interests as well. Moreover, it is an ***illusion*** that people would be capable of full rationality: brain power is a scarce commodity as well. Finally, it is not inefficient to stop searching through alternative actions once an acceptable threshold is met. Herbert Simon (1976), one of the Founding Fathers of

'behavioural economics', called stopping under these circumstances 'satisficing', a clever combination of to *satisfy* and to *suffice*. This chapter assumes that people, on the whole, are capable of ordering their preferences, but may benefit, here and there, from some guidance or prodding (Wolfson 2010: 39).

2. *Competition* in 'perfect' markets would drive out economic power; yet, in real life, competition is often far from perfect and does not constrain banks and other big business to extort fiscal and regulatory favours from governments.
3. *Market prices* reflect scarcities correctly; but this is false: crucial scarcities, such as environmental values, may remain *unpriced*.
4. *Market systems* even out demand and supply in a general equilibrium; false again. Markets may be 'not self-adjusting', as Keynes put it succinctly after the Great Depression. This observation has given rise to the distinction between micro-economics to analyse individual trades and macro-economics which looks at the more volatile way individual trades add-up in the performance of the economic system as a whole.

These four assumptions have lost most of their credibility as economic analysis became more sophisticated over time. Assumptions 5 and 6, below, still hold more or less:

5. Additional or 'marginal' *utility* or satisfaction derived from goods and services *declines* if we get more of the same and
6. People try to even-out the utility derived across the set of goods and services at their disposal.

Summing up, the *putative assumptions of traditional economics* are not good enough; we have got to go deeper. Game theory, for instance, has made an important contribution in raising our awareness that economic coordination may be frustrated by *information asymmetry*: 'that simple fact that different people know different things' (Stiglitz 2002: 469). However, the real breakthrough in our understanding of how people deal with scarcity came with the relatively recent emergence of a new field of *behavioural economics* (Kahneman 2000, 2012; Thaler 2015), which systematically gathers empirical evidence of how people form opinions and take decisions when managing their welfare. This development allows us to explore how more recent behavioural insights pave the way for an integration of bottom-up and top-down approaches in public administration. This will be our leading light in Sects. 10.3 and 10.4.

10.3 Discretion as the Hallmark of Professionalism

Many people have difficulties in coping with rapid changes in their economic and social situation and prone to 'national populism'. On both sides of the Atlantic, many are disgruntled, feel neglected and want to be heard, not spoken down to. Yet, every personal case is a story in its own right. The next section, therefore, will explore a way for politics to get closer to individual citizens by allowing for ***discretion*** and a personalized customization in public service delivery. In the present section, it will be argued that discretion is the hallmark of professionalism in governance, particularly in personalized social support. The twenty-first century may well be the 'age of the professional': an age in which an explosive growth of not necessarily reliable information requires vetting and structuring into useable knowledge. In this connection, it is telling that *The Economist*, in a leader of November 4, 2017: 9, cautions that 'Once considered a boon to democracy, social media have started to look like its nemesis'. This, too, calls for a professional attitude and mission to mediate between demand and supply of social services (Johnson 1972). ***Professionalism*** is here defined as a state in which agents in delivery can diagnose diverging needs and have the expertise to claim discretion in order to find appropriate and prudent solutions within the constraints of their professions' ethical codes of conduct and political guidance (Wolfson 2019). In the delivery of public support, we need front-line workers with professional expertise as what Evans (Chap. 23: 365) calls 'a mixture of thinking, acting and feeling' and skills that are social and improvisational. Think of a case worker who uses her social intelligence when deciding to give warning advice rather than applying a penalty in winning over an uncooperative client.

Following Culyer (1980: 70), ***need*** is defined as an externally determined demand, acknowledged by ***professional judgement***. If I am ill, my physician defines my needs; if unemployed, my case worker/job coach clarifies my options. Hence, professionals, throughout the process of policymaking and delivery, are seen as typically able to customize solutions in a creative, situational or contextual response to needs and as motivated by challenges and results, rather than by bureaucratic rules and regulation: professionals want to heal, to teach, to explore, to serve and protect human dignity or whatever they are called for. They deserve degrees of freedom to do their thing (Tummers and Bekkers 2014 and Chap. 11 of this edited collection) and to sustain their reputation *vis-à-vis* different audiences: their colleagues, clients and supervisors (Busuioc and Lodge 2016: 248).

Behavioural economics studies the effects of psychological, social, cognitive and emotional factors in the ways individuals deal with scarcity in their private life and in principal/agent relationships within and between institutions. Contemporary governance has a lot to learn from what psychology and behavioural economics have to say about principals and agents. Wherever there is a risk that information asymmetries may create scope for shirking (underperformance) or moral hazard (evasion of responsibility), behavioural insights show opportunities for trust management by principals, in an interactive and cooperative social exchange conception of principal/agent theory and a coaching style of leadership that nurtures the intrinsic motivations of their professional agents (Van Slyke 2007; Wolfson 2012; Dur and Zoutenbier 2014). The principal, as coach, can instruct and advise, change players and apply sanctions afterwards, but she does not play the game. Without fostering the intrinsic motivation and professional pride of her team, information asymmetry may lead to non-cooperative games in which actors may try to maximize individual welfare, rather than the common good. Section 10.4 will show how cooperative attitudes in the relation between principals and agents can be developed and *policy alienation*—tensions as described in Chap. 11—reduced.

With reference to professional attitudes, game theoretical assumptions of shirking or moral hazard of agents exploiting information asymmetry may be challenged. As Breton (1995) already pointed out, professional agents may be better informed about backgrounds and possible solutions of problems to be addressed, but are dependent on the resources of the principal. This mutual dependence offers an opportunity to link the agency of professionals with political guidance and support. Moreover, it answers the question why public managers would choose tools of collaborative and interactive governance (Scott and Thomas 2016: 2). Clearly, there is a trade-off between complexity and allowance for diversity (Calmar Andersen and Moynihan 2016). Hence, the five basic behavioural assumptions that underpin the analysis in the rest of this chapter are that

1. in a pluralist democracy, politicians (*political* principals) will be smart enough to have an interest in accommodating the diversity in preferences, capabilities and opportunities of their constituents where technically and politically possible, and to foster the expertise and agency of professionals in delivery;
2. public managers (*administrative* principals) and professional case workers (administrative agents) in delivery appreciate degrees of freedom to negotiate the best achievable fit between need and support;
3. network partners and individual beneficiaries or their representatives want to be recognized and heard;
4. showing respect for human dignity and acknowledging diversity by involving citizens or their voluntary associations as 'co-producers' of policies will improve targeting and help to foster trust in governance and
5. Hood cautions (in Chap. 3 of this volume) that *delegation* in the design of public policy might be inspired by *blame avoidance*. However, the situational mode is based on a combination of *mandates* approved by principals and accountability ('comply-or-explain') by agents. This, presumably, locates the buck.

Discretion in dealing with diversity and regaining trust in governance is a major challenge. Today's political reality appears to be that there is a growing awareness that the fruits of globalization, deregulation and technological development are distributed unevenly between the rich and the poor. In the US, the American Dream of equal opportunity seems broken by a combination of unequal access to higher education and a loss of social cohesion (Putnam 2015; Milanovic 2016). President Obama (2016: 21–4) noted that, in 1979, the top 1 per cent of American families received 7 per cent of all after tax income. By 2007, that share had more than doubled to 17 per cent. In Europe, inequality has increased as well. 'Brexit', moreover, and a growing populist sentiment are tokens of a structural failure to uphold common values.

Against this background, the next section of this chapter proposes a novel model of *situational contracting*, a cooperative mechanism design in which the content and the conditions or terms of trade of transactions concluded: (1) allow for diversity and discretion in customizing and personalizing public services, (2) *reveal* the values that a political system upholds on the supply side and the preferences of the beneficiaries on the demand side, (3) link the creativity of professionals with the commitment of politicians and citizens, (4) restore trust in governance and (5) regain control by principals over complexity in network management.

10.4 Discretion and the Case for Situational Contracting in Public Governance

In Sect. 10.2, Fig. 10.1 outlined the technical characteristics and normative considerations behind the choice between *markets* and *public provision or regulation* as facilitators in dealing with scarcity. Markets can 'customize' solutions. They are traditionally seen as organized by the 'hidden hands' of economic coordination, with prices paid in the process of exchange revealing reliable *information* about a presumably perfect match of the preferences of buyers and sellers. Yet, market coordination may be rigged by economic power or considered unacceptable when the distribution of income renders basic needs, such as security, shelter, health care or education unaffordable. The alternative of public provision by way of traditional bureaucracy and regulation, however, may stand in the way of *discretion* in dealing with diversity. Hence, it is time for a closer look at the potential for discretion in public governance in *customizing* public provision for the specific needs of individual citizens (see also Needham's Chap. 19 of this edited collection). What is needed is a format of *situational contracting* that combines the informational qualities of transactions with political guidance in matters of ethics, diversity, discretion and distribution. These considerations are elaborated upon in Sect. 10.5, but first, the situational format will be explained.

Situational contracting is an application of what Cornelisse and Thorbecke (2010: 5, 13, 88–90 and *passim*) call an *exchange configuration*, in which the three basic elements of transactions are brought together: (1) the *item* or *content* of what is exchanged (personalized public support, for instance, in exchange for specified efforts on the part of the individual beneficiary to cooperate in finding appropriate solutions); and also non-excludable public goods, in trades with representative organizations or advocacy coalitions, (2) the *actors* engaged in decisions relating to the exchange (at the different levels of policymaking and delivery or in horizontal networks of inter-agency cooperation); and (3) the *cultural, socio-economic, political and legal environment*—the informal and formal rules and regulations and the physical aspects, such as the climate, in which solutions are framed (Cornelisse and Thorbecke 2010: 86–90). The essence of the situational approach is that the combination of mutual dependence in defining the content and conditions of the exchange, as well as in achieving results, with excludability as a sanction on uncooperative attitudes, helps to align the preferences and incentives of the contracting parties.

Figure 10.2 shows how a format or *mechanism design* (Maskin 2008) of situational contracting holds the exchange configuration together in a set of principal/agent relationships.

It summarizes the vertical and horizontal relationships in situational contracting.

Layer 1: Political initiatives, presumably based on an electoral mandate

↕

Layer 2: Policy design

Inputs from outside ↔ Inputs from senior civil service ↔ Inputs from outside

↕

Output: Legislation and protocols of good practice in implementation

↕

Layer 3: Leadership in implementation

Inputs from outside ↔ interaction with case workers ↔ Inputs from outside

↕

Output: Mandates for implementation

↕

Layer 4: Delivery

Input: customization of support for preferences and capabilities

↕

Output: Results

↕

Layer 5: Feedback from experience, visitations and validation

Fig. 10.2 Situational contracting in a layered and interactive approach

Agents, when viewed from the top and layer by layer, assume the role of principal in the next layer, until the ultimate beneficiaries are reached who, in their role of citizen, are the principals of politicians in layer 1 again. In horizontal network relations, the demanding party is the principal.

While there seems to be a lingering conventional wisdom that principal/agent relationships in traditional top-down hierarchies are vulnerable to information asymmetries, shirking, moral hazard and power games, this chapter holds that *mutual dependence* links the agency of professionals in implementation with political guidance, in what Mascini (Chap. 9 of this edited collection) calls a socio-legal approach to discretion and Marston and Davidson (Chap. 7) refer to as 'relational case management'. Situational contracting is about exercising judgement within constraints of mandates, in responsiveness to citizens and working within a framework of promises (Needham, Chap. 19, and Evans, Chap. 23). Note that Carson, Madhok and Wu (2006) claim that while formal contracts are robust to ambiguity but not to volatility, 'relational contracting' in network management is robust to volatility but not to ambiguity. In the situational mode, however, mandates set the stage for volatility without ambiguity.

In *layer 1* of Fig. 10.2, politicians create a framework for collaborative governance and develop initiatives for a programme that, presumably, is based on a mandate obtained from citizens who have swapped support for electoral promises. Granted, this is a rather heroic assumption from the core of political theory about the way a democracy works, but that is exactly what the subsequent layers of civic involvement in collaborative governance aim to achieve. Involving a professional staff and citizens or their representatives as beneficiaries of public services in a levelled process of policymaking and delivery furthers an optimal use of information and introduces an element of *direct democracy*.

In *layer 2*, *political* principals interact with senior civil service as their agents in developing policies, drafting legislation and protocols of good practice for responsive policymaking, and implementation. In this process, inter-agency inputs may be negotiated with horizontal network partners in other departments of governance, other jurisdictions or voluntary organizations representing citizens.

Next, in *layer 3*, senior staff, now in their role of *administrative* principals, discuss data on actual performance as reported on by their agents and approve *mandates* for a situational or contextual mode of implementation, as developed *bottom-up* by professional agents in or, possibly, outside their own organization on the basis of their expertise in delivery. Mandates granted authorize case workers to *personalize* and *customize* support in *layer 4* of actual delivery for differences in *needs* and in *capabilities* of beneficiaries to improve their functionings (Sen 2009). This way, professionals in delivery are granted *discretion* to use their judgement in following mandates on the basis of *comply-or-explain*, in line with the argument developed earlier.

In *layer 4*, of service delivery, *content and conditions* or *terms of trade* of the situational contract concluded *show* what the caseworker has on offer and what the beneficiary is capable and prepared to do. Mandated degrees of freedom (comply-or-explain), moreover, drive the devil out of the details and help to align incentives, to further public service motivation on the part of case workers and trust on the part of beneficiaries. The situational mode creates scope for learning and innovation, as crucial conditions for collaborative governance (Koppenjan and Klijn 2004). Note, however, that discretion in delivery is feasible only when there is a need for customization on the part of beneficiaries and the possibility of exclusion to protect the state against non-cooperation. Administrative routines that do not require customization, such as issuing birth certificates or fishing licences, remain under traditional hierarchical control.

Layer 5, finally, closes the circle by providing feedback from results in learning loops of adjustment and continuous legitimation in the political process.

Excludability remains a standard requirement. It works two ways: first, degrees of freedom for *professional agents* in delivery may be withdrawn or, second, *access* to public facilities *for individual beneficiaries* in layer 4 denied in case of uncooperative behaviour. Note that excludability may be applied *vertically*, layer by layer, from losing a political majority or failure to build a coalition in layer 1 to the degrees of freedom for professionals in delivery to customize solutions and beneficiaries who do not cooperate, as well as *horizontally*, if network partners do not play game. In short, the risk of exclusion takes the guile out of self-interest. Yet, exclusion may be challenged through access to a second opinion or in a court of law.

Figure 10.1 (in Sect. 10.2) already showed that personalized support and individual exclusion on the demand side are not possible with regard to pure public goods in open access, such as protection or trade agreements. This means that voluntary associations and advocacy coalitions may have to stand in earlier on in the process, negotiating content on behalf of their constituents in the policy arenas of layer 2; their input, again, may be excluded in case of uncooperative behaviour.

The crux of the matter is that the discretion granted in layer 4 of actual delivery *emancipates* what Lipsky (1980) called the street-level bureaucrat. It presents the case worker not just as the interface between citizen and state, but also as the *face* of the state. This is more than a play with words: the human service element in co-production adds to the quality and productivity of solutions.

Another crucial contribution of situational contract is that content and conditions or terms of trade *reveal* the extent to which a government is prepared to render support and beneficiaries are ready to cooperate in finding appropriate solutions. No more hidden hands: the content or item to be exchanged and the conditions of the contract *show* the hand of governance. *Judgements* on the *content* (the first part of the exchange configuration), the *performance* of the actors engaged in the exchange (the second part); and the acceptability of these trades in terms of the cultural, economic and political *climate* (the third part; Cornelisse and Thorbecke 2010: 5) belong to the realm of ethics, politics and political theory. Monitoring by political and administrative principals may lead to *political* decisions to adjust the terms of trade, which distinguishes the situational mode from the market mode of privatization. Throughout the process of policymaking and delivery, moreover, the situational mode creates *transparency*. Guidance on the basis of comply-or-explain and customization in implementation endeavours to involve the parties concerned in a halfway house between the creativity of agency and the rigour of regulation.

Rules, however, remain paramount in situations where there is no risk of asymmetric information and discretion is not wanted or feasible, for instance in structuring the administrative routines mentioned before. Section 10.5 will elaborate on how contracts between principals and agents *reveal* the values that a society wants to uphold, pave the way for *discretion* in dealing with diversity and foster trust in governance. At first sight, all this may look complicated, but on closer inspection, it is possible to see this happening in our everyday encounters with public service. You have seen bits and pieces of it before: as a parent, you entrust your child to a teacher, who reports back on its progress to you and to her hierarchical principal and is prepared to *explain* her marks to you in a parent/teacher conference and to her hierarchical principal who, in turn, is an agent in relations with the school board and so we get on, upwards in the chain of responsibilities, to the minister of education who is the agent of Parliament. Or take your family doctor. He may, as your agent, refer you to a medical consultant who mails her report back to him, as her principal and explains her findings to the two of you. In summary, situational contracting, discretion, control and reputation building are framed within a system of mandating and reporting. If it works in education and health care, let us explore its potential in social security and other areas of (semi-) public administration in order to reduce information asymmetry and to involve citizens in dealing with their specific needs.

In the situational mode the principal/agent relationship involves all the relevant parties as interactive and creative agents, satisfying the criterion that governance structures, where possible, must enable, rather than constrain human agency. It is widely applicable in all areas where discretion and personalized service are appreciated and feasible as long as the *transaction costs* of deliberation remain below the alternative social costs of hard and fast rules imposed 'from above'.

Note however that, while the transaction costs of situational contracting are relatively easy to establish, the welfare gains in terms of effectiveness are more difficult to appreciate. The latter will depend on how people, professionals and politicians value discretion and customization of public support. Compared with the 'black boxes' of collaborative governance explored in the literature (Scott and Thomas 2016), the situational approach provides a 'modest' format, as it is based on degrees of freedom to customize solutions within a *given* and *monitored* structure of decision-making and accountability.

10.5 Notes About Values, Ideologies, Discretion and Revealed Preference

Any society needs precepts for living together. In the 'Western world', the leading precepts are representative democracy and the protection of human dignity and human rights under the rule of law. Yet, while people are seen as equal before the law, they *differ* widely in capabilities and preferences; hence the need for discretion in public governance. Capability theory was introduced by the welfare economist and philosopher Amartya Sen (1985, 2009); see also Wolfson (2015). Sen interprets well-being as not exclusively associated with affluence but also with an individual's capability to convert available resources and opportunities into actual *functionings*.

Discretion, in turn, calls for professionals who can transform an overload of information about facts, fiction, behaviour and values into useable knowledge for designing and implementing policies. As noted before, the terms of trade in the situational mode are value-loaded and monitored in the political process, but situational contracting as such does *not* provide us with a theory of justice. Its first and foremost contribution is that it creates *transparency*: it matches individualized demand and supply and—presumably—*reveals* the actual values as they transpire in the terms of trade of agreements reached and enforced with the sanction of exclusion, layer by layer and horizontally in the management of networks. That presumption does not necessarily imply that the deals concluded are rational (Kahneman 2012), fair or sustainable, but they show what's *happening* and reduce the gap between the *stated* ideologies, preferences and promises of politicians and what they *actually* have on offer, once elected. Note, moreover, that situational contracting can implement a range of ideologies, a characteristic of any good institutional or mechanism design. Rights and corresponding obligations may be periodically adjusted on the basis of feed-back from mandates and shifts in the political environment and the general stance of policy, for instance after elections. In short, the situational mode develops a picture of what a *community* apparently sees as the common good.

In a legal sense, public control moves from a *'compliance'* orientation in which success is measured by conformity to rules, towards a *'performance'* orientation, in which the focus is on reasonability in the achievement of goals (Noonan, Sabel and Simon 2009: 529) and on reputation in solving problems (Busuioc and Lodge 2016). In short, when people are not alike, discretion is an inevitable and useful part of the rule of law, as Mascini puts it in Chap. 9.

The values underlying situational contracting in any particular context are settled in 'choices of reasoning that we can reflectively sustain' (Sen 2009: 194): choices that weigh the *allocative* rationale of distributing the fruits of cooperation on the basis of individual contribution with the *ethical* recognition that the dice of opportunity and economic power are loaded. This is not an 'empty statement', as the terms of trade in the situational mode do indeed *reveal* the outcomes of an ongoing discourse on fairness and can serve a wide spectrum of ideologies.

In line with the theme of this edited collection, however, the most important contribution of situational contracting may well be that it identifies an economic rationale for ***discretion in public governance***. While people are equal in the narrow sense of equality before the law, it is recognized that they are not *alike*: not in their preferences and prejudices, not in their opportunities and capabilities to improve their life chances, not in their needs and not in their efforts (Sen 2009; Kahneman 2012; Putnam 2015; Thaler 2015). In today's complexity, we need a social system that introduces an element of direct democracy by involving citizens in the co-production and customization of support and that allows professionals to engage in a coaching style of public service that can regain trust in governance (Van Slyke 2007).

10.6 Applications

In earlier work (Wolfson 2012), I have introduced the operations of the International Monetary Fund (IMF) as an early example of the situational mode at the macro level. For 70 years, the Fund has arranged stabilization programmes with member countries, offering financial support on the basis of a letter of intent that specifies customized undertakings of the counterpart to put its economic house in order and restore its solvency. Customization takes account of the country's specific characteristics and the problems it faces, but drawing rights on loans are conditional on progress in meeting commitments made. In a similar vein, the European Council of Ministers, the political executive of the European Union, uses situational contracts in 'home-grown partnerships' with member countries as a way of developing plans for structural adjustment and is considering more conditionality in its budgeting. More generally, situational or relational contracts prove useful in forming 'coalitions of the willing', internationally as well as nationally. The situational mode is a proven instrument in diplomacy, where careful preparation and listening to your counterpart often are the keys to success. Yet, while international affairs and national covenants are usually conducted at the higher layers of Fig. 10.2, they may have or may be *presumed* to have considerable consequences for the relationship between public bodies and individual citizens and require a lot of canvassing at the micro-level, as the recent resistance to trade agreements indicates.

At the national level, situational contracting was pioneered in the Netherlands, in a major overhaul of the social security system at the beginning of this century. Employers, who increasingly used the relatively attractive benefits of disability insurance to lay-off surplus labour, are now obligated to contract private manpower agencies to monitor health and safety in working conditions and assist individual workers who lose their job. The manpower agencies operating in the situational mode help individuals to reskill if necessary and to find appropriate employment; they provide a competitive facilitating interface serving employers, claimants (employees) and political principals (who retain responsibility for the way the system works). A public agency provides insurance, funding for retooling programmes and operates as a 'gatekeeper' deciding on access to social security if credible efforts to find employment fail or are waived on situational grounds, such as lasting disability. Decisions may be challenged by second opinions and are contestable in a court of law, which uses a protocol of best reintegration practices as a frame of reference. As Euwals, de Mooij and van Vuren report (2009), the new approach replaces asymmetrically informed regulation by well-informed discretion and proves effective. The inflow in disability schemes, for instance, declined from almost 120,000 persons in 2000–2001 to less than 25,000 in 2006–2007, while over the period 2000–2008, the employment rate increased from 72.9 to 77.2 per cent in Europe, only second to Denmark. Results collapsed in 2009 when demand for labour evaporated as a result of the global financial crisis, but were beginning to pick up again in 2014. Fenger, van der Torre and van Twist (2011) also show how a situational mode can be helpful in structuring horizontal networks of cooperation between the various agencies involved in providing social support. More generally, Putters (2017: 51) notes how welfare state governance in areas such as social security and health care in the Netherlands and in public services in general, can be characterized by a 'mixed model of central government regulation, regulated market forces and professional autonomy', in a 'shift in focus from risk protection to investments in the resources that facilitate societal participation'.

10.7 Summary and Discussion

People are not alike. This chapter emphasizes the need for discretion to deal with diversity. Section 10.2 offered a brief introduction into the economic method and Sect. 10.3 highlighted the vital role of a professionalized public service with social and improvisational skills in managing discretion (more about that in Chap. 24). Section 10.4 introduced the notion of interactive governance in principal/agent relationships based on mutual interest, as inspired by recent contributions from an emerging field of behavioural economics. It explores the potential and limits of an incentive-compatible policy model of relational and situational contracting, in which public services, where possible, are personalized or customized for individual needs and civil servants and network partners are involved in the co-production of solutions with beneficiaries (Agranoff 2006: 61; Maskin 2008; Alford 2009).

The point of departure of this chapter is that welfare is not just a matter of efficiency and consumer sovereignty. Sovereign people also care about security, human dignity and human rights, fairness in distribution and sustainability. As citizens, they want recognition and to be heard, rather than told. They differ, however, in preferences as well as in capabilities and opportunities (Sen 2009). These differences call for discretion, prudence and customization in public support and for degrees of freedom for professionals to deal with diversity, as honest (and accountable) brokers between demand and supply.

Throughout the vertical column and the horizontal networks of policymaking and implementation sketched in Fig. 10.2, in Sect. 10.4, situational contracts create space for professionals to reduce information asymmetry and bring demand and supply together in areas where people or their non-governmental organizations, want to be heard, but non-cooperation is controllable by the sanction of exclusion.

Section 10.6 also gave some applications, but the situational mode is potentially useful in all situations where information about individual needs, corresponding obligations and professional know-how about possible solutions need to be disclosed. Its focuses on level 4 of service delivery in Fig. 10.2, where actors, content and conditions come together and reveal what your country can do for you and what you can do for your country (to paraphrase Kennedy's famous quote). Professional front-line workers—researchers, educators, health personnel, diplomats, job coaches and so on—all face their own challenges and generally have their own professional traditions and protocols. In addition, however, supplemental top-down guidance mandates discretion within a system of operational and political responsibility. Regional police services, for instance, face totally different 'situations' in urban areas and the country side; hence, they too should be managed 'bottom-up' and enabled to submit their own mandates for approval. Administrative routines, however, such as keeping records and reporting, remain standardized.

When, in Sect. 10.3, I called this century 'the age of the professional', I had five basic considerations in mind: (1) the typical sociology of *professions* (Johnson 1972; Evans in this edited collection, Chap. 23), (2) the availability of *talent*—in the Western World, nowadays, roughly half of the entrants in the labour market has a higher education and is presumably trained in creative thinking; (3) *preference*—many of the new generations of workers in the public and semi-public sector may be driven by public service motivation; they should be granted leeway to develop their professionalism in an interactive style of governance with room for initiative and innovation; (4) *leeway*, not framed in terms of outright *delegation*, but in the approval of *mandates, creating conditional freedom*, while maintaining the *primacy of politics*; and (5) advances in *information and communication technology (ICT)* that can facilitate, channel, monitor and control the exchange of information up and down the line and in horizontal network relations, while avoiding a management overload. Recording results, moreover, provides a wealth of data for research and innovation.

But how do we get away from traditional top-down hierarchies? How do we retool not just the case worker, but also the principals all the way up the hierarchy? Obviously, the case for discretion and for situational contracting, as its instrument, depends crucially on the underlying behavioural assumptions that were specified and referenced throughout this chapter and particularly on the *attitude* and the *public service motivation* of politicians and civil servants. Developing and fortifying attitudinal requirements requires a step-by-step approach, in careful preparation of a selective and gradual transition towards the situational mode of governance. *Selective*, in that traditional top-down control remains feasible in all those cases where there is no danger of strategic behaviour and regulation is broadly accepted (e.g., in keeping left, or right, in traffic). What helps is that modern behavioural research finds that professionals tend, on their own volition, to *sort* to occupations and styles of management that suit them best (Besley and Ghatak 2005; Dur and Zoutenbier 2014). Those who prefer to follow orders and be told what to do and those who value discretion and dialogue should be allowed to sort in different directions.

Summing up, this chapter suggests that the combination of transparency, control in the discussion and approval of mandates, accountability of beneficiaries and humanity of personal contact with caseworkers will promote citizenship and trust in governance. Note, finally, that the approval of mandates forces political and administrative principals to be specific about and responsible for the goals that they want to see pursued and that modern welfare economics tries to pave the way for a broader perspective than just efficiency.

10.8 Conclusion

This chapter explores how recent behavioural insights may pave the way for an integration of bottom-up and top-down approaches in public administration and proposes a model of situational contracting to implement discretion as an answer to the downside of globalization (Putnam 2015; Milanovic 2016) and the emergence of 'national populism' in the US and disturbing trends in large parts of Europe. Crucial contributions of the situational mode presented here are that it (1) synthesizes the top-down and the bottom-up approach in the policy process; (2) grants legitimate space for discretion in dealing with needs of people who are not alike; (3) involves citizens, civil servants and politicians in a continuous dialogue about ends, means, peer reviews, visitations and mandates; (4) specifies and controls everybody's role in the process of delivering social support in order to avoid incongruence in implementation (Hupe 2011); (5) reveals, in the content of its transactions and its mutual obligations, how a society trades efficiency with fairness and sustainability; (6) supports private initiatives and (7) fosters trust in governance. Lessons from applications remind us, however, that the situational mode cannot be introduced overnight. In developing a network of situational contracts, time is needed for trial and error and for the sorting hypothesis (Besley and Ghatak 2005; Dur and Zoutenbier 2014)—that some case workers will prefer to work with the hard and fast rules of traditional bureaucracy—to play out. Here again, diversity is the keyword.

Acknowledgements The author is very grateful to Peter Cornelisse for many helpful comments on earlier drafts of this chapter.

References

Agranoff, R. (2006). Inside collaborative networks. Ten lessons for public managers. *Public Administration Review*, 66, 50–56.

Alford, J. (2009). *Engaging public sector clients: From service delivery to co-production.* Oxford: Palgrave Macmillan.

Besley, T. & Ghatak, M. (2005). Competition and incentives with motivated agents. *American Economic Review*, 95(1–2), 94–105.

Breton, A. (1995). Organizational hierarchies and bureaucracies. *European Journal of Political Economy*, 11(3), 411–440.

Busuioc, E.M. & Lodge, M. (2016). The reputational basis of public accountability. *Governance*, 29(2), 247–263.

Calmar Andersen, S. & Moynihan, D.P. (2016). How leaders respond to diversity: The moderating role of information use. *Journal of Public Administration Research and Theory*, 26(3), 448–460.

Carson, S.J., Madhok, R. & Wu, T. 2006. Uncertainty, opportunism and governance: The effects of volatility and ambiguity on formal and relational contracting. *Academy of Management Journal*, 49(5), 1058–1077.

Cornelisse, P.A. & Thorbecke, E. (2010). *Exchange and development.* Cheltenham: Edward Elgar.

Culyer, A.J. (1980). *The political economy of social policy.* Oxford: Martin Robertson (1985).

Culyer, A.J. (1985). *Economics.* Oxford: Basil Blackwell.

Dur, R. & Zoutenbier, R. (2014). Working for a good cause. *Public Administration Review*, 74(2), 144–155.

Euwals, R., de Mooij, R. & van Vuren, D. (2009). *Rethinking retirement.* The Hague: CPB.

Fenger, M., van der Torre, L. & van Twist, M. (2011). *Uitvoeren naar vermogen [Implementation customized for capabilities].* Nijmegen: VOC Uitgevers.

Hennipman, P. (1995). *Welfare economics and the theory of economic policy.* Aldershot: Edward Elgar.

Hupe, P.L. (2011). The thesis of incongruent implementation: Revisiting Pressman and Wildavsky. *Public Policy and Administration*, 26(1), 63–80.

Johnson, T. (1972) *Professions and power.* London: Macmillan

Just, R.E., Hueth, D. & Schmitz, A. (2004). *The welfare economics of public policy.* Cheltenham: Edward Elgar.

Kahneman, D. (2000). *Choices, values and frames.* Cambridge: Cambridge University Press.

Kahneman, D. (2012). *Thinking, fast and slow.* London: Penguin Random House.

Koppenjan, J. & Klijn, E.-H. (2004). *Managing uncertainties in networks.* London: Routledge.

Lipsky, M. (1980). *Street level bureaucracy. Dilemmas of the individual in public services.* New York: Russell Sage Foundation.

Maskin, E.S. (2008). Mechanism design. How to implement social goals. (Nobel Lecture). *American Economic Review*, 98(3), 567–576.

Milanovic, B. (2016). *Global inequality. A new approach for the age of globalization.* Cambridge: The Belknap Press.

Noonan, K.G, Sabel, C.F. & Simon, W.H. (2009). Legal accountability in the service-based welfare state: Lessons from child welfare reform. *Law & Social Inquiry*, 34(3), 523–568.

Obama, B. (2016). The way ahead. *The Economist*, October 8th.

Putnam, R.B. (2015). *Our kids. The American dream in crisis.* New York: Simon and Shuster.

Putters, K. (2017). *Was getekend. Op weg naar een vernieuwd sociaal contract in de zorg (with English summary)*. Inaugural Lecture, Erasmus University Rotterdam.
Scott, T.A., Thomas, C.W. (2016). Unpacking the collaborative toolbox: Why and when do public managers choose collaborative strategies? *Policy Studies Journal* (early view).
Sen, A.K. (1985). *Commodities and capabilities* (Hennipman Lecture). Amsterdam: North-Holland Publishing Company.
Sen, A.K. (2009). *The idea of justice*. London: Allan Lane.
Sent, E.M. (2004). Behavioral economics: How psychology made its (limited) way back into economics. *History of Political Economy*, 36 (4), 735–760.
Simon, H. (1976). From substantive to procedural rationality. In S. Latsis (Ed.), *Method and appraisal in economics* (pp. 129–148) Cambridge: University Press.
Smith, A. (1759). *The theory of moral sentiments* (250th Anniversary Edition), with Introduction by A.K. Sen. London: Penguin Books.
Stiglitz, J.E. (2002). Information and the change in the paradigm of economics (Nobel Lecture). *American Economic Review*, 92, 460–501.
Thaler, R.H. (2015). *Misbehaving: The making of behavioural economics*. New York: W.W. Norton.
Tummers, L.G. & Bekkers, V. (2014). Policy implementation, street-level bureaucracy and the importance of discretion. *Public Management Review*, 16(4), 527–547.
Van Slyke, D.M. (2007). Agents or stewards; using theory to understand the government-non-profit social service contracting relationship. *Journal of Public Administration Research and Theory*, 17(2), 460–501.
Wolfson, D.J. (2010). Dreaming about a properly informed democracy. In R.J. In't Veld (Ed.), *Knowledge democracy: Consequences for science, politics and media* (pp. 37–48). London: Springer.
Wolfson, D.J. (2012). Situational contracting: Building reciprocity between rights and obligations. *Governance*, 25(4), 661–685.
Wolfson, D.J. (2015). Implementing fairness in social policy. *Journal of Human Development and Capabilities*, (16), 272–286.
Wolfson, D.J. 2019). Diversity and situational contracting in public governance (paper under review).
Yew-Kwang, N. (1979). *Welfare economics: Introduction and development of basic concepts*. Basingstoke: Macmillan.

CHAPTER 11

Discretion from a Psychological Perspective

Lars Tummers and Victor Bekkers

11.1 Introduction

In his book *Street-level bureaucracy: Dilemmas of the individual in public services*, Michael Lipsky (1980) analysed the behaviour of front-line staff in policy delivery agencies. These street-level bureaucrats—also called public service workers, public professionals or frontline workers—interact directly with citizens and have substantial discretion in the execution of their work. Examples are teachers, police officers, general practitioners and social workers. When doing their work they implement public policies. However, while doing this they have to respond to citizens with only a limited amount of information or time to make a decision. Furthermore, formal rules and regulations do not correspond to the specific situation of the involved citizen. How to apply general rules in concrete situations that are not covered by these rules? Or, how to apply rules 'by the book' when a street-level bureaucrat knows that this will be harmful to society? These questions arise as street-level bureaucrats have a certain degree of discretion—or autonomy—in their work (Lipsky 1980: 14). Put simply, they are not simple machines implementing rules, but have opportunities to make their own decisions. Following the work of Lipsky, the concept of discretion has received wide attention in the policy implementation literature (Vinzant and Crothers 1998; Hill and Hupe 2009; Brodkin 2011). More generally, as Evans and Hupe state in the introductory chapter of this edited

L. Tummers (✉)
Utrecht School of Governance, Utrecht, The Netherlands
e-mail: l.g.tummers@uu.nl

V. Bekkers
Department of Public Administration and Sociology, Erasmus University Rotterdam, Rotterdam, The Netherlands
e-mail: bekkers@essb.eur.nl

T. Evans, P. Hupe (eds.), *Discretion and the Quest for Controlled Freedom*, https://doi.org/10.1007/978-3-030-19566-3_11

collection, the concept of discretion is a 'commonplace idea', discussed extensively in fields like law, economics and Public Administration.

In this chapter, we will use a psychological perspective to study how street-level bureaucrats deal with their discretion in day-to-day encounters with citizens. Using insights from psychology to analyse public administration questions is in line with the recent development of Behavioural Public Administration. Behavioural public administration is the analysis of public administration from the micro-level perspective of individual behaviour and attitudes by drawing on insights from psychology on the behaviour of individuals and groups (Grimmelikhuijsen, Jilke, Olsen and Tummers 2017). Behavioural Public Administration complements traditional public administration, which is often less focused on the micro-level and more on macro-level topics such as governance systems and public management reforms (for instance Bevir, Rhodes and Weller 2003; Pollitt and Bouckaert 2004). Relating this to discretion, a psychological perspective analyses the attitudes and behaviours of street-level bureaucrats when they deal with discretion (for instance Thomann, van Engen and Tummers 2018b). The attitudes and behaviour of street-level bureaucrats are partly driven by macro-level developments (for instance Soss, Fording and Schram 2011). A psychological perspective does explicitly take such embeddedness into account to understand the attitudes and behaviour of street-level bureaucrats.

In this chapter, we use this psychological perspective on discretion by focusing on two concepts that combine insights from Public Administration and psychology. We do not intend to give a comprehensive discipline overview but instead want to take a close look at two concepts that explicitly combine insights from psychology and Public Administration: policy alienation and coping. First, we focus on *policy alienation* (we base our discussion primarily on Tummers 2011). Policy alienation is a psychological state of disconnection from the public policy. It occurs when street-level bureaucrats, such as social workers or teachers, cannot identify themselves with the policy they have to implement, for instance because they think it is not valuable for their clients. Policy alienation is an attitudinal concept. In other words, it is a psychological construct on what someone feels about a particular entity; in this case to what extent a street-level bureaucrat identifies with a particular policy. These attitudes towards a specific policy can impact how street-level bureaucrats use their discretion when implementing a policy. For instance, if they feel a policy is not beneficial for their clients, they can choose not to implement it or even try to sabotage the policy (Berkovich 2011).

The second concept—coping during public service delivery—also combines insights from Public Administration and psychology. Coping during public service delivery looks at behaviour that street-level bureaucrats show when interacting with clients. Ways of coping during public service delivery include working overtime for clients, rationing services (such as stating 'The office is very busy today, please return tomorrow') and bending or breaking rules for clients. In contrast to policy alienation, it is a behavioural construct: focusing on what street-level bureaucrats *do* (behaviour) instead of what they *feel* (attitude). We base the discussion primarily on the overview article by Tummers, Bekkers, Vink and Musheno (2015).

In the rest of this chapter we look more closely at policy alienation and coping during public service delivery. We end with theoretical, methodological and empirical research directions for scholars interested in studying discretion from a psychological perspective. We also discuss how managers can influence the way street-level bureaucrats use their discretion.

11.2 Discretion and Policy Alienation

Discretion is important. This, in part, is because various street-level bureaucrats have problems with new policies (Emery and Giauque 2003; Hebson, Grimshaw and Marchington 2003; Currie, Finn and Martin 2009). When street-level bureaucrats cannot identify with public policies, it becomes important to study how they use their discretion when implementing, adjusting or even sabotaging these policies. Hence, public policies are being shaped and re-shaped when street-level bureaucrats use their discretionary power (Pressman and Wildavsky 1973). The problems of street-level bureaucrats with new policies range from teachers striking against school reforms, to professors protesting against budget cuts and to physicians feeling overwhelmed by a constant flow of policy changes, resulting in conflicts with their professional ethos.

An illuminating example comes from the introduction of a new policy in Dutch mental healthcare. In one large-scale survey, as many as nine out of ten professionals wanted this new policy abandoned (Palm, Leffers, Emons, van Egmond and Zeegers 2008). Psychologists even went as far as to openly demonstrate on the street against this policy. A major reason for this was that many could not align their professional values with the content of the policy. The following quotation from a healthcare professional is illustrative: 'We experience the [new] policy as a disaster. I concentrate as much as possible on treating my own patients, in order to derive some satisfaction from my work' (quoted in Tummers 2012: 516).

This example is not unique. Overall, several studies show that street-level bureaucrats have difficulty identifying with public policies (Bottery 1998; Ball 2003). When street-level bureaucrats cannot identify with a policy, this may have severe consequences. It can negatively influence policy effectiveness, as street-level bureaucrats do not execute the policy or even try to sabotage it (Thomann 2015). Furthermore, street-level bureaucrats themselves can become dissatisfied with their work. Some professionals even experience burnout or quit their jobs entirely (Ball 2003).

These identification problems can be understood using the 'policy alienation' model as developed by Tummers, Bekkers and Steijn (2009). Policy alienation can be broadly defined as a general cognitive state of psychological disconnection from the policy programme to be implemented. Various scholars have used the policy alienation model (for instance Loyens 2016; van Engen

2017; Thomann *et al.* 2018a). In general, they showed that the policy alienation model can be useful for studying public administration topics. It has been shown that effects of high policy alienation include reduced change commitment (van der Voet, Steijn and Kuipers 2017) and even clear resistance and rule breaking of policies (Kerpershoek, Groenleer, and de Bruijn 2016). More generally, Thomann (2015) showed that policy alienation can lead to lower policy performance, while at the same time Loyens (2014, 2016) has showed that there are several—effective and ineffective—ways to cope with policy alienation.

Tummers (2011) identified two main dimensions of the policy alienation model, which can serve as explanations for low compliance with policies. First, street-level bureaucrats can feel *powerless* while implementing a policy. For instance, a police officer might be required by his superiors to issue a minimum number of tickets each day, with no room to deviate from this. Linked to this, it is also evident that professionals can feel that implementing a policy is *meaningless* if, for example, it does not deliver any apparent beneficial outcomes for society, such as safer streets. In making the dimensions more specific to the situation under study, the policy alienation model distinguishes between strategic, tactical and operational powerlessness and between societal and client meaninglessness. The definitions of these dimensions—including examples—are shown in Table 11.1.

Table 11.1 Defining the five dimensions of policy alienation

Dimension	*Definition*	*Examples of high scores*
Strategic powerlessness	The lack of perceived influence by street-level bureaucrats on decisions concerning the content of the policy, as is captured in rules and regulations	A professional feeling that the policy is drafted without the help of implementing professionals or professional associations
Tactical powerlessness	The workers' perceived lack of influence on decisions concerning the way policy is implemented within their own organization	Professionals stating that the managers in the organization did not consult them or their colleagues when designing the implementation process for the policy
Operational powerlessness	The perceived lack of freedom in making choices concerning the sort, quantity and quality of sanctions and rewards on offer when implementing the policy	Answering 'fully agree' to a survey question on whether the professional felt that their autonomy during the implementation process was lower than it should be
Societal meaninglessness	The perception of street-level bureaucrats concerning the lack of value of the policy to socially relevant goals	Stating in an interview that 'I agree with the policy goal of enhancing transparency, but I do not see how this policy helps in achieving this goal'
Client meaninglessness	The workers' perceptions of the lack of added value for their own clients in them implementing a policy	A professional who argues that a particular policy seriously impinges on their clients' privacy

Source: Based on Tummers (2011)

As can be seen from the definitions of the dimensions, operational powerlessness is highly related to the notion of discretion-as-used in the public administration literature. The main difference is the focus on *perceived* discretion. Hupe (2013: 34–5) makes a distinction between 'discretion-as-granted' and 'discretion-as-used'. We argue that, next to discretion-as-granted and discretion-as-used, there is also a key role for discretion-as-experienced: the degree to which street-level bureaucrats perceive to possess discretion. This notion of discretion-as-experienced adds a psychological lens to studying the topic of discretion.

The notion of 'discretion-as-experienced' can be connected to the Thomas theorem: 'If men [*sic*] define situations as real they are real in their consequences' (Thomas and Thomas 1928: 572 quoted in Merton 1995: 380). People often behave on the basis of their perceptions of reality, not on the basis of reality itself. For instance, employees can show lower work effort if they *think* that their boss does not like them, while this is not necessarily the case. The boss may value the employees highly, but she might be unable to show it clearly. Hence, perceptions of reality do influence behaviour and thus creates effects in reality. So, although street-level bureaucrats could have substantial granted discretion, they could still perceive themselves to have little, which subsequently influences their attitude and their concrete behaviour.

This psychological perspective on discretion highlights the importance of policy-related attitudes for frontline policy implementation. It is important to reveal what factors influence these attitudes, because individual street-level bureaucrats may experience different levels of discretion within the same policy. They experience them in different ways, because, (a) they possess more knowledge on (loopholes) in the rules; (b) their organization operationalized the policy somewhat differently; (c) they have a better relationship with their manager which enables them to adjust themselves to circumstances or (d) the personality of the street-level bureaucrats is more rule following.

11.3 Discretion and Coping During Public Service Delivery

Next to policy alienation, the concept of coping has also been linked to discretion. To understand how street-level bureaucrats could use their discretion, Lipsky (1980) used the concept of 'coping'. Related to this, Satyamurti (1981) talks in her book about 'strategies of survival' and Evans (2013) discusses how street-level bureaucrats 'approach' rules. We follow Lipsky and others and focus on the concept of coping to study how frontline workers use their discretion in day-to-day encounters with citizens (for criticisms of Lipsky and his view on coping and discretion, see for instance Evans 2011; see also Howe 1991).

Lipsky draws on the work of Richard Lazarus, who wrote the groundbreaking work on coping in 1966, entitled *Psychological stress and the coping process*. Based primarily on this work, coping evolved as a distinct research field.

The field of coping also inspired related discussions on emotional labour (Hochschild 1983; Korczynski 2003) and resilience (Egan 1993; Collins 2007) of street-level bureaucrats. Folkman and Lazarus (1980: 223) define coping broadly as 'the cognitive and behavioral efforts made to master, tolerate or reduce external and internal demands and conflicts among them'. Coping in this formulation is extremely broad. It can range from positive thinking, quitting one's job, to talking to one's partner about work problems. In this chapter, we focus on coping during the delivery of public services. That is, we concentrate on *behavioural* ways of coping that occur when *street-level bureaucrats interact with clients.* Coping during public service delivery can be defined as *behavioural efforts frontline workers employ when interacting with clients, in order to master, tolerate or reduce external and internal demands and conflicts they face on an everyday basis* (see Tummers, Bekkers, Vink and Musheno 2015: 1100).

We fully acknowledge that other ways of coping are important to frontline workers in responding to various forms of work-related stress (for an overview see Skinner, Edge, Altman and Sherwood 2003). Some are behavioural, but take place outside direct worker-client interactions, such as seeking comfort with colleagues, supervisors and family. Others are cognitive instead of behavioural, such as cognitive exhaustion and cynicism. These ways of coping have been studied extensively in literature streams like organizational behaviour and occupational health psychology. In Table 11.2 we introduce two dimensions for capturing coping types. We focus on type 1: behavioural coping during interactions with clients. We do recognize that the boundaries are not clear-cut and that there are potential connections. However, this distinction serves as a helpful analytical tool to focus on behavioural ways of coping that are embedded in direct frontline worker-citizen interactions.

In order to understand coping during public service delivery (type 1 as indicated in Table 11.1), Tummers, Bekkers, Vink and Musheno developed a classification of coping, which has been used quite extensively in the public administration field (see also Baviskar and Winter 2016; Cohen, Benish and Shamriz-Ilouz 2016; Hunter, Bretherton, Halliday and Johnsen 2016; Hyun,

Table 11.2 Classifying coping of street-level bureaucrats

	Behavioural coping	*Cognitive coping*
During client/ worker interactions	1. *Rule bending, rule breaking, aggression towards clients, routinizing, rationing, using personal resources to help clients*	2. Client-oriented cynicism, compassion towards clients, emotional detachment from clients
Not during client/ worker interactions	3. Social support from colleagues, complaining towards managers, turnover, substance abuse	4. Cognitive restructuring, cynicism towards work, work alienation

We focus on type 1
Source: Based on Tummers, Bekkers, Vink and Musheno (2015)

Post and Ray 2017; Liu, Tang, Lo and Zhan 2016; Møller 2016; Savi and Cepilovs 2016; Schillemans and van Twist 2016; Sowa and Lu 2016; Tummers 2017; Tummers and Rocco 2015; van Loon and Jakobsen 2017; Yang and Ortega 2016; Zang 2016). Here, we discuss this work. The coping classification is focused on the behaviour workers can display towards clients when confronted with stress. They show that during public service delivery there are three main families of coping (see also Horney 1945 and the work of Bekkers, Moody and Edwards 2011):

1. *Moving towards clients*: Coping by helping clients in stressful situations. An example is a teacher working overtime to help students.
2. *Moving away from clients*: Coping by avoiding meaningful interactions with clients in stressful situations. An example is a public servant telling a client that 'we cannot help you at the moment. There are 30 people waiting before you.'
3. *Moving against clients*: Coping by confronting clients. For instance, teachers who have/experience discretion can cope with stress when working with students by imposing very rigid rules, such as no cell phone use in class and sending everyone to the office when they use a cell phone.

Rule Bending, Rule Breaking and Rigid Rule Following

Tummers *et al.* (2015)'s systematic review provides an overview of 35 years of study regarding coping during public service delivery. We discuss the results that are particularly relevant in the discussion regarding discretion from a psychological perspective. We focus here on the notions of *rule bending*, *rule breaking* and *rigid rule following* as these are highly related to the notion of discretion.

Rule bending and rule breaking are often done to benefit the client. One can see them as a continuum, where rule breaking is less compliant than rule bending. Both are therefore classified as ways of coping under the coping family 'moving towards clients'. On the other hand, rigid rule following is defined as sticking to rules in an inflexible way, which may go against the client's demands. Hence, this way of coping is classified under the family 'moving against clients'.

Adjusting the rules to meet client demands (rule bending) is an often-mentioned way of coping in the family 'moving towards clients'. Rule bending describes how frontline workers adjust the rules to meet the clients' demands. In essence, they are experiencing a role conflict; the policy rules and requirements do not fit with the wishes and demands of their clients. In order to cope with this role conflict, they adjust the rules somewhat, so that the client can benefit. An example of rule bending is provided by Maynard-Moody and Musheno (2003: 113), who quote a teacher on his feelings about rules: 'I'll kind of use the system and tweak the system to get more benefits—not so much for me, but for the kids on my casework. [...] I like to do the best that I can, and I'll bend the system, and occasionally I'll snap it in half.'

Rule breaking is another often-mentioned way of coping. It is related to 'rule bending', but more extreme in that it deliberately goes *against* the rules rather than working *with* the rules. For an illustrative example, we refer to Anagnostopoulos (2003), who describes how American secondary school teachers coped with a new and stringent accountability policy on student failure. Many teachers were strongly opposed to this new policy. They could not see how this particular policy benefited society or their students. Hence, they were experiencing policy alienation, more specifically high societal and client meaninglessness. Where students were failing classes, many teachers tried to improve their instructional practices. However, some teachers indicated that they passed students who had not actually satisfied the course requirements. This is a clear example of rule breaking.

In terms of legitimizing rule bending and rule breaking, Evans (2013) argues that street-level bureaucrats often have mixed reasons for either following or breaking rules. Generally, rules are not to be broken, as indicated by a quote from a social worker, stating that '[you] can't be a maverick [...]. If you break the rules, you've broken the trust' (cited in Evans 2013: 749). However, good reasons can be found and are deemed 'good' in some situations but not in others. In line with the quote in Maynard-Moody and Musheno, Evans shows that a particular 'good reason' for bending or breaking rules is that this can be very meaningful for clients. One illustrating quote by a social worker was (cited in Evans 2013: 751): 'Saying "Mrs. Smith doesn't quite meet the criteria for getting this resource, but if you actually have a look at all this information you may wish to think that she should be getting the resource"—OK. You'd bend the rules there.'

Hence, situations are open to interpretation and ambiguous (see also Ellis, Davis and Rummery 1999; Evans and Harris 2004). Instead of bending or even breaking rules, frontline workers can also stick to the rules. Wright (2003: 137–8) refers to a welfare worker who tells a citizen who wants to apply for a well-suited job that the vacancy was suspended ten minutes ago and that the opportunity has passed. This shows the effects of the submissions limits, which are set by employers and enforced by staff. Soss *et al.* (2011: 220) comment that some officials view sanctioning as 'the most important process they have in terms of case management and producing results'. Some officials for instance choose the path of letting clients attend daily classes before having their application for benefits submitted. Missing a class or turning up inappropriately dressed means having to start over the following week.

One particular important reason for rigid rule following was that it could help street-level bureaucrats manage a very high workload. Anagnostopoulos (2003: 308–9) showed that American teachers used rules as a way to deal with overcrowded classes, noting that: 'One teacher used management time to check that students wore their school identification cards and to send those who didn't to the discipline office. This effectively reduced the number of students in the class by two or three students each day.'

11.4 Conclusion

This chapter shows how a psychological perspective can be beneficial when investigating discretion. This is firstly illustrated using the concept of policy alienation. Many street-level bureaucrats feel alienated from public policies. When they perceive they do not have enough discretion to implement the policy or feel that a policy is meaningless for society and clients, they experience policy alienation. Secondly this attitude can furthermore lead to different types of behaviours. These behaviours can be classified using the notion of coping during public service delivery. Coping can be grouped in three types: moving towards clients (for instance breaking rules for a client), moving away from clients (for instance by not answering emails from clients) and moving against clients (for instance by becoming aggressive to clients).

We end this chapter by considering future theoretical, methodological and empirical research directions that could be put forward by scholars interested in a psychological perspective on discretion. A first area for future research is the relationship between coping during public service delivery and managerial practices. More specifically, it is interesting to study whether and how managers can influence rule bending, rule breaking and rigid rule following by street-level bureaucrats. For instance, managers could adapt a very stringent leadership style, requiring that 'rules should not be broken' (Tummers and Knies 2016). Secondly, managers could require that street-level bureaucrats should follow the 'spirit' of the law, not the 'letter' of the law. They would require consistency in applying rules, but that this should be balanced against an equally important recognition of service users' complex individual circumstances, analysing who is 'deserving' of help (see also Maynard-Moody and Musheno 2003; Evans 2013; Jilke and Tummers 2018).

However, a potential downside of this approach is that it can threaten equality of treatment. Another avenue would be to study how these two different managerial strategies affect the degree of rule bending and rule breaking. This could be related to the specific context in which managers and street-level bureaucrats operate. Another potentially interesting avenue would be to study socialization processes: Do managers start as rigid enforcers of rules and become more flexible further in their career? What are the main drivers of this development? Here, scholars can combine sociological literature on socialization with street-level bureaucracy literature on discretion and coping (see for instance Oberfield 2010 and Chap. 12 of this edited collection).

A second area for research is the relationship between rigid rule following, rule bending and rule breaking to policy performance (Walker *et al.* 2010; Thomann 2015). A multimethod approach could be fruitful here. Researchers could use interviews or survey techniques to determine the degree of bending, breaking and rigid rule following by street-level bureaucrats. Using another source, researchers could then examine the actual policy performance of these public service workers when implementing the policy (Meier and O'Toole 2013). This observed policy performance could then be related to the level of rule bending, rule breaking and rigid rule following.

Alongside being of theoretical interest, this could also be very relevant for policymakers who need knowledge of the factors that affect policy performance.

A third area is examining coping during public service delivery in the interaction between street-level bureaucrats and clients. Up till now the attention of the psychological research literature has focused on coping mechanisms of workers, but at the same time citizens also develop coping mechanism when being confronted with all kinds of norms, also because citizens become more emancipated themselves (see for instance Mayer and Timms 1970). Hence, it is interesting to see if citizens develop coping strategies in which they move towards, against or away from the street-level bureaucrat. For instance, citizens could try to organize themselves in order to 'counterbalance' the discretionary power of the involved street-level bureaucrats or, when making use of open data or knowledge and information that is available on the internet, to question the decisions that are made by street-level bureaucrats. As a result of the coping mechanisms at the side of citizens, civil service workers are confronted with new and even more pressing demands and tensions. An interesting research line would be to study the interaction patterns of coping mechanisms and the mutually reinforcing nature of these patterns.

Next to connecting the literature on coping and discretion to other theoretical concepts, it could also be valuable to increase the methodological diversity of the field. The current literature is dominated by studies relying on cross-sectional studies and interviews. The value of these methods is that they are located in real organizational environments. However, these methods do not allow scholars to truly determine the causal direction of the relationships. Longitudinal studies and especially experiments—in the lab or in the field—can be useful here. A future study could for instance develop a field experiment showing how rigid rule following can be reduced by extensive communication or granting more autonomy to street-level bureaucrats. At a more general level, future studies can conduct such studies to address the concerns about causality. Scholars can follow guidelines on the use of experiments in the Public Administration discipline (for instance, Jilke, Van de Walle and Kim 2016).

The final suggestion for future research is empirical. Most studies on coping and discretion have been focused on Western countries, including the United States, the United Kingdom, Denmark and the Netherlands. Almost no studies have been conducted in the southern hemisphere or Asian countries (a recent interesting exception is Zang and Musheno 2017). It would be valuable to study these topics in such different settings. To what extent does a scale developed in one cultural context hold when applied in another? Are the same effects found? Are effect sizes comparable? In this way, the generalizability of the policy alienation model would be tested further. Furthermore, scholars can conduct replication studies (also in Western countries). Replication is one of the core tasks of science and has been increasingly recognized as important in the recent years (*Nature* editorial 2016).

In conclusion, it is of paramount importance to understand psychological processes underlying attitudes and behaviour of street-level bureaucrats.

Embracing a psychological perspective and developing this line of research should prove to be a timely and productive endeavour for both scholars and practitioners alike.

Acknowledgements We would like to thank Tony Evans and Peter Hupe for their constructive and insightful comments, significantly improving the chapter. Lars Tummers acknowledges funding by the NWO grant (Grant 016.VIDI.185.017). Furthermore, he acknowledges that this work was supported by the National Research Foundation of Korea Grant, funded by the Korean Government (NRF-2017S1A3A2067636).

References

Anagnostopoulos, D. (2003). The new accountability, student failure, and teachers' work in urban high schools. *Educational Policy*, 17(3), 291–316.

Ball, S.J. (2003). The teacher's soul and the terrors of performativity. *Journal of education policy*, 18(2), 215–228.

Baviskar, S. & Winter, S.C. (2016). Street-level bureaucrats as individual policymakers: The relationship between attitudes and coping behaviour toward vulnerable children and youth. *International Public Management Journal*, 20(3), 1–38.

Bekkers, V., Moody, R. & Edwards, A. (2011). Micro mobilization, social media and coping strategies: Some Dutch experiences. *Policy & Internet*, 3, 1–29.

Berkovich, I. (2011). No we won't! Teachers' resistance to educational reform. *Journal of Educational Administration*, 49(5), 563–578.

Bevir, M., Rhodes, R.A. & Weller, P. (2003). Traditions of governance: Interpreting the changing role of the public sector. *Public Administration*, 81(1), 1–17.

Bottery, M. (1998). *Professionals and policy: Management strategy in a competitive world*. London: Routledge.

Brodkin, E.Z. (2011). Policy work: Street-level organizations under new managerialism. *Journal of Public Administration Research and Theory*, 21(suppl 2), i253–i277.

Cohen, N., Benish, A. & Shamriz-Ilouz, A. (2016). When the clients can choose: Dilemmas of street-level workers in choice-based social services. *Social Service Review*, 90(4), 620–646.

Collins, S. (2007). Statutory social workers: Stress, job satisfaction, coping, social support and individual differences. *British Journal of Social Work*, 38(6), 1173–1193.

Currie, G., Finn, R. & Martin, G. (2009). Professional competition and modernizing the clinical workforce in the NHS. *Work, Employment & Society*, 23(2), 267–284.

Egan, M. (1993). Resilience at the front lines: Hospital social work with AIDS patients and burnout. *Social Work in Health Care*, 18(2), 109–125.

Ellis, K., Davis, A. & Rummery, K. (1999). Needs assessment, street-level bureaucracy and the new community care. *Social Policy & Administration*, 33(3), 262–280.

Emery, Y. & Giauque, D. (2003). Emergence of contradictory injunctions in Swiss NPM projects. *International Journal of Public Sector Management*, 16(6), 468–481.

Evans, T. (2011) Professionals, managers ad discretion: Critiquing street-level bureaucracy. *British Journal of Social Work*, 41(2), 368–386.

Evans, T. (2013). Organisational rules and discretion in adult social work. *British Journal of Social Work*, 43(4), 739–758.

Evans, T. & Harris, J. (2004). Street-level bureaucracy, social work and the (exaggerated) death of discretion. *British Journal of Social Work*, 34(6), 871–895.

Folkman, S. & Lazarus, R.S. (1980). An analysis of coping in a middle-aged community sample. *Journal of Health and Social Behavior*, 21(3), 219–239.

Grimmelikhuijsen, S., Jilke, S., Olsen, A. L. & Tummers, L. (2017). Behavioral public administration: Combining insights from public administration and psychology. *Public Administration Review*, 77(1), 45–56.

Hebson, G., Grimshaw, D. & Marchington, M. (2003). PPPs and the changing public sector ethos: Case-study evidence from the health and local authority sectors. *Work Employment and Society*, 17(3), 481–501.

Hill, M. & Hupe, P. (2009). *Implementing public policy: An introduction to the study of operational governance* (2nd ed.). London: Sage.

Hochschild, A.R. (1983). The *managed heart: Commercialization of human feeling*. Berkeley: University of California Press.

Horney, K. 1945. *Our inner conflicts: A constructive theory of neurosis*. New York: W.W. Norton & Company.

Howe, D. (1991). Knowledge, power and the shape of social work practice. In M. Davies (Ed.), *The sociology of social work* (pp. 202–220). London: Routledge.

Hunter, C., Bretherton, J., Halliday, S. & Johnsen, S. (2016). Legal compliance in street-level bureaucracy: A study of UK housing officers. *Law & Policy*, 38(1), 81–95.

Hupe, P. (2013). Dimensions of discretion: Specifying the object of street-level bureaucracy research. *Der moderne staat—Zeitschrift für Public Policy, Recht und Management*, 6(2), 425–440.

Hyun, C., Post, A.E. & Ray, I. (2017). Frontline worker compliance with transparency reforms: Barriers posed by family and financial responsibilities. *Governance*, 31(1), 65–83.

Jilke, S. & Tummers, L.G. (2018). Which clients are deserving of help? A theoretical model and experimental test. *Journal of Public Administration, Research & Theory*, 28(2), 226–238.

Jilke, S., Van de Walle, S. & Kim, S. (2016). Generating usable knowledge through an experimental approach to Public Administration. *Public Administration Review*, 76(1), 69–72.

Kerpershoek, E., Groenleer, M., & de Bruijn, H. (2016). Unintended responses to performance management in Dutch hospital care: Bringing together the managerial and professional perspectives. *Public Management Review*, 18(3), 417–436.

Korczynski, M. (2003). Communities of coping: Collective emotional labour in service work. *Organization*, 10(1), 55–79.

Lipsky, M. (1980). *Street-level bureaucracy: Dilemmas of the individual in public services*. New York: Russell Sage Foundation.

Liu, N., Tang, S.Y., Lo, C.W.H. & Zhan, X. (2016). Stakeholder demands and corporate environmental coping strategies in China. *Journal of environmental management*, 165, 140–149.

Loyens, K. (2014). Law enforcement and policy alienation: Coping by labour inspectors and federal police officers. In P. Hupe, M. Hill & A. Buffat (Eds), *Understanding street-level bureaucracy* (pp. 99–114). Bristol: Policy Press.

Loyens, K. (2016). How police detectives deal with policy alienation in the investigation of human exploitation crimes. In R. Burke (Ed.), *Stress in policing: Sources, consequences and interventions* (Chapter 8, pp. 137–152). New York: Routledge.

Mayer, J.E. & Timms, N. (1970). *The clients speaks*. London: Routledge and Kegan Paul.

Maynard-Moody, S.W. & Musheno, M.C. (2003). *Cops, teachers, counselors: Stories from the front lines of public service*. University of Michigan Press.

Meier, K.J. & O'Toole, L.J. (2013). Subjective organizational performance and measurement error: Common source bias and spurious relationships. *Journal of Public Administration Research and Theory*, 23(2), 429–456.

Merton, R.K. (1995). The Thomas theorem and the Matthew effect. *Social forces*, 74(2), 379–422.

Møller, M.Ø. (2016). "She isn't someone I associate with pension"—A vignette study of professional reasoning. *Professions and Professionalism*, 6(1), 1–20.

Nature editorial. (2016, August, 25). Go forth and replicate! *Nature*, 536, 373.

Oberfield, Z.W. (2010). Rule following and discretion at government's frontlines: Continuity and change during organization socialization. *Journal of Public Administration Research and Theory*, 20(4), 735–755.

Palm, I., Leffers, F., Emons, T., Van Egmond, V. & Zeegers, S. (2008). *De GGz ontwricht: Een praktijkonderzoek naar de gevolgen van het nieuwe zorgstelsel in de geestelijke gezondheidszorg*. Den Haag: SP.

Pollitt, C. & Bouckaert, G. (2004). *Public management reform: A comparative analysis*. Oxford: Oxford University Press.

Pressman, J. & A. Wildavsky (1973). *Implementation*. Berkeley: University of California Press

Satyamurti, C. (1981). *Occupational survival: The case of the local authority social worker*. Oxford: Blackwell Publishing.

Savi, R. & Cepilovs, A. (2016). Central decisions, decentralized solutions: Comparing the implications of central cutback policy for the agency level in Estonia and Latvia. *Journal of Comparative Policy Analysis: Research and Practice*, 19(2) 1–16.

Schillemans, T. & van Twist, M. (2016). Coping with complexity: Internal audit and complex governance. *Public Performance & Management Review*, 40(2) 1–25.

Skinner, E. A., Edge, K., Altman, J. & Sherwood, H. (2003). Searching for the structure of coping: A review and critique of category systems for classifying ways of coping. *Psychological Bulletin*, 129(2), 216–269.

Soss, J., Fording, R.C. & Schram, S. (2011). Disciplining the poor: Neoliberal paternalism and the persistent power of race. Chicago: University of Chicago Press.

Sowa, J. E. & Lu, J. (2016). Policy and management: Considering public management and its relationship to policy studies. *Policy Studies Journal*, 40(1), 74–100.

Thomann, E. (2015). Is output performance all about the resources? A fuzzy-set qualitative comparative analysis of street-level bureaucrats in Switzerland. *Public Administration*, 93(1), 177–194.

Thomann, E., Hupe, P. & Sager, F. (2018a) Serving many masters: Public accountability in private policy implementation. *Governance*, 31(2), 299–319.

Thomann, E., van Engen, N. & Tummers, L. (2018b). The necessity of discretion: A behavioral evaluation of bottom-up implementation theory. *Journal of Public Administration Research and Theory*, 28(4), 583–601.

Thomas, William I. & Dorothy Swaine Thomas. 1928. *The child in America: Behavior problems and programs*. Knopf.

Tummers, L. (2011). Explaining the willingness of public professionals to implement new policies: A policy alienation framework. *International Review of Administrative Sciences*, 77(3), 555–581.

Tummers, L. (2012). Policy alienation of public professionals: The construct and its measurement. *Public Administration Review*, 72(4), 516–525.

Tummers, L. (2017). The relationship between coping and job performance. *Journal of Public Administration Research and Theory*, 27(1), 150–162.

Tummers, L., Bekkers, V. & Steijn, B. (2009). Policy alienation of public professionals: Application in a new public management context. *Public Management Review*, 11(5), 685–706.

Tummers, L. & Rocco, P. (2015). Serving clients when the server crashes: How front-line workers cope with E-government challenges. *Public Administration Review*, 75(6), 817–827.

Tummers, L., Bekkers, V., Vink, E. & Musheno, M. (2015). Coping during public service delivery: A conceptualization and systematic review of the literature. *Journal of Public Administration Research and Theory*, 25(4), 1099–1126.

Tummers, L. & Knies, E. (2016). Measuring public leadership: Developing scales for four key public leadership roles. *Public Administration*, 94(2), 433–451.

van Engen, N.A. (2017). A short measure of general policy alienation: Scale development using a 10-step procedure. *Public Administration*, 95(2), 512–526.

van Loon, N.M. & Jakobsen, M.L. (2017, early view). Connecting governance and the front lines: How work pressure and autonomy matter for coping in different performance regimes. *Public Administration*, 96(3), 435–451.

van der Voet, J., Steijn, B. & Kuipers, B.S. (2017). What's in it for others? The relationship between prosocial motivation and commitment to change among youth care professionals. *Public Management Review*, 19(4), 443–462.

Vinzant, J.C. & Crothers, L. (1998). *Street-level leadership: Discretion and legitimacy in front-line public service*. Washington: Georgetown University Press.

Walker, R. M., Boyne, G. A., & Brewer, G. A. (Eds). (2010). *Public management and performance: Research directions*. Cambridge University Press.

Wright, S.E. (2003). *Confronting unemployment in a street-level bureaucracy: Jobcentre staff and client perspectives*. University of Sterling.

Yang, J.L. & Ortega, D. (2016). Bureaucratic neglect and oppression in child welfare: historical precedent and implications for current practice. *Child and Adolescent Social Work Journal*, 33(6), 513–521.

Zang, X. (2016). Research on street-level discretion in the West: Past, present, and the future. *Chinese Political Science Review*, 1(4), 610–622.

Zang, X. & Musheno, M. (2017). Exploring frontline work in China. *Public Administration*, 95(3), 842–855.

CHAPTER 12

Discretion from a Sociological Perspective

Zachary W. Oberfield

12.1 Introduction

As the chapters of this edited collection show, there are many approaches to understanding the origins and nature of bureaucratic discretion. No matter which lens we choose, studying discretion requires reckoning with officials and the social settings and contexts in which they act (Lipsky 1980; see also Weber 1947; Prottas 1979; Simon 1997). In other words, if we want to understand how bureaucrats behave, we need to understand who they are and how they are influenced by the social forces that they encounter.

The merits of this approach are plain: people are social animals, deeply connected to their surroundings. However, the trouble—at least in a relatively small space like this one—is what to exclude: a survey and synthesis of sociological scholarship on the factors that influence how people make judgements could form its own volume. As such, this chapter addresses a somewhat more narrow focus: organizational socialization. It asks how newcomers are shaped by the organizations that they enter and what this means for how they use their discretion. Organizational socialization is a useful point of entry for understanding sociological scholarship because it is something of a microcosm. The factors and explanations for how people are socialized mirror those used to explain how employees generally interact with their environments. As a result, focusing on organizational socialization can illuminate the utility of using a sociological approach to understanding discretion.

To guide this pursuit, the chapter begins by discussing a decision-making theory—the Logic of Appropriateness—articulated by James March and Johan Olsen (2006, 2009). The Logic of Appropriateness (LOA) is helpful as it directs our attention to a handful of socio-psychological outcomes—identities, attitudes

Z. W. Oberfield (✉)
Haverford College, Haverford, PA, USA

T. Evans, P. Hupe (eds.), *Discretion and the Quest for Controlled Freedom*, https://doi.org/10.1007/978-3-030-19566-3_12

and motivations—that form the heart of an individual's decision-making process (see also Rutz and de Bont's Chapter 18 of this edited collection). From the standpoint of organizational socialization, we want to understand what these views are and how they develop. As such, the chapter introduces and highlights two competing explanatory frameworks: the dispositional and institutional perspectives. Using these perspectives as a guide, the chapter then moves to discuss the findings from a research project about how entering street-level bureaucrats learn to use their discretion. It concludes with some suggestions for how future works might further our understanding of bureaucratic discretion.

12.2 A Logic of Decisions

As noted in this edited collection's introduction, discretion is 'the exercise of judgement and freedom to act within externally controlled limits' (p. 7). In practice, a moment of discretion may or may not be deliberate. In other words, discretion can be a stop-and-think moment of consciousness, which Daniel Kahneman (2011) calls 'System 2' or slow thinking. These are the decisions about which decision-makers are aware and fit more neatly into the classical economic view of people as *homo economicus* (Thaler and Sunstein 2008). From this perspective, decision makers are fully conscious of criteria, alternatives and consequences as they choose a course of action (Yoon and Hwang 1995).

Alternatively, a moment of discretion may be a decision that has been made hundreds of times previously, so that it now feels routine or second nature. Kahneman refers to this as 'System 1' thinking, fast thinking, or intuition. This type of thinking relies on unconscious shortcuts or heuristics, but is not innate. Just as people develop heuristics to navigate the entirety of their social lives, public servants, via 'prolonged practice' (Kahneman 2011: 22), develop heuristics to efficiently and, effectively conduct their work (Lipsky 1980).

Although slow thinking may feel or look more like discretion to decision makers and those observing them, we should be careful about overlooking the importance of fast-thinking discretion; even if a choice is obvious or automatic, that does not mean an actor had no agency. Although employees within a particular organization or office may develop similar routines, research since the 1950s has failed to show that employees are automatonic clones (Wilson 1989). Rather, they appear to adopt somewhat different approaches to their work based on differences in, for example, extra-organizational social identities, education and training (Maynard-Moody and Musheno 2003; Portillo and DeHart-Davis 2009).

With this in mind, this chapter distinguishes between 'routinized discretion', decision making that has been incorporated into daily patterns of behaviour and 'deliberate discretion', moments of conscious thought and response. To understand how these types of discretion unfold in practice, it is helpful to consider March and Olsen's Logic of Appropriateness theory (2006, 2009). For March and Olsen, at the centre of human behaviour is a reckoning with what is socially appropriate. As a result, understanding how organizations work requires studying how rules or norms of appropriateness are organized into institutions.

At the beginning of the Logic of Appropriateness are individuals who have multiple identities, which they choose from as they interact socially. When they arrive at a moment in which a decision is needed, individuals ask themselves a series of questions: What kind of situation is this? What kind of person am I? What does a person like me do in a situation like this? As they answer these questions, appropriateness is at the centre of their thinking. In the abstract, this process sounds onerous and odd but, in reality, March and Olsen suggest, it typically happens quickly and painlessly: people become adept at determining who they should be and how they should act depending on the situations that they are facing. Thus, as they choose among selves—and respond to situations and people—many decisions become nearly automatic. As such, this theory is obviously helpful for explaining routinized discretion. But even in moments of conscious thought and consideration, the Logic of Appropriateness is helpful: when existing scripts offer little guidance, decision makers start back at the beginning, assessing themselves, the situation and what is appropriate. Therefore, the Logic of Appropriateness also helps illuminate moments of deliberate discretion.

The Logic of Appropriateness is sometimes understood as standing in tension with economic or rationalistic approaches to decisions, which elevate the importance of consequences like costs and benefits over all other considerations. Thus, it is worth noting that the Logic of Appropriateness does not suggest that actors are unconcerned with outcomes. The difference between a cost/benefit approach and Logic of Appropriateness, March and Olsen would argue, is in the process by which decisions are made. According to cost/benefit approaches, agents are calculating machines, tallying up likelihoods and outcomes as they consider a course of action. According to the Logic of Appropriateness, outcomes matter, but they do not dominate the decision-making process.

For example, imagine a social worker at a child protective agency who cares about: her agency-wide reputation as a social worker, the wellbeing of the children on her caseload and minimizing paperwork when possible. Further, imagine that after investigating the home of an allegedly neglectful father, she chooses not to give him a written warning, saving herself considerable time spent on paperwork. According to a cost/benefit perspective, this action appears simple and typical: it is an example of an effort-minimizing bureaucrat at work. From the perspective of the Logic of Appropriateness, the decision is more complex: before choosing the outcome that minimized paperwork, she first needed to assess the facts and people associated with the case, her own identity as a social worker and what the appropriate action was in that instance. Thus, it is not that the Logic of Appropriateness ignores outcomes or consequences; rather, it is that the Logic of Appropriateness portrays them as one part of the decision-making process.

12.3 Appropriateness Under the Microscope

If the Logic of Appropriateness offers a useful approach to understanding routinized and deliberate discretion, what are the specific areas we should study if we want to foretell how employees might behave in a particular instance? Unfortunately, the Logic of Appropriateness does not put forward a coherent socio-psychological framework for understanding decision making. As such, this section argues that the term 'bureaucratic personality'—repurposed and reconceived from the mid-twentieth century understanding of the term (Wilson 1989)—offers a way in which we can use the Logic of Appropriateness to understand how bureaucrats use their discretion.

According to the Logic of Appropriateness, the decision-making process begins with the identities held by decision makers; put simply, if we want to understand how people act, we need to understand how they see themselves. There are social and individual perspectives on identities. On the social side, identities arise from interactions with others and help people sort themselves, or be sorted, into particular groups and roles. But identities are also unique: the purest expression of an individual's essence (March 1994: 62). The derivations and characteristics of identity across a population are of little concern here: we can assume that identities have social and individual components. The key point, insofar as the Logic of Appropriateness is concerned, is that we need to understand how individuals see themselves.

The second part of the Logic of Appropriateness (LOA) sequence is recognizing situations. As a result, we must grapple with how decision makers perceive the problems, issues, conditions or types of people with whom they interact. For example, if we were studying how Dutch health inspectors behave in a particular instance, we would want to grapple with how they perceive animal processing plants and types of violations (van Kleef 2016). Is a particular infraction a bad actor ignoring safety protocol or an honest mistake by a good-faith provider of a needed service? As this question shows, to understand how bureaucrats act, we need to understand their attitudes: their summary evaluations about an idea, group or thing (Ajzen 2001).

Stopping there, we would have two large, crucial sets of socio-psychological outcomes that are relevant to how bureaucrats make decisions according to the LOA. However, it would leave out a third part—motivation—that has been crucial to how public administration scholars have theorized bureaucratic behaviour. Specifically, the literature is full of works studying public service motivation (PSM)—a motivation that is basically associated with altruism or the sacrifice of some personal interest for a larger good (Perry and Wise 1990; le Grand 2003; Perry and Hondeghem 2008). Whether PSM motivates the lion's share of public sector behaviour or bureaucrats are motivated by more clichéd outcomes like sloth or indolence (Brehm and Gates 1997), is not important. The point is that if we want to understand bureaucratic behaviour, we need to think about motivation.

Putting these three elements together, bureaucratic personality consists of bureaucrats' identities, motivations and attitudes. For simplicity, the term can be defined as the psychological tendencies and structures that bureaucrats use to make sense of themselves and their work (Oberfield 2014). Returning to the Logic of Appropriateness, when bureaucrats move to take action in a particular moment, they use their bureaucratic personalities to determine what is appropriate. To see how this scheme works in practice, consider the example of a welfare caseworker processing applications for cash assistance benefits. Much of the processing is by rote. She may have control over the process but, because the appropriate thing to do is so obvious, she tends to follow the normal script (routinized discretion). But every once in a while the caseworker faces a moment of deliberate discretion: it is not clear how she should respond to a situation. For example, perhaps an applicant reports that she was fired from her job—and therefore is in need of assistance—because her supervisor was making unwanted sexual advances towards her. According to the state rules, the applicant must produce a letter from her supervisor proving that she is no longer employed at her former workplace. This puts the applicant in a terrible position: she must ask a man whose advances she rejected for help in getting welfare benefits for her family.

The caseworker in this situation faces a choice: stick with the standard protocol and tell the applicant that her case will not be approved until she documents that she is no longer working or waive the requirement for good cause. As the caseworker decides between these two options, she must reckon with how she understands the applicant: is she deserving of help? Is she trustworthy? The caseworker also has to grapple with who she is as a caseworker and what motivates her. Is she the type of worker who makes exceptions for people who deserve them? Is she motivated to help even if it means taking a reputational risk (if it turns out that the applicant was lying) or doing more work (placing a call to the employer to verify the information on her own)?

The deeper we go with this example, or consider how the Logic of Appropriateness would play out in practice, two things become obvious. First, there is an interconnectedness among the various aspects of bureaucratic personality. This does little harm to the above definition but it does imply that we need to look across these aspects of bureaucratic personality to understand behaviour. Second, thinking about how bureaucrats make decisions inevitably leads to questions about the origins of identities and attitudes. For instance, how did the caseworker in the example above form her views about who is deserving of her help? Questions like this suggest that if we want to understand how employees use deliberate or routinized discretion, we need to reckon with how they form their bureaucratic personalities. It is to that topic that we turn next.

12.4 The Origins of Bureaucratic Personality

How do bureaucrats develop the interrelated components of their bureaucratic personalities? March (1994: 60) notes that:

> Organizations select individuals with preexisting identities and rules. When an engineer, machinist, clerk, or truck driver is hired, the organization hires those identities, mixed as they are with an assortment of other identities that any one individual accepts—parent, friend, member of an ethnic or religious group. Organizations also define identities specific to themselves, train individuals in them and socialize individuals to adopt the identities as their own. Formal and informal organizational rules are woven into, utilize, and help define organizational identities and roles.

In other words, *who people are* in their official capacities is shaped by two factors: first, who they were when they arrived inside their workplaces; and, second, the organizational influences that they experience. To organize a consideration of these two explanations, this section labels them as the dispositional and institutional perspectives on organizational socialization (Oberfield 2014).

The dispositional perspective—which sees bureaucrats as remaining strongly connected to the ideas, roles and thinking that brought them to the door of their organizations in the first place—is a powerful narrative for explaining bureaucratic psychology and behaviour. Drawing from social psychological theories like person-organization fit theory and attraction-selection-attrition theory, this perspective envisions much of the heavy lifting of organizational socialization as being completed prior to entry (Schneider 1987; O'Reilly, Chatman and Caldwell 1991). Politically, this narrative has considerable currency in the wake of a bureaucratic crisis: using this logic, the failure of, for example, a public defender has less to do with systemic or institutional factors than she or he being a 'bad apple'.

But it would be wrong to dismiss the dispositional perspective as soft-headed or merely a convenient political excuse. In fact, crucial concepts from sociology (habitus) and psychology (personality) suggest that people have relatively durable patterns of thinking and acting throughout their lives (Bourdieu 1990; Costa and McCrae 1994). This is not to say that these concepts imply inert people, incapable of change. But the ideas and the empirical research supporting them, suggest that radical swings in thought and behaviour are relatively rare for most people. Supporting this perspective, research shows that bureaucrats remain strongly connected to identities (like race and gender) and motivations (like public service) that they formed early in life and certainly had prior to joining their organizations (Dolan 2000; see also Perry 1997; Wilkins and Williams 2008).

The institutional framework, points to a different set of factors that affect the thoughts and actions taken by organizational entrants. From this perspective, newcomers experience a cauldron of social forces when they step inside their organizations for the first time: culture, peers, training and leadership. Barnett (2003: 7) nicely articulates this perspective in discussing how newcomers are socialized at the United Nations (UN). For him, bureaucracies are more than the sum of their parts, they are 'orienting machines' and 'incubators of ethical claims'. As with the dispositional framework, this approach has considerable political resonance. Critics of a government policy or an instance of bureaucratic malfeasance will seek to frame their concerns as systemic rather than individual.

Again, there is empirical evidence supporting this perspective. For example, the organizational socialization literature suggests that training is a key period in which organizations have the capacity to shape how entrants think and act as organization members (Saks and Ashforth 1997). Similarly, the street-level bureaucracy literature shows that bureaucratic behaviour is affected by a range of intra-organizational factors, like caseloads, cultures and veteran role modelling (Ellwanger 2010; see also Lipsky 1980; Sandfort 2000).

The point of this overview is to delineate two roughly different perspectives on how entrants form their bureaucratic personalities, which are related to how they act in their official capacities. In doing so, we have an analytic framework for the chapter's next task: discussing the findings from a research project studying how two sets of street-level bureaucrats are socialized into their organizations.

However, before getting to that, it is important to emphasize that no one thinks that socialization is explained solely by either the dispositional or institutional perspective. In other words, although they point to different processes and sets of explanatory factors, we should not expect that one is right and the other wrong. Also, they do not work in isolation from one another; it is imperative for students of discretion to recognize and study the interactions and intersections between these explanations. For example, we would want to study how entrants with different rule-following identities (a dispositional factor) adapt to their organizations and develop similarly or differently; but we should not lose track of the fact that their development may depend on the institutional contexts of the organizations that they enter (like how much discretion they are expected to exercise). Thus, this framework is analytically helpful but the dispositional and institutional perspectives are not mutually exclusive.

12.5 Discretion and Development

With the dispositional and institutional perspectives in mind, I began a research project to understand how incoming street-level bureaucrats developed their views about discretion (and other aspects of their bureaucratic personalities) over the beginning of their careers. Specifically, I studied two sets of entrants—police officers and welfare caseworkers—in a large urban area and tracked them from their first few days on the job, through classroom and academy training and into the streets and their offices. That research project resulted in a book that studied their first two years on the job (Oberfield 2014). Subsequently, I got in touch with the police entrants at the ten-year mark in their careers.

This section highlights some of the identity-related findings from that book and presents initial findings about police discretion after a decade on the force. It begins by summarizing entrants' views about themselves and their discretion at the outset of their careers. Following that, it uses some descriptive statistical figures to characterize the trajectory of police entrants over the course of the study. It concludes by asking about why entrants may have remained the same or changed.

Before commenting on the findings, it is important to note that police cadets and caseworker trainees entered what Etzioni (1969) refers to as 'semi-professions'. Relative to professions like lawyer, doctor or accountant, they begin their workplace training with little to no professional training. Thus, we might expect that these entrants began their training more susceptible to organizational messages, relative to bureaucrats or street-level bureaucrats, who work as part of an established, esteemed profession. For example, one might surmise that joining a public defender office has less of an effect on entrants relative to the cases examined here, because entering public defenders begin their work after completing three years of professional schooling (law school).

In this way, police and welfare caseworker entrants are similar: neither group of entrants had prior professional training before beginning their work. However in other respects, prior research suggests, the fields that they entered were quite different. Police training is often described as a powerful experience, perhaps second in intensity only to military indoctrination, that regularly takes impressionable, unformed cadets and gives them a new purpose, identity and peer group (Rubinstein 1973; Van Maanen 1974). In comparison, caseworkers enter a far less totalizing institution; the work is intense but does not have the identity or behavioural implications analogous to joining the police (Lurie 2006; Watkins-Hayes 2009). Thus, as readers seek to situate these findings, the police represent an extreme case of organizational socialization—if any organization is likely to have a major effect on entrants, a police department would be the one—whereas the welfare caseworkers represent a more typical case (Yin 2003). It is also useful to recognize that this project used respondents' answers to survey and interview questions as its data. Although this is not uncommon in the literature, it is impossible to state the extent to which reported behaviour matched the actions taken by respondents.

At the Outset

When they began their work, both groups of entrants indicated fidelity to a rules-oriented vision of public administration. From this perspective, they would be neutral agents who approached people and situations the same. For instance, one police cadet, at the beginning of his career, noted: 'The main thing is just to be fair and impartial. You can't have any biases or prejudices or anything.' Similarly, an entering welfare caseworker said that she would be a 'by-the-book [...] compliance person'. Although this indicates some discomfort with discretion, most entrants did not see themselves as hamstrung by the rules or overly neutral. Even if they entered situations neutrally, they were comfortable responding to situations based on their read of it or how other people responded to them. For one officer this meant a shifting approach to interactions: 'you know, justice is supposed to be blind. So objectivity, it's pretty much what it is [...]. But, every situation is different and you've got to keep that in mind. You know, you can't talk to everyone the same way.'

To develop a more standardized view of entrants at the outset of their careers, I surveyed the entering cohort of each group. In this chapter I will highlight the findings from four questions asked of entrants:

1. 'I am someone who follows the rules even if I don't agree with them.'
2. 'People and situations are unique and should be treated on a case-by-case basis.'
3. 'It's important that things be done by the book no matter what.'
4. 'Sometimes it's okay to bend the rules for a person who deserves it.'[1]

An analysis of these surveys largely corresponded to the interview findings above. For example, nearly 70 per cent of police indicated that things should be done by the book and over 90 per cent indicated that they would follow rules that they did not agree with. On the welfare side, over half agreed that things should be done by the book and 70 per cent agreed that they would follow rules with which they did not agree. At the same time, there was strong agreement in both groups with the statement that situations and people are unique and should be treated on a case-by-case basis.

Training

After entering their organizations, both sets of newcomers began six-month training programmes in which they were schooled about different aspects of their work. In the organizational socialization literature—as well as in popular lore—experiences with training are thought to be some of the most important ways in which organizations affect the thinking and behaviour of newcomers (Wanous 1992). The police, as alluded to above, are reputed to be particularly good at this. For example, Van Maanen (1974: 84) quotes a chief of police as saying: 'The day the new recruit walks through the doors of the police academy he leaves society behind to enter a profession that does more than give him a job, it defines who he is.'

For the police, training took place at a municipal police academy, where they worked in classrooms, firing ranges and patrol cars. Welfare caseworkers reported to a centralized office building in which they learned about the various programmes that they would administer, mostly sitting behind computers and listening to lectures. In both settings, the instruction about the work and how entrants should handle it was led by experienced organization members, referred to as veterans.

One of the notable differences between the training formats was the deliberateness with which the organizations addressed discretion. For the police, academy instructors indicated to cadets that not all parts of their work were proscribed: they had and would need to understand how to use 'discretion'. In effect, they were told to follow their gut: discretion was described as a penumbra or grey area where different officers might choose different responses to the same situation. At the same time, there was clearly a 'hidden curriculum' (Hafferty 1998) in which the department made a strong effort to standardize discretion: they would tell them about a situation, indicate that there was no set way of handling it and then say which was the best way to proceed. For example, the instructors invoked a mythic 'working stiff' pulled over for speeding near his house. If he had all of his documents, was not going too fast and admitted to speeding, it was described as 'common sense' to give him a break.

Welfare training was a marked contrast: incoming caseworkers were told that there were no grey areas so they would never have to use their discretion. From this perspective, all questions should be resolved by agency policy. In fact, the trainers repeated a phrase so often it became almost a mantra 'policy states [...]'. Caseworker trainees were told that they could use the regulations as a scapegoat if a client was peeved by a decision. Nevertheless, as with police, the official message about discretion given to caseworker trainees was not easily aligned with the hidden curriculum: the actual stories and myths shared by trainers. For example, one trainer noted that 'a lot of this job is interpretation' of the rules and another noted that he 'took care of my elderly'. In these moments, it was clear, a different message was being communicated: there was some discretion in the job of being a caseworker. It was up to caseworkers, to some extent, when they would use policy as a foil.

Again, it is helpful to turn to the survey data to develop a more systematic understanding of how entrants viewed their discretion. It was twice during the training that I was able to survey cadets at the academy (it was not, unfortunately, possible to survey welfare caseworkers at that time). The results showed some evidence of change and a general acceptance of and comfort with discretion: the percentage of cadets who agreed that things should be done by the book dropped from nearly 70 per cent, at the outset of training, to around 40 per cent, after three and six months at the academy; there was also a large rise in the percentage of cadets who agreed that they could bend the rules for a deserving person—at the outset around 10 per cent agreed with this but after three and six months this rose to around 40 per cent.

In other respects, there was little evidence of the massive change predicted by the chief of police in Van Maanen's work: cadets continued to agree that situations and people should be handled case by case and that they would follow rules with which they did not agree. Also, when taking account of how entrants had answered questions about rule following at the outset, there was modest but not severe change. For each of the survey questions above, respondents were asked to indicate their agreement on a 5-point Likert scale. Therefore, the biggest possible change from the outset to a subsequent time would have been 4 points. Analysis showed that the average change after three and six months of training was around 0.75 of one point. Moreover, a multivariate statistical analysis, which explored cadets' experiences with various aspects of training and controlled for things like prior government or military service, revealed that their views about discretion were most strongly connected to their entering viewpoints on the topic. An entrant who was comfortable with discretion at the outset remained as such; another entrant who did not expect to use it a lot altered his or her outlook somewhat but not radically.

On the Streets and in the Office

While formal training is thought to be a time of major development for newcomers, few organizational socialization scholars suggest that entrants emerge from training fully formed. In fact, one might argue that as they leave training, entrants more fully enter their organizations: now they are among the veterans who, observers suggest, play a crucial role in socializing entrants (Rubinstein 1973; Ellwanger 2010). Also, they are now on the job, interacting with the public, superiors and figuring out who they will be in their official capacities.

Most of the police whom I interviewed after they began work indicated that they were using their discretion as they expected. For most, they saw themselves as entering situations neutrally and then responding based on the circumstances that they encountered. Their telling revealed that how they ended up behaving depended on the person with whom they were interacting. One officer commented that he needed a 'dual personality' one for the 'good, honest, hard-working people'—whom he treated respectfully—and one for the 'crackhead[s]' and 'assholes'—whom he treated with contempt and derision. Discretion, in this sense, was the decision about whom to enact in a particular moment. Caseworkers, after beginning work, appeared to embody the conflicted messages about discretion and rule following that they encountered during training. For example, one worker indicated that 'I'm always policy, whatever policy is.' Later, however, she said how she would diverge from the normal approach if she felt it necessary.

To provide a more systematic view of discretion and rule following after graduation, it is useful to turn to the surveys that both groups took and the questions discussed above. By the one- and two-year mark following entry, only around 25 per cent of police agreed that things should be done by the book. This was a radical drop from entry, where nearly 70 per cent had agreed with this statement. Similarly, there was a rise in agreement that rule bending was acceptable for a deserving person, from around 15 per cent at entry to 50 per cent by the end of the second year. For the two other questions—about following rules with which they disagreed and treating people on a case-by-case basis—there was less change.

Like police, caseworkers moved towards embracing discretion, but there was more consistency: at the outset 50 per cent indicated going by the book; after two years, this was at 40 per cent. They remained committed to treating people on a case-by-case basis, following rules with which they disagreed and not bending the rules for clients. In comparison, the police moved more decidedly towards an embrace of discretion. Again, a multivariate statistical analysis revealed that of all of the factors police and caseworkers encountered, their entering views about discretion and the rules were most strongly associated with their subsequent views.

Ten Years on the Force

Two years, of course, is just the beginning of a bureaucrat's career, which limited my earlier work and claims. To provide a longer term view, I was able to get back in touch with a number of the police entrants after they had been on the force for a decade (unfortunately, it was not possible to reestablish contact with the welfare caseworker entrants whom I studied). At that time, of the initial 84 officers in the entering group, 54 remained on the force (for a 36 per cent attrition rate). I reached out to all who remained and 35 responded to my request that they complete a survey (for a response rate of 65 per cent). To examine if there was any attrition or response bias, I studied whether there was evidence that different types of officers—based on demographic differences, like age, race or income; or identity-based characteristics, like strong rule-following—responded to surveys or left the force at different rates. In fact, there were few patterns based on these factors.

To describe police entrant development, Fig. 12.1 presents change histograms for only the officers who completed the beginning survey and the ten-year's later survey. In other words, the histograms show the differences between respondents' answers to each of the four questions analysed in this chapter at the outset of the project and at the ten-year mark. A difference of zero indicates no change over the ten-year period; a difference of negative or positive four indicates radical change (either towards or away from discretion depending on the question).

This figure reveals that, across each question, there is an unmistakable trend towards discretion usage: fewer agreed that they would follow rules with which they disagree, go by the book and so on. Additionally, we see that the scope of change is, for the most part, relatively minor: the modal difference between the 'by the book' and 'treat uniquely' questions was zero, indicating no change; the modal difference for the other two was one point of movement. For the 'follow rules' panel, only 2 out of 35 officers moved more than one point; for the 'treat uniquely' panel, only 3 out of 35 moved more than one point. In the other two panels there was more average change, but even there it was not massive: for the 'by the book', 6 out of 33 respondents moved more than one point; for the 'bend the rules' panel, 6 out of 35 respondents moved more than one point.

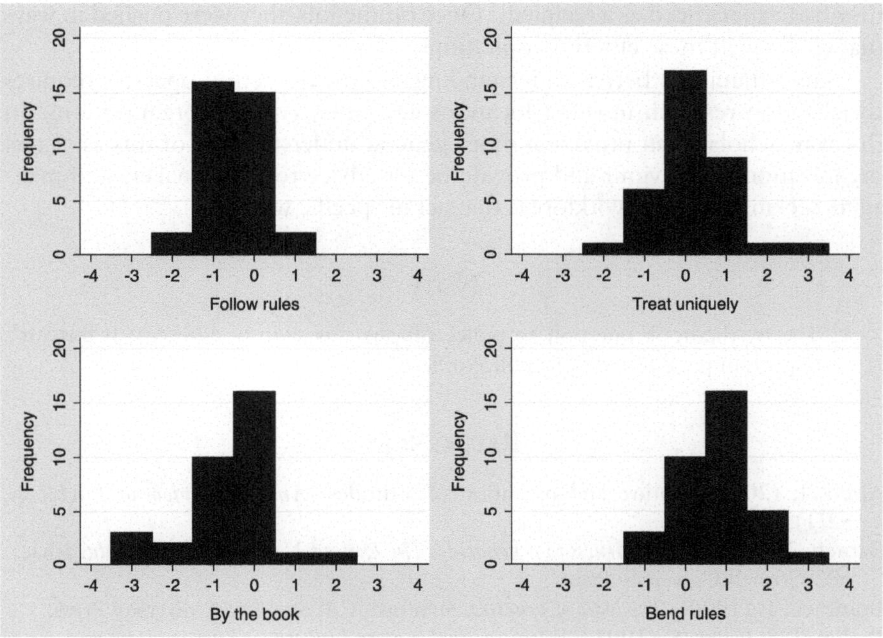

Fig. 12.1 Change and stability in police discretion over a ten-year period

12.6 Conclusion

The findings here suggest support for the institutional and dispositional perspectives on socialization. On the institutional side, we saw movement towards discretion across both groups of entrants; but we also see strong support for continuity and, therefore, the dispositional perspective: entrants remained tied to their beginning viewpoints about how discretion should be used. Also, they may have moved somewhat to the appropriate vantage point of their organizations, but the change was never radical.

If there is support for both perspectives, developing a general understanding of how discretion develops requires further study. To predict and alter the usage of discretion, we would need to know about what the prior entrants bring with them to their organizations and how they evolve during their organizational lives. For example, it was not surprising to find in my research that there were strong familial bonds connecting the police entering the department. Some had been told for years that they 'thought like a cop'. However, being a police officer, Fig. 12.1 suggests, pushed them somewhat away from these entering views. Similarly, in the welfare department, many entrants had experienced welfare offices first-hand: nearly three quarters had claimed welfare at one time in their life and a number went directly from claiming to administering benefits. For some entrants, their touchstone for becoming a caseworker was to be 'different' (by which they meant fair, calm and reliable) from those they had experienced as a recipient. Once on the job, they were pushed in ways that challenged these entering aspirations.

Thus, attaining a better understanding of how discretion operates requires socialization research in other locations and other types of organizations. In this way, scholars can provide a more general understanding of this aspect of organizational behaviour and provide better advice to policymakers and managers seeking to build workforces that act in specific ways.

Note

1. The by-the-book question to police officers was slightly different; before 'It's important [...]' it said 'As a police officer.'

References

Ajzen, I. (2001). Nature and operation of attitudes. *Annual Review of Psychology*, 52(1), 27–58.

Barnett, M. (2003). *Eyewitness to a genocide: The United Nations and Rwanda*. Ithaca, NY: Cornell University Press.

Bourdieu, P. (1990). *The logic of practice*. Stanford, CA: Stanford University Press.

Brehm, J. & Gates, S. (1997). *Working, shirking, and sabotage: Bureaucratic response to a democratic public*. Ann Arbor, MI: University of Michigan Press.

Costa, P. & McCrae, R. (1994). Set like plaster? Evidence for the stability of adult personality. In T. Heatherton & J. Weinberger (Eds) *Can personality change?* (pp. 21–40). Washington, DC: American Psychological Association.

Dolan, J. (2000. The senior executive service: Gender, attitudes, and representative bureaucracy. *Journal of Public Administration Research and Theory*, 10(3), 513–529.

Ellwanger, S. (2010). How police officers learn ethics. In M. Braswell, B. McCarthy & B. McCarthy (Eds), *Justice, crime and ethics* (pp. 45–70). New York: Elsevier.

Etzioni, A. (1969). Preface. In A. Etzioni (Ed.), *The semi-professions and their organization: Teachers, nurses, social workers* (pp. v–xvii). New York: Free Press.

Hafferty, F. (1998). Beyond curriculum reform: Confronting medicine's hidden curriculum. *Academic Medicine*, 73(4), 403–407.

Kahneman, D. (2011). *Thinking, fast and slow*. New York: Macmillan.

le Grand, J. (2003). *Motivation, agency, and public policy: Of knights and knaves, pawns and queens*. Oxford: Oxford University Press.

Lipsky, M. (1980). *Street-level bureaucracy: Dilemmas of the individual in public service*. New York: Russell Sage Foundation.

Lurie, I. (2006). *At the front lines of the welfare system: A perspective on the decline in welfare caseloads*. Albany, NY: State University of New York Press.

March, J. (1994). *A primer on decision making: How decisions happen*. New York: Free Press.

March, J. & Olsen, J. (2006). The logic of appropriateness. In M. Moran, M. Rein & R. Goodin (Eds), *The Oxford Handbook of public policy* (pp. 689–708). New York: Oxford University Press.

———. (2009). The logic of appropriateness. *ARENA: Centre for European Studies*.

Maynard-Moody, S. & Musheno, M. (2003). *Cops, teachers, counselors: Stories from the front lines of public service*. Ann Arbor, MI: University of Michigan Press.

Oberfield, Z. (2014). *Becoming bureaucrats: Socialization at the front lines of government service*. Philadelphia, PA: University of Pennsylvania Press.

O'Reilly, C., Chatman, J. & Caldwell, D. (1991). People and organizational culture: A profile comparison approach to assessing person-organization fit. *The Academy of Management Journal*, 34(3), 487–516.

Perry, J. (1997). Antecedents of public service motivation. *Journal of Public Administration Research and Theory*, 7(2), 181–197.

Perry, J. & Hondeghem, A. (2008). Editors' introduction. In J. Perry & A. Hondeghem (Eds), *Motivation in public management: The call of public service* (pp. 1–14). New York: Oxford University Press.

Perry, J. & Wise, L. (1990). The motivational bases of public service. *Public Administration Review*, 50(3), 367–373.

Portillo, S. & DeHart-Davis, L. (2009). Gender and organizational rule abidance. *Public Administration Review*, 69(2), 339–347.

Prottas, J. (1979). *People-processing: The street-level bureaucrat in public service bureaucracies*. Lexington, MA: Lexington Books.

Rubinstein, J. (1973). *City police*. New York: Hill and Wang.

Saks, A. & Ashforth, B. (1997). Organizational socialization: Making sense of the past and present as a prologue for the future. *Journal of Vocational Behavior*, 51(2), 234–279.

Sandfort, J. (2000). Moving beyond discretion and outcomes: Examining public management from the front lines of the welfare system. *Journal of Public Administration Research and Theory*, 10(4), 729–756.

Schneider, B. (1987). The people make the place. *Personnel Psychology*, 40(3), 437–453.

Simon, H. 1997. *Administrative behavior: A study of decision-making processes in administrative organizations*. New York: Free Press.

Thaler, R. & Sunstein, C. (2008). *Nudge: Improving decisions about health, wealth, and happiness*. New York: Penguin.

van Kleef, D. (2016). *Changing the nature of the beast: How organizational socialization contributes to the development of the organizational role identity of Dutch veterinary inspectors*. Doctoral thesis, Leiden University.

Van Maanen, J. (1974). Working the street: A developmental view of police behavior. In H. Jacob (Ed.), *The potential for reform of criminal justice* (pp. 83–130). Thousand Oaks, CA: Sage.

Wanous, J. (1992). *Organizational entry: Recruitment, selection, and socialization of newcomers*. Reading, PA: Addison-Wesley.

Watkins-Hayes, C. (2009). *The new welfare bureaucrats: Entanglements of race, class, and policy reform*. Chicago: University of Chicago Press.

Weber, M. (1947). *The theory of social and economic organization* (T. Parsons, Trans.). New York: Free Press.

Wilkins, V. & Williams, B. (2008). Black or blue: Racial profiling and representative bureaucracy. *Public Administration Review*, 68(4), 654–664.

Wilson, J. (1989). *Bureaucracy: What government agencies do and why they do it*. New York: Basic Books.

Yin, R. (2003). *Case study research: Design and methods*. Thousand Oaks, CA: Sage.

Yoon, K. & Hwang, C. (1995). *Multiple attribute decision making: An introduction*. Thousand Oaks, CA: SAGE Publications.

CHAPTER 13

Discretion from a Critical Perspective

Hannah Jobling

13.1 Introduction

Discretion is often discussed in terms of the authority conferred on, or exercised by, particular actors within various contexts and with varying effects. But what of the more nebulous drivers of discretionary activity? What bodies of knowledge do 'street-level' professionals draw upon when they intervene in the lives of the people they are working with? How do differing forms of knowledge enable or constrain professionals' ways of seeing and going about their work? The field of mental health provides fertile ground for an analysis of such questions for two interrelated reasons. Firstly, it is a field in which knowledge and the ensuing application of knowledge is contested. Secondly, as in many other 'street-level' settings, the consequences of professional intervention for those on the receiving end can be significant and far-reaching. As such, it provides an ideal case in which to address the operation of discretion from a critical perspective. 'Critical' in this sense refers to an analysis of power within the specific field of mental health, which interrogates the normative foundations of discretionary activity in mental health policy and practice, rather than a broader exposition of what the parameters to discretion might be. It should be noted therefore that this chapter does not set out to give an overview of the literature on discretion and apply it to the mental health field, but instead draws on specific aspects of the literature to illustrate a critical analysis of discretion in practice.

Analysis of the use of discretion in mental health services is typically oriented around how legal decisions on the restriction of individual liberty are enacted within a multi-professional context, taking into account the range of factors

H. Jobling (✉)
Department of Social Policy and Social Work, University of York, York, UK
e-mail: hannah.jobling@york.ac.uk

T. Evans, P. Hupe (eds.), *Discretion and the Quest for Controlled Freedom*, https://doi.org/10.1007/978-3-030-19566-3_13

that can influence professional judgement. In the UK,[1] these decisions involve a group of mental health professionals assessing whether: an individual has a legally defined mental disorder[2]; which poses risk to the health and safety of the individual or other people; and requires assessment and/or treatment in hospital; to which the individual is unable or unwilling to assent. The consequences of a decision to use mental health law can be profound for the individual in question, both in terms of their immediate experience of coercion and loss of liberty and the resultant impact on daily life (Katsakou and Priebe 2007). The professionals who make these decisions therefore wield significant statutory power. Peay (2003: ix) highlights the distinctive nature of such decisions being 'taken with the authority of the law, but in the absence of lawyers' and within a clinical rather than judicial remit. Indeed, it is worth noting that in England and Wales Approved Mental Health Professionals (AMHPs)—who are central actors in applying mental health law—are the only professionals aside from the Police and the judiciary who can lawfully deprive an individual of their liberty.

At the same time such decisions are typically complex, dependent as they are on situational and individual contingencies and within the context of mental health law that allows significant scope for interpretation. As Peay (2003: 118) notes, the application of mental health law in England and Wales is 'highly reliant on the judgement of the practitioners who are required to apply it'. As such, mental health professionals operate with a significant amount of discretion when applying the law. This combination of power and latitude means that legal decisions can be fraught with ethical dilemmas for the mental health professionals who enact them. In her influential study, Peay (2003) particularly focuses on how the multidisciplinary nature of decision-making in mental health law plays into these dilemmas, where a professional role can have a significant influence on final judgements. As has been noted elsewhere in this edited collection, the use of discretion in such scenarios is a collective endeavour and is thus dependent on the interaction between decision-makers; see Rutz and de Bont's Chap. 18. In mental health law, the involvement of more than one actor in decision-making has been described as a safeguard to wide-ranging powers, whereby 'two (or three) heads are better than one' (Laing 2004: 869). More specifically, the role of the AMHP[3] in Mental Health Act assessments is primarily aimed at ensuring that a social perspective is included in decision-making to act as a counter-balance to the medical approach embodied by the psychiatrist in attendance.

This deliberate counterpointing of different professional perspectives in legal decision-making draws attention to the central role of knowledge, alongside interpersonal dynamics and institutional factors, in informing discretion in mental health services. Mental health professionals rely upon a range of heuristic approaches and epistemological frameworks to interpret and respond to presenting dilemmas. For example, a concept such as 'insight' which is often used in mental health practice to support legal decisions, can be both a 'shorthand' formulation derived from clinical experience and a knowledge claim made on a scientific basis. The conscious drawing down of knowledge as a resource to support discretionary activity is associated with professional expertise (see Evans in Chap. 23 in this volume) and this is most clearly seen in a legal scenario, where decisions must be formally justified. Legal decisions are by their nature binary—they do or do not apply. Whilst they may be premised on contingent relations between actors and on contextual circumstances, there is an epistemological expectation of certainty about the course of action decided upon. The application of legal criteria in the mental health field thus foregrounds certain sources and kinds of knowledge which are relatively clear, nomological and tractable—namely knowledge derived from a biomedical conception of mental disorder.

Indeed, it has long been claimed that despite there being a broad biopsychosocial—a portmanteau term referring to the combination of biological, psychological and social perspectives—framework for mental health provision in advanced liberal societies such as the UK, biological explanations and medical solutions predominate (Tew 2011). Whilst most critical analyses of the biomedical model acknowledge that it has a role to play in mental health provision, it is also suggested that the biomedical model has colonized mental health provision and 'crowded out' other explanatory perspectives and approaches, leaving practitioners with a 'thin' and reductionist foundation from which to operate (Read, Bentall and Fosse 2009). An analysis of this claim lies at the heart of this chapter, which draws upon findings from an ethnographic study of mental health practice in England. The focus here is on how knowledge can both enable and constrain the application of practical-ethical reasoning by mental health professionals in *everyday* practice. In this context, knowledge is both a form of 'action prescription' and an 'action resource', which respectively can specify and enable professional conduct (Hupe and Buffat 2014). Moving the debate from 'rules-based' legal decision-making to the operation of discretion in informal judgements, allows for a more developed analysis of how knowledge influences professional thought and action in the 'greyer' realm of day-to-day practice. It is important to understand what professionals base 'micro-decisions' on, as these decisions shape the path taken by individuals within services and often mediate when and how formal decision-making under the law takes place. In sum, the questions explored in this chapter are: How does a biomedical model influence the scope and operation of discretion in mental health services? What capacity is there for mental health professionals to draw upon other kinds of knowledge and how does this manifest in the approaches they take when working together and with service users?

In surveying these questions, it is argued that although the 'bio' element of the biopsychosocial approach is often portrayed as hegemonic in critical academic writing on mental health service delivery, observations of everyday mental health practice suggest that practitioners make room for competing explanations and approaches. In particular, two aspects of practice are highlighted, which generate differentiated knowledge and subsequently shape discretionary action. Firstly, the generation of 'bottom-up' knowledge is presented in contrast to 'top-down' policy/service mandates. Here, notions of shared and co-created narratives, recognition and trust are explored in the context of the practitioner-service user relationship. Secondly, there is a discussion of the ways practitioners may position themselves as being *role* rather than *profession* oriented and the implications this has for the forms of knowledge they may draw upon when exercising discretion. These observations of 'street-level' mental health practice are placed in contrast to the dominant narrative of mental health services, in which professional freedom is described as being restricted by the prime position of the biomedical model. An account of this narrative is given in the next section, beginning with a brief overview of the history of the biomedical model in mental health. Moving to current times, the roles of vertical and horizontal knowledge integration in sustaining the biomedical model within the field of mental health are explored and in turn the potential effect of this on discretion in practice.

13.2 The Prevalent Position of the Biomedical Model in Mental Health Services

The current primacy of the biomedical model in mental health services was not inevitable, dependent as it is on historical contingency. In this sense, the biomedical model is a 'hardy perennial' (Pilgrim 2002: 590) which has exerted varying influence since its inception and has been perpetuated through particular ways of conceptualizing and structuring mental health provision and practice over time. In his historical treatment of madness, Foucault (1977) described how the Enlightenment period predicated a shift from the concept of 'madness' to 'mental illness'. The associated coalescence of theories and methods of individualism, containment, categorization and technical 'know-how', were inextricably linked to the biomedical model gaining traction in the management of mental disorder. It was through the developing discipline and profession of psychiatry (within the broader discipline of medicine) that these theories and methods became embedded in a particular scientific discourse of human cognition and behaviour. Scull's (1979) detailed historical analysis of Victorian asylums demonstrates how early modern psychiatry cemented its authority over both causes and treatment of mental disorder, specifically in its gradual unseating of 'moral management' approaches. Indeed, the containment of growing numbers of people in asylums during this period enabled psychiatry to flourish, providing a steady supply of subjects for observation and classification (Porter 1987). The ensuing rationalization of 'unreasonable' behaviour through reference to medical knowledge provided the means by which psychiatry became the lead discipline within the field of mental health.

It follows that from the beginning of psychiatry as a modern profession, it was positioned as being based on 'hard' science, where an empiricist conflation is made between the observable and the real and 'mindedness' is discounted (Schramme 2013). In this sense, biological psychiatry made (and continues to make) a distinction between subjectivist 'meaning-making' and a materialist ontology, with the latter given precedence. This perspective is encapsulated in early definitions of madness which emphasize its somatic nature. For example, an account from the early days of the modern profession, in a predecessor to the *British Journal of Psychiatry,* describes 'insanity [as] purely a disease of the brain' (Bucknill 1856). The dominance of this explanatory framework was challenged by the development of psychodynamic approaches in the early twentieth century. Soldiers' experiences of 'shell-shock' in the First World War particularly generated interest in therapies which considered the relationship between 'inner' and 'outer' life (Lester and Glasby 2006). However, a significant shift back to a biomedical perspective came in the 1950s and 1960s with the accidental 'discovery' of psychotropic medications and the concurrent development of ever evolving diagnostic tools.[4] Despite the genesis of anti-psychiatry in the 1960s and 1970s, most famously illustrated by R.D. Laing's work, the biomedical model continued to become entrenched in mental health research and provision over the following decades, with the promulgation of a spectrum of theories on the biomechanics of mental illness.

Although it has been suggested that the biomedical model in the UK has been increasingly competing with other approaches in recent years (Pilgrim and Rogers 2009), research on the increasing rates of medication usage in mental health services and the lack of alternative interventions indicate that it remains the prevailing policy and practice framework (Herrman and Harvey 2005; Domino and Swartz 2008). More generally, public belief in biological explanations for mental distress has grown steadily over the last 20 years, as has the perception that drug treatment is the appropriate first line of support (Schomerus, Schwahn, Holzinger, Corrigan, Grabe, Carta and Angermeyer 2012). Thus whilst a biopsychosocial approach is often referenced in research, policy and practice, the 'bio' element of that approach is pre-eminent. Biological explanations for mental illness are given causal precedence and medication is consequently the dominant intervention in mental health services, with medication compliance the primary aim. As with previous periods, there are contextualized theories about why this might currently be the case. The way that these approaches play out in practice may be understood in terms of *vertical* and *horizontal* integration (Hupe 2013) of biomedical knowledge, both of which can act to constrain the discretion of mental health practitioners:

The Vertical Integration of the Biomedical Model Through Policy Mandates

The vertical integration of the biomedical model in mental health refers to its being embedded via 'top-down' policy and institutional mandates. Conceptualizing the biomedical model as a form of 'dominant knowledge' (Dean 2010) means it can be understood as working 'through' other concepts to shape the rationalities of mental health practice. Specifically the biomedical model operates via the two current main policy drivers for mental health of *risk* and *recovery.* For risk, biomedically oriented perceptions of mental health status are linked to increased social distance and fear, based on notions of 'otherness' and deterministic pessimism about potential for change (Schomerus *et al.* 2012). Rose (2007) refers to 'biological citizenship' where rights and responsibilities are embedded in biological identity. In this way, differentiated forms of control are connected to 'distinctions between actual, potential, troublesome and impossible citizens' (Rose 2007: 132). In mental health, this manifests through interplay between actuarial and diagnostic categorizations which can reinforce each other. In other words, the biomedical model can provide clarity of cause and simplicity of action which enables risk assessment and management.

In contrast to the risk agenda, the service user generated idea of 'recovery' has often been characterized as challenging the biomedical model in mental health and allowing both practitioners and service users greater scope for creative and individualized approaches to mental distress (Bonney and Stickley 2008). Many proponents of recovery do not entirely reject the validity of 'clinical' recovery in terms of symptom reduction enabling better quality of life (Mountain and Shah 2008). However, the recovery literature generally positions medicalized approaches as being pathologizing, iatrogenic and dismissive of the value and meaning of service users' perceptions of their mental health related experiences (Thornton and Lucas 2011). Nonetheless, it has been argued that in the 'translation' of the recovery philosophy to mental health policy and practice, it has become subsumed into a biomedical framework (Slade, Adams and O'Hagan 2012). Returning to Rose's (2007) concept of biological citizenship, recovery in this context has been framed as a disciplinary mechanism for self-management, with the role of practitioners being to promote service user understanding and control of clinical state.

The biomedical model has been described here as an 'umbrella' framework in mental health, which has incorporated and been strengthened by other central concepts. Underpinning these knowledge assemblages are political concerns around resource management and rationing. The way that risk and recovery have been interpreted through a biomedical lens supports a minimalist approach to mental health provision which relies on medication. In turn this helps manage the 'doing more with less' dilemma that public sector managers and frontline workers are faced with by converting it to 'doing less with less' (Hupe and Buffat 2014). Furthermore, diagnostic certainty, the foregrounding of scientific principles and 'evidence-based' approaches also manage political risks related to charges of (cost)efficiency and effectiveness. If services are restricted to particular approaches (based on particular knowledge claims) then this limits the choices practitioners have in formulating the best way forward for an individual. It can be argued that recent policy and associated service changes support this trend. The continuing dissolution of specialist intensive services such as Assertive Outreach and Early Intervention in Psychosis, the introduction of Community Treatment Orders[5] and the development of care clustering and 'payment by results'[6] are (re)ordering mental health provision in ways which support a 'flatpack' approach based on specific precepts and the construction of predicated packages of care. There is the potential for this to limit possibilities of discretion for *all* mental health practitioners, but turning to the horizontal integration of the biomedical model, it can be argued that some practitioners may be more constrained than others.

The Horizontal Integration of the Biomedical Model Through Professional Status

The horizontal integration of the biomedical model refers to its 'on the ground' implementation across mental health services, specifically through its relationship to professional status. The role of knowledge in mental health services is strongly related to the position of professions. The biopsychosocial model as developed by Engel (1980) presupposes a pluralistic and systemic approach to mental disorder and uses a broadly critical realist framework to explain the emergence of mental health problems in context. It has had variable influence over mental health provision but its impact may most clearly be seen in the development of multidisciplinary teams which account for medical, psychological and social perspectives (DoH 2005). Colombo (1997, in Bailey and Liyanage 2012: 1122) suggests that ideally this means 'professionals with different disciplinary backgrounds should together, be able to solve a range of complex problems through an open exchange of skills and ideas.'

However as Pilgrim (2002) notes, the existence of multidisciplinary or integrated mental health teams do not necessarily lead to a biopsychosocial orthodoxy being shared within such teams. Instead, mental health teams—which can contain psychiatrists, mental health nurses, occupational therapists, psychologists and social workers—may operate as a pragmatic and hierarchical arrangement of different professions with distinct and mutually tolerated approaches. In their study of models of mental disorder in practice, Colombo, Bendelow, Fulford and Williams (2003) found an explicit link between the models different professional groups drew upon in shared decision-making and their training and that these differences were ingrained by institutional structures which exacerbated struggles for professional recognition and authority. As noted earlier, psychiatry has long retained a prime position within mental health services, with allied health and social work professions holding lesser status. Certainly, critical social work literature has made the case that the social perspective in mental health is poorly served by the marginal place of social work in mental health services, due in part to mental health social workers having to operate between health and social care systems (Bailey and Liyanage 2012; Nathan and Webber 2010). Morriss (2017) goes as far as to say that mental health social workers are an 'invisible' profession, taking on liminal tasks that fill the gaps left by professions such as psychiatry which have more defined roles. For psychiatry, a strong and clearly boundaried position comes through the presence of both a long history within the health service and a socially respected 'canonical' knowledge base. Conversely, social work traditionally has drawn from a more nebulous body of knowledge and has struggled to gain a stable position within health settings. It has been suggested therefore that professional anxiety—being felt of as an 'interloper'—has led to mental health social workers at times adopting the biomedical model rather than challenging it or supplementing it with an explicitly social orientation. Nathan and Webber (2010: 21) point out the important role of language in this process, whereby social workers are 'replicating the work of their mental health colleagues using medical idioms such as "patients" and "diagnosis", [and] formulating their work in terms of "treatment" [...]'. On this basis, there are two subtly different narratives presented in the literature: the former where mental health professionals are in constant competition, with psychiatry retaining dominance and the latter where psychiatry has transformed other professions in its own image, most evidently through the use of shared 'technical' language which is aligned to the biomedical approach. In either case, the result is a 'sick role' being imposed on service users, which may limit the choices for professionals and service users alike (Colombo *et al.* 2003).

13.3 Knowledge and Discretion in Everyday Mental Health Practice

Having set out the argument for the perpetuated dominance of the biomedical model in mental health provision and its vertically and horizontally realized influence on the scope of practitioner action, what can be said about room for manoeuvre in mental health practice? The study that is drawn on here consists of an ethnography of everyday mental health practice within two Assertive Outreach Teams (AOTs), each situated within a different Mental Health Trust in England, which took place over a period of eight months. The premise of Assertive Outreach is to work with individuals who have complex needs and require on-going support, but who services have struggled to maintain contact with. Practitioners in AOTs work with individuals in their environment, meeting frequently over a sustained period of time and using a needs-focused approach (Sainsbury Centre 2001). The individuals who access AOTs typically have long histories of severe mental health difficulties, which have led to frequent contact with services—contact which is often compulsory in nature, involving enforced treatment in the hospital and the community. As AOTs mainly work with people who have some form of psychosis-related diagnosis, treatment often takes the form of neuroleptic medication, with injections being a common method of administration in order to assist compliance (Patel, Matonhodze, Baig, Gilleen, Boydell, Holloway, Taylor, Szmukler, Lambert, and David 2011). If we consider discretion beyond the professional sphere, service users of AOTs can have very little opportunity for discretion over their medication regime. Consequently, individuals, who AOTs work with, can be defined as continuously on the 'edge' of medicalized compulsion, both through legal means and more informal leverage. The study's aim was to develop a deeper understanding of this dynamic as it unfolded in practice.

Eighteen service users were tracked over time with attention paid to how individual, relational and contextual factors informed the pathways that they took through services. A range of methods were used to gain a full picture of both practitioners' and service users' thoughts and actions in context. These included observations of key meetings and everyday processes, interviews with practitioners from different professional backgrounds[7] and service users ($n = 36$ and 18 respectively) and document analysis of practice-related sources. Thematic and narrative analytical approaches were combined (Floersch, Longhofer, Kranke and Townsend 2010) in order to generate service user 'story-lines' which encompassed contextual, interpersonal and individual factors.[8] AOTs provide a germane setting in which to observe the interaction between knowledge and discretion, as the work practitioners carry out is inevitably medically oriented, but also involves the sustainment of long-standing relationships with individuals, based on an understanding of their lives and situations 'in the round'. The following sections build on the discussion in this chapter thus far by illustrating: how practitioners perceived constraints on their discretion; how they adapted discretionary activity based on synthesizing different forms of knowledge, especially ground-level knowledge derived from their relationships with service users; and how discretion intersected with the ways practitioners acted in respect of their role in the team, as well as their profession.

Practitioner Perspectives on Constraints to Discretion

As has been noted in Marston and Davidson's Chap. 7 of this edited collection, accounts of policy implementation often highlight the multiple ways that practitioners interpret and act on policy at 'street level', dependent on 'policy preferences' (May and Winter 2009) and localized factors. This study was no different, in that the perceived moral principles that underpinned Assertive Outreach work and the ensuing ethical challenges that could arise for practitioners when they felt these principles were compromised were commonly referred to within interviews. Indeed, discretion was talked about largely in terms of defending the space available for what practitioners defined as ethical practice. Assertive Outreach work was seen as highly skilled, with a distinction drawn between being *assertive* and *coercive* in engaging service users. As a psychiatrist put it, the work of an AOT revolves around finding the *currency that engages* service users on an individualized basis. Practitioners described the 'bread and butter' of AOT work being that of managing individuals deemed as high-level risk and dealing with on-going crises, whilst maintaining the relationships necessary to do this work. Accordingly, practitioners described becoming accustomed to working with incremental change and handling uncertainty when making decisions in complex situations. In this sense, practitioners could be critical of policy initiatives they believed did not recognize the place of theorizing, understanding and relating in mental health practice. Many of the practitioners in the study gave a critical commentary on what they saw as the gap between what they believed to be ethical practice and what was possible within policy and service constraints. As one social worker commented:

> With Payment by Results, people are clustered into a pigeon hole; this is your illness, this is your type, so therefore your care plan will be prescribed and it might be quite minimal and quite restrictive.

There is a reflection here of what was noted earlier in relation to biomedically informed policy mandates reducing the sphere of possibility for practitioners and service users together. Practitioners highlighted how medicalized approaches were often aligned with coercion, with a mental health nurse describing how the team could act like *social police* in ensuring control over medication for risk management purposes, even when circumstances might call for a 'wait and see' approach to an individual's mental health state. In this sense, practitioners held a critical awareness of the biomedical framework whilst operating within it and in particular sometimes treating compliance with medication as both a means and an end. A social worker summed up these tensions:

> Decisions to recall [to hospital for enforced treatment] are made much more around ensuring ongoing medical treatment than 'what is the current state at this time?' It's really difficult to ... say 'I want you to have control, I want you to recover at your pace, I want you to set your goals ... oh and by the way, if you don't stick to these conditions, we're going to whip you back into hospital, you're going to stay on this medication, you can't have a choice in what you take'. It just feels ... sometimes it feels a bit odd.

This illustrates the implicit logic of policy frameworks and the difficulties practitioners sometimes faced in contesting such logic, even when they felt differently and indeed had the capacity to act differently. Evans and Harris (2004) make the point that an increase in rules and bureaucracy can paradoxically lead to more space becoming available for practitioners to operate with discretion. These findings demonstrate that in a mirror of this, possessing latitude meant practitioners could feel their range of choices became restricted and consequently their ability to act with discretion limited, especially in the face of external pressures for defensive decision-making.

Plural Knowledge in Practice

It may seem then that the filtering down of a biomedical model through policy does mean that practitioners are drawn into relying on particular rationalities and approaches, even when they hold some critical distance to them. However, this would be to paint too simple a picture. The interactions between practitioners and their service users could also be exercises of mutuality and shared understanding. When this occurred, practitioners drew upon elements of co-production, which they contextualized within a recovery discourse. In this way, a conscious attempt was made by some practitioners to develop a more equal partnership in order to bring about change. Hacking (2004) describes how individuals can be 'made up' via interrelational work which then constitute 'looping effects' whereby those on the receiving end of classification (consciously or not) augment or adapt their classification and in turn the knowledge that is held about them. In this way, 'rationalities which govern strategic interactions are not [solely] the pre-existing properties of the different actors involved, but are an emergent dimension of ongoing interaction itself' (Barnett, Clarke, Cloke and Malpass 2008: 632). Certainly, service user participants described their difficulties in varied terms, which were often not biomedically aligned and were embedded in a broader perception of self and self in relation to others. One individual, for example, talked about their diagnosis in the following terms:

> I think schizoaffective disorder sums it up, because one thing affects another thing affects another thing, affects your family, affects your relationships, the fact that your family and relationships are affected affects you again and there's … there's social consequences to this … it's not just a medical thing.

Where practitioners engaged with service user self-perceptions, service users reported feeling that their motivations and behaviours were understood and responded to as if they were a whole person, rather than solely through a diagnostic lens. This in turn led to service users feeling able to be more honest about their experiences and to ask for support when necessary. Practitioners described this kind of work in humanistic terms, with this mental health nurse talking about her aim with one service user being to enable them to 'see' each other beyond surface 'professional' and 'service user' identities:

> Irene did allow me to visit, but it had to be very tentative. She didn't want me mentioning medication, she didn't want me mentioning illness and it was more about building relationships so … I gradually built up a relationship with her over maybe 6 months or so and it started to get easier. It becomes more of an interpersonal thing rather than 'I must comply, I must attend the reviews, I must do this'. Maybe when it becomes seeing me as a person it's more, 'Rebecca is coming, that's okay because I know her', rather than an agent of the hospital is coming to check up on me and get me if I don't comply.[9]

Making the space to conduct such work allowed this practitioner to operate with some leeway in shaping the path through services that the service user took. For service users who felt that practitioners did not make a connection beyond diagnosis, the cumulative effect on self-conception and a sense of autonomy could be deleterious, as it magnified their perceived status as an 'irregular citizen' (Zedner 2010). In particular the invocation of the phrase 'lack of insight'—which is often conflated with resistance to diagnosis and medication—could create distance between practitioners and service users and subsequently hamper the development of open communication and mutual goal-setting. As noted earlier, insight is often used in mental health as a kind of technical short-hand which loosely represents a body of scientific knowledge. As such, it can be difficult for service users to challenge. The discussion of insight in decision-making forums could make service users feel that practitioners were acting in ways which did not account for their unique situation, as this service user expresses:

> The doctor who put me on the Treatment Order, I'm very wary of him because he didn't seem to take into account anything I said. He seemed to sit there and already have an idea of what he was going to do and he was going to do it regardless. I think if I had had it explained to me more in detail what was it about my life which he felt needed this intervention I could've accepted it more.

Conversely, when practitioners took a more situational and critical approach, it appeared that they were able to express—and act with—uncertainty, thus generating more choices on how to exercise discretion. Drawing on different ways of 'knowing' an individual and accepting the tensions that exist between such knowledge, allowed practitioners to move away from dichotomous 'quick-fixes' and take a more fluid approach to judgements. This in turn, relies on negotiated trust, which operates via a feedback loop between practitioner stance and service user response (Evans 2007). Brown and Calnan (2012) argue that a false opposition between rationality and irrationality underpins current thinking on decision-making and that choosing to trust is a necessary and effective way of managing uncertainty. For practitioners, being dependent on service users' accounts meant to a certain extent taking a 'leap of faith', thus integrating 'formal' logic and intuitive sense in deciding the way forward. Practitioner discretion thus begets service user discretion, in, for example, positive risk-taking through the removal of legal mandates so that service users are given greater choice over medication and engagement with services. This could involve a decoupling of practitioner understanding and action, with practitioners not necessarily agreeing with service user formulations on their difficulties, but still recognizing these formulations and integrating them into plans, as summed up by a social worker when talking about next steps with a service user: *We might not have shared ideas about what's wrong ... but we can have shared goals for plans for the future.* The concept of recognition (Honneth 1996) emphasizes the relational dimension to justice; 'only mutual recognition that grants others the status of an epistemic authority allows us to construct a normative space of reasons' (Mattias 2013). In turn, incorporating lay normativity into everyday practice enabled practitioners and service users together to expand notions of risk and recovery beyond the reductionist ways they are defined via a biomedical lens.

Professions and Roles

This kind of considered work does not take place in a vacuum. As noted, practitioners might struggle to orientate themselves within resource constraints and to negotiate risk-averse policy frameworks and institutions. However, a key factor which enabled practitioners to exercise latitude in their approach was their position in relation to the other professionals they worked alongside. Greater freedom to take different approaches appeared to be associated with practitioners acting on the basis of their acquired role at a meso level within a service, as well as at a micro level as an individual professional. A shift in the policy framework from distinct professions working together in the mental health field, to the advent of a more generic 'mental health practitioner' model (DoH 2005) has caused consternation across different professional groups. These concerns have been expressed in terms of removing essential professional boundaries (Craddock, Antebi, Attenburrow, Bailey, Carson, Cowen, *et al.* 2008) and subsuming all professionals in the same biomedicalized identity (Nathan and Webber 2010). However, the experiences of practitioners in this study belied these predictions. Observations of practice highlighted how role-based working can reduce power differentials and enable a more eclectic approach to the use of knowledge in practice. Greater autonomy seemed to come from the addition of an extra 'layer' to practitioner identity; operating within a professional *and* organizational role capacity appeared to diminish the strength of discrete professional norms in mediating practitioner approaches. In particular the role of care coordinator—which can be taken by mental health nurses, social workers and occupational therapists—demonstrated practitioners sharing a pluralistic perspective and approach regardless of professional background. Bailey and Liyanage (2012: 1127) reported similar findings, with practitioners in their study describing a shared and synthesized knowledge base via care coordination that meant 'professional boundaries are transcended and service user-focused care is the norm rather than the exception.'

Care coordinators carry out much of the day-to-day work with service users and are consequently the practitioners who are able to draw on in-depth knowledge of the service users in their case-load to inform decisions. This means that even though care coordinators do not have a formal role in legal decision-making, they still possess significant 'informal' power. By drawing on varied forms of knowledge, including an understanding of the individuals they worked with, care coordinators in the study were able to shape the parameters of practice. This was most often through playing a consultative part, as this mental health nurse describes when talking about decision-making on whether compulsory community treatment should be used: *So, if the AMHP asks me, 'no I don't think they should be on a community treatment order', if the psychiatrist asks me, 'I don't think they should be on a community treatment order'. And the likelihood is by me saying that they probably wouldn't.* Care coordinators also described being the mediator and advocate in treatment decisions on behalf of service users:

> I've always advocated for her, so I thought, this will either go one way or the other. If she does get a reduction [in medication] and it doesn't go right we're going to be back where we started but I'm going to have to show her that I trust her, how she feels and what she's saying to me. So I managed to talk the doctor into reducing it and after that she's been alright (Mental health nurse).

It also should be noted that assumptions about practitioners being aligned with the knowledge framework most redolent of their profession do not always reflect the realities of practice. The part that personalities played in the development of team cultures meant there was significant variation in how practitioners conceptualized and responded to service users' situations. For example, AMHPs (all of whom were social workers) were at times observed as the practitioners who advocated for medical treatment the most, with a mental health nurse describing *old school social work*ers as taking a paternalistic approach to medicalized control for *the good of the client.* Similarly, psychiatrists could at times be the professionals who were more willing to let events unfold and to resist requests by other professionals for them to use their authority to mandate treatment, as this psychiatrist commented: *my personal view is that care coordinators are usually too risk averse ... they are usually more cautious ... possibly for good reason, they know the patient better than I do.* It seems then that professional power could be bifurcated by organizational role and that accepted accounts of professional knowledge bases do not account for the variability of value judgements in everyday practice.

13.4 Conclusion

John Stuart Mill (1863: 23) said that 'it is [...] the complicated nature of human affairs, that rules of conduct cannot be so framed as to require no exceptions, and that hardly any kind of action can safely be laid down as either always obligatory or always condemnable'. The complexity of everyday practice in mental health provision requires an analysis of discretion that goes beyond understanding how decision-making operates within the framework of mental health law. Indeed, moral perplexity (Gibson 2003)—the lack of settled principles for dealing with a case—makes for a good starting point in considering how practitioners think, justify and go about their work. It is evident from the findings presented in this chapter that the significant degree of 'granted discretion' (Hupe 2013) in mental health practice leads to large variability in the use of discretion. At the same time, it should be acknowledged that knowledge frameworks can often act as implicit drivers within granted discretion, which generate institutionalized and internalized constraints on practitioner latitude. In mental health services, this is most clearly seen when the biomedical model is conjoined with policy frameworks and service models that support rationalization and resource management. Hupe and Buffat (2014: 554) argue that 'in most street-level bureaucracy studies, the nature of the macro-institutional setting involved and the impact of specific institutional factors are ignored.' The study referred to in this chapter cannot claim to be the thorough and comparative analysis they call for—indeed it is weighted towards 'micro' analysis. However, by sketching out the vertical and 'downwards' influence of biomedical knowledge on practice, the chapter has also highlighted the ethical tensions involved for practitioners who may be expected to do 'less with less' whilst still adhering to the tenets of risk management and recovery. As Brodkin (1997:

24) puts it, regardless of individual practitioner beliefs, 'caseworkers, like other lower-level bureaucrats, do not do just what they want or just what they are told to want. They do what they can'.

With that in mind, practitioners 'doing what they can' in the context of mental health services can still involve—and indeed given the nature of the work has to involve—operating with a certain amount of leeway and drawing on a spectrum of knowledge frameworks. For the majority of service users, the relational work they undertake with practitioners will be central to both maintaining stability and making positive change. It follows that accounting for service user mindedness and subjectivity is central to practitioner judgements, with service users and practitioners evolving and constituting their responses to each other together over time. The role of the service user thus brings with it a 'ground-up' dimension to discretion, which can combine with 'top-down' influences such as the biomedical model to shape practitioner action. The space necessary for this kind of approach is derived at least in part from the interplay between organizational role and professional role in mental health services. The kinds of tasks associated with roles such as care coordinator can make it possible for practitioners to 'step outside' professionally aligned knowledge frameworks; (see the tendency towards 'personalization' Needham describes in Chap. 19 of this edited collection). Furthermore, the relationship between power and professional standing may be inverted, as the kinds of knowledge generated through 'close-up' day-to-day work gives these practitioners informal yet influential sway in decision-making chains. The ability to act with discretion is often linked to professional status and associated claims to expertise, which in turn is based on well-defined bodies of knowledge. An analysis of roles rather than professions suggests that a differentiated construction of expertise can be called upon to support discretionary activity within the organizational context of mental health services. Whether this remains the case as mental health services—like other public services—continue to evolve their organizational structure to meet fiscal challenges is an open question.

Notes

1. For readers from outside the UK, it is worth noting that although there is a broadly similar basis for the use of mental health law across the UK, there is also regional differentiation. The legal framework for England and Wales is the Mental Health Act (1983, amended in 2007); for Scotland it is the Mental Health (Care and Treatment) (Scotland) Act (2003, amended in 2015); and for Northern Ireland it is the Mental Health (Northern Ireland) Order (1986). This chapter focuses on mental health provision in England and therefore further references to mental health law are to the framework for England and Wales.
2. Defined as 'any disorder of disability of the mind' as determined by relevant mental health professionals.
3. The role of the AMHP is usually taken by social workers (Mackay 2012), despite the Mental Health Act (2007) opening up the role to other allied mental health professionals (with the exclusion of psychiatrists to ensure the role remains

non-medical). To become an AMHP, mental health professionals must complete specialist training in mental health law.

4. The first Diagnostic Statistical Manual of Mental Disorders was published in 1952 by the American Psychiatric Association. It should be noted that it reflected both psychodynamic and biomedical frameworks, with the former being gradually superseded in later versions. Despite the USA now being at the forefront of biological psychiatry, psychodynamic approaches were more influential in American psychiatry than in the UK during the early to mid-twentieth century, and remained so for a longer period of time. There was significant scepticism towards psychodynamic approaches within the British psychiatry community (Tyrer and Craddock 2012).
5. Community Treatment Orders were enacted under the Mental Health Act (2007) and work by imposing conditions that clients have to adhere to (usually medication compliance) or face being recalled to hospital for enforced treatment.
6. Payment by Results (now called Mental Health Payment Systems) was introduced to UK mental health services in 2012. Essentially Payment by Results is a commissioning and service provision system where provider organizations are paid according to their ability to meet certain pre-determined outcomes. In mental health services, this entailed separating service users into 1 of 21 'care clusters', differentiated by diagnosis and level of need, for example, 'ongoing psychosis with high disability'. Each cluster has an associated care package and tariff which is paid to the provider per service user.
7. Including mental health nurses, social workers, occupational therapists and psychiatrists.
8. For a more detailed description of methodology, including selection, analysis and ethical issues/approval, see Jobling (2014).
9. Where names are used, they are pseudonyms.

References

Bailey, D. & Liyanage, L. (2012). The role of the mental health social worker: Political pawns in the reconfiguration of adult health and social care. *British Journal of Social Work*, 42, 1113–1131.

Barnett, C., Clarke, N., Cloke, P. & Malpass, A. (2008). The elusive subjects of neo-liberalism. *Cultural Studies*, 22(5), 624–653.

Bonney, S. & Stickley, T. (2008). Recovery and mental health: A review of the British literature. *Journal of Psychiatric and Mental Health Nursing*, 15, 140–153.

Bucknill, J.C. (1856). The diagnosis of insanity. *Journal of Asylum*, 2, 229–245.

Brown, P. & Calnan, M. (2012). *Trusting on the edge: Managing uncertainty and vulnerability in the midst of serious mental health problems*. Bristol: Policy Press.

Brodkin, E.Z. (1997). Inside the welfare contract: Discretion and accountability in state welfare administration. *Social Service Review*, 71(1), 1–33.

Colombo, A., Bendelow, G., Fulford, B. & Williams, S. (2003). Evaluating the influence of implicit models of mental disorder on processes of shared decision making within community-based multi-disciplinary teams. *Social Science and Medicine*, 56, 1557–1570.

Craddock, N., Antebi, D., Attenburrow, M.J., Bailey, A., Carson, P., Cowen, P. *et al.* (2008). Wake-up call for British psychiatry. *British Journal of Psychiatry*, 193, 6–9.

Dean, M. (2010). *Governmentality: Power and rule in modern society* (2nd ed.). London: Sage.
Department of Health (2005). *New ways of working for psychiatrists: Enhancing effective, person-centred services through new ways of working in multidisciplinary and multiagency contexts.* London: Department of Health.
Domino, M.E. & Swartz, M.S. (2008). Who are the new users of antipsychotic medications? *Psychiatric Services*, 59(5), 507–514.
Engel, G.L. (1980). The clinical application of the biopsychosocial model. *American Journal of Psychiatry*, 137, 535–544.
Evans, T. (2007). Confidentiality in mental health services. A negotiated order? *Qualitative Social Work*, 6(2), 213–229.
Evans, T. & Harris, J. (2004). Street-level bureaucracy, social work and the (exaggerated) death of discretion, *British Journal of Social Work*, 34(6), 871–895.
Floersch, J., Longhofer, J., Kranke, D. & Townsend, L. (2010). Integrating thematic, grounded theory and narrative analysis: A case study of adolescent psychotropic treatment. *Qualitative Social Work*, 9(3), 407–425.
Foucault, M. (1977). *Discipline and punish: The birth of the prison.* New York: Pantheon.
Gibson, K. (2003). Contrasting role morality and professional morality: Implications for practice. *Journal of Applied Philosophy*, 20(1), 17–29.
Hacking, I. (2004). Between Michel Foucault and Erving Goffman: Between discourse in the abstract and face-to-face interaction. *Economy and Society*, 33(3), 277–302.
Herrman, H. & Harvey, C. (2005). Community care for people with psychosis: Outcomes and needs for care. *International Review of Psychiatry*, 17(2), 89–95.
Honneth, A. (1996). *The struggle for recognition: The moral grammar of social conflicts.* Cambridge, MA: MIT Press.
Hupe, P.L. (2013). Dimensions of discretion: Specifying the object of street-level bureaucracy research. *Der moderne Staat: Zeitschrift für Public Policy, Recht und Management*, 6, 425–440.
Hupe, P.L. & Buffat, A. (2014). A public service gap: Capturing contexts in a comparative approach of street-level bureaucracy. *Public Management Review*, 16(4), 548–569.
Jobling, H. (2014). Using ethnography to explore causality in mental health policy and practice. *Qualitative Social Work*, 13(1), 49–68.
Katsakou, C. & Priebe, S. (2007). Patient's experiences of involuntary hospital admission and treatment: A review of qualitative studies. *Epidemiologia e Psichiatria Sociale*, 16(2), 172–178.
Laing, J. (2004). Peay: Decisions and dilemmas: Working with mental health law. *The Modern Law Review*, 67, 869–871.
Lester, H. & Glasby, J. (2006). *Mental health: Policy and practice.* London: Palgrave.
Mackay, K. (2012). A parting of the ways? The diverging nature of mental health social work in the lights of the new Acts in Scotland, and in England and Wales. *Journal of Social Work*, 12, 179–193.
Mattias, I. (2013). Recognition. In *The Stanford Encyclopedia of Philosophy.* Retrieved from https://plato.stanford.edu/entries/recognition/.
May, P.J. & Winter, S.C. (2009). Politicians, Managers, and Street-Level Bureaucrats: Influences on Policy Implementation. *Journal of Public Administration Research and Theory*, 19(3), 453–476.
Mill, J.S. (1863). *Utilitarianism.* London: Parker, Son and Bourn.
Mountain, D. & Shah, P.J. (2008). Recovery and the medical model. *Advances in Psychiatric Treatment*, 14, 241–244.

Morriss, L. (2017). Being seconded to a mental health trust: The (in)visibility of mental health social work. *British Journal of Social Work*, 47, 1344–1360.

Nathan, J. & Webber, M. (2010). Mental health social work and the bureau-medicalisation of mental health care: Identity in a changing world. *Journal of Social Work Practice*, 24(1), 15–28.

Patel, M.X., Matonhodze, J., Baig, M.K., Gilleen, J., Boydell, J., Holloway, F., Taylor, D.M., Szmukler, G., Lambert, T. & David, A. (2011). Increased use of antipsychotic long-acting injections with community treatment orders. *Therapeutic Advances in Psychopharmacology*, 1(2), 37–45.

Peay, J. (2003). *Decisions and dilemmas: Working with mental health law*. Oxford: Hart Publishing.

Pilgrim, D. (2002). The biopsychosocial model in Anglo-American psychiatry: Past, present and future? *Journal of Mental Health*, 11(6), 585–594.

Pilgrim, D. & Rogers, A. (2009). Survival and its discontents: The case of British psychiatry. *Sociology Of Health & Illness*, 31(7), 947–961.

Porter, R. (1987). *Mind-forg'd manacles: A history of madness in England from the Restoration to the Regency*. Cambridge, MA: Harvard University Press.

Read, J., Bentall, R.P. & Fosse, R. (2009). Time to abandon the bio-bio-bio model of psychosis: Exploring the epigenetic and psychological mechanisms by which adverse life events lead to psychotic symptoms. *Epidemiologia e Psichiatria Sociale*, 18(4), 299–310.

Rose, N. (2007). *The politics of life itself: Biomedicine, power, and subjectivity in the twenty-first century*. Princeton, NJ: Princeton University Press.

Sainsbury Centre for Mental Health. (2001). *Mental Health Topics. Assertive Outreach*. London: Sainsbury Centre for Mental Health.

Schomerus, G., Schwahn, C., Holzinger, A., Corrigan, P.W., Grabe, H.J., Carta, M.G. & Angermeyer, M.C. (2012). Evolution of public attitudes about mental illness: A systematic review and meta-analysis. *Acta Psychiatrica Scandinavica*, 125, 440–452

Schramme, T. (2013). On the autonomy of the concept of disease in psychiatry. *Frontiers in Psychology*, 4, 1–9.

Scull, A. (1979). *Museums of madness: The social organization of insanity in nineteenth-century England*. London: Allen Lane.

Slade, M., Adams, N. & O'Hagan, M. (2012). Recovery: Past progress and future challenges. *International Review of Psychiatry*, 24(1), 1–4.

Tew, J. (2011). *Social approaches to mental distress*. London: Palgrave.

Thornton, T. & Lucas, P. (2011). On the very idea of a recovery model for mental health. *Journal of Medical Ethics*, 37(1), 24–28.

Tyrer, P. & Craddock, N. (2012). The bicentennial volume of the *British Journal of Psychiatry*: The winding pathway of mental science. *British Journal of Psychiatry*, 200, 104.

Zedner, L. (2010). Security, the state, and the citizen: The changing architecture of crime control. *New Criminal Law Review*, 13, 379–403.

PART III

Discretion in Governance

CHAPTER 14

Discretion in Governance: An Introduction

Peter Hupe and Tony Evans

14.1 Introduction

Discretion is a generic and ubiquitous phenomenon. Perhaps in the most obvious way it is prevalent in the practice of governing. The theme of the third part of this interdisciplinary edited collection is discretion in governance. In the first three of the following chapters discretion is pictured in relation to some key elements of governance: bureaucracy as the institutional bedding; the policy process as 'path' for the directional part of governing and street-level practice as the locus of interactions with citizens where policy intentions ultimately are being shaped. The other three chapters of this part of the edited collection focus on important aspects of discretion in governance which so far have remained relatively understudied, headed as organized discretion, managerial discretion and automated discretion.

Making a case for bureaucracy, Paul du Gay and Kirstine Zinck Pedersen argue that discretion is intrinsic to public office (Chap. 15). Peter Hupe and Michael Hill show that the content of a public policy is stemming from various actors. A plurality of discretionary actors has been granted a mandate to implement the policy, while discretion may be exercised even beyond formal hierarchy (Chap. 16). Hendrik Wagenaar zooms in on the practice of such 'implementation' at the street level of public administration (Chap. 17). Suzanne Rutz and Antoinette de Bont point out that discretion may be granted as well as used in collective forms (Chap. 18). Catherine Needham shows how the phenomenon of personalization not only turns citizen-clients

P. Hupe (✉)
Public Governance Institute, Catholic University of Leuven, Leuven, Belgium
e-mail: pieter.hupe@kuleuven.be

T. Evans
Department of Social Work, Royal Holloway, University of London, Egham, UK
e-mail: Tony.Evans@rhul.ac.uk

T. Evans, P. Hupe (eds.), *Discretion and the Quest for Controlled Freedom*, https://doi.org/10.1007/978-3-030-19566-3_14

into co-producers of public services but also has consequences for managerial discretion (Chap. 19). And, finally, Stavros Zouridis, Marlies van Eck and Mark Bovens demonstrate the consequences of the ongoing development of information technology for discretion in public service delivery (Chap. 20).

14.2 Discretion and Bureaucracy

Paul du Gay and Kirstine Zinck Pedersen argue that discretion should be seen as both an inevitable and potentially highly beneficial feature of bureaucratic organization. The chapter starts with an exposition of 'the customary view' of bureaucracy. In that view, bureaucracy is associated with rule-bound inflexibility and a lack of unresponsiveness, fundamentally constraining the freedom of both public servants and the public they serve. Following Max Weber and Charles Perrow, the authors characterize this 'customary view' of bureaucracy and the relationship of bureaucracy and discretion expressed in it, as misleading.

While misleading, the view is at the basis of a widespread dichotomy between bureaucracy and discretion, as well as between bureaucracy and professionalism. Managerial reforms like those headed under the label of *New Public Management* often are identified with bureaucracy as opposed to professionalism. With professionals subjected to external rules and constraints instead of autonomous actors able to define their own conditions of work, professionalism then is cherished as a kind of resistance against bureaucratic control. A conflict between professional values and bureaucratic ones is presupposed, with discretionary freedom placed opposite of bureaucratic rigidity. However, much of the current control systems ('a tick-box mentality') is thoroughly anti-bureaucratic in nature when compared with Weber's classic account. After all, the Weberian stance acknowledges the inseparability of discretion and bureaucracy, while expressing the necessity of situation-specific judgement.

Like the *bureaucrat*, the *professional* is an office-holder. Professional discretion is closely connected to clear lines of authority, division of labour and equal treatment. The professional's discretionary capabilities are inseparably linked to the establishment of well-defined distribution of responsibilities and obligations through a system of offices, as well as a high degree of formalization and rule-based conduct. This means bureaucracy and professionalism have much in common. With both, discretion is seen as the exercise of casuistical, prudential judgement. Resolving indeterminacies inherent to the work concerned is not simply a technical matter; it requires public servants to prioritize certain values and interests over others—like professionals do. Hence, both exercise considerable discretion.

14.3 Discretion in the Policy Process

Peter Hupe and Michael Hill focus on discretion within the policy process. In many statements about discretion in governance, it is seen as stemming from a single source at the top of the hierarchy implied by the system of public administration. In connection to this supposition, discretion is also often seen as exclusively located and exercised at the bottom of that hierarchy; that is, in rule application at the street level.

In this chapter both suppositions are challenged. First, it is argued that the content of a public policy stems from a range of actors. A public policy therefore has a multiple character. Second, there are various *loci* where a plurality of actors exercise discretion. In other words, in a policy process there are many input producers and there are many inputs, which at the street level all function as 'action prescriptions' to reckon with.

Hence, when discretion is apparent, indeed a message is conveyed to exercise judgement while having the freedom to decide what to do, but there are two qualifying conditions. The first one is that this message may have multiple senders rather than a single one. Behind a policy statute much politics has been going on, implying a variety of views about what this policy means. In its implementation, this leads to less clarity about what exactly *the policy* entails. The other qualification is that the act of conveying can be performed from both horizontal and vertical directions. Therefore, at many spots in the policy process forces are working in ways which cannot easily be controlled by a single actor at the top.

It is important to recognize the institutional context in which discretion in public policy processes emerges. In most cases discretion will be formally mandated and delegated within a 'system of discretion'. Delegated legislation implies that an initial legislative act gives power to public officials to take further steps to translate it into action and that the exercise of those powers may create rules that define the discretionary powers of others. Hence, public policies may, in a more or less programmed way, be 'vertically co-produced' on the various layers of the system of public administration concerned.

Not all policies however are implemented within such a formal *hierarchy of discretions.* Discretionary powers may also be the less formal resultant of discretion exercised by other actors involved in the policy process concerned. This is the case, for instance, in situations of 'horizontal co-production' when citizen-clients are acknowledged in their role as contributors to the delivery of public services. This being so, also more in general, street-level tasks have a certain degree of indeterminacy. Even if there are relatively explicit tasks at stake, how and where they are to be performed depend on judgements—not in the least about the use of scarce resources. These are all reasons why the (varying) clarity of the mandates provided to street-level officials is important but not exclusively conclusive—implying further limits to absolute control.

14.4 Discretion and Street-Level Practice

Hendrik Wagenaar wants to know how the discretionary part of decentred administrative actions is shaped. Organizational routines, standard operating procedures and software architecture clearly are important, but they do not fully explain how public administration works. Aiming at the latter, Wagenaar offers the *practice approach* to administrative discretion.

The chapter starts with an exposition of the received view of administrative discretion. In that view, administrative discretion is considered the result of the individual's personal judgement to stick or deviate from the rules. As therefore deemed subjective, discretionary behaviour is regarded as a risk. The risk concerns cutting the relation with formal law, undermining the formal accountability dimension of public administration and, by consequence, hollowing out the legitimacy of the state within a democratic order.

This received view has a great intuitive appeal and normative power. Yet, the normative hold that this view has over academic and legal thinking about discretion, obscures its limited explanatory capacity. Discretion is not a deviation from the rules. It is inevitable and identical with the everyday administrative work of applying rules and of making formal rules work in the real world.

Wagenaar conceptualizes discretionary behaviour in terms of *practice*. Rules may be prescribed but they do not determine behaviour. Rules and their 'application' are part of the same practice. All administrative behaviour, including what appears to be the meticulous application of rules, is forged in the craft of practice. While open-ended and improvisational, that behaviour is neither arbitrary nor rule-less.

Grounding his *practice approach* on insights on rules and rule-following as developed by Ludwig Wittgenstein, Charles Taylor and other twentieth-century philosophers, Wagenaar challenges the assumptions underlying the received view of administrative work and administrative discretion as its corollary. In his alternative conceptualization, elements like practical judgements, the everyday routines, as well as tacit knowledge are central. In large administrative bureaucracies all these are mobilized towards mastering difficult human–emotional situations.

Wagenaar presents the case of a Dutch welfare officer who dispenses welfare benefits to the homeless, illustrating the argument unfolded in the chapter. An oral narrative analysis is given, illuminating the craft of navigating the complexities of the welfare programme concerned. He concludes that street-level practice, when properly organized, is the optimal way of safeguarding the democratic legitimacy of public administration.

14.5 Organized Discretion

Suzanne Rutz and Annette de Bont observe that the exercise of discretionary judgement in governance is increasingly being organized in teams or networks. To approach this new reality, they introduce a differentiation of the concept of discretion which captures those collective dimensions.

In the literature on street-level bureaucracy, discretionary judgement is seen as related to individual workers. As indicated in the introductory chapter and shown throughout this edited collection, discretion can be localized between the extremes of complete freedom and total control. The freedom to decide how to act is circumscribed by policymakers higher up in the system of public administration who define the worker's room for manoeuvre in rules, while the use of that freedom is controlled by managers.

Adopting Hupe's (2013) distinction between discretion-as-used and discretion-as-granted substantively, the authors specify it while suggesting different labels. With discretionary judgement as overarching concept in an individual and collective variant, they use the term *discretion* for discretion-as-used and *discretionary room* for discretion-as-granted. Collective discretionary room then is the freedom afforded to a team or a network to set the rules with which they can make a difference for citizen-clients. When discretionary room is made a collective resource, that fact changes the aim of afforded freedom from being responsive in individual situations, to improving policy designs and outcomes. At the same time this also offers more mechanisms for control; after all, workers may act outside the purview of managers and policymakers higher up.

Rutz and de Bont give an illustration of collective discretionary room by highlighting some of their empirical work done at the Joint Inspectorate Social Domain, a partnership of government inspectorates in the Netherlands. Their research shows how collective discretionary room as an organizational form highly determines how workers act. Teams carry responsibility for their joint judgements. They have to decide how to use their expertise and options, when to involve their managers and when to involve people from other organizations to broaden their repertoire. Hence, the work of teams is nested in a network of actors. The work of teams is also nested in a set of rules, which mainly entail decision-making processes that inspectors have to follow. Inspectors have the freedom within these boundaries to improve rules aimed at structuring the outcomes of decision-making.

In this way, the authors provide a differentiated conceptualization with which the involvement of others in discretionary judgement can be specified. While in the case of 'collective discretion' the involvement of others depends on the initiative of individual workers, in a situation of 'collective discretionary room' such involvement is organized. In both cases, the range of expertise, perspectives and options to take action that workers can draw on is broadened. Cooperation makes the additional information, values and interests and options to take action, available to all workers. Moreover, while it offers teams of workers the freedom to act, collective discretionary room also offers mechanisms to control and enhance the quality of the work concerned.

14.6 Managerial Discretion

Catherine Needham explores managerial discretion while particularly positioning it in the context of a move towards enhancing the 'person-centredness' of public services. Consumerist trends have led to the emergence of new norms of public service in which the dispositions and preferences of *the person* have become the focal point. In the UK, 'personalization' has shaped approaches to reform in the NHS, children's services, education, employment, housing and criminal justice. While the rhetoric flourishes, the question is how the new interplay between citizen-clients, service professionals and their managers works out. In particular, what does putting-the-person-central mean for discretion of the latter?

Needham focuses on three aspects of person-centredness as illustrative of new dilemmas relating to managerial discretion. The first aspect concerns the emergence of citizens as expert decision-makers and even budget holders. In policy settings in which the people who use services are considered to be experts, decision-making and discretion are relocated beyond the frontline. Personal health budgets, for instance, may be welcomed by the clients concerned as improving their situation, but professionals and managers may share an interest to avoid being blamed for the poor choices of users. They see their discretion reduced as more decision-making is devolved to the patient and user of care services. On the other hand, individual managers and professionals may also see their discretion enhanced, where the introduction of the person using services, as a 'third actor', may imply that they must sign off on user choices which do not fit into existing service options. In any case, when user preferences are privileged over both professional discretion and managerial authority, the position and role of managers are reframed.

Another aspect of the meta-policy of personalization is the pressure for more 'whole person' ways of working with citizens, requiring collaboration across service boundaries. This may get the form of multidisciplinary teams or lead professionals to support people with complex needs across care, health, employment and housing. A contrasting development has been the growth of 'one stop shops' on a call centre model. These are designed to support citizens with a range of issues through a protocol driven approach. Customer relationship management tools enable the profiling of callers so that support can be tailored to the caller—an algorithmic version of person-centredness. In both cases, frontline and managerial discretion may be minimal.

A final aspect of person-centredness concerns the rise of attention to the managerial self. In their work contacts with staff as well as—via social media—the public, managers are expected to share more of themselves. They should become more 'authentic' managers. Here then is a requirement for managers to exercise discretion in new ways, with rules and norms still in flux. Particularly the public nature of the interaction with the public via Twitter and other social media implies potentially high risks if the content is considered inappropriate. In the exercise of discretion, it creates new sorts of dilemmas for managers.

The legitimacy of a 'one size fits all' welfare state has vanished, Needham concludes. Person-centredness has become a characteristic of welfare reform across advanced democracies. Assertive citizens demand public services 'made to measure', while the technological possibilities enable such individually tailored services. The rise of a customer care ethos within public services can be seen as a shift from rule-following to the optimizing of outcomes for customers. As far as such a shift implies that services become more flexible and tailored to individuals, it may expand the scope for discretion. However, it is not necessarily managers that may see their discretion enhanced then.

14.7 Automated Discretion

Stavros Zouridis, Marlies van Eck and Mark Bovens observe that the use of information technology (IT) has caused the discretionary freedom within large-scale public executive organizations to shift from professional case managers to programmers and data analysts. This is particularly true of the 'decision factories', those large-scale bureaucracies that routinely make decisions on social benefits, licences, tax returns, fines, subsidies and permits. The same shift however can also be observed in law enforcement organizations. While such organizations formerly were approached as *street-level* bureaucracies, nowadays they are more properly understood as *system-level* bureaucracies.

This chapter describes how information technology has transformed large executive organizations into system-level bureaucracies. In the latter, the discretionary powers of the street-level professionals have been disciplined by digital systems. The locus of administrative discretion has shifted to those responsible for programming the decision-making process and translating the legislation into software.

When information technology was less developed, employees entered forms—pre-structured with text blocks—into the automated system and checked the decisions that the system spitted out. Later on, algorithms were developed for the decision-making process and included in the system as a tool for the professional. Those were the days of *screen-level* bureaucracy. Professionals became administrative screen-level bureaucrats. Now, however, we have entered the era of the *system* bureaucracy.

The introduction of decision-making systems has fundamentally changed this type of bureaucracy. No longer do the street-level bureaucrats form the core of the organization but, instead, those who build and refine the systems. One could say the latter have become the *new street-level bureaucrats*—although they never see an individual case. The management of the organization no longer primarily revolves around the legitimate processing of applications, but around the management of 'production'.

Zouridis, van Eck and Bovens distinguish three developments in system-level practice. In the first place, system-level bureaucracy has further expanded in scope and can now be observed in various fields. Most striking is the further extension of inter-organizational chains of system-level bureaucracies. In the chapter two cases are used to highlight how this works. One case has to do with establishing the right to and payment of child benefits by the Social Insurance Bank in the Netherlands; the other relates to establishing a citizen's taxable income and the corresponding assessment from the tax authorities. In the operational practice of the digitally connected organizations concerned, the computer makes most individual decisions.

A second development regards the phenomenon of self-organizing teams of IT engineers who continually make proposals on the implementation of smaller applications and links, about which the management next decides. In contrast to the large, managerial driven IT projects, this 'bricolage' approach, with software engineers at the wheel, is characterized by bottom-up ad-hoc software development. The third development is the rise of a new profession: data professionals. While the discretion of the IT developers has been expanded to the exchange of data in 'chains', in today's system-level bureaucracy there is another group of IT experts with considerable discretionary leeway: the data analysts.

The rise of system-level bureaucracies has replaced traditional professional routines by algorithms. In many respects, the authors claim straightforwardly, this has made the operation of these large production agencies more equitable and efficient. The processing of cases has become much faster and requires far less paperwork. Prejudices and biases of individual street-level bureaucrats no longer play a role in the allocation of public benefits.

What does this mean for discretion? In system-level bureaucracies, discretion does not result from scarcity and ambiguous standards. Rather, discretion is localized in operationalizing standards in parametrized variables in IT systems and in the use of software to manage administrative processes. No longer are the frontline professionals the ones with the power of discretion; this has shifted to the IT developers.

The authors hence sketch the reality of 'data chains', 'bricolage' by software engineers and data professionals exercising unforeseen discretion, as generic phenomena. While they picture an overall historical trend seen as sustained and inescapable, they are clear about the future: certainly, in the longer run—although not everywhere at the same pace, they add—the discretion exercised when making individual decisions relating to public administration is doomed. At the same time they acknowledge that these developments raise several novel normative concerns; the new types of discretion need matching modes of constraining and standardizing them. To what extent such new types of checks will be created and can be expected to be effective, remains open.

Reference

Hupe, P.L. (2013). Dimensions of discretion: Specifying the object of street-level bureaucracy research. *Der Moderne Staat. Zeitschrift für Public Policy, Recht und Public Administration*, 82(2), 279–299.

CHAPTER 15

Discretion and Bureaucracy

Paul du Gay and Kirstine Zinck Pedersen

15.1 Introduction

The place of discretion in formal organizations has shadowed discussions of bureaucracy in the social sciences since their inception. It has also played a significant role in debates about the reform of any number of areas of formally organized existence in public, private and, indeed, not-for-profit sectors.

What can be termed, following the organizational sociologist Charles Perrow (1972 [2014]), 'the customary view' of bureaucracy has carried and continues to carry enormous weight in the social sciences, not least in sociology, public administration and organization studies. Perrow noted that bureaucracy has largely been negatively coded and that many of the same criticisms of bureaucracy appear time and time again throughout the history of the social sciences. He pointed, in particular, to two enduring lines of criticism. The first associates bureaucracy with rule-bound inflexibility, inefficiency and, at times of rapid environmental change, with a lack of creativity and a pervasive unresponsiveness. The second, which he associates specifically with the humanistic tradition in sociology, represents bureaucracy as stifling the spontaneity, freedom and self-realization of those in its employ. Perrow noted too, that both lines of criticism are often combined by a single author and 'are echoed by such diverse groups as the radical right, the radical left, the man (*sic*) in the street, and the counterculture' (2014: 6).

This 'customary view' of bureaucracy is also based on a dichotomizing stance towards the relationship between discretion and bureaucracy. Discretionary capabilities and judgemental freedom then are often represented

P. du Gay (✉) • K. Z. Pedersen
Department of Organization (IOA), Copenhagen Business School, Frederiksberg, Denmark
e-mail: pdg.ioa@cbs.dk; kzp.ioa@cbs.dk

T. Evans, P. Hupe (eds.), *Discretion and the Quest for Controlled Freedom*, https://doi.org/10.1007/978-3-030-19566-3_15

as antithetical to bureaucratic attributes such as hierarchy, office-holding, formalization, rules and clear delineations of obligations and duties. What follows from this widespread dichotomy are some simplistic definitions of organizations and types of organizing based on either a routine/non-routine divide or a control/freedom distinction (or both). Hence it is argued that bureaucracy as an organizational form is only viable and efficient when tasks are predictable, repetitive and routine, whereas organizations that are in need of swift action, creative problem solving and expert decisions are difficult or near impossible to bureaucratize (Perrow 2014).

After many years of studying formal organization, Perrow concluded that, despite its enduring popularity and reach, the 'customary view' of bureaucracy and, not least, the relationship of bureaucracy and discretion it expresses, is very misleading. In particular, Perrow offered a reassessment of Max Weber's work on bureaucracy. In so doing, he indicated that contrary to the interpretation of his work offered by the 'customary view', Weber's stance towards bureaucracy was based on no such distinction between bureaucracy and discretion. Rather it demonstrated the impossibility of substituting an evaluatively neutral administrative science comprising universally valid rules of behaviour for the bureaucrat's practical judgement, in which questions of ends and means are inevitably intertwined (Storing 1998; du Gay 2000; Goodsell 2015; Zacka 2017).

Following Weber and Perrow, in this chapter we argue that discretion should be seen not only as an inevitable but also a potentially highly beneficial feature of bureaucratic organization, properly understood. Taking a Weberian 'stance' on bureaucracy as intrinsically connected with discretion, expertise, practical judgement and casuistical reasoning, we make two case-based arguments. First, we suggest that discretion is an invaluable characteristic of administrative office-holding to such an extent that, for example, the senior civil servant's instituted purpose can best be described as 'administrative statecraft'. As Barnard (1938) puts it, the 'functions of the executive' amount to the cultivation of 'organizational statesmanship'. Secondly—and coming from the other end of the supposed dichotomy—we argue with reference to the clinical hospital that office-holding and classic bureaucratic capacities are not located in opposition to the exercise of professional discretion. Rather, the professional's discretionary capabilities are inseparably linked to the establishment of clear lines of command, delineated and well-defined distribution of responsibilities and obligations through a system of offices, as well as a high degree of formalization and rule-based conduct. Hence bureaucratic discretion is seen as the exercise of casuistical, prudential judgement.

We end the chapter by arguing that attempts to curtail bureaucratic discretion—whether, for example, framed in terms of enhancing 'responsiveness' or 'performance'—carry with them a number of significant risks to the ability of specific bureaucracies to fulfil their instituted purposes—in public, private and professional domains alike. Such risks particularly concern restricting the capacity of those occupying particular offices—with their distinctive and nonreducible duties and obligations—to nurture, strengthen and indeed exercise administrative, executive and professional responsibility and statesmanship.

15.2 The Dichotomizing Stance on Bureaucracy and Discretion

Although the 'customary view' of bureaucracy can be found in research fields across the social sciences, the dichotomizing stance on bureaucracy versus discretionary freedom and flexibility has been particularly tenacious in discussions on expertise. According to Charles Perrow it was a footnote in Talcott Parsons' introduction to his translation of Weber's *Economy and society* that made the hard-lived conception of a discrepancy between expertise and classic bureaucracy famous. Here Parsons declared that Weber confused two types of authority, one based on technical competence and one based on legally defined office (Parsons 1947). Although Parsons made this distinction in his earlier writings (e.g. 1939: 460–2), Perrow declares that Parsons' well-known footnote is 'possibly the most important in the history of organizational theory' because with it the prevailing 'bureaucratic dilemma of expertise and discipline' was firmly established (Perrow 2014: 43; see also Toren 1976).

Perrow further notes that nowhere has this dilemma been as dominant as in 'the voluminous literature on professionals in organizations' (2014: 44–50). Thus, common accounts of professional organizations are often built on what Perrow describes as the supposed 'conflict between professional values and bureaucratic ones' (2014: 53). When studying the relation between bureaucracy and discretion it is therefore particularly interesting to turn to the organization of professionals, as this traditionally has been approached as an area in which bureaucratic rule and office-holding are represented as involving some kind of power struggle or conflict with discretionary freedom, expertise and professional autonomy. Since Parsons' footnote in 1947 and Perrow's observation in 1972, such an approach has gained thrust.

This dichotomy, which has been defined as the 'classic analytical grid' (Bezes, Demazière, Biamic *et al.* 2012: 6) in the sociology of professions, seems to have been solidified with the increased reform pressures on professional organizations. Thus, in its most simple and popular form this argument is found in the widespread critique of the documentation, control and performance management overload which have been the outcome of *New Public Management* inspired reform programmes in many public and professional organizations since the 1980s. In the popular press, in public discussions, among the professionals and even in scholarly work (e.g. Giauque 2003; Travers 2007) these new control regimes are often referred to as increased bureaucracy or rule-tyranny. Because of the simple thought-frame 'discretionary freedom versus managerial control' it is rarely noticed that rather than being bureaucratic, much of the current increase in control systems and tick-box mentality is thoroughly anti-bureaucratic in nature when compared with Weber's classic account.

The simple and popular image of professionalism as a kind of resistance against bureaucratic control is supported by a great deal of the most influential sociological studies of professional work that have followed from Parsons' seminal writings on professionalism (1939, 1951). An illustrative example of this is Eliot Freidson's widely cited *Professionalism, the third logic* (2001). In arguing for professionalism as an institutional logic that forms an alternative to both consumerism (the market) and bureaucracy (the state), Freidson broadly deploys the term professionalism to account for the institutional circumstances in which members of an occupation control their own work. Market then refers to circumstances in which consumers control work and bureaucracy to circumstances in which managers control work (2001: 12). In relation to this definition of professionalism, discretion is 'deserving of special status' (2001: 34) Freidson argues, because it is exactly the exercise of discretion that sets the professional organization apart from a more bureaucratic one: 'The ideal-typical ideology of professionalism stresses the lack of uniformity in the problems its work must contend with, therefore emphasizing the need for discretion' (2001: 111).

In the book's more specific discussions of bureaucracy, Freidson adds standardization to managerial and hierarchical control as key characteristics of the bureaucratic logic. While he acknowledges bureaucracy as a 'corrective to inappropriate or irresponsible discretion' (2001: 217–8), he simultaneously declares that:

> Fully realized, ideal-typical bureaucracy is intrinsically at odds with professionalism since its aim is to reduce discretion as much as possible so as to maximize the predictability and reliability of its services and products (Freidson 2001: 217).

Thus, Freidson outlines a position where the question of professionalism's relation to bureaucracy does not only form a dilemma but where the two are understood as inherently incompatible and mutually exclusive. In so doing, he became a prominent representative of a stance in which discretion and autonomy are related to management, formal rules and bureaucratic control as a kind of continuum where more of the one leads to less of the other in a zero-sum game (Numerato, Salvatore and Fattore 2012). This position appears to leave professionals with only two possible responses:

> as either subjected to external rules and constraints or agents with power to define their own conditions of work (Gleeson and Knights 2006).

As Numerato *et al.* (2012) have argued, even in recent scholarly discussions about the changed conditions of professional practice and its relation to management, this continuum is reproduced in a variety of theoretical approaches. The latter range from those proposing managerial hegemony at one end (where a colonization of professional autonomy is claimed), via theories of co-optation, negotiation and merging between professional and managerial cultures (for instance, in notions such as 'adaptive regulation' or 'hybrid managers'), to theories of strategic adaptation at the other (which describe a 'reverse colonization' where professionals strategically adopt management principles to strengthen their autonomy; e.g. Noordegraaf 2007; Ackroyd and Muzio 2008).

While Freidson's account suggests an 'intrinsic' opposition between bureaucracy and professionalism, less dichotomizing approaches can also be found. Of these, Henry Mintzberg's description of the Professional Bureaucracy as one of six organizational configurations in his classic *The structuring of organizations* (1979) has been particularly influential. Here, Mintzberg purposefully links bureaucracy and professionalism and describes the professional organization as one that relies on the standardization of skills through training and indoctrination. In a similar move to Perrow's definition of professionals as 'personnel who have complex rules built into them' (2014: 22) Mintzberg describes how rules and standards are inculcated into the professions; first during formal education in which 'skill and knowledge is formally programmed into the would-be professional' (1979: 350) and later during long periods of internship and on-the-job practical training in which professionals learn how to apply their formal knowledge—and to do so with discretion. It is this that Mintzberg famously refers to as 'the pigeonholing process' (1979: 352); the professional's method for categorizing and reducing complexities while containing uncertainty in their application of generalized and standardized knowledge to individual cases. With a glancing reference to Perrow (1970), Mintzberg notes that 'no matter how standardized the knowledge and skills, their complexity ensures that considerable discretion remains in their application' (Mintzberg 1979: 350). Therefore, he continues, no two professionals apply rules and standards in exactly the same way.

Mintzberg thus exhibits a keen eye for the importance of internalized rules and standardized practices for professional work, as well as for the necessary discretion that is needed in the case-based application of such rules. However, he simultaneously presupposes a conflict between professionalism and bureaucracy at various other levels of his analysis. This conflict is evident in Mintzberg's account of the Professional Bureaucracy as a distinct organizational form that is fundamentally different from another type of bureaucratic organization: the Machine Bureaucracy. In making this distinction, Mintzberg's account follows the direct trail of Parson's footnote and with it, classical components of bureaucracy—such as hierarchy, formal organization, written rules and office-holding—are either downplayed or absent from his conception of the Professional Bureaucracy. Mintzberg argues, for example, that '[t]he need for planning or the formalization of the work of professionals is very limited, so there is little call for a technostructure' (1979: 355). Hence, the Professional Bureaucracy is described as an organizational form with a flat, decentralized and democratic structure—combined, though, with a hierarchical structure for the administrative staff. Quoting Blau (1968), Mintzberg refers to professional bureaucracies as 'collegial organizations' based on an opposed and often conflicting relation between 'a professional orientation' towards service and 'a bureaucratic orientation' towards compliance with rules (1979: 360–1).

In line with this conception—and echoing Parsons' distinction between skill-based and office-based types of authority—Mintzberg (1979: 351) establishes an opposition between the professional organization and classic bureaucracy on their differing sources of authority:

> So whereas the Machine Bureaucracy relies on authority of a hierarchical nature—the power of office—the Professional Bureaucracy emphasizes authority of a professional nature—the power of expertise.

This means that while in the Machine Bureaucracy 'one salutes the stripes, not the man' (1979: 361), professionals should be approached not as part of a system of offices constituted by the particular organization of which they are part, but rather as experts or individual specialists defined by—in line with Freidson—their 'control over [their] own work' (1979: 349). Thus, the professional is understood as an extra-organizational self who only 'bothers to join an organization' to share resources and support services with other professionals or to get clients (1979: 357). This also suggests that when the professional does not get 'the autonomy he feels he requires he is tempted to pick up his kit bag of skills and move on' (1979: 357).

According to Mintzberg this loose coupling to the organization results in two major problems: A problem of coordination, because coordinating and controlling professionals can only be achieved through standardization and internalization of skills and knowledge, rather than through hierarchy and administrative office (1979: 361); and a connected problem of unhindered or misguided discretion caused by a lack of organizational control mechanisms and culture:

> Discretion not only enables some professionals to ignore the needs of their clients; it also encourages many of them to ignore the needs of the organization. Professionals in these structures do not generally consider themselves part of a team. To many, the organization is almost incidental, a convenient place to practice their skills (1979: 374).

To these two critiques—specific to the professional bureaucracy—Mintzberg (1979: 375) adds a third that the professional organization supposedly shares with the Machine bureaucracy: the problem of innovation.

> Like the Machine Bureaucracy, the Professional Bureaucracy is an inflexible structure, well suited to producing standard outputs but ill-suited to adapting to the production of new ones.

So, although Mintzberg appreciates the inseparability of rules and discretion in professional practice, he ends up reproducing what Perrow describes as one out of the two most common critiques of bureaucracy: its unresponsiveness and lack of flexibility.

15.3 The Weberian Stance: The Inseparability of Discretion and Bureaucracy

According to Perrow, the prevailing 'hiatus between expertise and the occupancy of an official position' (2014: 46) is highly problematic not least because when Parsons, for example, announces that the authority of office 'is not enjoyed by virtue of a technical competence' (Parsons 1939: 461), he conveniently forgets what Perrow describes as 'the technical character of administration' (2014: 46). While the scientist's authority and discretionary capacity are linked to her scientific technical competence and the doctor's to her medical technical competence, the administrative officer's is 'promoted on, and expected to exercise and increase, her *administrative* technical competence' (2014: 46). Thus, Perrow reminds us, '(i)t was Weber's simple but enduring insight to see how crucial expertise was a requirement for holding office throughout the hierarchy' (2014: 46).

For Weber, as a late, great exponent of the 'ethics of office', the bureau was a distinctive 'life-order' with its own ethos, one in which when 'in role' requires the bureaucrat not to act in an arbitrary, unpredictable or unlawful manner but which entitles and indeed requires her or him to make prudent use of their discretion in the performance of their 'official' duties (du Gay 2000, 2009; Wagenaar 2004; Zacka 2017). In other words, Weber's 'stance' towards bureaucracy expresses a casuistical insistence on the necessity of a principle of situation-specific judgement. For Weber, casuistry shadows the whole repertoire of practice. It constitutes a necessary, indeed, crucial, dimension of organizational reasoning and conduct, most significantly, when people are caught between conflicting patterns of duty in relation to the fulfilment of their official obligations. The ethos of bureaucratic conduct, then, far from 'disappearing' prudential judgement and the use of discretion, presupposes and depends upon their presence. Let us take a simple example to indicate exactly what we mean here. The text of the law is often ambiguous and riddled with conflicts, lending itself to various reasonable interpretations, which mean it can be 'operationalized' in a variety of ways. Resolving such indeterminacies is not simply a technical matter, but an ethical one, requiring public servants—no matter how lofty or lowly their station may be—to prioritize certain values and interests over others. In this way, moral and political decision-making takes place across all levels of bureaucratic agencies as the meaning of the law is clarified and given political countenance.

For Weber, the constant criticism of the bureau from both left and right in his own time—as at present—was indicative of a romanticism or principled certainty at odds with the reality of this particular 'life order'. It served to divert attention away from the need to cultivate and strengthen the bureaucrat's capacity for 'practical rationality and ethical seriousness'—their prudential judgement and situation-specific 'discretion'. Rather than the pre-eminent exponent of a 'politics/administration' dichotomy, Weber's work points in an entirely different direction altogether. Unlike his contemporary, Woodrow Wilson, Weber indicated that civil servants (most especially, but not exclusively, at senior levels) inevitably exercise considerable discretion in their daily work, also above and beyond the merely 'technical' question of finding the most efficient means of implementing the political directives of their elected superiors.

The continuing importance of this strand of thought is particularly evident in the work of a group of scholars who, in their different ways and in different contexts, have sought to build upon and extend Weber's insights on the positive and indeed irreducible importance of discretion in bureaucratic public administration (Schaefer and Schaefer 1992; Parker 1993; Uhr 1993; Storing 1998; Rohr 1999; Chapman 2000). Like Weber (1978, 1989), each has, again in their different ways, used what Thomas (1978) termed the 'British Philosophy of Administration' as a model and exemplar, to articulate the fundamental significance of 'discretion' in the conception of a bureaucratic apparatus that remains 'political' in the sense of fundamentally seeking to uphold and promote the ends of the regime it serves, without being tied to the policies and programmes of any one political party (which would serve to negate its capacity to serve other elected parties, 'without fear or favour'). Storing (1998), for example, argued that the very qualities that distinguish the civil servant from the elected politician—including their relatively long tenure in office, professional experience and expertise in 'the arts and business of government' and partial insulation from direct accountability to the electorate—enable them to serve a unique kind of political role, which can complement the skills of the latter and the operation and production of 'responsible government'. Borrowing a phrase from Sir Henry Taylor's (1836) classic *The statesman*, which like Weber's work prefigures much of the discussion of the theme of 'bureaucracy and discretion', Storing articulated a role for the senior civil servant as a 'closet statesman', exercising 'administrative statecraft'. The twin perils of 'populism', on one hand, and the various different reform programmes advocating variants of 'scientific management', on the other, could be mitigated or avoided by a realistic appreciation of bureaucracy à la Weber and by cultivating and strengthening the 'constitutional bureaucracy's' capacity to exercise 'administrative statecraft'.

Formality and Discretion: Wilfred Brown

As we indicated in the Introduction to this chapter, in his classic essay, *Complex organizations*, Charles Perrow (1972: 24–6 and 44) offered an acute reconsideration of bureaucracy as a potentially positive, if often fragile, organizational achievement. In so doing, he had cause to turn at certain points to the work of Wilfred Brown, an experienced and successful manager, executive, Minister of State and organizational analyst, who rose to prominence in the field of organizational theory as a result of his involvement in the first major research project undertaken by the Tavistock Institute of Human Relations in the UK after the Second World War: the Glacier Project, but whose work is now largely forgotten. Brown's experience of working within and empirically analysing the operations of bureaucratic hierarchy in a number of contexts had led him to argue, against the 'customary view', that bureaucracy was neither inherently pathological nor dysfunctional. Rather, in contrast, bureaucracy is something that could potentially enable an organization to employ large numbers of people and yet preserve both unambiguous work role boundaries and accountability for work conducted by those occupying those roles. In particular, Brown stressed that the very formalities or so-called rigidities of bureaucratic hierarchy were not antithetical to 'discretion' and 'flexibility', but rather their precondition (see also du Gay 2000; Stinchcombe 2001). Instead of being seen as mutually exclusive, as the 'customary view' had it, the one was seen as the condition of the other. For Brown, it was the relationship between the two that was important.

For Brown (1965: 308), all work, and thus all work roles, no matter how ostensibly routine or circumscribed, require 'decision-making' by those performing it. He defines work as 'the totality of discretion which a member is expected to exercise, and the proscribed acts he (sic) must discharge, in carrying out the responsibilities of the role he occupies' (1965: 308). By discretion, Brown refers to an act or course of action adopted by an organizational member in a specific role, where the policy set for that role leaves alternative courses of action from among which that member has to choose. By proscribed acts, Brown means an act or course of action performed by a member in undertaking their work role, where the policy set allows that member no choice. In framing employment work in this manner, Brown is keen to highlight that the main basis on which the assessment of the performance of such work is to be undertaken, is how an organizational member uses experience, knowledge and judgement in making decisions, rather than on the *apparent results* of their use of such experience, knowledge and judgement. As he puts it:

> We too readily agree that chief executives should be assessed on the basis of the profit and loss account, that the factory manager should be solely assessed on the volume of output, or the civil servant on the speed with which they can introduce arrangements that put into practice a change in Government policy. But these achievements—profit, volume of output, speed—are the end results of processes that involve not only the quality of the decisions made (…) but also a host of other variables outside their control. It would be very convenient if these were objective parameters of the performance of people, but they are not. Many find this so distressing that they sometimes fail to face up to it and go on trying to assess the work done by subordinates or others on a quite unreal basis. The reason for their distress is that instead of the relatively easy task of looking, for example, at the output volume achieved by the factory manager and accepting the figures as an index of their performance they must, instead, take their whole experience of their performance over a period of time into account and use their own judgment in coming to a decision as to whether their performance is good, bad, or

> indifferent. Judging the performance of subordinates is, in a very real sense, hard work (Brown 1974: 110–1).

This 'hard work' is a form of casuistical reasoning where practical judgement is crucial. The quality of assessment depends on judgements concerning the significance of situational factors. In the case of the chief executive, for instance, the profit and loss account is itself affected by variables outside the control of any one member of the organization, such as the state of the market, the changing costs of raw materials, changes in Government policy, the decisions of the Board about such things as capital investment and so on and so forth. The existence of these variables is obvious enough, so the question then is: exactly how useful or practical is it to undertake assessment of a chief executive's performance in terms of financial results alone? Quantitative indices such as profit, output, volume of sales and so on, are very important, but in using them as the basis of an assessment of performance, 'it is essential to consider the other variables that have affected them, and to assess how far they are a function of a manager's performance' (Brown 1974: 111).

Moreover, as Brown (1974: 112) continues, 'if one introduces the time element, the fallacy is compounded'. To the extent that profits are affected by the decisions of the chief executive, the effects virtually never show up during the year in which such decisions were made and for which the profit and loss account is constructed. The chief executive may take decisions in one year. The results may not appear until several years later. The larger the organization, the longer the time-span of the chief executive's discretion is likely to be. If it is decided to develop a new product line, for example, it may be some years before sales in volume result. In the intervening years the profit and loss account will include all the costs of a plan that has yet to introduce any revenue. How can it then be said that the chief executive's efforts can be assessed in terms of profits in those intervening years? Brown (1974: 112–3) argues that

> fallacious perceptions like this about how to assess an individual's work exist at all levels in employment hierarchies and are widespread in society. Factual results are very important, but they must be used intelligently. Their crude use as sole criteria of success not only results in injustice to individuals but can also bring about decisions that damage the future of companies.

However, he continues, if managers encourage their subordinates to discharge the tasks allotted to them by precisely cultivating and deploying their practical, situational judgement—their *discretion*—in for instance deciding how best to distribute work among their own subordinates, how to devise new methods of obtaining results when normal methods have failed, how to keep things on schedule, how to deal with personnel difficulties, how to train people to do their jobs, how to match changes in the environment in which they work that no one foresaw, with initiatives that nobody ordered them to take, then the fallacy can be avoided.

> If we realize that we have to judge subordinates on the way they use their judgment, then we will realize that our judgments of their work are based on experience over time and on our use of intuition and judgment. There is no easy formula (Brown 1974: 114).

For Brown, an effective and equitable assessment of a subordinate's performance must of necessity be mediated by a principle of situation-specific judgement.

> It is only by considering a subordinate's work in this way that a manager can help him. It is no help to him to say: 'Your output has fallen, there must therefore be something wrong about your approach to running the factory and you must do better.' You can help him only by pointing to examples of errors or marginal errors of judgment, and to do that you must have a pretty extensive knowledge of the types of decisions that his work involves (Brown 1974: 114).

As with Weber (1994), with whom, alongside Barnard, he is frequently compared (see Kelly 1968, Chapter 10), Brown roots almost everything in 'Fraglichkeit der Situation' ('the uncertainty of the situation'). As Weber's work can be seen to reside within both a classical tradition of political judgement and an 'ethics of office', so too can Brown's work be located within the classic stance of organizational theory as a practical science, where practical action and situational judgement are at a premium.

15.4 The Professional as an Office-Holder

The Case of Error-Management in the Clinical Hospital

From a Weberian stance, it is unviable to hold that 'the official is not an expert' (Perrow 2014: 46) who uses considerable discretion in exercising administrative and executive 'statesmanship'. It is, however, just as problematic to hold that the expert—or the professional more specifically—does not occupy an office with instituted official purposes and obligations. Or, relatedly, that the professional organization, such as the hospital, the university, or the school, is merely a 'collegial' organization that has little connection to bureaucracy. As Perrow (2014) suggests, professional discretion is rarely in opposition to, but often closely connected and interdependent with, clear lines of authority, formalization, division of labour, a high degree of rules and procedures, exact specification of duties and responsibilities, impartiality, equal treatment and so on.

In this section of the chapter we turn to the clinical hospital and the medical profession as a site to investigate the interrelations between bureaucracy and discretion. Traditionally, clinical judgement has been understood as a casuistical type of reasoning *par excellence* (Jonsen and Toulmin 1988; Pedersen 2018). The large degree of discretionary authority and freedom attributed to the medical profession has made the organization of medicine the preferred battleground for the discussion of the nature of professional discretion and expertise (e.g. Becker, Geer, Hughes and Strauss 1961; Freidson 1988). Thus, in Parson's aforementioned footnote to Weber, he discusses exactly the case of the physician to argue that the authority of expertise is radically different from the authority of office. The authority of the physician, Parsons suggests, is solely dependent on the patient's faith in their physicians' technical competences. Parsons further claims that when physicians are organized (in hospitals for instance), then

> instead of a rigid hierarchy of status and authority there tends to be roughly, in formal status, a 'company of equals', an equalization of status which ignores the inevitable gradation of distinction and achievement to be found in any considerable group of technically competent persons (Parsons 1947: 60).

Parsons thus articulates an idea of the collegial, democratic and equitable organization of the medical profession that has become dominant in large parts of the sociology of professions. This is a notion that Perrow opposes by noting 'that evidence from studies of hospitals indicates that medical staff are quite bureaucratic in their organizational functioning, with hierarchies that are apparent' and moreover, that hospitals indeed do seem to be environments that are sensitive to both gradations of distinction and achievement (2014: 43). While some of these early studies that Perrow referred to were undertaken by himself(1960, 1965), a number of important qualitative research studies dealing especially with the training of medical students also attested to the importance of hierarchy and office-holding in the clinical hospital—not least for the development and exercise of discretionary capabilities (e.g. Becker *et al.* 1961; Fox 1957, 1959).

A particularly thorough analysis of the interdependencies of bureaucracy and medical professionalism in the clinical hospital can be found in Charles Bosk's *Forgive and remember* (2003 [1979]) where he follows the training of resident surgeons in a US hospital in order to investigate the character of internal control and error-management in medical practice. Bosk comes to the conclusion that status (in the precise sense deployed by T.H. Marshall (2000), for instance), hierarchy and a clear distribution of responsibility and duty are preconditions for the identification and handling of failure within the clinical hospital understood properly as a system of offices through which both medical expertise and ethical attitudes are transmitted.

In the chapter 'Error, rank and responsibility', for example, Bosk describes how different types of error are judged differently according to their character, and according to the status and responsibilities of the person who commits them. As described, Mintzberg pictured professionals as extra-organizational selves that often do not 'consider themselves part of a team' and 'ignore the needs of the organization' (Mintzberg 1979: 374), with the associated problem of unhindered discretion caused by lack of coordination and organizational control through hierarchy and office-holding. In sharp contrast to this picture,

Bosk describes a fine-grained system of organized professional self-control transmitted by clear lines of authority, formal responsibility and division of labour. Here, the possibility of making what Bosk characterizes as 'independent judgements', as well as the disciplinary actions and the expected level of self-criticism in relation to judgemental errors, are strictly connected to one's particular place in the predetermined system of official roles in the hospital.

The prominence of role-morality in the clinical hospital is especially noticeable in what Bosk describes as *normative errors* that occur 'when a surgeon has, in the eyes of others, failed to discharge his role-obligations conscientiously' (Bosk 2003: 51). More specifically, that is an error in which the surgeon challenges what Bosk describes as the normative 'background assumptions' that govern clinical practices and that are 'drilled into' into clinicians since their first day as medical students (2003). This includes certain rules of conduct such as 'the rule of no surprises' (the rule of involving and informing superiors), 'the rule of full and honest disclosure' and the rule 'that one will not let personality intrude on clinical care' (2003: 51–61). The failure to follow these rules of conduct means crossing the boundaries of one's official duties and therefore such errors are taken to be much more serious and inexcusable that errors of judgement or technique. Consequently, they are strongly sanctioned by the medical community because while errors of judgement or technique are related to the surgeon's level of training and skill, the failure to live up to instituted purposes, duties and codes of conduct 'says something about the recruit himself' (2003: 60) and their willingness to take their role obligations seriously. It is the failure to forgive these errors by the medical community that establishes the normative boundaries of the profession. Thus, following Bosk's approach, it is hardly meaningful to separate the authority of expertise and the authority of office, or discretion and bureaucracy, not only because expertise and discretion are transmitted—given meaning and regulated through the complex system of offices that make up the clinical hospital—but also because the authority of clinicians in this system is closely linked to their technical competence as well as to their ethos and their ability and willingness to follow normative codes of conduct—including, for instance, taking responsibility for failure.

The interconnection between office and expertise in the clinical hospital cannot, however, be taken for granted. It would seem that today's intensive reforms of healthcare systems in important ways challenge some of the internal systems for distributing discretionary authority and responsibility to healthcare professionals. One example is the so-called blame-free approach to medical error promoted as part of a comprehensive international patient safety policy programme. Here, errors are approached not as questions of internal error-regulation distributed through the clinical hospital's official roles, duties and responsibilities, but rather as a policy problem and as an opportunity to system-optimize healthcare through developing a so-called learning culture in which 'blame and shame' is banned. With this, however, the classic distribution of responsibility for error and this distribution's importance for regulating expertise and discretion, for educating medical students in codes of conduct; and for defining the limits of office, is at risk of being neglected (for an overview, see Pedersen 2018).

15.5 Conclusion

Under the influence of the body of ideas collectively and popularly known as the *New Public Management*, since the 1980s public institutions have been subject to and incorporated a diverse range of managerial norms and practices drawn from a variety of locales—not least perceived 'best (private sector) practice'. Prominent among these is a focus on performance-based evaluation: the idea that the success of these organizations should be primarily assessed in relation to their capacity to 'deliver' on clear metrics ('set targets and track'). Focusing on clear objectives rather than rules and procedures or office-based duties and obligations and their casuistical spaces of discretion, for example, was meant to liberate these institutions from the negativities of red tape on one hand and from the presumed vagaries or inconsistencies of situation-specific judgements, on the other. The presupposed result was boosting efficiency while providing the public with an objective standard for accountability. These ambitions may well be laudable in the abstract, but they can and have become fetishized in ways that risk impoverishing the mandate of those subject to them and thus of distorting the overall purpose of the organizations and institutions which they serve.

For critics of these reforms, they are often represented as leading to 'increased bureaucracy' or 'rule-tyranny'—a presupposition that is supported by unspecific or faulty definitions of bureaucracy as, for instance, managerial control of work processes (Freidson 2001). These are accounts that together with the dichotomizing stance on discretion and bureaucracy cannot but help support the popular confusion of managerialism and bureaucracy. Contemporary reform programmes seeking to re-invent a 'politics/administration' dichotomy or aiming to create a 'blame-free' patient safety culture may have the effect of weakening internal systems for distributing discretionary authority to professionals. From a Weberian stance, such reform programmes are often strikingly anti-bureaucratic in nature.

References

Ackroyd, S. & Muzio, D. (2008). *Redirections in the study of expert labour: Established professions and new expert occupations.* London: Palgrave Macmillan.

Barnard, C.I. (1938/1968). *The functions of the executive.* Cambridge, MA: Harvard University Press.

Becker, H.S., Geer, B., Hughes, E.C. & Strauss, A. (1961). *Boys in white: Student culture in medical school.* Chicago: University of Chicago Press.

Bezes, P., Demazière, D., Biamic, T.L. *et al.* (2012). New public management and professionals in the public sector: What new patterns beyond opposition. *Sociologie du Travail,* 54(1), 152.

Blau, P.M. (1968). The hierarchy of authority in organizations. *American Journal of Sociology*, 1967–1968, 453–467.

Bosk, C. (2003, 1972). *Forgive and remember: Managing medical failure* (2nd ed.). London and Chicago: University of Chicago Press.

Brown, W. (1965). *Exploration in management.* Harmondsworth: Penguin.

Brown, W. (1974). *Organization.* Harmondsworth: Penguin.

Chapman, R.A. (2000). Ethics in public service for the new millennium. In R.A. Chapman (Ed.), *Ethics in public service for the new millennium* (pp. 217–231). Aldershot: Ashgate.

du Gay, P. (2000). *In praise of bureaucracy.* London: Sage.

du Gay, P. (2009). Max Weber and the ethics of office. In P. Adler (Ed.), *Oxford handbook of sociology and organizational studies: Classical foundations* (pp. 146–73). Oxford: Oxford University Press.

Fox, R. (1957). Training for Uncertainty. In R.K. Merton, G. Reader & P.L. Kendall (Eds), *The student-physician: Introductory studies in the sociology of medical education* (pp. 207–241). Cambridge, MA: Harvard University Press.

Fox, R. (1959). *Experiment perilous: Physicians and patients facing the unknown.* New Jersey: Transaction Publishers.

Freidson, E. (1988). *Profession of medicine: A study of the sociology of applied knowledge.* Chicago: University of Chicago Press.

Freidson, E. (2001). *Professionalism, the third logic: On the practice of knowledge.* Chicago: The University of Chicago Press.

Giauque, D. (2003). New public management and organizational regulation: The liberal bureaucracy. *International Review of Administrative Sciences*, 69(4), 567–592

Gleeson, D. & Knights, D. (2006). Challenging dualism: Public professionalism in 'troubled' times. *Sociology*, 40(2), 277–295.

Goodsell, C. (2015). *The new case for bureaucracy.* London: Sage.

Jonsen, A.R. & Toulmin, S. (1988). *The abuse of casuistry: A history of moral reasoning.* Berkeley: University of California Press.

Kelly, J. (1968). *Is scientific management possible? Critical examination of Glacier's theory of organization.* London: Faber & Faber.

Marshall, T.H. (2000). A note on "Status". In P. du Gay *et al.* (Eds), *Identity: A reader* (pp. 304–310). London: Sage.

Mintzberg, H. (1979). *The structuring of organizations: A synthesis of the research.* Saddle River, NJ: Prentice Hall.

Noordegraaf, M. (2007). From 'pure' to 'hybrid' professionalism: Present-day professionalism in ambiguous public domains. *Administration & Society*, 39(6), 761–785.

Numerato, D., Salvatore, D. & Fattore, G. (2012). The impact of management on medical professionalism: A review. *Sociology of Health and Illness*, 34(4), 626–644.

Parker, R.S. (1993). *The administrative vocation: Selected essays* (pp. xiii–xxiii). Sydney: Hale & Ironmonger.

Parsons, T. (1939). The professions and social structure. *Social Forces*, 17(4), 457–467.

Parsons, T. (1947). Introduction. In *Max Weber, theory of social and economic organization* (A.M. Henderson & T. Parsons, Trans. & Ed.). New York: Oxford University Press.

Parsons, T. (1951). *The social system.* Glencoe, IL: Free Press.

Pedersen, K.Z. (2018). *Organizing patient safety: Failsafe fantasies and pragmatic practices.* London: Palgrave Macmillan.

Perrow, C. (1960). *Authority, goals and prestige in a general hospital.* PhD thesis, University of California.
Perrow, C. (1965). Hospitals: Technology, structure and goals. In J.G. March (Ed.), *Handbook of organization.* Chicago: Rand McNally.
Perrow, C. (2014, 1972). *Complex organizations: A critical essay* (3rd ed.). Vermont: Echo Point Books.
Perrow, C. (1970). Departmental power and perspectives in industrial firms. In M. Zald (Ed.), *Power in organizations.* Nasville, TN: Vanderbilt University Press
Rohr, J.A. (1999). *Public service, ethics, and constitutional practice.* Lawrence: University Press of Kansas.
Schaefer, D. & Schaefer, R. (1992). Editors introduction: Sir Henry Taylor and the study of public administration. In D. Schaefer & R. Schaefer (Eds), *The Statesman by Sir Henry Taylor.* Westport, CT: Praeger.
Stinchcombe, A. (2001) *When formality works: Authority and abstraction in law and organizations.* Chicago and London: University of Chicago Press.
Storing, H. (1998). American statesmanship: Old and new. In J.M. Bessette (Ed.), *Toward a more perfect union: Writings of Herbert J. Storing* (pp. 403–28). Washington, DC: The AEI Press.
Taylor, Sir H. ([1836]/1992). In D.L. Schaefer & R.R. Schaefer (Eds), *The statesman.* Westport, CT: Praeger.
Thomas, R. (1978). *The British philosophy of administration: A comparison of British and American ideas, 1900–1939.* London: Longman.
Toren, N. (1976). Bureaucracy and professionalism: A reconsideration of Weber's thesis. *The Academy of Management Review*, 1(3), 36–46.
Travers, M. (2007). *The New Bureaucracy: Quality assurance and its critics.* Bristol: Policy Press.
Uhr, J. (1993). Administrative responsibility and responsible administrators: An introduction. In R.S. Parker (Ed.), *The administrative vocation: Selected essays* (pp. xiii–xxiii). Sydney: Hale & Ironmonger.
Wagenaar, H. (2004). 'Knowing' the rules: Administrative work as practice. *Public Administration Review*, 64(6), 643–655.
Weber, M. (1978). *Economy and society: Vols I and II.* Berkeley, CA: University of California Press.
Weber, M. (1989). Science as a vocation. In P. Lassman & I. Velody (Eds), *Max Weber's* AQ4 *science as a vocation.* London: Unwin Hyman.
Weber, M. (1994). In P. Lassman & R. Speirs. (Eds), *Weber: Political writings.* Cambridge: Cambridge University Press.
Zacka, B. (2017). *When the state meets the street: Public service and moral agency.* Harvard: Harvard University Press.

CHAPTER 16

Discretion in the Policy Process

Peter Hupe and Michael Hill

16.1 Introduction

In politics and government discretion has always been a contentious issue. It is usually seen as a necessary evil and sometimes therefore as something to be minimized. Where legislators or policymakers recognize the limits of their control, they may be willing to grant a certain degree of freedom of judgement and even decision-making to relevant others—although always only in a hierarchical relationship. The term *implementation gap* expresses the standard view on policy implementation, in which discretion is seen as a phenomenon to be curbed. In case of an acknowledged policy failure, that then is exactly the measure taken first: limiting the freedom within which implementation organizations or other actors identified as subordinate can act. In such a case, the target is to reduce the possibility of 'deviant' use of such freedom, by specifying the boundaries of legitimate authority more stringently. This being so, discretion may also be approached in positive terms: as facilitating the achievement of policy goals.

In many statements about discretion in the policy process it is seen as stemming from a single source at the top of a hierarchy and, secondly, as exercised generally at a single spot at the bottom of that hierarchy, that is, in rule application at the street level. Such a localization is enhanced by definitions of discretion like the one by Davis (1969: 4): 'A public officer has discretion wherever the effective limits on his power leave him free to make a choice among possible courses of action and inaction'.

P. Hupe (✉)
Public Governance Institute, Catholic University of Leuven, Leuven, Belgium
e-mail: pieter.hupe@kuleuven.be

M. Hill
University of Newcastle, Newcastle upon Tyne, UK

T. Evans, P. Hupe (eds.), *Discretion and the Quest for Controlled Freedom*, https://doi.org/10.1007/978-3-030-19566-3_16

Definitions like this one—widespread as they are—clearly stem from the context of law and legislation. Freedom here is connected to authority and formal rules. Hence the terminology is primarily a judicial one. The space of the 'hole in the donut' (Dworkin 1977: 31) is indicated as discretionary authority. The bit of circumscribed freedom at the bottom of a hierarchy is a derivation from the legitimate power exercised from the top.

Actually, this view is a particular one. When discretion is apparent, indeed a message is conveyed to exercise judgement while having the freedom to decide what to do, but there are two qualifying conditions. First, that message may have multiple senders rather than a single one. Therefore, it may be less clear what exactly the content of 'the message' entails. And second, the act of conveying can be performed from both horizontal ('sideward') and vertical ('downward') directions. Therefore, at many spots in the policy process forces are working, in ways which can hardly be directly controlled by a single 'Authoritative Actor' at the top.

In this chapter the following question is explored: *What is the meaning of discretion in the policy process and what are the consequences of that meaning for policy results?* In the next section, discretion will be defined, after an exposition of existing ways to circumscribe the phenomena to which it refers. Next, the question is addressed where in the policy process discretion is located and hence where 'discretionary actors' are to be found. The final section concludes with a summing up of the implications of the preceding analysis for an understanding of the role of discretion in the ultimate making of public policy.

16.2 Defining Discretion

Conceptualizations of Discretion

In the context of the study of public administration, public management and public policy the term 'discretion' refers to what implementers have—or rather 'do'—after the goals of a public policy have been formulated and decided upon. Of course, its substance entails some form of limited freedom and a certain room to make choices but, as such, discretion is seen as primarily and perhaps exclusively located at the street level. The variety of meanings the term discretion gets in the relevant literature is explored below. Apart from these conceptualizations, as a descriptive label of the object of street-level bureaucracy research, the term discretion has functional equivalents.

Traditionally, discretion has been a central object in the study of law. In his seminal work on this topic Galligan (1990: 2) begins:

> A noticeable feature of modern legal systems is the extent to which officials, whether they be judicial or administrative, make decisions in the absence of previously fixed, relatively clear, and binding legal standards.

Discretion for Galligan (1990: 2) is about:

> The vagaries of language, the diversity of circumstances, and the indeterminacy of official purposes are (...) considerations which guarantee discretion some continuing place in the legal order and make its elimination an impossible dream.

Thus, discretion has 'more central sense as an express grant of power conferred on officials where determination of the standards according to which power is to be exercised is left largely to them' (1990: 2). Hence the expanded role of the modern state has brought with it an increase in discretion, as 'control over a wide range of matters is delegated to officials with varying degrees of guidance as to the policy goals to be achieved or the standards by which they are to be achieved' (1990: 2).

Galligan treats discretion 'not just as a side-effect of having rules, but as a positive way of conferring powers where it is important that officials have more freedom as to the way they are to be exercised than a detailed set of rules might allow' (1990: 3). Discretion raises problems 'from the point of view of the official who has to translate a broad grant of power into specific courses of action' (1990: 3).

Galligan is quoted here at length, because on the first pages of his book he presents a whole range of issues that can be deemed relevant when the subject of the present chapter, discretion in the policy process, is considered. Those issues as expressed in the subsequent quotes regard, respectively, the abundance of discretion; its inevitability; the granting of power underlying it; a varying degree of guidance concerning policy goals and viable standards, while the 'conferring of powers' sometimes explicitly is intended and sometimes not. Hence there is a need but also difficulty of an appropriate translation towards what in given circumstances needs to be done.

Making such an 'appropriate translation' on the spot is one thing, analysing it is something different, while evaluating the appropriateness of the translation ultimately concerns a normative question. Reporting on an empirical study, Baker Collins (2016: 222–3) makes a distinction between discretion as interpretation or 'space in the rules' and discretion as 'space outside the rules'. The latter phrase indicates discretion as existing in those spaces which the rules do not cover (the hole in the donut). Such a space outside the rules is created when street-level bureaucrats are seen as deviating from, subverting, modifying or breaking the rules.

Baker Collins speaks of 'a workaround' and says that public employees 'may use discretion in ways which are responsive to the underlying intent of the policy and on other occasions in ways that prevent intended outcomes' (2016: 223). They 'decide which rules apply in situations where there may be different but equally valid interpretations of those rules' (2016: 222). Baker Collins speaks of intended discretion when, 'in situations where there is a gap between law and social reality, discretion allows for the adaptation of policies to individual circumstances and to changing conditions' (222). Such a flexibility is deemed necessary and assists in policy implementation. Baker Collins calls this dimension of discretion the 'space *in* the rules' (223) where 'Discretion is driven not only by the need to interpret the rules but by the need to negotiate between competing priorities and contradictions within the rules' (224).

Baker Collins claims that 'a straightforward equation of congruent policy implementation with democratic accountability is complicated by policy conflict, ambiguity and poor design' (224). Her empirical study of an income assistance programme in Ontario addresses how street-level bureaucrats, confronted with rules that make access to benefit difficult, may alternatively choose to be strict rule enforcers or use discretion to avoid undermining what they see as the ultimate objectives of the programme. Case managers spoke of 'black and white legislation', meaning policy directives seen as stringent (226) and of 'black and white implementation' when it would be possible to read the rules in a very restrictive way. Baker Collins argues 'that front line workers have a complicated and contradictory relationship with the policies they are required to implement. Often the policies, not the clients, are found wanting' (231). That last sentence of course entails a value judgement. In Brodkin's study (2011) of rather similar workers in Chicago one may find an example of enthusiastic operationalization of rules like these.

Baker Collins' study highlights four insights that have been gained in street-level bureaucracy research over the years. First, discretion and rules are intrinsically connected to each other. It is the hole that makes the donut a donut, while there is no freedom without some kind of force aimed at controlling it. It be noted, however, that in the context of public policy the term 'discretion' has a dual meaning. In the policy process, in street-level implementation discretion is *used*—a dimension of behaviour—but at the level of a ministry such discretion has been *granted*—as a characteristic of a public policy conceived as a set of rules (Hupe 2013).

Second, rules never come alone but neither do rule sets. At the street level there is almost always more than one public policy to be implemented. In general, there are various sources of *action prescriptions* adding up to the range of formal rules. In fact, action prescriptions come in various sorts; apart from formal rules also professional standards, societal expectations and sometimes market incentives as well have to be reckoned with (Hupe and Hill 2007; Thomann, Hupe and Sager 2018). Hence, at the street level of government bureaucracy—in the broad sense of agencies in the (semi) public sector—there is a multiplicity of both action prescriptions and related accountabilities.

Third, while Baker Collins (2016) speaks of 'bureaucratic discretion' (see also, for instance, Keiser, Mueser and Choi 2004), from the literature a diversity of 'discretions' arises. For example, 'value discretion', 'task discretion' and 'rule discretion' are distinguished by Taylor and Kelly (2006). At the same time discretion is used as an adjective, as in 'discretionary powers' (cf. the title of Galligan's book, 1990), 'discretionary authority' (Galligan 1990: 3), 'discretionary behaviour' and 'discretionary practices' (Garrow and Grusky 2013: 103). In the context of governance, the term 'discretion' primarily refers to what street-level bureaucrats do when implementing public policy; it is the subject of Chap. 17 of this edited collection. The present chapter explores not only the different meanings but also the various *loci* of discretion in the policy process. As a result, it is suggested there may be a need to use an adjective indicating the locus of discretion, as in street-level discretion (cf. Garrow and Grusky 2013). When referring to what happens at the street level, the term discretion is still robust, while it also has equivalents.

Fourth and finally, Baker Collins' work takes us away from a view that sees rules as essentially rational elements in the policy process regardless of the ways in which those rules have been formulated. As in Davis' (1969) influential book, such a view is embodied in perspectives that take it for granted that discretion is undesirable. There is a reminder here that rule interpretation itself may be seen as part of a power game, as in Gouldner's (1954) classic examination of rules within an industrial workplace analysed in terms of the functions they perform for different interests in different situations.

Framing What Happens at the Street Level

In this sub-section alternative conceptualizations of discretion will be explored. This is done in a twofold way; first, by exploring how the phenomenon 'discretion' is addressed in various disciplines. Secondly, this exploration entails looking at the different labels available within the study of public policy, public administration and public management indicating what happens at the street level, as alternatives to the term discretion.

In an article one of the present authors explored the variety of theoretical views on discretion in four academic disciplines (Hupe 2013). He distinguished between a *juridical* view, an *economics* view, a *sociological* view and a *political science* view on discretion (427–431). Since Lipsky (1980) coined the term, street-level bureaucracy has developed into a full-fledged scholarly theme (cf. Hupe, Hill and Buffat Eds 2015). In the ways it is studied, a strong social sciences orientation can be observed (Hupe Ed. 2019). This being so, a full understanding and explanation of what happens on the ground floor of government cannot do without the aspects central in the theoretical views of all four disciplines identified above. The juridical view highlights the interplay between rules and discretion. The economics view draws attention to issues about control over agents in contexts of divergent interests and the transaction costs involved. The sociological viewpoints at processes of social interaction within and at the borders of organizations. The political science view focuses on legitimacy, the working of power mechanisms and the significance of interest-driven behaviour.

This concise overview shows that across disciplinary borders different theoretical views and frames are being used while looking at similar phenomena. This finding, by the way, contributed to the present initiative to dedicate an interdisciplinary edited collection to this diversity of angles to discretion, as indicated in the introductory chapter. Particularly Part II of this collection shows the various disciplinary perspectives on discretion. On the other hand, the latter concept has equivalents within the study of government itself. Traditional labels for what public servants in the lower ranks of government bureaucracy do have a juridical connotation: 'law enforcement', 'compliance', 'rule application'. Apart from 'exercising discretion', the concept of 'street-level decision making' is used. Somewhat more recent may be scholarly emphases on 'coping behaviour' and 'styles of social interaction'. Bear in mind that here a historical 'succession' of terms is suggested, while actually all these different labels are being used next to each other. It can be noted, however, that the labels as sorted here can be ranged from ones with an explicit hierarchical connotation, via an empirically more focused one ('decisions'), to concepts with a neutral character and even a 'horizontal' connotation.

Echoing Lipsky's characterization of street-level bureaucrats as alienated (1980: 75–80) Tummers, Bekkers, Vink and Musheno (2015) go on to characterize their adaptations as 'coping'. This refers to dealing with stress through 'behavioural efforts frontline workers employ when interacting with clients, in order to master, tolerate, or reduce external and internal demands and conflicts they face on an everyday basis' (Tummers *et al.* 2015: 1101–2).

Tummers *et al.* distinguish behavioural from cognitive coping (2015: 1102) and use a classification of three 'families' of coping during public service delivery. They formulate the latter in terms of 'moving towards', 'away from' or 'against' clients (2015: 1104). Given, as indicated above, the emphasis in some of the literature on the undesirability of discretion, there is a tendency to interpret street-level bureaucracy negatively. That makes it important to note that this research found the 'largest number of coping instances is related to the coping family "moving towards clients" (43%)' (1108). It is argued that 'In sum, frontline workers seem to want to perform meaningful public service keying on their clients, even in stressful situations' (2015: 1112–3).

In this work and other contributions by Tummers, policy preferences are of key importance (Tummers 2012; Tummers, Steijn and Bekkers 2012; Tummers and Bekkers 2014; see also Chap. 11 of this edited collection). What is being highlighted is more than simply the fact that preferences vary. In fact, it is a starting point for the exploration of psychological factors. In this approach there is an emphasis on '*policy alienation*'. This needs to be explained but so too does its opposite '*policy fidelity*' as the default mode, apparently (Tummers *et al.* 2015: 1114).

Indeed, street-level bureaucrats may feel uneasy with certain policy goals and experience role conflicts. This being so, it can be assumed that public employees working 'at the frontline' do not break the rules often because most of the time they will find those rules, one way or another, meaningful for their clients. Reasoning can be pursued along the following lines. First, teachers—and, to a certain extent, public servants in general—like their work. They are not 'in it for the money', but realize a degree of self-fulfilment in doing their work properly. Second, they are aware of the societal relevance of their job. However stressful police work, for instance, may be, 'somebody has to do the job'. Third, although in varying degrees, teachers, police officers and other street-level bureaucrats have an *esprit de corps*. Independent of the degree of institutionalization of their occupation they see themselves as professionals. Being in public service makes them aware of the fact that the implementation of policy programmes is their essential task. Fulfilling that task in a professional way means implementing the public policies that need to be implemented—whether one likes the policy or not. Even if one is not enthusiastic about a particular new policy directive, one is professional enough to implement it—one way or another, even while the work load may be high. Then, however, with particular new political initiatives—for example, in respect of narrowly conceived quantifiable performance goals—'policy alienation' may come into play when the level of conflict with professional ideals is felt to be too high.

This practised *public service professionalism* implies a neutral stance, driven by the ethos of craftsmanship: doing one's job as good as one can. While resistance may be the exception, professionals in public service generally will tend to use the freedom of action they have in such a way that they can be held accountable for what they do—accountable in multiple directions: towards political-administrative authorities but also towards their colleagues and peers as well as their clients and the public at large. In other words, rather than the reduction of stress, an awareness of the need for an appropriate fulfilment of public tasks is guiding here. Dealing with constraints, as the essence of *coping*, then is no more and no less than part of professional conduct.

Positioning Discretion

The 'exercise of discretionary authority'—and certainly 'law enforcement' and 'rule application'— have a straightforward hierarchical connotation. Against this background, looking at 'behaviour' in the policy process can be welcomed as an empirically more neutral label. There is a chance, however, that this novel object description implies a reductive shift in focus to motivational aspects of behaviour rather than an extension to also consider the wider context of what needs to be taken into account. Garrow and Grusky (2013: 104) contend that 'because street-level research has not sufficiently accounted for broader environmental influences on discretion, it has overstated the agency of workers, who are viewed as exploiting the discretion as afforded to them to maximize their self-interest'.

In contrast, Garrow and Grusky start from the institutional theory axiom, that agency is institutionally embedded. Their analysis depicts street-level bureaucrats

> not as agents with objective interests and preferences, but rather as institutionally constructed actors whose values, interests, and practices are partially determined by the institutional logics that structure the organizational fields in which they

> operate. Thus, although workers may use their discretion to advance their interests in response to their shared conditions of work, their actions, intentions, and interests are themselves institutionally conditioned in systematic ways (2013: 104).

In their empirical research, Granow and Grusky test the idea that differences in discretionary behaviour are related to the underlying logic of the organizational field in which the work is embedded. In their research, they distinguish between four institutional logics—medical, public health, social movement and multi-service. They argue that particular institutional logics provide

> cultural and material repertoires that shape workers' understandings of the means and ends of their interests. Logics allocate the attention of workers by defining the purpose of their organization, the nature of the problems they face, appropriate organizational responses to these problems, the relevant attributes of clients (2013: 122).

The findings from Granow and Grusky's research suggest that

> worker agency, as expressed through discretionary practice, is embedded in an institutional system that shapes how discretion is exercised by providing institutionally defined means, ends, and interests (2013: 124).

and that

> (S)treet-level discretion (as well as the variation in organizational practices it enables) is bounded by the institution in which it occurs (2013: 124).

Addressing discretion in human service organizations, Sosin (2010) unfolds an institutional view with similar traits. He considers discretion particularly common in the human services, 'where workers and local organizations have the ability, willingness, or need to make choices in serving clients' (2010: 382). Discretion then concerns 'reactions to situations in which standards are complex and socially defined' (2010: 383). The term 'standards' adds a crucial element to the way the subject matter of the present chapter, discretion in the policy process, can be approached. Sosin's view is one from institutional theory: 'the culture frequently provides the expectations that drive the behaviour of organizations, and that cultural "standards", a term for norms, beliefs, and cognitions (…), do not always operate like concrete goals' (2010: 386).

Sosin stresses that 'discretionary behavior does not occur because of clear conflicts of interests or technical limits to monitoring. Rather, it reflects that social norms favor trust between providers and authorities, and also that legal requirements are tested by authorities as loose norms' (2010: 385–6).

It is clear that, certainly at the street level of human service organizations, employees have to deal with multiple social standards, stemming from 'local communities, professions, clients, and the nation as a whole' (2010: 387). However, these standards do not necessarily have to conflict directly in ways assumed in the literature about 'goal-related discretion' (388). Where multiple standards overlap, workers need to make choices. Which of the multiple standards in the situation at hand are they to follow and how are they to interpret them? Besides, there may be variation in the power to define the institutionalized standards. And then, culturally derived standards may be 'taken for granted and interpreted in loose ways' (389).

Patterns of discretion may vary with the social acceptance of the authority of the actors involved. '(D)iscretion can be socially sanctioned or granted by default' (2010: 395). Sometimes overlaps in standards are allowed, 'when multiple standards are deemed important' (2010: 397). At the street level, a balancing act is always involved. While the standards to be dealt with, coming from many sides, add up to a 'toolkit of prescriptions' (Swidler 1986), 'shaping discretion involves balancing the standards that apply to a situation' (Sosin 2010: 397). Policy programmes usually operate 'with a combination of myths, ceremonies, and various balanced institutional standards' (399).

How standards work as social constructs and how culture may affect street-level practice, is evidenced by Cohen (2016). In his article he shows how informal payments in Israeli healthcare are 'culturally based' and 'strongly correlated with the strength of the formal institutions' (2016: 16). At the same time, his study also indicates that using discretion while following action prescriptions involves more than the behaviour of particular individuals.

The emphasis here on the importance of standards brings us back to Galligan. As he points out, discretionary power is often characterized in terms of the authority to choose amongst alternative courses of action. This then implies a concern with the reasons for such choices (Galligan 1990: 6). This leads him to stress that discretionary choice is a function of standards. He argues '(T)here are three primary elements to the decision: (a) finding facts, (b) settling the standards, (c) applying the standards to the facts' (1990: 7).

Galligan positions discretion in the broader administrative system, in which both the rule of law and an accountable exercise of power are crucial so that a process occurs which gives meaning and context to standards. Hence reference here is to: '(…) powers delegated within a system of authority to an official or set of officials, where they have some significant scope for settling the reasons and standards according to which that power is to be exercised, and for applying them in the making of specific decisions' (1990: 15).

Accordingly,

> Firstly, discretion occurs in a context of standards, and although in the strongest cases of discretion these standards may be offer little guidance or discretion, there are usually some standards guiding, constraining, and influencing the way a discretionary decision is made. Secondly, discretionary powers may be thought of as subsystems of authority within which the official has some degree of freedom and autonomy in acting as he thinks best. (…). Thirdly, there is a characteristic of discretion which is especially pertinent in the administrative context. Here the idea is that the official should not simply formulate rules of decision-making and

> then apply them rigorously to situations as they arise, but must maintain a special relationship between the general standard and the particular case (1990: 15).

Perhaps the point of most importance for our present purposes is Dworkin's (1977: 27) insistence that officials exercising authority 'should be able to explain and justify their actions in terms of political principles and constitutional doctrines'.

When defining discretion in the context of the policy process is the objective, the following insights are relevant. First, discretion concerns the freedom to act as explicitly or implicitly granted in a set of rules formulated by a relevant actor, while the same term may also refer to the freedom to act as used, by weighing internalized action prescriptions. Second, *a rule is not its application*. The way a rule is being applied leaves the rule, as a rule, intact. Rule application belongs to the realm of action; rules to the realm of norms. As institutional theory shows, action and norms (Galligan's and Sosin's 'standards') have to be distinguished from each other. Therefore, when writers speak of 'rule bending' they are implying a challenge to the acceptance of a rule.

Third, norms as action prescriptions stem from various sources. They entail formal rules laid down in legislation, public policies and statements of organizational management, but also occupational standards, societal expectations and sometimes market incentives too—at various scales and in varying mixes. The multiplicity of norms ('action prescriptions', 'standards') to reckon with, makes it both inevitable and necessary to use the discretion at hand. Then, however, the latter is not conceived as a characteristic of one particular policy or other set of rules, but as an actor's attribute.

Fourth, as far as the 'behavioural turn' in studying public administration comes down to an exclusive focus on the motivation of individuals (a form of *subject centrism*), it tends to overlook the relevance of cultural standards and, more in general, the institutional context at large. Fifth, the common denominator behind the various meanings of the term discretion is 'controlled freedom', as highlighted in the introductory chapter. The rest is empirically open, while variety is multiple. The degree of legitimacy of practised discretion will vary, as well as the nature and degree of the efforts exercised to control that discretion. The sources of such control may be multiple, too.

16.3 A Plurality of Discretionary Actors

As we have shown, the analysis of discretion provided by legal scholars such as Galligan and Dworkin stresses the importance of seeing discretion in context and particularly noting the importance of rules for that context. At the same time, such an analysis is naturally focused upon the street-level end in the implementation part of the policy process and not particularly concerned with issues about how rules are made in agenda setting and policy formation, as the preceding 'stages'. This analysis may be contrasted with Huber and Shipan's (2002) study *Deliberate discretion*. Their interest is in questions about how legislative institutions design legislation. They set out to model ways to examine this subject comparatively. Interestingly, they never define 'discretion' and tend to treat it as synonymous with 'delegation'. Their central question is:

> At times legislatures adopt extremely detailed laws in an effort to micromanage the policymaking process. At other times, legislatures write astonishingly vague and general laws that cede substantial policymaking authority to the executive and bureaucrats. We want to understand the choice between these two possibilities (…) (2002: xiii).

In this very wide, essentially top-level, view Huber and Shipan brush aside the complexities of legislature/executive and executive/bureaucracy relationships. These are the subject of attention in public administration studies since Woodrow Wilson's (1887) essay on the relationship between politics and administration, raising pertinent issues about the origins of laws.

To explore this adequately would entail a substantial digression, but it is important to recognize that lower level discretion in public policy emerges within this overall context. In that sense it takes its cue from Huber and Shipan's interest in the origins of top-down policymaking. Simultaneously it acknowledges that, from an *output* perspective, the study of discretion concerns the question how laws or other norms 'work', in a constraining way or otherwise, when they are adhered to at or close to the street level.

Discretion and Delegation

Lawyers' interest in administrative discretion was in the past—at least certainly in British writings— particularly expressed in terms of a concern about arbitrary action by government. It meant not so much extensive discretion at street level as legislation that delegates uncontrollable powers to ministers (Dicey 1915; Hewart 1929). This was very tied up with an argument about the supremacy of the UK Parliament and particularly came from critics of welfare legislation that created extensive new powers. There was also a peculiar British element in this that resisted the creation of a body of constitutional law that could become a point of reference independently of the will of Parliament. Whilst exploring that would take us a long way from our topic here, it is relevant inasmuch as one of the origins of discretion may lie in political decisions, at the level of *high politics*.

However, modern writers on UK constitutional law take this point in another direction; see for example, Jowell and Oliver (2000), to the concerns of Dworkin and Galligan, discussed above, about the structuring of discretion. Such a perspective recognizes a reality of modern government, that statutes are likely to require interpretation and amplification. What is called *delegated legislation* has become an accepted part of the law-making process in the UK. Delegated discretion, in this legal context, refers to rulemaking consequent upon a need for the amplification or modification of originating statutes.

There is a debate about the extent to which this does or should involve reference back to or scrutiny by Parliament, which it is not appropriate to explore here.

Hence the lawyers' concern is with 'due process' in which discretionary powers are clear and ways in which their exercise may be challenged is identifiable. This brings the British approach much closer to that of countries where either a written constitution or an explicit body of written law may be the ultimate point of appeal where redress is sought (see further discussion below). A final note is appropriate here that the whole of this concern about discretion in a constitutional context rests in the first place upon an expectation of legitimate (democratic) government.

Systems of Discretion

The discussion in the last sub-section drew upon a British debate about delegated legislation. Just as the earlier discussion has stressed variation in the way discretion is manifest in different policy areas or from different professional perspectives, this discussion of systems of discretion needs to take into account the importance of institutional contexts different from country to country. Huber and Shipan (2002: 218) give some attention to this issue and write of 'a coherent and systematic relationship between the political and institutional contexts in which politicians find themselves and the way in which they use legislation to delegate authority to bureaucrats'. However, they are not able to take this further to indicate ways of comparing contexts. They give some attention to the distinction between presidential and parliamentary systems, suggesting greater autonomy to delegate in the former than in the latter. One cannot make too much of that without attention to the forms such autonomy takes.

The presidential/parliamentary dichotomy is but one of the distinctions that might be given attention. Another is the contrast between the *Westminster model*, with 'first past the post' electoral systems and the *consensus model* highlighted in the work of Lijphart (1999). Furthermore, both Huber and Shipan and Lijphart give some attention to the impact of federalism, whilst Lane and Ersson (2000, Chapter 4) suggest that any use of this as a variable needs to take into account its diverse forms and difficulties in distinguishing it from weaker forms of decentralization. This last issue is discussed further below. The problem remains with these distinctions that they are particularly used to characterize policymaking systems. They may imply forms taken by systems of delegation around questions about willingness to share power but no more than that. As such they have not been used—except by Huber and Shipan—in the exploration of discretion.

For our purposes there is perhaps more potential to be found in efforts to compare public administration systems. Three useful approaches to this are provided, respectively, by Pollitt and Bouckaert (2000), Painter and Peters (2010) and Kuhlmann and Wollman (2014). Each approach distinguishes 'families' of administrative systems and their groups have much in common. Pollitt and Bouckaert (2000) approach the task of classification by way of the identification of 'structural, cultural and functional elements' (40), going on to choose:

1. State structure—that is whether federal or unitary and the extent of co-ordination.
2. Nature of executive government at the central level—majoritarian, consensual or somewhere between.
3. The nature of 'minister/mandarin' relations.
4. Administrative culture: a complex categorization in which the notion of the *Rechtsstaat* is used. This involves the perspective that the administrative machine is in the service of the 'state' rather than simply the 'government'.
5. Diversity of sources of political advice.

Pollitt and Bouckaert's approach to classification suggests issues worth attention in comparing ways in which discretion is manifest, but their main concern in their study is with variation in approaches to 'modernization'. Their fourth element, linking issues about administrative culture to the idea of the *Rechtsstaat*, is the most pertinent here. Pollitt and Bouckaert (2000: 53) say of this perspective:

> (T)he state is a central integrating force within society, and its focal concerns are with the preparation, promulgation and enforcement of laws. It follows from this that most civil servants will be trained in the law (…). In such a culture the instinctive bureaucratic stance will be one of rule following and precedent.

The key contrast here is then with what Pollitt and Bouckaert call the 'public interest model' where the state is less dominant and government is 'regarded as something of a necessary evil' (2000: 53). This point is also emphasized by Kuhlmann and Wollmann (2014: 11).

There remain some intriguing issues for further research about the extent to which this distinction finds reflection in questions about discretion and its control at street level. One study that comes close to doing this is Jewell's (2007) examination of social assistance in Germany, Sweden and the United States, where certainly efforts to encourage rule following are prominent in the first named. This is not true of Sweden and here the limitations of generalization are perhaps highlighted by the fact that Kuhlmann and Wollmann put the Scandinavians in a special category where the *Rechtsstaat* ideal and decentralization seem to pull in different directions. In other words, in the Scandinavian system there may be a more relaxed approach to local discretion.

A Hierarchy of Discretions

The notion of delegated legislation implies that an initial legislative act gives power to a ministry to take further steps to translate it into action and that the exercise of those powers may create rules that define the discretionary powers of others. It suggests the possibility of speaking of a *hierarchy of discretions.* Knoepfel and Weidner use the term 'policy programming' (1982, see also Knoepfel, Larrue, Varone and Hill 2007, Chapter 8) to include:

- More precise definitions of policy objectives.
- Operational elements, which include the 'instruments' to be used to make the policy effective.
- 'Political-administrative arrangements', the specification of the authorities whose duty it will be to implement the policy and whom will need money and other resources to do that.
- Procedural elements, namely the rules to be used in the implementation of the policy.

Obviously, all of these elements may be present in the statute inaugurating the policy. The detail assumed by this formulation however suggests that any empirical search for them may need to recognize decisions that are consequent upon the initially specified objective. The term 'political-administrative arrangements' particularly highlights the fact that decisions may be delegated to other bodies: local governments or specific central government agencies. These may then be given powers to determine exactly how they will carry out their tasks.

Variation in these 'political-administrative arrangements' obviously follow from the national variety discussed in the previous sub-section, but more needs to be said about the manifold ways in which these may be constituted. Two particular aspects of this will be discussed here: federalism (and related forms of autonomy on the part of regional and local bodies) and the use of specific separate implementing agencies.

Elazar (1995: 474–5) defines federalism as 'a constitutionalized power sharing through systems that combine self-rule and shared rule'. What this means, for the purpose of this discussion is that actors within a federal system may find their powers specified by, using American terminology here, either the overriding 'federal government' or the specific 'state' level or some combination of the two. It is of course from the last that many of the sources of confusion and dispute about federalism emerge. Peter May has given extensive attention to this issue, writing about the extent to which states are 'mandated' in the United States and Australia (May 1995; May and Burby 1996). More recently he has developed what he calls the *policy regime perspective* (May and Jochim 2013). He applies this to President Obama's health reform where: 'The policy and implementation provisions call for a complex mosaic of actions to bring about the reform, illustrating the complexity of large-scale, multi-actor, intergovernmental policy' (May 2015: 432). The intergovernmental aspect here is particularly the requirement of the application of the policy in specific states, where it has to be integrated with pre-existing policies.

American federalism is the main focus in the remarks above, but the overall observations may be applied both in one direction to supra-national efforts to developed shared policies (e.g. in the European Union) and in the other to intergovernmental relationships not normally described as 'federal'. It is not appropriate to go further into supra-national arrangements; from the perspective of this chapter, it is the intergovernmental relationships that are most salient. Here the overriding point is that there may be *co-producing layers* within governmental systems. Expectations that 'lower' layers have roles to play in the policy formation part of the policy process then have been enshrined in taken for granted practices, in specific laws or even in the constitution (Hill and Hupe 2003; several chapters of this edited collection address the tasks assigned to professionals, while Chap. 7 focuses on the roles attributed to service users).

Also, without the latter dimension being present, the points about formal definitions of responsibility discussed here in terms of territorial divisions may apply. The second point noted above regards the role of specific implementing agencies. In Chap. 6 of this edited collection, an example of a quasi-independent agency is discussed. One of the reasons given for the establishment of a 'board' to administer social assistance was a need for issues about personal needs to be handled at 'arm's length' from the political system. That would today probably be regarded as a rather dated idea; nevertheless, the case for 'arm's length' implementation is still made in a variety of other ways. This is particularly found in the arguments for *New Public Management* where partial independence is justified in the cause of more efficient management (see Hood 1995 for an overview). This perspective is also closely connected with the idea of the creation of bodies where performance expectations comparable to those imposed by markets can be established, while perhaps actual competition can be required. Hence in a variety of areas—public utilities, transport, healthcare and so on—it is possible to identify delegation of discretionary powers. In relation to these powers, contracts are often important, establishing the terms and limits to this discretion, whilst also perhaps identifying how these organizations may be called to account in this respect.

The result of these various structural features (constitutional systems, systems of democracy, systems of intergovernmental relations, systems of political-administrative relations) and process factors (bureaucratic politics) in many cases will be public policies with a less than a 'single design' or 'programmed' character. Therefore, if a policy is looked at from the street level, while any discretionary powers may have been directly given by the initial statutes, they may also be the less formal resultant of discretion exercised by other actors involved in the policy process concerned.

There may be a process of structuring discretion through a hierarchical process. Those seeking redress against an act of discretion will see the legitimacy of the products of this process as their main practical concern, rather than the question about the extent to which a discretion has been specifically granted by the legislature. In this context, Jowell (1973: 178) distinguishes between two approaches to the control of discretion. One is *legalization*, the 'process of subjecting official decisions to predetermined rules' and thus, trying to minimize discretion. The other is *judicialization*, involving 'submitting official decisions to adjudicative procedures'. There are also important issues about the interaction between these two approaches. In that sense the issue is then about where ultimate decision-making power – as discretion – is to reside when there is conflict over official decisions. Then those adjudicative procedures may involve the exercise of discretion by courts and tribunals. There is an issue here that 'judicialization' may involve the shifting of discretionary powers to a judge or tribunal, with an assumption that such a body is better equipped to exercise discretion than the officials making the original decision.

A search for the provisions that manage discretion at the street level may not necessarily reveal an explicit mandate for action. A distinction may be made between 'agency' and 'individual' discretion (Bull 1980). The former has a recognizable legal definition whilst the latter is the object of managerial instructions to street-level workers. Formally specified discretionary powers may be interpreted and organizations may have rule books that specify these or it may even be left to first-line managers at the local level to brief their subordinates.

The distinction between agency and individual discretion may be important in a public policy context for the identification of responsibility if something goes wrong or a decision is challenged. There are contexts, particularly in regulatory policy, where individuals in the relevant law are identified as the decision makers. However, there will be others where individuals are just 'agents' of their organization. This is, however, not a simple dichotomy. The autonomous decision maker may operate in an organizational structure in which first-line managers provide advice and support. The subordinate one in a more strictly controlled situation may not be absolved of responsibility when things go wrong. Much may depend upon the clarity of the mandates provided to street-level officials. This is explored further in the next sub-section. In all cases, the issues about the limits to absolute control explored earlier will apply.

Discretion Beyond Hierarchy

The discussion of discretion in the previous sub-section pre-supposes a clarity about the way in which public policies delegate discretion, essentially following the principal/agent model in which discretion is seen to have a delegated character. The present sub-section explores a number of situations in which this may not be so:

1. When the initiator of a policy and its implementer are essentially the same.
2. Where implementation depends upon negotiation between different parties.
3. Where the case for professional autonomy has been conceded.

In the first case, there may be no delegation of discretion. Logically, that may occur in almost any context and is to some extent thus a function of scale. For example, decisions about social assistance payments or allocation of public housing or public employment may be made by members of the government. This applies where there are clientelist forms of politics with patronage through political favours. It may be seen today in various small nation states around the world, but lies at the roots of political party systems in many countries, including in particular the United States (Key 1942).

More generally, policy processes with high levels of discretion but little or no delegation are particularly evident in international relations (Allison 1971) and in macro-economic policy (Hall 1986). Actions may fall logically within the definition of discretion used here: declarations of war, the making or breaking of treaties, changes to bank interest rates, the granting of major public contracts. They differ however from the main concerns of analyses of discretion inasmuch as there are expectations that these belong within the remit of national political actors.

The second case overlaps with the first case inasmuch as the retention of discretion by the principal actors may be seen as necessary for negotiation with other actors. More generally it may be that decision-making by officials is embedded in a complex *governance* relationship in which results are achieved through interactions—negotiations, bargains and such—with other parties. The essential point here is made by Scharpf (1978: 347):

> (I)t is unlikely, if not impossible, that public policy of any significance could result from the choice process of any single unified actor. Policy formulation and policy implementation are inevitably the result of interactions among a plurality of separate actors with separate interests, goals and strategies.

That is putting the issue particularly strongly and linking formation and implementation. Nevertheless, there are many policymaking activities where interactions often within complex networks are important at the street level (see, for instance, Knoke 1990; Smith 1993; Klijn 1997; Koppenjan and Klijn 2004).

One feature of the analysis of networks is a recognition that these may contain not just the representatives of more than one public agency, but also that private interest groups may be incorporated into the network (In addition to the network literature the work of Sabatier and his colleagues (2007) on the 'advocacy coalition framework' is also relevant here). There is a wide general point applying to all of the analysis of discretion, that decisions are made in interactions with other parties—including those who gain or lose from those decisions—in what in fact is a relationship of *co-production* (Hanf 1993; Hupe 1993).

This leads to the third issue identified above: professional autonomy. This is a particularly salient issue where outcomes depend upon interactions between public officials and the public. The issues about professional autonomy in medicine, education and social work have been widely discussed (Freidson 1970; Johnson 1972; Harrison and Pollitt 1994; Evans 2015; see also several chapters of this edited collection). There have been efforts to constrain decision-making—recommended procedures and limits to activities that may be undertaken in medicine, defined curricula and rules about examinations in education. There are also supervisory and accountability arrangements. Nevertheless, considerable autonomy remains and many of the attempts to restrict discretion involve professional bodies as part of the controlling system (Harrison 2015). Those professional bodies, particularly in medicine, are themselves the subject of statutes in which their roles in respect of individual discretion are recognized. Another feature of this area of discretion, particularly in the case of medicine, is statutory provisions that determine decisions that should (or must) be made by professionals (e.g. the identification of disability).

Issues about professional discretion also apply in areas of regulatory policy. Here we may find extensive discretionary powers, exercised by experts in identifying and dealing with dangers to the public and other public nuisances. Jowell (1973) offers a useful analysis of these issues in terms of standards (as discussed above) where the strict application of rules would be inflexible, leaving no room for negotiation and difficult to change over time.

Finally, bearing in mind what was said earlier about the need to see decisions about resourcing of a policy as an important stage in the structuring of discretion, it is important not to lose sight of one of Lipsky's key issues about the determination of the street-level task:

> (T)he very nature of this work prevents them from coming close to the ideal conception of their jobs. Large classes or huge caseloads and inadequate resources combine with the uncertainties of method and the unpredictability of clients to defeat their aspirations as service workers (Lipsky 1980: xii).

Hence, even if there are relatively explicit tasks at stake, how and where they are to be performed depend on judgements about the use of scarce resources. This is something particularly evident in regulatory work and policing. Even workers with the most constrained rule-related tasks have to make operational decisions about how they use their time. Traffic wardens are charged to impose fines on illegal parkers. Even if aiming to be scrupulously officious, a warden has to decide which street to walk down and even which way to look.

There are therefore policy areas where extensive discretionary powers are granted, but it may be difficult to identify clear definitions and mandates for these. What we mean here is that an examination of the law may provide evidence that there is an expectation of a specific activity but no clarity about what that activity involves. This is an assertion which would be difficult to substantiate empirically, because it would require a detailed scrutiny of all the relevant laws and would have to be undertaken country by country. However, the characteristics of discretion identified in this chapter suggests that there are activities where what is to be done and the expertise upon which it will depend, will be difficult to subject to close specification. What is being talked about here are activities often defined in terms of the concept of professionalism.

16.4 Conclusion

In this chapter, discretion has been shown to be an inherent feature of public policy. A view of the relationship between rules and discretion that sees the former as sourced hierarchically and the latter as the issues that arise because of limitations to that process, has been demonstrated to be inappropriate. This is particularly so when attention to the issues is driven by a conception of discretion as something undesirable, regardless of its context.

In respect of that view, Dworkin's metaphor of discretion as the hole in the donut is helpful in indicating that discretion is exercised within a structure. The 'hole', however, conveys a notion of discretion as something entirely undetermined. He might instead have referred to it as a British rather than American donut in which there is jam in the hole. And, he could have taken his metaphor further to recognize that constituting the donut requires decisions on a balance between two elements, the dough and the jam, both of which are malleable.

Attention then needs to be given to the factors that determine these elements. The chapter has identified a number of significant considerations:

- the complexity of the activities concerned, particularly inasmuch as issues about 'standards' are involved;
- the insight that those who exercise discretion occupy a role in which they have to make judgements and effect compromises between alternatives and perhaps collaborate with others (about which they may have more or less strong views that influence their behaviour);
- that the transition of a complex policy aspiration into action depends upon a succession of decisions all which may be discretionary in some respects; and
- that, whilst many of the processes concerned may be hierarchical in character, this is not necessarily the case.

Such a perspective points us towards the political processes that determine policy. Behind formal public policy decisions, a lot of politics is hidden: democratic politics, party politics but also bureaucratic politics. Indeed, there are various views about what is meant by policy (see Hill and Varone 2017, Chapter 1). It is alternatively defined in very general terms as a 'stance' and in very specific terms. In many respects it may simply be seen as a 'claim', as in the ordinary usage embodied in the statement 'My policy is (…)', a view that becomes problematical when it is a product of a negotiated process. It may also be seen more as an outcome than as an input: a country's health policy or education policy and so on is what actually is being delivered in practice.

The fact of a *plurality of discretionary actors* is accompanied by the fact of a multiple character of a public policy as a 'message'. In other words, in a policy process there are many co-producers of inputs and there are many inputs, which at the street level all function as action prescriptions to reckon with (Hupe and Hill 2007). Much therefore depends on how the many actors perceive their roles when putting policies into practice.

References

Allison, G.T. (1971). *Essence of decision: Explaining the Cuban missile crisis*. Boston, MA: Little Brown.

Baker Collins, S. (2016). The space in the rules: Bureaucratic discretion in the administration of Ontario Works. *Social Policy and Society*, 15(2), 221–235.

Brodkin, E.Z. (2011). Policy work: Street level organizations under New Managerialism. *Journal of Public Administration Research and Theory*, 21(2), 253–277.

Bull, D. (1980). The anti-discretion movement in Britain: Fact or phantom? *Journal of Social Welfare Law*, 2(1), 65–83.

Cohen, N. (2016). How culture affects street-level bureaucrats' bending the rules in the context of informal payments for health care: The Israeli case. *American Review of Public Administration*, 1–18. https://doi.org/10.1177/0275074016665919.

Davis, K.C. (1969). *Discretionary justice: A preliminary inquiry*. Baton Rouge: Louisiana State University Press.

Dicey, A.V. (1915). *Introduction to the study of the law and the constitution* (8th ed.). London: Macmillan.

Dworkin, R.M. (1977). *Taking rights seriously*. Cambridge, MA: Harvard University Press.

Elazar, D.J. (1995). Federalism. In S.M. Lipset (Ed.), *Encyclopaedia of democracy*. London: Routledge.

Evans, T. (2015). Professionals and discretion in street-level bureaucracy. In P.L Hupe, M.J. Hill & A. Buffat (Eds), *Understanding street-level bureaucracy* (pp. 279–293). Bristol: Policy Press.

Freidson, E. (1970). *Professional dominance*. New York: Atherton.

Galligan, D.J. (1986). *Discretionary powers*. Oxford: Clarendon Press.

Galligan, D.J. (1990). *Discretionary powers: A legal study of official discretion*. Chapter 1 'Senses of discretion' retrieved from Oxford Scholarship Online https://doi.org/10.1093/acprof:oso/9780198256526.001.0001 Subscriber: Erasmus University Library. Date: 7 September 2015.

Garrow, E. & Grusky, O. (2013). Institutional logic and street-level discretion: The case of HIV test counseling. *Journal of Public Administration Research and Theory*, 23(1), 103–131.

Gouldner, A. (1954). *Patterns of industrial bureaucracy*. Glencoe, IL: Free Press.

Hall, P.A. (1986). *Governing the economy: The politics of state intervention in Britain and France*. Cambridge: Polity Press.

Hanf, K. (1993). Enforcing environmental laws: The social regulation of co-production. In M.J. Hill (Ed.), *New agendas in the study of the policy process* (pp. 88–109). Hemel Hempstead: Harvester Wheatsheaf.

Harrison, S. (2015). Street-level bureaucracy and professionalism in health services. In P.L. Hupe, M.J. Hill & A. Buffat (Eds), *Understanding street-level bureaucracy* (pp. 61–78). Bristol: Policy Press.

Harrison, S. & Pollitt, C. (1994). *Controlling health professionals*. Buckingham: Open University Press.

Hewart, L. (1929). *The new despotism*. London: Ernest Benn.

Hill, M.J. (Ed.) *New agendas in the study of the policy process*. Hemel Hempstead: Harvester Wheatsheaf.

Hill, M.J. & Varone, F. (2017). *The public policy process*. Abingdon: Routledge.

Hill, M.J. & Hupe, P.L. (2003). The multi-layer problem in implementation studies. *Public Management Review*, 5(4), 471–490.

Hood, C. (1995). Contemporary public management: A new global paradigm? *Public Policy and Administration*, 10(2), 104–117.

Huber, J.D. & Shipan, C.R. (2002). *Deliberate discretion? The institutional foundations of bureaucratic autonomy*. Cambridge: Cambridge University Press.

Hupe, P.L. (1993). The politics of implementation: Individual, organizational and political co-production in social services delivery. In M.J. Hill (Ed.), *New agendas in the study of the policy process* (pp. 130–151). Hemel Hempstead: Harvester Wheatsheaf.

Hupe, P.L. (2013). Dimensions of discretion: Specifying the object of street-level bureaucracy research. *Der Moderne Staat. Zeitschrift für Public Policy, Recht und Management*, 6(2), 425–440.

Hupe, P.L. (Ed.) (2019). *Research handbook on street-level bureaucracy: The ground floor of government in context*. Cheltenham: Edward Elgar Publishing.

Hupe, P.L. & Hill, M.J. (2007). Street-level bureaucracy and public accountability. *Public Administration*, 85(2), 279–299.

Hupe, P.L., Hill, M.J. & Buffat, A. (Eds) (2015) *Understanding street-level bureaucracy*. Bristol: Policy Press.

Jewell, C.J. (2007). *Agents of the welfare state*. New York and Basingstoke: Palgrave Macmillan.

Johnson, T.J. (1972). *Professions and power*. London: Macmillan.

Jowell, J. (1973). The legal control of administrative discretion. *Public Law*, 178–220.

Jowell, J. & Oliver, D. (Eds.) (2000). *The changing Constitution* (4th ed.). Oxford: Oxford University Press.

Keiser, L.R., Mueser, P.R. & Choi, S.-W. (2004). Race, bureaucratic discretion, and the implementation of welfare reform. *American Journal of Political Science*, 48(2), 314–327.

Key, V.O. Jr. (1942). *Politics, parties and pressure groups*. New York: Crowell.

Klijn, E.-H.. (1997). Policy networks: An overview. In W.J.M. Kickert, E.-H. Klijn & J.F.M. Koppenjan (Eds), *Managing complex networks: Strategies for the public sector* (pp. 14–34). London: Sage

Knoepfel, P. & Weidner, H. (1982). Formulation and implementation of air quality control programmes: Patterns of interest consideration. *Policy and Politics*, 10(1), 85–109.

Knoepfel, P., Larrue, C., Varone, F. & Hill, M.J. (2007). *Public policy analysis*. Bristol: Policy Press.

Knoke, D. (1990). *Policy networks: The structural perspective*. Cambridge: Cambridge University Press.

Koppenjan, J.F.M. & Klijn, E.-H. (2004). *Managing uncertainties in networks*. London: Routledge.

Kuhlmann, S. & Wollmann, H. (2014). *Introduction to comparative public administration*. Cheltenham: Edward Elgar.

Lane, J.-E. & Ersson, S.O. (2000). *The new institutional politics: Performance and outcomes*. London: Routledge.

Lijphart, A. (1999). *Patterns of democracy*. New Haven, CT: Yale University Press.

Lipsky, M. (1980). *Street-level bureaucracy: Dilemmas of the individual in public services*. New York: Russell Sage Foundation.

May, P.J. (2015). Implementation failures revisited: Policy regime perspectives. *Public Policy and Administration*, 30(3–4), 277–299.

May, P.J. & Jochim, A.E. (2013). Policy regime perspectives: Policies, politics and governing. *Policy Studies Journal*, 41(3), 426–452.

May, P.J. (1995). Can cooperation be mandated? Implementing intergovernmental environmental management in New South Wales and New Zealand. *Publius*, 25(1), 89–113.

May, P.J. & Burby, R.J. (1996). Coercive versus cooperative policies: Comparing intergovernmental mandate performance. *Journal of Policy Analysis and Management*, 15(2), 171–201.

Painter, M. & Peters, B.G. (Eds) (2010). *Tradition and public administration.* Basingstoke: Palgrave.

Pollitt, C. & Bouckaert, G. (2000). *Public management reform: A comparative analysis.* Oxford: Oxford University Press.

Sabatier, P.A. & Weible, C.M. (2007). The advocacy coalition framework: Innovations and clarifications. In P.A. Sabatier (Ed.), *Theories of the policy process* (pp. 189–220). Boulder, CO: Westview Press.

Scharpf, F.W. (1978). Interorganizational policy studies: Issues, concepts and perspectives. In K.I. Hanf & F.W. Scharpf (Eds), *Interorganizational policy making: Limits to coordination and central Control* (pp. 345–370) London: Sage.

Smith, M.J. (1993). *Pressure, power and policy.* Hemel Hempstead: Harvester Wheatsheaf.

Sosin, M.R. (2010). Discretion in human service organizations: Traditional and institutional perspectives. In Y. Hasenfeld (Ed.), *Human services as complex organizations* (2nd ed., pp. 381–403). London: Sage.

Swidler, A. (1986). Culture in action: Symbols and strategies. *American Sociological Review*, 51, 273–286.

Taylor, I. & Kelly, J. (2006). Professionals, discretion and public sector reforms in the UK: Re-visiting Lipsky. *International Journal of Public Sector Management*, 19(7), 629–642.

Thomann, E., Hupe, P. & Sager, F. (2018). Serving many masters: Public accountability in private policy implementation. *Governance*, 31(2), 299–319.

Tummers, L.L.G. (2012). Policy alienation of public professionals: The construct and its measurement. *Public Administration Review*, 72(4), 516–525.

Tummers, L.L.G., Steijn, A. & Bekkers, V.J.J.M. (2012). Explaining the willingness of public professionals to implement public policies. *Public Administration*, 90(3), 716–736.

Tummers, L.L.G. & Bekkers, V.J.J.M. (2014). Policy implementation, street-level bureaucracy, and the importance of discretion. *Public Management Review*, 16(4), 527–547.

Tummers, L.L.G., Bekkers, V.J.J.M., Vink, E. & Musheno, M. (2015). Coping during public service delivery: A conceptualization and systematic review of the literature. *Journal of Public Administration Research and Theory*, 24(4), 1099–1126.

Wilson, W. (1887). The study of administration. *Political Science Quarterly*, 2, 197–222.

CHAPTER 17

Discretion and Street-Level Practice

Hendrik Wagenaar

17.1 Introduction: The Seeming Conundrum of Administrative Discretion

The subject of administrative discretion in the literature gives rise to a certain inconclusiveness, a wavering between realism and normative anxiety. On one hand, public administration scholars are aware that effective policy implementation is more or less impossible when officials do not have the freedom to interpret rules in light of the person or situation they face. The reason is straightforward: general concepts, categories and conditions need to be related to concrete persons and situations (Bakker and van Waarden 1999: 19; translation HW):

> To be able to bridge the gap between general rules and specific situations and to diminish decision complexity and overload, implementing organizations and officials need a certain measure of discretion.

On the other hand, public administration scholars fear that rule deviation will be abused. The same authors state that officials and organizations can use their discretionary space to thwart or sabotage policy and make sure that policy goals with which they disagree are not attained (1999: 20).[1]

Underlying this anxiety is a strong normative dimension. A nation's laws, as well as the by-laws, regulations and administrative rules based on that body of law, represent the rule of law of a country. Together with an independent judiciary they form what in the continental legal and administrative tradition is called the *Rechtsstaat*. These 'lesser' rules derive their legitimacy from formal

H. Wagenaar (✉)
King's College London, London, UK

The University of Canberra, Canberra, ACT, Australia
e-mail: hendrik.wagenaar@kcl.ac.uk

T. Evans, P. Hupe (eds.), *Discretion and the Quest for Controlled Freedom*, https://doi.org/10.1007/978-3-030-19566-3_17

laws that have been deliberated and accepted by a majority of democratically elected members of parliament. Importantly, the rule of law implies that citizens can challenge the decisions and actions of administrative bodies. Hence, those decisions and actions need to be clearly and unequivocally based on the aforesaid democratically established laws (Hill and Hupe 2002: 22–28). Discretionary behaviour severs the crucial connection between democratically established law and administrative behaviour, thereby evoking the spectre of arbitrary, unjust and, ultimately, unlawful behaviour of the state. Thus, normatively, through the mechanism of the rule of law, the actions of administrators are irrevocably tied to the reach of formal rules. It does not matter how discretionary behaviour is explained: as a coping mechanism (Lipsky), as the input of multiple external sources (Vinzant and Crothers), as the outcome of moral judgement and peer pressure (Maynard-Moody and Musheno) or as political-administrative actors who are charged with making 'contextually appropriate' choices in complex governance networks (Hupe and Hill 2007). By definition, discretionary behaviour is regarded as a risk; the risk to cut the crucial relation with formal law that undergirds the legitimacy of the state and, ultimately, of the democratic order (Held 2006).

This received view has enormous intuitive and normative power. It informs ideals in the two dominant although contrasting public management strategies, public administration and new public management (Sandford 2000). Its normative claim concerns the constitutive principles of the democratic state, even in the fragmented formal and informal accountability configurations of contemporary governance (Hupe and Hill 2007: 289). In relation to this, administrative discretion is considered subjective: the result of the individual's personal judgement to stick or deviate from the rules. It risks undermining the accountability dimension of public administration and thereby the legitimacy of the whole political and administrative edifice of the state (Sandford 2000: 730).

Yet, the normative hold that the received view has over academic and legal thinking about discretion obscures a number of obvious aspects of administrative work; aspects that are hidden in plain sight as it were. For example, it fails to explain a number of commonly observed aspects of discretionary behaviour. Most administrators in a particular policy domain or government bureaucracy operate in broadly similar ways. While this is partly explained by the behavioural shaping by organizational routines, standard operating procedures and software architecture, it does not explain how the discretionary part of all these decentred administrative actions is shaped. Also, while citizens show high levels of distrust and dissatisfaction with elected officials, they are much more satisfied about their encounters with administrators, even in sensitive areas such as policing, welfare and teaching (Goodsell 2004; Amy 2017). This is even more remarkable as these areas of public administration often present officials with painful moral dilemmas (Wagenaar 2002). While the received view is unable to explain how officials resolve moral dilemmas, somehow officials usually manage to arrive at decisions that satisfy both the citizen and the organization. Also, citizens and officials alike have no trouble detecting and understanding unjust, ineffective and grievous administrative action, suggesting they countenance some unspoken moral standard. And, finally and perhaps most importantly, the received view fails to detect the sociological dimension of administrative discretion. Discretion is not a deviation from the rules; it is inevitable, ineludible (Hupe and Hill 2007). What is called 'discretion' is identical with the everyday administrative work of applying rules; of making formal rules work in the real world of poverty, welfare, policing and teaching.

In this chapter I will challenge the received view of administrative discretion as an undefined and undesirable space between formal rules and informal behaviour, as well as the implicit normative hierarchy between formal law and informal behaviour that it implies. Given its central position in the constitution of the democratic state I will not detract from the importance of parliamentary accepted formal law. Instead I will collapse the dualism between constitutionalism and realism by conceptualizing discretionary behaviour in terms of *practice*. Although the practice approach has made inroads in international relations, planning and organizational studies, it has been slow in influencing Public Administration and policy studies (Bartels 2018). In summary form the argument goes as follows.

Rules may be prescribed, but they do not, and inherently cannot, determine behaviour. Rules and their 'application' are part of the same practice. All administrative behaviour, including what appears to be the meticulous application of rules, is forged in the craft of practice. While open-ended and improvisational, it is neither arbitrary nor rule-less. Practice at the street level of public administration is bound by tradition, experience, norms, materialities (the tools and technologies that make the job possible), peer pressure and background knowledge. Street-level practice emerges in the course of discussing and narrating everyday experiences in organizational settings. To the outsider, practice may appear ephemeral and fleeting, which might put off researchers to engage with practice. However, the analysis of oral narrative is a robust methodological tool to understand how street-level practice unfolds in emerging time, what organizational, legal, moral and personal challenges it faces, how it harnesses these challenges and how in doing so it takes rules, laws and belief structures into account.

In the remainder of this chapter, I will give an overview of the practice approach to administrative discretion. First, I argue against the logical possibility of 'correct' rule application and instead suggest that what we perceive as rule following is in reality a form of, unacknowledged, practice. Then the theory and analysis of oral narrative will be introduced. Using the case of a Dutch welfare officer, I will show how narrative analysis illuminates the craft of navigating the complexities of the welfare programme. In the conclusions, I will argue that street-level practice, when properly organized, is the optimal way of safeguarding the integrity and democratic legitimacy of public administration.

17.2 Street-Level Practice and the Logical Impossibility of Rule Application

In the above paragraphs I invoked the concept of (administrative) work. What is (administrative) work?

> (B)y using the concept of work, I have in mind the hundreds of practical judgements, the everyday, taken-for-granted routines and practices, the explicit and tacit knowledge that is brought to bear on concrete situations, the moving about in the legal–moral environment of large administrative bureaucracies, the mastering of difficult human–emotional situations, the negotiating of discretionary space, and the interactive give and take with colleagues that, taken together, make up everyday public administration (Wagenaar 2004: 644).

My argument was that we tend to conceive of work in terms of its overt organizational processes, managerial interventions and visible outcomes. There are many reasons for that, but one of them is the taken-for-granted cognitive organization of a field—any field—into what is seen as important and unimportant; the field's signal to its irrelevant noise. In the above quote I attempted to redress this taken-for-granted carving up of the field of administrative work. My aim was to redeem the everyday experience of work in a large bureaucracy—the

> unthinking routines, the informal banter and gossip with colleagues during the coffee break, our sympathies and antipathies, our private doubts about the quality of our work, our affective responses to clients or colleagues, and our recurrent sense of stress or work pressure (2004: 644).

Put differently, my aim was to challenge the deep assumptions that underpin and shape our perception of administrative work and its corollary, administrative discretion. The decisions, reports, pronouncements and—at a higher level of institutional aggregation— the structures, legal rules, lines of authority and accountability procedures of the world of public authority are realized through—even constituted by—these fleeting, subjective, everyday experiences of administrative work. Taken together these are all elements of street-level practice.

To conceive of administrative work as practice is to follow in the footsteps of Wittgenstein's argument about rule following. The practice approach is the intellectual offspring of the non-foundational turn in twentieth-century philosophy by philosophers such as Martin Heidegger, Ludwig Wittgenstein, Henri Bergson, John Dewey, Mary Parker Follet, Maurice Merleau-Ponty and, in our days, Charles Taylor and William Connolly (Schatzki 1996; Nicolini 2012). These authors argued among other things that there are no ultimate intellectual foundations for our knowledge of the world and that at best we reach provisional understandings of some aspect of the world by acting upon it in emerging time and interpreting our actions and their effects (Taylor 1995a, b).

Wittgenstein developed his anti-foundational philosophy through an analysis of rule following. Pertinent to the topic of this chapter, he famously demonstrated in his lectures in the 1940s that there can be no such thing as a watertight, exhaustive explanation of *any* rule. Every rule, when 'applied' in real-world circumstances, may lead to misunderstanding. Even a simple rule such as 'Come to a full stop when the traffic light is red' or 'Acknowledge your colleague when she asks you: How are you?' can be open to various interpretations. In the first example, I might decide to ignore the red light when I rush to the hospital with my neighbour who suffered a cardiac arrest in the backseat. In the second example, the expected reaction will be different in the US (polite, noncommittal acknowledgement) than, let's say in the Netherlands (a full stop followed by a summary of the addressee's current personal situation) or in Vienna (a sarcastic answer: '*Noch immer slecht, danke*'). Rule following is either culturally dependent or shaped by unforeseen and unforeseeable external circumstances. This being so, we could reply, in the first case, that we all know what the right way to follow the rule is (after all, the driver knows that he just broke it), while in the second case, that the right way can be derived from grasping local cultural habits and understandings. However, that will not do, because the number of external circumstances or cultural prescriptions and therefore possible interpretations and misunderstandings are potentially endless (Taylor 1995c: 166). The problem resides in a certain, culturally institutionalized, conception of what it means to follow a rule. Wittgenstein gives the following example:

> Suppose I give this explanation: 'I take "Moses" to mean the man, if there was such a man, who led the Israelites out of Egypt, whatever he was called then and whatever he may or may not have done besides'—But similar doubts to those about the name 'Moses' are possible about the word of this explanation (what are you calling 'Egypt', whom the 'Israelites' and so forth?). These questions would not even come to an end when we got down to words like 'red', 'dark', 'sweet'.—But then how does an explanation help me to understand, if, after all, it is not the final one? (Wittgenstein 2009: (87) 45[e])

Wittgenstein argues that, although we might feel that we have exhaustive explanations to questions or we know for certain how to follow a particular rule, this feeling of certainty is misleading as it does not and cannot derive from the *inherent* structure of the premise or rule. Every attempt to explain a rule in real-world situations inevitably results in an infinite regress of terms that themselves require further explanation. What Wittgenstein does here is to radically question the realist foundation of several centuries of Western thought. (E.g. that qualifiers such as 'red', 'dark' or 'sweet' refer to self-evident empirical experiences.) He questions the intellectualist reflex that only explanations can provide a sufficient basis for human understanding and action, as he argues in a passage that immediately follows the one I quoted above:

> 'In that case the explanation is never completed; so I still don't understand what he means, and never shall!'—As though an explanation, as it where, hung in the air unless supported by another one. Whereas an explanation may indeed rest on another one that has been given, but none stands in need of another—unless *we* require it to avoid a misunderstanding (Wittgenstein 2009: (87) 45e.).

Wittgenstein's quotes provide both the diagnosis of the problem and a possible solution. The problem is that there is no final and decisive way of settling a disagreement or confusion caused by a rule by invoking another rule. Every explanation of a rule will inevitably run into the problem of infinite regress or further requests for explanation, extenuating external circumstances or cultural exceptions. For our topic, understanding administrative 'discretion'—and here the quotation marks are appropriate—this means that the premise that underlies the very concept is misguiding in itself: the premise that there is an obviously correct way to follow a formal law or rule. There will always be slippage between the law or rule and the real-world situation to which it pertains; slippage that follows from the recurrent problem that every explanation leaves potential issues unresolved (Taylor 1995c: 166). That, however, would erase the very distinction between rule following and discretionary behaviour and that would put the whole normative project of responsible and legitimate public administration that is embedded and guided by the precepts of the *Rechtsstaat* in doubt.

While the premise in the last sentence may be correct, the conclusion is surely absurd. What Wittgenstein says in the last quote is that people have other ways, besides explanations, of coming to an understanding. Surely there must be. After all, although misunderstanding and conflict are all too prevalent, we do not generally live in a world where no one, *ever*, understands another person. Wittgenstein says in effect that the imperative to explain is a misguided intellectualist dictate that we impose upon ourselves. What other ways of understanding do we as humans have at our disposal to move about more or less effectively, more or less adequately, in the world? Charles Taylor's answer is 'background understanding' (1995b, c); mine is 'practice'. In the end, both refer to the same fundamental human configuration or capacity to find our way and get things done in a world of uncertainty and conflict.

Public administration scholars have, in fact, *implicitly* understood this for many years. They argue that administrative discretion is inevitable because street-level bureaucrats 'work in situations that are too complex to reduce to programmatic efforts' (Lipsky 1980: 15). Also, street-level bureaucrats deal with the 'human dimension of situations' or 'the whole person' (Lipsky 1980: 15; Vinzant and Crothers 1998: 41; Maynard-Moody and Musheno 2003) and have to make judgements about intention and motives that are often unknowable and can only be inferred indirectly from the particulars of the situation at hand. These are strong attestations of the Wittgensteinian position on rule following. Nevertheless, according to these authors, administrative discretion is 'inextricably bound up' with questions of legitimacy. In other words, administrative legitimacy and by implication, the integrity of the democratic order, is not necessarily fatally compromised by discretionary behaviour. How does this work? The implicit answer is, by conceiving of discretionary decision-making as a practice. Administrative discretion is defined as a choice on how a goal is to be accomplished (preferred process) or to what end (desired outcome), in a situation of intrinsic uncertainty, that is constrained by external factors (laws, regulation, professional codes and standards, conventions, the opinion of colleagues), the appropriateness of which can be evaluated and which has consequences for the administrator (Vinzant and Crothers 1998: 37–8, 45). Administrators move in a field that is defined by responsibility and trust, where the first represents an accountability norm that puts certain constraints on the administrative process and the second represents the public power entrusted to administrators and professionals in a democratic system to put policies into effect (Lane 1987: 542). The trust aspect balances the autonomy (necessary for making the judgements to design and implement regulation) and accountability on one hand, with the constraints that follow from the intent of the rules and from a more generalized administrative ethos, on the other. Put differently: administrators make practical choices to which they are held accountable.

What is practice? There are many and varying accounts of practice (Gherardi 2012; Nicolini 2012), but most seem to agree on the following premises. The first—at the same time the most obvious yet the most far-reaching—is the primacy of interventionism. Reality (the environment in which we live and move about, that brushes against us from all sides, that we overwhelmingly experience as 'out there', independent of ourselves) is actually a product of our ongoing practical engagement with the world, the experience of our interaction with and interventions in the world (Pickering 1995; Cook and Wagenaar 2012) The second premise concerns temporal emergence and follows from the first. The constraints and affordances of the outer world only come to us through our experience of them in emergent time (within an 'eternally unfolding present' (Cook and Wagenaar 2012)). Practices, although recognizable and intelligible to practitioners and observers, always have a certain open-ended, improvisational quality. Our third premise is that the interpenetration of the human and the material is at the core of how we act on and understand the world (Pickering 1995; Pickering and Guzik 2008; Gherardi 2012; Shove, Pantzar and Watson 2012). In accordance with this relational, dynamic view of practice, our understanding of its dimensions must be seen as explanatory tools supportive of research, assessment and intervention—not as foundational claims about the 'objective' character of practice.

Arguably, these three premises rest on a fourth premise that is enormously significant for a proper understanding of the reach of the practice approach in social and political analysis and for our understanding of the nature of administrative work and the role of 'discretion': a focus on practices allows the analyst to reveal the unspoken, taken-for-granted, tacit, dimensions of our being-in-the-world. With this I mean the whole substructure of understanding, knowledge, experience, assumptions, as well as material and artefactual objects that is implicated by a particular practice, that shapes that practice, and that makes a practice into a social, not an individual, accomplishment. Charles Taylor calls this aspect of practice 'background understanding'. The importance of background understanding is that it lifts the actor's activities above the purely subjective and individual. Individuals do not own background understanding. Although it is experience it is not wholly subjective experience but shared by members of a community (Wagenaar and Cook 2011). Within the virtual boundaries of a practice, we think, feel and act 'as anyone does' (Taylor 1995b: 77). Or, as he continues: 'Bringing in the background allows us to articulate the ways in which our form of agency is nonmonological, in which the seat of certain practices and understandings is precisely not the individual but one of the common spaces in between' (1995b: 77).[2] Let us, by way of an example, see what practice means in the context of administrative behaviour and its discretionary qualities.

17.3 Understanding Street-Level Practice Through the Analysis of Oral Narrative

In the late 1990s, I was engaged in a series of studies in which I collected work stories of administrators, particularly those working at the street level of government bureaucracy—somewhat along the lines of Studs Terkel's famous *Working* (Terkel 1985). My aim with these interviews was to capture the everyday reality of the official's working life, with its challenges, doubts, boredom, achievements, irritations with clients and colleagues, conflicts at work and at home, small and large victories and ditto defeats and so on. The interviews yielded a treasure trove of rich, detailed ethnographic material (Rhodes 2011) that resulted in a number of papers on dealing with value conflict, the nature of street-level practice, the narrative structure of street-level practice and the methodology for capturing practice (Wagenaar 1997, 2002, 2004, 2006; Wagenaar and Hartendorp 2000). In this section, I illuminate the nature of street-level practice by introducing an example of these studies (Wagenaar 2006).[3]

The stories I had collected presented a major methodological problem: How to analyse them so that they yielded the practice element that they enclose. Analytically, we had concluded that the way administrators discuss their work is narratively structured (Wagenaar 1997, 2004; Wagenaar and Hartendorp 2000) and that administrative work had all the characteristics of practice:

> (A)dministrators use narrative to solve the ordinary problems and challenges that come up in the course of their work. These problems and challenges derive from the everyday, practical nature of administrative work. (…) Street-level practice (…) is action-oriented, open-ended, concrete, interactive, and beset with moral conflict. Stories somehow helped administrators deal with administrative practice.

The problem with these earlier publications was precisely in what was left unsaid in that ambiguous term 'somehow' (Wagenaar 2006: 43).

Part of the problem resides in the fluid, ephemeral and relational quality of practice and, by extension, of narrative knowing.[4] The relevant literature depicts practice, not as a straightforward, cerebral activity but as 'involving the whole person'. A typical statement is the following by Lave and Wenger when they describe what it means to think of practice as 'situated'. It implies an:

> (E)mphasis on comprehensive understanding involving the whole person rather than 'receiving' a body of factual knowledge about the world; on activity in and with the world; and on the view that agent, activity, and the world mutually constitute each other (Lave and Wenger 1991: 33).

This is conceptually rich language that emphasizes the personal and relational quality of situatedness as the space of practice. It also poses considerable methodological challenges in capturing this dynamic, interactive quality of situated practice. How does one empirically demonstrate this unpremeditated, reciprocal, simultaneous bringing-into-being of the problem, the situation and the solution? This problem is aggravated by the observation that actors often are unable to say why they acted the way they did, how they came upon a particular solution.[5] When actors 'understand' situations this understanding is often instantaneous and holistic, but also unarticulated, often even beyond the actor's awareness (Bourdieu 1977). When pressed on the issue, actors will say that it seemed the 'natural' or 'logical' thing to do in the situation at hand (Wagenaar 2006: 43)[6] The issue is crucial for the plausibility of practice studies in public administration. It is one thing to claim that administrators engage in practice and that this undercuts the very concept of administrative discretion and that this does not necessarily mean that crucial categories such as the rule of law or legitimate government are thereby invalidated. It is quite another to be able to show *how* administrators arrive at courses of action and solutions in difficult, polyvalent situations, that live up to acceptable legal, moral and democratic standards.

While the narrative structure of administrators' practice stories posed problems of analysis, it also suggested a solution. The literature on narrative, specifically sociolinguistics, makes a distinction between the literate and oral style. Sociolinguists consider them fundamental modes of linguistic expression. They are distinct ways of expressing and organizing experience and making sense of the world that cannot be reduced to one another (Ong 1982; Tannen 1982; Gee 1985; Ochs and Capps 2001). The literate style is the dominant mode of expression in our society. It is analytical, systematic, intellectual and explicit. It proceeds through arguments that derive their persuasive power by an appeal to causal mechanisms and logic. Syntactically it is well formed and complete. The literate mode of linguistic expression signals a universal, impersonal and authoritative quality that is independent of the speaker. It is, of course, the lingua franca of our societal institutions in the fields of government, public administration, economics, universities and education in general.

The oral style, on the other hand, is anecdotal and fragmented. Speakers jump from one topic to another, use incomplete and grammatically garbled sentences in a seemingly associative style. This is how we speak when we are 'off-duty'. This surface image of the oral style is, however, deeply misleading. Narrative scholars think that oral narrative is a 'primary genre', an 'ontogenetic starting point' for other forms of narrative (Ochs and Capps 2001: 3). It is a sense-making mechanism that is fundamental to human life (Bruner 1986; White 1981). Ordinary experience is the raw material of oral narrative. It is as much organized as literate narrative but in a more surreptitious way, employing different organization mechanisms. Prosodic means, the use of pitch, tempo, emphasis and hesitations, structure a text in flexible way, making it possible for the speaker to maintain an ongoing relationship with a continuously developing, polyvalent environment (Gee 1985). The orderliness of oral narrative is contingent, evolving with the development of the narrative and the reactions of other speakers (Ochs and Capps 2001: 6). In our official institutions the oral style is seen negatively because it lacks order, logic, polish and objectivity. It is not the authoritative language of experts; it is depreciatingly perceived as belonging to laymen, lower classes and indigenous cultures. We will see, though, that the oral style has infused formal institutions to the point that it makes the effective employment of the literate style possible.

We used James Gee's method of prosodic analysis to reveal the sense-making qualities of oral narrative.[7] It is sufficiently sensitive to register the fleeting, evanescent qualities of narrative spoken in practice. According to Gee, the communicative function of a spoken text is all about *sensefulness*. Sensefulness refers to the communication of meaningful statements, in which meaningfulness is inextricably bound to the situation at hand.[8] Gee proposes that sensefulness depends on the interaction of five subsystems of what he calls a 'discourse system'. These are *prosody* (the musical aspects of spoken language, such as pitch, loudness, emphasis, syllable length, rhythm, hesitations, pauses and highlighting), *cohesion* (the manifold ways that the sentences in a spoken text hang together thematically through devices such as contrast, parallelisms and rhythmic speech patterns), *discourse organization* (the way that sentences are organized into higher order units, such as plots, episodes or genres),[9] *contextualization signals* (indications distributed throughout the text 'as to what the speaker takes the context to be and how the speaker wants the hearer to construct that context' (Gee 1985, 1991: 105)). Narratives of personal experience are not purely descriptive but always present a particular perspective (Ochs and Capps 2001: 45). An important dimension of this perspective is the moral stance that the speaker communicates to her audience. As Ochs and Capps (2001: 45) put it:

> Rooted in community and tradition, moral stance is a disposition towards what is good or valuable and how one ought to live in the world. Human beings judge

themselves and others in relation to standards of goodness: they praise, blame, or otherwise hold people morally accountable for their comportment. Philosophers from Aristotle to Alisdair MacIntyre propose that moral judgements are based on standards for social roles, practices, and the good life in relation to person and community.

The moral dimension of oral narrative is particularly important for the analysis of administrative discretion. Far from being a mere subjective disposition, 'discretionary' behaviour presents a moral stance that is understood as such, as well as reacted to and commented on, by a relevant audience. Stories of administrative behaviour construct moral frameworks that are interpreted by the speaker's embedding community.[10]

A final element of a discourse system is *thematic organization*, the way in which themes (images, contrasts larger issues) are developed throughout the text with the help of the four other subsystems (Gee 1991: 105–7). According to Gee, speakers organize their spoken text prosodically in lines, stanzas and sections. The end of a line is marked by an increase in pitch and the end of a stanza by a noted decrease. Apart from its methodological significance, the importance of the line/stanza/section structure is that, concurrent with the open-ended, evolving nature of oral narrative, meaning is produced prosodically.

Oral narrative analysis gives the scholar an empirical handle on the development of practice and, by extension, on administrative discretion. It shows in detail the interactive, fluid, emergent nature of practical judgement, which is at the heart of every form of practice (Beiner 1983). In a number of publications, we have used this method of oral narrative analysis to analyse the way that Dutch officials negotiate the challenges of administering welfare, disability and immigration programmes (Wagenaar 1997, 2002, 2004, 2006; Wagenaar and Hartendorp 2000). The restrictions of a book chapter do not allow for the presentation of a detailed extended case. What follows here is a summary of one case to wrap this chapter up by illustrating administrative discretion as an evolving, emergent practice.

The case is that of Joanna, a Dutch welfare administrator who dispenses welfare benefits to the homeless.[11] The central theme of her story was her struggle with the dilemma between the ordered world of the Dutch welfare law and the chaotic lifestyle of her homeless clients. It is a genuine dilemma because the programme is in effect more or less powerless to attenuate the situation of the homeless without compromising the institutional integrity of the welfare law. The text below falls apart in two parts each consisting of between six and eight paragraphs. In the first part, Joanna explains the regulations of the welfare programme and the organization of her unit. The style is clear and expository, with well-formed sentences and few hesitations. The second part consists of the stories of a succession of clients. Each client is a vignette of a distinct problem (the violent client, the drug addicted client, the client that plays the system) that she—and the welfare programme—encounter when they meet the real world of homelessness. The text in these paragraphs is syntactically garbled, full of hesitations and pauses, with lines of irregular length.

The text shows a clear pattern in which clear, prosodically well-organized 'programme'—stanzas and prosodically garbled 'homeless' stanzas alternate. This suggested to us the juxtaposition of two distinct voices in the text. As we saw earlier, one of the devices that speakers use to construct and convey meaning is the adoption of a plot. Joanna's story showed much affinity with the plot structure of Sophocles' tragedy *Antigone*. Similar to the play, Joanna's story presents two points of view, each of them equally reasonable and persuasive but in the end wholly irreconcilable. One is the voice of administrative order; the Weberian world of the administrative professional who applies precisely worded formal rules in an efficient and equitable way. The other one is the voice of the homeless, representing a world of unremitting chaos and upheaval, of people suffering from serious personality disorders, who are impervious to therapeutic or administrative intervention (Wagenaar, Vos, Balder, and van Hemert 2015). Each of these two perspectives is incomplete, defective, in that they provide only a limited, partial view of the world (Nussbaum 1986). It is important to be reminded that this plot structure is not imposed on the text from the outside but emerges in the course of the telling, by 'a process of incremental addition' (Gee 1991: 122), from the prosodic and stylistic characteristics of the oral narrative. Joanna is very likely not even aware that she structures her story by borrowing a particular culturally available, semantic resource.

I want to draw attention to one more aspect of Joanna's story that is particularly pertinent to the problem of administrative discretion. One of the problems that Joanna faces is that the programme rules enable her to dispense an emergency allowance of 90 guilders to her homeless clients. The emergency payment can only be dispensed once in a three-month period. Because of the risk that beneficiaries might play the system by applying for it in different cities, the rules stipulate that they have an address, if only an administrative address such as a shelter. Some of Joanna's clients are, however, too disorganized to even have, or know, the address of a shelter. The dilemma this creates for Joanna is illustrated in the following stanzas:

Stanza 67
Actually you can't really give them the ninety guilders
Because she's not as a real homeless
... uh ... she doesn't have any residence
yet well she isn't a wandering homeless
so that is quite difficult then

Stanza 68
And then you often try
Well to work out something
So that she will get the ninety guilders.

Joanna goes on to say that when the whereabouts of the beneficiary are unknown, she starts making calls:

> *Stanza 71*
> Colleagues of mine always say dear why are you always calling for
> But I really do make a lot of calls
> You know
> Every now and then I find a couple of them who turn out to have additional income
>
> *Stanza 72*
> But then I think yeah after all it is tax money
> It comes from the coffers of the state so you cannot just
> Even if it is only ninety bucks
> You cannot just that money
> ... provide it
>
> *Stanza 73*
> But yeah ... sometimes .... It also depends
> How do you interpret it yourself
> How do you deal with the story
> Huh ... what ....

Despite the halting, seemingly inept quality of the language, this series of stanzas is a clear illustration of the richness of oral narrative and the way it conveys its meaning on different levels simultaneously. First, it is an illustration of the power of contextualization signals. Joanna presents herself as an official who is aware of the dilemma that is inherent in the programme rules and who is willing to go the extra mile in attempting to find a solution. Because the lives of some homeless are too disorganized, decisive information of their whereabouts is simply not available, while these are the people who are probably most in need of an emergency payment. All we have to go by are their own stories and our interpretation of them, she says in stanza 73. And then, in the space of these few stanzas, she both constructs a moral framework and a strategy for implementing the framework. On one hand, she appeals to the value of accountability. The emergency payment represents taxpayers' money that should be accounted for. On the other hand, she appeals to the values of compassion and solidarity. These people are deserving of our assistance. (In stanza 74 she talks of her clients as 'human misery incarnate sitting at your desk' (Wagenaar 2006: 59)).[12] The best Joanna can do to navigate the poles of this dilemma is to do her utmost to obtain information among other things by calling other colleagues. Calling colleagues is not just a means to obtain information but also a way to implicitly elicit colleagues' judgements of her strategy to deal with the dilemma. (Am I too strict or too lenient? (stanza 69) Do I go too far in my inquiries? (stanza71)).

17.4 Conclusion: Organizing for Street-Level Practice

Rulemaking operates in an inescapable tension between formality and contingency. Legal and administrative rules are the depositories of the experiences, aspirations, fears and wisdom of a social and administrative community. In this sense, rules represent a society's ideals and conscience. Rules are also an attempt to finalize and universalize these experiences and aspirations. This inevitably results in a reification and de-contextualization of rules; the loss of the shared memories and experiences that are the unspoken conditions of applicability of any rule. Every experienced politician, administrator and professional whose work involves rule application is aware of this essential tension and adopts ways to negotiate it. What all these attempts at adequate rule application have in common is the reintroduction, to a greater or lesser extent, of necessary context; necessary in the sense that without that context the rule would not make sense in the situation at hand. This bringing together of formal rules with real-world persons and situations, with the purpose of resolving the situation in an effective and equitable way, is the substance of street-level practice.

Despite the unremarkableness of street-level practice, a discrepancy exists between the unofficial, taken-for-granted and the official face of the discipline. In the discourse about effectiveness, equality, legitimacy, accountability and democracy in the administrative state, we foreground the codification and universalism of formal rules (Taylor 1995a). Although accountability, in the complex, negotiated environment of the contemporary state, operates in different registers—political-administrative, professional and participatory (Hupe and Hill 2007) —this is not just mere talk. Formal law and bureaucratic rule are, in the final analysis, still the bedrock of accountability. This is an epistemological, not a practical, stance. It is the reply to the question: On what grounds did you come to this decision? This epistemological position—disengaged, finite, rational, individualistic—is deeply embedded in our collective self-image and institutional designs (Taylor 1995a: 7, c: 169; Sandford 2000: 735).[13] It is from this hegemonic epistemic ideology that the concept and problem of administrative discretion arises. This chapter concerns an attempt to reframe the received view of administrative discretion as the deviation—warranted or unwarranted—from formal legal rules. In effect, I have supplemented an alternative epistemology of discretion as practical judgement that is commensurate with the fragmented, decentred reality of public accountability in contemporary situations of governance. Taking twentieth-century philosophy, which demonstrated the logical impossibility of immanently conclusive rule application, seriously, I suggested that discretionary behaviour could more fruitfully be seen as a form of street-level practice. Arguably, this raises the spectre of arbitrary behaviour and the violation of the rule of law with the ensuing loss of the legitimacy of the state and the democratic order. While we know that in most democratic administrative states this dystopian vision has not materialized, the practice framework needs to be sufficiently precise and robust to explain why and how the activities of administrators usually do not slip into injustice and arbitrariness.

To this end an oral narrative analysis was presented, as a method to trace with some measure of precision the way that administrators make sense of the challenges and dilemmas they face and the courses of action they embark on. Oral narrative is particularly suited to understand ordinary practical judgement. It is not only a 'primary genre' from which other linguistic genres derive; oral narrative's function is to navigate a landscape of action (Bruner 1986). We tell stories to solve problems of action in situations where an obvious solution to the situation at hand is not available (Ochs and Capps 2001: 4; Wagenaar 1997). Through the largely unconscious, habitual, employment of various narrative tools actors simultaneously make sense of the problems and challenges they face in a non-reductionist, meaningful way and make pragmatic suggestions of how to resolve it. Using oral narrative analysis, I presented the case of a Dutch welfare official who administers welfare to the homeless. The case gives rise to three observations.

The first is that rules are not all-important in the work of these officials. It would be a stretch of the imagination to characterize Joanna's work as 'rule-application'. Officials do not apply knowledge (as in the received view of 'applying rules') but, routinely or haltingly, find their way in and through situations by trying to make sense of them. They face real persons with complex issues and often serious personality problems, situations that are full of uncertainty and unpredictability, budgetary and time constraints, demanding bosses, supportive or indifferent colleagues, private situations that need attention, as well as the necessity to maintain the proper balance between distance and engagement that enables the official to sustain herself in the job (Lipsky 1980; Vinzant and Crothers 1998; Wagenaar and Hartendorp 2000; Maynard-Moody and Musheno 2003; Wagenaar 2004; Wagenaar *et al.* 2015). Rules play a role and an important one at that. Joanna repeatedly refers to the rules of the welfare programme. In her story, they structure and constrain the situation at hand; they function as quality standards and reminders of the wider goals of the programme and organization.

The second observation is the intense moral quality of the narrative. The unmistakable moral tenor of the story is intimately connected with the story's relational, outward-reaching character. Joanna has an urge to communicate her moral judgements, to bring them out in the open, to ask the audience: Am I the person that I claim to be? Is this reasonable behaviour on my part? Am I missing something? Perhaps Joanna is an especially sensitive, morally conscious official, but that is not the point here. Joanna demonstrates a structural feature of oral narrative and, by implication, practice: its essential other-directedness (Wagenaar 2004: 650). We tell stories for and with others to enable us to better make sense of baffling situations and to better navigate the ambiguity and open-endedness of everyday life in cases in which there is no obvious solution to the situation. To engage in street-level practice does not mean to lose sight of the moral dimension of public administration. On the contrary. Most administrators are acutely aware that their actions have consequences. In the first place for the client but also for their personal reputation and, as Joanna made clear, for the integrity of the programme and the organization. Through its essential relational nature, practice is full of safety mechanisms in the shape of the advice and judgements of bosses, peers and important others (Maynard-Moody and Musheno 2003).

The third conclusion is that, despite our uneasiness in the face of the received view, there is no alternative to street-level practice. Practice is not an alternative frame but a 'primary genre' on which the very possibility of rule application depends. Even if we apply simple formal rules in a seemingly automatic, non-controversial manner, the practice element has simply been effaced. Practice is no guarantee against abuse, but neither is legalistic rule application. In fact, legalism is often a form of punitive policy implementation. The facilitation of excellence and the avoidance or redress of abuse requires organizational set-ups and procedures that allow practice to flourish. This suggests open, horizontal, decentralized, competence-centred and recursive organizations that foster a problem-solving attitude, deliberation, reflexivity and evolutionary learning.[14] The conclusion is that administrative discretion should not be seen in terms of a deficit. It is not a second-best form of administration or a retreat from vital administrative and democratic ideals. On the contrary, taking street-level practice seriously is a powerful heuristic towards more effective, responsive and democratic public organizations.

Notes

1. It is telling that the book cover shows a person looking through the spread fingers of his hand. To every Dutch person this is an obvious visual reference to the saying: '*iets door de vingers zien*', literally 'to see something through the fingers', to let bad behaviour pass for once.
2. See Wagenaar (2018) for an example of how the concept of background understanding helps to explain a remarkable consistency in policy practices over time and across geographical space. For the use of practice theory in explaining policy change, see Shove *et al.* (2012).
3. For a similar study, although using a theoretical framework that flirts with the practice approach but does not embrace it, see Sandford (2000).
4. See Cook and Wagenaar (2012) and Wagenaar and Cook (2011) for a more extended discussion of the nature of knowing in practice.
5. The habitual, unaware nature of much human action is a central theme in theories of tacit knowledge (Polanyi 1958) Bourdieu also elevates it to a key feature of his concept of 'habitus'.
6. Wittgenstein was very clear about the inarticulate and even inarticulable nature of rule-following. He argues that at some point explanations for our actions reach a dead end and we act without reasons (2009 90e: 211). When pressed on the matter, we say 'This is simply what I do' (2009 91e: 217). This is not a retreat into subjectivity. Following a rule is a practice; a shared activity that can never be wholly private (2009 87e: 202).

7. For a more complete explanation of Gee's method of oral narrative analysis, see Wagenaar and Hartendorp (2000) and Wagenaar (2006).
8. An important dimension of sensefulness is appropriateness. Sensefulness is about effective communication in different situations. By way of example: a well composed, logical statement about the causes of right-wing populism in Europe would be perfectly appropriate in the context of an academic conference but hopelessly out of place in a rowdy speakeasy. In contrast to the literate style the oral style always links language to its social environment.
9. Plots and genres are powerful communicative devices. They suggest a larger cultural meaning above and beyond the directly spoken or written word. Narrative theorists surmise that there are only a limited number of basic plots in circulation that are easily recognized by people (Wagenaar 2011).
10. This is another example of oral narrative as a primary genre that is constitutive of derivative narrative genres. While literate narrative is careful to erase value judgement to present the speaker as objective and dispassionate, individuals need value judgment to make practical judgments about, and find their stance towards, the issue that is the object of a narrative. The result is that value positions have not been erased from the literate style but have been made implicit.
11. For the full extended analysis see Wagenaar (2006).
12. In this and the next stanza Joanna revisits the moral dilemma at the heart of the emergency payment system. While she trenchantly describes the plight of the homeless in stanza 74, in stanza 75 she describes a homeless person who, upon further inquiry, turned out to have already received an emergency payment in the preceding three months without telling her.
13. This deep-seated bias towards formality and codification was also evident in a recent discussion about value pluralism in public administration in the journal *Administration & Society.* See for example, Overeem and Verhoef (2014), Talisse (2015) and my reply, Wagenaar (2015).
14. It would far exceed the boundaries of this chapter to discuss these organizational principles in this place. A particularly rich resource is Ansell (2011). Ansell himself makes use of Follet (2013 [1951]). For an application of this pragmatist approach to the organization of public services, see Wagenaar *et al.* (2015)

References

Amy, D.J. (2017). Government is good. An unapologetic defense of a vital institution. http://governmentisgood.com/articles.php?aid=20&print=1.pdf. Accessed 18 January 2018.

Ansell, C. (2011). *Pragmatist democracy. Evolutionary learning as public philosophy.* Oxford: Oxford University Press.

Bakker, W. & van Waarden, F. (1999). Discretionaire Ruimte bij de Formulering en Handhaving van Regelgeving. In W. Bakker & F. van Waarden (Eds), *Ruimte rond regels: Stijlen van regulering en beleidsuitvoering vergeleken.* (pp. 13–40). Amsterdam: Boom.

Bartels, K. (2018) Policy as practice. In R. Hoppe & H. Colebatch (Eds), *Handbook on policy, process and governing* (pp. 68–89). Cheltenham: Edward Elgar.

Beiner, R. (1983). *Political judgement.* London: Methuen.

Bourdieu, P. (1977). *Outline of a theory of practice.* Cambridge: Cambridge University Press.

Bruner, J. (1986). *Actual minds, possible worlds.* Cambridge, MA: Harvard University Press.

Cook, S.D.N. & Wagenaar, H. (2012). Navigating the eternally unfolding present: Toward an epistemology of practice. *American Review of Public Administration*, 42(1), 3–38.

Follet, M.P. (2013 [1951; 1924]). *Creative experience.* Mansfield Centre, CT: Martino Publishing.

Gee, J.P. (1985). The narrativization of experience in the oral style. *Journal of Education*, 167(1), 9–36.

Gee, J.P. (1991). *Social linguistics and literacies: Ideology in discourses.* Milton Park, Abingdale: Routledge Falmer.

Gherardi, S. (2012). *How to conduct a practice-based study: Problems and methods.* Cheltenham: Edward Elgar.

Goodsell, C. (2004). *The case for bureaucracy: A Public Administration polemic* (4th ed.). Washington, DC: CQ Press.

Held, D. (2006). *Models of democracy* (3rd ed.). Oxford: Polity Press.

Hill, M. & Hupe, P. (2002) *Implementing public policy: Governance in theory and practice.* Thousand Oaks, CA: Sage.

Hupe, P. & Hill, M. (2007). Street-level bureaucracy and public accountability. *Public Administration*, 85(2), 279–299.

Lane, J.E. (1987). Implementation, accountability and trust. *European Journal of Political Research*, 15(5), 527–546.

Lave, J. & Wenger, E. (1991). *Situated learning: Legitimate peripheral participation.* Cambridge: Cambridge University Press

Lipsky, M. (1980). *Street-level bureaucracy: Dilemmas of the individual in public service.* New York, NY: Russell Sage Foundation.

Maynard-Moody, S. & Musheno, M. (2003). *Cops, teachers, counselors: Stories from the frontlines of public service.* Ann Arbor, MI: University of Michigan Press.

Nicolini, D. (2012). *Practice theory, work, and organization.* Oxford: Oxford University Press.

Nussbaum, M.C. (1986). *The fragility of goodness: Luck and ethics in Greek tragedy and philosophy.* Cambridge: Cambridge University Press.

Ochs, E. & Capps, L. (2001). *Living narrative: Creating lives in everyday storytelling.* Cambridge, MA: Harvard University Press.

Ong, W.J. (1982). *Orality and literacy: The technologizing of the world.* London: Methuen.

Overeem, P. & Verhoef, J. (2014). Moral dilemmas, theoretical confusion: Value pluralism and its supposed implications for Public Administration. *Administration & Society*, 46(8), 986–1009.

Pickering, A. (1995) *The mangle of practice. Time, agency and science.* Chicago, IL: The University Of Chicago Press.

Pickering, A. & Guzik, K. (Eds) (2008). *The mangle in practice. Science, society and becoming.* Durham, SC: Duke University Press.

Polanyi, M. (1958) *Personal knowledge: Towards a post-critical philosophy.* Chicago, IL: The University of Chicago Press.

Rhodes, R. (2011). *Everyday life in British government.* Oxford: Oxford University Press.

Sandford, J.R. (2000) Moving beyond discretion and outcomes: Examining public management from the front lines of the welfare system. *Journal of Public Administration Research and Theory*, 10(4), 729–756.

Schatzki, T.R. (1996) *Social practices. A Wittgensteinian approach to human activity and the social.* Cambridge: Cambridge University Press.

Shove, E., Pantzar, M. & Watson, M. (2012) *The dynamics of social practice: Everyday life and how it changes.* Thousand Oaks, CA: Sage.

Talisse, R.B. (2015). Value pluralism: A philosophical clarification, *Administration & Society*, 47(9), 1064–1076.

Tannen, D. (1982). The oral/literate continuum in discourse. In D. Tannen (Ed.), *Spoken and written language: Exploring orality and literacy* (pp. 1–17). Westport, CT: Praeger.

Taylor, C. (1995a). Overcoming epistemology. In C. Taylor. Philosophical arguments (pp. 1–19). Cambridge, MA: Harvard University Press.

Taylor, C. (1995b). Lichtung or lebensform: Parallels between Heidegger and Wittgenstein. In C. Taylor. *Philosophical arguments* (pp.61–79). Cambridge, MA: Harvard University Press.

Taylor, C. (1995c). To follow a rule... In C. Taylor. *Philosophical arguments* (pp. 165–181). Cambridge, MA: Harvard University Press.

Terkel, S. (1985). *Working people talk about what they do all day and how they feel about what they do.* New York, NY: Ballantine Books.

Vinzant, J.C. & Crothers, L. (1998). Street-level leadership: Discretion and legitimacy in front-line public service. Washington, DC: Georgetown University Press.

Wagenaar, H. (1997). Beleid als fictie: Over de rol van verhalen in de bestuurlijke praktijk. *Beleid & Maatschappij*, 24(1), 7–21.

Wagenaar, H. (2002). Value pluralism in Public Administration: Two perspectives on administrative morality. In J.S. Jun (Ed.), *Rethinking administrative theory. The challenge of the new century* (pp. 105–131). Westport, CT: Praeger.

Wagenaar, H. (2004). 'Knowing' the rules. Administrative work as practice. *Public Administration Review*, 64(6), 643–655.

Wagenaar H. (2006). Bureaucratic order and personal order: The narrative analysis of administrative practice. In M. van den Brink & T. Metze (Eds), *Words matter in policy and planning: Discourse theory and method in the social sciences* (pp. 43–65). Utrecht: Koninklijk Nederlands Aardrijkskundig Genootschap.

Wagenaar, H. (2011). *Meaning in action: Interpretation and dialogue in policy analysis.* Milton Park, Abingdale: Routledge.

Wagenaar, H. (2015). Administrative decision making: A practical clarification. *Administration & Society*, 47(9), 1087–1093.

Wagenaar, H. (2018). Policy as practice: Explaining persistent patterns in prostitution policy'. *The Howard Journal of Crime and Justice*, 57(3), 379–400.

Wagenaar, H. & Hartendorp, R. (2000). Oedipus in the welfare office. In H. Wagenaar (Ed.), *Government institutions: Effects, changes and normative foundations* (pp. 147–178). Dordrecht: Kluwer Academic Press.

Wagenaar, H. & Cook, S.D.N. (2011). The push and pull of the world: How experience animates practice. *Evidence and Policy*, 7(2), 193–212.

Wagenaar, H., Vos, J.J., Balder, C. & van Hemert, A.M. (2015) Overcoming conflicting logics of care and justice: Collaborative innovation in dealing with habitual offenders in the Netherlands. In A. Agger, B. Damgaard, A.H. Krog & E. Sørensen (Eds), *Collaborative governance and public innovation in Northern Europe* (pp. 111–133). Sharjah: Bentham Science Publishers.

White, H. (1981). The value of narrativity in the representation of reality. In W.J.T. Mitchell (Ed.), *On narrative.* Chicago, IL: University of Chicago Press.

Wittgenstein, L. (2009). *Philosophical investigations* (Rev. 4th ed., P.M.S. Hacker & J. Schulte, Eds). Chichester, West Sussex: Wiley Blackwell.

CHAPTER 18

Organized Discretion

Suzanne Rutz and Antoinette de Bont

18.1 Introduction

Discretionary judgement—defined as the freedom to decide how to act within controlled limits; see the introductory chapter of this edited collection—is increasingly being organized in teams or networks. Therefore, we introduce the notion of collective discretionary room. As we explain in this chapter, this concept provides insight into new ways of affording the freedom to act and new mechanisms to control that freedom. Moreover, it reshapes the relation between actors who use freedom and actors who grant a degree of freedom and/or control it. When discretion becomes a concerted effort, it becomes nested not only in a set of rules but also in an extended network of actors.

The literature has described discretionary judgement as freedom either used by or granted to an individual frontline worker. An important argument in establishing this freedom is enhanced responsiveness; it allows workers to tailor their judgements and actions in everyday interactions. It is about the freedom to go beyond and outside a prescribed set of rules to achieve the rule's purpose. Yet, this freedom of workers is subject to control of managers and policymakers higher up in the system of public administration. An important argument in establishing control on the use of discretion is the consistent application of rules as improper use of discretionary judgement could result in unwanted variation and differences between policy design and policy delivery (Bannink, Six and van Wijk 2016; see also Lipsky 2010; Brodkin 2016). Consequently, uncontrolled freedom may have a negative impact on fairness. The characteristics of workers (such as their moral values, training and personal experience)

S. Rutz • A. de Bont (✉)
Erasmus School of Health Policy & Management, Erasmus University Rotterdam, Rotterdam, The Netherlands
e-mail: rutz@eshpm.eur.nl; debont@eshpm.eur.nl

T. Evans, P. Hupe (eds.), *Discretion and the Quest for Controlled Freedom*, https://doi.org/10.1007/978-3-030-19566-3_18

and the characteristics of the persons they are regulating (such as demography, behaviour and knowledge of rules) influence the judgements and may tip the balance for or against 'big-hearted' or 'mingy' judgements (Rice 2013). Likewise, the use of discretionary judgement may lead to a lack of democratic control (Davis 1969).

Here we elaborate on the collective aspects of discretionary judgement. The use of discretionary judgement is increasingly considered to be embedded in and the result of relations with colleagues and workers of other organizations rather than an individual accomplishment (e.g., Hupe and Buffat 2014; see also Evans 2011; Silbey 2011). Workers cooperate with colleagues and people from other organizations working on the same subject and function in teams and networks, such as regional partnerships and multi-agency teams (Hupe and Hill 2007; Noordegraaf 2011; Rice 2013). Hence, workers pool discretionary judgement (see also Hood's Chap. 3 of this edited collection) and exercise judgement in interaction (see also Wolfson's Chap. 10). In other words, judgements are made in collectives.

When discretionary judgement is granted to collectives, the relation between freedom and control changes as well as the role of the actors who exercise that freedom and control. While freedom and control are often presented as two opposite ends of a continuum, our argument is that organizing the collective use of discretion and creating the conditions in which the collectives operate lead to more freedom and more control. Collective discretionary room also results in a shift of focus from rules to the outcomes of rules, as it is not only used for policy delivery but also offers feedback that may lead to new policy designs (see also the layers Wolfson identifies in Chap. 10 of this edited collection).

To illustrate this, we will consider the provision of integrated services. To provide integrated services, workers from different disciplines cooperate to make multidisciplinary judgements for which they combine their expertise and various sector-related rules. When workers cooperate on making multidisciplinary judgements, discretionary judgement is no longer an individual's resource, giving a worker the freedom to act within controlled limits of policy-makers and managers.

To underline the need to consider the collective aspects of discretionary judgement, we first describe the need for multidisciplinary judgements stemming from the provision of integrated services and then the motives and challenges for collective decision making. This is followed by a concise overview of the literature on discretion, about how workers develop policy while implementing it and what freedom and control entail according to this literature. Next, we discuss how the collective aspects of discretion influence freedom and control. We also discuss possible differences in how workers change policy and function as co-makers of policy when they use discretion individually or in teams or networks. We illustrate this with an example from our empirical work at the Joint Inspectorate Social Domain in the Netherlands where collective discretionary room is organized in terms of decision-making procedures put in place to use teamwork as mechanism for freedom and control. Finally, we discuss the consequences of viewing discretionary judgement as a concerted effort and draw conclusions.

18.2 Towards Collective Discretionary Judgement

In recent years, many European countries have made major reforms in the social welfare and health sectors. The emphasis has been on integrating services that put the needs of their users centre stage (Montero, van Duijn, Zonneveld, Minkman and Nies 2016). Integrated services involve coordination to ensure that a continuum of services is delivered (WHO 2015; Minkman 2017). User-centredness means personalized holistic support; various services providing integrated support that is tailored to the needs of a specific person or target group (Montero *et al.* 2016). Consequently, the reforms represent a considerable shift in the way public policies are planned and delivered.

A prominent aspect of providing user-centred integrated services is multidisciplinary cooperation in networks that cross organizations and sectors (Montero *et al.* 2016; Minkman 2017). When a user needs particular services that exceed what the worker and the worker's organization have to offer, the worker has to involve others that can provide the alternative or additional services. Hence, networks consist of workers from various disciplines, providing a range of expertise and options to handle various situations. Workers that offer integrated services in networks have to share decisions on what a user needs and what has to be done to meet those needs; they make multidisciplinary judgements. Legislation and policy are usually sector-related. This means that workers cooperating in multidisciplinary networks often need to balance, stretch and deviate from varying sector-related rules in order to develop a suitable, combined approach. Hence, they need discretionary room to make decisions together.

The pros and cons of collective decision making have been described in the literature (Janis 1982, 1989; 't Hart 1998). The first advantage is that groups are better able to process information to analyse complex problems and make decisions on how to tackle these problems. Group members have access to different information. They collect, scan and critically weigh all the information relevant to the problem at hand to come to rigorous decisions. The second advantage is that groups can reach compromises between competing values. Groups are supposed to make sure that all relevant values and interests are adequately represented, articulated and incorporated in the decision-making process. A third advantage is that groups are viewed as a source of legitimacy. The institutionalization of groups, their authority and the processes they undertake to reach agreement aim to raise the confidence of outsiders in the group's judgements.

The main disadvantage of collective judgements is groupthink (Janis 1982, 1989; 't Hart 1998). Groupthink occurs when the desire for conformity becomes so dominant that group members reach a consensus without taking into account possible alternative courses of action. Group pressures prevent contradictory views from being expressed and subsequently evaluated (Janis 1982). As a consequence, groupthink may lead teams to selectively neglect or misinterpret crucial information. It may also lead to the suppression of minority views and restricted access to advocates that hold different values. And it may result in groups that are no longer viewed as legitimate when their consensus judgements turned out to have problematic consequences ('t Hart 1998).

Scholars offer a diversity of recommendations to improve the quality of group decisions; from putting in place prescriptions, opening up the group deliberation process to outsiders, to institutionalizing devil's advocacy and ensuring that all members of the group can be individually held to account (Janis 1982; 't Hart 1998). All these recommendations have in common that they organize decision-making processes. In other words, organized group work is established to improve the quality of the decisions.

We will compare and contrast the collective aspects of discretionary judgement with the literature on street-level bureaucracy and with how the literature views discretion, cooperation between workers, as well as freedom and control. But first, we summarize the most important insights from the literature.

18.3 Discretionary Judgement, Freedom and Control

In the literature on street-level bureaucracy, Lipsky has drawn attention to the place of the individual frontline worker who delivers public policy and, more specifically, the worker who judges whether citizens are eligible for public services. Lipsky argued that not only top-level policymakers at departments do policymaking, but the workers who deliver the policy to citizens also make it. Street-level bureaucrats have relatively high degrees of discretion to make decisions. In sum, their decisions effectively become the public policies they carry out (Lipsky 2010). Hence, the actions of street-level bureaucrats are part of the policymaking process, as they randomly influence distribution and content of policy delivery (Brodkin 2016). In short, street-level bureaucrats function as policy co-makers (Hupe, Hill and Buffat Eds 2016).

Discretionary judgement is an important concept in the literature on street-level bureaucracy and often figures as a broad term with multiple meanings (Hupe 2013). A classic formulation, originally derived from the study of law, stems from Davis (1969: 4; used e.g., in Evans 2011; Tummers and Bekkers 2014; Hupe *et al.* 2016): 'whenever the effective limits on his [the worker's] power leave him free to make a choice among possible courses of action or inaction.' The limits on the worker's power are determined by rules and regulations. Whereas the literature originally seems to presume that workers have to deal with one set of rules at the time, more recently it is acknowledged that rules and regulations can arise from multiple sources and that a worker's decision on what to do may be based not only on formal rules but also on other guidance, such as professional norms and societal expectations (Ellis 2016). Taking this variety into account, Hupe and Hill (2007) speak of 'action prescriptions' as an umbrella term. Exercising discretionary judgement then stands for using the freedom to balance a plurality of action prescriptions (see also the introductory chapter of this edited collection). Above we have shown that when workers make multidisciplinary judgements to deliver integrated services it is necessary to juggle action prescriptions that stem from different sectors.

Hupe (2013) distinguishes between discretion-as-granted and discretion-as-used. Discretion-as-granted is associated with the freedom given to workers which permits them to make a decision. Rules and regulations specify when and to what extent a worker is allowed to decide between various courses of action. Discretion-as-used is associated with the behaviour of workers who use the freedom to make a decision. The worker takes the initiative to interpret, balance or deviate from rules and regulations. In this chapter, we adopt Hupe's distinction. To highlight the difference between the two, we use *discretion* for discretion-as-used and *discretionary room* for discretion-as-granted. We use discretionary judgement as an overarching concept.

Discretionary judgement is connected to two interacting dimensions; the use of freedom and the exercise of control. Freedom and control are often presented as belonging to different actors. While the individual worker is using or is afforded freedom, another actor controls the use of discretion. The actor who controls the worker's freedom to act can be a rule-maker or policymaker that formulates laws and other formal rules and regulations. In these rules, they can grant freedom to the worker who is supposed to apply them. In addition, managers act as controlling actors, as highlighted in the literature (Evans 2011; see also Lipsky 2010). They check that organizational goals are met, regulate the duties of their subordinate workers, survey the assessment criteria that workers use, control expenditure and manage the use of discretion.

The use of discretion is often described in a context of conflict between actors who want to use freedom and actors who want to control the use of discretion (Moscovici and Doise 1994). Freedom and control are then presented as two opposite ends of a continuum. While workers strive for the freedom to act, as they feel the need to be responsive to the specific case, managers and policymakers 'higher up' in vertical administration want to limit and control the use of discretion to encourage workers to act consistently (Noordegraaf and Steijn Eds 2013; see also Durose 2011; Evans 2011; Lipsky 2010; Pires 2011). Yet, the conflict between freedom and exercising control is not a black-and-white issue. For instance, research has shown that workers do not always use the freedom granted to them. Rather, they rely on clear and specific guidance on how to interpret and balance the rules to deal with complex situations (Osiander and Steinke 2016; see also Ellis, Davis and Rummery 1999). In other words, workers may welcome rules and do not always want more freedom to act. In addition, managers and workers often share the same professional background. Consequently, managers are committed to values that inform responsiveness to specific cases and may encourage discretion where it works for the organization (Evans 2011). Hence, workers may enjoy greater freedom to act as their managers will not focus their control on constraining the use of discretion. Research shows that the effectiveness of control on discretion via managers and via the definition of rules is limited as street-level bureaucrats often work outside the purview of others. This is especially true for workers who have to act in complex and ambiguous situations (Bannink *et al.* 2016; Hupe *et al.* 2016; see also Evans 2011).

To summarize, in the literature on street-level bureaucracy discretionary judgement is seen as related to an individual worker. Individual workers *use* freedom to make a decision (*discretion*) or *are granted* freedom to make a decision (*discretionary room*). This freedom is controlled by managers and also by policymakers higher up who define the worker's room for manoeuvre in rules. In this literature, rules are seen as a given; workers may interpret, balance and deviate from the rules, but do not define them. Yet, at the same time, workers are seen as unofficial policy co-makers as their decisions determine what the policy will look like in practice. In the next section we will elaborate on this and add a new perspective that views discretion as a concerted effort instead of the accomplishment of an individual worker. Adopting this collective perspective influences the allocation of freedom and control over the use of discretion.

18.4 Collective Discretionary Judgement

The collective aspects of discretionary judgement can be defined in terms of a grid based on two axes. The first axis marks the distinction between discretion and discretionary room. The second axis adds a new distinction between individual and collective. This results in a four-square grid (see Table 18.1).

We apply the notion of individual discretion to the ways individual workers use their own 'logic of appropriateness' (March and Olsen 2004), interpreting, balancing and deviating from the rules to reach judgements and take action. We apply the label 'individual discretionary room' when discretion is formally granted to individual workers. Similarly, we use the notion of 'collective discretion' to refer to how pragmatic individual workers take the initiative to involve

Table 18.1 Organized discretion

	Discretion *(used)*	Discretionary room *(granted)*
Individual	Individual discretion Individual behaviour of a worker interpreting, balancing and deviating from rules to reach judgements to take action	Individual discretionary room Degree of freedom formally granted to individual workers to reach judgements to take action
Collective	Collective discretion Ways individual workers pragmatically involve others on their own initiative to interpret, balance and deviate from rules to reach judgements to take action	Collective discretionary room Degree of freedom formally granted to teams or networks to reach judgements to take action

Source: Based on Rutz, Mathew, Robben and de Bont (2017). The distinction between discretion-as-used and discretion-as-granted stems from Hupe (2013)

others to interpret, balance and deviate from the rules to reach judgements and take action. Consequently, we use 'collective discretionary room' to label teams of workers that have been granted the freedom to reach judgements together.

Collective discretion and collective discretionary room both entail group decision making. In collective discretion, individual workers involve others on their own initiative. The inclusion of others depends on the relations and networks that an individual worker has. Workers may involve colleagues or people from other organizations when they need additional information, when they want to include alternative perspectives (values and interests) or when they are looking for actions outside their own repertoire that are related to the authority and tasks of others. By involving others, they create opportunities to broaden their view and own repertoire of options. This may strengthen the decisions that are made. However, controlling collective discretion is difficult because workers often include others covertly, outside the purview of their managers.

Collective discretionary room also enables workers to include new information, multiply the values and interests related to the subject under scrutiny and broaden the repertoire of options to handle situations. However, unlike collective discretion, in collective discretionary room, this broader view and repertoire is available not only to workers with good relations with colleagues and workers at other organizations; other workers may also draw on these relations and gain access to this information and these values, interests and options to handle the situation. Hence, collective discretionary room facilitates the ability to make complex decisions—balancing rules, information, values, interests and contexts of the subject—for the organization. Various authors argue that in complex and ambiguous situations it is vital that rules are not a given but that groups are entitled to transform and improve on them (Perez 2014; see also Piore 2011; Pires 2011; Sabel and Zeitlin 2012a). Collective discretionary room opens up the possibility of adjusting and redefining rules, goals, strategies and tools, making them more practicable and effective. While the team makes judgements, they may learn about the applicability and feasibility of the rules, methods, actions and goals and discover in which situations they deviate from rules. In other words, collective discretionary room may enhance learning and the development of more effective ways of working.

The way in which collective discretionary room is organized offers mechanisms to control the judgements. This control may come in three ways. The first mechanism of control is peer review: while working together in teams or networks, workers gain insight into and discuss each other's work. Lipsky (2010) describes this as a way to enable qualitative evaluations of how workers handle cases and to enable the development of assessment criteria for the quality of workers' judgements and actions. The second control mechanism relates to the adjustment and redefinition of rules, goals, strategies and tools to develop more effective ways of working. Teams of workers develop a shared perspective upon which they interpret the rules and discuss in which situations they have to use their discretion. This may enhance consistent ways of working.

The third control mechanism encompasses procedures that specify how the group makes decisions, who to involve in judgements and the situations in which rules and regulations may be adjusted. In the first two mechanisms, control is not done by managers and rules; workers control their own use of discretion and can be held to account for this. In the third mechanism, control is done by procedures that may be made by workers, managers or rule-makers. These procedures structure decision-making processes but not their outcomes, which differs from the traditional rules for street-level bureaucrats that aim to structure the outcomes of decision making.

In sum, the involvement of others in discretionary judgement broadens the range of expertise, perspectives and options to take action that workers can draw on. The main difference between collective discretion and collective discretionary room is that whereas in the former the involvement of others depends on the initiative of individual workers, in the latter the involvement of others is organized. Cooperation between workers is part of the organizational form. This makes the additional information, values and interests and options to take action available to all workers. Moreover, while it offers teams of workers the freedom to act, collective discretionary room also offers mechanisms to control and enhance the quality of the working methods (judgements and rules).

18.5 A Dutch Illustration of Collective Discretionary Room

In this section, we illustrate how the Joint Inspectorate Social Domain (JISD) has organized collective discretionary room for their inspectors. The JISD is a partnership of government inspectorates in the Netherlands (before 2017 this partnership was known as the Joint Inspectorate for Youth). We have studied the JISD since 2009, using participant observations, interviews and document analysis, focusing on inspectors' daily practices; how they conduct inspections and reach their judgements (for more information see: Rutz 2017).

JISD involves four cooperating inspectorates: the Health and Youth Care Inspectorate, the Inspectorate of Education, Inspectorate for Justice and Safety and the Inspectorate of Social Affairs and Employment. JISD's inspections are mainly theme-based, focusing on public problems concerning young people or vulnerable adults that cannot be solved by one organization or sector, but require integrated services with contributions from many sectors. Examples of inspection themes are child abuse, youth offences, women in refuges and access to services for people with learning disabilities. These problems are often surrounded by uncertainty and ambiguity. There is a lack of comprehensive knowledge and what the problem means to those affected and what action should be taken are both controversial (WRR 2006; see also Koppenjan and Klijn 2004). In addition to theme-based inspections, since 2012 inspectors also investigate complex critical incidents. JISD's intention is to help find options to deal with the social problems that are the themes of the inspections and to contribute to the provision of integrated services at the local level (STJ/TSD 2015). To achieve this, inspectors examine a broad range of local services in all sectors providing services to children and vulnerable people, including health, youth care, education, police and social affairs.

JISD can be characterized as a mission-led regulator that measures performance to stimulate improvement and regards legislative provisions as a set of tools for enacting the wider mission and purpose. The inspectors use informal and quasi-legal powers and the leverage they gain from their positional authority, professional standing and the like to achieve their mission (Walshe and Pipps 2013). At the same time, their inspections contain the three activities often done in regulatory work; set standards and criteria, collect information to assess whether services comply with the criteria and take action to meet criteria and make improvements (e.g., Koop and Lodge 2015; see also Hood, James and Scott 1999; Nutley, Levitt, Solesbury and Martin 2012).

Inspectors have been described as 'street-level bureaucrats', doing their jobs outside the purview of their managers in interaction with non-voluntary clients and using discretion in their work (e.g., Mascini and Van Wijk 2009; see also May and Wood 2003). In the JISD, multidisciplinary teams of three to eight inspectors from various inspectorates conduct the inspections. The teams have been granted discretionary room to reach collective judgements. The teams enjoy the freedom to develop inspection plans that match the specificities of the inspection theme and to develop new methods or tools to conduct the inspections.

Cooperation and deliberation are key characteristics of the work of inspectors. One inspector described his input into developing an inspection framework with assessment criteria on which the inspectors base their judgements as contributing to a dialogue with others[1]:

> Interviewer: 'Do you think that you were able to contribute to the development of the framework? Because hat took a lot of deliberation, didn't it?'
>
> Inspector: 'Yes, yeah, of course it was developed in a dialog with the others. My contribution came about through the discussion. So I can't tell you which part of the inspection framework is based on my input.'

The inspectors have various backgrounds (e.g., social work, teaching, legal, youth care, criminology and epidemiology). Consequently, they can draw on a range of expertise. As the inspectors come from different inspectorates, they may use the authority of the different inspectorates that constitute the team and have a range of options to handle situations, related to the particular enforcement capabilities of the various inspectorates. Inspectors also recommend options to professionals and organizations to handle a situation. For instance, they ask local municipalities to impose conditions on quality in the subsidies they provide to services providing care to vulnerable people.

The JISD teams use this range of expertise and options not only to act responsively to separate situations, but also to change and improve their rules and procedures. For instance, during an inspection one team discovered that an inspection criterion they used to assess care and assistance for vulnerable families could have a negative impact on the families. Several inspectors on the team felt that the inspection framework should be adjusted. But, because developing the framework had taken a lot of discussion, they were afraid that the team would not immediately agree. Therefore, they decided to have a small delegation prepare a proposal for the whole team:

> We discussed that proposal at our team meeting. In preparation, we asked the team to reflect [on their experiences with the current criteria]. Everybody agreed straight away [that the changes were necessary]. Because on our inspection we saw how care for vulnerable families was delivered in practice and it was really an eye-opener.

Following what the team had learned, they adapted the inspection framework and applied the new criterion to assess other situations as well. Inspectors consider this flexibility an important virtue, as it enables them to continuously improve their approach and act responsively. At the same time, deliberating and reaching consensus in teams requires significant effort from team members even if individual input is often not discernible.

The teams conduct their inspections outside the purview of their managers. However, the inspectors involve their managers in situations where there are high stakes, for instance, when the team wants to make major changes to the inspection plan or when they decide to make major revisions to the regulatory framework. In the example given above, the inspectors involved the manager and a chief inspector in confirming the changes made.

JISD has procedures in place that structure decision-making processes, for instance on whom to involve in each phase of the inspection. Another example is that before distributing an inspection report outside the JISD, the content of the report must be approved by the team manager, managing director, chair and one of the chief inspectors in the programme committee. Procedures can be considered as the boundaries of the inspectors' discretionary room. It is not acceptable for inspectors to cross these boundaries. When a colleague sent a report to an inspected service before the team manager and managing director had approved it, one inspector commented:

> That is against how we want to work and against our procedures. An inspector cannot do this on his own without involving others.

The action had serious consequences. The inspection was terminated and the inspector concerned was no longer allowed to work at the JISD.

This example from the Joint Inspectorate Social Domain illustrates that collective discretionary room is an organizational form which highly determines how workers act. Teams carry responsibility for their joint judgements. They have to decide how to use their expertise and options, when to involve their managers and when to involve people from other organizations to broaden their repertoire. Hence, the work of teams is nested in a network of actors. The work of teams is also nested in a set of rules, which mainly entail decision-making processes that inspectors have to follow. Inspectors have the freedom within these boundaries to improve rules aimed at structuring the outcomes of decision making.

18.6 Individual Versus Collective Discretionary Room

As discussed above, the notion of collective discretionary room builds upon the literature on individual discretionary room. To understand the added value of the notion of collective discretionary room in relation to the literature, we now describe the differences between the two.

The first difference relates to the aim of afforded freedom. While the aim of individual discretionary room is to tailor general rules to individual situations, the aim of collective discretionary room is to add information, values, interests and options to deal with the situation. That is, collective discretionary room multiplies perspectives and repertoires.

The second difference is about both the work and the timing of the work involved in granting freedom to reach judgement and take action. In collective discretionary room, including others is deliberate and organized; it requires extensive a priori deliberation. Most of the effort is invested in granting a degree of freedom rather than organizing control mechanisms. Yet, despite its focus on freedom, collective discretionary room may lead to more standardized practices as teams and networks adjust and improve the rules.

The third difference has to do with the distribution of tasks. The notion of individual discretionary room implies a distribution of tasks between workers and managers or policy makers. It distributes freedom to the former and control to the latter. In contrast, the notion of collective discretionary room implies the merging of these tasks. Using granted freedom and controlling this freedom by peer review, discussion on when to use discretion and when to adjust rules are all in the hands of the team. Hence, the distinction between actors that use freedom and actors that control that freedom gets blurred. While the notion of discretionary room implies a dichotomy between freedom and control, the notion of collective discretionary room reconceptualizes the relation between freedom and control as a continuum.

The fourth difference lies in control mechanisms. Rather than specifying rules or exercising managerial control, the control mechanisms for collective discretionary room are based on reflection and learning with others. Freedom is conceptualized as the possibility—and requirement—to tailor actions to the specifics of the situation while adjusting the rules in such a way that policy purposes are realized more effectively. Hence, a collective discretionary room implies a shift from compliance to outcome.

The fifth difference concerns the role of workers in policymaking. As mentioned before, workers who use discretion act as policy co-makers. They decide how to apply a set of rules in practice; in effect their work shapes the policy and unofficially changes the rules. Like individual workers, teams also apply rules in practice. The difference is that the teams use their experiences to also adjust the rules and institutionalize the adjusted rules; they use feedback to design official new policies.

18.7 Discussion and Conclusion

We explored the notion of collective discretionary room to conceptualize the differences between how individuals and teams use freedom to decide how to act within controlled limits. The notion of collective discretionary room emphasizes the relational nature of discretionary judgement (see also Chap. 1 of this edited collection). Controlled freedom to make decisions is the result of a network of workers, managers and stakeholders outside the organizations. Conditional to the use of collective discretionary room are both team composition and group decision-making procedures.

In contrast to other forms of discretionary judgement, collective discretionary room is exercised at all steps of the policy cycle: agenda setting, policy design and decision making, implementation, delivery and evaluation. It is not limited to policy implementation and delivery. Making and applying rules happens simultaneously. Collective discretionary room entails exploring the goals and the activities to pursue it. In fact, collective discretionary room includes a commitment to pursue a general goal that accords with society's moral values and ideas of justice, such as that children receive 'adequate' education or that water is of 'good' quality. Thereby, the joint exploration may well give new meaning to the original intent (Sabel and Zeitlin 2012b). Thus, rules and regulations may change, as well as the room for manoeuvre.

The work of engaging others, weighing various perspectives and reaching consensus is time-consuming and constrains the speed with which organizations can react. Therefore, a collective discretionary room should not replace other forms of discretionary judgement. In straightforward situations, individual workers can make judgements themselves (based on the rules) because involving others would only delay action. Moreover, in situations that need a swift response, the worker's individual discretion and using their relations via collective discretion may prove invaluable in acting responsively. Organizing a collective discretionary room is especially valuable in uncertain or ambiguous situations; when the best way to handle a situation is unknown or still under debate. Therefore, collective discretionary room can never replace the individual use of discretion. In fact, discretionary judgement relies on the combination of, first, the individual use of discretion; second, discretion granted to individuals; third, cooperative work on the worker's initiative to use discretion collectively and, fourth, discretion granted to teams give organizations and workers a broad repertoire to act in the wide variety of situations they encounter.

This chapter theoretically elaborates on the collective aspects of discretionary judgement. We illustrated our conception of a collective discretionary room with our empirical findings about the partnership of the Joint Inspectorate Social Domain in the Netherlands. We chose to give one example to be able to describe more thoroughly how such a collective discretionary room can be organized. However, this example fits into a trend towards teamwork within organizations. Other inspectorates, in Scotland and Northern Ireland for instance, are also starting to cooperate and establish inspection teams that are granted the freedom to select inspection topics and are developing a regulatory framework and regulatory strategies (Ehren, Janssens, Brown, McNamara, O'Hara and Shevlin 2017; see also Janssens and Ehren 2016). In various other organizations, there is a trend towards self-steering teams in the social welfare and health sector and also in education. Self-steering teams make joint decisions on the provision of care in neighbourhoods, for instance (Johansen and van den Bosch 2017). Hence, the collective aspects of discretionary room are relevant in a variety of organizational contexts. Future research should focus on the diverse ways in which discretionary room is organized and how its organizational form affects the relationship between freedom and control.

Collective discretionary room is the freedom afforded to a team or a network to set the rules with which they can make a difference for users. When discretionary room is made a collective resource, the use of freedom and the mechanisms for control are changing. Collective discretionary room changes the aim of afforded freedom (from being responsive in individual situations to improving policy designs and outcomes), offers more mechanisms for control when workers act outside the purview of managers and policymakers higher up, merges granting and controlling freedom and, last but not least, facilitates an even greater role of practice in rulemaking.

Note

1. The quotes presented in this chapter stem from a research into the collective aspects of inspectors' discretionary judgments in which interviews were combined with a document analysis and a comparison was made between two inspectorates (Care Quality Commission in England and the Joint Inspectorate Social Domain (previously the Joint Inspectorate for Youth) in the Netherlands). The study design and methods have been described in an article that has been published previously (Rutz *et al.* 2017). The three quotes we use in this chapter are all derived from interviews at the Joint Inspectorate Social Domain. Two of the three quotes have been used before in the previous article.

References

Bannink, D., Six, F. & van Wijk, E. (2016). Bureaucratic, market or professional control? A theory on the relation between street-level task characteristics and the feasibility of control mechanisms. In P. Hupe, M. Hill & A. Buffat (Eds), *Understanding street-level bureaucracy* (pp. 205–225). Bristol: Policy Press.

Brodkin, E.Z. (2016). The inside story: Street-level research in the US and beyond. In P. Hupe, M. Hill & A. Buffat (Eds), *Understanding street-level bureaucracy* (pp. 25–42). Bristol: Policy press.

Davis, K.C. (1969). *Discretionary justice: A preliminary inquiry*. Baton Rouge, LA: Louisiana State University Press.

Durose, C. (2011). Revisiting Lipsky: Front-line work in UK local governance. *Political Studies*, 59(4), 978–995. https://doi.org/10.1111/j.1467-9248.2011.00886.x.

Ehren, M.C.M., Janssens, F.J.G., Brown, M., McNamara, G., O'Hara, J. & Shevlin, P. (2017). Evaluation and decentralised governance: Examples of inspections in polycentric education systems. *Journal of Education Change*, 18(3), 365–383.

Ellis, K. (2016). Personalisation and adult social work: Recasting professional discretion at the street level? In P. Hupe, M. Hill & A. Buffat (Eds), *Understanding street-level bureaucracy* (pp. 187–202). Bristol: Policy Press.

Ellis, K., Davis, A. & Rummery, K. (1999). Needs assessment 'street-level bureaucracy' and the new community care. *Journal of Social Policy and Administration*, 33(3), 262–280.

Evans, T. (2011). Professionals, managers and discretion: Critiquing street-level bureaucracy. *British Journal of Social Work*, 41(2), 368–386. https://doi.org/10.1093/bjsw/bcq074.

Hart, P. 't. (1998). Preventing groupthink revisited: Evaluating and reforming groups in government. *Organizational Behavior and Human Decision Processes*, 73(2), 306–326.

Hood, C., James, O. & Scott, C. (1999). *Regulation inside government*. Oxford: Oxford University Press.

Hupe, P.L. (2013). Dimensions of discretion: Specifying the object of street-level bureaucracy research. *Der Moderne Staat: Zeitschrift Für Public Policy, Recht Und Management*, 6(2), 425–440.

Hupe, P. & Buffat, A. (2014). A public service gap: Capturing contexts in a comparative approach of street-level bureaucracy. *Public Management Review*, 16(4), 548–569.

Hupe, P. & Hill, M. (2007). Street-level bureaucracy and public accountability. *Public Administration*, 85(2), 279–299. https://doi.org/10.1111/j.1467-9299.2007.00650.x.

Hupe, P., Hill, M. & Buffat, A. (Eds). (2016). *Understanding street-level bureaucracy*. Bristol: Policy Press.

Janis, I.L. (1982). *Groupthink*. Boston: Houghton Mifflin.

Janis, I.L. (1989). *Crucial decisions*. New York: Free Press.

Janssens, F.J.G. & Ehren, M.C.M. (2016). Toward a model of school inspections in a polycentric system. *Evaluation and Program Planning*, 56(Supplement C), 88–98.

Johansen, F. & van den Bosch, S. (2017). The scaling-up of neighbourhood care: From experiment towards a transformative movement in healthcare. *Futures*, 89(Supplement C), 60–73.

Koop, C. & Lodge, M. (2015). What is regulation? an interdisciplinary concept analysis. *Regulation & Governance*, 11(1), 95–108. https://doi.org/10.1111/rego.12094.

Koppenjan, J. & Klijn, E.H. (2004). *Managing uncertainties in networks. A network approach to problem solving and decision making*. London: Routledge.

Lipsky, M. (2010). *Street level bureaucracy. Dilemmas of the individual in public service* (Updated ed.). New York: Russell Sage Foundation.

March, J.G. & Olsen, J.P. (2004). *The logic of appropriateness. ARENA working papers*. (No. WP 04/09). Oslo: Arena, Centre for European Studies.

Mascini, P. & Van Wijk, E. (2009). Responsive regulation at the Dutch food and consumer product safety authority: An empirical assessment of assumptions underlying the theory. *Regulation & Governance*, 3(1), 27–47. https://doi.org/10.1111/j.1748-5991.2009.01047.x.

May, P.J. & Wood, R.S. (2003). At the regulatory front lines: Inspectors' enforcement styles and regulatory compliance. *Journal of Public Administration Research and Theory*, 13(2), 117–139. https://doi.org/10.1093/jpart/mug014.

Minkman, M. (2017). *Innovatie van organisatie en governance van integrale zorg.: Verlangen naar integraliteit.* Tilburg: Tilburg University.

Montero, A., van Duijn, S., Zonneveld, N., Minkman, M. & Nies, H. (2016). *Integrated social services in Europe. A study looking at how local public services are working together to improve people's lives.* Brighton: European Social Network.

Moscovici, S. & Doise, W. (1994). *Conflict and consensus.* London: Sage Publications.

Noordegraaf, M. (2011). Risky business: How professionals and professional fields (must) deal with organizational issues. *Organization Studies*, 32(10), 1349–1371. https://doi.org/10.1177/0170840611416748.

Noordegraaf, M. & Steijn, B. (Eds). (2013). *Professionals under pressure. The reconfiguration of professional work in changing public services.* Amsterdam: Amsterdam University Press.

Nutley, S., Levitt, R., Solesbury, W. & Martin, S. (2012). Scrutinizing performance: How assessors reach judgements about public services. *Public Administration*, 90(4), 869–885.

Osiander, C. & Steinke, J. (2016). The moment of the street-level bureaucrats in a public employment service. In P. Hupe, M. Hill & A. Buffat (Eds), *Understanding street-level bureaucracy* (pp. 295–311). Bristol: Policy Press.

Perez, O. (2014). Courage, regulatory responsibility, and the challenge of higher-order reflexivity. *Regulation & Governance*, 8(2), 203–221. https://doi.org/10.1111/rego.12038.

Piore, M.J. (2011). Beyond markets: Sociology, street-level bureaucracy, and the management of the public sector. *Regulation & Governance*, 5(1), 145–164. https://doi.org/10.1111/j.1748-5991.2010.01098.x.

Pires, R.R.C. (2011). Beyond the fear of discretion: Flexibility, performance, and accountability in the management of regulatory bureaucracies. *Regulation & Governance*, 5(1), 43–69. https://doi.org/10.1111/j.1748-5991.2010.01083.x.

Rice, D. (2013). Street-level bureaucrats and the welfare state: Toward a micro-institutionalist theory of policy implementation. *Administration & Society*, 45, 1038–1062. https://doi.org/10.1177/0095399712451895.

Rutz, S., Mathew, D., Robben, P. & Bont, A. de (2017). Enhancing responsiveness and consistency: Comparing the collective use of discretion and discretionary room at inspectorates in England and the Netherlands. *Regulation & Governance*, 11, 81–94. https://doi.org/10.1111/rego.12101.

Rutz, S.I. (2017). *Practicing reflexive regulation.* Rotterdam: Erasmus University Rotterdam.

Sabel, C.F. & Zeitlin, J. (2012a). Experimentalist governance. In D. Levi-Faur (Ed.), *Oxford handbook of governance.* (pp. 169–183). Oxford: Oxford University Press.

Sabel, C. F. & Zeitlin, J. (2012b). Experimentalism in the EU: Common ground and persistent differences. *Regulation & Governance*, 6(3), 410–426. https://doi.org/10.1111/j.1748-5991.2012.01157.x.

Samenwerkend Toezicht Jeugd/Toezicht Sociaal Domein (STJ/TSD). (2015). *Meerjarenvisie 2016–2019*. Utrecht: STJ/TSD.

Silbey, S.S. (2011). The sociological citizen: Pragmatic and relational regulation in law and organizations. *Regulation & Governance*, 5(1), 1–13. https://doi.org/10.1111/j.1748-5991.2011.01106.x.

Tummers, L.G. & Bekkers, V.J.J.M. (2014). Policy implementation, street-level bureaucracy and the importance of discretion. *Public Management Review*, 16(4), 527–547.

Walshe, K. & Phipps, D. (2013). *Developing a strategic framework to guide the Care Quality Commission's programme of evaluation*. London: CQC.

Wetenschappelijke Raad voor het Regeringsbeleid (WRR). (2006). *Lerende overheid. een pleidooi voor probleemgerichte politiek*. Den Haag: WRR.

World Health Organisation (WHO). (2015). *WHO global strategy on people-centred and integrated health services*. Geneva: WHO Document Production Services.

CHAPTER 19

Managerial Discretion

Catherine Needham

19.1 Introduction

This chapter focuses on exploring managerial discretion, identifying the distinctive features and dilemmas of discretion for people working in managerial positions. In particular the objective of this chapter is to position managerial discretion in the context of a move towards public services which are more 'person-centred'. Person-centredness, and the associated policy of personalization, is a theme of welfare reform across advanced democracies, as the technological possibilities of individually tailored services mesh with the rise of 'assertive citizens', less willing to settle for 'one size fits all' welfare (Griffiths, Foley and Prendergrast 2009). The chapter begins by discussing managerial discretion more broadly and then focuses on the specific dilemmas and challenges generated by services in which primacy is given to a recognition of personhood.

19.2 Discretion as a Manager

If discretion is seen as a key concept in implementation theory, then it is notable that managers get little explicit attention from proponents of either top-down or bottom-up approaches to implementation research (Hill and Hupe 2008). In the top-down view of implementation, a manager's role is to ensure fidelity with the policy issued by government and to minimize variance by front-level staff. This account of managers as a buffer layer, seeking to minimize staff deviation from central policy, is replicated in bottom-up accounts of

C. Needham (✉)
Public Policy and Public Management, Health Services Management Centre,
University of Birmingham, Birmingham, UK
e-mail: c.needham.1@bham.ac.uk

T. Evans, P. Hupe (eds.), *Discretion and the Quest for Controlled Freedom*, https://doi.org/10.1007/978-3-030-19566-3_19

policy implementation, in which attention is given to the spaces for creativity and discretion at the frontline. In the classic work of Lipsky (1980/2010), for example, managers are characterized as little more than 'the disinterested servants of policy' (Evans 2011: 373) (although Lipsky does acknowledge this lapse in the 2010 update of the book, with additional content on management; see Lipsky 1980/2010).

There is more focus on managerial discretion within theoretical approaches of the 'managerial state' (e.g. Clarke and Newman 1997; Exworthy 1998) which chart the increased dominance of managers within public services since the emergence of new public management (NPM) approaches. Here managers are recognized to be both more numerous and more powerful than in the past, setting performance targets, gathering performance data, rewarding and disciplining staff, and maintaining tight cost control (Clarke and Newman 1997). An explicit aspect of the NPM approach was that managers be given more autonomy from central state control to determine how best to meet the broad goals of public policy, expanding the spaces for managerial discretion (James 2003). Power is seen as zero-sum, with control shifting from frontline professionals to a new cadre of managers (Exworthy 1998).

This zero-sum account of power shifting from frontline staff to managers, with an attendant transfer of discretion, is limited in a number of ways. Implementation of these managerialist approaches has been patchy and contradictory, such that workers have been able to retain substantial discretion over their work (Evans 2010). In relation to understanding discretion there is also a limitation to discussing management as a homogeneous layer, sitting between government and the frontline. This misrepresents the complex structures of public service organizations and the manifold relationships within it (Ringquist 1995). Multiple tiers of management must exercise discretion as they interpret instructions from above and pass them on to their own team as well as sending signals back up the line. Managers must also look to develop horizontal working relationships with managers in related services, through which discretion may be enhanced or reduced.

Evans (2011) has highlighted the extent to which focus on managers as a distinct cadre underestimates the extent to which managers may identify more strongly with the professional identity of frontline staff than with their own organizational role. Most managers will have been drawn from that professional group (Freidson 1994). Contra Lipsky, Evans (2011: 383) found in a study of management and professional identities in social work that 'local managers largely expressed a professional commitment, distancing themselves from senior managers and identifying more with their fellow professionals'. Evans (2010) suggests that rather than 'dominant managerialism' or 'street-level bureaucracy' there can be a 'discursive managerialism' at work in welfare services, in which shared professional identities broker local constructions of discretion between managers and frontline staff. This dual identity is particularly the case with junior managers who may still retain a case load (Evans 2010).

Rather than approaching managerial discretion through location in a hierarchy, a functionalist account of what makes managers distinctive in relation to discretion is explored by Evans (2012). He draws on Oakeshott's (1991) distinction between nomocracy (a focus on rules) and teleocracy (a focus on goals) as a key dividing line in public service management. Rules are often said to be the domain of managers whilst goals are the focus of professionals. However, Evans' (2012) research with social work managers and frontline staff highlights that this distinction breaks down in practice, with rule adherence or a focus on goals being distributed among staff in a way that does not map onto organizational positions. His research suggests that some staff are by disposition more inclined to prioritize rules or goals regardless of their status in the organization.

An alternative way to utilize the rules/goals distinction is to shine a light on the contradictions within managerialism itself. What is evident from 30 years of managerial reforms of public services is that they have contained within them a number of tensions and contradictions, for example, increasing managerial oversight whilst cutting 'red tape' (Kirkpatrick, Ackroyd and Walker 2005). In relation to discretion, managers have had to blend rule-following with a commitment to user choice and flexibility which is antithetical to standardized rule-bound services (Pollitt 1993: 43; Gray and Jenkins 1995: 81). Consumerist trends within public services have seen the emergence of new norms of public service in which the person—their dispositions and preferences—is the focal point for attention (Needham 2007). Echoing Evans' distinction between rules and goals, the rise of a customer care ethos within public services can be seen as a shift from rule-following to the optimizing of outcomes for customers (Needham 2006).

In a UK context, this shift is particularly associated with the incoming New Labour government in the late 1990s, which explicitly rejected 'monolithic' public services in favour of more tailored support (Needham 2007). The cross-party appeal of person-centred services was evident when the Conservatives took power from 2010, as David Cameron's vision of a 'post-bureaucratic' age was translated into a variety of more 'personalized' approaches to public services in the Conservative manifesto for the 2010 general election (Conservative Party 2010). Personalization has shaped approaches to reform in the National Health Services (NHS), children's services, education, employment, housing and criminal justice (Needham 2011). Indeed it is possible to argue that within public services, personalization constitutes a new valence issue: like economic growth, it is hard to argue against being person-centred and the main point of contention is over which party can implement it most effectively. Mansell and Beadle-Brown (2005: 21) suggest, 'There is now no serious alternative to the principle that services should be tailored to individual needs, circumstances and wants.'

In some service sectors, this approach has been in part a rhetorical flourish, while its impact has been mitigated by countervailing forces. In education and medicine, for example, professional expertise about the appropriate intervention continues to be the primary force shaping frontline practice, leavened with input from regulators and ministries, but with limited scope for the individual to personalize their experience. In housing and employment services, expert interpretations of deservingness and punitive compliance regimes, again undercut a rhetoric of person-centred approaches. More substantive progress has been made in personal social services such as care for older people and people with disabilities. Here some of the countervailing pressures that militate against user control in other sectors—professional expertise, notions of desert, regulatory standardization—have been weakened by sustained campaigning by disability rights groups (Glasby and Littlechild 2016). Since much of social care is about intimate personal care and how people spend their day, the case for people to be 'experts on their own lives' (Poll 2007) has been more strongly argued here than in other sectors. Shifts towards forms of self-directed support are evident in a wide range of countries (Izuhara 2003; Glasby and Dickinson 2009; Alakeson 2010; Grit and de Bont 2010; Christensen and Pilling 2014; Dickinson, Needham and Sullivan 2014). Examples of this include personal budgets in England, Nurse Family Partnerships in the US, Buurtzorg nurses in the Netherlands and Local Area Coordination (LAC) in Australia and parts of the UK (Olds 2006; Bartnik 2007; Bartnik and Chambers 2007; Needham 2011; Laloux 2014; Gray, Sarnak and Burgers 2015).

Three aspects of person-centredness are looked at below as illustrative of new dilemmas relating to managerial discretion. The first relates to the emergence of citizens as expert decision-makers and budget holders. The second is the pressure for more 'whole person' ways of working with citizens, requiring collaboration across service boundaries. The third focuses on the rise of the managerial self, in which managers are expected to share more of themselves—with staff and via social media—in order to be more authentic managers.

19.3 Person-Centredness: Citizen Experts

A first tension between managerial discretion and person-centredness relates to the extent to which managerial discretion is preserved in a policy setting in which the people who use services are considered to be experts. Arguably this policy shift is relocating decision-making and discretion beyond the frontline, privileging user preferences over both professional discretion and managerial authority. Self-directed care involves an affirmation of the legitimacy of user knowledge (Poll 2007). Person-centred planning by social workers is seen as recognizing 'the authority of the service user's voice', rather than the professional's and focuses on 'aspirations and capacities' of the service user 'rather than needs and deficiencies' (Mansell and Beadle-Brown 2005: 20). Conventional accounts of knowledge and evidence are challenged as the authenticity of the user experience is privileged and forms of informal peer support come to be valued (Cutler, Waine and Brehony 2007: 851). Griffiths *et al.* (2009: 92) note the shift: 'As expertise is increasingly regarded as being constructed as much from self-awareness, achievement and lived experience as from professional or educational background, so there are inevitable implications for the professional/user relationship.' The notion of the individual as the expert on their own life evokes a teleological logic: *what matters is what works for the person with care needs.* It implies impatience with rule-bound approaches which curtail user freedoms (Glasby and Littlechild 2016). In a context of person-centred approaches, the primacy given to goals over rules creates potential problems for managers, who must ensure that the support given meets expected risk thresholds and constitutes an appropriate use of public money.

This tension is perhaps most intense where budgets are transferred to individuals—as it is for some health and care service users—and the key managerial role of gate-keeping resources is diluted. Whilst managers may still decide the overall allocation of money received by an individual, it may well be that the individual is given much more control than in the past over how that money is spent. Such an approach is evident in English social care services, where there has been a move over a decade to ensure that all people using care services are entitled to receive their money as a personal budget, which they can hold themselves (as a direct payment) or which can be managed for them by the local authority or a third party (Needham 2011). Personal health budgets are also being introduced into the National Health Services for people with continuing health care needs (i.e. who need long-term care) and some English localities are introducing them for a wider range of conditions. Some variant of individualized care funding has also been developed in the Netherlands, Canada, Belgium, France, Austria, Finland, Sweden and Germany (e.g. Alakeson 2010; Gadsby 2013).

Hutchinson, Land and Salisbury (2006: 76) argue that whilst direct payments in social care are only a means to an end of more individualized planning and support, there is something distinctive about the payments themselves, namely,

> the changed relationship between the person with learning disabilities and their staff. Instead of being controlled by support staff, direct payments gave people the opportunity to 'be the boss'. This is such a dramatic and complete reversal of roles, and is probably a key to other changes in people's lives.

Similarly, a report on housing and personal budgets argues, 'We must understand that at the heart of the personalization agenda is a cultural shift which requires providers and professionals to be accountable to customers or risk losing their business' (Taylor Knox 2009: 4). This language of customer has become more prevalent in public services as symbolic of the power shifts that decentred budgets are designed to trigger (Needham 2006, 2011).

There has been extensive discussion of the need for professionals and people who use services to develop new relationships in this context, whilst much less is said about how it reframes managers. According to Boyle, Clark and Burns (2006: ix), 'the role of the professional needs to shift from being fixers who focus on problems to becoming catalysts who focus on abilities'. New professional roles of broker and support planner are starting to proliferate and to insert themselves into the space between the service user and the social worker or clinician. Hutchinson *et al.* (2006: 58) describe the role of independent planner and facilitator as 'listening, assisting individuals to dream and express their own voice, supporting family involvement and being skilful about planning and implementation of those dreams'. Elsewhere the new public service professional brought to life by personalization has been called a 'Sherpa' (British Medical Journal 2003—cited in Griffiths, Foley and Prendergrast 2009: 100). Relationships with professionals are expected to be more co-productive (Parker 2007: 107; see also Callaghan and Wistow 2008: 166; Coulson 2007; Cummins and Miller 2007). For example, the *Personal Health Budgets* document, launching the pilots, also calls for a co-productive approach: 'Personalisation of healthcare embodies co-production. It means individuals working in partnership with their family, carers and professionals to plan, develop and procure the services and support that are appropriate for them' (DH 2009: 23).

The manager of person-centred and co-produced services is a less scrutinized role, although the challenges it poses are no less profound than they are for frontline professionals (and of course the manager and the frontline professional may in practice be the same person). Managers are usually charged with overseeing resources and minimizing risks to service users and staff. Personalization challenges both of these positionings. Resource decisions are devolved to people using services, even if the overall allocation remains a management decision (and managers must still sign off on users' spending decisions). Efforts by professionals and managers to safeguard clients through avoidance of risky situations have been condemned by advocates of personalization for placing too many limits on individuals' freedoms (Carr 2014). Rather than this negative view of risk, social care managers are invited to embrace a positive version of risk, which is much more permissive in relation to individual choices.

Looking at social care services in England, in practice personalization has been applied very differently by managers in different local settings. Some local areas have retained risk committees to sign off user spending choices and have imposed clear limits on what can be purchased. Other localities have become much more liberal in allowing services users a high degree of discretion over spending choices, even if those span far beyond what might normally be considered a health or social care service (with the appropriate evidence base to back that up) (Glasby and Littlechild 2016).

At issue here is partly a concern about risk, but partly also concerns of managers about the difficulties of defending eccentric spending choices to the media and elected councillors. In interviews with social care commissioners for an earlier project by the author, it was clear that there were different attitudes to what it was and was not appropriate to pay for through an individualized care budget. Purchases such as a walk-in bath have an obvious link to care, but spending on a family holiday, a TV sports package, a laptop or a massage are much more contestable and may expose managers to critical media scrutiny (Needham 2011).

In interviews with social care managers, there was a range of views on how far individuals and families should have discretion over spending choices. As one director of adult social care said:

> We aren't bothered what people spend their unemployment or social security on. When people raise concerns about disabled people misusing funds I just see it as an example of prejudice (Cited in Needham 2011: 120).

However, another director felt that unconditional payments would diminish 'the professional raison d'être' [...] and 'just isn't affordable. We're focusing on what's realistic and being honest with people' (cited in Needham 2011: 120). Another interviewee highlighted the economic and outcome benefits of taking a permissive approach:

> Some people with direct payments are going to a nice hotel for respite [...] which is cheaper for us, going to Centre Parcs or whatever. People's needs are met in a much more uplifting and creative way – not just going to a grotty place to play bingo (Cited in Needham 2011: 125).

Writing about holding a personal health budget for his father with dementia, Royle sets out how his family used the money to get his father out of the day centre, where they felt he was deteriorating: 'Nine months since first attending the daycentre, my dad's medication had been tripled, his anxieties were continuing [...] [and he] frequently verbalised how he wished to stop attending the daycentre and spend more time at home' (Royle 2014: 123). The personal health budget was used to purchase a Sky TV package, so that he could watch his favourite shows at home. As well as giving them more choice over how resources were used, Royle (2014: 125) reports:

> What we also noticed as a family was the change in relationship between ourselves and the professionals involved in my dad's care. No longer were we attending appointments and our opinions being overlooked. Instead, we were now being treated as the experts we were with regard to my dad's condition and his ever-changing behaviours.

From the family's perspective, this seemed like a sensible switch of resourcing. However, for managers charged with defending public expenditure on a high-end satellite TV package, this can be an awkward position. An article in *Pulse*, the magazine for General Practitioners, in September 2015 exemplified the resistance to individualized funding among some health professionals. It was headlined, 'Revealed: NHS funding splashed on holidays, games consoles and summer houses'. The article went on: 'the scheme to give "patients more control over their care" has been used to buy many un-evidenced treatments at the expense of long-established services which have been defunded' (Price 2015). The article exemplifies a number of points of professional resistance to personal health budgets, including the way in which patients choose treatments which lack a conventional evidence base and the extent to which this is reducing funding for collectively provided services. Professionals and managers may share a common imperative to avoid being blamed for the poor choices of users.

It could be argued that the challenge in relation to evidence constitutes a particular threat to professional authority, whereas the financial implications reflect a challenge to managerial authority (although in practice these aspects will be blurred). Writing about individualized care funding in Australia, Dickinson, Needham and Sullivan (2014) identify three particular accountability challenges in relation to personalized funding: accountability for outcomes, accountability for public money and accountability for the welfare of care workers. Each of these forms of accountability is likely to be felt acutely by managers who need to report to senior officials and elected councillors within localities, but who also will be held accountable by national government, regulatory agencies and potentially by hostile media.

In sum then we can see that a person-centred narrative within health and social care, including personalized budgets in some cases, disrupts the binary of managerial versus professional discretion by introducing a third actor—the person using services, along with their families. For managers and professionals this may involve a reduction in their discretion as more decision-making is devolved to the patient and user of care services. However, it may also involve more discretion than previously, as individual managers and professionals must sign off on user choices which do not fit into existing service options and may not meet conventional evidence thresholds.

19.4 Person-Centredness: Managing for the Whole Person

A second way in which person-centredness may be in tensions with managerial discretion is through requiring more generic ways of working to support 'whole person' approaches. Two distinct and contrasting examples are discussed in relation to this. The first is the development of multi-disciplinary teams or lead professionals to support people with complex needs across care, health, employment and housing. The second (contrasting) development has been the growth of 'one-stop shops' on a call centre model, which are designed to be able to support citizens with a range of issues through a protocol-driven approach in which frontline and managerial discretion may be minimal. These two examples are discussed in turn.

Collaborative Management

As public services become more person-centred there have been efforts to join up fragmented public services to support people in a more holistic way. This may entail the formation of multi-disciplinary teams to support people with complex needs or the use of lead professions who can support people across care, health, employment and housing (Needham, Mastracci and Mangan 2017). These ways of working bring together different sets of managers, while they will deploy discretion in ways that can complement or clash with each other. For example, in the commissioning and delivery of social care services, managers from the statutory sector will need to collaborate with managers from third sector and private organizations providing services or advocacy/information/advice. Thus managerial discretion needs to be understood not just as a link in a vertical chain from policy-makers higher up through managers to the frontline, but also horizontally, as managers across different sectors exercise discretion in ways that may complement or disrupt each other.

Governments have created a range of roles which explicitly cross traditional professional boundaries, as people are appointed to posts such as care coordinators (AHRQ 2016), navigators (UCL 2016) and brokers (Tually, Slatter, Oakley and Faulkner 2015). The Local Area Coordination (LAC) model was developed in Western Australia to support people with disabilities and their families (Bartnik 2007; Bartnik and Chambers 2007). It seeks to deliver a pro-active and person-centred approach to support which combines elements of community development with care management. The Coordinator is expected to give wide-ranging assistance rather than splitting care, health, housing and other issues into separate service streams (Lord and Hutchison 2003; Glasby 2012; Laragy, Fisher, Purcal and Jenkinson 2015). Recruitment to such a role emphasizes the cross-cutting nature of the job where 'Coordinators also provided information, assisted people in building their support networks, and helped people to purchase their own supports via direct consumer funding' (Lord and Hutchison 2003: 98).

These roles are quasi-professional, in that authority comes from proximity to the setting and the community rather than from traditional forms of professional knowledge. Supporting people across a range of services is assumed to bring an increase in frontline discretion, as emphasis is placed on pragmatic problem-solving (and trust-building) rather than observance of professional boundaries and service distinctions. Such initiatives seem premised on 'freeing up' frontline workers and minimizing the imposition of managerial rules. Flexibility is a key element of what is on offer, as the Local Area Coordinator Network website makes clear:

> Local Area Coordinators support individuals and their families and are based in their local communities as a local, accessible, single point of contact for people with disabilities, mental health needs, older people and their families. This enables the support provided by Local Area Coordinators to be personalised, flexible and responsive, within the context of their family and community life. They take time to get to know and build positive, trusting relationships with individuals, families and local communities and develop a more personal relationship with a wide range of people and their families (LAC Network n.d.).

A similar key worker approach has been used in the UK's Family Intervention projects which morphed into the Troubled Families approach (Hayden and Jenkins 2014; Crossley 2016). The Troubled Families Initiative in England was established in 2012 by the Department for Communities and Local Government with the aim of 'turning around' the lives of 120,000 families with multiple disadvantages (PAC 2016). The intervention is built around the principles of a single key worker supporting a family across a range of support needs, relating to, for example, health, parenting, employment, housing and substance misuse. An evaluation of the Troubled Families scheme report found,

> It was perceived to have enhanced family intervention practice by enabling key workers to: work intensively with all family members; to dig deeper than other professionals and to get to the roots of deeply entrenched problems; to understand the whole family more effectively; to be more closely aligned with partners, to take a more assertive and challenging approach; and to incorporate training and employment as part of the intervention (NIESR 2016).

However the high political profile of Troubled Families has led to dispute about the extent to which frontline staff were freed from managerial imperatives and allowed to support families to address problems in a long-term and sustainable way. A recent Public Accounts Committee report was highly critical of the ways in which the 'payment by results' approach used to incentivize local authorities to support so-called troubled families led to a focus on short-term goals rather than 'providing the support necessary to tackle deep rooted problems' (PAC 2016: 5). This suggests that discretion for both managers and frontline staff was sabotaged by the re-imposition of performance indicators in a project where too much political capital rested on being able to demonstrate quick success.

Automized Management

A second (contrasting) manifestation of more holistic ways of supporting citizens has been the growth of 'one-stop shop' call centres to respond to a range of citizen queries and problems. Local and central government in many countries now use online or telephone-based contract centres to handle citizen queries (PWC 2012; see also Askim, Fimreite, Moseley and Pedersen 2011). As Askim *et al.* (2011: 1452) observe: 'Like other "frontline" forms of partnership working, the one-stop shop aims to make services feel seamless for service users by providing a single entry point into the welfare system.' Call centre operatives are expected to be able to offer a holistic service to citizens, only referring on to specialized, service-specific teams in particularly complex cases. The call centres are staffed by 'generically skilled officers', who have a script and protocol to structure engagement with the citizen and to build rapport in the absence of professional role legitimacy (Richter and Cornford 2008). They must negotiate legitimacy with citizens through observing the display rules of the call centre encounter (Needham *et al.* 2017). Customer relationship management (CRM) tools enable the profiling of callers so that support can be tailored to the caller—an algorithmic version of person-centredness.

Such contexts are often heavily monitored by managers, curtailing the scope for frontline discretion and creating new dilemmas around relationships between managerial oversight and the street-level worker (Bovens and Zouridis 2002; Zapf, Isic, Bechtoldt, and Blau 2003; Alferoff and Knights 2008; see also Chap. 20 of this edited collection). Call centre workers, for example, are closely monitored to ensure that their emotional displays are appropriate (Zapf *et al.* 2003: 334). As Dormann and Zijlstra write, 'Call centre employees should make customers feel as if they are really interested in the customers' problems, and be friendly as if they are happy to talk to them' (2003: 308). Research with call centre workers has found that they experience high levels of emotional dissonance (i.e. a gap between felt emotions and emotional display), as they must maintain courtesy and stick to the script even when dealing with angry or abusive customers (Lewig and Dollard 2003: 367).

Limiting frontline discretion therefore may be said to be a key managerial goal within the call centre setting. Alferoff and Knights (2008: 33), drawing on case study work in five call centre settings, argue:

> [T]he manipulations of data by managers in call centers is increasingly designed to master and maintain the content of service and sales encounters that might otherwise become 'off-limits' in terms of management control.

However, as well as closing down frontline worker discretion, the call centre mode of operating is also a limit on managerial discretion, as managers must oversee these tightly scripted performances and remain accountable upwards for adherence to required conventions of timeliness and consistency. As Alferoff and Knights put it, 'The "gaze" of the electronic boards displaying their unceasing demands on staff combined with tele-computing and the automatic distribution of calls (ACD) ensures that backlogs are always driving performance' (Alferoff and Knights 2008: 31).

19.5 Person-Centredness: The Managerial Self

Putting the personhood of users in public services at the forefront, disrupting managerial and frontline discretion, as discussed above can be seen as an expression of a broader trend towards '*subject centrism*' (Hupe 2017). With this concept Hupe characterizes the inclination to consider the individual as the centre of the universe. Managerialism has increasingly discovered the 'self' in relation to managers, which poses a new set of dilemmas for discretion. The rise of the 'authentic leadership' movement (Gardner, Cogliser, Davis and Dickens 2011) has drawn attention to the value of management which builds strong and genuine interpersonal connections (George 2010). In place of the machine metaphors of Weberian bureaucracy, managers are expected to engage and inspire workers through personal storytelling and empathetic connections (Ganz 2010). The 'bring your whole self to work' approach emphasizes vulnerability and the creation of a nurturing environment for staff (Robbins 2015).

These more personalized, informal and 'authentic' encounters are facilitated by new social media technologies, in which citizens as well as staff can be engaged. In these encounters the interaction becomes more informal and less rule-driven, while managers must take a view of what constitutes discretion in both senses of the word: being discrete in this new medium, as well as how much to constrain or free up the social media activities of team members.

Public service delivery organizations increasingly interface with the public via social media. Local authorities, health providers, police and fire services have active twitter feeds which citizens can use to interact with frontline staff, as well as organizations using these streams to publicize their activities (Jeffares 2014). A research project by Needham and Mangan (2016) on the *twenty-first-Century Public Servant*, focusing on English local government, reported the difficulties that senior local officials—in managerial rather than frontline roles—found in utilizing social media to engage with citizens. As public services change the ways in which they interact with residents, interviewees reported that they are being expected to be more visible, available and prepared to interact in a rapid and more informal way with residents than they had done in the past.

Twitter in particular provides a space for discourse which is supposed to be authentic in the sense of being spontaneous and unrehearsed (Margaretten and Gaber 2012). As Margaretten and Gaber (2012: 337) put it in discussing the communicative norms that shape Twitter behaviours: '[A]uthenticity involves identifying themes of being a genuine person, one who is unrehearsed, available and respectful.' Spicer (2014) discusses pressures to be 'authentic' in the workplace as part of a broader challenge to worker identity: 'Because employees are asked to bring themselves to work, there is a very blurry line between personal issues and professional issues. Because you should be passionate about what you do, it is not clear when you are working and when you are not. This often means work begins to bleed out into people's personal lives.'

This expectation can be a cause of anxiety as managers struggle to find time for this new demand and to find an appropriate blend of the public and the personal in how they present themselves through social media. Organizations have developed different protocols for the use of social media by employees, with some instituting a blanket ban and others taking a more permissive approach. One interviewee for the *twenty-first-Century Public Servant* project (a manager in a large social housing provider in England) expressed the tension between being encouraged to be 'authentic' by her organization and the fear that she might get into trouble if she was too frank:

> A lot of public sector organizations fall into the trap of putting out this bland stuff […]. We're talking about personality now. [The communications team] are saying you need to be blogging as yourself. But when I do get the time, fitting it

> into the day job, what guarantees do I have that no one is going to say you've overstepped the mark here? (Cited in Needham and Mangan 2016: 269).

Another said, 'You have to be careful with Twitter. It's difficult to draw the line between personal and professional life. I tend to retweet things but without a value statement attached. We are in politically restricted posts so we have to be careful' (cited in Needham and Mangan 2016: 269).

Here then is a requirement for managers to exercise discretion in new ways, with rules and norms still in flux and the public nature of the interaction creating high risks if the content is considered inappropriate. Jeffares' work examining how the police use Twitter is explicitly framed in relation to discretion, arguing that social media 'open[s] up a new space for discretionary behaviour at the interface between public and public servants' (2016: 1). He identifies a range of discretionary practices engaged in by police communication teams when on Twitter, which range from friendly 'banter' to more classic authoritative positionings, noting also the surveillance of these communication practices by managers. However, as he points out, 'The question of bending or indeed breaking the rules is a moot point, given that the rules of the game of social media continue to evolve both formally (through revised social media policies) and informally in terms of what is accepted, tolerated or for that matter known' (Jeffares 2016: 18). This reflection highlights the fluid, emerging and spontaneous nature of Twitter interactions, creating new sorts of dilemmas for managers in the exercise of discretion.

19.6 Conclusion

Ranging across various examples of *subject centrism* in public services, the chapter has highlighted a number of challenges in relation to the scope and type of discretion that managers deploy. Person-centredness disrupts the binary of professional goals versus managerial rules by bringing in people who use services and their families. These groups can set their own goals to a degree and may not accept the legitimacy of existing rules or forms of authority. When budgets are devolved to individuals, the tensions relating to who and how discretion can be exercised are particularly intense. Managers then must reconcile the requirement to offer service users wide discretion over their support, with being accountable to senior managers and political leaders for user outcomes and safety.

A second facet of person-centred approaches is the growth of generic professional or quasi-professional roles and the increase in multi-disciplinary working, which create new challenges for staff and for managers in establishing legitimacy and exercising discretion. Technological developments have created scope for new kinds of person-centred relationships between public service workers and citizens. Some of these, such as social media, privilege authenticity and spontaneity; for managers this creates new demands about how to manage the challenges of discretion for themselves and their workers. Other technologies such as call centres close down spontaneity and authenticity in favour of protocol-based encounters, in which there is little scope for discretion for frontline staff or managers.

Person-centredness disrupts the notion of rule-bound and standardized public services in ways that expand the scope for discretion. The legitimacy of a 'one size fits all' welfare state has vanished (Needham 2007). However, as services become more flexible and tailored to individuals, it is not necessarily managers that have enhanced discretion. Claims to lived experience or proximity to the setting means it may be citizens or frontline staff who determine what 'person-centredness' means in a particular case. However, managers remain accountable for the use of public money, for the performance metrics that result from citizen support and for ensuring that the public duty of care is discharged. Being accountable whilst also maintaining an authentic, open and informal style, in which managers project their own personhood and encourage staff and citizens to do the same, is the core management challenge.

References

Alakeson, V. (2010). International development in self-directed care. *Issue Brief (Commonwealth Fund)*, 78, 1–11.

AHRQ (Agency for Healthcare Research and Quality) (2016). *Care Coordination.* Rockville, MD: AHRQ. https://www.ahrq.gov/professionals/prevention-chronic-care/improve/coordination/index.html. Accessed 12 February 2017.

Alferoff, C. & Knights, D. (2008). Customer relationship management in call centers: The uneasy process of re(form)ing the subject through the 'people-by-numbers' approach. *Information and Organization*, 18(1), 29–50.

Askim, J., Fimreite, A. L., Moseley, A. & Pedersen, L.H. (2011). One-stop shops for social welfare: The adaptation of an organizational form in three countries. *Public Administration*, 89(4), 1451–1468.

Bartnik, E. (2007). *Local area coordination in the Australian capital territory. External evaluation summary report.* Western Australia.

Bartnik, E. & Chambers, R. (2007). It's about more than the money: Local area coordination supporting people with disabilities. *Research Highlights in Social Work: Co-Production and Personalisation in Social Care Changing Relationships in the Provision of Social Care*, 49(1), 19–38.

Bovens, M. & Zouridis, S. (2002). From street-level to system-level bureaucracies: How information and communication technology is transforming administrative discretion and constitutional control. *Public Administration Review*, 62(2), 174–184.

Boyle, D., Clark, S. and Burns, S. (2006). *Hidden work: Co-production by people outside paid employment.* York: Joseph Rowntree Foundation.

British Medical Journal (2003). Doctors as Sherpas: BMJ round table debate. The BMJ Patient issue, 14 June. www.bmj.com/content/vol326/issue7402/. Accessed 12 February 2017.

Callaghan, G. & Wistow, G. (2008). Can the community construct knowledge to shape services in the local state? A case study. *Critical Social Policy*, 28(2), 165–186.

Carr, S. (2014). Making it real: From putting people first to think local act personal. In C. Needham & J. Glasby (Eds), *Debates in personalisation* (pp. 27–42). Bristol: Policy Press.

Christensen, K. & Pilling, D. (2014). Policies of personalisation in Norway and England: On the impact of political context. *Journal of Social Policy*, 43(3), 479–496.
Clarke, J. & Newman, J. (1997). *The managerial state*. London: Sage.
Conservative Party (2010). *Invitation to join the government of Britain: The Conservative manifesto 2010*. London: Conservative Party.
Coulson, S. (2007). Person-centred planning as co-production. *Research Highlights in Social Work*, 49, 105.
Crossley, S. (2016). The troubled families programme: In, for and against the state? *Social Policy Review: Analysis and Debate in Social Policy*, 28.
Cummins, J. & Miller, C. (2007). *Co-production, social capital and service effectiveness*. London: Office for Public Management.
Cutler, T., Waine, B. & Brehony, K. (2007). A new epoch of individualization? Problems with the 'personalization' of public sector services. *Public Administration*, 85(3), 847–855.
Department of Health (DH) (2009). *Personal health budgets: First steps*. London: Department of Health.
Dickinson, H., Needham, C. & Sullivan, H. (2014). Individual funding for disability support: What are the implications for accountability? *Australian Journal of Public Administration*, 73(4), 417–425.
Dormann, C. & Zijlstra, F. (2003). Call centres: High on technology—High on emotions. *European Journal of Work and Organizational Psychology*, 12(4), 305–310.
Evans, T. (2010). *Professional discretion in welfare services: Beyond street-level bureaucracy*. Farnham: Ashgate.
Evans, T. (2011). Professionals, managers and discretion: Critiquing street-level bureaucracy. *The British Journal of Social Work*, 41(2), 368–386.
Evans, T. (2012). Organisational rules and discretion in adult social work. *British Journal of Social Work*, 43(4), 739–758.
Exworthy, M. (Ed.). (1998). *Professionals and new managerialism*. McGraw-Hill Education (UK).
Freidson, E. (1994). *Professionalism reborn: Theory, prophecy, and policy*. University of Chicago Press.
Gadsby, E.W. (2013). *Personal budgets and health: A review of the evidence*. Kent: Policy Research Unit in Commissioning and the Healthcare System.
Ganz, M. (2010). Leading change: Leadership, organization and social movements. In N. Nohria, & R. Kurana (Eds), *Handbook of leadership theory & practice* (pp. 505–550). Cambridge, MA: Harvard Business School.
Gardner, W.L., Cogliser, C.C., Davis, K.M. & Dickens, M.P. (2011). Authentic leadership: A review of the literature and research agenda. *The Leadership Quarterly*, 22(6), 1120–1145.
George, B. (2010). *True north: Discover your authentic leadership* (Vol. 143). John Wiley & Sons.
Glasby, J. (2012). The controversies of choice and control: Why some people might be hostile to English social care reforms. *British Journal of Social Work*, 44(2), 252–266.
Glasby, J. & Dickinson, H. (Eds). (2009). *International perspectives on health and social care: Partnership working in action*. John Wiley & Sons.
Glasby, J. & Littlechild, R. (2016). *Direct payments and personal budgets: Putting personalization into practice*. Bristol: Policy Press.
Gray, A. & Jenkins, B. (1995). From public administration to public management: Reassessing a revolution? *Public Administration*, 73(1), 75–99.

Gray, B.H., Sarnak, J.S. & Burgers, J.S. (2015). Case study: Home care by self-governing nursing teams: The Netherlands' Buurtzorg model. *The Commonwealth Fund*. www.commonwealthfund.org. Accessed 12 February 2017.

Griffiths, S., Foley, B. & Prendergrast, J. (2009). *Assertive citizens: New relationships in the public services*. London: Social Market Foundation.

Grit, K. & de Bont, A. (2010). Tailor-made finance versus tailor-made care. Can the state strengthen consumer choice in healthcare by reforming the financial structure of long-term care? *Journal of Medical Ethics*, 36(2), 79–83.

Hayden, C. & Jenkins, C. (2014). 'Troubled families' programme in England: 'Wicked problems' and policy-based evidence. *Policy Studies*, 35(6), 631–649.

Hill, M.J. & Hupe, P.L. (2008). *Implementing public policy: An introduction to the study of operational governance*. London: Sage.

Hupe, P.L. (2017). Capturing what happens 'after a bill became a law': The ongoing quest of implementation research. Valedictory lecture and first chapter in *liber amicorum* for Peter Hupe. In V.J.J.M. Bekkers, H.J.M. Fenger, & P.W.A. Scholten (Eds), *Public service as practice* (pp. 11–29). Rotterdam: Erasmus School of Social and Behavioural Sciences, Erasmus University Rotterdam.

Hutchinson, P., Land, J. & Salisbury, B. (2006). North American approaches to individualised planning and funding. In J. Leece and J. Bornat (Eds), *Developments in direct payments* (pp. 49–62), Bristol: Policy Press.

Izuhara, M. (2003). Social inequality under a new social contract: Long-term care in Japan. *Social Policy & Administration*, 37(4), 395–410.

James, O. (2003). *The executive agency revolution in whitehall*. Basingstoke: Palgrave Macmillan.

Jeffares, S. (2014). *Interpreting hashtag politics: Policy ideas in an era of social media*. Basingstoke: Palgrave.

Jeffares, S. (2016). *Tweet level bureaucrats: Interpreting public encounters on Twitter between cops and citizens*. Paper presented at Interpretive Policy Analysis Conference, University of Hull, pp. 1–21.

Kirkpatrick, I., Ackroyd, S. & Walker, R. (2005). *The new managerialism and public service professions*. Basingstoke: Palgrave.

LAC Network (n.d.). Local area coordination: How does it work? http://lacnetwork.org/local-area-coordination/how-does-it-work/. Accessed 12 February 2017.

Laloux, F. (2014). *Reinventing organizations: A guide to creating organizations inspired by the next stage in human consciousness*. Nelson Parker.

Laragy, C., Fisher, K. R., Purcal, C. & Jenkinson, S. (2015). Australia's individualised disability funding packages: When do they provide greater choice and opportunity? *Asian Social Work and Policy Review*, 9(3), 282–292.

Lewig, K.A. & Dollard, M.F. (2003). Emotional dissonance, emotional exhaustion and job satisfaction in call centre workers. *European Journal of Work and Organizational Psychology*, 12(4), 366–392.

Lipsky, M. (1980/2010). *Street-level bureaucracy: Dilemmas of the individual in public service*. New York: Russell Sage Foundation. (2010= 30th anniversary edition).

Lord, J. & Hutchison, P. (2003). Individualised support and funding: Building blocks for capacity building and inclusion. *Disability & Society*, 18(1), 71–86.

Mansell, J. & Beadle-Brown, J. (2005). Person centred planning and person-centred action: A critical perspective. In P. Cambridge and S. Carnaby (Eds), *Person centred planning and care management with people with learning disabilities* (pp. 19–33). London: Jessica Kingsley Publishers.

Margaretten, M. & Gaber, I. (2012). The crisis in public communication and the pursuit of authenticity: An analysis of the Twitter feeds of Scottish MPs 2008–2010. *Parliamentary affairs*, 67(2), 328–350.

Needham, C.E. (2006). Customer care and the public service ethos. *Public Administration*, 84(4), 845–860.

Needham, C.E. (2007). *The reform of public services under new labour: Narratives of consumerism*. Springer.

Needham, C.E. (2011). *Personalising public services: Understanding the personalisation narrative*. Bristol: Policy Press.

Needham, C.E. & Mangan, C. (2016). The 21st-century public servant: Working at three boundaries of public and private. *Public Money & Management*, 36(4), 265–272.

Needham, C.E., Mastracci, S. & Mangan, C. (2017). The emotional labour of boundary spanning. *Journal of Integrated Care*, 25(4), 288–300.

NIESR (2016). *Troubled families evaluation synthesis report*. http://www.niesr.ac.uk/sites/default/files/publications/Troubled_Families_Evaluation_Synthesis_Report.pdf

Oakeshott, M. (1991). *On human conduct*. Oxford: Clarendon Press.

Olds, D.L. (2006). The nurse–family partnership: An evidence-based preventive intervention. *Infant Mental Health Journal*, 27(1), 5–25.

PAC (Public Accounts Committee) (2016). *Troubled families*. London: The Stationery Office.

Parker, S. (2007). Participation: A new operating system for public services? *Participation Nation: Reconnecting Citizens to the Public Realm. Involve*, 103–112.

Poll, C. (2007). Co-production in supported housing: KeyRing Living Support Networks and neighbourhood networks. *Research Highlights in Social Work: Co-production and Personalisation in Social Care Changing Relationships in the Provision of Social Care*, 49, 49–66.

Pollitt, C. (1993). *Managerialism and the public services*. Oxford: Blackwell.

Price, C. (2015). Revealed: NHS funding splashed on holidays, games consoles and summer houses. *Pulse*, 1 September, http://www.pulsetoday.co.uk/news/commissioning-news/revealed-nhs-funding-splashed-on-holidays-games-consoles-and-summer-houses/20010960.fullarticle. Accessed 12 December 2015.

PWC. (2012). *Transforming the citizen experience: One stop shop for public services*. Australia: Price Waterhouse Coopers.

Richter, P. & Cornford, J. (2008). Customer relationship management and citizenship: Technologies and identities in public services. *Social Policy and Society*, 7(2), 211–220.

Ringquist, E. J. (1995). Political control and policy impact in EPA's Office of Water Quality. *American Journal of Political Science*, 336–363.

Robbins, M. (2015). Bring your whole self to work. *Huffington Post*, https://www.huffingtonpost.com/mike-robbins/bring-your-whole-self-to_b_6993358.html. Accessed 12 February 2017.

Royle, C. (2014). Managing a personal health budget: Malcolm's story(book). In C.E. Needham & J. Glasby (Eds), *Debates in personalisation*. Bristol: Policy Press.

Spicer, A. (2014). Goodbye to bosses: Zappos is biting off more than it can shoe'. https://theconversation.com/goodbye-to-bosses-zappos-is-biting-off-more-than-it-can-shoe-21821. Accessed 12 February 2017.

Taylor Knox, H. (2009). *Personalisation and individual budgets: Challenge or opportunity*. York: Housing Quality Network (HQN).

Tually, S., Slatter, M., Oakley, S. & Faulkner, D. (2015). *The role of private rental support programs in housing outcomes for vulnerable Australians.* AHURI Positioning Paper No. 162. Melbourne: Australian Housing and Urban Research Institute.

UCL (University College London) (2016). *Feasibility trial of an intervention to increase community connections and reduce loneliness for people with complex anxiety or depression.* London: Community Navigator Study. https://www.ucl.ac.uk/psychiatry/research/epidemiology/community-navigator-study. Accessed 12 February 2017.

Zapf, D., Isic, A., Bechtoldt, M. & Blau, P. (2003). What is typical for call centre jobs? Job characteristics, and service interactions in different call centres. *European Journal of Work and Organizational Psychology*, 12(4), 311–340.

CHAPTER 20

Automated Discretion

Stavros Zouridis, Marlies van Eck and Mark Bovens

20.1 Introduction: 'Computer Says No'

The film *I, Daniel Blake*, directed by Ken Loach, describes the administrative struggles of an elderly carpenter who suffered from a heart attack. After taking a work capability assessment he is deemed fit for work, even though his doctor does not allow him to return to work. He gets lost in the bureaucracy, because he is a computer illiterate and most of the forms have to be filled in online and are processed digitally. His case managers, bound by their pre-programmed decision systems, are unwilling and unable to empathize with him and to do justice to his personal circumstances.

The story of Daniel Blake is a rather dramatic illustration of a general trend. The use of information technology (IT) has caused the discretionary freedom within large-scale public executive organizations to shift from professional case managers to programmers and data analysts. This is particularly true of the 'decision factories', those large-scale bureaucracies that routinely make decisions on social benefits, licences, tax returns, fines, subsidies and, to an increasing extent, permits. The same shift also seems to occur in law enforcement

S. Zouridis (✉)
Tilburg University, Tilburg, The Netherlands
e-mail: s.zouridis@tilburguniversity.edu

M. van Eck
eLaw—Center for Law and Digital Technologies, Leiden University, Leiden, The Netherlands

M. Bovens
Utrecht University School of Governance, Utrecht, The Netherlands
e-mail: m.bovens@uu.nl

T. Evans, P. Hupe (eds.), *Discretion and the Quest for Controlled Freedom*, https://doi.org/10.1007/978-3-030-19566-3_20

organizations that apply data science to optimize their resources and intervention strategies. Whereas previously, these organizations employed massive amounts of 'street-level bureaucrats', today these organizations are more properly understood as 'system-level bureaucracies' (Bovens and Zouridis 2002). In these 'system-level bureaucracies', the basic principle of 'unit production', which involved human judgement for each individual case, has been replaced by 'continuous process production' (Woodward 1958/1975). Decision-making by automated decision systems based on algorithms has pushed aside human judgements based on rules of thumb. In colloquial terms: it is the computer that says 'yes' or 'no'.

This chapter describes how information technology, such as automated decision systems and big data analysis, has transformed large executive organizations into system-level bureaucracies. In these system-level bureaucracies, the discretionary powers of the street-level professionals have been disciplined by digital systems, while the locus of administrative discretion has shifted to those responsible for programming the decision-making process and translating the legislation into software.

Our analysis is limited to large 'production agencies' (Wilson 1989), such as internal revenue services, departments for work and pensions and social security agencies. We make no claims about more traditional street-level bureaucracies, such as the police, social work, schools or courts—although some of the trends we describe can be observed there too. Intelligent and predictive policing is already transforming police organizations and shifting policing from street-level bureaucrats to systems designers and data analysts (e.g. Guilfoyle 2013). Even though police professionals still do street-level work, computer algorithms decide on where police capacity is being sent to and how police officers work. Data science allows these organizations both to zoom out and analyse patterns on the macro level and to zoom in and focus on particular cases. For example, doppelganger search using big data analysis is used by Amazon to personalize the offer for individual clients, but it also can be used to detect citizens who commit tax fraud (see Stephens-Davidowitz 2017). These shifts have raised and will raise fundamental questions about constitutional and democratic checks and balances (Bovens and Zouridis 2002).

We first discuss, in the next section, the rise of system-level bureaucracies, based on our own work and on recent research. In Sects. 20.3, 20.4 and 20.5 we outline observable changes in the system-level bureaucracy. These are explored in greater detail, based on two recent case studies. In Sect. 20.6, we take stock of our findings. Have the developments described given rise to a 'new' phase in the development of large-scale administrative organizations and, if so, does this not evoke new questions about checks, balances and accountability? We also explore the significance of IT for the future of discretion in public administration.

20.2 The Rise of 'System-Level Bureaucracies'

From Street-Level to System-Level Bureaucracy

In 2002, Bovens and Zouridis (2002) first presented the 'system-level' bureaucracy as the tentative result of a transformation of a series of large 'decision-making bureaucracies', such as tax departments, social security agencies and agencies that collect traffic fines. Inspectorates and regulatory authorities, charged with the supervision of permits, benefits and taxes, also come under this heading. The core of the executive tasks of these organizations consists of making decisions that concerned individual situations—good examples would be a tax return, a traffic fine, an exemption, a building permit, a social security benefit or a decision on whether or not to prosecute a crime suspect.

For a long time, these organizations exhibited many of the features of what Lipsky (1980) called a *street-level bureaucracy*. In a street-level bureaucracy, the operational activities—which involve directly interacting with individual citizens and making decisions—constitute the core of the organization. Street-level bureaucrats, who perform their jobs at 'street level', operate in conditions that are shaped by scarcity and discretion.[1] There is scarcity due to the shortage of resources, compared to the task to be done. In order to fully check each individual tax return, far more people would be needed than the tax authorities have available. To gather all the information about each building permit would demand far more capacity than the municipality could muster. Conducting a full assessment of the personal situation of an individual applying for welfare benefits would require more of the social services' time and attention than is available. In short, scarcity is the order of the day, which means that choices must be made.

A second characteristic of street-level bureaucracy is that the rules and regulations leave room for professional discretion at the executive level of the organization. Hence this means that one and the same situation can be weighed differently. For example, is the failure to comply with the fire safety regulations in a permit serious enough to warrant the revocation of the permit?

The 'street-level bureaucracy' has been characterized by Mintzberg (1983) as a professional bureaucracy. The operating core is the most powerful part of the organization. Its job is mainly the deployment of pre-defined standard repertoires, such as a welfare benefit, permit, exemption, fine, tax assessment, prosecution and adjudication. The professionals 'fight' to secure their power to make decisions. In the course of a few decades IT has changed this type of organization dramatically. That transformation began with the introduction of early and rather primitive forms of IT in the 1960s and 1970s. At the time, decision-making on such matters as individual benefits, levies and permits was still predominantly the domain of street-level bureaucrats within municipal services and other public institutions. Street-level bureaucrats formed the core of the implementing organization. They worked on a case-by-case basis and usually knew the person applying for benefits or a permit personally. In many cases, there was also personal contact between the street-level bureaucrat and the individual citizen about the benefit, permit or levy.

For a number of reasons street-level bureaucrats enjoyed a great deal of discretion. There were at that time virtually no detailed rules in many policy areas in the Netherlands and a minimum of external checks (Ringeling 1978). In the Netherlands, up to and including the 1980s, there was no independent judge for administrative affairs, extensive audit systems were lacking, while external accountability was largely absent. There were some hierarchical constraints, as the immediate superior of the street-level bureaucrat either supervised the process or signed the decision. Staff positions and senior line positions were limited and played no role of significance in day-to-day activities. It was primarily the culture of the organization that circumscribed the discretionary power of these bureaucrats. Informal codes shaped the interpretation of the discretionary space—women students, for example, received a lower study grant, because they were supposed to be able to sew their own clothes.

Initially, the primitive level of IT served mainly to set down on paper the decisions of the street-level bureaucrats neatly and legibly with the help of word processors and printers. Over the course of time, IT systems were able to handle more and more tasks: for example, the motivations became standard blocks of text. Later on, algorithms were developed for the decision-making process and included in the system as a tool for the professional. Yesterday's street-level bureaucrat thus evolved into a *screen-level* bureaucrat, mainly engaged in entering forms into the automated system and in checking the decisions that the system spits out. Discretion, to the extent available at all, was applied in the interpretation of the information on the form and the input process itself. What remained was the manipulation of the information to achieve the desired outcome. In the course of the 1990s, the input of the forms was also automated. And with the arrival of the internet, citizens increasingly had to fill in the forms themselves, online, as had Daniel Blake.

The introduction of decision-making systems has fundamentally changed this type of street-level bureaucracy. No longer do the street-level bureaucrats form the core of the organization, but those who build and refine the systems. They have, as it were, become the new street-level bureaucrats, although they never see an individual case. The management of the organization no longer primarily revolves around the legitimate processing of applications, but around the management of 'production'. The substantive content of the decisions made is controlled via detailed rules and regulations that correspond, as far as possible, with the algorithms in the systems. Where necessary, the law is adapted or concepts are harmonized in the rules and regulations. No longer is there frontline control via the hierarchical structure. The management only checks the 'production' in the quantitative sense. In complex legal contexts street-level bureaucrats can still manipulate the way they feed the system with information and keep discretion with regard to individual cases. In these legal contexts, management will preserve some control on the content of the cases or only focus on the hard cases that cannot be dealt with by the information technology. In general the technostructure controls the systems and an independent judge reviews the individual decision in case of appeal. Because of the detailed regulation that is necessary in order to automate decision-making processes the independent judge also has limited discretion.

We therefore referred to the organization that evolved at the start of the new millennium as a *system-level* bureaucracy, alluding to the fact that the IT system may be regarded as the core of the bureaucracy. In system-level bureaucracies the human organization is built around the information system that implements the core task of the organization. As Mintzberg (1983) put it, the organizations have been transformed into machine bureaucracies: no longer is the operating core the most powerful part of the organization—this role has been taken over by the technostructure, which structuralizes the work to be performed. From the point of view of Wilson's (1989) framework, organizations have become mere 'production agencies'. Discretion of the kind previously available has transformed. First, it shifted to discretion exercised in designing the IT systems. Second, as noted, in some cases the professionals still feed the IT systems and they can thus still control their inputs.

Recent Research

The studies on system-level bureaucracies published since 2002 have, in part, confirmed the conclusions drawn back then. Research into 'e-enforcement' by inspectorates has demonstrated, for example, that information technology curtails the discretionary leeway enjoyed by inspectors. However, inspectors still exhibit strategic behaviour, thus safeguarding their discretionary powers (Koopmans-van Berlo and de Bruijn 2004). Moreover, research conducted by Jorna and Wagenaar (2007) has revealed that in system-level bureaucracies, leeway for interpretation and freedom of choice is preserved at the operational level. Discretion, instead of shifting, is concealed. Deploying IT causes the personal ties between operational practice and other, more technostructure-oriented, practices to be severed. The monitoring of operational practice by legal advisers, the drafting of rules by policymakers, management by middle-level and top-level officials, the judicial reviews of the administrative court and the internal checking process following from objection procedures, all serve to illustrate this. In the analysis framework developed by Argyris (1994), these practices may be connected in two ways: by means of 'artefacts' and with 'participatory boundary practices'. 'Artefacts' are, for example, work instructions, reports or management information systems. 'Participatory boundary practices' require human interaction. IT replaces 'participatory boundary practices' with 'artefacts' and this, according to Jorna and Wagenaar, touches on the fundamental significance of IT. On the basis of two Dutch cases, Jorna and Wagenaar demonstrate that, with IT, the personal ties between the said practices are replaced by artefacts, which not only affects 'managerial' practice but can also lead to the disintegration of the organization.

The disintegration theory has been confirmed by the work performed by Marston (2006). Further disintegration can arise in the organization and especially between the bureaucracy and the citizens if IT is combined with outsourcing. The combination of outsourcing and the introduction of automated 'job classification schemes' has led to the de-individualization of income support and helped to combat long-term unemployment in Australia, according to Marston. Note that the organization he describes was one we would call a 'screen-level' bureaucracy—in which bureaucrats engage in making decisions about individual situations, but solely through the entry of data or forms in the automated system. A comparison of Australia with Denmark confirms this conclusion (Caswell, Marston and Larsen 2010). Following the introduction of the automated systems, professionals 'feel' more like administrative screen-level bureaucrats than professional street-level bureaucrats. Breit and Salomon (2015) have described the introduction of IT in large-scale implementing organizations as the replacement of the 'dyadic relationship' between citizens and bureaucracy by a complex web of relationships between citizens, the bureaucracy and IT. And finally, Wong and Welch (2004) showed, on the basis of their 14-country comparative study, that 'Web-based' service delivery does not lead to more or enhanced accountability.

20.3 Chains and Other New Developments

Over the past decades, the system-level practice has continued to develop. There are at least three developments in typical system-level bureaucracies that bear mentioning. In the first place, system-level practice has further expanded in scope. It has now been implemented in various public administration fields; specifically, the inter-organizational chains have been further extended. We describe and explicate this development in the light of two recent Dutch case studies.

In the second place, the way in which the software is built would also seem to have changed, at least if we re-examine the case study on the enforcement of traffic regulations (Bovens and Zouridis 2002). The endless tinkering with IT systems, which has in fact become the core of the organization, remains a valid description of the organization. However, instead of developing new, large-scale systems, today, self-organizing teams of IT engineers continually make proposals on the implementation of smaller applications and links, about which the management then decides. The discretionary powers of these IT engineers would appear to have increased, not decreased, since 2000.

In the third place, a new profession has come into being in the system-level bureaucracy stimulated by the rise of 'big data'. We are referring to the rise of the data professionals. These data professionals also focus on the production process and not on individual cases, exactly as Woodward predicted and which she termed 'continuous process production'. The data professionals approach the production process from a different perspective entirely than system developers. Data analysts generate information for policy development by means of large-scale analyses: What are the most important trends in the target group, what kind of cases make up the risk category, what are the effects of small nudges on the behaviour of clients or the target group? Just as was formerly the case for the system engineers, these 'data cowboys' have more than ample discretionary leeway. The first stirrings in the direction of regulation on the discretionary freedom enjoyed by data analysts are already being felt.

Chains of System-Level Bureaucracies

As an organizational form, 'system-level bureaucracy' is a true 'millennial': born in the 1980s, growing up and coming of age in the 1990s and 2000s. Since then, these bureaucracies have been further refined and expanded. We illustrate this in the light of two examples. In 2015 and 2016, two operational practices were studied in the Netherlands, both of which could qualify as system-level bureaucracies (van Eck 2018). In these operational practices, the computer makes the lion's share of the individual decisions and in fact implements these. The one case has to do with establishing the right to and payment of child benefits by the Social Insurance Bank. The other relates to establishing a citizen's taxable income and the corresponding assessment from the tax authorities.

Case A Implementation of Child Benefits

Dutch citizens with children under the age of 18 are entitled to the payment of child benefits. In the implementation of the child benefit scheme, the Social Insurance Bank largely builds on the personal data of citizens that have been recorded in other processes by other government bodies. Following the registration of a birth with the municipality in which the child was born, a birth certificate is generated and the birth is registered in the Municipal Personal Records Database (BRP). The child is assigned an individual, unique, number and the birth of the child and corresponding data are submitted to the Social Insurance Bank in the form of a recurring subscription. An automated application is then prepared and the parents are given the opportunity to verify the application. In standard situations, this is the sole activity citizens need to undertake.

On receipt of the application, the decision is made by the computer in the majority of cases—in 2014, in 77% of all cases. The remainder is made by a civil servant either because the case has been tagged as a potential fraud risk or because there are international aspects concerned and insufficient data are available in the database. In subsequent years, the computer does all the work in the background. When legal milestones are reached, such as when the child turns 6 or 12 years old, the entitlement and the amount change, although the citizens do not receive the underlying decision unless they so request. After the birth of a second or next child, the benefit automatically rises. In 2014, there were just under 2 million claimants in the Netherlands. Notice of the decision as to whether or not a claimant is entitled to receive child benefit payments is then given to the administrative body charged with the payment of an eventual means-tested supplement. The computers of that administrative body then commence with the preparation of the application for this supplementary benefit. Already, this brings the number of links in the chain of system-level bureaucracies to three.

Case B Establishing a Citizen's Income

To enable the tax authorities to levy salaries tax and national insurance contributions, the Netherlands Tax and Customs Administration has branches that extend in various directions. In the first place, the tax administration cooperates with employers, benefits agencies and the statistics office. A large part of the task of calculating, withholding and payment of the wage tax owed is performed automatically by the employers and their software packages. The data are then broken down per individual employee. When these data are forwarded to the tax authorities via the Uitvoeringsinstituut Werknemersverzekeringen (Employee Insurance Agency), a social security organization, they can be used to prepare the annual income tax assessment. From then on, the procedure resembles that in the case of the child benefits. All the information available to the tax authorities is filled in on the return and the amount of tax payable is calculated. Citizens subsequently only need to check the data on the form and to make any changes necessary, after which the digital return is verified by means of a digital signature.

Some 90% of the 11 million tax returns submitted annually are decided by the computer. Based on a pre-defined set of fraud risk rules, the rest are set aside for manual handling by a tax official. The decision both determines the amount of tax owed and establishes a citizen's official income. This is subsequently included in a national income database. In this way, other government bodies that are charged with implementing means-tested schemes have access to these data. For those who are not required to submit a tax return, the data are determined per individual and automatically included directly in a national database with individual data on a person's income. The number of people who are not required to submit a return but who do pay wage tax is estimated to be 3.5 million. In addition, we see that in determining the income, the administrative body relies on data generated by other organizations and that the automated decision taken on the basis of these data is a determining factor for decisions taken by other public bodies.

The Algorithms

In both cases, decision-making is solely a matter of applying algorithms to data provided by citizens or other organizations. These algorithms have not been developed with the aim of processing knowledge or performing analyses, but for calculations, in which the data are applied as variables in the mathematical formulas. They are more like administrative systems than expert systems (Koers 1990: 262). Both practices strongly resemble Bing's (2005: 204) description of the implementation of the right to 'housing aid' in Norway: 'A trivial type of legal decision fully automated, containing what has been the objective of many knowledge-based systems in the legal domain, though nobody would like to characterise this very conventional system as an example of artificial intelligence'.

The information managers determine which data are used; they program the algorithms. Individual judgements and interference on the part of citizens are seen as disruptions and therefore avoided as far as possible. The content of the decision rules is virtually untraceable in both case studies. The decision rules cannot be isolated from the administrative process even by IT experts. The reason for this is that both cases concern relatively old IT applications, implementations that have grown throughout the years, which have been added to and maintained, with only the outside being given a more modern look. Also, algorithms are built into the digital forms that are completed by the citizens.

An important factor in the use of automated processing systems is the distinction between hard and easy cases. An 'easy' case is easily processed by the system by straightforward subsumption of facts under rules (Koers 1990: 262). The hard cases are processed by civil servants. At the Tax and Customs Administration, these are identified on the basis of the so-called fraud risk rules that have been built into the system: could the tax return be inaccurate and does it need to be checked manually? It has been announced that in the future, data analyses will also replace these fraud risk rules. At the Social Security Bank, the difference is mainly due to the practical impossibility of having the computer take decisions in cases where international aspects play a role, such as the birth of a child abroad. Often, the data are not available digitally or it is simply too complicated or expensive to translate valid interpretations of the law into programming code.

The Data

The data that constitute the raw material for the decision were found, in both implementation practices, largely to derive from the primary processes of other public and private organizations. By-products of one process can in some cases be determining factors for the decision in another process. Laws are harmonized to make chain collaboration possible. Uniform definitions are developed to ensure that data are 'inter-operable'. But even without shared definitions, data are reused if they mean approximately the same thing or if something may be derived from these. As, increasingly, pre-filled forms are being used, citizens can view the data and request that changes be made before the decision is taken. In most situations, the data are not substantively checked but are directly included in the administrations of the recipient party.

The 'system-level' bureaucracy expects citizens to respond in the case of errors and regards this as a means to improve the quality of the data. At the same time, the process citizens must go through to effectuate a change in his or her personal information is not always an effective one.

Also important is the fact that a decision affects the processes of other administrative agencies. The result is a chain reaction, plus that the process is required to be managed with a view to the interests of those other administrative agencies. A disruption in one organization, can lead to a temporary halt of the 'production' in another one.

This also creates a different problem, namely the problem of retroactive effect. Most IT systems have difficulty in giving retroactive effect to a decision. In law, giving retroactive effect to a decision is an important mechanism in rectifying errors. However, in the systems studied, retroactive effect is sometimes difficult to achieve. A decision that is standardized in a piece of data—for example, by assigning this a two-digit code—and that is subsequently retracted proves impossible to delete. The only technological alternative is to insert a note of the inaccuracy.

20.4 System Development: Bricolage with Software Engineers at the Wheel

Both the system-level bureaucracy and the screen-level bureaucracy evolved during a period in which public organizations were building large systems. In the Netherlands, many 'large' systems have become well known, such as SAGITTA, used by the customs services; the Wet Studiefinanciering (Student Finance Act) system for student grants; the Bedrijfsprocessensysteem (Business Process System) used by various police departments; and the Gemeentelijke Basisadministratie Persoonsgegevens (Municipal Personal Data Administration) for population registration.[2] The organizations aimed at completely automated decision-making processes with large-scale information systems that are linked to huge registers with personal data. National systems have been developed, for example, to distribute funds across educational institutions, but also to generate tax assessments and to collect taxes. Ultimately, these large-scale systems were to lead to the achievement of the 'e-government ideal', in which all communication and transactions between government and citizens could take place digitally.

With the initial large-scale systems in place came the criticism of the megalomaniac ambitions, followed by the first fiascos. Large sums were spent on the development of systems, projects which, by their very size, posed huge risks, while the governance of these projects was difficult, if not impossible. Various major revisions of systems were abandoned, leading to substantial financial losses. In the Netherlands, criticism of this approach to software development even led to a parliamentary enquiry.[3] The committee of enquiry drew a number of important conclusions, including the fact that the IT enthusiasm of the political world and among policymakers was not matched by the IT realism; that building large-scale systems takes a long time; that policy has the tendency to change and that the development of large-scale systems cannot remain continuously flexible; and that this combination of factors could explain a number of IT fiascos.

In response, in system-level bureaucracies we can see the rise of a different approach to software development. It is an approach championed years ago by

Ciborra (2002), who pointed to the need of 'bricolage' in the development of information systems. In contrast to the large, managerial-driven IT projects, this is characterized by bottom-up ad-hoc software development.

A typical example is that of the Central Judicial Collection Agency (CJIB), the Dutch organization tasked with the collection of traffic fines and punitive orders. This is a typical system-level bureaucracy, with information being supplied to the system by the police, then processed, after which the fine is sent—these days even by digital mail—to citizens, with the payment process being monitored completely automatically. The core of this organization is a set of automated systems, while the system is a classic example of what Woodward called 'continuous process production'. Within the organization, the core of the operations is known as the 'business'. Next to the 'business', a small group of creative software developers have deliberately been set apart from the organization. They are housed in a building at a walking distance from the 'business' and have been given the freedom to develop their own ideas for new applications and for improving the existing systems. Periodically, they suggest (small) ideas for applications and changes to refine the 'business'. These ideas are presented to the management, after which agreements are made about their implementation.

Characteristic of this approach is the use of the creativity of the software developers, the distance from the core of the organization and the small-scale enhancements. In short, 'bricolage' *avant la lettre* or, as this is called today, 'agile' IT development. This group of creative software developers has no formal decision-making authority, but it does have considerable discretion when it comes to applications development. *De facto*, therefore, these software developers steer much of the software development.

20.5 Unforeseen Discretion: Data Analysts

The core of the transformation from street-level to system-level bureaucracy is the transfer of discretion from the handling of individual cases to the design of IT. As this case study shows, it is a shift that has gained further force throughout the past decades. The discretion of the IT developers has been expanded to the exchange of data in 'chains'. They determine which links are made between systems, which data are used and which 'loopholes' in the legislation are acceptable and which need to be repaired. Rather than being subjected to hierarchical control, these IT developers are given the space to propose their own new applications and links and to implement these.

In today's system-level bureaucracy, there is another group of IT experts with considerable discretionary leeway: the data analysts. They do not modify the system, but they analyse the data in the system, looking for patterns. Based on these patterns, they suggest improvements or develop 'nudges' to gently push citizens in the direction desired by the system-level bureaucracy.[4]

When it comes to data analysis, the most sophisticated organization around in the Netherlands is probably the Dutch Tax and Customs Administration.

This department not only has access to large volumes of data on all taxpayers in the Netherlands, but, as we described above, the tax department is closely linked, both in and outside public administration, with other information sources. These data are increasingly used by data analysts to uncover patterns for various purposes. For example, data analyses can serve to help detect fraud, whether or not in combination with other government agencies such as the police department, municipalities or benefits agencies. Notorious and possibly apocryphal examples are more than amply available. The OECD has compiled an overview of the sources of big data that could be used by the tax authorities to profile citizens and enterprises. These not only include the data in their own databases but also data on citizens' use of the available digital facilities (their browsing behaviour on the website, how long it takes for a person to complete their tax return, how is the app used) and even the data that can be read out via the internet of things.[5]

Data analyses can also be used to distinguish between many commonly made errors and instances of possible fraud, so that the inspection capacity of the tax department can be more efficiently utilized. The above-mentioned Central Judicial Collection Agency (CJIB) uses data analyses to winnow out the more promising collection claims from the total non-starters to avoid the inefficient use of, for example, debt collectors. The Tax Administration also utilizes data analyses for quite the opposite reason, for example, by creating green lanes for taxpayers whose track record or profile reveals a minimal risk of their committing fraud or attempting to evade taxes. Data analysts can also be tasked with 'risk management': which pattern, for example, is likely to point to a case of VAT fraud? They can serve too to enhance the degree of effectiveness. When does it make sense to pursue redress, which returns should be checked with extra thoroughness and in which cases is there a real chance of deliberate errors?

The Tax and Customs Administration and the major administrative agencies in the field of social security and the municipalities—which in the Netherlands have been increasingly tasked with implementing the social security legislation—all take part in a broader network known as System Risk Indication (WRR 2016). As the privacy laws do not allow the large-scale, direct coupling of the files of these public organizations with those of private organizations such as water works or rental car agencies, a special procedure has been developed. A risk analysis can therefore be initiated by one of the partners, but is then performed by a national information agency. This agency links and encrypts the files supplied at the request of the participants and decrypts any results indicating a heightened risk (WRR 2016: 57). These potential 'hits' are forwarded to the Ministry of Social Affairs and Employment, which assesses the data and informs the requesting organizations of the reported risks. The organization can then institute a further enquiry into the case in question.

As the examples illustrate, data analysts enjoy a considerable measure of latitude in their activities. Although checks on the discretion of the data analysts were present in the latter example, they would nonetheless clearly appear to have very considerable margins of discretion.

20.6 Disciplining Digital Discretion

Democratic Control of System Development

For various reasons, the theoretical framework of the system-level bureaucracy is helpful to understand contemporary discretion in large public bureaucracies. The first and most important reason for this is purely theoretical. This concept offers a better understanding of modern practice in large decision factories than does the concept of street-level bureaucracy. The street-level bureaucracy was a useful concept through which to understand the dirty work carried out by the 'frontline professionals' in direct contact with citizens. The system-level bureaucracy makes it clear how the humming, interconnected, computers operate as an organization in large production agencies such as the internal revenue service.

However, the concept is more than a mere heuristic tool, as it also has a normative dimension. There has long been great concern about the democratic and constitutional control of large-scale government bureaucracies.[6] Obtaining the best possible understanding of how these bureaucracies function is a key condition for their control. Lipsky's street-level bureaucracy showed how discretion evolved in the 'frontlines'. The combination of resource scarcity due to, among other things, the work load and ambiguous standards, yielded discretionary freedom that became filled with professional routines.

The rise of system-level bureaucracies has replaced these professional routines and rules of thumb by algorithms. This has made it more difficult to empathize with hard cases, such as Daniel Blake. In many other respects, it has made the operation of these large production agencies more equitable and efficient. The processing of cases has become much faster and requires far less paperwork. Prejudices and biases of individual street-level bureaucrats no longer play a role in the allocation of public benefits.

In system-level bureaucracies, discretion does not result from scarcity and ambiguous standards, but by operationalizing standards in parametrized variables in IT systems and by the use of software to manage administrative processes. No longer are the frontline professionals the ones with the power of discretion; this has shifted to the IT developers. This raises several novel normative concerns.

The first issue is whether and, if so, to what extent the democratic checks on the IT developers have been toughened up since the rise of the system-level bureaucracy. This has not yet been systematically explored. The parliamentary enquiry in the Netherlands shows that political control of IT and IT specialists still is quite limited, mainly because of the logic of IT development. Moreover, far more data are exchanged between many different organizations than in the past, a phenomenon in which IT developers play a leading role. Additionally, in the ensuing 'bricolage pattern', the IT developers acquire more space for the development of applications and refinement of systems.

It would appear that the new types of discretion that are evolving in the digital era are accompanied by new needs for constraining and standardizing these. Whether and, if so, the extent to which these new types of constraint are able to effectively guide the work of the 'data chains', 'bricolating' software engineers and data professionals into democratic and constitutional channels, remain to be seen. And, of course, we have not even touched on the application of Artificial Intelligence, which will lead to computers replacing today's software engineers and data analysts, in turn (Powles 2017; Brauneis and Goodman 2017).

Conclusion: The End of Decision-Making Discretion?

The scope of our study was limited to large decision-making organizations and the introduction of IT in support of the executive tasks of these organizations. As analysed, IT leads to a loss of discretion in making individual decisions, as the discretionary power shifts to the development of the software. Does this mean that the discretion exercised when making individual decisions relating to public administration is doomed? This certainly looks to be the case in the longer run, although not everywhere at the same pace. Already, the tax assessments of individuals in the Netherlands have been almost completely automated, while those of medium-sized and small businesses are still partly the responsibility of implementing staff, who have discretionary powers (Raaphorst 2018). However, the ratio of automated decision-making to people is changing, as the taxation of medium-sized and small businesses also becomes increasingly automated.

And even in cases where people are still responsible for making decisions, increasingly, the process is being pre-structured by IT. In the first place, because IT determines which cases are to be dealt with automatically and which not. Hence, the personnel working at these implementing agencies only handle whatever the system rejects. A second reason is because the IT system indicates which cases require handling by personnel. In other words, it is a process that is not determined by humans, but on the basis of parameters that determine whether the automated system or a data analyst flags a case as being questionable. Tax assessments of small- and medium-sized businesses in the Netherlands are still dealt with by humans with discretionary powers, but the computer algorithm decides what cases are attributed to human decision-making and what cases are dealt with by the IT system. Strictly speaking, the available discretionary leeway lessens through this use of IT for 'risk management'. For example, the use by the police force of sensing technology will probably curb the discretionary powers of police agents or at least pre-structure these powers. If the system should note a combination of anomalies in the continuous data analysis, for example, by means of camera images with facial recognition, a police officer is sent to investigate.

Hence, IT both draws off discretionary powers and structuralizes those remaining, at least at the level of the individual decision. What remains is the discretionary leeway in the organization of the IT—what should be automated and what not? Which decision-making algorithms should be used via which links and with which other organizations and using which algorithms for data analysis? In a formal legal sense the structures of authority and power do not change. Data scientists and software engineers operate under the formal powers of ministers and top-level managers as do street-level bureaucrats. Whatever new application or inter-organizational link is proposed by the software engineers, it still requires a decision by a minister or top-level managers in order to be implemented. A new nudge based on data analysis requires a decision to adopt it; hence, the overall managers formally still control the discretion of the data scientists.

In order to assess the new patterns of discretion in these types of public bureaucracies we need more in-depth empirical research on the interactions between data scientists, software engineers and the overall management as well as the politico-administrative relations that result from the new technologies. Instead of studying a steadily declining group of administrative personnel with decision-making discretion, far more academic and practical attention should be directed at the way IT is organized in the democratic constitutional state. In the near future, most discretion is indeed 'digital discretion'.

Notes

1. Although research into street-level bureaucracies, their management and the context of the tasks of street-level bureaucrats has been considerably augmented since Lipsky's original work (see, for example, Hupe, Hill and Buffat Eds 2015), these organizational features continue to be relevant.
2. SAGITTA as an acronym stands for: 'Systeem voor Automatische Gegevensverwerking met betrekking tot Invoeraangiften met Toepassing van Terminals voor het doen van Aangifte. It is a data system used by customs.
3. Tweede Kamer, vergaderjaar 2014–2015, 33, 326, nr. 5.
4. In a report on 'big data', the Netherlands Scientific Council for Government Policy describes a number of practices of data analysts (WRR 2016).
5. Technologies for Better Tax Administration, Using big data in tax administrations, OECD (2016: 49).
6. See, for example, Weber (1922) and Hayek (1944), but also Waldo (1948).

References

Argyris, C. (1994). *On organisational learning*. Cambridge, MA: Blackwell.
Bing, J. (2005). Code, access and control. In M. Klang & A. Murray (Eds), *Human rights in the digital age*. London: Cavendish Publishing.
Bovens M.A.P. & Zouridis, Z. (2002). From street-level to system-level bureaucracies: How information and communication technology is transforming administrative discretion and constitutional control. *Public Administration Review*, 62(2), 174–184.

Brauneis, R. & Goodman, E.P. (2017, August 2). Algorithmic transparency for the smart city. *Yale Journal of Law & Technology*. Forthcoming; GWU Law School Public Law Research Paper; GWU Legal Studies Research Paper. Available at SSRN. Retrieved from https://ssrn.com/abstract=3012499; https://doi.org/10.2139/ssrn.3012499.

Breit, E. & Salomon, R. (2015). Making the technological transition: Citizens' encounters with digital pension services. *Social Policy and Administration*, 49(3), 299–315. https://doi.org/10.1111/spol.12093.

Caswell, D., Marston, G. & Larsen, J.E. (2010). Unemployed citizen or 'at risk' client? Classification systems and employment services in Denmark and Australia. *Critical Social Policy*, 30, 384–404.

Ciborra, C. (2002). *The labyrinths of information. Challenging the wisdom of systems.* Oxford: Oxford University Press.

Guilfoyle, S. (2013). *Intelligent policing: How systems thinking methods eclipse conventional management Practice.* Axminster: Triarchy Press.

Hayek, F. (1944). *The road to serfdom*. London: Routledge.

Hupe, P., Hill, M. & Buffat, A. (Eds). (2015). *Understanding street-level bureaucracy.* Bristol: Policy Press.

Jorna, F. & Wagenaar, F.P. (2007). The 'iron cage' strengthened? Discretion and digital discipline. *Public Administration*, 85(1), 189–214.

Koers, A. (1990). Delphi revisited: The mythology of the lawyer's electronic workbench. In H.W.K. Kaspersen & A. Oskamp (Eds), *Amongst friends in computers and law: A collection of essays in remembrance of Guy Vandenberghe*, Deventer and Boston: Kluwer Law and Taxation Publishers.

Koopmans-van Berlo, M. & de Bruijn, H. (2004). When e-government is opposed by unwilling clients; Case studies on e-enforcement. *Electronic journal of e-Government*, 2(1), 65–74.

Lipsky, M. (1980). *Street-level bureaucracy: Dilemmas of the individual in public services.* New York: Russell Sage.

Marston, G. (2006). Employment services in an age of e-government. *Information, Communication, & Society*, 9(1), 83–103. https://doi.org/10.1080/13691180500519555.

Mintzberg, H. (1983). *Structures in fives; Designing effective organizations.* Englewood Cliffs, NJ: Prentice Hall.

OECD. (2016). *Technologies for better tax administration: A practical guide for revenue bodies.* Paris.

Powles, J. (2017, December 20). New York City's bold, flawed attempt to make algorithms accountable. *The New Yorker*. Elements. Retrieved from https://www.newyorker.com/tech/elements/new-york-citys-bold-flawed-attempt-to-make-algorithms-accountable.

Raaphorst, N. (2018). How to prove, how to interpret and what to do? Uncertainty experiences of street-level tax officials. *Public Management* Review, 20(4), 485–502. https://doi.org/10.1080/14719037.2017.1299199.

Ringeling, A.B. (1978). *Beleidsvrijheid van ambtenaren: Het spijtoptantenprobleem als illustratie van de activiteiten van ambtenaren bij de uitvoering van beleid.* Alphen aan den Rijn: Samsom H.D. Tjeenk Willink.

Stephens-Davidowitz, S. (2017). *Everybody lies: Big data, new data, and what the internet can tell us about who we really are.* New York: Harper-Collins Publishers.

van Eck, B.M.A. (2018). *Geautomatiseerde ketenbesluiten & rechtsbescherming: Een onderzoek naar de praktijk van geautomatiseerde ketenbesluiten over een financieel belang in relatie tot rechtsbescherming*. Doctoral dissertation, Tilburg University, Tilburg.

Waldo, D. (1948). *The administrative state: A study of the political theory of American public administration*. New York: Ronals Press Co.

Weber, M. (1922). *Wirtschaft und Gesellschaft*. Tübingen: J.C.B. Mohr.

Wilson, J.Q. (1989). *Bureaucracy: What government agencies do and why they do it*. New York: Basic Books.

Wong, W. & Welch, E. (2004). Does E-Government promote accountability? A comparative analysis of website openness and government accountability. *Governance: An International Journal of Policy, Administration, and Institutions*, 17(2), 275–297.

Woodward, J. (1958/1975). *Management and technology*. London: H.M. Stationery Office.

WRR (De Wetenschappelijke Raad voor het Regeringsbeleid). (2016). *Big data in een vrije en veilige samenleving*. WRR rapport 95, WRR, The Hague.

PART IV

Practising Freedom and Control

CHAPTER 21

Practising Freedom and Control: An Introduction

Tony Evans and Peter Hupe

21.1 Introduction

In the fourth and final part of this interdisciplinary edited collection, authors look at how discretion is applied and experienced in often complex, dynamic and challenging situations of practices in public services. For public service workers, particularly those who are professionals, discretion is seen as synonymous with who they are and the work they do. However, the nature of professional discretion is not fixed but varies, depending on the intersection of notions of knowledge and relations of power that obtain for particular professions in specific situations. While discretion can be characterized as a negative phenomenon, to be contained and constrained by a proliferation of rules, a strong theme of this part of this collection is that it can have a positive role as a solution to key challenges that inhere in human services. Authors in this part of the edited volume identify discretion as a more positive space. For instance, it is a recognition of the limitations of rules, a place where actors have to improvise and invent new insights. Discretion can also be an arena of creativity, where, at the street level, policy becomes a human encounter between practitioner and citizen, while discretion is a site for solving problems arising from the impersonal nature of policies. Public services are also replete with moral challenges and discretion provides a space for ethical discernment in balancing ethical principles with sensitivity to individual circumstances.

T. Evans (✉)
Department of Social Work, Royal Holloway, University of London, Egham, UK
e-mail: Tony.Evans@rhul.ac.uk

P. Hupe
Public Governance Institute, Catholic University of Leuven, Leuven, Belgium
e-mail: pieter.hupe@kuleuven.be

T. Evans, P. Hupe (eds.), *Discretion and the Quest for Controlled Freedom*, https://doi.org/10.1007/978-3-030-19566-3_21

21.2 Discretion and Expertise

Part IV 'Practising Freedom and Control' opens with Michael Luntley's exploration of a particular aspect of discretion—freedom where the rules run out. The focus on discretion as freedom between the rules, he argues, tends to ignore the role of discretion as a response to the absence of rules where one has to craft new ideas, new processes, new attitudes. He challenges the central place given to rules in the analysis of discretion and the way in which discretion is thought of as the domain only of experts with specialist knowledge and skills.

Luntley unpicks the distinction that is often drawn between propositional knowledge, characterized as hard, clear-cut statements of what we know, and expertise, characterized as intuitive know-how. Expertise is often the basis upon which professions claim discretion; it is only those who have this esoteric know-how who can do the job, understand what they do and regulate their work. One of the problems with this argument is that it places expertise beyond challenge and accountability. However, more fundamentally, the distinction drawn between propositional know-what and intuitive know-how, Luntley argues, collapses propositional knowledge into a limited and narrow idea of propositions as formal statements. It hence ignores the way in which our ideas and concepts can also be expressed in symbols, attention to aspects of contexts, gesture and physical expression, and so on. It confuses these inchoate and developing propositions with intuitive and inexplicable understanding.

It is with this contrast between knowledge as explicit general statements and specific embodied contextual propositions that claims to discretion are generally located. However, for Luntley, this is a rather pared-down notion of the role of discretion. Discretion is not just about negotiating general rules and specific local practices; it is also—and perhaps more importantly—about crafting new thoughts and perceptions and developing new ways of working, where existing practices and established ways of working make no sense in the situations we now encounter.

For Luntley, we need to engage with discretion as the area where we have to respond to what is new, confusing and challenging: established ideas and practices no longer help, or just do not seem to fit. This is an area in which discretion takes on a particular character. It involves an aesthetic sense: a recognition that there are things outside our current frame of understanding and an ability to make insightful leaps, extending our attention to new areas and crafting new ways of engaging with our environment. Importantly, this is not a dimension of expertise as we understand it in the division of labour. It is not a unique skill possessed by a particular occupation. Rather, it is a dimension of our common potential to be playful and open to experience and experiment, hence crafting new knowledge.

21.3 Discretion and Professional Work

Professions are occupations that are often seen as synonymous with discretion. In the second chapter of this part of the interdisciplinary edited collection, Tony Evans points out that 'profession' is a difficult term to pin down. Ideas of professions and professionalism have often been mystified, particularly in early studies, as special and privileged occupations. Early analysis of professions focused on identifying the specific traits that identify these occupations. However, analysts failed to agree on the characteristics of a profession. An alternative and, Evans argues, more fruitful way to look at professions is by seeking to understand how occupations attain and sustain professional status and control by considering them in a broader social and economic context. Evans returns to two classic texts in this critical tradition—Jamous and Pelliole's and Johnson's seminal studies of professional discretion—to consider the intersection of knowledge and power that characterizes professional occupations.

Jamous and Pelliole examine the nature of professions' claims about what they know, contrasting claims to determinate procedural knowledge and indeterminate intuitive expertise. They argue that professionals often use claims to indeterminate knowledge to mystify their work and sustain the profession's discretion. Evans is concerned that the distinction they draw between forms of professional knowledge is too sharp. It fails to recognize that there are aspects of professional knowledge that, while difficult to express as rules and procedures, are not designed to mystify but simply reflect the fact that knowledge is often fast-moving and is often inchoate in the processes of being expressed more precisely or of being changed because it is no longer helpful.

Johnson—the second text Evans considers—draws on Jamous and Pelliole's analysis to underline the view of expertise as a strategy of professional occupations to control their work. For Johnson, professionals are able to claim extensive discretion when they can exert power through their perceived expertise and dominate those who want to buy their skills. However, where a profession's expertise is less valued or buyers are more organized and can exert their power, these buyers can resist expert control and constrain professional discretion. Johnson also identifies a third possibility, where another party—usually the state—intervenes in the relationship between producer and consumer to regulate the freedom of movement available to the occupation and the control that may be exercised by purchasers.

If professional expertise is more fluid than is suggested by Jamous and Pelliole's distinction between indeterminate and technical knowledge, we need to reconsider Johnson's analysis of the dimensions of control of professional discretion. First, the experience of individual professionals (and subgroups) within a profession may be that their discretion is constrained by an idea of appropriate freedom and judgement within the profession as a whole. Second, any systems of buyer control constraining professional discretion has to constantly struggle with the emergence and development of new forms of knowledge and expertise in day-to-day practice. Third, this form of control also raises the question why professionals accept the control of their practice entailed in being members of a profession and the constraints put on them by buyers of their services. Is it just an issue of an economic imperative? Might it also be a more constructive balance between negative freedom—the absence of constraint—and positive freedom—the ability to carry out one's goals?

Finally, Evans suggests that Johnson's third form of professional control—the intervention of the state—is not a separate form of control but a key constant factor influencing the terms of trade between professionals and those buying their services. It frames the terms of trade between professional and buyer, privileging the role of one or other party and various points in between.

21.4 The Art of Discretion

In the third chapter of this part of the interdisciplinary edited collection, Tony Evans also develops the theme of discretion as a positive attribute by looking at discretion and creativity. He is especially interested in creativity as a way of viewing discretion in a particular area of public services—human services—where a significant part of the service provided is the human encounter, where the skills and insights of workers are intrinsic to the provision of services themselves.

In this context, Evans argues, a narrow conception of discretion as scripted in procedures and rules misrepresents the nature and role of discretion. From this narrow perspective, discretion is a problem that needs to be either eliminated by more complete rules or procedures or closely supervised and directed. In directing our attention to an alternative approach to discretion, he draws an analogy between policy and frontline practitioners, on one hand, and dramatic texts and actors, on the other. A policy, he argues, is like a text. It is not just open to interpretation: it only comes to life with its enactment. Practitioners, like actors in a theatre, have to use their creative skills to achieve this.

Underpinning this analogy and recognizing the positive role of discretion is an idea that service, rather than production, best characterizes human services. Human services cannot be delivered mechanically, as products and predetermined outputs. Instead, they are services crafted in their delivery, constituted in the relationship between citizen and practitioner within a policy framework of resources and expectations.

Creativity is central to services, Evans argues. He draws on two related aspects of creativity to explore discretion in human services: imaginative problem-solving; and creativity as imaginative understanding. Creativity moves from routine processes to solutions, often by pushing, augmenting or adapting existing frameworks. Creativity also involves an ability to engage with, to value and to imagine others' particular points of view and to use these insights to craft human and humane responses. For Evans, the need for these two factors explains the role of freedom, as well as the particular nature and value of creative judgement as discretion in human services. He also points to the idea of affordances as a way to capture key aspects of the way creativity in discretion operates. The idea alerts us to the way in which actors interact pragmatically with their environment—the role and nature of things in the context are perceived and adapted (as far as they can be) to the purposes of the actor. A log, for instance, can be a bridge if one wants to cross a river, but it can also be a pole if one wants to string up a telephone wire. Performance, then, is not predetermined by text, but involves the imagination of the actor, who sees the potential of the text and other objects to achieve the dramatic purpose. An object is not only physical; an object can also be a symbol, or conventions and rules that structure social interaction. In human services, for instance, these rules can be used in different ways to provide different services and also the way in which these services. Symbols can also communicate and establish constructive or unproductive relationships in services in the interaction between practitioner and citizen.

21.5 Discretion as Ethical Practice

Gideon Calder concludes this fourth part of the interdisciplinary edited collection by considering ethics and discretion. Discretion and ethics, he argues, are closely tied together. The extent of discretion afforded to actors (and accepted by them) is an ethical judgement. The discretionary space within which they have the freedom to act is replete with ethical questions requiring discretionary judgement. His concern in this chapter is not with applying moral formulae to decide the correct extent of discretion and specify the right way in which it can be used. Instead, his interest is to understand how actors on the ground can understand discretion and use it to negotiate ethical decisions in practice.

He explores these issues by considering the practices of social professionals—social workers, teachers, nurses and so on—not because they are particularly ethical but because they provide a good illustration of the issues of considering the role of ethics in a challenging aspect of public services.

Like other authors in this collection, Calder emphasizes the way in which discretion runs together ideas of freedom and judgement. He also notes that the ethical tension within discretion is reflected in the many different shades of grey between the black-and-white of freedom as arbitrary action (which is unstructured and unpredictable) and control as detailed mechanical rule-following (which is unthinking and inflexible). Discretion is the exercise of ethical discernment; a balanced approach, a middle way where people may start at different points—freedom is paramount over rules. But when examined closely, these approaches are often more subtle, recognizing that freedom is contained by looser conventions and a sense of broader responsibilities; rules can be flexed when the circumstances call for this. There is give-and-take in ethical thinking that reflects the need to balance a range of considerations. This is also reflected in different approaches to the broader context within which this discernment is exercised. One view sees the ethical environment as fixed and stable, in which the spaces for and the need to apply discretion arise from gaps in the rules—a prescriptive environment. The alternative view is one of a dynamic, evolving environment in which discretion describes the continuing interaction of action and environment—more of an improvisational setting.

For Calder, Aristotle's notion of practical wisdom—*phronesis*—is central to understanding the ethical skill of negotiating the tensions between general standards and particular circumstances. This is a picture of a crafts-person who has both to attend to the fine detail of the work and to stand back, take in and understand the work, taking the wider/longer view. Practitioners deploy practical wisdom to move effectively between general standards and particular issues in the deployment of discretion. They need to understand their role in its broader context and use insights to do the right thing. This is not, he argues, a routine or easy task. In fact, if it becomes habitual, there is probably something wrong—the exercise of practical ethical judgement is a continuing struggle to do the best one can in balancing the changing and evolving relationships, tensions and pressures within practice.

CHAPTER 22

Expertise and the Space for Discretion

Michael Luntley

22.1 Introduction

Whatever else is meant by 'discretion', I shall assume the idea of exercising discretion includes the idea of having the legitimate option to perform, whether in action or in judgement, in a way that is outwith some recognized standard either by breaching the standard or acting in a manner not covered by the standard. Put simply, discretion concerns our legitimate option to act in ways that breach or ignore standards for performance. The discretion in which I am interested exploits this option when it arises in virtue of the epistemic standing of the agent. That is to say, what makes discretion possible for an agent concerns something they know, something that equips them with the resources to act outwith standards. One way of unpacking this idea is this.

Suppose the standards for performance are articulated in propositions—something that can be known as a body of propositional know-that. Then you might think of discretion as made available when the agent confronted with situations that are not covered by the propositional knowledge of standards exploits a body of know-how that, as it were, covers the gaps left by the articulate propositional know-that. So, know-how covers the spaces left untouched by propositional know-that. And then you might add, it is this know-how that is the mark of the expert actor whose expertise gives them licence to act in ways that are, from the point of view of the propositions that govern novice actors, invisible. There is, I think, something right in this idea, but it needs unpacking if we are to have a positive picture of what goes into acts of discretion.

The last point matters. I am interested in getting a positive account of discretion. It is not enough just to think of discretion as something that operates

M. Luntley (✉)
University of Warwick, Coventry, UK
e-mail: Michael.Luntley@warwick.ac.uk

T. Evans, P. Hupe (eds.), *Discretion and the Quest for Controlled Freedom*, https://doi.org/10.1007/978-3-030-19566-3_22

in the gap where standards run out. That would be a negative account of discretion. Dworkin (1977: 31) famously refers to discretion as akin to the hole in a doughnut; it is the space where formal and prescribed rules give out. That is a case of what I mean by discretion understood negatively as the absence of such rules. My own view is that the focus on formal rules as the contrast for discretion only makes sense if a clear account can be given to the know-how/know-that distinction and how that helps make space for the discretion of expertise. I have doubts about this that I note in Sect. 22.3. So I think it more useful to focus on the idea of a space where rules-as-such give out. And by 'rules-as-such' I mean the patterns that define an order bound by semantic regimentation, an order subject to truth, falsity and allied concepts. The rules that matter for propositional knowledge are the rules that map out the structures by which truth applies to the thinking that shapes action—knowing that such-and-such action is required in the light of so-and-so piece of theoretical knowledge. This is not to deny that discretion operates within an arena of experience that exhibits patterns, but only to raise the possibility that such patterns are not the patterns exploited in pursuit of truth. In which case, we need a positive account of the patterns that inform the space of discretion and how they figure in making sense of expertise and its discretion. My interest is in a positive account of what happens in the space beyond rules. From Dworkin's point of view, my position is that it is holes all the way down. That is, however, too negative. I want to provide a positive account of the space for discretion. I think we learn something fundamental about ourselves when we start to provide such an account.

On a common view about expertise, experts constitute a special class of epistemic actors whose enhanced cognitive stance places them beyond the epistemic standards that govern non-expert actors, novices (Benner 1984; Dreyfus and Dreyfus 1986).[1] On this view, the epistemic standing of the novice is bound by standards, rules that prescribe performance. In contrast, the epistemic standing of the expert is commonly assumed to include a licence to act in ways that fall outwith the prescriptions that bind the novice. In this sense, the epistemic standing of the expert exhibits discretion, for their epistemic standing licenses performances that are not available within the rules that govern the novice.

The idea that experts have licence to exercise discretion due to their epistemic standing is, however, questionably coherent and potentially dangerous. I want to develop a viable notion of discretion, but it is important to acknowledge what makes the concept challenging. What is interesting about the idea is the claim that a special epistemic standing makes it legitimate to breach, ignore or simply act outwith the standards that govern those with a more limited cognitive achievement. This might amount to no more than a relative sense of discretion: experts are not bound by the rules that prescribe performance for the lower cognitive skill sets of novices. That relative claim of discretion is compatible with thinking that with regard to their own cognitive standing, the performance of the expert is bound by standards, albeit standards that are not salient to the novice. On this relative account, discretion does not require performance outwith standards, just performance outwith the common standards that apply to non-experts. One might think, however, that experts are still subject to standards—expert standards—with respect to which discretion is not an option. That is to say, we expect experts to perform correctly, to do the right thing and it would be epistemically dangerous to ignore the normative force of the idea of correct performance. So even if the expert's performance, when measured against the standards applicable to novices, appears to exhibit discretion—they act outwith those normal standards—nevertheless they are still required to perform correctly in their field. That is to say, there is scope for judging their action as right and the beliefs on which it is based as true. The action responds to appropriate facts regarding what is the case in a way that conforms to the standards and goals of the activity. What some present as a 'hole' outside the scope of extant rules is, nevertheless, a site for action that can be judged as done well and appropriate to how the facts lie and answerable to a notion of proper conduct. Where such notions of proper performance apply, there must be some account of what it is to perform correctly, and whatever that is, it is a standard.

That last point seems compelling. It is the point that fuels a natural concern about the terminology often used in characterizing the way that experts are supposedly free of the standards applicable to novices. On the Dreyfus and Dreyfus (1986) model of the trajectory from novice to expert, the inarticulacy of expert knowledge that lifts it beyond the regulatory standards of the novice is badged by calling it 'intuitive knowledge'. This is a dangerous label, for without some notion of that to which intuition is answerable, there is a real danger that 'intuition' is just a tag for an ill-defined bunch of hunches, guesses and epistemic what-nots. Intuition becomes a dangerous ragbag category of epistemic ill-repute (Benner 1984; Dreyfus and Dreyfus 1986).[2]

The crunch issue is: How can something be exempt from standards of correctness and still deliver a cognitive achievement that guides correct performance? Suppose discretion targets cognitive correctness. That is to say, it targets the truth of the beliefs on which performance relies and, by so doing, it delivers a correct performance—one that results in action that fits the demands of the situation given whatever concerns, desires and goals the agent may have. But then it is *prima facie* a mystery how discretion can be excused the need to be answerable to standards of truth and appropriate deployment. There must be things that can and should be said in its defence, for if it is not defendable, its entitlement to the epithet 'correct' is suspect.

The point being pressed here is a constitutive one; it concerns what constitutes the idea of discretion. If it is constitutive of the exercise of discretion that the cognitive standing of the knowledge and the actions it delivers fall outwith any notion of regulatory standard, then it is doubtfully coherent that discretion is a proper part of expert performance. One response to this challenge is to deflate the notion of discretion to little more than the exercise of judgement that falls outwith familiar routines, but that does not make it something outwith routines *tout court*; only that its routines have not yet been fully formulated. One might then think that, had we time, we could in principle formulate the routines revealed in the operation of discretion: discretion just marks the site where we have more work to do in giving an account of what we are doing; it is not in itself a distinct type of cognitive doing.[3]

In contrast, what I want to explore in this chapter is the idea that there is something real at stake in the idea of discretion that picks up on a genuine and deep open-endedness to our cognitive endeavours. I want to explore a constitutive sense in which discretion can mark the site of cognitive operations that work outwith rules. Furthermore, I shall suggest that this sense of discretion is endemic to a proper understanding of our common cognitive projects rather than being the special preserve of experts.

22.2 Where the Rules Give Out

My interest is in the idea that discretion operates in the spaces where the rules 'give out'. This idea seems implicated in the common view about the trajectory from novice to expert. On the common view, novices follow rules and procedures; their knowledge is articulatable in rules that regulate performance. In contrast, experts are distinguished by their deployment of knowledge that resists full articulation. One of the hallmarks of the expert on this view is that the knowledge characteristic of expertise cannot be codified in advance in rules and procedures. Hence it is classed as 'intuitive', 'tacit' or 'implicit' knowledge. On this view, the trajectory from novice to expert is a developmental trajectory from forms of performance in which discretion is absent to cases where the gaps between the rules exploited by advanced performers permit discretion. The performance of the novice is prescribed and codified; the performance of the expert is, to some degree, open-ended. And in that open-endedness lies the opportunity for discretion. Although I think the idea of discretion is important, I think its placing within this common view is in large measure mistaken. The common view encourages a model of learning that is topsy-turvy.

On the common view, open-endedness in concept deployment and the discretion for judgement, where that involves some sense of freedom from the rule-governed application of concepts, are characteristics of expert practitioners. Open-endedness and discretion are elements of the repertoire of advanced cognitive agents. That is the idea that I think is topsy-turvy. I want to suggest that open-endedness and the scope for discretion is, when properly acknowledged, endemic to human cognition. On the common view, the novice is the commonplace agent and the expert the rare achievement, the agent with a specialized role. On my view, the open-endedness and discretion often attributed to the expert is a mark of a basic common cognitive orientation and it is the idea of the novice that marks a construct, a role constructed, in large part, by the regimentation of cognitive life into the specialist occupational roles of modern industrial societies.[4]

I have argued elsewhere (Luntley 2011b) that what is really distinctive of expertise is not that experts exploit novel forms of inarticulate knowledge, but that they have an ability to generate new concepts. The idea of novel forms of inarticulate knowledge is appealed to in response to an alleged datum about the phenomenology of expert thinking in the moment: the expert cannot articulate all that they know in the moment. There is, however, an alternative explanation of this apparent inarticulacy. On my theory, oftentimes such inarticulacy arises because the expert is noticing new opportunities in conceptual space. Their thinking is difficult to codify in a patterned way because they are in the process of making new patterns in the moment, constructing new concepts whose form—let alone, appropriate form of expression—has yet to be settled. I suggest that it is this constructive activity that marks the site of discretion. Rather than see discretion negatively as operating in a field marked by what we do not know, in my view discretion is the positive carving out of new fields for cognitive exploration.

One of the devices used in arguing for the special status of expert knowledge is the distinction between know-how and know-that. The latter is often taken as the hallmark of the novice, for it is the form of knowledge found in fully coded sets of rules and instructions for guiding performance. Propositional know-that can be pinned down in language and by such encoding deployed in managing standardized performance. There is now a large debate about the stability of the know-how/know-that distinction that concentrates on the issue whether know-how can be captured in know-that. I discuss this debate briefly below, but much of it is orthogonal to my focus on discretion and open-endedness. There is, however, a central point about the idea of 'know-how' that matters for what I want to say about the place of discretion. I review that point in the following section.

If the common view about expertise is topsy-turvy, this suggests a quite different sense of the role of discretion and why it matters. Drawing on ideas from recent work on Dewey (Luntley 2016), I want to develop further the idea that what is distinctive of experts is their capacity for learning, for generating new concepts. This is an ability for open-endedness that arises from the subject's imaginative responses to the aesthetics of experience. Open-endedness has its roots in the imaginative games we play with the aesthetic structures and patterns of experience (cf. also Luntley 2015). Experts are enquirers *par excellence*, but the key to understanding enquiry is not a body of rules or procedures that carve out a methodology for hypothesis framing and testing; it lies in the open-ended know-how of being inquisitive, knowing how to explore and interrogate. This is the open-ended 'craftiness of know-how'. My main aim in this chapter is to explore this idea of the craftiness of know-how and to make the case for seeing this as a basic component of cognition, rather than the special preserve of a cognitive elite. Once that thought is made clear, it suggests the developmental trajectory from novice to expert has things upside down. Novices, as commonly characterized, are not beginners; they are subjects whose learning has been stunted, whose role has been regimented and codified. And that raises some quite general issues about the role and value of discretion across the board, not just for 'experts', for on this inversion of the common view, we all start as experts, as rapid learners and crafty pattern-makers.

In so far as experts de facto are a separate category, on my view it is because they are the minority who have been left to engage in enquiry in its proper Deweyan sense, an open-ended exploration of what is possible in bringing adaptive order to the contingencies of experience. In contrast, the cognitive majority have been marshalled, regimented to follow the propositionally coded for rules for conduct. The alternative to the familiar expert/novice distinction is to see it as an artifice that stands in the way of recognizing that open-ended adaptiveness of cognition applies to all. And, of course, from a Deweyan perspective, any sense this open-endedness is appropriate only for 'the few' is anathema. Discretion is the better part of sensible judgement for any serious enquirer.

22.3 Know-How to Open-Endedness

Although many theorists have appealed to the know-how/know-that distinction in trying to differentiate between the cognitive abilities of expert and novices, the distinction has been subject to extensive critique in recent years. It is unclear that it can bear the weight placed upon it. I think that there is a role for 'know-how' in understanding the open-endedness of discretion, but that we will not find that role simply by comparing know-how with know-that.

Some writers reach for 'know-how' as a label for the indeterminate inarticulacy of rapid in-the-moment thought in action. The trained medical diagnostician or trained baker has a hands-on grasp of what they are doing and why they are doing it that is difficult to put into words. So whatever it is, it is not a know-that, knowledge as relation to a proposition, for they cannot identify the proposition. But knowledge is at play nevertheless seems legitimate: hence, the appeal to 'know-how' to pick up the phenomenon.

I want to briefly note two concerns regarding this appeal to know-how before turning to the issue that I think is central. First, there is a methodological concern with the appeal to know-how. The claimed inarticulacy of the expert actor in the moment, even if it is accepted as a datum to be reckoned with, cannot be taken at face value, for it distorts theorizing about how experienced actors think in the moment. The fact that from the first-person point of view the experienced actor can find no proposition as object of their thought is poor ground for concluding that their thinking is not propositional in form. It is simply unclear why we should grant what the subject is able to avow of their thought processes an overriding consideration in the determination of what their thought processes are. Being expert in some activity does not mean that you are expect at surveying, cataloguing and theorizing the character of your thought processes that govern the activity. For example, for an expert baker, paying detailed attention to the precise differentiation of the feel of dough might well stand in the way of being able to pay detailed attention to the delineation of the thought processes involved. The baker is focused on the dough, not her thinking. We do well to defer to her judgement regarding the state of the dough, but it is not obvious why we should defer to her account of her own cognitive processes in making that judgement.[5]

Second, if we take the task of cataloguing the character of the expert baker's thought processes as a serious theoretical undertaking, bound by questions of theoretical consistency, format and so on, then there are a number of powerful reasons for disregarding the apparent obviousness of the phenomenology that says that the baker's orientation to the dough is not propositionally constituted.

A general strategy has emerged for understanding most, if not all, instances of know-how as being propositional in form. I call it the 'kidnapping strategy' (Luntley 2009, 2011a). This provides a general strategy for kidnapping all cases of 'know-how' and rendering them as 'know-that'. The strategy exploits an idea, commonplace in contemporary philosophy of mind, that provides a way of individuating propositions without identifying them with linguistic strings. There are many propositions to which we can form attitudes of belief, knowledge, interrogation and so on that are partially individuated by language and partially individuated by contextual features of the way in which the thinking subject is located by perception and agency in the environment.

Suppose you are out walking and someone asks if you know the way home. You reply, 'It's that way'. You know the way home, but might have no way of formulating what it is you know—the proposition that is the object of your cognitive attitude—that articulates that proposition fully in language. The proposition you know is only expressible as, 'That is the way home' uttered as you point in the right direction. This is a proposition. It is a case of know-that. For sure, you know how to get home and you know how to get home because you know that the perceptually indicated route is the way home. You cannot fully express the proposition you know other than by using the context-sensitive expression, the perceptual demonstrative 'that' used *in situ* to pick out a way to go home. That this is propositional knowledge is clear, for the proposition that you express with 'that is the way home' is a candidate for truth and falsity. If you are right, then the proposition you expressed with 'that is the way home' is true. And if that proposition is false, then you are probably lost.

Propositions are structured contents capable of being true or false. The component parts of propositions are concepts. It is because concepts are repeatable component parts of propositions that propositions stand in inferential linkages to one another and the truth value of one can bear on the truth value of another. Inference trades on the recurrence of identifiable parts (concepts) in different composite wholes (propositions). But nothing in this set of familiar reminders requires that propositions or their component parts be items that can be fully individuated in language. Many concepts, if not most, are not fully expressible without remainder in language. If this is right, then our attitude to propositions should not be modelled in terms of attitudes to sentences, for there are few sentences that, qua symbol strings, fully encode the proposition expressed on any given utterance of the sentence. Here is a very simple example to conclude the point.

The experienced baker uses the sentence, 'this dough is ready', many times a day, but arguably uses it to express a different proposition on each occasion. This is because each time she utters it, she is perceptually demonstrating a different sample of dough. You cannot count propositions by counting sentences. The example generalizes. When pressed to explain why the dough is ready the baker might say: 'the dough is ready because it feels like this'. In the second proposition, the perceptual demonstrative is used to pick out a quality of the dough—it feels like this. This concept, the concept of a way a dough feels when it is ready, might be deployed many times during a day. Its repeatability turns not on the repeatability of the linguistic string 'feels like this', but on the repeatability of the particular kind of perceptual/agential engagement with dough that the baker enjoys when she says it feels like this. That kind of engagement is only available to actors who have acquired a considerable amount of experience in handling dough. And it is because of that last point that the concept expressed by '[…] feels like this' is typically opaque to those who lack the extensive perceptual and agential history of the experienced baker who handles the dough. There is little the baker can say to express what they know—the dough is ready because it feels like this—but it does not follow that what they know is not propositional.

The above sketches the outline of a now familiar argument to show that there is no basis for thinking that the seemingly inarticulate knowledge of the expert who thinks well in the moment is anything other than familiar propositional knowledge-that.[6] All the knowledge that the expert calls upon is conceptually articulated knowledge, answerable to truth and falsity and thereby inferentially bound to the whole domain of human knowledge-that. Perhaps experts exploit a higher percentage of perceptually contextual knowledge and perhaps they deploy perceptual skills of discrimination that outreach the resources of less experienced actors?[7] None of this makes a case for thinking that their knowledge is anything other than propositional knowledge.

If the above line of argument goes through, then all talk of intuition, tacit knowing, implicit knowing and so on picks out no more than aspects of how things can seem to the expert performer acting well in the moment. The knowledge they exploit might seem to them inarticulatable and even inchoate, but, for all that, it might be no more than good old-fashioned propositional knowledge. On this view, because the account of conceptual structures is released from the demand that they be fully expressible (without remainder) in language, then such structures expand to overrun the whole domain of human intelligent behaviour. Wherever agency is shaped by knowledge, the door is open to seeing that knowledge as conceptual through and through.

This is a powerful and compelling line of thought. It is not without its critics (cf. Brockmann, Clarke and Winch 2011; see also Winch 2010, 2015). It is an argument well placed in confronting the ease with which theorists have tended to proliferate forms of knowledge on no better basis than a reminder that it often seems to those who act well in the moment that the knowledge they draw upon in so acting is difficult to express.

Notwithstanding this argument for kidnapping know-how in know-that, it seems plausible to think that know-how is somehow more basic than know-that. It can seem natural to think that although the expert baker's know-how with regard to the condition of the dough as felt can be captured and adequately expressed with the concept of '… feels like this', the availability of this concept is dependent upon the know-how acquired in the repeated exposure to handling the dough. The know-how comes first and only later comes to provide an ingredient for propositional thinking (Wiggins 2012).[8]

The thought here seems to arise from thinking that there ought to be an answer to the question: What makes these context-sensitive concepts available to the agent? Take the concept of the way the dough feels when it is proved, the concept that the expert baker expresses by saying, 'It feels like this'. You might be tempted to say that it is in virtue of their repeated experience of handling different samples of dough that they gain the conceptual take on the feel of the dough. This might suggest that the know-how is somehow more basic than the know-that. Construed simply as a question about the genesis of the concept, the point is not, however, compelling.

To say that the possession of the concept '[…] feels like this' depends on the availability of a history of experiencing the dough does not require that the history of experiences be experiences that deliver an irreducible know-how, for perhaps the development of know-how is contemporaneous with the development of the concept? That, after all, is surely the line that the advocate of propositionalism will take. The idea that know-how is somehow more basic than know-that is not obvious. So here is another respect in which the idea that know-how is more basic might be explored.

One of the features that Wiggins (2012) emphasizes in his account of know-how is the open-endedness and indeterminacy of know-how. This might not apply to all cases, but the idea of an indeterminate open-endedness seems applicable for many cases of know-how. And such open-endedness then suggests the site for discretion. But what role does this play in a case for the relative primitiveness of know-how compared to know-that? Wiggins does not supply a clear account here. One suggestion would be that if know-how is not conceptually articulated, then it is not bound by the rules that govern concept deployment. The underlying intuition is that concept use is rule-governed. If know-how is not conceptually articulate, then it is excused the rules that govern or shape the formation and deployment of know-that. But that point only goes through if the kidnapping argument does not work. Wiggins does not challenge the kidnapping argument as such, but that leaves the case for open-endedness still to be made. It cannot simply arise as a datum regarding the phenomenology of know-how.

My suspicion is that Wiggins' claim regarding the primacy of know-how is onto something real, but that the point he is after reflects something more general than merely the contest for priority between know-how and know-that. I suspect it reveals something deep about cognition in general and how knowledge claims across the board reflect deeper facets of our mental lives.

22.4 Open-Endedness

The case for propositionalism relies on kidnapping know-how in propositional know-that form by deploying context-sensitive expressions—the perceptual demonstratives—that express contextual concepts in contextualized propositions. Know-how gets expressed in contextual know-that. Know-how is a knowing-how to do something and the range of things 'to do' are found within experience and agency.[9] Know-that can seem different; it can be deployed in isolation, in contemplation. The contrast in focusing on the connection between know-how and experience and activity can encourage the idea of the genetic primitiveness of know-how, for this makes know-how connected with those areas that figure as sources for cognition in a traditional empiricist framework. If the focus on know-how is on experience and action, then it is tempting to try to factor out the contribution of these as the primitive element that then gets picked up by thought and rendered into a contextualized content. But that move is just a re-fashioned empiricism, the attempt for some sort of given; something of questionable coherence (*locus classicus* McDowell 1994, 2013). Furthermore, having factored out the contribution of experience and action to know-how, it is unclear that one would find a real open-endedness to knowing how to tell when the dough is ready, for it is ready when it feels like this. And what it is for it to 'feel like this' is determined in part by the meaning of the words and in part by what the perceptual context supplies in completing the sense of the contextualized expression—'feels like this'. The expression as such does not fully determine a meaning, but that does not make the expression open-ended; it just makes it incomplete. It is, however, complete-able with the addition of the contextual information supplied by perception. There is, once word and context are combined, a complete and determinate meaning for the proposition as compiled: the dough feels like this.

Trying to factor out the experiential and agential contribution to know-how does not therefore help us in pursuit of the idea of open-endedness. The point about open-endedness is, I think, different to the simple point that know-how often implicates experience and action in completing the account of what we know. The point about open-endedness occurs in cases of know-how that are generally accepted to be equally expressible in terms of know-that.

If know-how is open-ended, this is not a matter of inarticulacy, a matter akin to the inarticulacy of a contextual proposition expressed with a perceptual demonstrative; for example, the dough feels like this. The words do not articulate the proposition at stake here; it is the words as used in a context that articulate the proposition. There is no real open-endedness; there is only an incompleteness in the linguistic representation of what is known. The linguistic representation only captures part of what is known; the rest is provided by the perceptual and agential context. But there is nothing about such examples that suggests that what is provided by context to complete what is known is anything other than a determinate concept, albeit one the determinacy of which is not captured in language. What is known in such cases is context-dependent, but it is not thereby indeterminate, for in many cases what context provides is exactly enough to determine, in tandem with the linguistic expression, a determinate knowing. And, for sake of argument, let us assume that where there is a determinate meaning, there is a rule governing application of the expressions used to express that meaning. Context-sensitivity poses no obvious challenge to that idea of rules and thereby provides no model for a cognitive operation that exhibits or licenses a kind of freedom or discretion that operates where the rules give out.

There is, however, a different kind of open-ended indeterminacy to know-how that does not turn on the above idea of context-dependency. It depends on the phenomenon that Travis calls occasion-sensitivity (Travis 2008, 2011). This is a more radical sense of context, one in which context provides not the 'completion' to the otherwise incomplete linguistic expression, but one in which the very idea of a completed case of what is known is undermined. Consider Wittgenstein's example—'This is a game'. In this proposition, there is the demonstrative 'this' that only makes a clear contribution to the proposition in the context of perceptual demonstration. That idea is clear and provides, to all intents and purposes, a rule-governed deployment of language to express a clear concept—the concept that picks out the instance of behaviour identified with the 'this'. What fascinated Wittgenstein was the word 'game', the word that prima facie exhibits no context-sensitivity, for, surely, the word game is used to express a familiar concept and, as such, is rule-governed. But, notoriously, what Wittgenstein suggests is that we have no clear sense of what the rule might be that governs our use of this word.

Knowing the meaning of 'game' is knowing how to use the word and that know-how might be expressed in the semantic rule: knowing that 'game' is satisfied by activity α if and only if α is a game. Such kidnapping of know-how by know-that is not, however, what matters with regard to Wittgenstein's key insight. His insight is that there is an open-endedness to the meaning of 'game' regardless of your favoured expression of what it is to know that meaning in terms of know-how or know-that. Howsoever you think it is best expressed, what is expressed is a knowing-how to go on with using the word in a way that permits real open-endedness and discretion.

That's the claim I want to turn to. I want to flesh out the suggestion that there is an open-endedness in this example that reveals a sense of discretion at the heart of our cognitive endeavours. Travis traces the open-endedness of occasion-sensitivity to a thesis that Descartes expresses in the *Discourse on method*. Descartes says that what distinguishes the distinctive mindedness of human cognition is a feature of what it is to be responsive to reasons. For Descartes, human responsiveness to reasons is essentially open-ended.

Now, our responsiveness to reasons reflects our ability to find rules in our behaviour. When someone offers us a claim as a reason for behaviour, we find it compelling because it instantiates some general pattern. Suppose we agree that what Alfie is doing is a game, but I am unsure whether what Bella is doing is a game. My interlocutor then points out that Bella's activity is like Alfie's. For this to count as a reason for saying that Bella is playing a game, there must be some generality that covers these two cases, something they have in common. What Wittgenstein argues is that we have no determinate way of expressing what that generality amounts to. The point here is not just the lack of a clear linguistic representation of the generality, something that requires completion by a contribution from perceptual or agential context. The point is more basic than that. The point, as Wittgenstein develops it in his rule-following considerations, seems to enjoin a real open-endedness, an actual indeterminacy that leaves the speaker with licence for discretion in employing the word. You might think that this is a local point peculiar to the concept 'game' and certain other peculiar concepts for which the family-resemblance metaphor has some point.[10] But Travis' suggestion about the Cartesian roots of all this suggests a more radical picture.

We are prone to think that it is because we are responding to a rule that our responsiveness to the similarity between the Alfie and Bella cases is a reason for saying that the latter is a game. The rule provides a general pattern that somehow commands our allegiance. So, in responding to reasons we are responding to patterns found in experience and this makes us passive responders to patterns. No wonder that we are tempted to reify these patterns into platonic Forms or ethereal Ideas that determine the general form to which our reasoned responses show our allegiance. But the Cartesian insight to which Travis appeals has an altogether different image at its core. It is the image of a responsive that comes from the following core ability that is the mark of a *res cogitans*: the unboundedness of the ability to place oneself under the sway of reason.

We are not passive responders to the rules and patterns of reason; we actively place ourselves under the bondage of such patterns. When presented with a pattern provided as reason for word use, we have the option of placing that pattern under some other pattern. For any given appeal to a pattern as reason for action we can always step back and ask if that pattern should be applied in the current case. In doing so, we explore and test the possibility of alternative patterns. This is why there is an open-endedness to the use of the word 'game', for any pattern offered as reason for using the word can be subsumed under another that might change the way we go on. Knowing how to go on with the word 'game' is not a matter of responding to some pattern; it is to share in the responsibility for shaping and sustaining the patterns of reasonable word use.

That last thought can sound radically constructivist. To acknowledge that the patterns by which we deploy words in our discourse (and by which we deploy ideas in our thinking) are in part our patterns that we can help shape and sustain looks to undermine the very idea of correctness that we rightly take to constrain our use of meaningful words. We arrange words (and ideas) for many purposes, but a key purpose that we cannot disregard when thinking about our actions as epistemic actors is the purpose of using words correctly. The correctness that matters in word use is the correctness of truth. Truth is not for us to shape or sustain; it is the measure of whether our shaping is right or wrong. What then is the type of pattern in word use of which it makes sense to say we have a role in its shaping and sustenance? In the broad, the answer is: those patterns that figure in the aesthetic of experience, the patterns we manipulate by acts of imagination.

Descartes' idea about the unboundedness of our ability to place ourselves under reasons picks up on the following sort of occasion. We are offered a pattern of thinking, a pattern of word use, that looks to govern what we do next. I have agreed to a series of events being called 'game' and that pattern seems to govern what I do next when considering the next event I observe. The pattern of use thus far gives me reason to call the next item 'game', but the pattern does not fully determine that this is the case. It is possible that I find another way of continuing the pattern that licenses that I withhold the word 'game' from the next occasion. It looks as if meaningful word use is bendy and that undermines the idea that the use is subject to constraint for being used in a way that is semantically correct.

I think there are two things going on here. First, there is a role for the actor in shaping the patterns of word use, but that is not the same as determining whether a word is used correctly. Whether a word is used correctly is not down to us; it is down to how things are.[11] Semantic correctness is, if you like, a matter of how the world responds to what we say. But that of itself does not fully determine how we use words, what the shape of their meaning is. The pattern of previous use shapes the options for what we do next, but it does not do this mechanically and neither does it determine it fully. That last thought can seem incoherent. Put simply, it amounts to the idea that there can be a case of some object or event available to us in thought—we notice it—but which has not previously been brought into thought with the concept 'game'. The range of that concept is being extended.[12]

But that now raises a further problem: how do we hold two things in thought—the new event and the concept 'game'—and bring them together without exploiting the conceptual patterns required for holding things in thought? The danger is that the suggestion requires a level of cognition, the nonconceptual, in terms of which the new items can be 'held in thought' prior to being conjoined in concepts. But that is to accept a bifurcation of abilities that has been repeatedly critiqued as unstable, the bifurcation typical of traditional empiricism between a nonconceptual given and the conceptual forms of thought.

What I want to suggest is that the inarticulacy we find in expert encounters with novelty (that they employ in developing the shape of concept use) arises from encounters that exploit patterns of experience that have a shape and fit, but whose shape is not the generalized pattern distinctive of semantic fit; it is the fit that accrues to aesthetic patterns. The point is not to posit a basic level of experience—the aesthetic—that is the playground of the imagination and forever below and out of reach of concept use. The point is that the aesthetic and imagination run throughout human cognition. It is what makes us the kind of language users that we are; it is part of the basic kit that makes us language-using cognitive agents, always on the move and making our way in our cognitive endeavours.

We use words to speak truthfully, but we also use them in all sorts of other ways, imaginatively with a sense of play and aesthetic fit. Aesthetic fit is the notion of correctness that we find in the often formal patterns of aesthetic experience—rhythm, rhyme, repetition and cadence (Ginsborg 2011, 2012). These are patterns that give us a sense of things fitting in place or sequence, but where the sense of fit is subjective. To say it is subjective is just to say that my sense of the fit of words in the rhythm of a phrase does not give me warrant to insist that you find them fit too. You might, but the sense of fit, unlike the sense of correctness at stake with truth, does not automatically generalize over persons. Semantic fit is insensitive to the beholder of fit; if I use 'game' truthfully of a situation, its truthfulness is not a function of *my* using it; it would be equally true if you used it. Aesthetic fit is not like this. If I find a colour combination resonates and you do not, the fact that it works for me does not, of itself, give reason for you to find it so.[13] Nevertheless, aesthetic patterns and their sense of fit can be ways in which we open up new options for truthful uses. It is the uses of words in the service of aesthetic fit that can provide judgement in the sense of creating a conceptual form upon experience and offering it to the tribunal of truth.[14] That, I suggest, is what happens when I extend the use of the word 'game' to a new case by exploiting similarities akin to aesthetic fit and use the word in a way that is not bound to be seen as a truthful way. When that happens, it is, in part, up to us whether to treat this new use as a continuation of the old and thereby bound by the sense of correctness due to words with semantic content.

22.5 From Noticing to Thinking: Judgement and Discretion

It is often said that experts exercise judgement and that is the site of discretion. Consider the idea of judgement as an activity that places a conceptual form upon experience. But what does this activity of judgement operate upon? If it operates upon conceptual components to form a propositional content and take it to be true, then the only sense of open-endedness in discretion concerns the issue whether a given pair of concepts have previously been brought together. But that does not sound like discretion so much as just noticing something that had not previously been noticed.

So, consider the judgement that things are thus and so (broadly speaking, forming and taking to be true a propositional content of the form '*something is so-and-so*'). If forming such a judgement is the model for the exercise of discretion, then all it seems to capture is the notion of the expert putting together the concepts '*something*' and '[...] *is so-and-so*' when these have not been previously combined and it is difficult to see what kind of activity this could amount to beyond something as banal as noticing that '*something is so-and-so*', a fact previously not observed by others. On this model, all discretion captures is a novel compiling of concepts into compound wholes. This produces new propositions, but no extension to the expressive power of the conceptual system being used. The model of 'new judgement' here is simply new compiling. It is unclear why novelty in compiling might count as something especially interesting, let alone the key to the idea of exercises of discretion.

Here's an intuitive way of trying to capture a more radical sense of discretion as the site of judgement where the activity is not just the novel compiling of conceptual components already available within the conceptual system in use. The intuitive thought is that expert discretion occurs when the expert notices a phenomenon that falls outwith the range of the extant conceptual system and by exercising judgement brings that phenomenon within the reach of conceptual understanding. So that means that the expert notices something that has not previously been conceptually located (perhaps, 'not previously been fully conceptually located'). Then, having noticed this, they provide a way of conceptualizing the phenomenon—they bring it to judgement.

The above claim might seem obvious. Is not it just the thought that what is distinctive of expertise is oftentimes the ability to 'see more' than the novice? The expert notices things that the novice misses; they are marked out by the superiority of their perceptual skills. That sounds plausible, but there are two ways of taking this idea of 'noticing more'. On one reading, that fits with the expertise-as-superior-conceptual-achievement model—it provides no insight on the idea of discretion and freedom; on the other reading, that fits with my model of expertise—the idea of 'noticing more' is part of the general cognitive endowment applicable to all even if, under modern models of the division of labour, we tend to regiment the activities of some (novices) to blank out such 'noticing more'.

We need to distinguish between two notions of 'noticing more': one construed as a cognitive operation that can transform the subject's capacity for judgement and thought, and the other construed as a cognitive operation that exploits extant capacities for judgement and thought. The latter is the simpler and less interesting notion.

The former notion is quite different. It is the notion of a way of engaging with things that can make them salient without determining what concept they fall under. It is this, I suggest, that can be achieved by exploiting the forms of experience typically found in the aesthetics of experience—the often formal properties of rhythm, cadence, rhyme and simple association. This is, I suggest, the site of what I called the craftiness of know-how. This is the know-how that resists capture by know-that, for it is a know-how in the domain of patterns where the 'fit' of the patterns involves a correctness different to semantic correctness. It is a know-how that operates outwith what I called 'rules-as-such'; it operates outwith those rules that describe the patterns involved in the pursuit of truth. The know-how implicated in the patterns of fit is a know-how within the aesthetics of experience. These aesthetic patterns do not determine truth, but they can be ways by which we extend the domain of truth into new areas,

areas of experience not previously picked up in judgement and held before the tribunal of semantic correctness. And we pick them up when we have the freedom to explore and play with the aesthetic forms of experience, when we have the option to do more than just apply rules already determined, when we have the discretion to imaginatively explore the aesthetics of our encounters and in so doing find new ways of going on and using words truthfully.

Notes

1. For some more recent work in the same territory, see Beckett and Hager (2005), Eraut (1994), Hager (2000) and Collins (2010); see also Gascoigne and Thornton (2014).
2. Current researchers are still appealing to the inarticulacy of expert knowing as a mark of something beyond the realm of ordinary propositional knowing, for example, appealing to the Polanyi claim 'we know more than we can tell'; see Varpio, Grassau and Hall (2016).
3. The present point is comparable to the case often made against particularist account of moral judgement; see Jackson, Pettit and Smith (2000).
4. This is not to denigrate the fluid regimentation of action in the skilled professional operating at speed, for example, paramedics in the resuscitation room. But even established and well-rehearsed routines still bear the scrutiny of the imagination that is open to spotting that in this situation at this time something a bit different might be called for. The imagination that remains open to the possibility that this case might be different is, I think, the hallmark of the site of discretion.
5. This is not to deny the fascination with the descriptive enterprise of logging the phenomenology of the first-person point of view of acting well in the moment. The phenomena are interesting. But this phenomenological project at best amounts to a descriptive task, and even on the matter of getting an accurate description of acting well in the moment, it is, at most, a first draft of that task. There is a serious methodological issue regarding the extent to which we should grant the subject's first-person take on what they are thinking when acting in the moment as the trump consideration in cataloguing accurately what they are thinking and doing. And when we move to an explanatory project of trying to theorize and understand the processes involved in acting well in the moment, it is quite unclear why that theoretical project should be in thrall to the descriptive offerings obtained from the first-personal in-the-moment description.
6. Some key items in this literature: Stanley (2005, 2011), Stanley and Williamson (2001), Luntley (2009, 2011a), Gascoigne and Thornton (2014) and Schear (2013).
7. For details on an empirical project that tracked some of the role of attention in expert practice, see Ainley and Luntley (2005a, b, 2007).
8. This genetic claim is part of what Wiggins (2012) has in mind when he speaks of know-that as the step-child of know-how.
9. It includes mental agency, knowing how to think, to ponder, to interrogate, muse and so on.
10. On such a reading, the lack of an essence to the meaning of 'game' is a peculiarity of a limited range of concepts whose meaning is given by an overlapping set

of characteristics like the similarities in appearance one finds across members of a family, rather than seeing the point as an instance of a general anti-essentialism about meaning, one that sees meaning as what is revealed in ongoing use and where 'use' is something we contribute to, create and sustain.

11. Of course, some of the things that fall under 'how things are' are the things we do, but that does not block the thought that there is a clear sense in which it is true that what we have done cannot be undone.
12. This is the limit case of developing a new concept.
13. 'Aesthetic fit' is a large topic. I take the idea from Ginsborg's work (2011, 2012). It is the idea that there can be a notion of correctness in using a sign that falls short of the generalizable notion of correctness that is at stake when signs are used in ways subject to semantic assessment. I use 'fit' to signal that simpler notion of correctness; it is the notion of correctness that governs, for example, the placing of signs in nonsense rhymes. See Luntley (2015, 2016, 2017) for further detail on aesthetic fit and how it figures in both Wittgenstein and Dewey.
14. The idea that aesthetic fit has a role in learning and conceptual development is implicit in Carey's (2009) account of the developmental trajectory of concept acquisition. Her key example uses the idea of numeral sequences as meaningless strings, the sense of place therein not unlike the sense of place or fit of words in nonsense rhymes; these are sequences that ex hypothesis bear no semantic content. And yet learning the sequence '2, 4, 6, 8' as a unit with rhythm and cadence is still, in Carey's account, the starting block to acquiring a sense of that sequence as expressive of a semantic content where position in the sequence is now representative of a state of affairs.

References

Ainley, J. & Luntley, M. (2005a). The role of attention in classroom practice: Developing a methodology. In P. Clarkson, A. Downton, D. Gronn, M. Horne, A. McDonough, R. Pierce & A. Roche (Eds), *Proceedings of the 28th Annual Conference of the Mathematics Education Research Group of Australasia* (Vol. 1, pp. 73–80).

Ainley, J. & Luntley, M. (2005b). What teachers know: The knowledge bases of classroom practice. In *Proceedings of 4th Conference European Society for Research in Mathematics Education*, Barcelona.

Ainley, J. & Luntley, M. (2007). The role of attention in expert classroom practice. *Journal of Mathematics Teacher Education*, 10(1), 3–22.

Beckett, D. & Hager, P. (2005). *Life, work and learning*. London: Routledge.

Benner, P. (1984). *From novice to expert: Excellence and power in clinical nursing practice*. London: Addison Wesley.

Brockmann, M., Clarke, L. & Winch, C. (2011). *Knowledge, skills and competence in the European labour market*. Abingdon: Routledge.

Carey, S. (2009). *The origin of concepts*. Oxford: Oxford University Press.

Collins, H. (2010). *Tacit and explicit knowledge*. Chicago: University of Chicago Press.

Dreyfus, H. & Dreyfus, S. (1986). *Mind over machine: The power of human intuition and expertise in the era of the computer*. Oxford: Blackwell.

Dworkin, R. (1977). *Taking rights seriously*. Cambridge, MA: Harvard University Press

Eraut, M. (1994). *Developing professional knowledge and competence*. London: The Falmer Press.

Gascoigne, N. & Thornton, T. (2014). *Tacit knowledge*. London: Routledge.
Hager, P. (2000). Know-how and workplace practical judgement. *Journal of Philosophy of Education*, 34, 281–296.
Ginsborg, H. (2011). Rule-following and primitive normativity. *Journal of Philosophy*, CVIII(5), 227–254.
Ginsborg, H. (2012). Meaning, understanding and normativity. *Proceedings of the Aristotelian Society, Supplementary Volume*, 86(1), 127–146.
Jackson, F., Pettit, P. & Smith, M. (2000). Ethical particularism and patterns. In B. Hooker & O. Little (Eds), *Moral particularism* (pp. 79–99). Oxford: Clarendon Press.
Luntley, M. (2009). Understanding expertise. *Journal for Applied Philosophy*, 26(4), 356–370.
Luntley, M. (2011a). What do nurses know? *Nursing Philosophy*, 12, 22–33.
Luntley, M. (2011b). Expertise: Initiation into learning, not knowing. In L. Bond, D. Carr, C. Clark & C. Clegg (Eds), *Towards professional wisdom* (pp. 27–44). Farnham: Ashgate Publishing.
Luntley, M. (2015). *Wittgenstein: Opening investigation*. New York: Wiley-Blackwell.
Luntley, M. (2016). What's the problem with Dewey? *European Journal of Pragmatism and American Philosophy*, (*Special number on centenary of Dewey's Education and Democracy)*, VIII(1) 77–99.
Luntley, M. (2017). Wittgenstein and the path of learning. In M. Peters & J. Stickney (Eds), *A companion to Wittgenstein on education: Pedagogical investigation* (pp. 437–451). Springer: Singapore.
McDowell, J. (1994). *Mind and world*. Cambridge, MA: Harvard University Press.
McDowell, J. (2013). The myth of the mind as detached. In J. K. Schear (Ed.), *Mind, reason and being-in-the-world: The McDowell-Dreyfus debate*. London: Routledge.
Schear, J.K. (Ed.). (2013). *Mind, reason and being-in-the-world: The McDowell-Dreyfus debate*. London: Routledge.
Stanley, J. (2005). *Knowledge and practical interests*. Oxford: Oxford University Press.
Stanley, J. (2011). *Know how*. Oxford: Oxford University Press.
Stanley, J. & Williamson, T. (2001). Knowing how. *Journal of Philosophy*, 98, 411–444.
Travis, C. (2008). *Occasion-Sensitivity*. Oxford: Oxford University Press.
Travis, C. (2011). *Objectivity and the parochial*. Oxford: Oxford University Press.
Varpio, L.K. Grassau, P., & Hall, P. (2016). Looking and listening in arts- and humanities-based creations. *Medical Education*, 51, 136–45
Wiggins, D. (2012). Practical knowledge: Knowing how to and knowing that. *Mind*, 121, 97–130.
Winch, C. (2010). *Dimensions of expertise*. London: Continuum.
Winch, C. (2015). *Teachers' knowledge and know-how: A philosophical investigation*. Oxford: Wiley.

CHAPTER 23

Discretion and Professional Work

Tony Evans

23.1 Introduction

When we think about professionals and professions, a number of ideas seem to follow one another. Professionals are people who have expertise and skills. We also associate them with their training and the professional institutions that valorize and promote their expertise and skills. And discretion—a degree of freedom to work in line with your judgement—is also closely tied to the idea of professional practice.

All frontline workers in welfare services—including professionals—have some freedom in their day-to-day work, not least because of the limitations of managerial control (Hupe, Hill and Buffat Eds 2015). However, professional discretion is of a different quality to this pervasive and systemic discretion in welfare organizations and it also tends to be more extensive (Evans 2016). The discretion available to professionals is particularly associated with their belonging to an occupation whose identity is knitted into their specialist knowledge and skills. In this sense professionals are more 'cosmopolitan' (Gouldner 1957) than other public servants; their occupational identity stands at a critical distance from any particular role they occupy or organization that employs them (Wilson 1989).

The nature of the work in which professionals are engaged and the nature of their skills and expertise mean that they are often given freedom by senior policymakers and by the organizations within which they work. This may be because the work is politically sensitive and it is useful to shift responsibility for decisions to non-political experts (Hood, Rothstein and Baldwin 2001; see also Chap. 3 of this edited collection), or it may be formal recognition of the

T. Evans (✉)
Department of Social Work, Royal Holloway, University of London, Egham, UK
e-mail: Tony.Evans@rhul.ac.uk

T. Evans, P. Hupe (eds.), *Discretion and the Quest for Controlled Freedom*, https://doi.org/10.1007/978-3-030-19566-3_23

need for informed expert judgement rather than dehumanized rule-following. Policy (and law-making) is complex and policymakers often assume, even if they do not explicitly recognize, existing specialist knowledge when they are framing procedures and regulations, and require that only specified professionals occupy particular service roles (see, for instance, Jobling's Chap. 13 of this edited collection).

Professionals are key actors in public services (and beyond), but pinning down what we mean by the terms 'profession' and 'professional'—and the discretion they exercise—is a challenge. One option is to look to lists of professional characteristics which categorize and prioritize occupations as professions. However, under examination these lists often contradict each other and come down to the assertion that identifying a role as professional is obvious to those who know (see, for instance, Etzioni 1969[1]). In this chapter I suggest that a more productive route is to look to more critical approaches. Heeding Gan's (1992) advice to avoid academic amnesia I will revisit Jamous and Pelliole's (1970) and Johnson's (1972) seminal studies of professional discretion. It seems to me that amnesia can take two forms—outright forgetting and simply acknowledging without engaging with the logic and evidence that underpin the arguments they put forward. Jamous and Pelliole (1970) and Johnson (1972) clearly have not been forgotten in that they continue to be widely cited. My concern rather is to re-engage with their arguments and consider the insights they still have to offer us. Jamous and Pelliole examined the idea of professional expertise and argued that it is made up of two broad elements: technical knowledge and indeterminate knowledge. Johnson (1972) drew on Jamous and Pelliole's distinction, arguing that expertise is a source of power. Expertise puts professionals at an advantage because they can set the terms of trade in encounters with their clients—unless, that is, economic or political power intervenes to alter these terms of trade. For Johnson, whichever power prevails—the expertise of professions, consumer clout or political intervention—relates to particular patterns of professional discretion in particular situations. Neoliberalism and the rise of public management have challenged professional discretion across welfare services over the past 30 years. In the remainder of the chapter I will explore the themes of professional knowledge and power, and consider their continued relevance to understanding professional discretion.

23.2 Professions and Professionals

Trait Approaches

Interest in 'professions' reflects a particular aspect of the division of labour along the lines of expertise that developed in the late nineteenth and early twentieth centuries. Professions have existed (at least) since the Middle Ages, when the development of medicine, law and theology, for instance, was closely associated with the establishment of the medieval universities. In the late nineteenth century, there was an explosion of expert occupations such as journalism, engineering, dentistry, pharmacy and accountancy, providing services in the quickly expanding market economy (Carr-Saunders 1928). In the twentieth century professions such as nursing, teaching and social work crystallized in the context of the post-war welfare state.

Pinning down what precisely is meant by 'profession' is fraught with problems. The term carries such emotive and evaluative weight that you may already be baulking at my inclusion (or exclusion) of some occupations in the preceding paragraph.

This problem of definition is not new. It can be seen in interrelated—and still influential—strands of the early analysis of professions. One characterizes 'professional' as a eulogistic term fixed to a bundle of attributes—often drawn from medicine—and uses these to set clear criteria, distinguishing professional sheep from non-professional goats. Abraham Flexner (2001: 158), for instance, a major figure in American medical education in the early twentieth century, explained that professions 'involve personally responsible intellectual activity; they derive their material immediately from learning and science; they possess an organized and educationally communicable technique; they have evolved into definite status, social and professional; and they tend to become, more and more clearly, organs for the achievement of large social ends'.

A strong thread in early sociological work on professions reflected this view of professions as bundles of (primarily positive) attributes—traits—and sought to explore the relationship between these attributes to explain professional status. This approach sought to explain attributes—such as freedom to control and manage work—in terms of variables such as knowledge and commitment. Goode (1961: 307–8), for instance, reviewing this literature, noted that while detailed definitions of 'professional' varied, they shared the sense that any profession 'is autonomous, is organized in professional associations, its members receive higher incomes than most workers and occupy a high proportion of the governing posts in our society, and so on. Two traits, conspicuous because they seem to be found in all definitions, are sociologically central, because they are the main determinants of the others [...] (1) prolonged specialized training in a body of abstract knowledge, and (2) a collectivity or service orientation'.

Trait analysis became less influential in the 1960s in the face of increasing criticism. There was concern, for instance, that Trait approaches tended not to interrogate of the role that professions play in modern society, and their relationship to economic and political interests. Looking back to Durkheim, Trait approaches tended to see the role of professions in society as necessarily positive. This, though, ignored long-standing concern that professions in a free market for their services focus on advancing their own interests rather than the needs of their clients (and wider society), concerns captured in Bernard Shaw (1909)'s Preface to *The doctor's dilemma*:

> Anyone who has ever known doctors well enough to hear medical shop talked without reserve knows that they are full of stories about each other's blunders

> and errors, and that the theory of their omniscience and omnipotence no more holds good among themselves than it did with Molière and Napoleon. But for this very reason no doctor dare accuses another of malpractice. [...] I do not blame him: I should do the same myself. But the effect of this state of things is to make the medical profession a conspiracy to hide its own shortcomings. No doubt the same may be said of all professions. They are all conspiracies against the laity.

Shaw (1909) was concerned that the lionizing of medical expertise reflected a political agenda resisting a more sociological public health perspective. However, advancing a professional position can also include a strategy of criticism—but this is criticism of others' claims as inappropriate or misplaced. One professional group is often only too happy to criticize the assumed expertise of another. Arguments about the validity of different points of view and forms of expertise can provide the basis for advancing the interests of a particular profession. Abbott (1988), for instance, points to the role of conflicts between systems of knowledge and turf wars in interprofessional relations.

Under scrutiny, key traits associated with 'real' professions by Trait theorists seem to melt away. Flexner and Goode, for instance, emphasize the nature of professional knowledge as abstract and intellectual. Hafferty (1998: 404), though, examining medical education, highlights the role of tacit, intuitive and local expertise in medical training. He points out that 'a great deal of what is taught—and most of what is learned—in medical school takes place not within formal course offerings but within medicine's "hidden curriculum"'. The hidden curriculum—daily routines, demeanour and dress, assumptions, the organization of space and so on—enables students to understand and practise the aspects of medicine that are often not talked about but simply shown or performed. Professional expertise goes beyond a narrow technical idea of abstract intellectual knowledge.

The essentially evaluative and conservative nature of Trait approaches is reflected in Etzioni's (1969)[2] deployment of an idea of 'semi-professional' to berate 'a group of new professions whose claim to the status of doctors and lawyers is neither fully established nor fully desired' (1969: v). He drew the distinction between professional and semi-professional on the basis of three ('real') professional characteristics: longer training (five years or more), work that entails life and death matters or privileged communication, and the creation or application of knowledge (rather than being told what to do). Why is five-years-plus training so significant? Barristers, for instance, the highest status group within the legal professional in England and Wales, can qualify after just three years' training. In what ways are nurses less concerned with life and death than doctors? Lawyers are required to follow the interpretation of law that are given down to them by the courts. Doctors are often instructed by pharmacists on the correct dosage of a medicine to administer. Trait criteria of professionalism, when interrogated, are essentially arbitrary.

Critical Approaches

In response to these concerns, the focus of study shifted amongst many sociologists to examining how occupations sought to use attributes (their expertise and skills) to claim professional status and how, and for what purposes, powerful social actors might promote an occupation's claim to professional privileges. This resulted in a shift in focus in study 'from the false question "Is this occupation a profession" to the more fruitful one "what are the circumstances in which people in an occupation attempt to turn into a profession and themselves into professional people?"' (Hughes 1971a: 340).

Critical approaches are diverse, but they share a concern with questioning what is taken as 'natural' and 'normal' in society. Social enquiry involves identifying the ways in which society is organized and how this is sustained by particular groups to reflect their interests in society. In relation to the study of professions, they tend to be concerned with the role of power—of occupations and other social actors—in their analysis of professions and professionalism. But there is not just one critical approach. Macdonald and Ritzer (1988), for instance, point out that there has been a trans-Atlantic divergence in examining the relationship between power and professions. American approaches, they argue, focus on power as a professional attribute. In contrast, the UK literature has tended to view professional power in relation to the wider social, political and economic context.

In looking at discretion and professionals, a key issue is the relationship between professionals and the organizations that employ them: firms in the private sector and agencies in the public sector. Macdonald and Ritzer (1988) note that US authors tend to emphasize the idea of independent 'free professionals', whereas UK authors view professions primarily as organizationally based and organizationally constrained. Organizations now play a significant role in the lives of most professionals, and are central to the analysis of professional practices (Brock, Leblebici and Muzio 2014). Accordingly, my focus here will be the approach developed within the UK literature and I will revisit two essays published in the early 1970s that set the tone characterizing the analysis. Jamous and Pelliole's essay (1970) analysed the nature of professional expertise and the relationship between expert occupations and powerful social actors in promoting professional status. Johnson (1972) identifies the control of esoteric professional knowledge as the key factor in understating the variety of institutional arrangements managing professional practice.

Both approaches draw distinctions between professions as expert occupations and the social arrangements that control their practice. They share a concern with the idea of a profession as an expert occupation and how it can support or undermine claims to discretion and how the social and economic forces influence institutional arrangements of control and freedom that structure professional practice. Importantly, Johnson's analysis draws explicitly on Jamous and Pelliole's argument about the centrality of indeterminacy in understanding professional expertise.

23.3 Expertise and Power

Expertise

For Jamous and Pelliole (1970) the first task of examining professionals is to clear away the dead wood of detailed specifications of the characteristics and attributes of professionalism associated with Trait analysis. Many professional traits, they argue, are contingent and reflect the particular attributes of occupations we recognize as professions at a particular historical point; but they are not essential to understanding the nature of professions. They present a pared-down definition of professions as 'occupations or activities whose I/T ratio, intrinsic to the system of production, is generally high' (113). The I/T ratio refers to the nature of an occupation's expertise: 'I' refers to indeterminate expertise that is seen as reflecting factors such as the virtues of the practitioners, their training or the reputation and standing of their occupations' institutions; 'T' relates to technical expertise that can be expressed in clear statements and rules that are used to manage practice and train and assess practitioners. Professions are occupations with a high level of expertise characterized as a mixture of indeterminate and technical knowledge.

Expertise is a necessary element of a profession. But Jamous and Pelliole argue, there is more. Achievement of the freedom often associated with being a profession is not a given but relates to the way in which an expert occupation presents the relationship between indeterminacy (work characterized by uncertainty and unpredictability of outcome) and technicality in its work. They argue that there is no one right balance: only a dilemma. To train practitioners and to demonstrate to powerful social sponsors (e.g. policymakers, academic institutions, etc.) that they can intervene effectively, a profession needs technical knowledge that explains the problems with which it works, makes them predictable and shows that positive outcomes are not just good luck but reflect expertise and judgement. However, where technical expertise can be specified and formulated in precise terms, expertise becomes procedures that anyone (and now this must include a computer) can acquire and use, and with which non-professionals can measure/assess and manage professional practice. If professional expertise is seen as primarily a set of techniques, this can undermine the occupation's claims to special qualities and skills. Indeterminacy is central to an occupation's claim to control its own work: the greater the degree of indeterminacy it can claim in its expertise (which the wider world will accept), the more reason it can give to be left to its own devices; only fellow professionals can understand and assess this work. However, an occupation cannot overplay this hand and remain credible. Emphasizing indeterminacy enhances an occupation's own exclusivity, but it might also undermine it, straining credibility and calling into question the integrity of its skills and expertise.

Power

Johnson (1972: 42–3) draws on Jamous and Pelliole's idea that indeterminacy can be used as a manipulative professional strategy 'to increase the social distance and his autonomy and control over practice by engaging in a process of "mystification"'. This assumed expertise puts professions in a position of power in relation to their customer. This is the basic problem of the terms of trade of professional service. But these terms are not fixed; they can be changed in the interplay of wider social, economic and political factors. The equation between freedom and expertise is altered by market relations. A professional has skills to sell, but her control over her work depends on whether the occupation producing the service or the consumers receiving the service have the upper economic hand.

Where demand for expertise outstrips supply, an occupation is in a strong position *vis-à-vis* potential buyers, particularly where they are not a homogenous group but are diffuse and weak. Buyers become supplicants for service (even though they pay), cast as clients who should give up control to the experts in order to receive help: 'the producer-consumer relationship will normally be a fiduciary, one-to-one relationship initiated by the client and terminated by the professional' (Johnson 1972: 52–3). This is collegiate control—the occupation is coherent and self-conscious and organizing and regulating its own work.

When consumers are strong—acting as a coherent economic force—a different form of occupational control arises: patronage control. The consumer's perspective sets the terms of trade regarding what is expected and what the focus of work should be. The modern corporation is a prime example of a powerful and homogenous consumer (group) dominating professional practice—for instance, the relationship between the big four accountancy firms and financial services professionals. The professionals become 'housed' within the organization. Their loyalty and expertise focus on local corporate concerns (rather than broader professional commitments) and their practice is managed hierarchically, within the organization.

Collegiate control reflects the classic ideal-type idea of a profession as an occupation in control and with extensive discretion. In the patronage system of control, professional freedom is suppressed by consumer control. However, it is not that occupations in systems of collegiate control are more professional than those in systems of patronage control. They are both professions in the sense of being occupations with expertise. But the systems of control under which they practise afford different degrees of freedom to act and allowances to exercise judgement.

A study by Fournier (1999) illustrates how these two different forms of control can operate. Drawing on the work of Michel Foucault, she argues that professionals are influenced by ideas of professionalism in relation to how they think about and are expected to deploy their expertise and skills. Professionalism is tied up with ideas of knowledge and skills—techniques to understand and manage feelings, thoughts and behaviours; and these ideas become ingrained in professionals—how they think and how and what they do—and are 'inscribed' in their practice. Fournier looks at the way in which the idea of 'professionalism' has been extended beyond professional occupations to describe particular attributes expected of all employees by their employers—a move intended to facilitate greater management control of work. First, there is the more established discourse in which professionals have managed to invest their expertise and worldview with status and power (in Johnson's terms, a collegiate perspective). Second, there is a more recent managerial discourse of professionalism as a strategy to control occupations by imposing expectations of 'professionalism' in their work, for example, 'customer care' and prioritizing of organizational objectives (an example, when applied to professions, of Johnson's patronage control).

Johnson adds that the control of expertise is often also of interest to broader social and political interests. Leaving the problem to the free market is one political response. Another is to intervene to manage the relationship between the producer (professional) and the consumer in some way. Johnson identifies this as a third type of control of professional work—which he calls 'mediated'. In this situation, a third party (usually the state) intervenes in the relationship 'to remove from the producer or the consumer the authority to determine the content and subjects of practice' (Johnson 1972: 77). Mediation can take a number of forms, including licensing and regulation, funding to occupations or consumers, or direct provision by state agencies such as the National Health Services (NHS) or local authority services such as education or social services in the UK.

Jamous and Pelliole's (1970) and Johnson's (1972) analysis have an economy and elegance that avoids the elaborate lists of professional attributes in many accounts. They both look at professions as expert occupations whose expertise is a powerful resource. However, Jamous and Pelliole's (1970: 117) view of indeterminate expertise as an ideological strategy to protect professional control of practice needs interrogation, not least because Johnson's analysis of professional control draws on the idea of indeterminate expertise as mystification and a professional power grab.

23.4 Dimensions of Professional Discretion

Indeterminacy

Jamous and Pelliole (1970:117)'s account of professional expertise contrasts the clear and rational nature of technicality with indeterminate expertise, which they characterize as a social strategy in which professions deploy an array of symbols designed to mystify their work. Professions, they argue, have

> either to act with a view to greater and greater control of their practice by making it more technical, by codifying it [...]. Or on the other hand to make use of their

> qualities in order to continue to monopolize their field by ideological rationalizations about its nature, its functions, and so to avoid all possibility of intervention and reappraisal from outside.

But is this all there is to indeterminacy? Is it just a manipulative strategy, a power grab? It would be naïve not to accept that professions can use knowledge to carve out and protect territory: 'People of the same trade seldom meet together, even for merriment and diversion, but the conversation ends in a conspiracy against the public, or in some contrivance to raise prices' (Smith 2013 bk1, Chap. 10: II). In so far as this is the case, technicality, as well as indeterminacy, can potentially be used to mystify professional expertise.

What then can we make of 'indeterminacy'? It is possible to see it in a more constructive—and balanced—light when we recognize that professional expertise is a mixture of thinking, acting and feeling. It is the idea that there are important elements to expertise that are difficult to formulate and that are learnt and developed through practice. It is not just about applying abstract ideas but also about being innovative and creating knowledge and skills in practice (see Luntley's Chap. 22 and Evans' Chap. 24 of this edited collection). This view of professional expertise chimes with observations of professional expertise as developed and sustained through continuing use. Hughes, for instance, talks about the tension between new surgeons and experienced surgeons who fought over opportunities to carry out specific techniques—the new surgeons to learn them, and the experienced surgeons to maintain their knowledge and skills in the deployment of the technique (Hughes 1971b).

As we saw in the idea of a hidden curriculum (see Hafferty 1998), there are aspects of professional knowledge that are social and improvisational and cannot simply be expressed as a set of technical procedures. Frey and Osborne (2013), looking at the future impact of computerization on employment, note that there are three 'engineering bottlenecks' frustrating the proceduralization of many professional roles: highly complex manual and perceptual tasks, human creativity and social intelligence. The challenge to proceduralization, in complex manual and perceptual tasks, relates to the way these skills cannot be divorced from the context in which they are used and have to be understood as a dynamic relationship between the actor and the object of action. Frey and Osborne also note that psychologists have found it difficult to specify what human creativity involves. A particular problem is not just creativity as a process but also as a set of values: 'values are highly variable, it follows that many arguments about creativity are rooted in disagreements about value' (Frey and Osborne 2013: 26) In relation to social intelligence, they note: 'While algorithms and robots can now reproduce some aspects of human social interaction, the real-time recognition of natural human emotion remains a challenging problem, and the ability to respond intelligently to such inputs is even more difficult' (26–7).

An aspect of Luntley's analysis of expertise also helps us understand not only why expertise is difficult to proceduralize but also that expertise exists and can be communicated, even though it cannot always be pinned down in abstract statements. Many aspects of expertise are expressed in activity-dependent concepts: 'concepts the grasp of which depends on your activities on and with things, including the activities of perceptually attending to things [...] The words alone do not reveal what she is thinking. You need to attend to the fine details of her actions to understand' (Luntley 2011a: 24–5).

This is the state of professional knowledge, not because professionals want to make what they know unclear or are unwilling to share their expertise, but because their expertise is closely related to doing the work and constantly developing and changing in practice. Expertise can often 'outrun the expressive power of ordinary language' (Luntley 2011b: 32). Explanations often entail metaphors, similes and examples. Sometimes technical statements can take their place, but at the cost of sensitivity and nuance. And such explanations are after the event, and the risk is in formulating expertise into a set of procedures and rules, when knowledge in practice is constantly in the process of being created (Luntley 2011a; see also Luntley's Chap. 22 of this edited collection).

Professions may sometimes take advantage of the fact that they have expertise that cannot be fully proceduralized to resist external control, but this should not prevent us from recognizing that there are aspects of expertise that are difficult to articulate or which shift and change in use. This may be contained in gut feelings, images and metaphors or physical movements or the tacit recognition of social mores, which cannot be captured in abstractions or set out in techniques, but which are learnt and emerge in practice. This indeterminate expertise does not exist in isolation from or opposition to technical knowledge, but complements it.

Control

Johnson's (1972) starting point is the problem of professional expertise and sees the solutions as either accepting the mystification and leaving the professional to it—collegiate control—or, if the consumer has the power, imposing rational common sense and directing professional work—patronage control. However, when we recognize the complex nature of the indeterminate dimension of professional expertise (often shifting between the inarticulable and the inchoate, and sometimes in the process of translation into technical specificity), we need to consider how this can complicate and have a significant impact on these systems of control in practice.

Collegiate control describes a form of professional practice in which discretion is overt and predominant. If we think of discretion in both its senses—as freedom from external restrictions and as the exercise of judgement—at a collective level, the idea of this form of control as professional freedom makes sense. However, if we look at it from the perspective of individual practitioners within the occupation, questions arise of the nature and extent of control and restriction on freedom, particularly when we take into account the idea that professional expertise is more diverse and dynamic than can be captured in the notion of abstract rational technical knowledge.

Collegiate control is potentially fragile. Johnson's analysis emphasizes the importance of occupational homogeneity in holding this form of control together. If the occupation's work is fragmented into sub-specialisms, this is a threat to the occupation's identity and coherence. If its social make-up diversifies, this can undermine the sense of shared identity. The indeterminate nature of much expert knowledge is also a constant threat to professional homogeneity. It points to the role of the profession itself as an institution to police homogeneity of practice within and to present uniformity to the outside world. However, the dynamism and creativity inherent in indeterminate expertise suggest that it is helpful to look at professional practice as what Wittgenstein calls a 'game', an activity structured by ideas and rules which are not static but which change and develop in their application (see Luntley, Chap. 22 and Evans, Chap. 24). Each participant is playing the same game, but in playing is generating new slightly different ways of playing, which will feed back into its development. Accordingly, we should not look for an essence of professional expertise but rather recognize a 'family resemblance', where 'you will not see something that is common to all, but similarities, relationships, and a whole series of them at that [...] we see a complicated network of similarities overlapping and criss-crossing: sometimes overall similarities, sometimes similarities of details' (Wittgenstein 2001: 27e).

Collegiate control, though, looks more rigid, rather like Kuhn (1970)'s idea of a paradigm: it is a system to focus individual practice; a mechanism for identifying particular problems and specifying the acceptable way to solve them. The paradigm establishes a collective freedom but constrains individual practitioners within acceptable and established ways to practise from the point of view of those committed to the paradigm. It also functions as a way of structuring work and of enforcing an idea of the right way to approach the world. The collective nature of the occupation and freedom comes at the cost of 'the individualistic elemental nature of professionalism—its basis of individuals' professionality as a singular unit, and the inherent diversity that this imposes upon it' (Evans 2008: 35). As a system of control, collegiality frames the discretion of individual practitioners: it is a system of peer control to conform to accepted ways of practising and accepted ways of seeing the problems and issues with which the occupation should engage. But as Jobling (in Chap. 13) notes, individual professionals can use the liminal area at the intersection of professional and bureaucratic roles to step outside the constraints of the professional paradigm and work more effectively with individual service users.

There are two observations here about collegiate discretion. The first thing is that collegiate strategies to marshal professional practice have to tread a fine line between technicality and indeterminacy, not only in making themselves seem credible to powerful social actors, but also to hold the profession together while not suppressing the dynamic aspect of professional knowledge bubbling up in indeterminate expertise. Technicality, as well as indeterminacy, can potentially be used to mystify professional expertise. Evidence-based practice is a case in point. Many professions are now promoting the evidence-based credentials of their expertise, but this is often based on a claim of the potential of evidence and how it will make practice more rational and technically sophisticated in the future—while the promised future is, however, constantly delayed (Evans and Hardy 2010). Here the promise of technicality becomes a rational myth to promote legitimacy (Meyer and Rowan 1991). The introduction of evidence-based practice was contentious in medicine (e.g. Williams and Gardener 2002) and current moves by the *British Medical Journal*, for instance, to marginalize qualitative research (BMJ 2016), as well as moves to introduce evidence-based algorithms to direct general practice in the UK (e.g. Copperfield 2016), have resulted in increasing dissent within the profession.

Professionals within a particular profession may see their expertise as different in extent or emphasis than that specified by their professional body. The point here is not that one side is right or wrong, but that establishing a collegiate idea of right practice entails curtailing individual practitioner freedom to specify the professional activity. The discretion associated with collegiate control involves some constraints on individual discretion and, potentially, resistance to these constraints. I will return to this point below.

In contrast to collegiate control, patronage control is a regime within which (collective) occupational freedom is externally limited. The focus of professionals' work and the approach they take depend on the direction they are given by their patron—predominantly public bodies and corporations in the contemporary setting. Collective professional freedom is limited and constrained: in this context, discretion is constructed within the idea of principal and agent, in which organizational managers direct employees to carry out instructions.

However, scratch the surface and the role of indeterminate expertise is again bubbling underneath—in the exercise of professional judgement and skills to adapt and shift the application of policies—tacitly accepted, or even required, to make sense of policies and to make policies and procedures work (as mentioned above).

The constrained nature of discretion within this form of control would seem to undermine claims of expert occupations to discretion. In this respect, professionals are just workers alongside other workers whose discretion is simply de facto. Within welfare organizations, they are street-level bureaucrats (Lipsky 1980/2010). Their discretion arises from organizational mess: gaps in management control, the vagueness of policy direction and the mismatch of resources and work requirements. However, their indeterminate expertise, the aspects of their knowledge that are difficult to express clearly in language, which depend on practice knowledge (often the practical expertise acquired in doing the job) to understand the situation and which reflect an understanding of the context within which rules may be applied, significantly enhances for professionals the extent and nature of the *de facto* discretion that permeates welfare organizations (Evans 2016).

Within the patronage regime, the way patrons specify situations takes precedence over how experts themselves define them. This is not particularly problematic if, to do the job, one just needs technical, proceduralized knowledge. Others can learn what to do by following the script—they do not have to rely on the professional to do it for them. However, there are often gaps that require (expert) professional expertise to fill. For example, professionals have to use their judgement to interpret procedures and decide when they apply. Who, for instance, decides when circumstances require a shift from the practitioner's discretionary judgement to procedures? Professional expertise seems to be a strong basis to claim and justify discretion in doing this. Furthermore, procedures often assume a complex, interrelated body of back-knowledge to understand and decide how they should be applied; rules of practice entail a context of interpretation and background knowledge (Evans and Hardy 2010). Procedures, criteria, tick-charts and so on, by themselves, are meaningless: they require expert knowledge to make them usable (Munro 1998). In patronage systems, professional discretion is often taken for granted and hidden in plain sight.

Negative and Positive Freedom

Johnson's account of both collegiate and patronage systems of control emphasizes negative freedom: the constraints which are put upon (or not put upon) an occupation in the exercise of its expertise. On this account, professions are located within a particular system of control, because they are powerful, or because they are powerless, or because of the intervention of a powerful third party. There may also be another factor at play. There may be a dimension of freedom which is a calculation by the profession(al) of the balance between positive and negative freedom—a P/N ratio perhaps—whereby, in order to gain access to resources to do the job, professionals accept some constraint on their freedom from control, and recognize accountability to others. Negative freedom is the absence of constraint, freedom to act without interference. But being free from restrictions does not mean that you can act. There is also a positive dimension to freedom, which is having the opportunity and resources to act (Carter 2016).

In relation to collegiate and patronage forms of control we need to consider that a P/N ratio may also operate, alongside the I/T ratio—which effectively involves individual members of an occupational accepting a self-denying ordnance to practice within a certain range of expertise at a particular time within a certain balance of technical and indeterminate skills—giving up their freedom not to be controlled—in order to obtain and deploy the collective credibility and licence: positive freedom. This calculation can also be seen in the construction of discretion in patronage systems. Professional practice tends to be more than just dispensing expertise: it is about acting, changing things and intervening in the world. This is particularly the case in relation to welfare professionals, for instance. Doctors want to address health problems. Teachers want to educate pupils. Social workers want to address structural inequalities. Welfare organizations, potentially, offer these professions freedom as a positive quality—access to the resources and facilities that enable them to act. A doctor does not just want to be able to diagnose: she also wants to be able to have the prescribed medicines dispensed, and the patient's health and care closely monitored by nursing staff in a clean and efficient environment. Historically the NHS in the UK, for instance, has offered doctors control of day-to-day service provision within a policy framework set by the government (Elston 2009).

Context

Up to this point I have not examined Johnson's (1972) third 'mediated' form of control of professional discretion, where a powerful third party inserts itself into and influences the producer-consumer power dynamic. He talks about three forms of control: collegiate, patronage and mediated. These are read as three different types of occupational control. However, empirically, it is difficult to imagine pure examples of any one of these types of control, particularly when we think of mediated control. The same profession, for instance, can be subject to degrees or forms of control at the same time; for example, collegiate control may operate amongst an elite group, while the majority of the profession is subject to close patronage control (Leicht and Fennell 2001) and any dispensation will also operate within a system mediated by state regulation.

In fact, rather than seeing the three forms of control as three distinct types, it seems to be more productive to see them as overlapping and blurring, as dimensions of a dynamic matrix of control and freedom that can be used to understand the particular form of a profession's discretion in a particular place at a particular time.

Conceptually it is difficult to imagine mediated control as a stand-alone form. It operates to recalibrate the balance of collegiate and patronage control in a situation; it does not fully replace either—it adjusts the balance of power of market actors, and itself can be a market intervention to change the nature of the market. Looking at the systems of control of professions as interacting systems also helps us to identify the dynamic nature of discretion, how it changes over time and in different settings to reflect the shifting interaction of ideas of professional expertise, consumer power and the actions of social and political institutions.

For Johnson, writing in the 1970s, mediation was exemplified by the position of many welfare professional services within the framework of the British welfare state (1972: 79). The post-war welfare state was a move by the state to provide social services in a context of the failure of the market or charitable patronage to meet fundamental citizenship needs (77). Many professional services—teaching, medicine, nursing, social work and so on—were incorporated directly into the local and national state to ensure their provision. While services were provided within bureaucracies, these were bureau-professional organizations animated by professional cultures which reflected a collegiate idea of control (e.g. Parry and Parry 1979). Local authority education and social services, for instance, were professional-led services emphasizing ideas of professional authority and values. Mediation was a state intervention to provide services by addressing problems of demand within a system of delivery that viewed professions through a largely collegiate lens. In fact it is difficult to imagine collegiate or patronage control without some idea of society: the market and professions seem to be 'polis-dwelling' entities; they rely on social institutions setting their bounds and enabling them to operate, such as trust, law, conventions and so on.

However, the situation analysed by Johnson (1972) has changed. There has been a sea-change in the organizational culture and a shift in the political culture from the 1980s onwards, reflecting neoliberal suspicion of experts' role in delivering public services (Stedman-Jones 2012). Where possible, services were returned to the market, and regulation restricted to enhance consumer power—a promotion of patronage forms of control constraining traditional collegiate professional discretion. Outside direct provision of welfare services, for instance, funding for legal advice to citizens (legal aid) was reduced and restricted, and legal practices in England and Wales were liberalized to 'free' the market and promote consumer choice (Alaszewski and Manthorpe 1990). In areas of welfare provision where a return to the market has not (yet) looked practical, the state's role as a mediator has also changed. A prime example of this in the UK is adult social care, where a bureau-professional culture has been replaced by a management/business culture (e.g. Harris 2002), promoting a more patronage form of control over professionals and advocacy of consumer 'empowerment'. The emphasis has been on promoting consumerism and professional accountability in the development of organizational complaints procedures, a service culture that emphasizes consumer-specified 'wants' rather than professionally defined 'needs' and a shift from services provided 'in kind' to services 'in cash', 'empowering' service users as consumers to take responsibility for their 'personalized' services (Ferguson 2007; see also Chap. 19 of this edited collection).

This is mediation, but it also looks like (state) patronage control, designed to reduce occupational freedom and promote a consumer of consumer service. In this case, it seems the state has taken the role of patron/mediator—perhaps a new 'tutelage' form of control?—to re-educate and re-engineer welfare professions and citizens to better fit them for the marketplace. The state has used mediation—as the rebalancing of the relationship between professionals and consumers (in welfare services)—to recalibrate the relationship between professional work and service users, which itself was created by earlier mediation by the state. Over the past 30 years in welfare, policy has not only sought to reconfigure professional discretion, but sought to remake professions in welfare services to fit the job of remaking citizens as consumers in a welfare market/responsible citizens independent of the state (Evans 2018). There has been an emphasis in policy (state patronage control) on changing the culture and nature of professional practice ('modernization'), which has sought both to rebalance the producer-consumer relationship (state mediation control promoting patronage control, 'personalization') and to re-engineer professions to transform citizens into consumers, emphasizing the entrepreneurial role of the professions in using their discretion to make things happen (state promotion of collegiate control).

This mediator/patron/tutelage/collegiate intervention of the state in welfare services gives rise to a complex and seemingly contradictory landscape of professional discretion. It has seen the imposition of a regime of managerial control, constraining traditional collegiate, professional freedom (in the bureau-professional institutional setting). Alongside attempts to direct collegiate professional freedom, there has been a process of reorienting professional attention to focus on priorities and costs, managing demand, drawing in resources and making citizens into responsible consumers of welfare services (rather than simply having a right to services). Over the past decade, particularly, there has been a shift to a more positive organizational attitude to discretion in social care, but it is quite unlike the collegiate discretion in the earlier welfare state: it is a mode of discretion that is entrepreneurial: economically entrepreneurial in terms of a flexibility towards standards to accommodate resource constraints; and ethically entrepreneurial, where professionals are expected to deploy moral management to make citizens more responsible and independent (Evans 2015, 2018; Slasberg and Beresford 2017).

23.5 Conclusion

Professions are expert occupations whose work is controlled in particular ways. Examining how expertise is understood and how expert occupations are managed and controlled is central to understanding their discretion. Discretion starts with expertise and control chimes in; it acknowledges, regulates, modifies and directs it. Looking at discretion in this way is to approach it from a different angle from deficit accounts—such as Davis' description of discretion as a failure of external control: 'whenever the effective limits on his [a public officer's] power leave him free to make a choice among possible courses of action or inaction' (Davis 1971: 4).

Approaching discretion in this way poses important questions about the nature and valorization of professional expertise. It raises questions not only about the impact of control on professional knowledge and skill, but also about its role in establishing accountability. Professional expertise is wider and more variegated than traditional ideas of expertise suggest. It can have an abstract intellectual dimension, but it is also closely related to its environment, dynamic and embodied in practice. Professional discretion is not a fixed quotient of freedom: it is more fluid and contextual. Expertise, freedom and control are interrelated and draw our attention to different levels of analysis of professions practice. Within professions, for instance, practitioners are faced with a tension between the standards and uniformity (that establish the profession's collective credentials) and individual practitioner's innovation and creativity (that keep professional expertise alive and relevant). Constraints on professional discretion within organizations can be about imposition or about accountability;

they can undermine professionals' ability to deploy their expertise or contain and channel it to consider others' interests too—or both. Discretion also tends to be viewed from the perspective of (negative) freedom from external control without also considering a possible dimension of (positive) freedom in terms of access to resources (to do the job or advance professional commitments it would not otherwise be able to do or make). And how these different aspects of professional discretion play out—in its shape and operation—cannot be understood in isolation from the broader context of the social, economic and political environment within which any profession operates.

Notes

1. 'The correct observation is that although the borderlines are not sharply delineated, the parties involved are not prevented from recognising those who are manifestly, on several accounts, on one side or the other' (Etzioni 1969: vii).
2. Etzioni recognizes that his idea of 'semi-professions' relates to occupations that are predominantly female (vi). His aim, he tells us, is to help members of these occupations to recognize their place in the occupational pecking order to avoid them getting frustrated by unrealistic aspirations and feeling dissatisfied with their lot. He is concerned: 'As semi-professionals see it, they obviously are "more" than secretaries, salesgirls, or office clerks. Unable to find a niche between these white collar statuses and the professions, and not wishing to identify with lower-status group, they cling to the higher aspiration of being a full professional' (1969: vi). However, he continues: 'even in the best of all worlds there will still be differences resulting from the division of labour between those with no professional knowledge, those with highly specialized knowledge, and those who are in between. Once it is recognized that there is middle ground, inauthentic aspirations and positions are more likely to be renounced and the dysfunctional consequences of attempts to pass will tend to disappear' (1969: vii).

References

Abbott, A (1988). *The system of professions.* Chicago: University of Chicago Press.

Alaszewski, A. & Manthorpe, J. (1990). Literature review: The New Right and the professions. *British Journal of Social Work*, 20, 237–251.

British Medical Journal. (2016). 352, i563.

Brock, D., Leblebici, H. & Muzio, D. (2014). Understanding professionals and their workplaces: The mission of the Journal of Professions and Organization. *Journal of Professions and Organization*, 1, 1–15.

Carr-Saunders, A. (1928). *Professions: Their organization and place in society.* Oxford: The Clarendon Press.

Carter, I. (2016). Positive and negative Liberty. In E. Zalta (Ed.), *The Stanford encyclopedia of philosophy.* Retrieved from https://plato.stanford.edu/archives/fall2016/entries/liberty-positive-negative/.

Copperfield, T. (2016). Replace me with an app? Just try it. *Pulse.* Retrieved from http://www.pulsetoday.co.uk/replace-me-with-an-app-just-try-it/20032813.blog.

Davis, K. (1971). *Discretionary justice: A preliminary inquiry.* Urbana, IL: University of Illinois Press.
Elston, M. (2009). Remaking a trustworthy medical profession in twenty-first century Britain. In J. Gabe & M. Calan (Eds), *The new sociology of the Health Service* (pp. 17–36). London: Routledge.
Etzioni, A. (1969). Preface. In A. Etzioni (Ed.), *The semi-professions and their organization: Teachers, nurses, social workers* (p. 328). New York: Free Press.
Evans, L. (2008). Professionalism, professionality and the development of education professionals. *British Journal of Educational Studies*, 56(1), 20–38.
Evans, T. (2015). Street-level bureaucracy, management and the corrupted world of service. *European Journal of Social Work*, 19, 602–615.
Evans, T. (2016). *Professional discretion in welfare services.* Abingdon: Routledge.
Evans, T. (2018). Orientations of Professional Discretion in the Welfare Service State. *Social Work and Society.* Available at: https://socwork.net/sws/article/view/564
Evans, T. & Hardy, M. (2010). *Evidence and knowledge for practice.* Cambridge: Polity Press.
Ferguson, I. (2007). Increasing User Choice or Privatizing Risk? The Antinomies of Personalization. *British Journal of Social Work*, 37, 387–403
Flexner, A. (2001). Is social work a profession? *Research on Social Work Practice*, 11, 152–165.
Fournier, V. (1999). The appeal to 'professionalism' as a disciplinary mechanism. *The Sociological Review*, 47, 280–307.
Frey, C. & Osborne, M. (2013). *The future of employment: How susceptible are jobs to computerisation?* Oxford: Oxford Martin Programme. Retrieved from http://www.oxfordmartin.ox.ac.uk/downloads/academic/The_Future_of_Employment.pdf.
Gans, H. (1992). Sociological amnesia: The noncumulation of normal social science. *Sociological Forum*, 7, 701–710.
Goode, W. (1961). The librarian: From occupation to profession? *The Library Quarterly*, 31, 306–318.
Gouldner, A. (1957). Cosmopolitans and locals: Towards an analysis of latent social roles. *Administrative Science Quarterly*, 2, 281–306.
Hafferty, F.W. (1998). Beyond curriculum reform: Confronting medicine's hidden curriculum. *Academic Medicine*, 73(4), 403–407.
Harris, J. (2002). *The social work business.* London: Routledge.
Hood, C., Rothstein, H. & Baldwin, R. (2001). *The government of risk: Understanding risk regulation regimes.* Oxford: Oxford University Press.
Hughes. E. (1971a). Work and self. In *The sociological eye.* Chicago: Aldine Atherton.
Hughes. E. (1971b). Mistakes at work. In *The sociological eye.* Chicago: Aldine Atherton.
Hupe, P., Hill, M. & Buffat, A. (Eds). (2015) *Understanding street-level bureaucracy.* Bristol: Policy Press.
Jamous, H. & Pelliole, B. (1970). Changes in the French university-hospital system. In J.A. Jackson (Ed.), *Professions and professionalization* (pp. 111–152). Cambridge: Cambridge University Press.
Johnson, T. (1972). *Professions and power.* London: Macmillan.
Kuhn, T. (1970). *The structure of scientific revolutions.* Chicago: University of Chicago Press.
Leicht, K.T. & Fennell, M.L. (2001). *Professional work: A sociological approach.* Blackwell: Oxford.

Lipsky, M. (1980/2010). *Street-level bureaucracy. Dilemmas of the individual in public service.* New York: Russell Sage Foundation (2010 = thirtieth anniversary edition).

Luntley, M. (2011a). What do nurses know? *Nursing Philosophy*, 12, 22–33.

Luntley, M. (2011b). Expertise: Initiation into learning, not knowing. In L. Bondi, D. Carr, C. Clark & C. Clegg (Eds), *Towards professional wisdom: Practical deliberation in the people professions* (pp. 27–44). Aldershot: Ashgate.

Macdonald, K. & Ritzer, G. (1988). The sociology of professions: Dead or alive? *Work and Occupations*, 15, 251–272.

Meyer, J., & Rowan, B. (1991). Institutionalized organizations: Formal structure as myth and ceremony. In W. Powell & P. DiMaggio (Eds), *The new institutionalism in organizational analysis* (pp. 41–62). Chicago: University of Chicago Press.

Munro, E. (1998). Improving social workers' knowledge base in child protection. *British Journal of Social Work*, 28, 101–102.

Parry, N. & Parry, J. (1979). Social work professionalism and the state. In N. Parry, M. Rustin & C. Satyamurti (Eds), *Social work, welfare and the state* (pp. 21–47). London: Edward Arnold.

Shaw, B. (1909). *The doctor's dilemma: Preface on doctors.* Retrieved from http://www.gutenberg.org/files/5069/5069-h/5069-h.htm.

Slasberg, C. & Beresford, P. (2017). Strengths-based practice: Social care's latest Elixir or the next false dawn? *Disability & Society*, 32(2), 269–273.

Smith, A. (2013). *An inquiry into the nature and causes of the wealth of nations.* Retrieved from http://www.gutenberg.org/ebooks/3300.

Stedman-Jones, D. (2012). *Masters of the universe.* Princeton, NJ: Princeton University Press.

Williams, D. & Gardener, J. (2002). The case against "the evidence": a different perspective on evidence-based medicine. *British Journal of Psychiatry*, 180, 8–12.

Wilson, J. (1989). *Bureaucracy: What government agencies do and why they do it.* New York: Basic Books.

Wittgenstein, L. (2001). *Philosophical investigations.* Oxford: Blackwell (trans: G.E.M. Anscomb, page number followed by 'e' refers to English translation).

CHAPTER 24

The Art of Discretion

Tony Evans

24.1 Introduction

Several years ago I saw a performance of Shakespeare's *King John*. I had not seen the play before and one scene (Act 4, Scene 2) jumped out at me because it connected with material I had been looking at in the course of my studies of discretion. King John is a monarch striving (and failing) to control a restive feudal court. In one scene Hubert, the king's gaoler, is told by John to kill the king's young cousin, Arthur, a possible rival to the throne. Subsequently, it becomes clear that Arthur's death could threaten John's own position and the king berates Hubert for following his orders. (In fact, he has not followed them—he did not have the heart.) In this scene Shakespeare presents a visceral portrayal of the shifting threads of power and authority, risks and responsibilities that characterize discretion—and how these can be deployed in a febrile political environment to manage blame. Looking back, the play helped me realize how drama helps one recognize feelings and ideas underpinning action and understand the situation in the round—a process Aristotle (undated) describes in the Poetics as 'Anagnorisis'.

I saw a second, quite different, production of *King John* around ten years later. Both productions were by the same company—the Royal Shakespeare Company (RSC)—and on the same stage—the Swan Theatre in Stratford. The earlier production was in traditional dress, presenting John as a Machiavellian figure failing to negotiate the internecine conflicts of a medieval court (RSC 2001). In contrast, the 2012 production was in modern dress, locating the king in a court characterized as hedonistic and riven with family conflicts (RSC

T. Evans (✉)
Department of Social Work, Royal Holloway, University of London, Egham, UK
e-mail: Tony.Evans@rhul.ac.uk

T. Evans, P. Hupe (eds.), *Discretion and the Quest for Controlled Freedom*, https://doi.org/10.1007/978-3-030-19566-3_24

2012). The play—and the scene that had first caught my attention—still examined the politics of authority and discretion, but the two performances did this in very different ways, while still being the same play.

Thinking about this, I was struck by two things. First, the play did not just provide some insight into discretion in the flesh; performance is itself an exercise of discretion. Performance necessarily involves the balance of authority (the text) and freedom (interpretation). Second, if the director, cast and production team had approached the play in the same way that commentators assume policy should be implemented—as fixed and inviolable—I would have been very disappointed. The production team had played with the play, yet while the second version was a very different production, it was also clearly the same play—and just as good. Its difference was not a problem. Furthermore, I could see that, in their differences, the productions sought to bring out different aspects of the play to reflect different social and political concerns of their times and to speak to different concerns: the first in the age of spin and the second in the age of financial collapse, disillusionment and social excess (RSC 2001, 2012). Within the constraints of the play, the company had been driven to create something new, something that resonated with contemporary concerns.

In this chapter, I want to explore the relationship of creativity and discretion. Stereotypically, creativity is associated with the image of the lone genius, the Romantic hero, the artist; whereas discretion is a more prosaic problem of ill-fitting cogs in machines of law, policy and practice—in Davis's classic formulation, it is a deficit in policy, a hole, that occurs 'whenever the effective limits on his [a public officer's] power leave him free to make a choice among possible courses of action or inaction' (Davis 1971: 4).

However, creativity is often far from the stereotype of the 'lone genius'; creativity is more widespread—it is not only in 'the arts' but also in many other aspects of our lives, crucially, here, in the humdrum of public services (e.g. Friedrich 1940, Titmuss 1971). In recognizing this we can better understand the role of discretion in practice—and recognize the drawbacks of Davis's equation of discretion with a problem of control. Creativity, I will argue, offers a fruitful way to look at frontline discretion in the policy process as problem-solving and innovation, which in turn can help us to recognize discretion as a site where creativity is used to make services work.

In the first part of this chapter, I consider creativity as an integral but under-recognized aspect of discretion in human services. Seeing discretion through the lens of creativity draws our attention to its role in crafting services around policies. In the main body of the chapter, I explore problem-solving, imagination, and understanding and engaging with other people's perspectives, as aspects of creativity. Creativity, I will argue in the later part of the chapter, enables practitioners to recognize discretion as a positive dimension of their practice; to find space to provide services and breathe life into policy on the ground; and it translates bloodless documents and protocols into human services.

24.2 Creativity and Discretion

Descriptively, creativity and discretion bear a strong similarity. One way of understanding this connection is by recognizing how they are both constituted in the tension between freedom and limitation. Exercising judgement within constraints is a common experience across the different domains of policy and arts practice. Within welfare services, for instance, professionals operate within rules, policies and procedures to deliver services that are intended to be responsive to citizens. In performance, actors and musicians are often working with texts and manuscripts. In both settings, we would be disappointed if actors (in the general sense) unthinkingly followed a rule or replicated words and notes. In both areas, we want them to make sense of the task before them, work with the material to express their understanding through their own performances, making the material they are presented with work for their respective audiences/communities.

We are often prevented from seeing this fundamental similarity by the different ways in which policy and text and practice and performance are perceived. Frontline practitioners tend to be characterized as operatives who, in turn, seem to approach policy as a burden; whereas in the arts practitioners are seen as active agents and any text as resonant with opportunities. From the point of view of many welfare professionals, policy tends to be thought of as an alien and external constraint on practice, and a detrimental limit on their freedom. In contrast, in performance, the manuscript and text are recognized as opportunities for creativity and interpretation that can bring out new meanings and life in different contexts. (There are of course exceptions in both cases, but as a general contrast I think this point is useful to consider.) It is not just that the relationship between practice/performance and policy/text is understood and evaluated in very different ways on the front line. It is also that there are different external expectations of actors in policy and performance. Policymakers imagine that their policy prescriptions are precise and detailed; that they should and can be followed on the ground (e.g. Hupe 2017).

In welfare services, then, the creative dimension of frontline discretion tends to be constrained by the sense of indifference or alienation on the front line and the authoritative rhetoric of policy. In contrast, in stage performance, the manuscript and text are recognized as opportunities for creativity and interpretation. But why is 'creativity' a problem when thinking about professional practice and policy work? The problem stems from the way in which policy is conceived; the assumption that policy is what Elmore calls 'forward mapping'—the idea that policymakers at the top can specify their intent in more and more detail and that this is how the service should be provided on the front line. But, Elmore points out: 'The notion that policymakers exercise, or ought to exercise, some kind of direct and determinate control over policy implementation might be called the "noble lie" of conventional public administration and policy analysis' (1979: 603).

It is a lie that distorts the nature of public service provision and the role of policy within it. Osborne, Radnor and Nasi (2012: 136), for instance, argue that public management is framed in terms of manufacturing but, they argue,

> the business of government is, by and large, not about delivering pre-manufactured products. Nor are most relationships between public service users and public service organisations characterised by a transactional or discrete nature […]. On the contrary, the majority of 'public goods' (whether provided by a government, the non-profit and third sector or the private sector) are in fact not 'public products' but rather 'public services' […] they are intangible, process driven and based upon a promise of what is to be delivered. Public services can, of course, include concrete elements (health care or communications technology, for example). But these are not 'public goods' in their own right—rather they are required to support and enable the delivery of intangible and process driven public services.

There is a different logic of service provision from product delivery. Services are created on the ground in the interaction of the person providing the service and the person receiving it, working within a framework of promises. Public servants and citizens work together to negotiate, educate each other and create the service in the 'moment of truth' (Norman quoted in Osborne *et al.* 2012: 139).

What is lost in policymakers' 'noble lie' is the role of creativity. We miss the basic idea from creative disciplines such as drama—the play is not the performance; policy is not the service. When we go to the theatre we expect more than to hear a text parroted mechanically. We afford leeway for directors and actors to bring life to a play, to make it work, to communicate with us—to engage in a human enterprise. We are tolerant of divergence because we do not see the difference between the play and the performance as a problem, but as the result of creativity. Similarly, in the context of personalization of public services, service users expect services to be tailored and adapted to their situation (see also Needham's Chap. 19 of this edited collection).

24.3 Understanding Creativity: From Exception to Everywhere

The idea that creativity is a narrow and restricted phenomenon—a quality of an exceptional person who transcends rules and acts with intuition and imagination to produce what is novel and original—is dated and deeply ideological (Banaji and Burn with Buckingham 2010). It is a powerful but fundamentally unhelpful stereotype. Its power is its default quality when 'creativity' is mentioned. However, contemporary ideas of creativity have moved away from it, seeing it as a product of a particular cultural moment—Romanticism—and as a stereotype which promotes an exclusive, elitist and essentially unrealistically isolating characterization of creativity (Banaji *et al.* 2010). In its place, contemporary approaches have developed a picture of creativity that emphasizes its ubiquity and the role of inventive thinking and problem-solving that it entails. Central to this rethinking of creativity is imagination: 'refusing to be stumped by circumstances but being imaginative in order to find a way around a problem' (Craft 2000: 3–4).

There are two broad approaches that can help here in understanding the link between creativity and imagination. The first is drawn from work on creativity and information technology. The second is imagination, making links and connections that are not only cognitive but also emotional.

A particularly influential area of current work on creativity is computer science, where there is increasing interest in the possibility (or not) of computerizing creativity. A key figure here is Boden (1994), for whom creativity is about newness, difference and what has not gone before. In one way we can see echoes of the lone genius idea here—particularly in the emphasis of the originality—but she goes on to argue that creativity is, in fact, a widespread phenomenon in the sense that we all, to a lesser or greater degree, do things that are new, different and unexpected (to us, at least). Here she distinguishes two forms of creativity that help us to understand the power of the Romantic creative stereotype but also its limitation. All creativity involves making things that are new or different to oneself—this is what Boden calls 'psychological' (P) creativity—but sometimes individuals also do some things that are new, different or unexpected not only to themselves but also to all those around them. These situations reflect creativity, but the second has an additional feature of wider recognition. Boden calls this 'historical' (H) creativity. It is this idea of H creativity that tends to dominate our thinking about what creativity involves, but it is essentially problematic—it is historically and culturally unstable. Shakespeare is a case in point. While he was celebrated alongside other playwrights during his lifetime, his reputation declined over the following two centuries, and his work was characterized as ill-wrought, crude and vulgar. When his plays were performed, they were heavily edited and 'corrected' (Shakespeare Birthplace Trust). It was only in the early nineteenth century that our current view of Shakespeare, as a particular genius, became widespread (although some major cultural figures, such as Tolstoy and Shaw, dismissed 'bardolatry'). H creativity is essentially evaluative—it is a judgement made by peers or posterity that reflects their concerns and priorities—and it is something that can shift and change over time. It is a form of creativity, but not the only form.

Boden also argues that creativity is essentially context-bound—it is more newish than brand new—often pushing against/building on what already exists. In fact, she observes: 'constraints, far from being opposed to creativity, make creativity possible. To throw away all constraints would be to destroy the capacity for creative thinking' (Boden 1995).

Another strand in understanding creativity is the role of imagination in recognizing what is often ignored, hidden or taken for granted and making connections that are insightful or challenging. Creativity is also about finding ways to express and explore ideas and emotions, recognizing and reflecting what we may not notice or acknowledge. At an individual level, it is the imaginative ability to step into others' shoes—to try and see the world through others' eyes—or imagine new situations, releasing yourself from the immediate context and concerns to imagine future possibilities or past achievements, what it feels like to be in another position and how those feelings would affect you. In any stage performance, for instance, an actor is not just reciting prepared words; he or she has to make sense of those words in that context—what they say about the character and how the character might use them in that situation—and convey this to their audience. The Russian director, actor and theorist Stanislavski identifies a key aspect of any actor's performance as an understanding and connection with the character—using the actor's own experiences and empathic understanding to flesh out and bring a character to life (Stanislavski 2003).

The role of imagination in art is also fundamental in making connections between individual experiences and broader perspectives. Imagination is a fundamental tool for making connections between individuals and conceiving of them as social actors and subject to social influences. Anyone who has read George Eliot's *Middlemarch*, one of the greatest novels in English, cannot fail to recognize her observation: 'there is no creature whose inward being is so strong that it is not greatly determined by what lies outside it' (undated: Chap. 87). It is also about appreciating that: 'instead of seeing one world only, our own, we see that world multiply itself and we have at our disposal as many worlds as there are original artists, worlds more different one from the other than those which revolve in infinite space' (Proust 2000: 254).

As Negus and Pickering (2004) remind us, creativity is a skilful response to a dynamic situation that involves recognizing 'the intrinsic connections between creative practice and everyday life, for it's important that we don't forget how the heightened moments of creativity are always linked to routine and the daily round' (44–45). Creativity, understood in this way, echoes the nature of the delivery of welfare services where frontline professionals carry through 'central government's grand designs and use their knowledge to adapt the intentions into workable forms through local bargaining' (Glennerster, Korman and Marslen-Wilson 1983: 6). This is a situation occasionally recognized, in England, by governments calling for frontline creativity to improve service efficiency, quality and sensitivity to individual needs and preferences. In a review of innovation and change in the National Health Services (NHS), for instance, Darzi proposed greater frontline freedom to achieve this: 'setting frontline staff, both providers and commissioners, free to use their expertise, creativity and skill to find innovative ways to improve quality of care for patients' (Darzi 2008: 60). Similarly, in social care in England, senior officials and user policy advocates have criticized overly prescribed services in which 'social care workers find themselves operating as part of an institutional machine, using only a fraction of their skills, experience, empathy, respect, and knowledge. This can mean that most of the limited time a social worker has available is concentrated on deciding whether the person is eligible for support, with little scope for creative planning' (Gollins, Fox, Walker, Romeo, Thomas and

Woodham 2016: 9) and have called for the 'unleashing of social workers' creativity' (9). What seems to be advocated here is not that professionals should be maverick lone geniuses, but rather that they can be allowed to be imaginative, empathetic problem-solvers working with their clients to make services (work) on the ground. In the rest of this chapter I want to consider what this sort of creativity in practice looks like.

24.4 Creativity in Service Delivery and Professional Practice

I have already mentioned the problems of a 'manufacturing' idea of public services as the delivery of a specified product in line with central instructions. This manufacturing model misrepresents the nature of services. Services are not fixed and predetermined products; they are continually made and remade in the process of delivery:

> [N]o service is ever produced identically to two people—a meal in a restaurant is as much a product of the interaction between the customer and the waiter as it is of the quality of the food, as is a consultancy intervention by the consultant and client, while a surgical procedure is influenced just as much by the individual pathology of a patient as by the skills of the doctor. (Osborne *et al.* 2012: 139)

Providing services involves imagining human needs and adapting and creating services on the front line. It is about being able to understand others, and making and recognizing connections. The sociologist Ervin Goffman (1990), for instance, describes the essentially dramatic and performative nature of social life and how we imagine and reimagine others and ourselves in the ways in which we create and act out our social persona. He talks about the ways in which we, as social actors, are given and take roles which we manipulate to create and manage (or fail to manage) our identity in the performance of everyday life; and how the way we imagine people, the names we give them, the groups we put them in can have profound effects not only in our private lives but also in public roles such as those of professionals or policy actors. It is also present in apparently impersonal processes such as professional categories and policy criteria, which imagine people and services in particular ways, and by these means create and limit possibilities (Hacking 1986). As a trainee social worker, a memorable experience of mine was helping a man fill in a disability benefit claim and realizing that the questions I asked him (from the form) were undermining his own sense of himself—forcing his life into a category that did not reflect his reality. It became clear that I needed to shift my explanation of the process from one focusing on his dependency to one recognizing his needs as rights to services.

While this is a practical observation, it also reflects an ethical imperative in public services in favour of creativity; see also Chap. 25 of this edited collection. Frontline workers should question a requirement of unquestioning uniformity and obedience. Accountability has to be fluid and there is certainly no ethical basis for undeviating adherence to instructions. At the extremes, there have to be limits to obedience (Arendt 2006; see also the concluding Chap. 26 of this edited collection). In the UK, the idea that organizational and managerial commitments should silence professionals' ethical concerns and present challenges to organizational priorities, where these impede the provision of service users' needs, has been roundly criticized in a major public report (Francis 2013).

Here, creativity engages us with the idea that frontline staff often have to play with policy to provide 'good' services. The problem is that 'bending rules' is often thought of as either the subversion of policy *(the implementation gap)* or a challenge to policy (resistance). More often, however, it is improvisation (see also Wagenaar's Chap. 17 of this edited collection). In education, for instance, in contrast to 'scripted teaching', which prescribes routines that teachers have to follow (and which also assumes a passively receptive and uncritical audience), Sawyer (2004) points out that teachers have to think on their feet and work creatively with their classes to educate. To do this, teachers have to take from policy and expert knowledge and improvise, to adapt and create material that will engage the class. This does not mean that teaching is chaotic. There has to be a structure, but it needs to be loose and flexible to allow for innovation: 'shifting between scripts, scaffolds, and activity formats as the material and the students seem to require. These shifts in themselves are improvisational responses to the unique needs of that class' (Sawyer 2004: 17).

24.5 Creativity, Constraint and Affordance

Thinking about creativity as an amalgam of notions (newness, useful solutions and imagination) and as a social, as well as an individual, phenomenon focuses our attention on the fluidity that is required to energize policy and practices. It is a fluidity that is channelled and constrained by policy but which also allows policy to be shaped in practice in a way that enables it to be relevant and evolve on the ground.

At its most radical and disruptive, creativity is fundamental change, when basic concepts and ideas about the nature of a domain and how one operates within it are transformed. More typically, and much more widespread, creativity is less dramatic: it is an exploratory process, where ideas, assumptions and principles are interrogated, refined and developed. It is an exploration of possibilities and potential within an area of practice (Boden 1994). Here, the idea of 'affordance', an idea used widely in design, theatre and literature, is helpful in understanding the process and, I would argue, offers a helpful way to understand the nature and potential of creativity in thinking about discretion.

Affordance is the idea of the possibilities offered for action to an actor by an object in a context:

> The *affordances* of the environment are what it *offers* the animal, what it *provides* or *furnishes*, either for good or ill … If a terrestrial surface is nearly horizontal (instead of slanted), nearly flat (instead of convex or concave), and sufficiently extended (relative to the size of the animal) and if its substance is rigid (relative to the weight of the animal), then the surface *affords support* (Gibson 1986: 127—original emphasis).

An object in an environment is perceived as a way of achieving an actor's purpose—a tired person passing a fallen tree sees it as a surface on which to sit; a person who wants to cross a stream sees it as a potential bridge.

An object's 'affordance' is not fixed in the object. The object can offer many possibilities, but these arise through action. The object in the environment enables the action but does not predetermine it. A stick, for example, can be many things, but it is a particular thing for a particular person with a particular purpose at a particular juncture. If you sprain your ankle while out walking, a stick is a potential support that can bear your weight. If you are in a wood and you hear a noise, a stick can be seen as a rudimentary weapon to beat off your imagined pursuer. If you are worried about getting lost, a stick, stuck in the ground, can be a way-marker. Depending on a person's different purposes, the same object can be seen in different ways. I am worried that I am being pursued in the wood; I remember the stick I put in the ground as a way-marker and go back to pick it up as a defence. To me the stick affords defence (weapon), despite its original informative purpose (signpost), because my current need to protect myself is pressing and has elicited this recognition. Once this need passes I may focus once more on my need to find my way and replace the stick in the ground, returning it to its original purpose (for me) as a sign. (I have of course accumulated in the process different ways of thinking about and using the same object—and new situations are likely to add to this.)

Affordance can also relate to the way the social and cultural environment offers opportunities and affords actors the ability to express their needs and their creativity. It is an idea that highlights agency in social action through the role of imagination, reinvention, improvisation and ingenuity in local action, and through the contribution this makes to continuing processes of reinvention and development of the ideas, assumptions and conventions (Cave 2016: 62). In this way the idea of 'affordance' involves the recognition of possibilities within an environment to create or adapt meaning and open up new possibilities that can change the environment itself. As an example, following the implementation of the NHS & Community Care Act 1990, many local authorities introduced eligibility criteria as a way of rationing services. Eligibility criteria were widely seen as constraining practitioner judgement and restricting access to services (Carey 2003). However, in a context of austerity and a mismatch between political rhetoric and resources, eligibility criteria now have the potential to hold policymakers to account, and to act as the basis for the assertion of citizens' rights (even though criteria often only set down minimum requirements) (Evans 2016).

24.6 Creativity and Discretion

In the preceding section I have looked at the idea of creativity as an activity embedded in rule-infused environments and considered the idea of affordance as a helpful way of understanding how this creativity can operate on a day-to-day basis. In this section I want to look at how discretion itself can be understood as a creative domain and how the approaches to creativity outlined above can help explain and delineate the extent of discretion.

Earlier I referred to Davis's account of discretion—as a problem that arises from policymakers' inability to control every aspect of how policy is put into effect. It is the residual freedom that has been retained by policy implementers. However, there are several problems with this deficit account of discretion. It prejudges the situation, seeing control through explicit rules as possible and as necessarily better than freedom in all policy contexts. It also fails to recognize the positive potential of discretion to make policy work by making sense of policy imprecision, making policy injunctions practical and humanizing mechanical policy blueprints. Ronald Dworkin (1978) offers an alternative view of discretion. This provides a more nuanced framework within which to recognize, understand and assess the operation of discretion.

Dworkin's account of discretion locates it within a context of assumptions and expectations in which actors exercise discernment and judgement—exercising freedom against a background set of standards that form the basis against which these acts are understood and assessed (Dworkin 1978).

In considering the nature of these restrictions, he distinguishes different degrees of discretion: the application of a pre-existing standard to a set of facts where this cannot just be done mechanically but calling for some judgement in the application (e.g. do the facts make this a case of neglect or of abuse?), taking all the facts and different rules into consideration in making the final decision (choosing within the gamut of the rules), and finally making a judgement in the absence of formal and prescribed rules—while recognizing in doing so 'certain standards of rationality, fairness, and effectiveness. We criticise each other's acts in terms of these standards, and there is no reason not to do so when the acts are within the centre rather than beyond the perimeter of the doughnut of special authority' (Dworkin 1978: 33).

In relation to Dworkin's first two (more specifically formal rule-informed) dimensions of discretion, the idea of affordance offers insights into how discretion can operate creatively and how a belt of rules and regulations, while in some ways restricting options, may also offer previously unimagined possibilities in new situations, through new interpretations of existing rules, and avoid seeing rules and regulations as inevitably an iron cage of restriction (see also du Gay and Pedersen's Chap. 15 of this edited collection). When I started working as a social worker I asked a solicitor how to approach a lawyer for advice. She told me the best thing was to decide how I wanted to approach the situation and have a clear idea of what I wanted to do and to ask: 'Can I do this or not?' I was told that asking 'What are the options?' or 'What does the law say about this?' would just create confusion, as more often than not there are different but equally defensible answers to these sorts of questions.

The third, strong, sense of discretion seems to offer even more striking similarities to the approaches to creativity considered above and insights into the operation of discretion in practice. A significant aspect of service provision, particularly in human services, comes down to adaptation, improvisation, imagination and judgement within the purposes of policy frameworks—which have already been touched on above (see also Wolfson, Chap. 10, and Needham, Chap. 19, of this edited collection).

In practice, providing a service often entails working out what the problem is and what is the best thing to do in the circumstances. Professional expertise about problems, solutions and the ethical thing to do entails making judgements within a wide-ranging system of routines, ideas, assumptions and conventions which are shared but which allow exploration, new insights and development in practice in coming up with practical responses in the situation. While professionals often talk about their expertise as fixed and firm in guiding their practice, the reality is that practitioners, faced with the imperative to do something, have to draw on disparate aspects of knowledge to create their own practical understanding of and response to the situations they face (Evans and Hardy 2010). An area where one might expect creativity to be less prevalent is in relation to identifying the ethically right course of action. However, apart from a narrow set of regulations relating to professional registration, ethics is not a hard-and-fast set of rules. Ethical decision-making entails creativity in relation to

> the range of ethical ideas, principles and feelings that frontline practitioners draw on; how they combine and deploy them in particular situations; how they learn from situations—or not—in terms of extending and developing their ethical perspectives, and how they hold the tension between recognizing particular rights, the consequences of action and retaining their own sense of their professional character and project (Evans and Hardy 2017: 8).

24.7 Creativity and Discretion as Human Services

Human services—education, medicine, social care and so on—focus directly on working with people as pupils, patients, clients, service users and the like. Their aims are broadly about realizing potential—such as learning, health and well-being and so on—through working with individuals and groups. They are typically a subset of broader welfare services: those services that are, to a significant degree, human encounters (Zins 2001) between pupil and teacher, health work and social care practitioner and service user. In these services, the nature of the encounter is intrinsic to the service. Practitioners do not just provide resources; they themselves *are* also the resource, deploying their skills, knowledge, humanity and expertise in their encounters with the service users. In these situations it is not possible to predetermine what the service user needs and how support can best be provided. The immediate or obvious problem may not be the underlying issue and the obvious solution may not work in that place, at that time, for that person or family. If I go to the doctor or nurse with a backache, it may be a basic problem or it may be a symptom of something else. A significant aspect of the encounter is working out what the problem is and how I want to be helped with it (Zins 2001).

These sorts of services are structured around the idea that needs can be complex: that they cannot be simply isolated, but are interconnected, dynamic and multilayered. In education, for instance, as Sawyer (2004) noted earlier, lessons cannot be delivered according to an inflexible plan; the teacher has to improvise and adapt the pace and content of material to the needs, mood and circumstance of the class and its members. A doctor who simply gives out a painkiller without investigating what the pain may indicate is not doing her job or meeting her professional obligation. In social work, the practitioner needs to 'understand and extend the way people construct and interpret their effective world, and these constructions and interpretations are always unique' (English 1986: 105). In fact, English (1986) argues that social workers have to use their own creativity to build up their own picture of the client's world, including making imaginative connections between broad culture and individual actions to develop insights into behaviour.

These services cannot be pre-programmed and manufactured. Their content, aims and process cannot be specified in precise detail, without undermining the service itself—these services are fundamentally constituted through the discretion of the staff involved and negotiation with the people with whom they are working (see also Needham in this edited collection, Chap. 19). The skills practitioners deploy to negotiate and meet needs and to provide services are difficult to specify and are liable to change and shift as culture, demography and individuals change. Particularly, in diverse modern societies, any intervention models that assume a fixed notion of human motivation or need are inherently problematic (Evans and Hardy 2010). Human services professionals—social workers, physicians, teachers, nurses and so on—have to use creativity, social intelligence and imagination in their work and these are characteristics that resist proceduralization and pre-programming (Frey and Osborne 2013).

While recognizing that discretion can be a practical response to the problem of exercising control, there is also a political/ethical dimension in considering the extent of discretion. This relates to the perspective from which the nature of human services is viewed—as a set of procedural/mechanical or technical acts or as an organic process of human interaction and co-creation at the service level.

The procedural manufacturing/mechanical/technical view tends to privilege compliance with and conformity to a detailed plan and characterize discretion as the problem of constraining frontline practice: rules should be drafted as tightly as possible and then only at the edges can there be freedom, where it is not currently possible to specify any further. According to this point of view, it is important to deliver the product as specified and for those on the receiving end to receive, as far as possible, the same—regardless of who is involved in receiving or delivering this service.

An alternative viewpoint is that discretion is not what is (reluctantly) left out, the residual freedom in the system. Rather, it is recognition of the positive role of creativity to make services delivered by different people work for the different people who receive them. This is seeing public services not as mass-produced but as co-created, reflecting the need to tailor and adapt what is given by policymakers to the circumstances of the people who need or want this help (see Wolfson in this edited collection, Chap. 10, and Needham, Chap. 19).

We can also see different emphases in thinking about justice at play within these different approaches to welfare services and the role of discretion: on the one hand, justice as uniformity (equal treatment means the same treatment); and, on the other, a focus on calibrating justice to the situation—treating similar cases in a similar way, but, where there are differences, recognizing this and treating difference differently.

Equal treatment, on the face of it, seems perfectly just, but scratches the surface of the idea, and problems emerge. People have different needs. Treating everyone equally fails to recognize these differences and any equal treatment risks preferring some people's needs to others. Similarly, persons with different needs will experience equal help very differently. For instance, tax breaks on health insurance will benefit someone who can afford the premiums, but for another person, who cannot afford premiums, they will be of no help at all. The problem with equal treatment is that it fails to recognize diverse needs and different resources. This is a long-standing problem which goes back millennia and was captured in Aristotle's formulation of the idea of formal justice—that justice is not just treating things similarly; it is treating similar things in the same way and different things differently (1976). Practically, this is recognized in administrative law, in the principle that a policy should never be applied so rigidly that discretion was fettered—the general rules of policy should not constrain flexibility (Government Legal Department 2016).

24.8 Conclusion

Discretion in welfare services tends to be seen through a narrowly legalistic lens as a problem (see discussions in Chaps. 9 and 16 of this edited collection). This negative view of discretion is often buttressed by an emphasis on services as predetermined products manufactured in the process of policy implementation. However, engaging with discretion as a creative process challenges the taken-for-granted nature of these views. Considered discretion, through the lens of creativity, shows us how it provides the space to bring services to life and helps us imagine the relationship between practitioners, people who use services and policymakers in a different way. In identifying creativity as an important, but often underrated, dimension of discretion, I do not want to claim that it is the essential or most important aspect of discretion. There are some situations in which it is appropriate for creativity to be regarded in the foreground of discretion, but there are also others in which it is not. The situation where, I have argued, creativity plays a central role is in the provision of 'human services'. Here creativity is an essential dimension, humanizing policy and making services real and more responsive. Recognizing its creative dimension directs our attention to discretion as a positive attribute of frontline practice, translating policies into services.

References

Arendt, H. (2006). *Eichmann in Jerusalem: A report on the banality of evil.* London: Penguin.

Aristotle. (1976). *Ethics* (J. Thomson, Trans.). London: Penguin Books.

Aristotle. (undated). *Poetics.* Public Domain Book: Kindle.

Banaji, S. & Burn, A. with Buckingham, D. (2010). *The rhetorics of creativity: A literature review* (2nd ed.). Newcastle: Creativity, Culture and Education.

Boden, M. (1994). What is creativity? In M. Boden (Ed.), *Dimensions of creativity* (pp. 75–117). Boston: MIT Press.

Boden, M. (1995). Creativity and unpredictability. *Stanford Electronic Humanities Review*, 4, 2. Retrieved from https://web.stanford.edu/group/SHR/4-2/text/boden.html.

Carey, M. (2003). Anatomy of a care manager. *Work, Employment and Society*, 17, 121–135.

Cave, T. (2016). *Thinking with literature: Towards a cognitive criticism.* Oxford: Oxford University Press.

Craft, A. (2000). *Creativity across the primary curriculum.* London: Routledge.

Darzi. (2008). *High quality care for all—NHS next stage review final report.* Retrieved from https://www.gov.uk/government/publications/high-quality-care-for-all-nhs-next-stage-review-final-report.

Davis, K. (1971). *Discretionary justice: A preliminary inquiry.* Urbana, IL: University of Illinois Press.

Dworkin, R. (1978). *Taking rights seriously.* London: Duckworth.

Eliot, G. (undated). Middlemarch. *George Eliot complete works.* Minerva Classics: Kindle.

Elmore, R. (1979). Backward mapping: Implementation research and policy decisions. *Political Science Quarterly*, 94, 601–616.

English, H. (1986). *Social work as art: Making sense for good practice.* London: Harper Collins.

Evans, T. (2016). Street-level bureaucracy, management and the corrupted world of service. *European Journal of Social Work*, 19, 602–615.

Evans, T. & Hardy, M. (2010). *Evidence and knowledge for practice.* Cambridge: Polity Press.

Evans, T. & Hardy, M. (2017). The ethics of practical reasoning: Exploring the terrain. *European Journal of Social Work.* Retrieved from http://www.tandfonline.com/doi/abs/10.1080/13691457.2016.1278524.

Francis, R. (2013). *Mid Staffordshire NHS Foundation Trust public inquiry*. Retrieved from https://www.gov.uk/government/publications/report-of-the-mid-staffordshire-nhs-foundation-trust-public-inquiry.

Frey, C. & Osborne, M. (2013). *The future of employment: how susceptible are jobs to computerisation?* Oxford: Oxford Martin Programme. Retrieved from http://www.oxfordmartin.ox.ac.uk/downloads/academic/The_Future_of_Employment.pdf.

Friedrich, Carl J. (1940). Public policy and the nature of administrative responsibility. *Public Policy*, 1, 1–20.

Gibson, J. (1986). *The ecological approach to visual perception*. Hillsdale, NJ: Erlbaum, Lawrence & Associates.

Glennerster, H., Korman, N. & Marslen-Wilson, F. (1983). *Planning for priority groups*. Oxford: Martin Robertson.

Goffman, E. (1990). *The presentation of self in everyday life*. Harmondsworth: Penguin.

Gollins, T., Fox A., Walker B., Romeo L., Thomas J. & Woodham, G. (2016). *Developing a well-being and strengths-based approach to social work practice: Changing culture*. England: Think Local Act Personal.

Hacking, I. (1986). Making up people. In T. Heller, M. Sosna & D. Wellbery (Eds), *Reconstructing individualism: Autonomy, individuality, and the self in Western thought* (pp. 222–236). Stanford: Stanford University Press.

Hupe, P.L. (2017). Implementation and the policy process. In W.R. Thompson, R. Dalton, N. Kauppi, F. Laursen, K. Lippert-Rasmussen, B.G. Peters, K. Rasler, and L. Breshear Tiede (Eds), *Oxford research encyclopaedia of politics*. Oxford: Oxford University Press. Retrieved from https://doi.org/10.1093/acrefore/9780190228637.013.125.

Negus, K. & Pickering, M. (2004). *Creativity, communication and cultural value*. London: Sage.

Osborne, S., Radnor, Z. & Nasi, G. (2012). A new theory for public service management? *American Review of Public Administration*, 43, 135–158.

Proust, M. (2000). *In search of lost time VI: Time regained* (Mayor & Kilmartin, Trans.). London: Vintage.

Royal Shakespeare Company. (2001). *King John: Programme*. Stratford: RSC.

Royal Shakespeare Company. (2012). *King John: Programme*. Stratford: RSC.

Sawyer, R.K. (2004). Creative teaching: Collaborative discussion as disciplined improvisation. *Educational Researcher*, 33, 12–20.

Shakespeare Birthplace Trust. (undated). Into the 18th century: Shakespeare in performance. Retrieved from https://www.shakespeare.org.uk/explore-shakespeare/blogs/18th-century-shakespeare-performance/.

Stanislavski, C. (2003). *Building a character*. New York: Routledge.

Titmuss, R. (1971). Welfare "rights", law and discretion. *The Political Quarterly*, 42 (2), 113–132.

The Government Legal Department. (2016). *Judge over your shoulder*. Retrieved from https://www.gov.uk/government/publications/judge-over-your-shoulder.

Zins, C. (2001). Defining human services. *The Journal of Sociology & Social Welfare*, 28(1), Article 2. Retrieved from https://scholarworks.wmich.edu/jssw/vol28/iss1/2.

CHAPTER 25

Discretion as Ethical Practice

Gideon Calder

25.1 Introduction

The moral philosopher Bernard Williams once wrote of reaching the realization, after a glass of bourbon, that his work 'consisted largely of reminding moral philosophers of truths about human life which are very well known to virtually all adult human beings except moral philosophers' (Williams 2005: 52). Looking at how discretion is treated in the 'official channels' of ethics gives what seems a good example of what he was getting at. In everyday terms, discretion might seem *obviously* tied up with ethics and vice versa. Ethics has to do with standards of conduct and discretion with when it is legitimate to act outside or irrespective of such standards. So it might seem that to take up a position on one is necessarily to have some kind of stance on the other.

Strikingly, though, questions of discretion as such—what it is and when it is appropriate—get little attention in the classics of ethical theory, right down from Aristotle through Kant to modern utilitarianism. At least, this specific term does not intrude in discussions of practical reason, where we might most expect it. Nor do they feature explicitly in guidelines on professional ethics—in the 'real-world' codes by which people whose job it is to make decisions affecting others are supposed to operate.[1] It is not that such codes or those canonical texts have nothing to say about anything related to discretion or have no relevance to how we understand its nature, place and scope; or negotiate it through practical reason. On the contrary: they teem with points and implications inviting interpretation in light of just those factors. So while discretion is not analysed in its own right, it is implied, or invoked, in more distant or indirect ways. This makes its place in the architecture of ethics more obscure than it should

G. Calder (✉)
Social Sciences and Social Policy, Swansea University, Swansea, UK
e-mail: g.j.calder@swansea.ac.uk

T. Evans, P. Hupe (eds.), *Discretion and the Quest for Controlled Freedom*, https://doi.org/10.1007/978-3-030-19566-3_25

be. This itself reinforces the case for defending those lay assumptions just referred to and for regarding discretion as quite crucial, both in our framing of ethical values and in their application. Discretion needs attention in itself and setting in its rightful place.

This chapter offers such a case. I aim to do this not by re-theorizing ethics in some grand way or devising new guidelines for its deployment in this or that professional field or other context—but rather by showing how discretion both informs our understanding of ethical judgement in important respects and is an area in which any ethical practitioner will already have achieved a certain kind of competence. Doing this will also help in addressing how discretion should be situated, both in the wider scheme of ethics and in the institutions through which individual agents are held to ethical account. While points made may apply more widely, I am thinking chiefly about organizations based around dealing directly with individuals' well-being—the 'social professions', as they are sometimes called, including teaching, social work, counselling and work across sectors providing key public services such as housing, health and social care. This is not to imply that, somehow, the ethics/discretion relationship emerges in the same patterns across all such fields. However, rather than picking out particular professional contexts, it makes sense, in terms of the level at which the discussion rolls out, to keep the focus general. It is worth stressing too that in what follows, our main focus is on discretion as the exercise of discretionary judgement, rather than in the sense of withholding information.[2]

The chapter proceeds like this. Section 25.2 outlines a contextual approach to ethics as one dimension of the space in which we act (e.g. in professional life), suggesting that this offers a helpful line of approach when addressing discretion in particular. The following section looks at the equivocal relationship between ethics and discretion, by exploring how both its presence and its absence may seem *prima facie* problematic. In Section 25.4 I look at two distinct conceptions of ethical standards and show how each allows space for discretionary action. The following section explores the nature of that space—and Section 25.6, the nature of the work which goes on there. I suggest that Aristotle's notion of *phronesis* is a particularly helpful resource for understanding and evaluating that work. The overall case is that the role of discretion is important to *all* sensible understandings of the role of ethical standards in professional practice, that like other aspects of practice, discretion involves skills, but also that those skills are not perfectible. From an ethical perspective we should seek proficiency, in the work of discretion—but not perfection or expertise.

25.2 A Line of Approach

As with any discussion, there are various available directions from which we might approach the place of discretion in ethics. One would be to start from examples of ethical standards or rules; or accounts in normative ethics (Kantianism, utilitarianism, virtue ethics, etc.) and then explore how they may or may not leave room for this or that version or degree of legitimate discretion.

However, I will be arriving from a different, in some ways opposite, trajectory—starting from the front line of practice and invoking particular rules or perspectives in moral philosophy only when this helps shed light on a given issue or case. In so doing, it helps to declare an interest, reflected in the story from Williams, with which we began. I start out from the assumption that ethics involves our navigation and negotiation of a particular kind of space—both between subjects and between them and the rest of reality (which, for most purposes, means the circumstances in which they are acting). This 'in-between', as Hannah Arendt calls it, is difficult to map or measure, because of its qualities:

> [I] t is not tangible, since there are no tangible objects into which it could solidify; the process of acting and speaking can leave behind no such results and end products. But for all its intangibility, this in-between is no less real than the world of things we visibly have in common. We call this reality the 'web' of human relationships (Arendt 1958: 163).

Yet 'intangible' does not mean elusive or remote. For this 'web' is something we always inhabit and so already 'know' in the sense that Williams refers to. It is both something we are stuck with—we cannot somehow extricate ourselves from it and locate ourselves somewhere else—and something which we cannot help shaping, as agents, insofar as we act. It is, in part, a product of what we do:

> Action, [...] no matter what its specific content, always establishes relationships and therefore has an inherent tendency to force open all limitations and cut across all boundaries (Arendt 1958: 163; 170).

This view resonates strongly with a shift in the academic treatment of professional ethics, well charted in her recent work by Sarah Banks (see e.g., 2013, 2016). Across various strands of recent literature, Banks identifies a shift from 'professional ethics' to 'ethics in professional life'—meaning by this an expansion of parameters away from the analysis of dilemmas, codes and the application of principles, and towards a 'situated ethics [...] that places dilemmas and decision in a broader social, political and cultural context and sees responsibility in a wider, more relational sense, beyond the isolated individual decision-maker' (Banks 2016: 36). Thus too heavy or exclusive a focus on principles and abstract puzzles and thought experiments—so often a staple of professional ethics teaching—diverts us from what it is to encounter ethical demands amid the messier 'real-world' dynamics of everyday practice (Calder 2007b, 2015).

For reasons we will hear more about as the chapter moves on, this view of the dynamics between relationships and action proves especially illuminating when we consider discretion. Discretion is both a feature of the space in which we 'do' ethics and something we deploy in trying to navigate that space—and to some degree altering it, by 'forcing open limitations'. The relationship between ethics and discretion is not incidental, we might say, but one way of understanding the opportunities, tensions and dilemmas with which we are confronted in our actions towards others—saliently so in roles in the social professions.

25.3 Discretion's Ethical Equivocality

Even if we have an everyday sense that discretion and ethics seem mutually tied up, their relationship is not clear-cut. So when we hear that someone in a position of power has 'used her discretion', the news may be received with relief or alarm, depending on the orientation of the hearer. For the sake of drawing a stark contrast, the use of discretion may appear as the following:

(a) The mark of an advanced, confident, skilled and authoritative decision-maker.
(b) A sign of inconsistency, ignorance, weakness of will or double standards.

Under (a), discretion is compatible with ethical conduct—and, indeed, is an indicator of a special kind of proficiency in ethical decision-making. For (b), discretion runs counter to ethics: perhaps one necessarily disrupts the other, or (more strongly) the two are altogether incompatible. Adherents to (a) may tend towards an agent-centred view of ethics—one for which matters of character and reflection are key to our weighing of judgements and actions. From this point of view, what we seek are skilled ethical decision-makers, rather than followers of rules as such. Ethical behaviour may be seen in terms of attributes accrued through practice, so that the capacity to exercise due discretion is something we attain through getting better at the kind of work which ethics requires of us. Those drawn towards (b) are likely to see ethics in terms of categorical rules—which, if conceived aright, will by definition apply evenly across all like cases. Viewed this way, ethics is underwritten by procedural frameworks that must transcend the particular, apply universally and comprehensively; and so bestow consistency. For the strongest version of this view, the exercise of any substantial degree of discretion is by its nature unwarrantedly transgressive—and hence, an 'ethics of discretion' is a contradiction in terms.

This basic contrast between ordinary 'takes' on the ethics/discretion relation shows, at least, that any deeper exploration builds on uneven and contested ground. Discretion can be plausibly couched either as a necessary part of a full and consistent conception of the ethical or as something which defeats it. The implications of (a) and (b) can be unpacked (and thus critiqued or reinforced) via quick negative caricatures. Depending on the case, the agents in question could be professionals or parents, CEOs or frontline workers. The term 'standards' here might, if this is helpful, also be read as 'rules' (although for reasons which we will arrive at shortly, 'standards' is a more inclusive term). Figure 25.1 shows some possibilities.

The 'unbending' characters in the left-hand column show the ethical worth of discretion: of the freedom to exercise judgement, versatility, taking each

The unbending *Reinforcing (a), critiquing (b)*	**The loose cannon** *Reinforcing (b), critiquing (a)*
The mechanically standard-observant The agent so rigid in their application of the (generally accepted) standards that they stick to them even when anyone reasonable would make an exception, or bend them, in this case.	*The randomly maverick* The agent so inconsistent and erratic in their handling of each case that there is no discernible pattern or rationale behind their actions.
The insincerely compliant The agent who fully conforms to standards but without believing them, or without any genuine motivation to act ethically.	*The consciously biased* The agent who consciously bends or suspends the usual standards for the benefit of preferred groups but not others, without clear ethical grounds.
The uncomprehendingly compliant The agent who fully conforms to standards but without really understanding their implications, or why they have been adopted.	*The unconsciously biased* The agent who unconsciously bends or suspends the usual standards for the benefit of preferred groups but not others, while believing themselves to be 'doing the right thing'.

Fig. 25.1 Discretion and standards: Six kinds of agents

case on its merits and a confidence in one's own interpretation of the spirit of rules when the letter of them seems not to apply. Their 'loose' counterparts in the right-hand column show ethical dividends deriving from the removal of discretion: consistency, humility, the suspension of one's own prejudices and the avoidance of discrimination. Of course, such cartoon examples may be regarded as unhelpful just to the extent that they are cartoons. However, to the extent that each of these six figures occupies a problematic position, totting up the negatives in each column is instructive about why discretion can seem both required by, and disruptive of, ethical practice. As so often with cartoon oppositions, the apparent contradictions between the unbending and the loose cannons are less stable than they seem—and there is value in reflecting on why this is.

25.4 Two Conceptions of Ethical Standards

For its defenders—and those for whom the 'unbending' figures above are *especially* egregious—exercising discretion implies *both* that one is fluent in the language of standards *and* that one has the moral confidence to do what is not anticipated by those standards. It is the mark of suppleness and deliberation, rather than a lapse or a lack of grip. Like its opposite, this view of discretion hinges importantly on what counts as a standard in the first place.

Here are two alternative conceptions of 'standards'. In the discussion so far, we may have been playing on a possible slippage between the two. In part, they reflect the ambiguity of the word 'norm', which may mean either 'principle' or 'convention'.

Conception (1): Standards as Rules

If we understand standards in terms of formal or a priori rules, principles or codes of practice, then to be legitimate, discretion will consist in operating in the space between those norms or their creative interpretation or adaptation, rather than departing from them. The next questions are: how big is that space? How open for adaptation can a rule be, and still be a rule? For those with strong 'incompatibilist' intuitions, the answers here will be 'negligible' and 'not at all'. Rules, to *be* rules, must be both strictly universal and reach all the way down. This view, however, has far fewer friends in philosophy than adherents might expect. Everywhere we think we find it—for example, in Kant's discussion of whether it is permissible to lie to a murderer at the door, enquiring as to whether his intended victim is at home, where Kant's own ostensible answer is famously 'no' (Kant 1949: 427)—we find that the sharpest sympathetic treatments of such positions steer them away from the calamitous implication that rules such as a prohibition on lying are so sacred that they render us powerless to act in the face of evil (see e.g. Korsgaard 1986; Wood 2011). On such views, the mechanically standard-observant figure really is a caricature: a misreader of the nature of rules and their force.

Indeed in the most developed expositions of the rule-based conception of ethics, the agent's room for manoeuvre is crucial, rather than denied. From this point of view, mere mechanical deployment of the rules or channelling them into one's actions without reflection or sincerity—so that 'just following orders' becomes the paradigm case of ethical behaviour—is itself a kind of corruption of them. To put it another way, discretion may be *required* by the fact that rules do not interpret or apply themselves and always admit exceptions. They are not, as Onora O'Neill puts it, algorithmic: they leave room for judgement and deliberation (O'Neill 1988: 55–61). O'Neill writes this as a defender of rule-based ethics. There is no direct line between an appeal to rules as the basis for ethics and caricatures of the 'unbending', because no coherent defender of the value of rules could argue that they somehow enact themselves or adapt themselves seamlessly to the contours of every context in which they are applied. Similarly, Eileen Gambrill has made the case that codes of ethics require professionals (she refers specifically to social workers) to exercise discretion for the benefit of service users (Gambrill 2010: 35–7). The question at stake is: to what extent does a justified set of rules allow for different kinds of interpretation in different circumstances? Given that those—like O'Neill—keenest to defend a rule-based conception of ethics preserve a key role for judgement, there seems no entailment that their conception offers any solace to our 'unbending' figures. In principle, their exercising discretion may make them more authentic followers of rules, truer to their spirit.

Conception (2): Standards as Conventions

If we understand standards in terms of established or a posteriori patterns of expected behaviour ('the way we do things'), then discretion consists in a reinterpretation or amendment of such conventions: not a wholesale overhaul, but an incremental reshaping. We find the strongest exponents of this view among those—like the neo-pragmatist Richard Rorty—who cheerfully embrace the contingency of our language of moral deliberation (Rorty 1989; cf. Calder 2003). Because standards are a product of time and chance, not fixed but evolving, they are already fluid and adaptive and indeed need to be redescribed in fresh contexts in order to be kept vibrant—and for what the earlier pragmatist John Dewey (1991: 184) called the 'crust of conventionalized and routine consciousness' to be broken. From this point of view, what we call discretion is an inevitable and vital part of this creative process. Whether or not discretion is acceptable in any given context is ultimately a matter of whether an action can be accommodated within—or at least tacked onto—the existing moral self-identity of the institution in question. Different 'takes' on acceptable behaviour are tried out in the flux of practice; some 'stick' and become part of convention. However, this is only provisional: conventions should never imprison practice, or ossify.

Standards on these terms, being open to revision, might seem definitively more elastic, so more hospitable than their rule-based counterpart to a positive affirmation of the ethical contribution which discretion might make. This being so, we should tread carefully here. Conventions, being grounded in what counts as acceptable 'around here' or at this particular historical juncture, may wield more force than any rule (see Calder 2007a, Chap. 3). Usually, the cultural dynamics of a workplace will carry more influence on the actions of practitioners than the rulebook ever could, by itself. Under some such cultures, discretion will be especially unlikely to wield the kind of creative, constructive input suggested in the more optimistic depictions. Cultures can close down debate and in ways which—precisely because their conventions are informal—can be hard to specify, appeal to or question. What counts as creative, or constructive, may seem arbitrary in the absence of any independent or a priori ethical parameter. When institutions fail most badly in ethical terms, we are unsurprised to find that subsequent enquiries find that the 'crust of convention' has been unbroken: that patterns of bad practice have become entirely normal. For example, the Francis Report into sustained failures at Mid-Staffordshire National Health Services (NHS) Trust in the UK between 2005 and 2009 described an institution in the grip of a negative culture, over-tolerant of poor standards, neglectful of patients' needs and inattentive to the raising of concerns about malpractice (Francis *et al.* 2013). Here is a case where discretion—working outside of locally established standards—would have been especially valuable, but was rendered especially unlikely by the cultural habits of the organization. The mere fact that conventions are not by definition fixed or rigid does not make them easy to budge or evade.

The point of comparing (1) and (2) is to show that standards may be conceived in different ways, and that there is no simple hierarchy in terms of their relative receptiveness or resistance to an ethical case for the use of discretion. A tenable account of rules will allow for their reflexive interpretation and application by agents. A tenable account of conventions will acknowledge the value of allowing for—indeed encouraging—well-justified departures from the norm at the level of practice. What emerges from either conception is the importance of 'give and take' between standards and frontline practice: wriggle room in which standards might be challenged, reinterpreted or adapted in light of pressing situational factors. Both allow for, and arguably require, the space for (to use Arendt's phrasing) action to force open the boundaries imposed by the standards informing the web of human relationships.

25.5 The Space for Discretion

The nature of that space is important. Here again, the contrast between conceptions (1) and (2) is instructive about the relationship of ethical standards and discretion.

Under (1), the space in which we might legitimately act outside of standards is synchronic: it consists in the gaps in between a priori (and so fixed) parameters or side constraints. Being bound by more than one such rule, we judge and act in the space afforded by the way they relate to each other. Sometimes this runs more fluently than others; sometimes rules sync readily with each other or apply to a context in, for the agent, a relatively smooth and seamless way. At other times, there will be tensions between them. Because rules do not tell us exactly what to do, and because they do not themselves resolve their mutually conflicting messages when these arise, these tensions may be experienced the more sharply the more one is in tune with the rules at stake—the more one has internalized them.

Under (2), the space in which discretion does its work is diachronic: it consists in the relationship between established conventions and what is permissible in light of those precedents. On these terms, discretion again requires fluency in the rules—again, perhaps optimally their internalization (though on this, more shortly). However, it operates not in the gaps in between multiple ethical rules taken as ultimately governing practice, but the gaps in between rules in general and the context in which one finds oneself. It requires, specifically, a kind of mediation between the general and the particular: between rules of thumb and the specific case.

Again, however, just as with our earlier columns of caricatures, the value of the opposition between conceptions (1) and (2) lies partly in its highlighting of its own limitations. My point here is not that there is a false dichotomy here between two ways of thinking of standards—or that the task of discretion emerges in distinct ways, in connection with each. Rather, it is that arguably, the negotiation of discretion—being 'good' at it—requires a similar kind of disposition either way. The space of discretion is underdetermined by standards: it is a place of uncertainty, slippage and imprecision. If it were certain, fixed and precise, then it would already have been accounted for by the general standards by which practitioners are expected to operate. Rather than the work of discretion being cut out in somehow fundamentally different ways, according to how one conceives of ethical standards, it requires similar skills and orientation and similar kinds of practical wisdom, under both conceptions (1) and (2).

Before saying more about those skills, it is worth pausing to take stock of where our discussion so far has taken us. Ethics involves the navigation and negotiation of the space between subjects, and between subjects and their circumstances. Discretion involves an understanding of standards and their limits. Both adhering mechanically to standards and disregarding them are readily portrayed as ethically problematic—and it is not obvious that any coherent approach to ethics could endorse either. While standards (and their limits) may be understood in different ways and while this makes for different framings of the space in which discretion is enacted, the work of discretion itself consists in mediation, which, arguably, requires similar kinds of practical reasoning. This last point needs further elaboration.

25.6 Discretion as Skilled Work

I am suggesting that we view discretion as an orientation required of professionals to meaningfully apply ethical standards in their work and thus as a kind of practice we might be competent in—and that the appeal to an orientation or set of skills is present in different understandings of the nature and scope of standards. Viewed this way, what makes someone (to return to our caricatures) mechanical, maverick, biased or—alternatively—a sensitive interpreter of the space for discretion, pertains to their attributes as an agent. In one sense this is stating the obvious: as we paint such figures as exaggerated personalities, it is their personality traits that attract our attention. There is a wider implication, however. Whether a judgement qualifies as (acceptable) discretion or as, for example, flawed, unfounded, oblivious, incoherent or whimsical depends definitively on how the agent stands in relation to the discretionary space in which they are operating.

And the western ethical canon has a good deal to tell us about this relationship. Indeed among the fullest and most resonant resources are found early in the story, in Aristotle's notion of *phronesis*—'practical wisdom'. This is a reliable capacity to make good judgement calls—to exercise what Aristotle calls 'sympathetic judgement' (Aristotle 1998: Book VI). As Alasdair MacIntyre (1998: 74) paints it, we might be more comfortable in calling this 'prudence' were the latter term not now largely associated with financial thrift:

> Prudence [...] is the virtue of practical intelligence, of knowing how to apply general principles in particular situations. It is not the ability to formulate principles intellectually, or to deduce what ought to be done. It is the ability to act so that principle will take a concrete form.

Phronesis is embodied in 'practical knowledge of what criteria are relevant to this or that situation' (MacIntyre 2006: 4). It is practical knowledge, consisting in a certain kind of skill in mediating between the general and the particular. This is the space of discretion. We find *phronesis* (or prudence) where we find a practitioner skilled in negotiating the relationship between, for example, a general standard and a particular context—the facility that 'discriminates what is equitable and does so correctly' (Aristotle 1998: 152). This means sensitivity, a sense of relevance and 'fit'—summed up by Aristotle's reference to the flexible ruler used by builders on Lesbos: 'the rule adapts itself to the shape of the stone and is not rigid, as so too the decree is adapted to the facts' (1998: 133). The space of ethics does not adapt to a straight ruler, or a fixed prescription. It is uneven—and to navigate it, we need to adapt our means of measurement. So we reach instead for the tailor's tape measure. As Joseph Dunne puts it: 'In every fresh actuation [of general knowledge] there is an element of creative insight through which it makes itself equal to the demands of a new situation' (Dunne 2011: 18). It is in such moments that the work of discretion gets done.

Accepting this prompts further questions. What kind of work is this, how does it typically get done and what are the marks of a skilled practitioner? It is worth giving our remaining space to a brief consideration of each of these questions.

What Kind of Work Is This?

Consisting as it does in adaptation to the situation, discretion work will require different kinds of capacity: assessment of the terrain and of the nature of the issues, sensitivity in engaging with others, care, courage, a sure sense of purpose, an eye for the correct course of action and confidence in justifying the course taken. Banks (2013, 2016) has developed a general account of 'ethics work', geared towards the context of the social professions. Like the list just given, it covers a range of different attributes. To them she adds the need for what she calls 'role work', defined as 'playing a role in relation to others (advocate, carer, critic); taking a position (partial/impartial; close/distant); negotiating roles; responding to role expectations' (Banks 2016: 37). A good 'role worker' thus judges each of these things in a balanced, reflexive and appropriate way. What does this look like? Well, one way of answering this is to consider why each of our caricatures earlier on seemed problematic. Each picked out a flaw and made a one-dimensional figure of it. Each of those figures embodies—amongst other things—a lapse in their sense of role: a poor situation of themselves with regard to the specifics of the terrain, the others involved, their professional responsibilities and the overall standards at stake. However, the ethical weight of roles sits alongside, and is qualified by, those other factors crucial to ethics work. The mechanical rule-follower is not licensed as such by their role, and indeed shows the limits of any one-dimensional understanding of the ethical basis of work. 'Role work' in Banks's sense is thus important in understanding discretion both because it reflects the orientation of the practitioner to the space in which they act and because its limitations show the complexity of the space in which discretion is exercised.

How Does It Happen in Practice?

Other chapters in this edited collection have far more to say on this question than can be done justice to here. And to an extent, it is artificial to make ethics a special case. It is unlikely that the work of discretion in ethical terms takes place in ways significantly different from the other angles from which it might be understood, or involves separate challenges. *Inter alia*, the background against which discretion plays out will be defined by the contours of the law (Chap. 9), the economy (Chap. 10), policy (Chaps. 6 and 16), bureaucracy (Chap. 15) and particular professional purposes and identities (Chap. 23). Ethics stands in complex relations with each of these—and many of the concerns raised by the nature, scope and limits of discretion across those spheres have an ethical quality to them. For example, the conflicting pressures with which street-level bureaucrats must cope (Chap. 11; see also Chap. 17) have special relevance when it comes to ethics—because coping itself is a means by which we mediate between context and standards. The terrain of ethics and discretion may appear differently when looked at from the point of view of standards themselves and goals such as the pursuit of social justice compared to the point of view of the deliberating agent. Thus the debate about universalism versus means testing in social security (see Chap. 6, particularly the discussion of Rothstein and Titmuss) gives one way of weighing this up. However, one could simultaneously hold a universalist position on the provision of child benefit while also seeking to preserve and validate the role of discretion in the handling of particular parents by workers for social security agencies—just because decisions on the distribution of resources form only one aspect of the responsiveness to individuals' circumstances required for judicious execution of that role. The need for *phronesis* is invoked regardless of whether the overall parameters in which one works and the degree to which they are themselves ultimately justifiable in ethical terms. Thus bureaucratic settings are a key, inevitable embodiment of the way 'standards' are shaped and constrained in practice. Such settings may facilitate discretion, or thwart it. To assume that somehow discretion would be freer or truer without such constraints, however, is to misread what the ethics of discretion involves and the kind of space it occupies. That is precisely, between the general and the particular; between overarching standards and the specific situation or case. 'The light dove', as Kant famously wrote, 'in free flight cutting through the air the resistance of which it feels, could get the idea that it could do even better in airless space' (Kant 1999: 129). The administration of standards is part of what makes the ethical challenges of discretion what they are.

Who Is Our Skilled Practitioner?

One version of the expert decision-maker, familiar from Dreyfus and Dreyfus (1986—covered critically in Chap. 22 of this edited collection and in Calder 2014 and 2015), has them as so immersed in skilful performance that they are untroubled by problems or dilemmas. This finds an echo in Mintzberg's (1979) stress on the importance of internalized rules for professional practice; see also this edited collection, Chaps. 12, 15 and 23. We might imagine that the expert navigator of the space of discretion is one for whom it does not pose challenges at all or interrupt the confident rhythm of their ongoing work. This, though, seems a mistake. In ethical terms, there are serious risks in any assumption that the navigation of that space gets easier to the point where, like driving a car, it comes naturally. On Aristotelian terms, practice in the work of discretion does not diminish the extent to which it feels like work. The space in between standards and situations does not dissolve away and neither does the need to travel, in mediating between the two. What will accrue over time in the skilled proponent of *phronesis* will be factors such as their perception of the space; their sense of their own role in relation to it; their capacity to relate to others involved in that space and affected by any emerging judgement or action; their capacity to justify and communicate the terms on which the judgement is made. We do not arrive in any role already equipped with the fullest extent of these skills. There is a sense, however, in which nobody becomes 'expert' at this work. On the Dreyfus understanding of the steps from 'novicehood' to 'expertise', skilled ethics work seems epitomized by 'proficiency'—the stage prior to the achievement of 'expertise'. Here, practice combines a considerable stock of sedimented 'know-how' with the careful, conscious, stepping back and analysing of what to do (Dreyfus and Dreyfus 1986: 27–30). The space of discretion is by its nature uncertain, imprecise and messy. While we may get better at the ethics of discretion, we do not perfect it.

25.7 Conclusion

This chapter has offered an account of discretion's role in ethics where it is not only compatible with the achievement of ethical standards, but required by them—and required however we understand the nature of ethical rules. The particular kinds of practical wisdom involved in negotiating the challenges of discretion will develop as a role unfolds—but do not stop being challenging. The degree to which they are successfully negotiated will depend importantly on the environment in which one works—or in Arendt's more specific terms, the nature of the space in which one acts. Other chapters in this edited collection have a great deal to say about such environments and (of particular importance) when and why they may facilitate discretionary judgement and action or thwart them. My case here has been that discretion is at the core of good professional practice rather than peripheral and is enacted through practice rather than learned abstractly via a manual or textbook. If this seems convincing so far, an obvious next step would be to explore how ethics informs frontline practice in the social professions, what makes for 'good' discretionary practice and how it compares from setting to setting.

Acknowledgements I am grateful for their input to all present at a meeting held for contributors to this volume at All Souls College, Oxford in September 2017—and particularly to Mark Hardy, as respondent to my own presentation. However, the faults here are all my own work.

Notes

1. The (US) National Association of Social Workers Code of Ethics does state: 'Social workers should be alert to and avoid conflicts of interest that interfere with the exercise of professional discretion and impartial judgment' (NASW 2017: 10). That is the only mention: neither discretion itself, nor its relation to impartial judgement or the code in general is unpacked further.
2. Discretion in the sense of 'being discreet' is less distinctive as an ethical issue, falling closer to 'regulation' discussions in normative and applied ethics on whether and when full disclosure is required, when lying is permissible and so on. There are oft-cited discussions in Kant (1949, 2012) and Mill (1861, Chap. 2) on this, and across a wide range of professional ethics literature. So my assumption here is that it is less demanding of treatment in its own right. There are, though, clear overlaps between those two senses of discretion—and part of what Kant and Mill are concerned with in their own discussions might indeed be characterized in terms of the kinds of 'discretionary judgement' dwelled on here.

References

Arendt, H. (1958). *The human condition*. Chicago: University of Chicago Press.

Aristotle. (1998). *The Nichomachean ethics* (D. Ross, Trans.). Oxford: Oxford University Press.

Banks, S. (2013). Negotiating personal engagement and professional accountability: Professional wisdom and ethics work, *European Journal of Social Work*, 16(5), 587–604.
Banks, S. (2016). Everyday ethics in professional life: Social work as ethics work. *Ethics and Social Welfare*, 10(1), 35–52. https://doi.org/10.1080/17496535.2015.1126623.
Calder, G. (2003). *Rorty and redescription*. London: Weidenfeld and Nicholson.
Calder, G. (2007a). *Rorty's politics of redescription*. Cardiff: University of Wales Press.
Calder, G. (2007b). Theory, practice and 'teaching' professional ethics. In S. R. Smith (Ed.), *Applying theory to policy and practice* (pp. 87–102). Aldershot: Ashgate.
Calder, G. (2014). Values-based practice, competence and expertise. In M. Loughlin (Ed.), *Debates in values-based practice: Arguments for and against* (pp. 108–120). Cambridge: Cambridge University Press.
Calder, G. (2015). Competence, ethical practice and professional ethics teaching. *Ethics and Social Welfare*, 9(3), 297–311. https://doi.org/10.1080/17496535.2015.1031263.
Dewey, J. (1991–orig. 1927). *The public and its problems*. Athens, OH: Swallow Press.
Dreyfus, H.L. & Dreyfus, S.E. (1986). *Mind over machine: The power of human intuition and expertise in the era of the computer*. New York: The Free Press.
Dunne, J. (2011). 'Professional wisdom' in 'practice'. In L. Bondi, D. Carr, C. Clark & C. Clegg (Eds), *Towards professional wisdom: Practical deliberation in the people professions* (pp. 13–26). Farnham: Ashgate.
Francis, R. *et al.* (2013). *Report of the mid Staffordshire NHS Foundation Trust public inquiry February 2013: Executive summary*. London: The Stationery Office. Retrieved September 10, 2017, from http://www.midstaffspublicinquiry.com/report.
Gambrill, E. (2010). Evidence-based practice and the ethics of discretion. *Journal of Social Work*, 11(1), 26–48. https://doi.org/10.1177/1468017310381306.
Kant, I. (1949–orig. 1797). On a supposed right to lie from altruistic motives. In L.W. Beck (Ed.) *Immanuel Kant: Critique of practical reason and other writings in moral philosophy* (pp. 346–50). Chicago: University of Chicago Press.
Kant, I. (1999–orig. 1781). *Critique of pure reason* (P. Guyer, Trans.). Cambridge: Cambridge University Press.
Kant, I. (2012–orig. 1785). *Groundwork of the metaphysics of morals* (M. Gregor & J. Timmermann, Eds). Cambridge: Cambridge University Press.
Korsgaard, C. (1986). The right to lie: Kant on dealing with evil. *Philosophy and Public Affairs*, 15(4), 325–349.
MacIntyre, A. (1998). *A short history of ethics* (2nd ed.). London: Routledge.
MacIntyre, A. (2006) Aristotle against some renaissance Aristotelians. In his *Ethics and Politics: Selected Essays, Volume 2*. Cambridge: Cambridge University Press.
Mill, J.S. (1962–orig. 1861). Utilitarianism. In M. Warnock (Ed.), *Utilitarianism*. London and Glasgow: Collins.
Mintzberg, H. (1979). *The structuring of organizations: A synthesis of the research*. Saddle River, NJ: Prentice Hall.
NASW (National Association of Social Workers). (2017). Code of ethics. Retrieved September 12, 2017, from https://www.socialworkers.org/About/Ethics/Code-of-Ethics.

O'Neill, O. (1988). Abstraction, idealization and ideology in ethics'. In J.D.G. Evans (Ed.), *Moral philosophy and contemporary problems* (pp. 55–69). Cambridge: Cambridge University Press.
Rorty, R. (1989). *Contingency, irony, and solidarity.* Cambridge: Cambridge University Press.
Williams, B. (2005). The liberalism of fear. In *In the beginning was the deed: Realism and moralism in political argument* (pp. 52–61). Princeton: Princeton University Press:
Wood, A.W. (2011). Kant and the right to lie. *Eidos* 15, 96–11.

CHAPTER 26

Controlled Freedom: Dealing with Discretion

Peter Hupe and Tony Evans

26.1 Introduction

Legislators and policymakers may recognize the limits of their control. They may also grant discretion as a useful strategy to avoid difficult decisions and to shift potential responsibility for the consequences of those decisions. In many cases political authorities and policy advisers may see discretion of street-level bureaucrats as a necessary evil. Until signals of failure, they remain indifferent to the way the latter exercise freedom. Whether deliberately, strategically or just 'turning a blind eye', these public actors grant a certain degree of freedom of judgement and even decision-making to others.

At the street level itself, too, the view on discretion can be complex and feelings about it ambivalent. The public servants working there may consider discretion as an inherent and necessary feature of their work. Some of them may cherish their freedom to make judgements, while others may practise 'self-binding' in order to make their freedom manageable for themselves. This being so, at the street level of government bureaucracy the discretion granted usually will be used in an accountable manner—even when on the spot supervision is absent or top-down control is flawed.

These are the general messages that can be drawn from this interdisciplinary edited collection. Of course, in an edited volume there will be a range of insights; in this chapter we will seek to draw them out. In the next section the rather pertinent consequences of the juridical view on discretion are explored.

P. Hupe (✉)
Public Governance Institute, Catholic University of Leuven, Leuven, Belgium
e-mail: pieter.hupe@kuleuven.be

T. Evans
Department of Social Work, Royal Holloway, University of London, Egham, UK
e-mail: Tony.Evans@rhul.ac.uk

T. Evans, P. Hupe (eds.), *Discretion and the Quest for Controlled Freedom*, https://doi.org/10.1007/978-3-030-19566-3_26

That view may limit an appropriate understanding and explanation of what happens in and around government, when discretion is exercised. Instead, a broader and more empirical view, circumscribed in the variety of insights gained in the chapters of this edited volume, may capture empirical reality more fully. In the final section, implications for the ways discretion is to be treated as an object of analysis are considered, before a conclusion is drawn.

26.2 The Juridical View and the Eichmann Paradox

Within the various academic literatures, perhaps the most influential approach to conceptualize 'discretion' has been drawn from law and jurisprudence. The legal approach is reviewed in Chap. 9 and as the contributions to this edited collection indicate, key elements of that juridical view have been adopted across a range of disciplines and scholarly themes. In many statements about discretion in the context of governance, discretion is seen as stemming from a legitimate source at the top of a hierarchy that is delegated down to a single spot at the bottom of that hierarchy; that is, in rule application at the street level.

Galligan (1990: 2), for instance, sees discretion 'as an express grant of power conferred on officials where determination of the standards according to which power is to be exercised is left largely to them'. The expanded role of the modern state has brought with it an increase in discretion as

> control over a wide range of matters is delegated to officials with varying degrees of guidance as to the policy goals to be achieved or the standards by which they are to be achieved.

In contrast, Davis sees discretion as a failure to control. Discretion is a problem. It occurs where the rules run out and leave room for movement:

> A public official has discretion where the effective limits on his power leave him free to make a choice among possible courses of action and inaction (Davis 1969: 2).

And when Dworkin (1977: 31) speaks of the 'hole in the donut', he points at discretionary authority as a freedom deliberately left to designated others—which is informed by the belt of rules around it. Those rules can range from formal regulation in some cases to broader norms of reasons and purpose, in others.

The various versions of the juridical view on discretion, as Mascini pointed out in Chap. 9, have important characteristics in common. First, discretion is based on rules; actually it is itself an element of a set of rules. Second, there is an extent of freedom but it is both connected to and limited by legitimate authority and formal rules as inherent to a hierarchical relationship. Third, the extent of granted freedom at the bottom of that hierarchy is a derivation from the legitimate power exercised from the top. As such, discretion is a circumscribed residual.

The juridical view of discretion begs the question whether discretion involves a confined set of situations where the rules have ended and individual judgement begins. Such an assumption is ingrained in the standard perspective on discretion so well captured in Davis' (1969: 4) definition mentioned above, stating that discretion occurs 'whenever the *effective limits* on the (public officer's) power *leave him free to make a choice* among possible courses of action and inaction' (italics added). This is a picture of discretion as a left-over.

The central focus of the juridical view is the rule set in which a degree of granted freedom is circumscribed. The view implies that the exercise of discretion begins where the formal rules end. This ending can take the form of a deliberate and explicit granting of freedom by the rule maker to a—not always specified—rule applier, to act in line with the rules in situations more or less described. It can also be a hiatus, where the rule maker just remains silent—sometimes deliberately, perhaps for reasons of blame avoidance (see Hood's Chap. 3) or perhaps deferring to expertise (see Evans' Chap. 23).

When discretion is apparent, indeed a message is conveyed to exercise judgement while having the freedom to decide what to do, but a problem of control is inherent here. As du Gay and Pedersen indicate in Chap. 15, even in the Weberian model of modern bureaucracy the public administrator explores a *range of considerations* when deciding about the appropriate way to use the freedom granted in the case at hand. Understanding the usage of that freedom implies an empirical question (Hawkins Ed. 1992). For the analysis of discretion this means that the primary focal point becomes practices, rather than a given set of rules.

Examining discretion empirically allows us to uncover additional dimensions beyond the application of the rules as formulated. A key dimension is the acknowledgement of a *plurality of action prescriptions.* At the level of individual actors, sets of rules are 'piling up'. It is, for instance, hardly ever one single public policy programme that has to be implemented or one law that needs to be enforced. Developing a typology of accountability regimes, Hupe and Hill (2007) point out that 'action prescriptions' come in various sorts. Apart from the formal rules stemming from a range of laws, public policies, regulations and management directives, there are also occupational norms (professional standards, protocols), as well as societal expectations (individual clients' preferences, media exposure, public opinion) to reckon with. In some cases, additionally, also market requisites have to be taken into account (Thomann, Hupe and Sager 2018).

The point is that every maker of a set of action prescriptions considers his or her set as the only one—and certainly the one to be given priority. However, viewed from a street-level perspective, actors are confronted with a multiplicity of action prescriptions and related accountabilities, as well as a multiplicity of mandates, which they have to manage. Paradoxically, in this way rule saturation itself can create discretion by requiring actors to choose between prescriptions (Evans and Harris 2004). Discretion inheres in the multi-dimensional nature of a public actor's role in a particular setting. In such a setting, actors perform a particular public task, balancing the various action prescriptions they have to deal with and assessing which ones need to prevail here and now.

The difference between these two grand contrasting views can be illustrated by the Eichmann case. In Chap. 3 Hood mentioned this case as, in a very dark way, exemplary. E.'s response during his trial ('I was only following orders') expresses the formal-juridical view on discretion in its most narrow sense. The rules as formulated were technical instructions and E. 'just' applied them that way. Discretion was *not* exercised, because the set of rules were detailed and could not be misunderstood. From an alternative view, however, one could say, even a 'servant of the state' has professional standards to reckon with and must acknowledge wider ethical considerations. E. could have made a different decision than he did, if he had judged it appropriate to make the weight of ethical and/or professional considerations preponderant. In other words: allowing 'bureaucratic' considerations (in the narrow sense) to prevail, E. *did* exercise discretion.

In this latter case E., stating 'I was only following orders', was choosing to follow a particular set of orders. In doing this he was culpable because he chose to ignore alternative sets of action prescriptions in his deliberation and to account for his act in a particular way. Recognizing this has consequences for the question whether 'discretion' only begins where 'rule application' ends. A broader view needs to be adopted, in which 'exercising discretion' refers to deliberation and behaviour. Discretion then is no longer conceptualized as a left-over—the 'hole in the donut'. Rather it is a site where rules intersect. It is granted—explicitly and implicitly—from a variety of sources, while only in understanding this range of granted *discretions* (plural) and how they are understood and balanced by actors, we can capture the conduct of discretionary actors overall. When using his discretion to stick with the rules as 'just' technical instructions, E. was responsible. Paradoxically, E. hiding behind 'the rules' suggested he did not make a decision, while he actually did.

26.3 Dealing with Discretion in Practice

In this section we want to consider some of the themes that have emerged as key insights from the social sciences perspectives on discretion put forward in this edited collection. We will do so, by structuring those insights under three different headings: the politics, the organization and the practices of discretion. We will close by considering how these themes interact.

Discretion and Politics

Politics is concerned with power. Discretion is a site of power to make decisions and to choose; as such it is often considered to be sought-after and desired by actors. Hood, however, points out that, while we often think discretion is sought, this is not always the case—because with power comes responsibility, blame and, potentially, criticism (Chap. 3). Political authorities choose to delegate power for a number of reasons and one reason that should not be discounted is that they want to protect themselves from having to decide on a contentious issue. Brodkin, in fact, sees political gridlock and failure amongst politicians to make decisions about social provision resulting in political decisions about who gets what, when and how, being taken by default by senior administrators (Chap. 5). In designing welfare services, these senior public administrators create structures which make these political decisions seemingly administrative ones, by providing an ordered framework for the delivery of services.

Such processes of sometimes shifting responsibility and being put in the position of making 'political' decisions by default are often observed at the level of senior civil servants working as policy advisers at a department. It is an open question how far considered 'political' decision-making is limited to this organizational stratum. Zimmerman (1971), in his classic ethnographic study of practicalities of rule use, points to the thoughtful way in which street-level actors bend and break rules to realize the purpose behind those rules: '[t]o coordinate applicants (who typically cooperated) and bring off the day's work with respect to the constraints of timing, pacing, and scheduling represented by the described "actual task structure"' (237). These front desk workers were not just coping with or automatically reacting to situations. They used discretion thoughtfully to adapt vague and general statements to deliver the services to citizens. They sought to do this in a way that was as ordered and fair as possible in the circumstances and in a way that met the (political) spirit, if not the letter, of the administrative rules involved.

Politics may not just be reflected in formal procedures and processes and the practices that bring them to life, but also in the promotion of certain ways of thinking and practising over others. Hardy, in Chap. 4, considers discretion from the perspective of the surveillance state. This is the idea that the state organizes and uses society—often through the exercise of discretion based on ideas of expert knowledge—to categorize, monitor and manage its members. Jobling, in Chap. 13, also considers the relationship between power and systems of expert knowledge. She examines different professional discourses within mental health and points out that some can be promoted in a way that pushes out other alternative forms of knowledge to highlight certain social and political perspectives reflecting political interests.

Discretion and Organization

Welfare is provided through organizations. These may be purely governmental, but they may also be for profit or not-for profit, while often they will have a hybrid character. We will return later to the question of how these different forms of agency raise issues of discretion. Here, we will focus on a characteristic that captures the general nature of these organizations: bureaucracy. It is a term that can be used abusively, meaning a slow-moving, red-tape-bound behemoth—especially in relation to the public sector—in contrast to 'business methods' and 'office organization' in the private sector (Williams 1976: 41). However, bureaucracy as a form of organization applies equally to corporate business and non-profit sectors. In this sense, it is used to characterize administrative systems peopled by career office holders, appointed on merit, whose work is governed by rules and managed within a hierarchical system of command and control (Beetham 1987). In Chap. 15, du Gay and Pedersen challenge the opposition which is often put up between bureaucracy and discretion. They point out that discretion is actually the life-blood of bureaucracies, allowing the exercise of an 'administrative statecraft' to maintain the bureaucracy's agility and prudent judgement in the application of general rules to particular circumstances by officers within a bureaucracy.

The ideas of administrative statecraft and of administrative politics offer insights into the complexity underlying many of the organizations within which discretion is exercised. Looking back to Hood's observation about the use of discretion and risk-shifting helps us understand how organizations may operate for a range of different motives and reasons that can create tensions and contradictions. Hill also outlines debates about the formal and informal role of discretion in the British welfare payments system over the past century (Chap. 6). Systems of welfare change for many reasons and the reasons are often in tension, while they may be more or less publicly acknowledged (Lewis and Glennerster 1996). The reforms of public funding for adult welfare in England in the 1990s, for instance, was driven by government concern about growing costs for providing care for an ageing population. Responsibility was transferred by central government from the welfare benefits system to local authorities and, within those, to professionals such as social workers. On one hand, this can be seen as a transfer of decision-making to local bodies with better knowledge of local needs and, within these, to experts who could bring dispassionate knowledge to bear on the allocation of services. From another perspective, it could be seen as a process of government shifting the risk of rationing a service from the centre to local government and, within public services, transferring this responsibility from politicians to experts. Organizationally, the situation was created of a mixture of logics: of rationing, of customizing services, of blame, of expert judgement and of bringing in a consumer voice. This produced a complex terrain within which policies were implemented and services delivered (Evans 2016). A similarly complex terrain is described by Needham in her analysis of the conflicting demands and layers of accountability faced by managers in contemporary social care services (Chap. 19).

Different forms of organization are likely to privilege different relations of control, freedom and judgement in the construction of discretion. This suggests that we need to consider discretion not just within the broad context of bureaucratic organizations, but also to look more closely at different forms of organization covered by the 'bureaucratic' rubric. Beetham (1987: 20) captures this sense of organizational diversity by examining the notion of bureaucratic effectiveness, pointing out that 'the criteria for effective operation will vary systematically with the purposes, technology and environment of that organization', concluding that 'We shall need to talk both of bureaucracy as such, and of particular types' (44).

Contributors to this book do this, for instance, in considering the increasingly important role of information technology. In Chap. 20 Zouridis, van Eck and Bovens underline the changing nature of welfare provision in the context of developments in information technology systems. Questions of discretion and information technology, they point out, not only relate to the extent of freedom within computerized procedures and systems. Increasingly, such questions also concern the role of judgement and the replacement of human judgement by algorithms. They see these developments particularly in certain forms of welfare organizations which they characterize in terms of Wilson's (1989) primarily rule-based 'production agencies'. Hill also notes that commentators have expressed concerns about a similar process in aspects of the welfare benefits payments systems in the UK (Chap. 6). Hardy points out that information systems are being introduced across a wide range of public services but that, while there is a lot of focus on their potential for good or ill, their actual impact is still unclear. Evans also points to the limitations of applying logic of information technology in human services organizations (Chap. 23). Wolfson, examining changing economic approaches to principal/agent relations and developments in situational contracting and Needham, looking at the cross-cutting responsibilities of managers in the personalization of public services, point to other directions of development in the relationship between discretion and information. They argue that it can support greater flexibility and agility in providing tailored services to people (respectively, Chaps. 10 and 19).

Discretion and Practice

The main focus of the contributions to this book has been on the practices of discretion: the freedom that actors have and how they use this; and the judgements they exercise. From the perspective of organizations, these questions tend to be answered in terms of roles and organizational rules. Oberfield considers the role of social norms that inform the exercise of discretion. In Chap. 12, he examines the extent to which discretionary practices are the result of socialization to the norms of the organization or whether they reflect patterns of distributions and attributes that actors bring in to the organization. Tummers and Bekkers identify another dynamic, which focuses on understanding discretion in terms of actors' responses to the psychological pressures of work, where actors feel alienated from policy goals (Chap. 11). The authors identify different strategies that actors adopt towards using rules—for instance, bending or breaking them—to help reduce psychological stress.

Wagenaar characterizes organizational rules as a scaffolding around the substance of practice, which gives form and regularity to the operation of the organization (Chap. 17). This practice reflects the collective patterns of behaviour built up within the organization and transformed in the process of use and contained within habits, norms and the material environment of the organizational culture. In Chap. 9 Mascini identifies the role of parallel decision systems within organizations. Looking at judicial decision-making, he points out that judgements often cannot be understood simply as a result of the application of formal legal rules. Rather, they draw on socio-psychological processes and heuristics, which run alongside and influence the understanding of the situation and the choice of legal approach to be taken. One way of looking at this is to see it as two discourses which run alongside each other.

Jobling describes a similar situation in mental health, where different professional discourses can operate and may be drawn on in different ways and, additionally, official credence may be given to one particular approach over another (Chap. 13). This brings to the fore the role of judgement both in understanding the use of discretion and also in its application and evaluation. Organizational rules are often the most immediate way to grasp the extent of discretion and what is understood as its legitimate use. However, as many contributors to this volume emphasize, these rules operate within the context of norms and draw on different forms of knowledge, which can work to clarify and specify the meaning of vague, general rules and give them vitality and resonance.

Discretion and Complexity

We cannot necessarily assume that formal rules and underlying norms sit comfortably with each other. They may; but they may work in different directions. Organizations change over time; underlying practices may not change at the same pace. Hupe and Hill set out the complexity of policy implementation by specifying the range and layers of organizations and actors involved in the policy process and the various forms of discretion they deploy (Chap. 16). Organizations are seldom monochrome, built on *terra nova*. They function while using given paths. They are the accretion of policies, cultures and roles. Organizations are more like a multi-coloured geological map of overlaid and exposed geological strata. It may also be that organizational rules project a picture of practice which presents it in a particular—legitimate—way, but does not capture the reality of balancing a range of factors or having to order decision-making in different ways.

Another dimension of this complexity of discretion is brought out by the role of professions. Evans, for instance, talks about the way certain expert occupations with their own structure may operate with a form of expertise that does not necessarily fit comfortably into the formal rules of a bureaucracy (Chap. 23). These professional occupations have an idea of their role, but one that may also differ from the characterization of their role as employees by the organization. A fundamental set of questions about discretion, then, are posed by the way in which actors and organizations see roles, view rules and understand the expertise, skills and knowledge which should operate in the situation. To what extent should these be prescribed by the organization? By the actors? And on what basis do researchers stand in evaluating the extent and use of discretion?

In Chap. 22, Luntley focuses on the role of discretion where rules give out. This, in a sense, is a radical area of freedom; not only because of the absence of rules, but also because of the need to think about and imagine how to respond to situations. Luntley sees the ability to do this as a general human attribute, but one which has been increasingly specialized in the division of labour. This conception of discretion may serve as the dynamo of innovation and change. Evans looks at approaches in the arts which help us to conceptualize this form of freedom. This may lead to understanding problems in different ways and hence to understand the processes that may be deployed in developing new strategies of work (Chap. 24).

A possible danger with this characterization of discretion, though, is that it can be individualized; it seems to lack a social dimension. However, identifying imagination or creativity as individual activities does not exclude such a dimension. This perhaps is illustrated by Hume's observation that shared practices in communities often develop implicitly through collective individual actions: 'Since the actions of each of us have a reference to those of the other, and are performed upon the supposition, that something is to be performed on the other part. Two men, who pull the oars of a boat, do it by an agreement or convention, though they have never given promise to each other' (Hume n.d.: loc.: 7007). In this way, these seemingly individual developments contribute to the dynamic processes which Wagenaar, drawing on Wittgenstein, identifies as social practices (Chap. 17). In Chap. 18, Rutz and de Bont look at more formal strategies where discretion has to do with the reframing of rules. This discretionary space they identify as an organizationally sanctioned area within which participants—they were looking at regulatory teams—review and revise both formal regulations and norms which govern practice. The relationship between informal, individual and collective developments and more formal, specified reviews and changes raises questions about the authority and range of discretionary decision-making that clearly require further examination and offer the opportunity to explore the comparison and contrast between formal and informal developments. For instance, to what extent do formal developments build on, recognize and seek to specify the pragmatic responses to situations that emerge from informal innovation and creativity?

Ethical issues run through discussions of discretion. In Chap. 25, Calder examines discretion from the perspective of ethics. He focuses on managing the productive tensions between standards and freedom and deploying practical reasons to negotiate this tension in different situations. Ethical discussion often centres around on actors within organizations. The perspectives of citizens and service users, though, are increasingly recognized as central to ethical debates about discretion. Marston and Davidson identify empowerment as a critical criterion by which uses of discretion should be examined (Chap. 7). Also Needham, in relation to managers, and Jobling, in relation to professionals, highlight the voices of service users in evaluating discretion (respectively, Chaps. 19 and 13).

26.4 Dealing with Discretion as Object of Analysis

What do the insights gained in this edited collection mean for the further analysis of discretion? Individual contributors have identified their own research agendas; here we want to stand back and consider the broad contribution of this interdisciplinary collection for further academic research. Those consequences will be differentiated along the lines of the themes indicated in the previous section. Hence, successively the implications for the study of discretion in its relation with politics, organization and practice will be looked at.

Exercising Discretion Means Exerting Influence

In every-day language 'politics' is often used to indicate a particular part of the public domain: the place where authoritative decisions are made about who gets what, when and how (Lasswell 1936). Frequently the term more specifically points to the place where this happens—*Westminster*, Brussels, Washington and so on—and to political actors who make the authoritative decisions. Interestingly, this language tends not to differentiate between government actors (the executive branch) and members of legislative assemblies—nationally and locally.

These two meanings both refer to a locus: where politics takes place and the people involved in it. There is, however, also a more fundamental meaning of the term politics, tied up with the use of power. When someone who just attended a meeting says: 'It was all politics, you know', then she refers to the *wheeling and dealing* she observed. *Politics* entails struggle—explicit and implicit—between actors, each asserting specific agendas, having particular stakes, pursuing certain values and following strategies to realize their goals. This is the predominant sense when we talk about party politics, bureaucratic politics and social politics. We are interested in these locations because we are focusing on the way power is played out in them.

However, power is more widespread. Laws, policy statutes and similar official documents seldom speak for themselves. They need to be interpreted and in these interpretations, implementing actors also deploy power and bring their own stakes and values into play (Hupe, Hill and Nangia 2014). And in a policy programme it often remains open which of several actors are supposed to take the lead in implementing that programme, let alone how the actors involved relate to each other. The social interaction between them necessarily takes the form of a struggle. As Hood notes in Chap. 3 (p. 24), the terms 'discretion' and 'influence' sometimes merge:

> [P]ower struggles within governments, bureaucracies and organizations might normally be expected to consist of groups or individuals trying to reduce or restrict the discretion of others, while increasing or maintaining their own discretionary space.

And these struggles can be implicit as well as explicit. Forms of knowledge are not neutral technical stances. They reflect assumptions and can promote some interests and downplay others (Evans and Hardy 2010). Jobling, for instance, shows how conflicts about expertise can also be read as conflicts about the nature of services and the role and rights of service users. Furthermore, in the process of implementation, policy accumulates meanings and interpretations as it percolates through an organization. Recognition of administrative politics can lead hierarchical subordinates to question their hierarchical superiors' interpretation of the original policy (Evans 2016). In this context the effective exercise of the top-down control of discretion is practically impossible.

The study of discretion needs to take ambiguity and conflict into account, as is the case in implementation studies generally (Matland 1995). The analysis of discretion is a 'political' analysis. Hood, for example, describes situations in which actors pursue strategies of blame avoidance by shunning or limiting their own discretion. It is clear that 'blame/discretion trade-offs' are part of the 'political' analysis of discretion. Brodkin also distinguishes a range of dimensions of the politics of discretion, stating that when shaping social provisions, structuring opportunities for exercising clients' rights and managing the consequences of their practices, organizations at the street level of government bureaucracy *de facto* function as political institutions. 'Discretion', Brodkin states in Chap. 5 (p. 71), 'can be understood to be politically significant to the extent that its exercise both reflects and refracts the broader political environment, sometimes in unanticipated ways.'

Discretion Is Used in Given Settings and Contexts

The development of the social sciences reflects a tension between specialization and generalization. Within and between the major mono-disciplines like economics, sociology and political science a variety of sub- and inter-disciplines have emerged, sometimes around a particular object of research. Other approaches focus on the interaction and application of broader bodies of knowledge around a specific scholarly theme, like social work or social policy.

The study of *executive government*, to adopt Hood's umbrella term, occupies territory that crosses the borders of disciplines and scholarly themes. This being so, focused attention to dimensions of this broad empirical object is given under headings such as (the study of) public administration, public management and public policy. The analysis of the policy process has enabled the development of identifiable scholarly themes each representing a separate 'stage' in that process, such as implementation.

Lately, a 'behavioural turn' in policy analysis has been signalled. Government officials give attention to ways of influencing citizens' conduct via 'nudging' (John 2018). In the wake of the Cambridge Analytica disclosures, such 'nudging' sensitizes us to the political and ethical questions when policy actors characterize themselves as 'choice architects'. Some authors have made a case for a 'Behavioural Public Administration' (Grimmelikhuijsen, Jilke, Olsen and

Tummers 2017; see also Chap. 11). These developments offer interesting perspectives on the practice of policymaking including critical contributions that point to its political as well as technical dimensions.

It is important to underline that discretion is always exercised in a specific organizational setting and a particular context. As the range of chapters of this edited collection indicates, such settings and contexts may vary greatly, on several dimensions. Even when one formal rule is concerned, how it is understood by different actors or to be applied in different situations can vary. Moreover, the actual mode of application may vary too, within the room set by the rule maker. Equal treatment does not mean uniform treatment. Circumstances differ, clients vary and street-level bureaucrats have to calibrate their responses to the circumstance and people they encounter.

At a macro level it is clear that the way in which institutions differ has consequences for the ways discretion is granted. For instance, as Chaps. 5 and 6 of, respectively, Brodkin and Hill, indicate, the welfare state of an American type has different traits than its British counterpart—while belonging to the same category of Esping-Andersen's (1990) typology of welfare state regimes. Depending on one's focus, similarities and differences in any comparison may advance and recede in any analysis. Similarly, when looking at how discretion is exercised at the meso level (by organizations) and at the micro level (by individuals) alongside variations it is also important to attend to the possibility of commonalities and similar patterns.

There is an external context in which discretion is exercised but there is also an internal environment. As Oberfield in Chap. 12 suggests, the ways in which public servants have been educated, trained and socialized have effects on their dispositions and, by consequence, on the ways they are dealing with discretion. Here, as well, institutional context does matter. Internationally, the training programme of marines, for instance, will have a different character in the US and the Netherlands—despite similarities that may arise from their joint participation in NATO.

For future research Hupe (2017: 21) observed a major challenge: 'to combine an eye for personal traits with an explicit positioning and further embedding of the behaviour of public officials working at the street level, within the "bigger picture" of government-in-action'. While this challenge applies to the study of governance in general, here it suggests the need to engage with the ways discretion is granted and exercised as well as how it is positioned within its institutional and political context (Frederickson 1997; Peters 2012).

Modes of Dealing with Discretion Need Contextual Comparison

A Multi-Dimensional Phenomenon

In undertaking empirical research of the exercise of discretion, it is necessary to identify the 'discretionary actors' concerned. In the preceding sections, we have considered discretion in its relationship with politics and organization. In looking at actors, we are not using this idea to suggest a hierarchical distinction. Researchers and theorists have offered valuable insights into the attributions, skills and practices of actors working in direct interaction with citizens and we will draw on these insights. However, 'actors' refers to actors at all levels—political and organizational as well as 'at the front line'. Research into discretion in the latter locus can offer insights into other actors' dealing with discretion—and vice versa. If, as we have argued, politics infuses discretion, understanding political factors and thinking is as relevant in the analysis of discretion at the street level, as it is in examining the discretion of senior public officials and political authorities. Similarly, as Tummers and Bekkers note in Chap. 11, the exploration of psychological factors in discretion is as applicable to the study of senior administrators, as it is to the study of street-level employees.

Actors are seldom one-dimensional; they often occupy several social and institutional roles at the same time. A manager of a local authority social work team, for instance, may be a registered social worker, a mental health survivor, have an MBA and be a member of a trade union, as well as fulfilling the role of manager. Furthermore, identities overlap. The manager's job description will require the office holder to have both professional status and a management qualification. She may have chosen work as a manager because of her identity as a mental health survivor; as a manager, she can be an advocate for service users within the organization. One of the challenges in research therefore is to engage with actors in a rounded way.

In research, empirical strategies are guided by concepts and ideas, but researchers also have to retain a sceptical stance towards these ideas and be open to revise and challenge them in the light of evidence. Researchers always run the risk of reifying concepts and forcing the facts to fit their theory, rather than being open to revise and change assumptions in the light of the evidence—for instance, approaching this manager using a fixed idea about conflicts between managers and professionals; or seeing service users and practitioners as necessarily at loggerheads.

Dimensions of Variety

Some questions propose themselves here. First, given the variety of such actors, what justifies an equal analytical treatment and indicates a common denominator of comparability? Second, what dimensions highlight the variety of categories? Third, what makes a difference for performance, as the result of exercising discretion? And, related to the preceding question, on what basis is discretion evaluated?

What can be called 'the public sphere' is inhabited by government ('the state'), business corporations and organizations in the civil society as major institutional actors—present in all kinds of forms and mixtures and interacting more or less intensively (Hupe and Meijs with cooperation of Vorthoren 2000). Lately, internet and social media have enhanced a more or less autonomous role of individual citizens. In this edited collection, the primary focus has been, one way or another, on the exercise of discretion by people working in the public and semi-public sector as important parts of that broader public sphere. This is a wide spectrum of employees, including people in many different roles. The claim that they function under an overall umbrella label is a point here, but one can observe a range of labels varying from just plain 'bureaucrats', via 'public servants' or 'public administrators', to 'professionals'. This cake can be cut in any number of ways depending on one's research focus.

A common distinction is made between, on one hand, policy advisers mainly interacting with other policy advisers and having a 'vertical' orientation to their political superiors and, on the other, public servants working at the street level of government. The *street* locus implies that they interact with citizens in various roles, hence having a 'horizontal' orientation. This being so, we have to be aware that professionals working in that locus can also be frequently drawn into policy work bringing not only their expertise but also valuable experience of doing the job to policymaking.

Workers in the *street* locus—Lipsky's street-level bureaucrats—may well be captured under the heading of 'professionals in public service' (Hupe 2010). The common features are that they are, first, working in direct contact with citizens as clients, patients, pupils and in other roles. Next, they are in public service. Moreover, they have got a level of education and training required for the job (Hupe, Hill and Buffat 2015b: 16). The fact of contact with citizens makes these professionals in public service different from policy advisers working at a department. However, as noted above, alongside commonalities there are also significant differences amongst street-level workers—most obviously their professional status (Evans 2011). Kallio and Saarinen (2014), for instance, in a major study of Finnish welfare services identified significant differences in orientation to role and approach to benefit recipients between non-professional staff and professionals. This makes these authors question the utility of 'street-level bureaucrat' as an analytic category. Furthermore, while these services are paid for by taxpayers, taxpayers are likely to be shocked if political or senior administrative officials interfere in clinical or individual professional decisions while they accept their intervention in individual administrative decisions.

The cake can be cut in another way to focus on a different issue, for instance, the nature of work within different types of agencies. In his book, *Bureaucracy*, Wilson (1989/2010) highlights relevant dimensions of the variety of 'what government agencies do and why they do it' (the subtitle of the book). He distinguishes between the visibility of activities of the various categories and the visibility of the results of those activities. Wilson speaks of a production agency, like the Tax Office, of which both the activities and their results are visible. Apart from a procedural agency, like an environmental inspectorate and a craft agency, like an army at war, he identifies a coping agency, like a social welfare organization. In an agency of the latter type, both the activities and their results are relatively invisible. In each of such agencies, Wilson sees 'executives', 'managers' and 'operators' at work. Although Wilson's conceptualization can be criticized, his book demonstrates—along with classics such as Gouldner's

(1954) *Patterns of industrial bureaucracy*—the variety of forms of public agencies and discretionary actors working under the broad label of 'bureaucracy'.

Another question is: what makes a difference for performance, as the result of exercising discretion? Of course, many answers are possible here. From a juridical perspective, the clarity of rules will be stressed, as well as the willingness of the discretionary actor to properly apply those rules. At the other end of the spectrum, ethical commitments and responsibilities are emphasized in terms of one's ethical autonomy (Applbaum 1999). Often in focusing on either hierarchical control or practitioner autonomy, advocates of either position invoke images of unrestrained and arbitrary practice (advocates of bureaucracy) or of a Kafkaesque nightmare of inhumane bureaucracy (advocates of autonomy) to support their respective positions. Embedded in these positions—and running across arguments about discretion throughout—are essentially evaluative claims about the value (or not) of discretion. We do not want to claim that there is one right position. Rather, for the evaluation of discretion we distinguish two types of approaches complementing each other.

Dealing with Variety

On what basis is discretion evaluated? In one type of approach, it is key that the empirical analysis of discretion avoids a one-sided stress on either the 'bureaucracy' or the 'profession' side of the equation. Exercising discretion as formulated in a set of rules implies more than just following instructions and hence will lead to empirical variation. Similarly, such a variation may be observed in the way recognized professionals do their work. There may be *good* and *bad cops* but there may also be better and less skilled doctors. *Practising craftsmanship* is what makes someone a 'professional', rather than the latter label itself. And clearly, the degree of that practising may empirically vary—as it does. However, it does so across settings and occupational borders, but also within one occupation and even one team of peers.

Professionals in public service simultaneously fulfil three roles. Being teachers, environmental inspectors, doctors working at the National Health Service—they all have, first, a particular occupation. Secondly, at the same time they are public officials. Willy nilly, they represent the state; as professionals they may be 'client agents' but they are 'state agents' as well (Maynard-Moody and Musheno 2000). And finally, they are citizens interacting with fellow citizens. They are public actors embedded in society (Hupe, Hill and Buffat Eds 2015a).

One does not have to adopt the negative qualification of one-sided dispositions as 'reductive pathologies' (Zacka 2017), to acknowledge that aiming at a balance is a norm here. Perhaps the most important indicator for the craftsmanship practised by Lipsky's (1980/2010: 12) 'street ministers' is the degree to which they manage to weigh prevalent considerations. It is the constant seeking of a dynamic but justifiable equilibrium that forms the essence of *practised professionalism in public service*. And as such, also of practised accountability, as well as of an accountable dealing with discretions (plural) in practice.

An appropriate analysis of discretion then takes into account the context-bound variation in the craftsmanship practised. How discretion is being used cannot be read-off from the formulation with which such discretion has been granted. Likewise, the degree of practised craftsmanship does not coincide with the label of the occupation concerned. Both deserve to be researched empirically, in the context at hand.

In a complementary type of approach to the empirical analysis of discretion, the recognition of significant difference amongst actors, as well as similarities, is the starting point. Take, for instance, the idea of street-level bureaucrats:

> teachers, police officers and other law enforcement personnel, social workers, judges, public lawyers and other court officials and many other public officials who grant access to government programs and provide services within them (Lipsky 1980/2010: 3).

In most welfare states this list would also include a wide range of health professionals. Within this expansive category, it is possible to differentiate between those street-level bureaucrats with a background of a more institutionalized profession and those with a less institutionalized profession. While a continuum of such institutionalization can be observed, some occupations more than others are associated with ideas of having expertise and being required to operate certain standards that are set externally from the organization within which the person works.

The underlying point here is that the shape of discretion and ideas about how it should be used and evaluated are likely to differ across public service occupations as well as contexts. Identifying a group of occupations which is perhaps in a stronger position than others to claim some freedom from top-down control in its work (or to assert it), allows researchers to explore an important dimension of discretion. This enables comparisons of similarities and differences within a specific category of public sector workers, but it will also allow the identification of similarities and differences with other categories of public sector workers. This approach suggests a process of theory-building and revision which involves a series of comparisons and contrasts. At stake is the tentative and nuanced identification of commonalities and differences across a range of discretionary actors.

The other aspect of such an approach is to recognize that there is a range of theoretical perspectives from which discretion can be understood and assessed. A particular issue here is the need to investigate actors' own ideas of why they have discretion and why they should use it, to bring them into the critical dialogue about its use. In terms of the process of research this involves understanding how these actors see the world, understand their situation and the meaning they give to their actions. Blumer (1998: 86) explains that

> [r]emaining aloof as a so-called 'objective' observer and refusing to take the role of the acting unit is to risk the worst kind of subjectivism—the objective

> observer is likely to fill in the process of interpretation with his [*sic*] own surmises in place of catching the process as it occurs in the experience of the acting unit which uses it.

Drawing on Becker (1971), Evans and Hardy (2018: 955) argue that engaging actors' interpretive worlds involves being open to both actors' idealism and cynicism. This implies:

> challenging the default cynical pose of the social researcher and probing and pushing beyond immediate and obvious answers to draw out underlying ideas and arguments. To balance this, it also entails a heightened sense of micro-ethics in social research, knowing when to stop pushing, recognizing when the interviewee has gone as far as he or she can. The other side of this is that researchers themselves need to bring into clearer understanding their own ethical perspective through a process of unsentimental reflection and reflexivity, to be aware of their own ethical assumptions and to seek to articulate them so that they are aware of their own particular commitments and how these may influence and sometimes close off others' opportunities to express their point of view and challenge their own commitments.

Understanding how these actors see the world, understand their situation and the meaning they give to their actions is not to condone a perspective. Rather it provides the basis to engage with that view point and then engage with it critically.

26.5 Conclusion: Revisiting Crassus' Engineer

In the introduction to this edited collection, we referred to Montaigne's (1958) story of the Roman general Crassus and the engineer. Crassus had instructed the engineer to fetch a particular mast he had seen so that it could be used as a battering ram. The engineer, however, chose another mast which in his judgement was better suited to the purpose.

Reflecting on this event, Montaigne (1958: 51) states: 'We corrupt the function of command when we obey through discretion, not subjection.' He explains that Crassus had the engineer whipped for disobeying his order. However, Montaigne (1958: 51) notes: 'I have in my time known people in command be reprimanded for having obeyed the King's letter rather than the demands of the situation they were in.'

Discretion is caught in a field of tensions—control and freedom, command and judgement, obedience and challenge, punishment and praise. Montaigne's story of Crassus and the engineer encapsulates the structure of discretion we have sought to sketch in this concluding chapter—and the risks entailed in using or avoiding it.

Firstly, the engineer employed his influence. He moved beyond the general's strict command to consider the command's purpose. In doing this, the engineer opened up space where his role was not just to follow orders but to use his judgement in executing them. The goal was to find the mast most suited to the general's purpose and to use his expertise to do this.

Secondly, discretion is situated. It is about making decisions, choosing between options, in the situation at hand. The engineer translated Crassus' instructions into action by looking at what was possible, what the options were available and then deciding how best to act.

And, thirdly, in using and exercising discretion he was using craftsmanship to weigh up the range of factors—the command, the purpose behind it, his expert knowledge, the materials he needed and the materials available and so on—to understand his role and decide how to act within it.

Discretion is a process of constructing space within which one decides and acts. It is also a confusing and frightening setting within which to operate, accompanied by ambiguities. Is not Crassus right to expect his orders to be followed—no ifs, no buts? On the other hand, was it not a fair assumption for the engineer—an expert in the matter—to assume that Crassus, in consulting him, was inviting him to exercise and act on his expert judgement? Both injunctions stand together in the same situation. Which one to choose? Which is the safe option, which is the right option? How will others react?

One can observe here what can be called a 'fear of ultimate freedom', actually on both sides. General Crassus expects his orders to be simply obeyed and punishes disobedience in case of what he sees as an illegitimate use of freedom. The engineer, on the other hand, does exercise the discretion granted to him but he does so in a highly responsive and responsible way, keeping an orientation on what the general had in mind. This shows how the control and freedom perspectives can be observed as occurring simultaneously. Total control is an illusion—as indicated in the introductory chapter—and so too is unconstrained freedom. The fear of ultimate freedom can be seen in actors using discretion as well as in actors granting discretion, both among professionals and among bureaucrats—to use that dichotomy one more time.

References

Applbaum, A. (1999). *Ethics for adversaries*. Princeton: Princeton University Press.

Becker, H. (1971). *Sociological work: Method and substance*. London: Allen Lane.

Beetham, D. (1987). *Bureaucracy*. Milton Keynes: Open University Press.

Blumer, H. (1998). *Symbolic interactionism: Perspective and method*. Berkeley and Los Angeles: University of California Press.

Davis, K.C. (1969). *Discretionary justice: A preliminary inquiry*. Baton Rouge: Louisiana State University Press.

Dworkin, R.M. (1977). *Taking rights seriously*. Cambridge, MA: Harvard University Press.

Esping-Andersen, G. (1990). *The three worlds of welfare capitalism*. Cambridge: Polity Press.

Evans, T. (2011). Professionals, managers and discretion: Critiquing street-level bureaucracy. *British Journal of Social Work*, 41(2), 368–386.

Evans, T. (2016). *Professional discretion in welfare services: Beyond street-level bureaucracy.* London: Routledge.

Evans, T. & Hardy, M. (2010). *Evidence and knowledge for practice.* Cambridge. Polity Press.

Evans, T. & Hardy, M. (2018). The ethics of practical reasoning: Exploring the terrain. *European Journal of Social Work*, 20(6), 947–957.

Evans, T. & Harris, J. (2004). Street-level bureaucracy, social work and the (exaggerated) death of discretion. *British Journal of Social Work*, 34(6), 871–895.

Frederickson, H.G. (1997). *The spirit of public administration.* San Francisco: Jossey-Bass Inc.

Galligan, D.J. (1990). *Discretionary powers: A legal study of official discretion.* Chapter 1 'Senses of discretion' retrieved from Oxford Scholarship Online https://doi.org/10.1093/acprof:oso/9780198256526.001.0001 Subscriber: Erasmus University Library. Date: 7 September 2015.

Gouldner, A.W. (1954). *Patterns of industrial bureaucracy.* Glencoe, IL: Free Press.

Grimmelikhuijsen, S., Jilke, S., Olsen, A.L. & Tummers, L. (2017). Behavioral Public Administration: Combining insights from Public Administration and psychology. *Public Administration Review*, 77(1), 45–56.

Hawkins, K. (Ed.). (1992). *The uses of discretion.* Oxford: Clarendon Press.

Hume, D. (n.d.). *Treatise of human nature.* Kindle Edition.

Hupe, P.L. (2010). The autonomy of professionals in public service. In Th. Jansen, G. van den Brink & J. Kole (Eds), *Professional pride: A powerful force* (pp. 118–137). Amsterdam: Boom.

Hupe, P.L. (2017). Capturing what happens 'after a bill became a law': The ongoing quest of implementation research. Valedictory lecture and first chapter in *liber amicorum* for Peter Hupe. In V.J.J.M. Bekkers, H.J.M. Fenger & P.W.A. Scholten (Eds), with cooperation of R. Simonse, *Public service as practice* (pp. 11–29). Erasmus University Rotterdam: Erasmus School of Social and Behavioural Sciences.

Hupe, P.L. & Hill, M.J. (2007). Street-level bureaucracy and public accountability. *Public Administration*, 85(2), 279–299.

Hupe, P.L. & Meijs, L.C.P.M., with cooperation of M.H. Vorthoren. (2000). *Hybrid governance: The impact of the non-profit sector in the Netherlands.* Baltimore, Rotterdam and The Hague: Johns Hopkins University, Erasmus University Rotterdam and The Netherlands Institute for Social Research (SCP).

Hupe, P.L., Hill, M.J. & Nangia, M. (2014). Studying implementation beyond deficit analysis: The top-down view reconsidered. *Public Policy and Administration*, 29(2), 145–163.

Hupe, P.L, Hill, M.J. & Buffat, A. (Eds). (2015a). *Understanding street-level bureaucracy.* Bristol: Policy Press.

Hupe, P.L., Hill, M.J. & Buffat, A. (2015b). Introduction: Defining and understanding street-level bureaucracy. In P.L. Hupe, M.J. Hill & A. Buffat (Eds), *Understanding street-level bureaucracy* (pp. 3–24). Bristol: Policy Press,

John, P. (2018). *How far to nudge: Assessing behavioural public policy.* Cheltenham: Edward Elgar.

Kallio, J. & Saarinen, A. (2014). Street-level bureaucrats' attitudes towards the Finnish labour market allowance. *International Journal of Sociology and Social Policy*, 34, 817–834.

Lasswell H.D. (1936). *Politics: Who gets what, when, how.* Cleveland, OH. Meridian Books.

Lewis, J. & Glennerster, H. (1996). *Implementing the new community care*. Buckingham: Open University Press

Lipsky, M. (1980/2010). *Street-level bureaucracy: Dilemmas of the individual in public services*. New York: Russell Sage Foundation. (2010 = thirtieth anniversary edition).

Matland, R.E. (1995). Synthesizing the implementation literature: The ambiguity-conflict model of policy implementation. *Journal of Public Administration Research and Theory*, 5(2), 145–174.

Maynard-Moody, S. & Musheno, M. (2000). State agent or citizen agent: Two narratives of discretion. *Journal of Public Administration Research and Theory*, 10(2), 329–358.

Montaigne, M. (1958). *The complete essays of Montaigne* (Frame, Trans.). Stanford, CA: Stanford University Press.

Peters, B.G. (2012). *Institutional theory in political science: The new institutionalism* (3rd ed.). New York: The Continuum International Publishing Group.

Thomann, E. Hupe, P.L. & Sager F. (2018). Serving many masters: Public accountability in private policy implementation. *Governance*, 31(2), 299–319.

Williams, R. (1976). Bureaucracy. *Keywords*. London. Croom Helm.

Wilson, J.Q. (1989/2000). *Bureaucracy: What government agencies do and why they do it*. New York: Basic Books.

Zacka, B. (2017). *When the state meets the street: Public service and moral agency*. Cambridge, MA: The Belknap Press of Harvard University Press.

Zimmerman, D. (1971). The practicalities of rule use. In J. Douglas (Ed.), *Understanding everyday life* (pp. 221–238). London: Routledge and Kegan Paul.

Index[1]

[1] Note: Page numbers followed by 'n' refer to notes.

T. Evans, P. Hupe (eds.), *Discretion and the Quest for Controlled Freedom*, https://doi.org/10.1007/978-3-030-19566-3

The manufacturer's authorised representative in the EU is Springer Nature Customer Service Centre GmbH, Europaplatz 3, 69115 Heidelberg, Germany. If you have any concerns regarding our products, please contact ProductSafety@springernature.com

Printed and bound by CPI Group (UK) Ltd, Croydon, CR0 4YY
30/09/2026
02225661-0019